road
atlas

USA | CANADA | MEXICO

ROAD MAPS are organized geographically. United States, Canada, and Mexico road maps are organized in a grid layout, starting in the northwest of each country. To find your way, use either the **Key to Map Pages** inside the front cover, the **Listing of State and City Maps** on page 3, or the **index** in the back of the atlas.

COUNTRY COLORS

Colors represent countries throughout the atlas.
Red → Canada
Green → Mexico
Blue → United States
Purple → United States (Northeast Corridor)

MAP SCALES

Scale bars are shown at a constant length throughout the atlas for quick and easy scale comparison between regions.

DRIVING DISTANCES

Use this chart to check driving distances between major cities within each map. Refer to distance and driving time information at the back of the atlas for travel over greater distances.

LOCATOR MAPS

A quick glance at this miniature map lets you check which states and/or provinces are shown on each page.

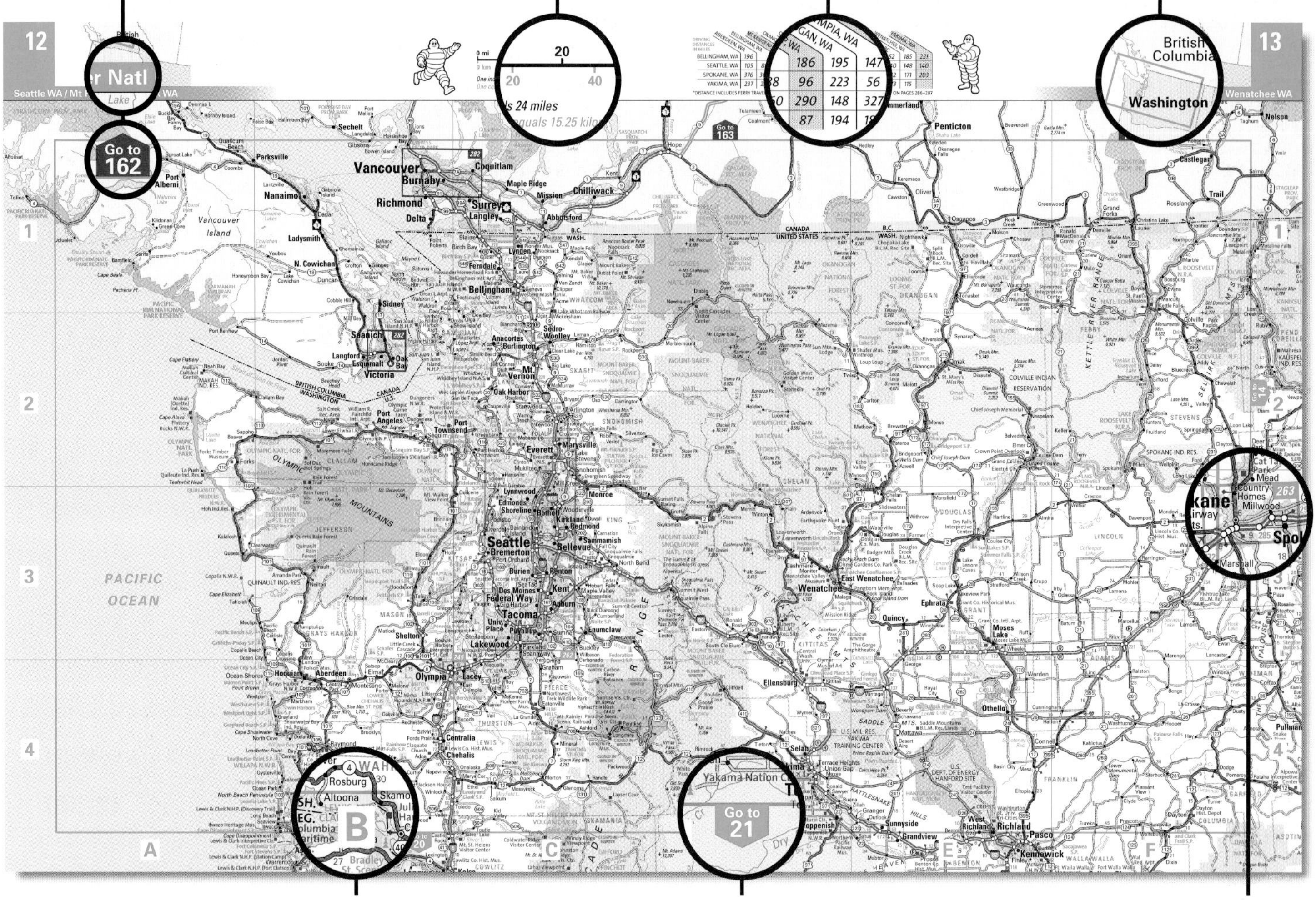

GRID REFERENCES

Use grid references to locate places listed in the index. For instance, Rosburg WA is listed in the index with "12" and "B4", indicating that the town may be found on page 12 in grid square B4.

"GO TO" POINTERS

Handy page tabs point the way to the next map, making navigation a breeze.

INSET MAP BOXES

These color-coded boxes outline areas that are featured in greater detail in the index section. The tab with "263" (above) indicates that a detailed map of Spokane may be found on page 263 (below).

HOW THE INDEX WORKS

Cities and towns are listed alphabetically, with separate indexes for the United States, Canada, and Mexico. Figures after entries indicate population, page number, and grid reference. Entries in bold color indicate cities with detailed inset maps. The U.S. index also includes counties and parishes, which are shown in bold black type.

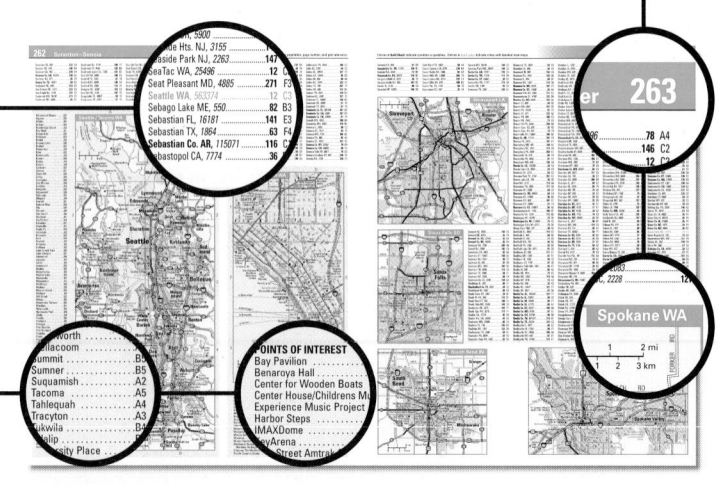

INSET MAP INDEXES

Many inset maps have their own indexes. Metro area inset map indexes list cities and towns; downtown inset map indexes list points of interest.

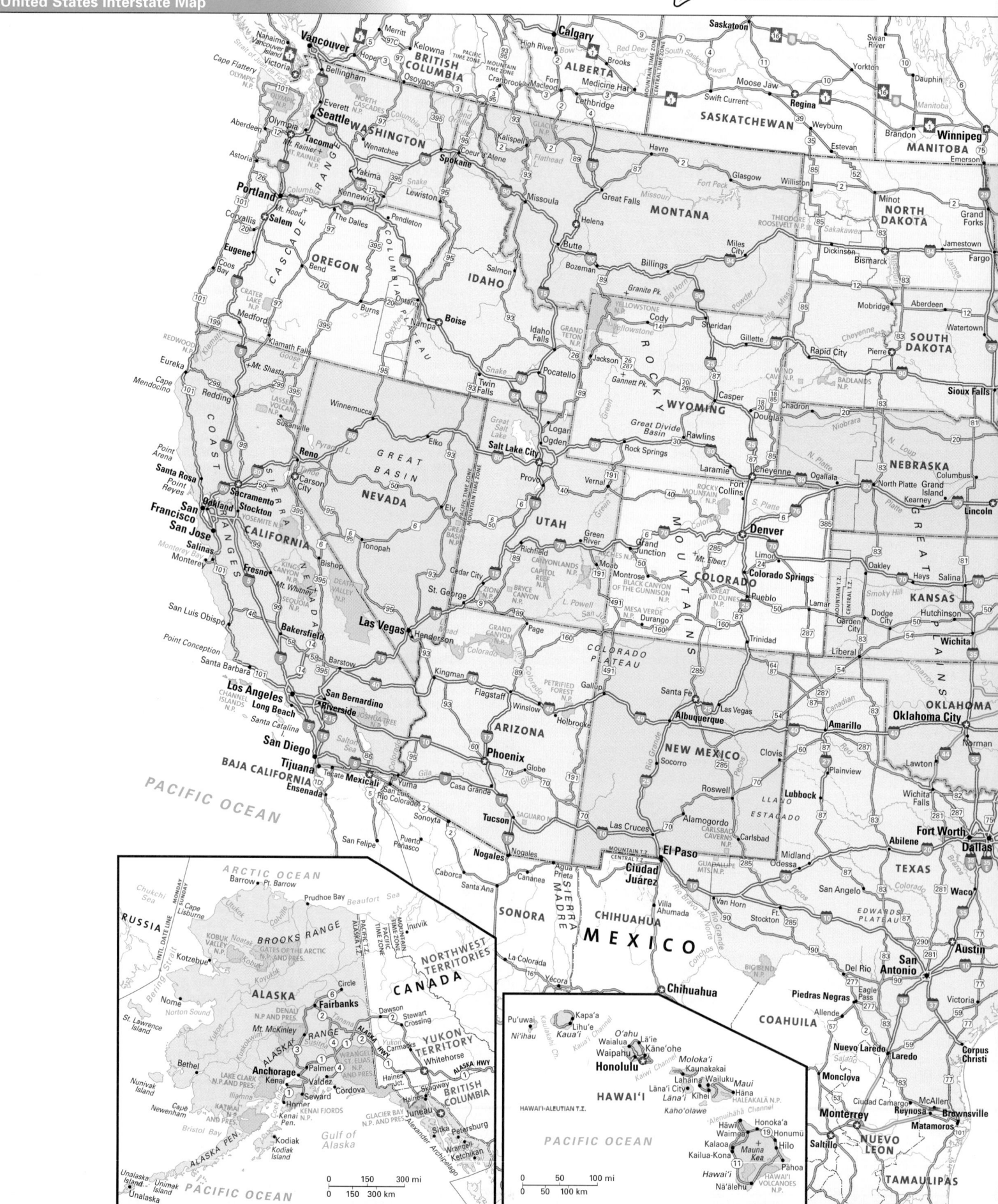

0 mi   125   250   375

0 km   125   250   375   500

One inch equals 204.6 miles
One centimeter equals 129.4 kilometers

CANADA
ONTARIO
QUÉBEC
NEW BRUNSWICK
MINNESOTA
WISCONSIN
MICHIGAN
IOWA
ILLINOIS
INDIANA
OHIO
PA.
NEW YORK
VT.
N.H.
MAINE
MASS.
R.I.
CT.
N.J.
DEL.
MD.
WEST VIRGINIA
VIRGINIA
KENTUCKY
TENNESSEE
NORTH CAROLINA
SOUTH CAROLINA
GEORGIA
FLORIDA
ALABAMA
MISSISSIPPI
LOUISIANA
ARKANSAS
MISSOURI
BAHAMAS
CUBA
ATLANTIC OCEAN
GULF OF MEXICO
Lake Superior
Lake Michigan
Lake Huron
Lake Erie
Lake Ontario
EASTERN TIME ZONE
CENTRAL TIME ZONE
Thunder Bay
Kenora
Dryden
Fort Frances
International Falls
Nipigon
Geraldton
Hearst
Kapuskasing
Timmins
Kirkland Lake
Wawa
Marathon
Sault Ste. Marie
Sudbury
North Bay
Rouyn Noranda
Val-d'Or
Matagami
Chibougamau
Chicoutimi
Alma
Baie-Comeau
Rimouski
Matane
Mont-Joli
Percé
Campbellton
Bathurst
Miramichi
Edmundston
Presque Isle
Houlton
Woodstock
Fredericton
Saint John
Québec
Trois-Rivières
Drummondville
Sherbrooke
St-Georges
Montreal
Ottawa
Pembroke
Maniwaki
Mont-Laurier
Kingston
Peterborough
Toronto
Oshawa
Barrie
Orillia
Huntsville
Parry Sound
Owen Sound
Tobermory
Manitoulin Island
Brampton
Hamilton
Kitchener
London
St.Catharines
Niagara Falls
Sarnia
Chatham
Windsor
Duluth
Superior
Bemidji
St. Cloud
St. Paul
Minneapolis
Rochester
Winona
Eau Claire
Wausau
Green Bay
Appleton
Sheboygan
Milwaukee
Madison
Racine
La Crosse
Mason City
Escanaba
Traverse City
Alpena
Muskegon
Grand Rapids
Lansing
Flint
Saginaw
Detroit
Ann Arbor
Jackson
Kalamazoo
Toledo
Cleveland
Akron
Youngstown
Canton
Erie
Buffalo
Rochester
Syracuse
Utica
Albany
Watertown
Binghamton
Scranton
Williamsport
State College
Altoona
Harrisburg
Pittsburgh
Allentown
Philadelphia
New York
Newark
Trenton
Bridgeport
New Haven
Hartford
Springfield
Worcester
Boston
Providence
New Bedford
Cape Cod
Nantucket Island
Martha's Vineyard
Manchester
Concord
Portsmouth
Portland
Augusta
Bangor
Bar Harbor
Calais
Burlington
Montpelier
Rutland
Sioux City
Fort Dodge
Waterloo
Dubuque
Cedar Rapids
Des Moines
Davenport
Rock Island
Council Bluffs
Omaha
Ottumwa
Chicago
Gary
South Bend
Joliet
Rockford
Peoria
Bloomington
Champaign
Springfield
Quincy
Decatur
Fort Wayne
Lafayette
Indianapolis
Terre Haute
Lima
Mansfield
Columbus
Dayton
Cincinnati
Wheeling
Morgantown
Cumberland
Parkersburg
Huntington
Charleston
Baltimore
Washington
Annapolis
Dover
Wilmington
Atlantic City
Cape May
Salisbury
Charlottesville
Richmond
Hampton
Norfolk
Virginia Beach
Newport News
Petersburg
Roanoke
Danville
St. Joseph
Kansas City
Topeka
Lawrence
Emporia
Columbia
Jefferson City
Hannibal
St. Louis
Rolla
Springfield
Joplin
Cape Girardeau
Poplar Bluff
Evansville
Owensboro
Louisville
Frankfort
Lexington
Pikeville
Paducah
Cairo
Bowling Green
Clarksville
Nashville
Knoxville
Johnson City
Bristol
Asheville
Mt. Mitchell
Winston-Salem
Greensboro
Durham
Raleigh
Charlotte
Fayetteville
Jacksonville
Wilmington
Cape Fear
Cape Hatteras
Pamlico Sound
Spartanburg
Greenville
Columbia
Myrtle Beach
Charleston
Augusta
Savannah
Brunswick
Tulsa
Muskogee
Fayetteville
Jonesboro
Ft. Smith
McAlester
Little Rock
Hot Springs N.P.
Pine Bluff
El Dorado
Texarkana
Durant
Paris
Memphis
Jackson
Tupelo
Columbus
Greenville
Meridian
Jackson
Hattiesburg
Natchez
Monroe
Shreveport
Longview
Nacogdoches
Alexandria
Lake Charles
Lafayette
Baton Rouge
New Orleans
Houma
Beaumont
Huntsville
Houston
Galveston
Chattanooga
Huntsville
Decatur
Gadsden
Birmingham
Tuscaloosa
Montgomery
Selma
Mobile
Biloxi
Pensacola
Panama City
Dothan
Albany
Columbus
Macon
Atlanta
Marietta
Tallahassee
Valdosta
Lake City
Gainesville
Ocala
St. Augustine
Daytona Beach
Orlando
Cape Canaveral
Melbourne
Tampa
St. Petersburg
Sarasota
Ft. Pierce
West Palm Beach
Fort Myers
Naples
Fort Lauderdale
Miami
Key West
Florida Keys
Dry Tortugas N.P.
Everglades N.P.
Biscayne N.P.
Straits of Florida
Havana
Grand Bahama
Freeport
Abaco Island
Nassau
New Providence
Eleuthera
Andros Island
Great Guana Cay
Cat Island
San Salvador
Rum Cay

0 mi 200 400
0 km 200 400 600
One inch equals 235.8 miles/Un pouce équivaut à 235.8 milles
One cm equals 149.3 km/Un cm équivaut à 149.3 km

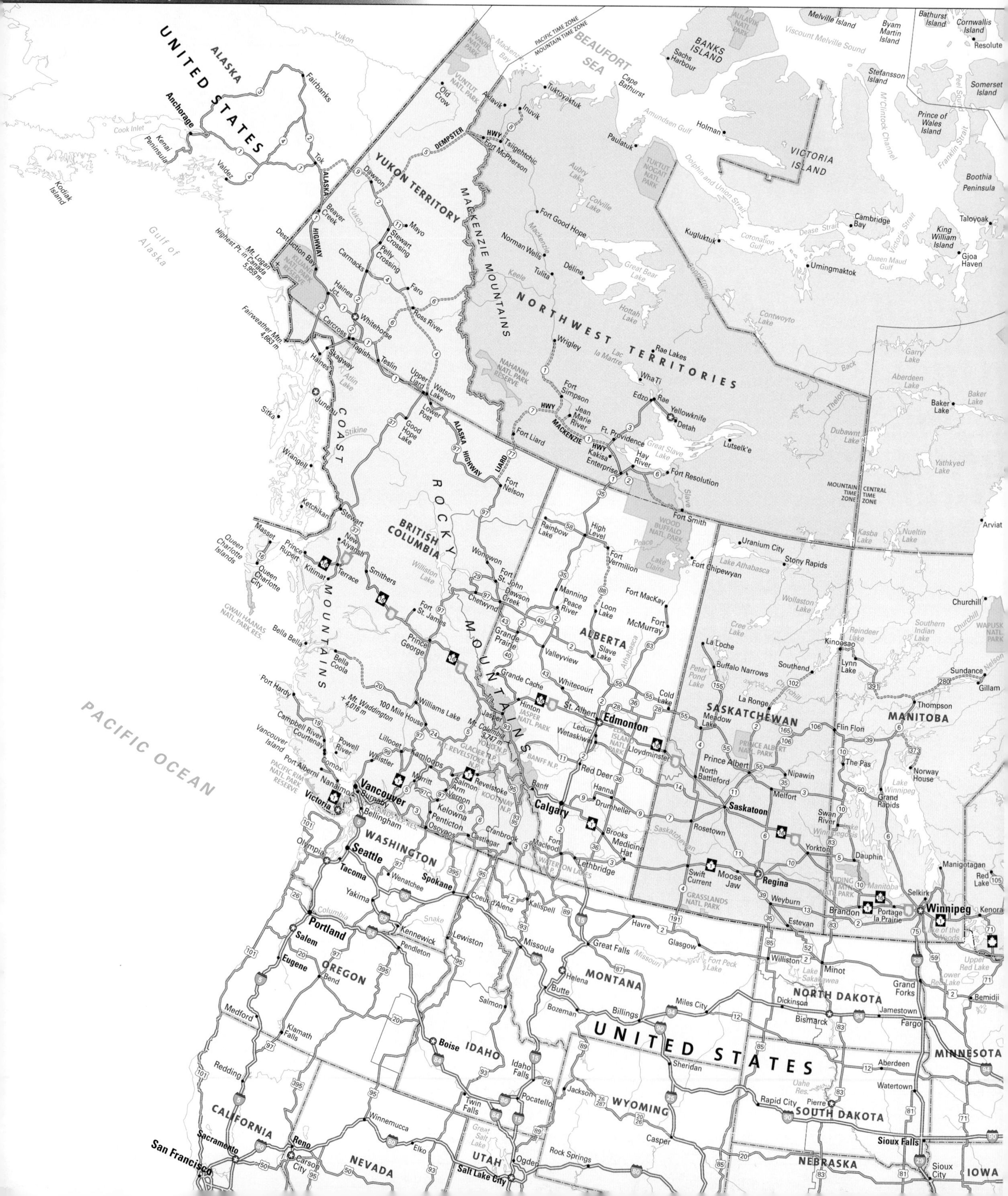

Experience the thrill of the open roads of North America with these great Scenic Drives from Michelin. The famous star ratings highlight natural and cultural attractions along the way.

  ★★★   **Highly recommended**
  ★★   **Recommended**
  ★   **Interesting**

Michelin Scenic Drives are indicated by a green and yellow dashed line (▬▬▬▬) on corresponding atlas maps for easy reference. The following 17 drives are also plotted for your use.

A Calendar of Events on page 290 shows popular festivals for several cities in the scenic drives.

ABBREVIATIONS

N	North	NHS	National Historic Site
E	East	NL	National Lakeshore
S	South	NM	National Memorial/
W	West		National Monument
NE	Northeast	NMP	National Military Park
NW	Northwest	NP	National Park
SE	Southeast	NPR	National Park Reserve
SW	Southwest	NRA	National Recreation Area
Hwy.	Highway	NWR	National Wildlife Refuge
Pkwy.	Parkway	PP	Provincial Park
Rte.	Route	SHP	State Historical Park
Mi	Miles	SHS	State Historic Site
Km	Kilometers	SP	State Park
Sq Ft	Square Feet	SR	State Reserve
		VC	Visitor Center

For detailed coverage of the attractions, and for suggestions of places to dine and stay overnight, see Michelin's North America **Regional Atlas Series**, designed for the way you drive, and Michelin's **Green Guide Collection**, the ultimate guidebooks for the independent traveler.

NORTHWEST

Anchorage/Fairbanks/Denali★★★

892 miles/1,436 kilometers   Maps 189, 154, 155

From **Anchorage★**, Alaska's largest city, take Rte. 1 (Glenn Hwy. and Tok Cutoff) N and then E through the broad Matanuska Valley to the small town of **Tok**. The route passes agricultural communities, the **Matanuska Glacier** and the Wrangell Mountains before heading up the Copper River Basin. From Tok, take the Alaska Hwy. (Rte. 2) NW to **Fairbanks★**, a friendly town with a frontier feel. The road passes the **Trans-Alaska Pipeline** and **Big Delta SHP** then parallels the Tanana River. From Fairbanks, opt for Rte. 3 W that crosses the river at Nenana, then veers S to **Denali NP★★★**, home of spruce forests, grassy tundra, grizzlies, moose and North America's highest peak, **Mount McKinley** (20,320ft). Return S to Anchorage via Rtes. 3 and 1.

Badlands NP

Badlands★★

164 miles/264 kilometers   Maps 253, 26

From **Rapid City★**, South Dakota, drive SE on Rte. 44 through Farmingdale and Scenic, then east to Interior to enter **Badlands NP★★**. Take Rte. 377 NE 2mi to Cedar Pass and stop at the park's **Ben Reifel VC**. From there, **Cliff Shelf Nature Trail★★** (.5mi) is popular for its shady juniper trees and **Castle Trail★★★** (4.5mi) is spectacular in early morning when the moonscape valley and pointed spires get first light. Turn left onto Rte. 240, **Badlands Loop Road★★★**, along the northern rim, where prairie grasslands give way to buttes and hoodoos. **Pinnacles Overlook★★** is a sweeping viewpoint to the south. Drive N to I-90, and cross the Interstate N to Wall. On Main St. visit **Wall Drug★**, a "drug store" with over 20 shops filled with historical photos, 6,000 pairs of cowboy boots, wildlife exhibits and Western art displayed in five dining rooms. In the backyard a roaring, 80ft **Tyrannosaurus** sends toddlers running. Leave Wall on I-90, driving W. Take Exit 66 to Ellsworth Air Force Base, where the **South Dakota Air and Space Museum** displays stealth bombers and other aircraft. Continue W on I-90 back to Rapid City to conclude the tour.

Black Hills★★

244 miles/393 kilometers   Maps 253, 26, 25

From **Rapid City★**, drive S on US-16 then US-16A S past Keystone. Take Rte. 244 W to **Mount Rushmore NM★★★**. Continue W on Rte. 244 to the junction of US-16/385. En route S to Custer, **Crazy Horse Memorial★** honors the famous Sioux chief. From Custer, head S on US-385 through Pringle to the junction of Rte. 87. Take Rte. 87 N through **Wind Cave NP★★** and into **Custer SP★★**. Follow **Wildlife Loop Road★★** (access S of Blue Bell, across from Rte. 342 junction) E and N to US-16A. Then travel W to join scenic **Needles Highway★★** (Rte. 87) NW to US-16/385 N. Where US-16 separates, continue N on US-385 to **Deadwood★★**, a former gold camp. Turn left onto US-14A, driving SW through **Lead★**, site of the former **Homestake Gold Mine★★**, to Cheyenne Crossing. Drive N on US-14A to I-90, turning SE back to Rapid City.

Columbia River Gorge★★

83 miles/134 kilometers   Maps 251, 20, 21

From **Portland★★**, Oregon's largest city, take I-84 E to Exit 17 in Troutdale. There, head E on the winding **Historic Columbia River Highway★★** (US-30), which skirts the steep cliffs above the river. For great **views★★**, stop at **Vista House at Crown Point**. You'll pass the 620ft **Multnomah Falls★★** and moss-draped **Oneonta Gorge**. At Ainsworth State Park (Exit 35), rejoin I-84 and travel E to Mosier (Exit 69), where US-30, with its hairpin turns, begins again. Continue E on US-30, stopping at **Rowena Crest Viewpoint★★** for grand vistas—and wildflowers. Just past the Western-style town called **The Dalles**, take US-197 N to conclude the tour at **The Dalles Lock and Dam VC★★**.

Grand Tetons/Yellowstone★★★

224 miles/361 kilometers   Map 24

Note: parts of this tour are closed in winter.
From **Jackson★★**, drive N on US-26 to Moose. Turn left onto Teton Park Rd. to access **Grand Teton NP★★★** and **Jenny Lake Scenic Drive★★★**. From Teton Park Rd., drive N to the junction of US-89/191/287 (**John D. Rockefeller Jr. Memorial Pkwy.**) and follow the parkway into **Yellowstone NP★★★** to **West Thumb**. Take Grand Loop Rd. W to **Old Faithful★★★**, the world's most famous geyser. Continue N on the Grand Loop Rd., passing **Norris Geyser Basin★★** en route to **Mammoth Hot Springs★★★**. Turn E on Grand Loop Rd. to Tower Junction, then S into **Grand Canyon of the Yellowstone★★★**. Continue S from Canyon Village through **Hayden Valley★★** to Lake Junction. Head SW, back to West Thumb, to conclude to tour.

Pacific Coast/Olympic Peninsula★★★

419 miles/675 kilometers   Maps 245, 12

From the state capital of **Olympia**, drive N on US-101 to Discovery Bay. Detour on Rte. 20 NE to **Port Townsend★★**, a well-preserved Victorian seaport. From Discovery Bay, head W on US-101 through **Port Angeles** to the **Heart O' the Hills** park entrance for **Olympic NP★★★** to see **Hurricane Ridge★★★**. Back on US-101, head E then S to the park entrance that leads to **Hoh Rain Forest★★★**. Follow US-101 S, then E after Queets to **Lake Quinault★**, home to bald eagles, trumpeter swans and loons. Continue S on US-101 to Aberdeen, taking Rte. 105 to the coast. At Raymond, return to US-101 heading S to **Long Beach**. Follow Rte. 103 N past the former cannery town of **Oysterville** to **Leadbetter Point★** on Willapa Bay, where oysters are still harvested. Return S to **Ilwaco** and drive E and S on US-101 to Astoria, Oregon, to end the tour.

The Oregon Coast★★

368 miles/592 kilometers   Maps 20, 28

Leave **Astoria★**, Oregon's first settlement, via US-101, heading SW. **Fort Clatsop National Memorial★★** recalls Lewis and Clark's historic stay. **Cannon Beach★** boasts a sandy **beach★** and tall coastal rock. At the farming community of **Tillamook★**, go west on 3rd St. to **Cape Meares** to begin **Three Capes Scenic Drive★★**. Continue S, rejoining US-101 just beyond Pacific City. Drive S on US-101 through **Newport★**, then **Yachats★**, which neighbors **Cape Perpetua Scenic Area★★**. From **Florence** to **Coos Bay★** stretches **Oregon Dunes National Recreation Area★★**. At Coos Bay, take Cape Arago Hwy. W to tour the gardens of **Shore Acres State Park★**. Drive S on the highway to rejoin US-101. Pass **Bandon★**, known for its cheese factory, and **Port Orford**, with its fishing fleet. Farther S, **Boardman State Park★** shelters Sitka spruce, Douglas fir and **Natural Bridge Cove**. End the tour at **Brookings**.

Oregon Coast at Bandon

SOUTHWEST

Big Bend Area★★
581 miles/935 kilometers   Maps 211, 56, 57, 62, 60

Head S from **El Paso★** via I-10, then E to Kent. Take Rte. 118 S to Alpine, passing **McDonald Observatory★** (telescope tours) and **Fort Davis NHS★★**. Continue S to Study Butte to enter **Big Bend NP★★★**, edged by the Rio Grande River and spanning 1,252sq mi of spectacular canyons, lush bottomlands, sprawling desert and mountain woodlands. The park has more species of migratory and resident birds than any other national park. Travel E to the main VC at **Panther Junction** in the heart of the park (US-385 and Rio Grande Village Dr.). Then take US-385 N to Marathon. Turn E on US-90 to Langtry, site of **Judge Roy Bean VC★**. Continue E to **Seminole Canyon SP★★**, with its 4,000-year-old pictographs. Farther E, **Amistad NRA★** is popular for water sports. Continue on US-90 to conclude the tour in Del Rio.

Canyonlands of Utah★★★
481 miles/774 kilometers   Maps 39, 40

From **St. George★**, drive NE on I-15 to Exit 16. Take Rte. 9 E to Springdale, gateway to **Zion NP★★★**, with its sandstone canyon, waterfalls and hanging gardens. Continue E on Rte. 9 to Mt. Carmel Junction, turn left onto US-89 and head N to the junction with Rte. 12. Take Rte. 12 SE to **Bryce Canyon NP★★★**, with its colored rock formations. Continue SE on Rte. 12 to Cannonville, then S to **Kodachrome Basin SP★★**, where sandstone chimneys rise from the desert floor. Return to Cannonville, and drive NE on Rte. 12 through Boulder to Torrey. Take Rte. 24 E through **Capitol Reef NP★★**—with its unpaved driving roads and trails—then N to I-70. Travel E on I-70 to Exit 180, then S on US-191 to Rte. 313 into **Canyonlands NP★★★** to **Grand View Point Overlook**. Return to US-191, turning S to access **Arches NP★★★**—the greatest concentration of natural stone arches in the country. Continue S on US-191 to **Moab★** to end the tour.

Arches NP

Central Coast/Big Sur★★★
118 miles/190 kilometers   Maps 236, 44

From **Cannery Row★** in **Monterey★★**, take Prescott Ave. to Rte. 68. Turn right and continue to Pacific Grove Gate (on your left) to begin scenic **17-Mile Drive★★**, a private toll road. Exit at Carmel Gate to reach the upscale artists' colony of **Carmel★★**, site of Carmel **mission★★★**. The town's **Scenic Road** winds S along the beachfront. Leave Carmel by Hwy. 1 S. Short, easy trails at **Point Lobos SR★★** line the shore. Enjoy the wild beauty of the **Big Sur★★★** coastline en route to San Simeon, where **Hearst Castle★★★**, the magnificent estate of a former newspaper magnate, overlooks the Pacific Ocean. Continue S on Hwy. 1 to **Morro Bay**, where the tour ends.

Colorado Rockies★★★
499 miles/803 kilometers   Maps 209, 41, 33, 40

Note: Rte. 82 S of Leadville to Aspen is closed mid-Oct to Memorial Day due to snow.

From **Golden★★**, W of **Denver★★★**, drive W on US-6 along Clear Creek to Rte. 119, heading N on the **Peak to Peak Highway★★** to **Nederland★**. Continue N on Rte. 72, then follow Rte. 7 N to the town of **Estes Park★★**. Take US-36 to enter **Rocky Mountain NP★★★**. Drive **Trail Ridge Road★★★** (US-34) S to the town of **Grand Lake★**. Continue S to Granby, turn left on US-40 to I-70 at Empire. Head W on I-70 past **Georgetown★** and through **Eisenhower Tunnel**. You'll pass ski areas **Arapahoe Basin**, **Keystone Resort★** and **Breckenridge★★**. At Exit 195 for **Copper Mountain Resort★**, take Rte. 91 S to **Leadville★★**, Colorado's former silver capital. Then travel S on US-24 to Rte. 82 W over **Independence Pass★★** to **Aspen★★★**. Head NW to I-70, passing **Glenwood Springs★★** with its **Hot Springs Pool★★**. Drive E on I-70 along **Glenwood Canyon★★** and the Colorado River to **Vail★★**. Continue E on I-70 to the old mining town of **Idaho Springs** to return to Golden via Rte. 119.

Lake Tahoe

Lake Tahoe Loop★★
71 miles/114 kilometers   Map 37

Begin in **Tahoe City** at the intersection of Rtes. 89 and 28. Drive S on Rte. 89. **Ed Z'berg-Sugar Pine Point State Park★** encompasses a promontory topped by **Ehrman Mansion★** and other historic buildings. Farther S, **Emerald Bay State Park★★** surrounds beautiful **Emerald Bay★★**. At the bay's tip stands **Vikingsholm★★**, a mansion that resembles an ancient Nordic castle. At **Tallac Historic Site★★**, preserved summer estates recall Tahoe's turn-of-the-19C opulence. From Tahoe Valley, take Rte. 50 NE. **South Lake Tahoe**, the lake's largest town, offers lodging, dining and shopping. High-rise hotel-casinos characterize neighboring **Stateline** in Nevada. Continue N to Spooner Junction. Then follow Nevada Rte. 28 N to **Sand Harbor** (7mi), where picnic tables and a sandy beach fringe a sheltered cove. Continue through Kings Beach to end the tour at Tahoe City.

Maui's Hana Highway★★
62 miles/100 kilometers   Map 153

Leave **Kahului** on Rte. 36 E toward **Paia**, an old sugar-plantation town. Continue E on Rte. 36, which becomes Rte. 360, the **Hana Highway★★**. The road passes **Ho'okipa Beach Park**, famous for windsurfing, and **Puohokamoa Falls**, a good picnic stop, before arriving in **Hana**, a little village on an attractive bay. If adventurous, continue S on the Pulaui Highway to **Ohe'o Gulch★★** in Haleakala **NP★★★**, where small waterfalls tumble from the SE flank of the dormant volcano Haleakala. Past the gulch the grave of aviator **Charles Lindbergh** can be found in the churchyard at Palapala Hoomau Hawaiian Church. End the tour at Kipahulu.

Redwood Empire★★
182 miles/293 kilometers   Maps 36, 28

In **Leggett**, S of the junction of Hwy. 1 and US-101, go N on US-101 to pass through a massive redwood trunk at **Chandelier Drive-Thru Tree Park**. To the N, see breathtaking groves along 31mi **Avenue of the Giants★★★**. **Humboldt Redwoods SP★★** contains **Rockefeller Forest★★**, the world's largest virgin redwood forest. From US-101, detour 4mi to **Ferndale★**, a quaint Victorian village. N. along US-101, **Eureka★** preserves a logging camp cookhouse and other historic sites. The sleepy fishing town of **Trinidad★** is home to a marine research lab. **Patrick's Point SP★★** offers dense forests, agate-strewn beaches and clifftop **views★★**. At **Orick**, enter the **Redwood National and State Parks★★**, which protect a 367ft-high, 600-year-old **tree★**. The tour ends in **Crescent City**.

Santa Fe Area★★★
267 miles/430 kilometers   Maps 189, 48, 260, 49

From **Albuquerque★**, drive E on I-40 to Exit 175 and take Rte. 14, the **Turquoise Trail★★**, N to **Santa Fe★★★**. This 52mi back road runs along the scenic Sandia Mountains and passes dry washes, arroyos and a series of revived "ghost towns." Continue N on US-84/285, turning NE onto Rte. 76, the **High Road to Taos★★**. East of Vadito, take Rte. 518 N to Rte. 68 N into the rustic Spanish colonial town of **Taos★★**, a center for the arts. Head N on US-64 to the junction of Rte. 522. Continue W on US-64 for an 18mi round-trip detour to see the 1,200ft-long, three-span **Rio Grande Gorge Bridge** over the river. Return to Rte. 522 and take this route, part of the **Enchanted Circle★★** Scenic Byway, N to **Questa**, starting point for white-water trips on the Rio Grande. Turn onto Rte. 38, heading E to the old mining town of **Eagle Nest**. There, detour 23mi E on US-64 to **Cimarron**, a Wild West haunt. Back at Eagle Nest, travel SW on US-64, detouring on Rte. 434 S to tiny **Angel Fire**. Return to Taos on US-64 W to end the tour.

Sedona/Grand Canyon NP★★★
482 miles/776 kilometers   Maps 249, 54, 47, 213

Drive N from **Phoenix★** on I-17 to Exit 298 and take Rte. 179 N toward **Sedona★★** in the heart of **Red Rock Country★★★**. The red-rock formations are best accessed by four-wheel-drive vehicle via 12mi **Schnebly Hill Road★** (off Rte. 179, across Oak Creek bridge from US 89A "Y" junction), which offers splendid **views★★★**. Then head N on Rte. 89A through Sedona to begin 14mi drive of **Oak Creek Canyon★★**. Continue N on Rte. 89A and I-17 to **Flagstaff★**, commercial hub for the region. Take US-180 NW to Rte. 64, which leads N to the **South Rim★★★** of **Grand Canyon NP★★★**. Take the shuttle (or drive, if permitted) along **West Rim Drive★★** to **Hermits Rest★**. Then travel **East Rim Drive★★★** (Rte. 64 E) to **Desert View Watchtower★** for **views★★★** of the canyon. Continue to the junction with US-89 at Cameron. Return S to Flagstaff, then S to Phoenix via I-17.

Grand Canyon NP

NORTHEAST

The Berkshires★★★
57 miles/92 kilometers   Map 94

From **Great Barrington**, take US-23 E to Monterey, turning left onto Tyringham Rd., which becomes Monterey Rd., to experience scenic **Tyringham Valley★**. Continue N on Main Rd. to Tyringham Rd., which leads to **Lee**, famous for its marble. Then go NW on US-20 to **Lenox★**, with its inviting inns and restaurants. Detour on Rte. 183 W to **Tanglewood★**, site of a popular summer music festival. Return to Lenox and drive N on US-7 to **Pittsfield**, the commercial capital of the region. Head W on US-20 to enjoy **Hancock Shaker Village★★★**, a museum village that relates the history of a Shaker community established here in 1790. Rte. 41 S passes West Stockbridge, then opt for Rte. 102 SE to **Stockbridge★★** and its picturesque **Main Street★**. Follow US-7 S to the junction with Rte. 23, passing **Monument Mountain★** en route. Return to Great Barrington.

Cape Cod★★★
164 miles/264 kilometers   Maps 151, 95

At US-6 and Rte. 3, cross **Cape Cod Canal** via Sagamore Bridge and turn onto Rte. 6A to tour the Cape's **North Shore★★**. Bear right onto Rte. 130 to reach **Sandwich★**, famous for glass manufacture. Continue on Rte. 6A E to **Orleans**. Take US-6 N along **Cape Cod National Seashore★★★**, with its wooded and marshland trails, to reach **Provincetown★★**, a resort town offering **dune tours★★** and summer theater. Return to Orleans and take Rte. 28 S through **Chatham★**, then W to **Hyannis**, where ferries depart for **Nantucket★★★**. Continue to quaint **Falmouth★**. Take Surf Rd., which becomes Oyster Pond Rd. to nearby **Woods Hole**, a world center for marine research and departure point for ferries to **Martha's Vineyard★★**. Take Woods Hole Rd. N to Rte. 28. Cross the canal via Bourne Bridge and head E on US-6 to end the tour at Rte. 3.

Maine Coast★★
238 miles/383 kilometers   Maps 82, 251, 83

From **Kittery**, drive N on US-1 to **York★**, then along US-1A to see the 18C buildings of **Colonial York★★**. Continue N on coastal US-1A to **Ogunquit★**. Rejoin US-1 and head N to Rte. 9, turn right, and drive to **Kennebunkport**, with its colorful shops. Take Rte. 9A/35 to **Kennebunk**. Then travel N on US-1 to **Portland★★**, Maine's largest city, where the **Old Port★★** brims with galleries and boutiques. Take US-1 N through the outlet town of **Freeport**, then on to **Brunswick**, home of **Bowdoin College**. Turn NE through **Bath★**, **Wiscasset**, **Rockland**, **Camden★★**, **Searsport** and **Bucksport**. At Ellsworth, take Rt. 3 S to enter **Acadia NP★★★** on **Mount Desert Island★★★**, where **Park Loop Road★★★** *(closed in winter)* parallels open coast. From the top of **Cadillac Mountain★★★**, the **views★★★** are breathtaking. The tour ends at **Bar Harbor★**, a popular resort village.

Bar Harbor from Cadillac Mountain

Mohawk Valley★
114 miles/184 kilometers   Maps 188, 94, 80

From the state capital of **Albany★**, take I-90 NW to Exit 25 for I-890 into **Schenectady**, founded by Dutch settlers in 1661. Then follow Rte. 5 W along the Mohawk River. In Fort Hunter, **Schoharie Crossing SHS★** stretches along a canal towpath. Near Little Falls, **Herkimer Home SHS** (Rte. 169 at Thruway Exit 29A) interprets colonial farm life. Rte. 5 continues W along the Erie Canal to **Utica**. From Utica, drive W on Rte. 49 to **Rome**, where the river turns N and peters out. The tour ends in Rome, site of **Fort Stanwix NM★**.

South Shore Lake Superior★
530 miles/853 kilometers   Maps 211, 64, 65, 69

From **Duluth★**, drive SE on I-535/US-53 to the junction of Rte. 13 at Parkland. Follow Rte. 13 E to quaint **Bayfield**, gateway to **Apostle Islands NL★★**, accessible by boat. Head S to the junction of US-2, and E through Ashland, Ironwood and Wakefield. There, turn left onto Rte. 28, heading NE to Bergland, and turning left onto Rte. 64. Drive N to Silver City and take Rte. M-107 W into **Porcupine Mountains Wilderness SP★**. Return to Rte. 64 and go E to Ontonagon. Take Rte. 38 SE to Greenland, then follow Rte. 26 NE to Houghton. Cross to Hancock on US-41 and continue NE to Phoenix. Turn left onto Rte. 26 to Eagle River and on to Copper Harbor via **Brockway Mountain Drive★★**. Return S to Houghton via US-41, then travel S and E past Marquette, turning left onto Rte. 28. Head E to Munising, then take County Road H-58 E and N through **Pictured Rocks NL★**. End the tour at Grand Marais.

Villages of Southern Vermont★★
118 miles/190 kilometers   Map 81

Head N from the resort town of **Manchester★** by Rte. 7A. At Manchester Center, take Rte. 11 E past **Bromley Mountain**, a popular ski area, to Peru. Turn left on the back road to **Weston★**, a favorite tourist stop along Rte. 100. Continue to **Chester**, turning right onto Rte. 35 S to reach **Grafton★**, with its **Old Tavern**. Farther S, Rte. 30 S from Townshend leads to **Newfane** and its lovely village **green★**. Return to Townshend, then travel W, following Rte. 30 through West Townshend, passing **Stratton Mountain** en route to Manchester. S of Manchester by Rte. 7A, the crest of Mt. Equinox is accessible via **Equinox Skyline Drive** (fee). Then continue S on Rte. 7A to end the tour at **Arlington**, known for its trout fishing.

The White Mountains★★★
127 miles/204 kilometers   Map 81

From the all-season resort of **Conway**, drive N on Rte. 16 to **North Conway★**, abundant with tourist facilities. Continue N on US-302/Rte. 16 through **Glen**, passing **Glen Ellis Falls★** and **Pinkham Notch★★** en route to Glen House. There, drive the **Auto Road** to the top of **Mount Washington★★★** (or take guided van tour). Head N on Rte. 16 to Gorham, near the Androscoggin River, then W on US-2 to Jefferson Highlands. Travel SW on Rte. 115 to Carroll, then S on US-3 to Twin Mountain. Go SW on US-3 to join I-93. Head S on I-93/Rte.3, passing scenic **Franconia Notch★★★** and **Profile Lake★★**. Bear E on Rte. 3 where it separates from the interstate to visit **The Flume★★**, a natural gorge 90ft deep. Rejoin I-93S to the intersection with Rte. 112. Head E on Rte. 112 through **Lincoln** on the **Kancamagus Highway★★★** until it joins Rte. 16 back to Conway.

SOUTHEAST

Blue Ridge Parkway★★
574 miles/924 kilometers   Maps 102, 112, 111, 190, 121

From **Front Royal**, take US-340 S to begin **Skyline Drive★★**, the best-known feature of **Shenandoah NP★★**. The drive follows former Indian trails along the **Blue Ridge Parkway★★**. **Marys Rock Tunnel to Rockfish Entrance Station★★** passes the oldest rock in the park and **Big Meadows★**. The Drive ends at **Rockfish Gap** at I-64, but continue S on the Parkway. From Terrapin Hill Overlook, detour 16mi W on Rte. 130 to see **Natural Bridge★★**. Enter NC at **Cumberland Knob**, then pass **Blowing Rock★**, **Grandfather Mountain★★** and **Linville Falls★★**. Detour 4.8mi to **Mount Mitchell SP★** to drive to the top of the tallest mountain (6,684ft) E of the Mississippi. At mile 382, the **Folk Art Center** stocks high-quality regional crafts. Popular **Biltmore Estate★★** in **Asheville★** (North Exit of US-25, then 4mi N) includes formal **gardens★★**. The rugged stretch from **French Broad River to Cherokee** courses 17 tunnels within two national forests. **Looking Glass Rock★★** is breathtaking. The Parkway ends at **Cherokee**, gateway to **Great Smoky Mountains NP★★★** and home of Cherokee tribe members.

Central Kentucky★★
379 miles/610 kilometers   Maps 230, 100, 214, 227, 110

From **Louisville★★**, home of the **Kentucky Derby★★★**, take I-64 E to **Frankfort**, the state capital. Continue E to **Lexington★★**, heart of **Bluegrass Country★★** with its rolling meadows and white-fenced horse farms. Stop at the **Kentucky Horse Park★★★** (4089 Iron Works Pkwy.) for the daily **Parade of Breeds**. Then head S on I-75 through Richmond to the craft center/college town of **Berea★**. Return to Lexington and follow the Blue Grass Parkway SW to Exit 25. There, US-150 W leads to Bardstown, site of **My Old Kentucky Home SP★**, immortalized by **Stephen Foster** in what is now the state song. Drive S from Bardstown on US-31E past **Abraham Lincoln Birthplace NHS★**. Turn right onto Rte. 70 to Cave City, then take US-31W to Park City, gateway to **Mammoth Cave NP★★★**, which features the world's longest cave system. Return to Louisville via I-65 to end the tour.

Florida's Northeast Coast★★
174 miles/280 kilometers   Maps 222, 139, 141, 232

From **Jacksonville★**, drive E on Rte. 10 to **Atlantic Beach**, the most affluent of Jacksonville's beach towns. Head S on Rte. A1A through residential **Neptune Beach**, blue-collar **Jacksonville Beach** and upscale **Ponte Vedra Beach** to reach **St. Augustine★★★**, the oldest city in the US and former capital of Spanish Florida. Farther S, car-racing mecca **Daytona Beach** is known for its **international speedway**. Take US-92 across the Intracoastal Waterway to US-1, heading S to **Titusville**. Take Rte. 402 across the Indian River to **Merritt Island NWR★★** to begin **Black Point Wildlife Drive★**. Return to Titusville and follow Rte. 405 to **Kennedy Space Center★★★**, one of Florida's top attractions, to end the tour.

Florida Keys★★
168 miles/270 kilometers   Maps 143, 142

*Note: Green **mile-marker** (MM) posts, sometimes difficult to see, line US-1 (Overseas Hwy.), showing distances from Key West (MM 0). Much of the route is two-lane, and traffic can be heavy in December to April and on weekends. Allow 3hrs for the drive.* Crossing 43 bridges and causeways (only one over land), the highway offers fine views of the Atlantic Ocean (E) and Florida Bay (W). Drive S from **Miami★★★** on US-1. Near **Key Largo★**, **John Pennekamp Coral Reef SP★★** harbors tropical fish, coral and fine snorkeling waters. To the SW, **Islamorada** is known for **charter fishing**. At **Marathon** (MM 50), **Sombrero Beach** is a good swimming spot, but **Bahia Honda SP★★** (MM 36.8) is considered the best **beach★★** in the Keys. Pass **National Key Deer Refuge★** (MM 30.5), haven to the 2ft-tall deer unique to the lower Keys. End at **Key West★★★**, joining others at **Mallory Square Dock** to view the **sunset★★**.

Florida Keys

The Ozarks★
343 miles/552 kilometers   Maps 227, 117, 219, 107, 106

From the state capital of **Little Rock**, take I-30 SW to Exit 111, then US-70 W to Hot Springs. Drive N on Rte. 7/Central Ave. to **Hot Springs NP★★** to enjoy the therapeutic waters. Travel N on Rte. 7 across the Arkansas River to Russellville. Continue on **Scenic Highway 7★** N through **Ozark National Forest** and across the **Buffalo National River** to Harrison. Take US-62/65 NW to Bear Creek Springs, continuing W on US-62 through **Eureka Springs★**, with its **historic district**, to **Pea Ridge NMP★**, a Civil War site. Return E on US-62 to the junction of Rte. 21 at Berryville. Travel N on Rte. 21 to Blue Eye, taking Rte. 86 E to US-65, which leads N to the entertainment hub of **Branson**, Missouri, to end the tour.

River Road Plantations★★
200 miles/323 kilometers   Maps 239, 134, 194

From **New Orleans★★★**, take US-90 W to Rte. 48 along the Mississippi River to Destrehan. At no. 13034, **Destrehan★★** is considered the oldest plantation house in the Mississippi Valley. Continue NW on Rte. 48 to US-61 to Laplace to connect to Rte. 44. Head N past **San Francisco Plantation★**, built in 1856. At Burnside, take Rte. 75 N to St. Gabriel. En route, watch for **Houmas House★** (40136 Hwy. 942). Take Rte. 30 to **Baton Rouge★**, the state capital. Then drive S along the **West Bank★★** on Rte. 1 to White Castle, site of **Nottoway★**, the largest plantation home in the South. Continue to Donaldsonville, then turn onto Rte. 18. Travel E to Gretna, passing **Oak Alley★** (no. 3645) and **Laura Plantation★★** (no. 2247) along the way. From Gretna, take US-90 to New Orleans, where the tour ends.

CANADA

Gaspésie, Québec★★★
933 kilometers/578 miles   Maps 178, 179

Leave **Sainte-Flavie** via Rte. 132 NE, stopping to visit **Reford Gardens★★** en route to **Matane**. After **Cap-Chat**, take Rte. 299 S to **Gaspésie Park★** for expansive **views★★**. Back on Rte. 132, follow the **Scenic Route from La Martre to Rivière-au-Renard★★**. Continue to **Cap-des-Rosiers**, entrance to majestic **Forillon NP★★**. Follow Rte. 132 along the coast through **Gaspé**, the administrative center of the peninsula, to **Percé★★★**, a coastal village known for **Percé Rock★★**, a mammoth offshore rock wall. Drive SW on Rt. 132 through **Paspébiac** to **Carleton**, which offers a **panorama★★** from the summit of **Mont Saint-Joseph**. Farther SW, detour 6km/4mi S to see an array of fossils at **Parc de Miguasha★**. Back on Rte. 132, travel W to Matapédia, then follow Rte. 132 N, passing **Causapscal**—a departure point for salmon fishing expeditions—to end the tour at Sainte-Flavie.

North Shore Lake Superior★★
275 kilometers/171 miles   Map 169

From the port city of **Thunder Bay★★**—and nearby **Old Fort William★★**—drive the Trans-Canada Hwy. (Rte. 11/17) E to Rte. 587. Detour to **Sleeping Giant PP★**, which offers fine **views★** of the lake. Back along the Trans-Canada Hwy., **Amethyst Mine** (take E. Loon Rd.) is a rock hound's delight (fee). Farther NE, located 12km/8mi off the highway, **Ouimet Canyon★★** is a startling environment for the area. Just after the highway's Red Rock turnoff, watch for **Red Rock Cuesta**, a natural formation 210m/690ft high. Cross the Nipigon River and continue along **Nipigon Bay★★**, enjoying **views★★** of the rocky, conifer-covered islands. The **view★★** of Kama Bay through Kama Rock Cut is striking. Continue to Schreiber to end the tour.

Nova Scotia's Cabot Trail★★
338 kilometers/210 miles   Map 181

From **Baddeck★**, follow Hwy. 105 S to the junction with the road to **North East Margaree** in salmon-fishing country. Take this road NW to Margaree Harbour, then N to **Chéticamp**, an enclave of Acadian culture. Heading inland, the route enters **Cape Breton Highlands NP★★**, combining seashore and mountains. At Cape North, detour N around Aspy Bay to **Bay St. Lawrence★★**. Then head W to tiny **Capstick** for shoreline **views★**. Return S to Cape North, then drive E to South Harbour. Take the coast road, traveling S through the fishing villages of **New Haven** and **Neils Harbour★**. Rejoin Cabot Trail S, passing the resort area of the **Ingonishs**. Take the right fork after Indian Brook to reach St. Ann's, home of **Gaelic College★**, specializing in bagpipe and Highland dance classes. Rejoin Hwy. 105 to return to Baddeck.

Capstick

Lake Louise

Canadian Rockies★★★
467 kilometers/290 miles   Map 164

Leave **Banff★★** by Hwy. 1, traveling W. After 5.5km/3.5mi, take **Bow Valley Parkway★** (Hwy. 1A) NW within **Banff NP★★★**. At **Lake Louise Village**, detour W to find **Lake Louise★★★**. Back on Hwy. 1, head N to the junction of Hwy. 93, turn W and follow Hwy. 1 past **Kicking Horse Pass** into **Yoho NP★★**. Continue through **Field**, and turn right onto the road N to **Emerald Lake★★★**. Return to the junction of Rte. 93 and Hwy. 1, heading N on Rte. 93 along the **Icefields Parkway★★★**. Pass **Crowfoot Glacier★★** and **Bow Lake★★** on the left. **Peyto Lake★★★** is reached by spur road. After **Parker Ridge★★**, massive **Athabasca Glacier★★★** looms on the left. Continue to **Jasper★** and **Jasper NP★★★**. From Jasper, turn left onto Hwy. 16 and head into **Mount Robson PP★★**, home to **Mount Robson★★★** (3,954m/12,972ft). End the tour at Tête Jaune Cache.

Vancouver Island★★★
337 kilometers/209 miles   Maps 282, 163, 162

To enjoy a scenic drive that begins 11mi N of **Victoria★★★**, take Douglas St. N from Victoria to the Trans-Canada Highway (Hwy. 1) and follow **Malahat Drive★** (between Goldstream PP and Mill Bay Rd.) for 12mi. Continue N on Hwy. 1 past Duncan, **Chemainus★**—known for its murals—and Nanaimo to Parksville. Take winding Rte. 4 W (Pacific Rim Hwy.) passing **Englishman River Falls PP★** and **Cameron Lake**. Just beyond the lake, **Cathedral Grove★★** holds 800-year-old Douglas firs. The road descends to **Port Alberni**, departure point for cruises on Barkley Sound, and follows Sproat Lake before climbing Klitsa Mountain. The route leads to the Pacific along the Kennedy River. At the coast, turn left and drive SE to Ucluelet. Then head N to enter **Pacific Rim NPR★★★**. Continue to road's end at **Tofino★** to end the tour.

Yukon Circuit★★
1,485 kilometers/921 miles   Map 155

From **Whitehorse★**, capital of Yukon Territory, drive N on the **Klondike Hwy.** (Rte. 2), crossing the Yukon River at **Carmacks**. After 196km/122mi, small islands divide the river into fast-flowing channels at **Five Finger Rapids★**. From Stewart Crossing, continue NW on Rte. 2 to **Dawson★★**, a historic frontier town. Ferry across the river and drive the **Top of the World Hwy.★★** (Rte. 9), with its **views★★★**, to the Alaska border. Rte. 9 joins Rte. 5, passing tiny **Chicken**, Alaska. At Tetlin Junction, head SE on Rte. 2, paralleling **Tetlin NWR**. Enter Canada and follow the **Alaska Highway★★** (Rte. 1) SE along **Kluane Lake★★** to **Haines Junction**, gateway to **Kluane NPR★★**, home of **Mount Logan**, Canada's highest peak (5,959m/19,550ft). Continue E to Rte. 2 to return to Whitehorse.

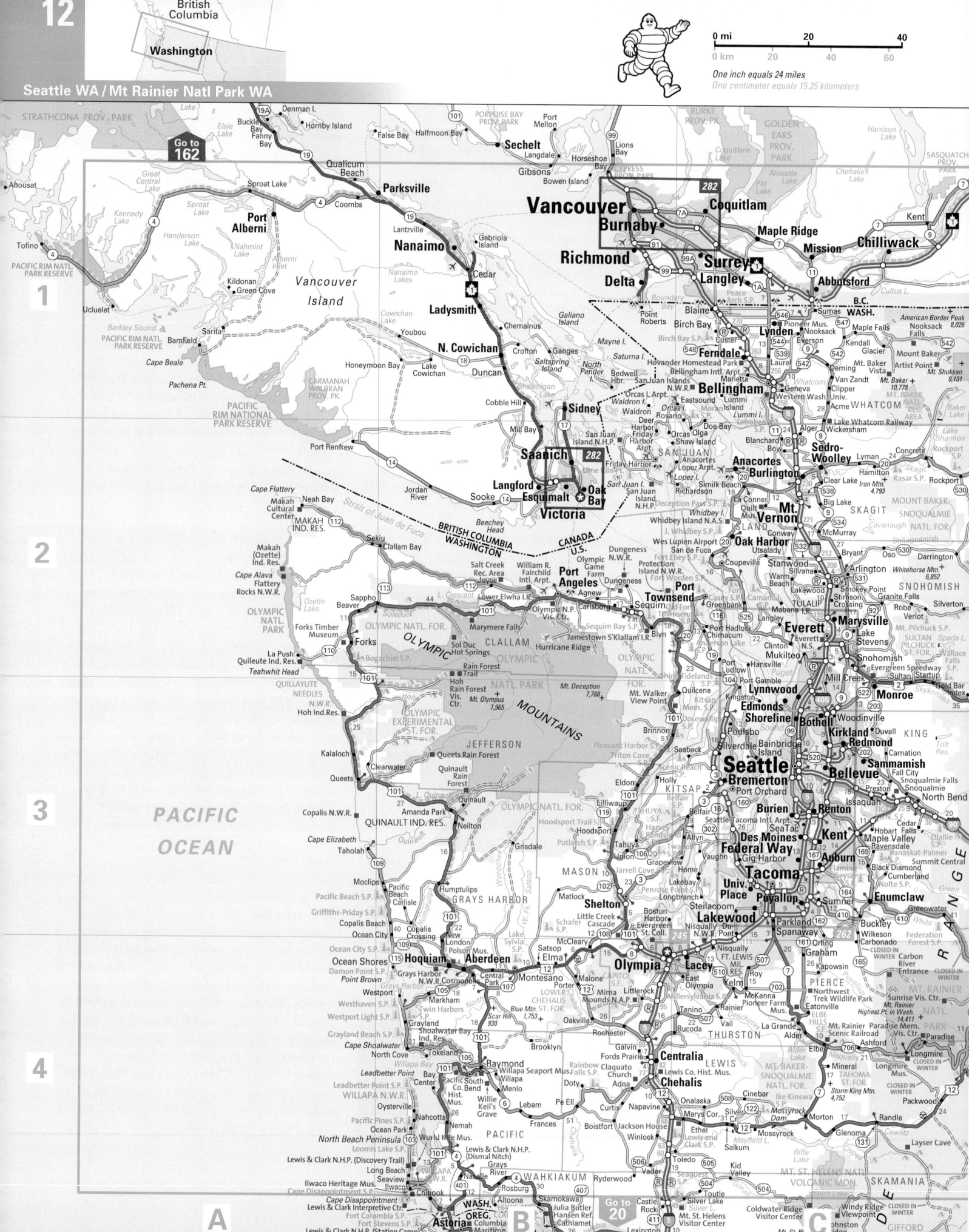

One inch equals 24 miles
One centimeter equals 15.25 kilometers

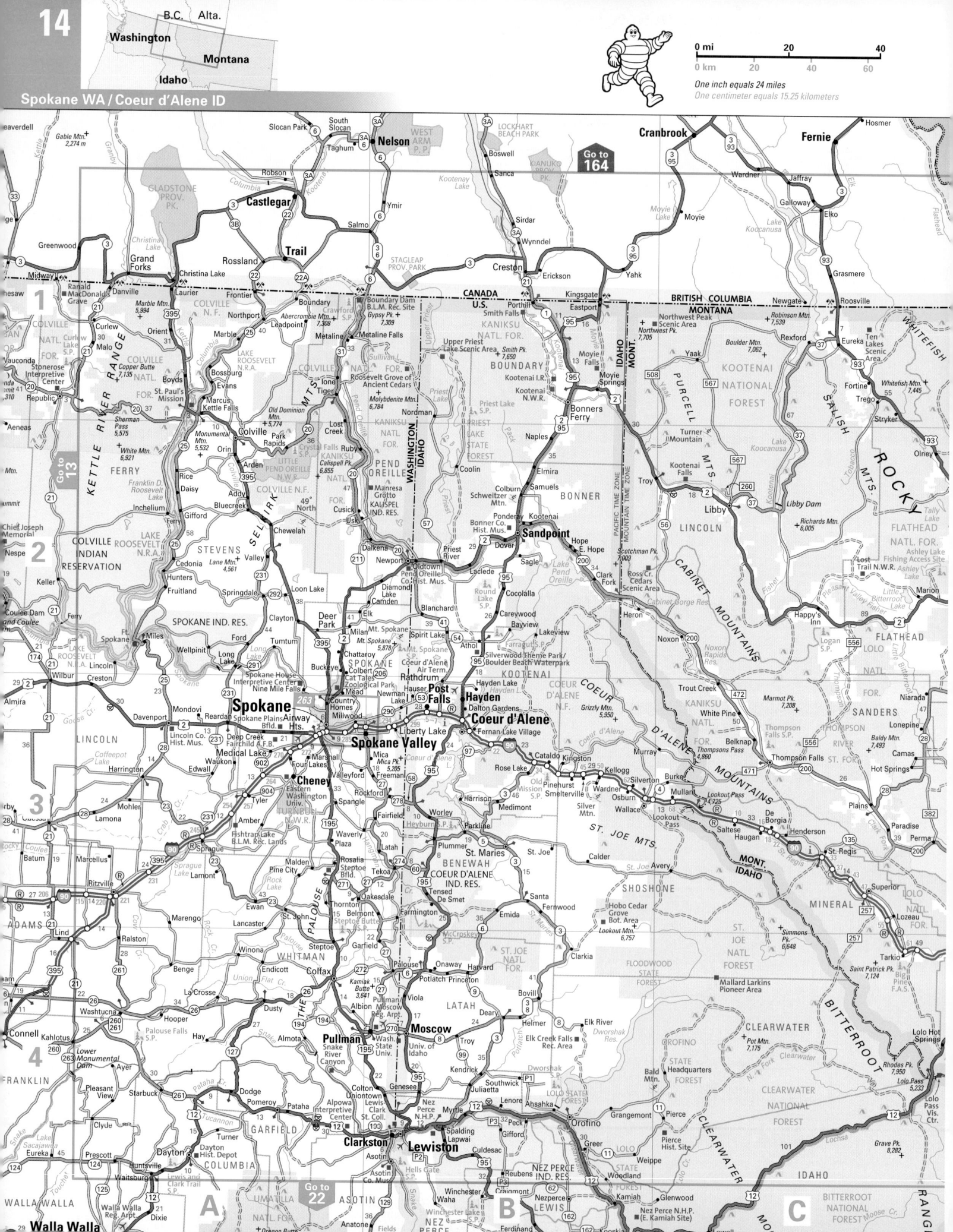

Go to 164

Go to 13

Go to 22

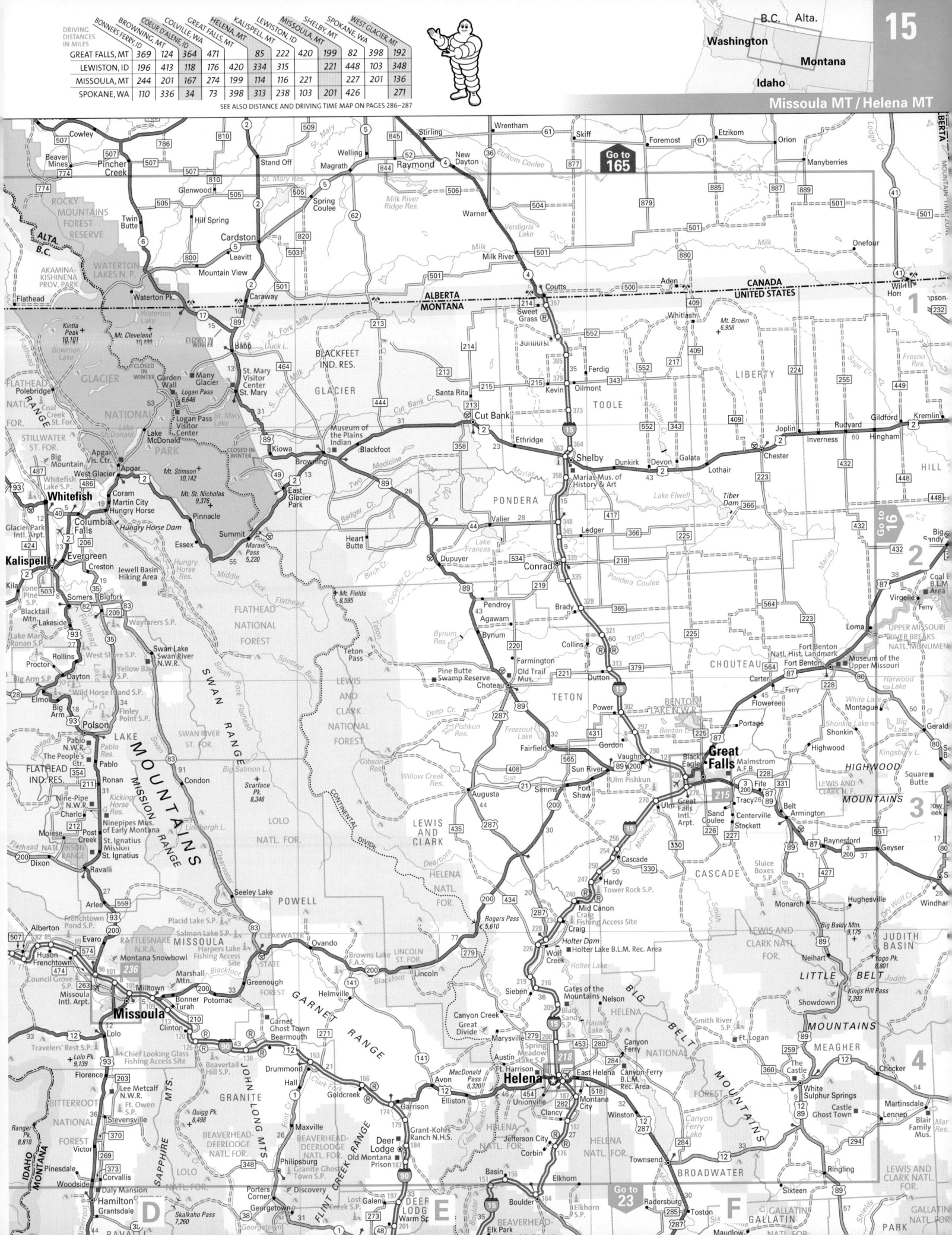

One inch equals 24 miles
One centimeter equals 15.25 kilometers

DRIVING DISTANCES IN MILES	GLENDIVE, MT	GREAT FALLS, MT	HARLOWTON, MT	HAVRE, MT	LEWISTOWN, MT	MALTA, MT	MILES CITY, MT	ROUNDUP, MT	SHELBY, MT	WILLISTON, ND	WOLF POINT, MT
GLENDIVE, MT	147		351	309	306	242	217	74	219	408	106	98
GREAT FALLS, MT	277	351		133	118	90	207	329	183	82	422	326
HAVRE, MT	159	306	118		210		175	89	345	198	102	304	208
WILLISTON, ND	145	106	422	415	304	324	215	180	325	406		96

SEE ALSO DISTANCE AND DRIVING TIME MAP ON PAGES 286–287

Sask.   Manitoba

North Dakota   Minnesota

0 mi   20   40
0 km   20   40   60

One inch equals 24 miles
One centimeter equals 15.25 kilometers

DRIVING DISTANCES IN MILES	BOTTINEAU, ND	DETROIT LAKES, MN	DICKINSON, ND	FARGO, ND	GRAND FORKS, ND	JAMESTOWN, ND	MINOT, ND	PEMBINA, ND	RUGBY, ND	THIEF RIVER FALLS, MN	WILLISTON, ND
BISMARCK, ND	189	244	97	199	274	105	116	347	153	319	229
FARGO, ND	199	271	45		291	79	97	268	152	221	424
GRAND FORKS, ND	274	198	125	367		79	173	212	77	148	61	340
MINOT, ND	116	76	313	178	268	212	171		238	64	276	128

SEE ALSO DISTANCE AND DRIVING TIME MAP ON PAGES 286–287

0 mi 20 40
0 km 20 40 60

One inch equals 24 miles
One centimeter equals 15.25 kilometers

PACIFIC OCEAN

Go to 12

WASHINGTON

LEWIS

WAHKIAKUM

COWLITZ

SKAMANIA

Pacific Pines S.P.
Ocean Park
North Beach Peninsula (103)
Loomis Lake S.P.
Long Beach
Seaview
Ilwaco Heritage Mus.
Ilwaco
Cape Disappointment
Cape Disappointment S.P.
Lewis & Clark Interpretive Center
Fort Columbia S.P.
Fort Stevens S.P.
Warrenton

Astoria
Astoria Column
Astoria Reg. Arpt.

Seaside
Gearhart
Seaside Nat. Area
Tillamook Head
Ecola S.P.
Tolovana Beach St. Rec. Site
Cannon Beach
Arcadia Beach St. Rec. Site
Hug Point St. Rec. Site
Arch Cape
Cape Falcon
Oswald West S.P.
Manzanita
Nehalem Bay S.P.
Manhattan Beach St. Rec. Site
Rockaway Beach
Rockaway Beach St. Rec. Site
Garibaldi
Tillamook Bay
Bay City

Cape Meares N.W.R.
Cape Meares St. Scenic Viewpoint
Oceanside
Three Arch Rocks N.W.R.
Netarts
Netarts Bay

Tillamook
Tillamook N.A.S. Mus.

Cape Lookout S.P.
Cape Lookout
Sandlake
Cape Kiwanda St. Natural Area
Cape Kiwanda
Pacific City
Hebo
Nestucca Bay N.W.R.
Robert Straub S.P.
Neskowin
Cascade Head
Neskowin Beach St. Rec. Site
Roads End St. Rec. Site
Neotsu
Otis

Lincoln City
Siletz Bay N.W.R.
Gleneden Beach St. Rec. Site
Fogarty Creek St. Rec. Area
Government Point
Depoe Bay
Otter Crest St. Scenic Viewpoint
Devil's Punchbowl St. Nat. Area
Beverly Beach S.P.
Yaquina Head Lighthouse
Otter Rock
Siletz

Newport
Oregon Coast Aquarium
Yaquina Bay
South Beach
South Beach S.P.
Lost Creek St. Rec. Site
Ona Beach S.P.
Lost Creek St. Rec. Site
Seal Rock St. Rec. Site
Seal Rock
Gov. Patterson Mem. St. Rec. Site
Beachside St. Rec. Site
Waldport
Alsea Bay
Tidewater
Smelt Sands St. Rec. Site
Yachats
Yachats St. Rec. Area
Cape Perpetua Scenic Area
Neptune St. Scenic Viewpoint
Stonefield Beach St. Rec. Area
M.O. Ponsler Mem. St. Scenic Viewpoint
Carl G. Washburne Mem. S.P.
Heceta Head Lighthouse St. Scenic Viewpoint
Sea Lion Caves
Darlingtonia St. Wayside
Heceta Beach

Florence
Cushman
Jessie M. Honeyman Mem. S.P.
Dunes City
Siltcoos
Siltcoos Recreation Corridor
OREGON DUNES NATL. REC. AREA
Bolon Island Tideway St. Scenic Corr.
Winchester Bay
Gardiner

Reedsport
Dean Cr. Elk Viewing Area
Scottsburg
William M. Tugman S.P.
Lakeside
OREGON DUNES NATL. REC. AREA
Hauser
North Bend Mun. Arpt.

North Bend
Coos Art Mus.
Coquille Ind. Res.

Coos Bay
Barview
Charleston
Sunset Bay S.P.
Shore Acres S.P.
Cape Arago S.P.
Seven Devils St. Rec. Area
Bullards Beach S.P.
Ile R. Lighthouse
Bandon March N.W.R.
Coquille
Riverton
Fairview
Dora

Longview
Kelso
Castle Rock
Silver Lake
Mt. St. Helens Visitor Center
Coldwater Ridge Visitor Center
Windy Ridge Viewpoint
Johnston Ridge Vis. Ctr.
Mt. St. Helens 8,366

St. Helens
Warren
Columbia City
Scappoose

Vancouver
Portland
Gresham
Beaverton
Hillsboro
Forest Grove
Tigard
Tualatin
Sherwood
Lake Oswego
West Linn
Wilsonville
Oregon City
Canby
Newberg
Dundee
Lafayette
McMinnville
Amity
Sheridan
Willamina
Dallas
Salem
Keizer
Four Corners
Independence
Monmouth
Stayton
Jefferson
Scio

Albany
Corvallis
Philomath
Lebanon
Sweet Home
Cascadia
Harrisburg
Junction City
Santa Clara
Coburg
Eugene
Springfield
Goshen
Creswell
Cottage Grove
Lorane
Drain
Yoncalla
Sutherlin
Oakland
Roseburg

Go to 28

CASCADE RANGE

COAST RANGES

WILLAMETTE NATL. FOREST

SIUSLAW NATIONAL FOREST

UMPQUA NATL. FOREST

Mt. Hood 11,239
Mt. Jefferson 10,497
Mt. Washington 7,794
Three Sisters
Mt. Bachelor 9,065

CLACKAMAS
MARION
LINN
LANE
BENTON
POLK
YAMHILL
TILLAMOOK
CLATSOP
COLUMBIA
LINCOLN
COOS
DOUGLAS

DRIVING DISTANCES IN MILES	ASTORIA, OR	BEND, OR	BURNS, OR	COOS BAY, OR	EUGENE, OR	KENNEWICK, WA	LA GRANDE, OR	NEWPORT, OR	PORTLAND, OR	SALEM, OR	THE DALLES, OR	WALLA WALLA, WA
BEND, OR	252		142	227	115	245	295	183	158	134	137	276
EUGENE, OR	216	115	257	105		328	377	101	112	65	198	359
KENNEWICK, WA	306	245	256	440	328		111	328	212	264	131	49
PORTLAND, OR	97	158	299	224	112	212	261	116		48	82	243

SEE ALSO DISTANCE AND DRIVING TIME MAP ON PAGES 286–287

Washington
Montana
Oregon
Idaho
Wyoming

One inch equals 24 miles
One centimeter equals 15.25 kilometers

DRIVING DISTANCES IN MILES	BOISE, ID	BOZEMAN, MT	BUTTE, MT	GRANGEVILLE, ID	HAMILTON, MT	IDAHO FALLS, ID	JACKSON, WY	LA GRANDE, OR	ONTARIO, OR	SALMON, ID	SUN VALLEY, ID	W. YELLOWSTONE, MT
BOISE, ID		485	486	202	339	288	378	170	58	247	163	395
BUTTE, MT	486	81		290	103	203	275	566	541	150	312	162
IDAHO FALLS, ID	288	199	203	483	272		92	455	342	168	153	109
W. YELLOWSTONE, MT	395	90	162	451	264	109	128	562	449	244	252	

SEE ALSO DISTANCE AND DRIVING TIME MAP ON PAGES 286–287

DRIVING DISTANCES IN MILES	BILLINGS, MT	BOZEMAN, MT	BUFFALO, WY	CODY, WY	GILLETTE, WY	JACKSON, WY	MILES CITY, MT	RAPID CITY, SD	SHERIDAN, WY	SPEARFISH, SD	W. YELLOWSTONE, MT	WORLAND, WY
BILLINGS, MT		141	165	111	233	287	144	379	131	333	232	161
BUFFALO, WY	165	306		180	70	342	237	216	34	170	396	91
SPEARFISH, SD	333	474	170	350	100	512	186	53	202		564	261
W. YELLOWSTONE, MT	232	90	396	147	464	128	376	610	363	564		236

SEE ALSO DISTANCE AND DRIVING TIME MAP ON PAGES 286–287

Montana | North Dakota
Idaho
Wyoming | South Dakota

SEE ALSO DISTANCE AND DRIVING TIME MAP ON PAGES 286–287

North Dakota · Minnesota · South Dakota · Iowa

Oregon

California Nevada

0 mi | 20 | 40
0 km | 20 | 40 | 60
One inch equals 24 miles
One centimeter equals 15.25 kilometers

TRAVEL NOTE: California has started numbering freeway exits using a mileage-based numbering system (shown here). Full implementation is expected to take several years.

PACIFIC OCEAN

Go to 20

Go to 36

Major places and labels:

North Bend, Coos Bay, Charleston, Barview, Bunker Hill, Sumner, Fairview, Coquille, Riverton, Bandon, Norway, Myrtle Point, Bridge, Gaylord, Powers, Remote, Camas Valley, Riddle, Tri-City, Days Creek, Milo, Canyonville, Anchor, Drew, Tiller, Azalea, Glendale, Wolf Creek, Sunny Valley, Merlin, Hugo, Leland, Galice, Grants Pass, Wilderville, Murphy, Williams, Applegate, Ruch, Jacksonville, Central Point, Medford, Phoenix, Talent, Ashland, White City, Eagle Point, Lakecreek, Butte Falls, Trail, Prospect, Union Creek, Fort Klamath, Chiloquin, Klamath Falls, Altamont, Keno, Midland, Merrill, Dorris, Macdoel, Tennant, Weed, Mount Shasta, McCloud, Dunsmuir, Castella, Lamoine, Lakehead, Shasta Lake, Redding, Anderson, Cottonwood, Red Bluff, Yreka, Montague, Grenada, Gazelle, Edgewood, Etna, Fort Jones, Greenview, Callahan, Cecilville, Sawyers Bar, Forks of Salmon, Somes Bar, Orleans, Weitchpec, Hoopa, Willow Creek, Salyer, Denny, Burnt Ranch, Big Bar, Helena, Junction City, Weaverville, Lewiston, Douglas City, Hayfork, Hyampom, Peanut, Mad River, Ruth, Platina, Crescent City, Smith River, Gasquet, Klamath, Requa, Orick, Trinidad, McKinleyville, Arcata, Blue Lake, Korbel, Samoa, Eureka, Loleta, Ferndale, Fortuna, Hydesville, Carlotta, Bridgeville, Rio Dell, Scotia, Redcrest, Weott, Myers Flat, Miranda, Phillipsville, Honeydew, Petrolia, Redway, Garberville

COAST RANGE, KLAMATH MTS., SISKIYOU MTS., SISKIYOU NATL. FOR., KLAMATH NATL. FOR., SHASTA-TRINITY NATL. FOR., TRINITY NATL. FOR., SIX RIVERS NATL. FOR., REDWOOD NATL. PARK, WINEMA NATL. FOR., ROGUE RIVER NATL. FOR., UMPQUA NATL. FOR., CASCADE RANGE, DOUGLAS, JACKSON, JOSEPHINE, CURRY, COOS, DEL NORTE, HUMBOLDT, TRINITY, SHASTA, SISKIYOU, KLAMATH, TEHAMA

CALIFORNIA / OREGON

DRIVING DISTANCES IN MILES	ALTURAS, CA	CRATER LAKE NP, OR	CRESCENT CITY, CA	EUREKA, CA	KLAMATH FALLS, OR	LAKEVIEW, OR	LASSEN VOLCANIC NP, CA	MEDFORD, OR	REDDING, CA	ROSEBURG, OR	SUSANVILLE, CA	WINNEMUCCA, NV
LAKEVIEW, OR	56	153	282	332	98		192	171	199	265	161	212
MEDFORD, OR	176	80	111	192	76	171	208		148	94	221	383
REDDING, CA	143	198	189	133	141	199	63	148		242	114	364
SUSANVILLE, CA	105	226	303	247	170	161	74	221	114	315		250

SEE ALSO DISTANCE AND DRIVING TIME MAP ON PAGES 286–287

Wyoming
South Dakota
Nebraska
Utah
Colorado

0 mi   20   40
0 km   20   40   60
One inch equals 24 miles
One centimeter equals 15.25 kilometers

DRIVING DISTANCES IN MILES

	CASPER, WY	CHEYENNE, WY	CRAIG, CO	FORT COLLINS, CO	KEMMERER, WY	LANDER, WY	LARAMIE, WY	PINEDALE, WY	RAWLINS, WY	ROCK SPRINGS, WY	SCOTTSBLUFF, NE	VERNAL, UT
CASPER, WY		175	234	217	297	144	148	271	117	214	173	322
CHEYENNE, WY	175		221	44	342	276	52	355	151	260	111	367
CRAIG, CO	234	221		194	257	221	171	269	117	149	331	123
ROCK SPRINGS, WY	214	260	149	273	86	118	210	98	110		370	111

SEE ALSO DISTANCE AND DRIVING TIME MAP ON PAGES 286–287

Go to 29
Go to 30
Go to 38
Go to 45

DRIVING DISTANCES IN MILES

	AUSTIN, NV	CHICO, CA	MERCED, CA	RENO, NV	SACRAMENTO, CA	SAN FRANCISCO, CA	SAN JOSE, CA	S. LAKE TAHOE, CA	STOCKTON, CA	TONOPAH, NV	UKIAH, CA	YOSEMITE VIL., CA
RENO, NV	171	164	243		132	217	245	59	177	237	261	199
SACRAMENTO, CA	302	88	118	132		87	115	100	48	329	153	170
SAN FRANCISCO, CA	387	182	131	217	87		43	185	82	352	116	183
YOSEMITE VIL., CA	280	257	79	199	170	183	168	180	123	199	289	

SEE ALSO DISTANCE AND DRIVING TIME MAP ON PAGES 286–287

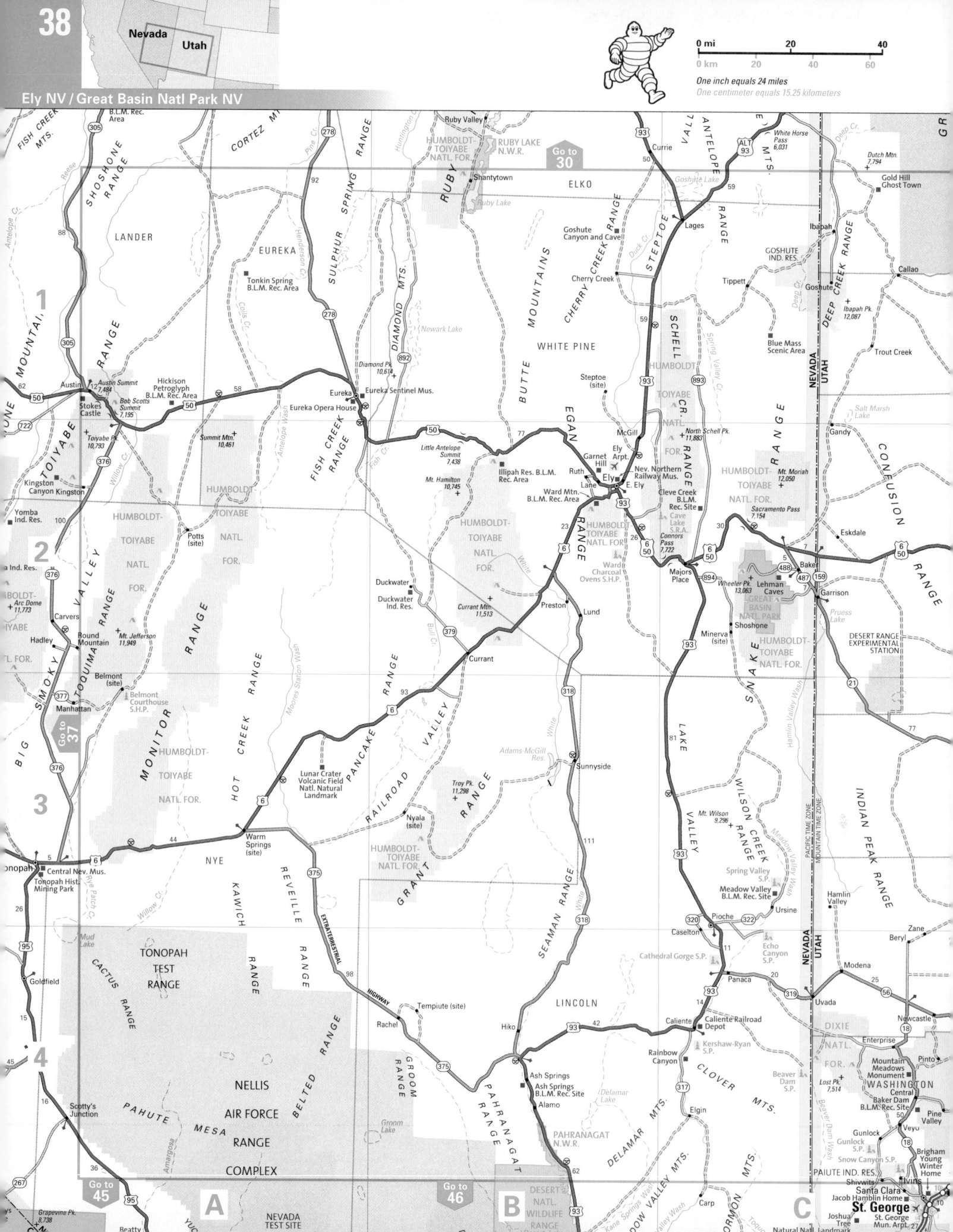

0 mi · 20 · 40
0 km · 20 · 40 · 60
One inch equals 24 miles
One centimeter equals 15.25 kilometers

FISH CREEK MTS.

B.L.M. Rec. Area

305

CORTEZ MTS.

278

SULPHUR SPRING RANGE

Ruby Valley

HUMBOLDT-TOIYABE NATL. FOR.

RUBY LAKE N.W.R.

Go to 30

White Horse Pass 6,031

ALT 93

93

Currie

ANTELOPE VALLEY

ANTELOPE RANGE

Dutch Mtn. 7,794

Gold Hill Ghost Town

SHOSHONE RANGE

92

Pine Cr.

Shantytown

Ruby Lake

ELKO

RUBY MTS.

50

Goshute Lake

GOSHUTE MTS.

Ibapah

Callao

LANDER

EUREKA

Henderson Cr.

DIAMOND MTS.

Goshute Canyon and Cave

Cherry Creek

CHERRY CREEK RANGE

Lages

59

Tippett

GOSHUTE IND. RES.

Goshute

DEEP CREEK RANGE

Ibapah Pk. 12,087

88

Tonkin Spring B.L.M. Rec. Area

278

Newark Lake

892

Diamond Pk. 10,614

WHITE PINE

BUTTE MOUNTAINS

59

Duck Cr.

STEPTOE VALLEY

93

SCHELL CR. RANGE

HUMBOLDT-TOIYABE NATL. FOR.

Steptoe (site)

893

North Schell Pk. 11,883

Blue Mass Scenic Area

NEVADA UTAH

Trout Creek

Salt Marsh Lake

62

50

305

Austin

Austin Summit 7,484

Hickison Petroglyph B.L.M. Rec. Area

58

Eureka

Eureka Sentinel Mus.

Eureka Opera House

50

77

Egan Cr.

Ely Arpt.

Nev. Northern Railway Mus.

McGill

Gandy

722

Stokes Castle

Bob Scotts Summit 7,195

50

Little Antelope Summit 7,438

Garnet Hill

Ruth

Ely

Lane

E. Ely

Mt. Moriah 12,050

Eskdale

CONFUSION RANGE

Toiyabe Pk. 10,793

Summit Mtn. 10,461

FISH CREEK RANGE

Mt. Hamilton 10,745

Illipah Res. B.L.M. Rec. Area

93

Cleve Creek B.L.M. Rec. Site

Sacramento Pass 7,154

HUMBOLDT-TOIYABE NATL. FOR.

6 50

Kingston Canyon Kingston

376

HUMBOLDT-TOIYABE NATL. FOR.

100

Ward Mtn. B.L.M. Rec. Area

EGAN RANGE

23

HUMBOLDT-TOIYABE NATL. FOR.

Cave Lake S.R.A.

Connors Pass 7,722

26

6 50

30

SNAKE RANGE

5

488

487

159

Baker

Yomba Ind. Res.

HUMBOLDT-TOIYABE NATL. FOR.

Potts (site)

Duckwater

Ward Charcoal Ovens S.H.P.

Majors Place

894

Wheeler Pk. 13,063

Lehman Caves

7

Garrison

Arc Dome 11,773

376

TOQUIMA RANGE

MONITOR RANGE

Duckwater Ind. Res.

Currant Mtn. 11,513

Preston

Lund

GREAT BASIN NATL. PARK

Minerva (site)

Shoshone

Pruess Lake

DESERT RANGE EXPERIMENTAL STATION

Carvers

Round Mountain

Mt. Jefferson 11,949

379

Currant

318

HUMBOLDT-TOIYABE NATL. FOR.

21

Hadley

BIG SMOKY VALLEY

SMOKY VALLEY

6

93

81

WILSON CREEK RANGE

Mt. Wilson 9,296

77

Belmont (site)

Belmont Courthouse S.H.P.

Adams-McGill Res.

LAKE VALLEY

Manhattan

377

Go to 37

376

HUMBOLDT-TOIYABE NATL. FOR.

6

PANCAKE RANGE

Lunar Crater Volcanic Field Natl. Natural Landmark

RAILROAD VALLEY

Sunnyside

Troy Pk. 11,298

GRANT RANGE

111

White R.

Spring Valley S.P.

Meadow Valley B.L.M. Rec. Site

Hamlin Valley

INDIAN PEAK RANGE

44

5

6

Warm Springs (site)

Nyala (site)

HUMBOLDT-TOIYABE NATL. FOR.

320

Pioche

322

Ursine

Zane

Beryl

Tonopah

Central Nev. Mus.

Tonopah Hist. Mining Park

NYE

KAWICH RANGE

375

REVEILLE RANGE

SEAMAN RANGE

Caselton

11

Echo Canyon S.P.

Modena

25

56

26

95

EXTRATERRESTRIAL HIGHWAY

98

318

Cathedral Gorge S.P.

Panaca

20

319

Uvada

DIXIE NATL. FOR.

Newcastle

18

15

Goldfield

Mud Lake

CACTUS RANGE

BELTED RANGE

Tempiute (site)

Rachel

LINCOLN

93

14

Caliente

Caliente Railroad Depot

317

Kershaw-Ryan S.P.

Enterprise

Pinto

45

5

Scotty's Junction

267

16

TONOPAH TEST RANGE

PAHUTE MESA

NELLIS AIR FORCE RANGE COMPLEX

Amargosa R.

GROOM RANGE

Groom Lake

Hiko

Ash Springs

Ash Springs B.L.M. Rec. Site

Alamo

375

Delamar Lake

PAHRANAGAT RANGE

PAHRANAGAT N.W.R.

DELAMAR MTS.

Rainbow Canyon

Elgin

93

42

CLOVER MTS.

Beaver Dam S.P.

Lost Pk. 7,514

MOUNTAIN MEADOWS MONUMENT

Mountain Meadows Monument

WASHINGTON

Central

Baker Dam B.L.M. Rec. Site

Veyo

Pine Valley

Gunlock

Gunlock S.P.

Snow Canyon S.P.

Brigham Young Winter Home

Santa Clara

Ivins

PAIUTE IND. RES.

St. George

St. George Mun. Arpt.

Shivwits

Jacob Hamblin Home

Joshua Tree

Natural Natl. Landmark

Grapevine Pk. 8,738

36

95

Go to 45

Go to 46

NEVADA TEST SITE

DESERT NATL. WILDLIFE RANGE

62

93

18

50

A · B · C

1 · 2 · 3 · 4

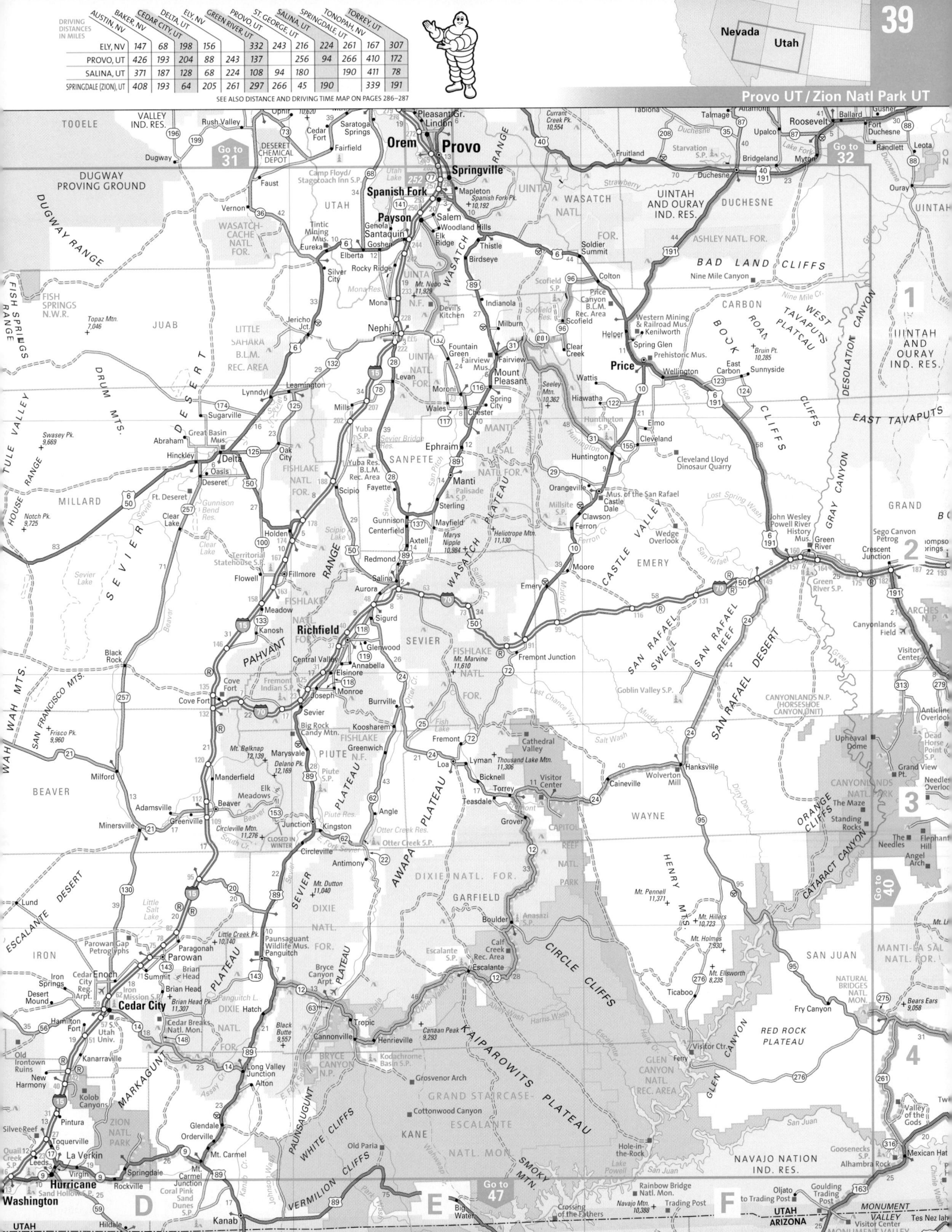

DRIVING DISTANCES IN MILES	AUSTIN, NV	BAKER, NV	CEDAR CITY, UT	DELTA, UT	ELY, NV	GREEN RIVER, UT	PROVO, UT	ST. GEORGE, UT	SALINA, UT	SPRINGDALE, UT	TONOPAH, NV	TORREY, UT
ELY, NV	147	68	198	156		332	243	216	224	261	167	307
PROVO, UT	426	193	204	88	243	137		256	94	266	410	172
SALINA, UT	371	187	128	68	224	108	94	180		190	411	78
SPRINGDALE (ZION), UT	408	193	64	205	261	297	266	45	190		339	191

SEE ALSO DISTANCE AND DRIVING TIME MAP ON PAGES 286–287

Utah
Colorado

0 mi ____ 20 ____ 40
0 km __ 20 __ 40 __ 60
One inch equals 24 miles
One centimeter equals 15.25 kilometers

DRIVING DISTANCES IN MILES	ASPEN, CO	ALAMOSA, CO	COLORADO SPRS., CO	CORTEZ, CO	DENVER, CO	DURANGO, CO	GRAND JUNCTION, CO	GREEN RIVER, UT	MOAB, UT	MONTROSE, CO	PUEBLO, CO	TRINIDAD, CO
COLORADO SPRS., CO	162	157		359	70	314	318	404	236	43		127
DENVER, CO	230	164	70	452		337	250	350	337	277	111	196
DURANGO, CO	152	244	314	45	337		169	214	160	107	271	260
GRAND JUNCTION, CO	261	135	318	203	250	169		102	88	62	360	444

SEE ALSO DISTANCE AND DRIVING TIME MAP ON PAGES 286–287

Utah Colorado

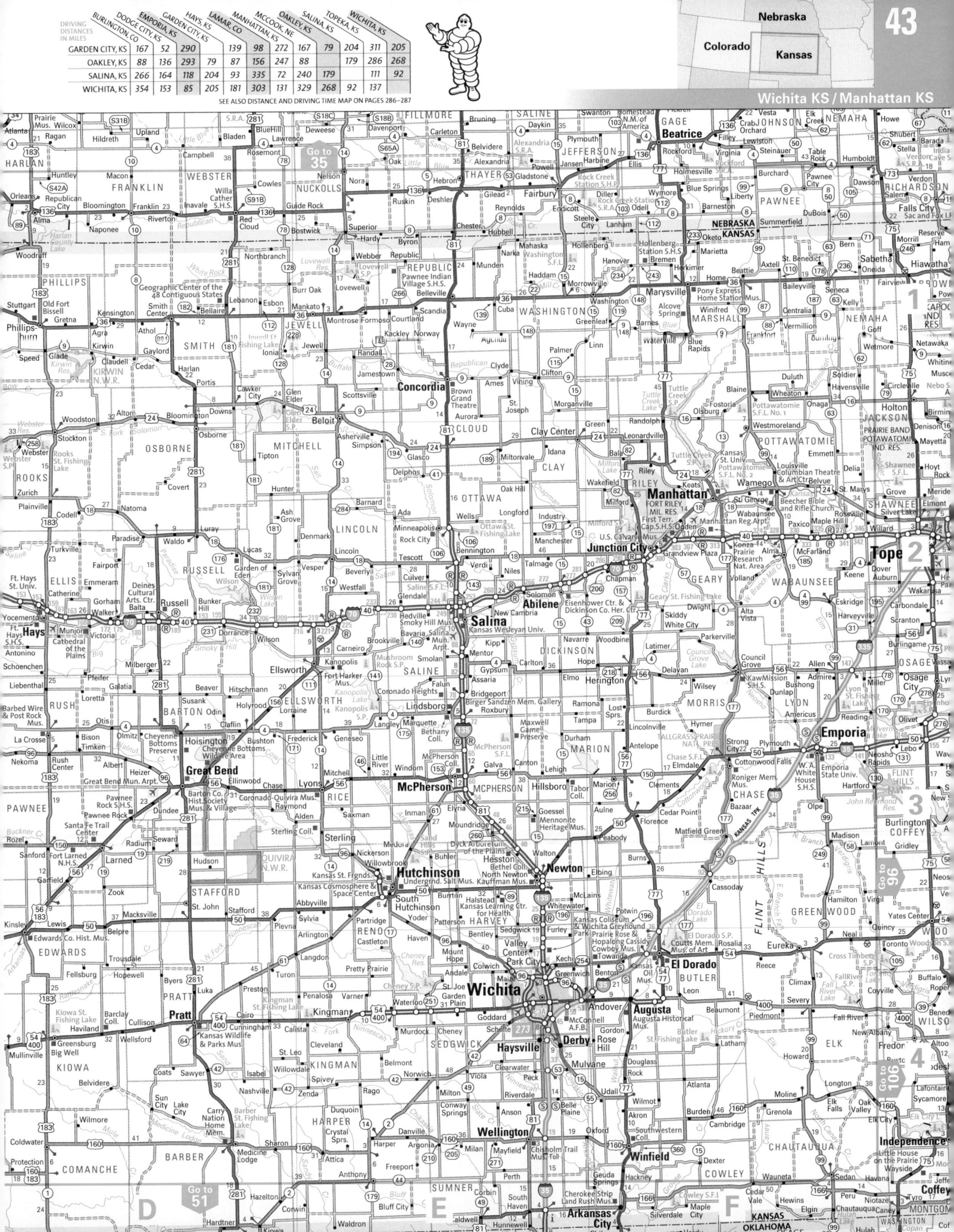

Go to 35
Go to 96
Go to 106
Go to 51

DRIVING DISTANCES IN MILES	BURLINGTON, CO	DODGE CITY, KS	EMPORIA, KS	GARDEN CITY, KS	HAYS, KS	LAMAR, CO	MANHATTAN, KS	McCOOK, NE	OAKLEY, KS	SALINA, KS	TOPEKA, KS	WICHITA, KS
GARDEN CITY, KS	167	52	290			139	98	272	167	79	204	311	205
OAKLEY, KS	88	136	293	79	87	156	247	88		179	286	268
SALINA, KS	266	164	118	204	93	335	72	240	179		111	92
WICHITA, KS	354	153	85	205	181	303	131	329	268	92	137	

SEE ALSO DISTANCE AND DRIVING TIME MAP ON PAGES 286–287

Nebraska
Colorado Kansas

Nevada

California

0 mi 20 40
0 km 20 40 60
One inch equals 24 miles
One centimeter equals 15.25 kilometers

PACIFIC OCEAN

TRAVEL NOTE: California has started numbering freeway exits using a mileage-based numbering system (shown here). Full implementation is expected to take several years.

Go to 36

Rohnert Park, Vacaville, Dixon, Elk Grove, Nevada
Petaluma, Sonoma, Napa, Fairfield, Galt, Ione, Jackson, Amador City, Sutter Creek, Pine Grove
Novato, Suisun City, Rio Vista, Lodi, San Andreas, Murphys, Angels Camp, Columbia, Sonora
Vallejo, Benicia, Pittsburg, Antioch, Stockton, Manteca, Copperopolis, Jamestown, Tuolumne
San Rafael, Richmond, Concord, Brentwood, Lathrop, Escalon, Oakdale, Groveland, Mather
Mill Valley, Berkeley, Walnut Creek, Danville, Tracy, Salida, Riverbank, Waterford, El Portal
San Francisco, Oakland, San Leandro, San Ramon, Modesto, Ceres, La Grange, Coulterville, Mariposa
Daly City, Pacifica, Hayward, Livermore, Pleasanton, Turlock, Patterson, Denair, Hornitos, Midpines
San Bruno, San Mateo, Fremont, Redwood City, Palo Alto, Milpitas, Delhi, Livingston, Winton, Merced
Half Moon Bay, Los Altos, Sunnyvale, Cupertino, Saratoga, San Jose, Newman, Gustine, Atwater, Le Grand
Los Gatos, Morgan Hill, Santa Clara, Los Banos, Chowchilla, Madera
Scotts Valley, Gilroy, Santa Cruz, Capitola, Dos Palos, Firebaugh, Clovis, Fresno
Watsonville, Aptos, Hollister, San Juan Bautista, Mendota, Kerman, Malaga
Castroville, Prunedale, Tres Pinos, Kettleman City
Marina, Salinas, Gonzales, San Benito, Tranquillity, San Joaquin, Easton
Pacific Grove, Monterey, Seaside, Carmel-by-the-Sea, Soledad, Greenfield, Lemoore, Riverdale
Big Sur, King City, Huron, Coalinga, Avenal
San Simeon, Bradley, San Miguel, Cholame, Devils Den, Lost Hills
Cambria, Paso Robles, Templeton, Atascadero, Shandon, Blackwells Corner
Morro Bay, Los Osos, San Luis Obispo, Santa Margarita
Pismo Beach, Grover Beach, Arroyo Grande, Oceano

PACIFIC OCEAN
STANISLAUS NATIONAL FOREST
POINT REYES NATL. SEASHORE
FARALLON N.W.R.
Farallon Islands
SAN JOAQUIN VALLEY
COAST RANGES
DIABLO RANGE
GABILAN RANGE
SANTA LUCIA RANGE
LOS PADRES N.F.
TEMBLOR RANGE
LA PANZA RANGE
CARRIZO PLAIN
TULARE LAKE BED
KETTLEMAN HILLS
MARIPOSA
MADERA
MERCED
STANISLAUS
CALAVERAS
TUOLUMNE
SAN BENITO
MONTEREY
KINGS
SAN LUIS OBISPO

Nevada

California

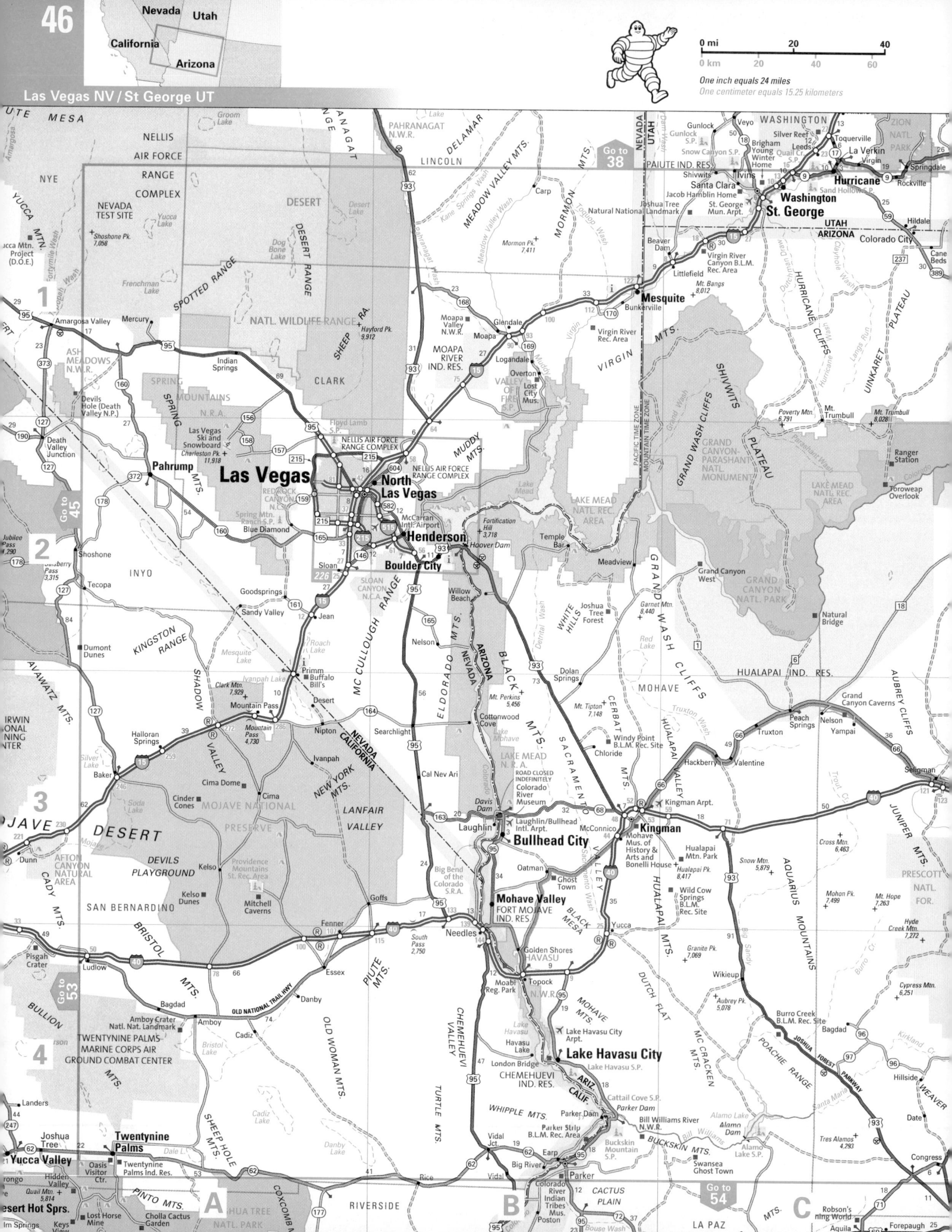

DRIVING DISTANCES IN MILES

SEE ALSO DISTANCE AND DRIVING TIME MAP ON PAGES 286–287

	CHINLE, AZ	FLAGSTAFF, AZ	GRAND CANYON, AZ	HOLBROOK, AZ	KAYENTA, AZ	KINGMAN, AZ	LAKE HAVASU CITY, AZ	LAS VEGAS, NV	LAUGHLIN, NV	PAGE, AZ	PRESCOTT, AZ	ST. GEORGE, UT
FLAGSTAFF, AZ	216		89	93	152	148	209	249	182	135	89	271
GRAND CANYON, AZ	232	89		182	153	175	236	276	209	136	131	272
LAS VEGAS, NV	465	249	276	341	374	103	154		94	277	251	118
ST. GEORGE, UT	358	271	272	353	255	221	272	118	212	159	369	

Nevada Utah
California
Arizona

Utah Colorado
Arizona New Mexico Okla.
Texas

One inch equals 24 miles
One centimeter equals 15.25 kilometers

0 mi   20   40
0 km   20   40   60

Go to 40
Go to 47
Go to 56

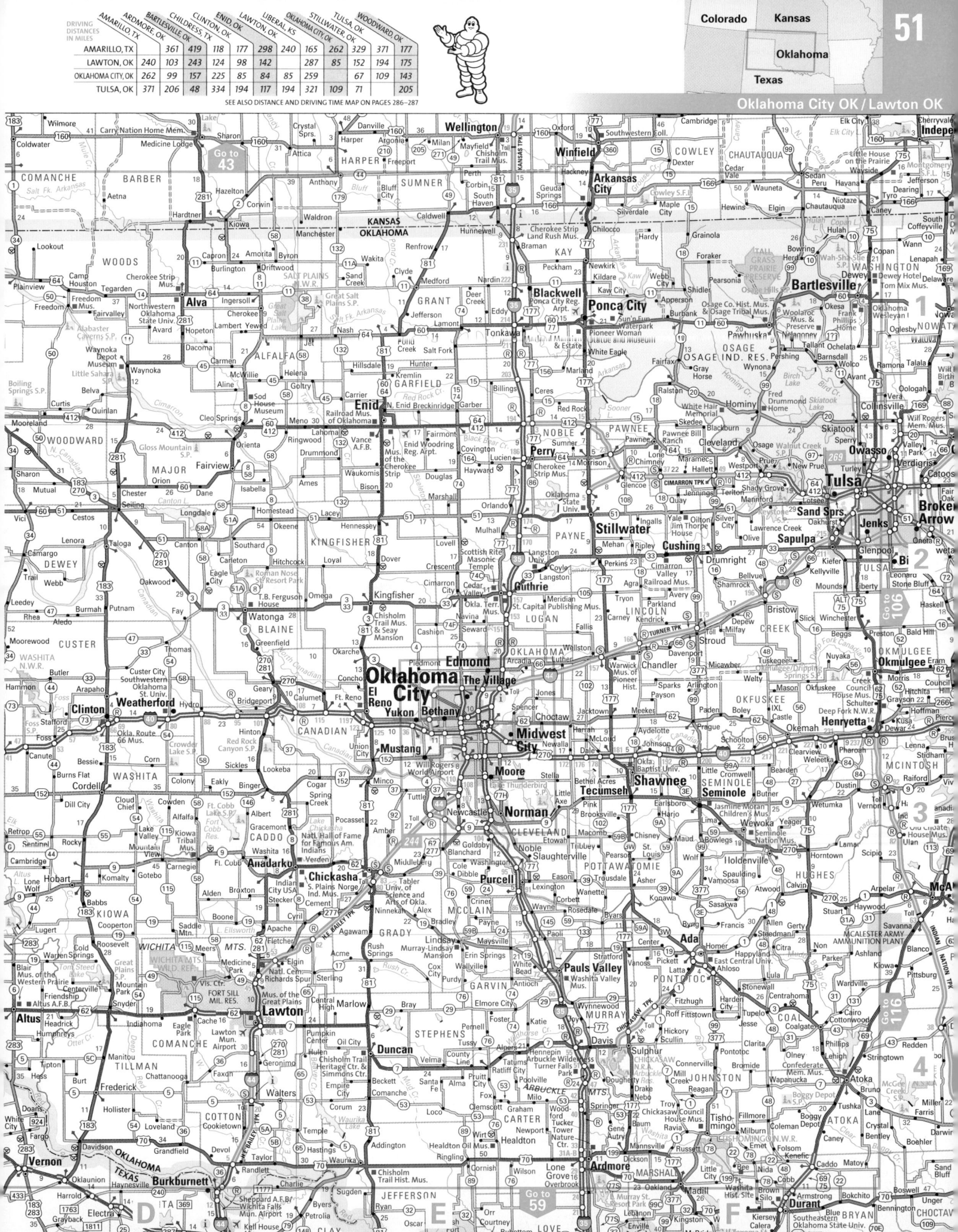

Nev.
California Arizona
Mexico

0 mi   20   40
0 km   20   40   60
One inch equals 24 miles
One centimeter equals 15.25 kilometers

Go to 44
Go to 45

PACIFIC OCEAN

Cambria
San Simeon
Harmony
Pt. Estero
Cayucos
Morro Bay
Morro Strand St. Beach
Los Osos
Camp San Luis Obispo
Montaña de Oro S.P.
Los Osos Oaks S.R.
Avila Beach
Pismo Beach
Grover Beach
Oceano
Pismo St. Beach
Oceano Dunes S.V.R.A.
Guadalupe-Nipomo Dunes N.W.R.
The Dunes Center
Guadalupe
Point Sal
Point Sal St. Beach
Casmalia
VANDENBERG A.F.B.
Purisima Pt.
Vandenberg Village
Surf
Lompoc
Pt. Arguello
Jalama Beach Co. Park
Pt. Conception
Gaviota
Gaviota S.P.
Refugio St. Beach
El Capitan St. Beach
Isla Vista
Santa Barbara Mun. Arpt.
Santa Barbara
S.B.
Carpinteria
Banana Garden

Atascadero
Templeton
Creston
Santa Margarita
Cuesta Ridge Botanical Area
Cal. Poly. State Univ., S.L.O.
Pozo
Pozo Summit 2,635
San Luis Obispo
Co. Reg. Arpt.
Mission S.L.O. de Tolosa
San Luis Obispo
Arroyo Grande
Nipomo
Santa Maria
Santa Maria Public Arpt.
Orcutt
Sisquoc
Los Alamos
La Purisima Mission S.H.P.
Mission Santa Inés
Los Olivos
Santa Ynez
Buellton
Solvang
Las Cruces
Nojoqui Falls Co. Park
Lake Cachuma
Lower Santa Ynez Rec. Area
Figueroa Mtn. Rec. Area
Wheeler Sprs.

SAN LUIS OBISPO
TEMBLOR RANGE
CARRIZO PLAIN NATIONAL MONUMENT
LA PANZA RANGE
Sode Lake
Simmler
California Valley
Goodwin Educ. Ctr.
SIERRA MADRE MTS.
SANTA BARBARA
SAN RAFAEL MTS.
PADRES
LOS PADRES N.F.
Cuyama
New Cuyama
McPherson Pk. 5,749
Ventucopa
Big Pine Mtn. 6,828
Dry Lakes Ridge Botanical Area
HOPPER MTN. N.W.R.

Lost Hills
Buttonwillow Raceway Park
Buttonwillow
McKittrick
Derby Acres
Tupman
Fellows
Taft
Ford City
Maricopa
Bitter Creek N.W.R.
Cuyama

Wasco
Shafter
Famoso
Calif. State Univ. Bakersfield Greenacres
Oildale
Calif. Living Mus.
Mesa Marin Raceway
Edison
Bakersfield
Old River
Pumpkin Center
Lamont
Di Giorgio
Arvin
Lakeview
Mettler
Wheeler Ridge
Ft. Tejon S.H.P.
Mt. Pinos Rec. Area
Frazier Park
Lebec
Mt. Pinos 8,831
Tejon Pass 4,183
Gorman
Three Point
Pyramid Lake Rec. Area
Castaic Lake S.R.A.
Castaic
Val Verde Park
Six Flags California
Fillmore & Western Railway
Piru
Fillmore
Santa Paula
Calif. Oil Mus.
Moorpark
Somis
Camarillo
Oxnard Arpt.
Oxnard
Port Hueneme
Point Mugu Naval Air Warfare Center Weapons Division and Naval Air Weapons Station
Point Mugu S.P.
McGrath St. Beach
El Rio
Ventura
Ojai
Oak View
Casitas Sprs.
Meiners Oaks
Montecito

GREENHORN
Miracle Hot Springs
Lake Isabella
Bodfish
Havilah
Bodfish Piute Cypress Botanical Area
Meadows Field
Caliente
Keene
Loraine
Tehachapi
Tehachapi Loop Viewpoint
Tomo-Kahni S.H.P.
Monolith
Mojave
KERN
PIUTE MTS.
TEHACHAPI MTS.
PACIFIC CREST N.S.T.
ANTELOPE VALLEY

Ridgecrest
Go to 45
Johannesburg
Garlock
Randsburg
Red Mountain
Atolia
Cantil
Koehn L.
RED ROCK CANYON S.P.
SEQUOIA N.F.
Desert Tortoise Natural Area
California City
North Edwards
Boron
NASA Dryden Flight Research Ctr.
Edwards Flight Test Center Mus.
EDWARDS A.F.B.
Rogers Lake
Rosamond
Rosamond Lake
Willow Springs
Hi Vista
Lancaster
Antelope Valley Calif. Poppy Reserve
Antelope Acres
Quartz Hill
Palmdale Reg. Arpt.
El Mirage
Wilsona Gardens
Antelope Valley Indian Mus.
Saddleback Butte S.P.
Lake Hughes
Elizabeth Lake
Green Valley
Leona Valley
Vasquez Rocks Co. Park
Palmdale
Littlerock
Pearblossom
Llano
Pinon Hills
Valyermo
Ski Sunrise
Acton
Vincent
Santa Clarita
Placerita Canyon S.P.
San Fernando
Burbank
Glendale
Pasadena
ANGELES NATIONAL FOREST
Mt. Baldy
Wrightwood
LOS ANGELES
Los Angeles
Beverly Hills
Santa Monica
Los Angeles Intl. Airport
SANTA MONICA MTS. N.R.A.
Malibu
Westlake Village
Thousand Oaks
Simi Valley
Inglewood
Downey
Compton
Norwalk
Whittier
Ontario
Pomona
Torrance
Long Beach
Santa Ana
Anaheim
Fullerton
Orange
ORANGE
Irvine
Huntington Beach
Newport Beach
Mission Viejo
Laguna Beach
San Juan Capistrano
Dana Point
Doheny St. Beach
San Clemente
Norco

CHANNEL ISLANDS NATL. PARK
San Miguel I.
Santa Rosa Island
Santa Cruz Island
Anacapa Islands
Santa Barbara Channel
Santa Cruz Channel
Anacapa Passage

Santa Barbara Island
CHANNEL ISLANDS NATL. PARK

San Nicolas Island

PACIFIC OCEAN

San Pedro Channel
Santa Catalina Island
Avalon
Catalina Island Mus.
Outer Santa Barbara Passage
Gulf of Santa Catalina
U.S. NAVAL RES.
San Clemente Island

TRAVEL NOTE: California has started numbering freeway exits using a mileage-based numbering system (shown here). Full implementation is expected to take several years.

DRIVING DISTANCES IN MILES	BAKERSFIELD, CA	BARSTOW, CA	BLYTHE, CA	EL CENTRO, CA	LOS ANGELES, CA	NEEDLES, CA	PALM SPRINGS, CA	SAN BERNARDINO, CA	SAN DIEGO, CA	SAN LUIS OBISPO, CA	SANTA BARBARA, CA	YUMA, AZ
LOS ANGELES, CA	111	118	230	234		263	110	62	124	190	97	294
SAN DIEGO, CA	234	181	211	117	124	326	143	111		314	221	177
SANTA BARBARA, CA	150	213	325	330	97	358	205	157	221	93		391
YUMA, AZ	403	294	103	65	294	187	171	225	177	483	391	

SEE ALSO DISTANCE AND DRIVING TIME MAP ON PAGES 286–287

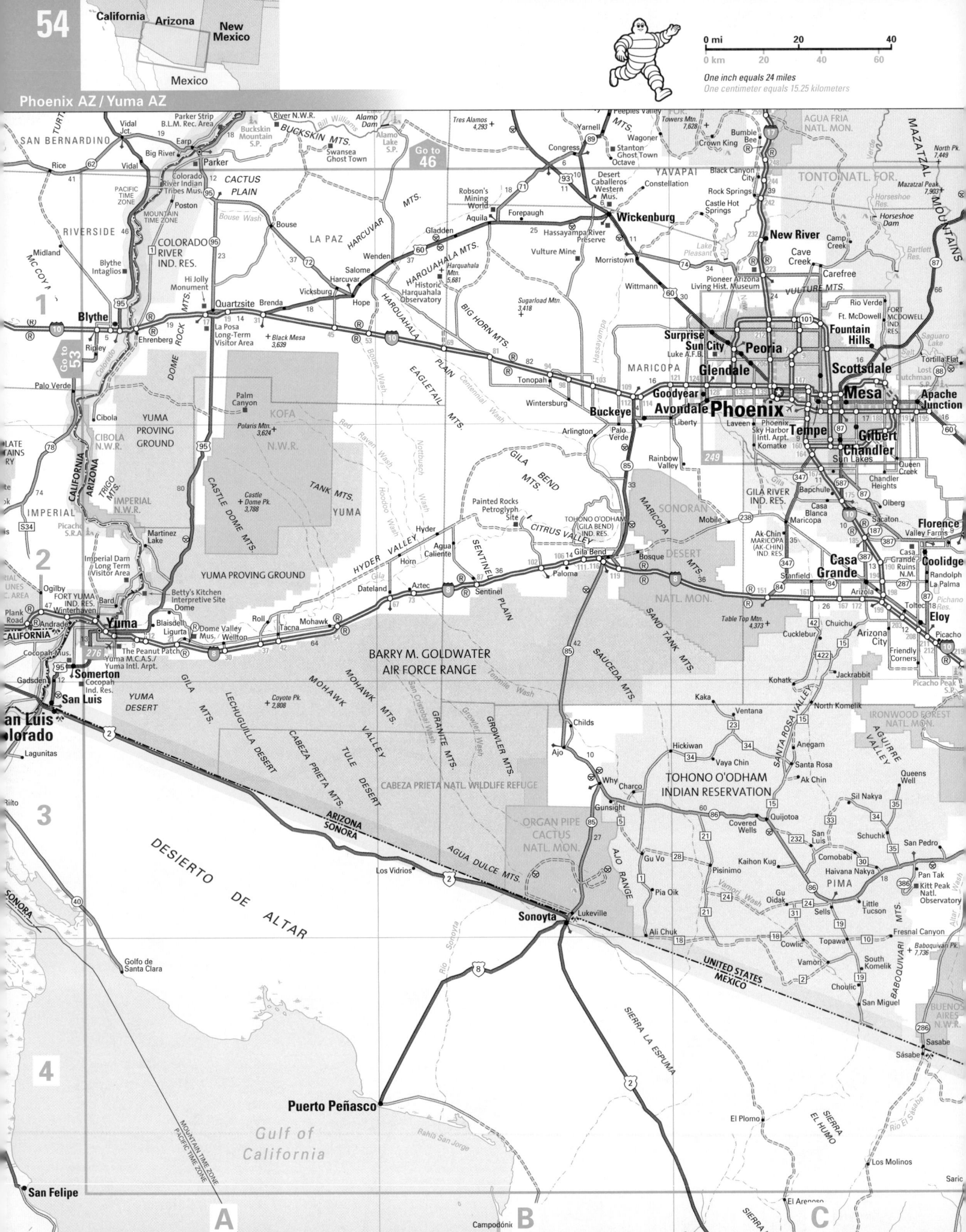

0 mi   20   40
0 km   20   40   60

One inch equals 24 miles
One centimeter equals 15.25 kilometers

DRIVING DISTANCES IN MILES

SEE ALSO DISTANCE AND DRIVING TIME MAP ON PAGES 286–287

	BLYTHE, CA	CASA GRANDE, AZ	DOUGLAS, AZ	EAGAR, AZ	GLOBE, AZ	LORDSBURG, NM	NOGALES, AZ	PHOENIX, AZ	SAFFORD, AZ	SILVER CITY, NM	TUCSON, AZ	YUMA, AZ
LORDSBURG, NM	417	228	101	184	155		185	278	77	45	161	401
PHOENIX, AZ	140	50	237	227	92	278	181		169	322	118	183
TUCSON, AZ	258	68	120	242	106	161	65	118	128	205		241
YUMA, AZ	103	179	360	401	265	401	304	183	368	446	241	

New Mexico
Texas
Mexico

DRIVING DISTANCES IN MILES	ALAMOGORDO, NM	EL PASO, TX	HOBBS, NM	LAS CRUCES, NM	LORDSBURG, NM	ODESSA, TX	PECOS, TX	PORTALES, NM	ROSWELL, NM	SILVER CITY, NM	SOCORRO, NM
CARLSBAD, NM	144		162	70	203	321	137	87	168	76	311	241
EL PASO, TX	86	162		232	42	160	285	209	295	203	150	190
LAS CRUCES, NM	65	203	42		250	122	325	250	274	182	111	146
ROSWELL, NM	117	76	203	117	182	304	201	163	92	293	164

SEE ALSO DISTANCE AND DRIVING TIME MAP ON PAGES 286–287

Oklahoma

Texas

0 mi · 20 · 40
0 km · 20 · 40 · 60
One inch equals 24 miles
One centimeter equals 15.25 kilometers

Go to 50
Go to 57
Go to 62
Go to 60

	BIG SPRING, TX	BROWNWOOD, TX	DALLAS, TX	FORT WORTH, TX	LUBBOCK, TX	ODESSA, TX	SAN ANGELO, TX	SHERMAN, TX	TEMPLE, TX	WACO, TX	WICHITA FALLS, TX
ABILENE, TX	110	78	191	153	166	176	91	249	194	235	144
DALLAS, TX	191	298		32	354	364	265	64	130	94	141
LUBBOCK, TX	166	106	247	354	317		142	185	322	358	399	207
WACO, TX	235	343	124	94	87	399	409	219	159	40	201

SEE ALSO DISTANCE AND DRIVING TIME MAP ON PAGES 286–287

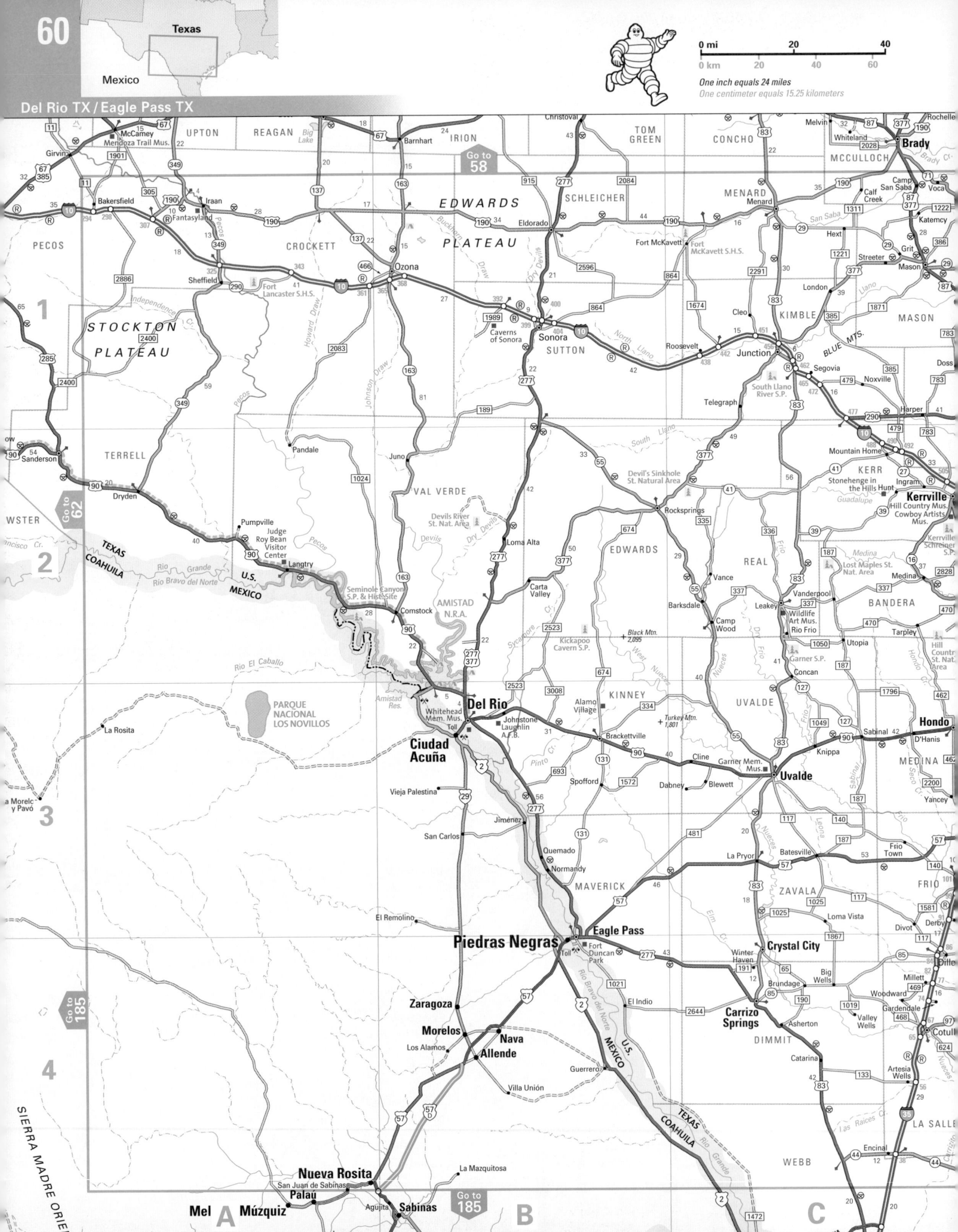

Texas

Mexico

0 mi   20   40
0 km   20   40   60

One inch equals 24 miles
One centimeter equals 15.25 kilometers

Texas

Mexico

DRIVING DISTANCES IN MILES

	ALPINE, TX	BIG BEND NP, TX	FORT STOCKTON, TX	ODESSA, TX	PECOS, TX	VAN HORN, TX
ALPINE, TX		97	65	151	96	110
FORT STOCKTON, TX	65	123		86	58	119
ODESSA, TX	151	209	86		76	163
VAN HORN, TX	110	207	119	163	87	

SEE ALSO DISTANCE AND DRIVING TIME MAP ON PAGES 286–287

One inch equals 24 miles
One centimeter equals 15.25 kilometers

0 mi   20   40
0 km   20   40   60

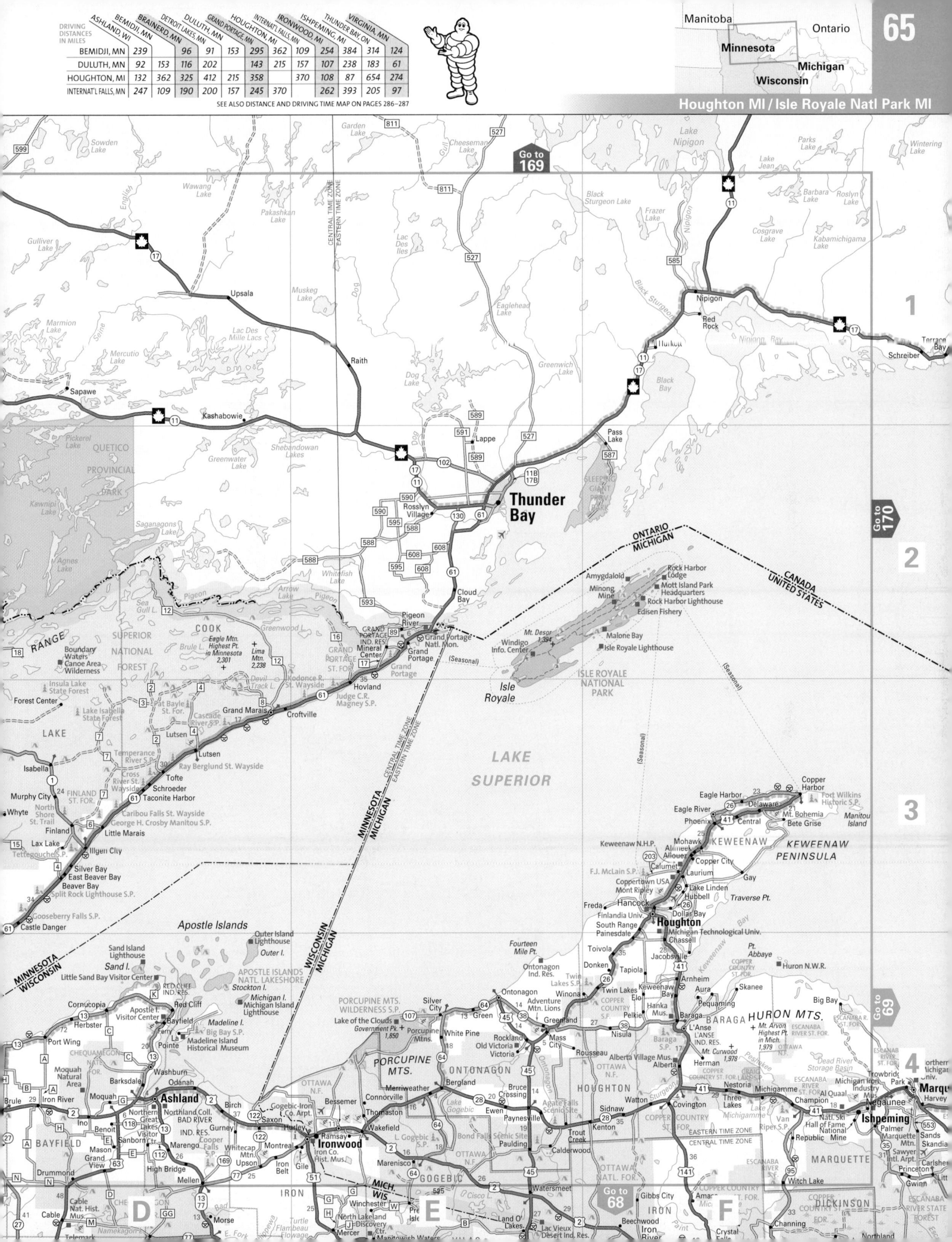

Go to 169

Go to 170

Go to 69

Go to 68

DRIVING DISTANCES IN MILES	ASHLAND, WI	BEMIDJI, MN	BRAINERD, MN	DETROIT LAKES, MN	DULUTH, MN	GRAND PORTAGE, MN	HOUGHTON, MI	INTERNAT'L FALLS, MN	IRONWOOD, MI	ISHPEMING, MI	THUNDER BAY, ON	VIRGINIA, MN
BEMIDJI, MN	239		96	91	153	295	362	109	254	384	314	124
DULUTH, MN	92	153	116	202		143	215	157	107	238	183	61
HOUGHTON, MI	132	362	325	412	215	358		370	108	87	654	274
INTERNAT'L FALLS, MN	247	109	190	200	157	245	370		262	393	205	97

SEE ALSO DISTANCE AND DRIVING TIME MAP ON PAGES 286–287

Wisconsin

Michigan

One inch equals 17.4 miles
One centimeter equals 11 kilometers

0 mi 10 20 30 40
0 km 10 20 30 40 50 60

LAKE SUPERIOR

Go to 65

Go to 67

Go to 74

1

2

3

4

A B C

Ashland · Washburn · Odanah · Barksdale · Sanborn · Marengo · High Bridge · Mellen · Morse · Clam Lake · Glidden · Butternut · Park Falls · Fifield · Phillips · Lugerville · Prentice · Catawba · Kennan · Brantwood · Tripoli · Ogema · Westboro · Rib Lake · Whittlesey · Chelsea · Medford · Stetsonville · Dorchester · Athens · Abbotsford · Colby · Unity · Spencer · Stratford · Marshfield · Chili · Granton · Neillsville

Hurley · Montreal · Gile · Ironwood · Bessemer · Ramsay · Wakefield · Marenisco · Mercer · Manitowish · Manitowish Waters · Boulder Jct. · Winchester · Presque Isle · Land O' Lakes · Watersmeet

Rhinelander · Tomahawk · Merrill · Wausau · Schofield · Rothschild · Kronenwetter · Mosinee · Weston · Stevens Point · Plover · Wisconsin Rapids

Antigo · Shawano · Green Bay · Howard · Ashwaubenon · De Pere · Bellevue · Suamico · Little Suamico · Pulaski · Seymour · Oconto Falls · Gillett

Iron Mountain · Kingsford · Iron River · Crystal Falls · Florence · Niagara · Pembine

PORCUPINE MTS. · HURON MTS. · COPPER COUNTRY S.F. · BARAGA · OTTAWA N.F. · GOGEBIC · IRON · VILAS · ONEIDA · FLORENCE · FOREST · MARINETTE · LANGLADE · MENOMINEE · SHAWANO · OCONTO · WAUPACA · PORTAGE · WOOD · MARATHON · CLARK · TAYLOR · PRICE · ASHLAND · SAWYER · LINCOLN · RUSK · JACKSON · BROWN · OUTAGAMIE

DRIVING DISTANCES IN MILES	ESCANABA, MI	GREEN BAY, WI	IRON MOUNTAIN, MI	IRONWOOD, MI	L'ANSE, MI	MANISTIQUE, MI	MARINETTE, WI	MARQUETTE, MI	RHINELANDER, WI	STEVENS POINT, WI	TRAVERSE CITY, MI	WAUSAU, WI
ESCANABA, MI		111	52	178	134	54	57	65	132	185	252	171
GREEN BAY, WI	111		96	202	178	165	54	175	124	87	363	93
MARQUETTE, MI	65	175	79	145	70	86	122		147	238	269	204
WAUSAU, WI	171	93	133	121	176	225	112	204	58	35	423	

SEE ALSO DISTANCE AND DRIVING TIME MAP ON PAGES 286–287

Go to 170

LAKE SUPERIOR

LAKE MICHIGAN

Go to 70

Go to 75

Go to 2

Ontario

Michigan

0 mi   10   20   30   40
0 km   10   20   30   40   50   60

One inch equals 17.4 miles
One centimeter equals 11 kilometers

LAKE SUPERIOR

Go to 170

CANADA / U.S.

ONTARIO / MICHIGAN

Sault Ste. Marie
Sault Ste. Marie
Soo Locks
S.S. Valley Camp

Searchmont
Heyden
Goulais
Echo Lake
Echo Bay
Gros Cap
Desbarats
Richards Landing
Hilton Beach
Kentvale
Neebish
St. Marys
Sugar I.
Lake George
Rosedale
Barbeau
Raco
Brimley
Bay Mills Ind. Res.
Dafter
Kinross
Rudyard
Chippewa Co. Intl. Arpt.
Fibre
Pickford
Stalwart
Goetzville
Cedarville
Les Cheneaux Islands
De Tour Village
Drummond I.

PICTURED ROCKS NATIONAL LAKESHORE
GRAND ISLAND NATL. REC. AREA
Grand Island
Miners Castle
Chapel Basin
Trout Bay
Christmas
Munising
Munising Falls
Melstrand
Au Sable Pt.
Grand Sable Dunes
Grand Marais
Deer Park
Muskallonge Lake S.P.
Lower Falls
Upper Falls
TAHQUAMENON FALLS S.P.
Paradise
Whitefish Point
Whitefish Pt. N.W.R. & Bird Observatory
Great Lakes Shipwreck Museum
Point Iroquois Light
Natl. Fish Hatchery
Bay Mills
Brimley S.P.

LUCE
LAKE SUPERIOR STATE FOREST
CHIPPEWA
HIAWATHA
NATIONAL
FOREST
MACKINAC

Newberry
McMillan
Seney
SENEY N.W.R.
Germfask
Helmer
Curtis
Gilchrist
Engadine
Naubinway
Epoufette
Brevort
Blaney Park
Gould City
Moran
Allenville
St. Ignace
Gros Cap
Father Marquette Natl. Mem.
Fort Mackinac
Mackinac Island S.P.
Mackinac Island
Round Island Scenic Area
Straits of Mackinac
Colonial Michilimackinac
Mackinaw City
Historic Mill Creek
Pointe Aux Pins
Bois Blanc I.

LAKE HURON

Manistique
Indian Lake S.P.
Thompson
Cooks
Garden Corners
Garden
Fayette Historic S.P.
Nahma
Big Bay De Noc
Pt. aux Barques
Portage Bay

Go to 69

LAKE MICHIGAN

Beaver Island
Michigan Islands N.W.R.
St. James
Beaver Island Marine Museum
High I.
Garden I.
Hog I.
MACKINAW ST. FOR.
Sturgeon Bay
WILDERNESS S.P.
Cross Village
Good Hart
Harbor Springs
Boyne Highlands
Wequetonsing
Petoskey
Bay View
Conway
Oden
Alanson
Pellston
Brutus
Pleasant View
EMMET

Cheboygan
Mullett Lake
Aloha
Indian River
Burt Lake
Topinabee
Afton
CHEBOYGAN
Tower
Onaway
Millersburg
Hawks
PRESQUE ISLE
MACKINAW STATE FOREST
Clear Lake S.P.

North Fox I.
South Fox I.
North Manitou I.
South Manitou I.
SLEEPING BEAR DUNES NATL. LAKESHORE
Pierce Stocking Scenic Drive
Glen Haven
Glen Arbor
Empire
Leland
Northport
Omena
Suttons Bay
LEELANAU
Peshawbestown
Old Mission
Grand Traverse Lighthouse
Cathead Pt.
Leelanau S.P.

CENTRAL TIME ZONE / EASTERN TIME ZONE

Washington Island
Green Bay N.W.R.
Rock Island S.P.
WISCONSIN / MICHIGAN

Charlevoix
Fisherman's Island S.P.
Lake Charlevoix
Boyne City
East Jordan
Ironton
Norwood
Atwood
Ellsworth
Central Lake
Eastport
Torch Lake
Bellaire
Alba
Mancelona
Kewadin
Elk Rapids
Alden
Rapid City
CHARLEVOIX
ANTRIM
OTSEGO
Gaylord
Vanderbilt
Johannesburg
Vienna
Atlanta
MONTMORENCY
Lewiston
Hillman
Fletcher Pond

Traverse City
Clinch Park Zoo
Cherry Capital Arpt.
Acme
Williamsburg
Mt. Holiday
Kalkaska
GRAND TRAVERSE
KALKASKA
Darragh
Grayling
Frederic
Lovells
CAMP GRAYLING ARMY & AIR NATL. GUARD TRAINING CTR.
Hartwick Pines Logging Mus.
HARTWICK PINES S.P.
CRAWFORD
OSCODA
Luzerne
Mio
McKinley
Fairview
Comins
Red Oak
Kirtland's Warbler N.W.R.
MACKINAW ST. FOR.

Pt. Betsie
Crystal L.
Frankfort
Elberta
Beulah
Benzonia
Benzie Area Hist. Mus.
Honor
Interlochen
BENZIE
PERE MARQUETTE S.F.
Thompsonville
Copemish
Buckley
Mayfield
Fife Lake
South Boardman
Kingsley
Arcadia
MANISTEE
WEXFORD
Manton
Kaleva
Sherman
Meauwataka
MISSAUKEE
Lake City
Lake Missaukee
Houghton Lake
Higgins Lake
Roscommon
ROSCOMMON
St. Helen
OGEMAW
HURON NATL. FOR.
Rose City

Go to 75
Go to 76

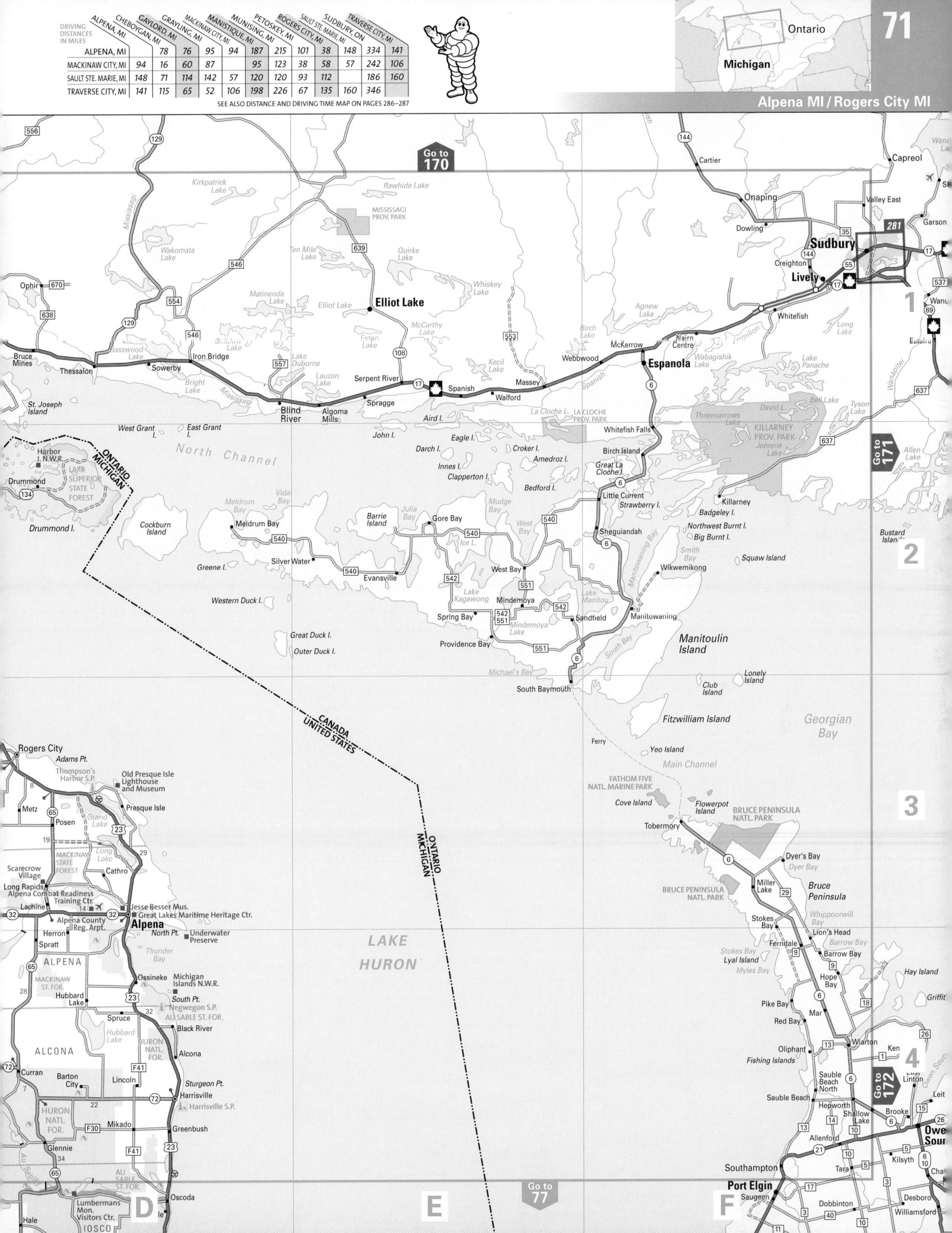

Alpena MI / Rogers City MI

0 mi 10 20 30 40
0 km 10 20 30 40 50 60
One inch equals 17.4 miles
One centimeter equals 11 kilometers

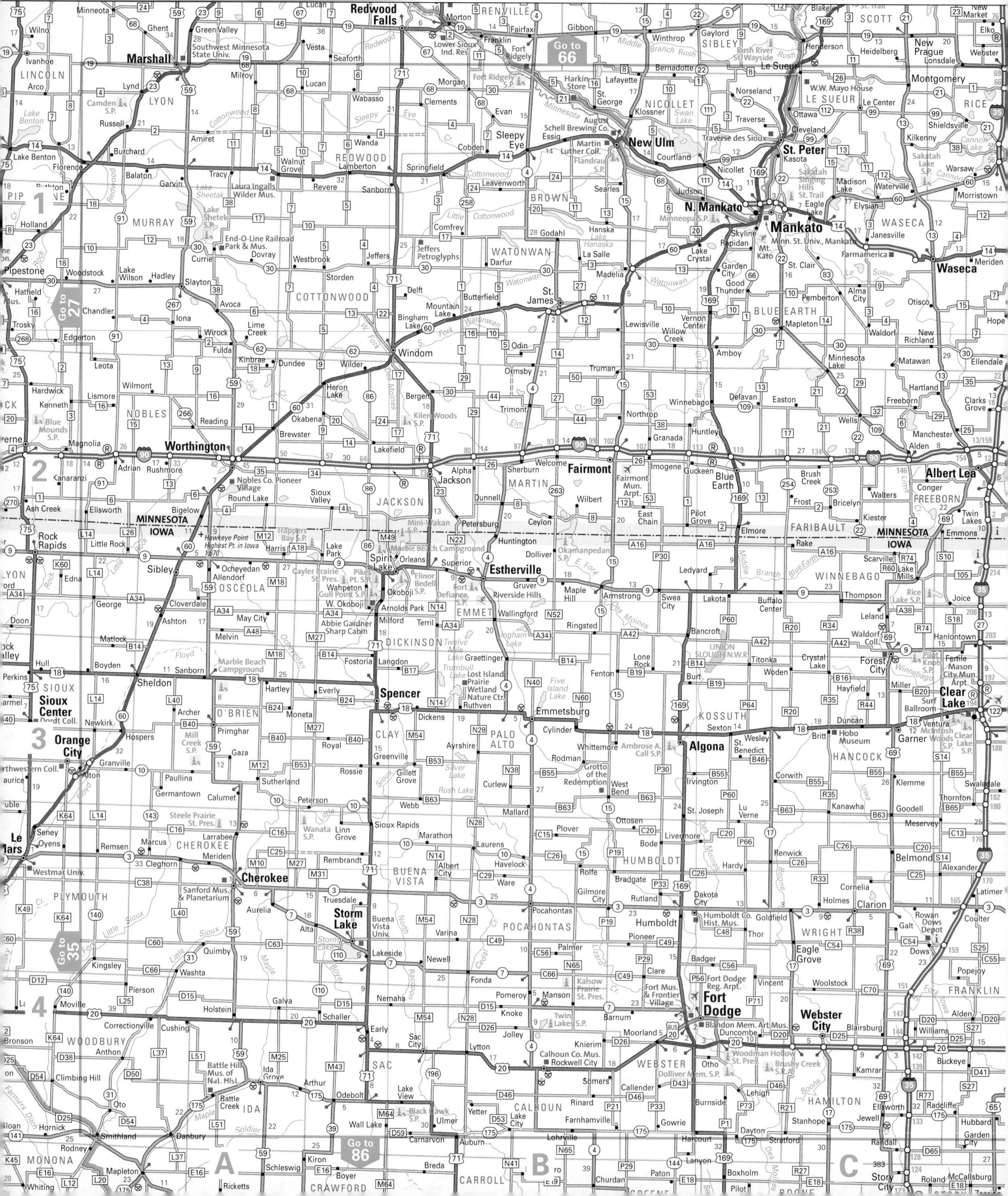

Go to 66
Go to 27
Go to 35
Go to 86

Redwood Falls — Marshall — New Ulm — N. Mankato — Mankato — St. Peter — Le Sueur — Waseca — Albert Lea

Worthington — Fairmont — Blue Earth — Sleepy Eye — Windom — St. James — Madelia

MINNESOTA
IOWA

Sioux Center — Orange City — Spirit Lake — Estherville — Spencer — Algona — Forest City — Clear Lake

Cherokee — Storm Lake — Fort Dodge — Webster City — Le Mars

LINCOLN · LYON · MURRAY · COTTONWOOD · NOBLES · REDWOOD · BROWN · WATONWAN · NICOLLET · LE SUEUR · RICE · BLUE EARTH · WASECA · MARTIN · FARIBAULT · FREEBORN

SIOUX · O'BRIEN · CLAY · PALO ALTO · EMMET · DICKINSON · OSCEOLA · KOSSUTH · WINNEBAGO · HANCOCK · CERRO GORDO

PLYMOUTH · CHEROKEE · BUENA VISTA · POCAHONTAS · HUMBOLDT · WRIGHT · FRANKLIN

WOODBURY · IDA · SAC · CALHOUN · WEBSTER · HAMILTON

MONONA · CRAWFORD · CARROLL · GREENE

DRIVING DISTANCES IN MILES

	ALBERT LEA, MN	DECORAH, IA	DUBUQUE, IA	FORT DODGE, IA	LA CROSSE, WI	MANKATO, MN	MASON CITY, IA	ROCHESTER, MN	SPENCER, IA	WATERLOO, IA	WINONA, MN	WORTHINGTON, MN
FORT DODGE, IA	124	186	200		245	138	97	183	95	108	225	148
MANKATO, MN	56	151	253	138	149		100	80	123	186	128	108
ROCHESTER, MN	62	68	170	183	71	80	103		189	116	51	174
WATERLOO, IA	130	79	93	108	138	186	79	116	189		144	244

SEE ALSO DISTANCE AND DRIVING TIME MAP ON PAGES 286–287

Ontario

Michigan

0 mi   10   20   30   40
0 km 10 20 30 40 50 60
One inch equals 17.4 miles
One centimeter equals 11 kilometers

LAKE HURON

Go to 70

Go to 75

Go to 90

Detroit

Windsor

Lansing

E. Lansing

Flint

Saginaw

Bay City

Midland

Mt. Pleasant

Cadillac

Ann Arbor

Battle Creek

Jackson

Marshall

Albion

Alma

Owosso

Pontiac

Sterling Hts.

Troy

Warren

Rochester Hills

Southfield

Livonia

Westland

Dearborn

Taylor

Wyandotte

Lincoln Park

Mount Clemens

St. Clair Shores

Grosse Pointe Woods

Marysville

Bad Axe

Sandusky

Lapeer

Lake St. Clair

DRIVING DISTANCES IN MILES	ANN ARBOR, MI	BAD AXE, MI	BATTLE CREEK, MI	CADILLAC, MI	DETROIT, MI	FLINT, MI	HAMILTON, ON	LANSING, MI	LONDON, ON	MT. PLEASANT, MI	PORT HURON, MI	SAGINAW, MI
DETROIT, MI	42	107	116	209		62	203	86	128	149	58	97
LANSING, MI	63	140	56	131	86	53	270		191	67	117	86
PORT HURON, MI	101	81	175	211	58	64	154	117	75	155		100
SAGINAW, MI	87	64	142	116	97	36	253	86	174	60	100	

SEE ALSO DISTANCE AND DRIVING TIME MAP ON PAGES 286–287

Ontario

New York

One inch equals 17.4 miles
One centimeter equals 11 kilometers

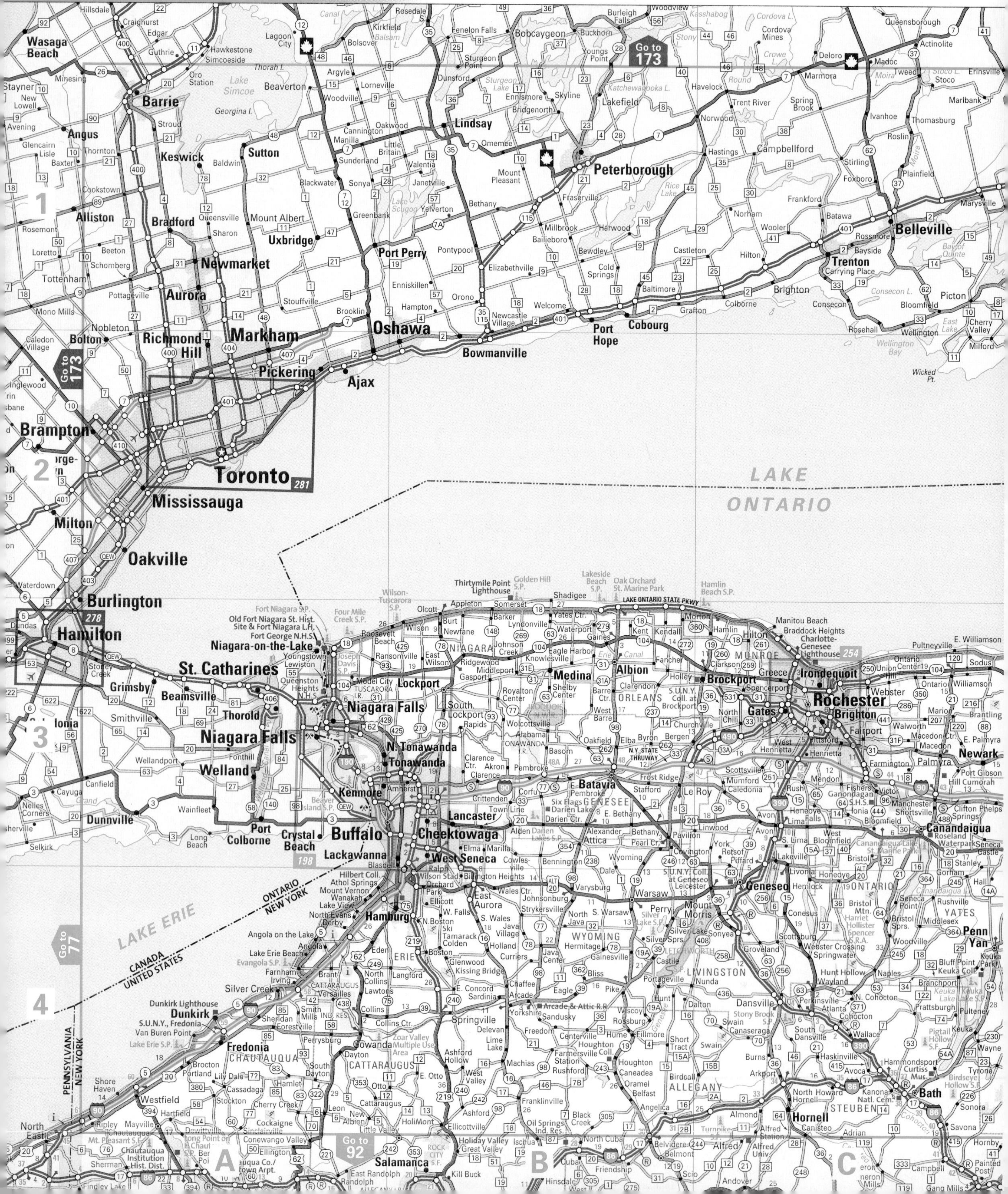

0 mi   10   20   30   40
0 km   10   20   30   40   50   60

LAKE ONTARIO

LAKE ERIE

CANADA
UNITED STATES

PENNSYLVANIA
NEW YORK

ONTARIO
NEW YORK

Go to 173
Go to 92
Go to 77

Toronto
Mississauga
Hamilton
Burlington
Oakville
Milton
Brampton
St. Catharines
Niagara Falls
Buffalo
Rochester
Peterborough
Belleville
Trenton
Oshawa
Cobourg
Barrie
Newmarket
Aurora
Markham
Pickering
Ajax
Bowmanville
Port Hope
Batavia
Geneseo
Canandaigua
Penn Yan
Bath
Hornell
Dunkirk
Fredonia
Salamanca
Hamburg
Lockport
Medina
Albion
Brockport
Irondequoit
Brighton

One inch equals 17.4 miles
One centimeter equals 11 kilometers

DRIVING DISTANCES IN MILES	BURLINGTON, VT	CONCORD, NH	LAKE PLACID, NY	OGDENSBURG, NY	PLATTSBURGH, NY	RUTLAND, VT	ST. JOHNSBURY, VT	SARATOGA SPS., NY	SYRACUSE, NY	UTICA, NY	WATERTOWN, NY	WHITE RIVER JCT., VT
BURLINGTON, VT		150	68	208	51	69	76	115	230	183	195	91
CONCORD, NH	150		215	357	198	104	104	173	280	228	312	59
LAKE PLACID, NY	68	215		96	49	133	141	106	192	148	126	156
WATERTOWN, NY	195	312	126	68	167	244	319	179	65	86		289

SEE ALSO DISTANCE AND DRIVING TIME MAP ON PAGES 286–287

One inch equals 17.4 miles
One centimeter equals 11 kilometers

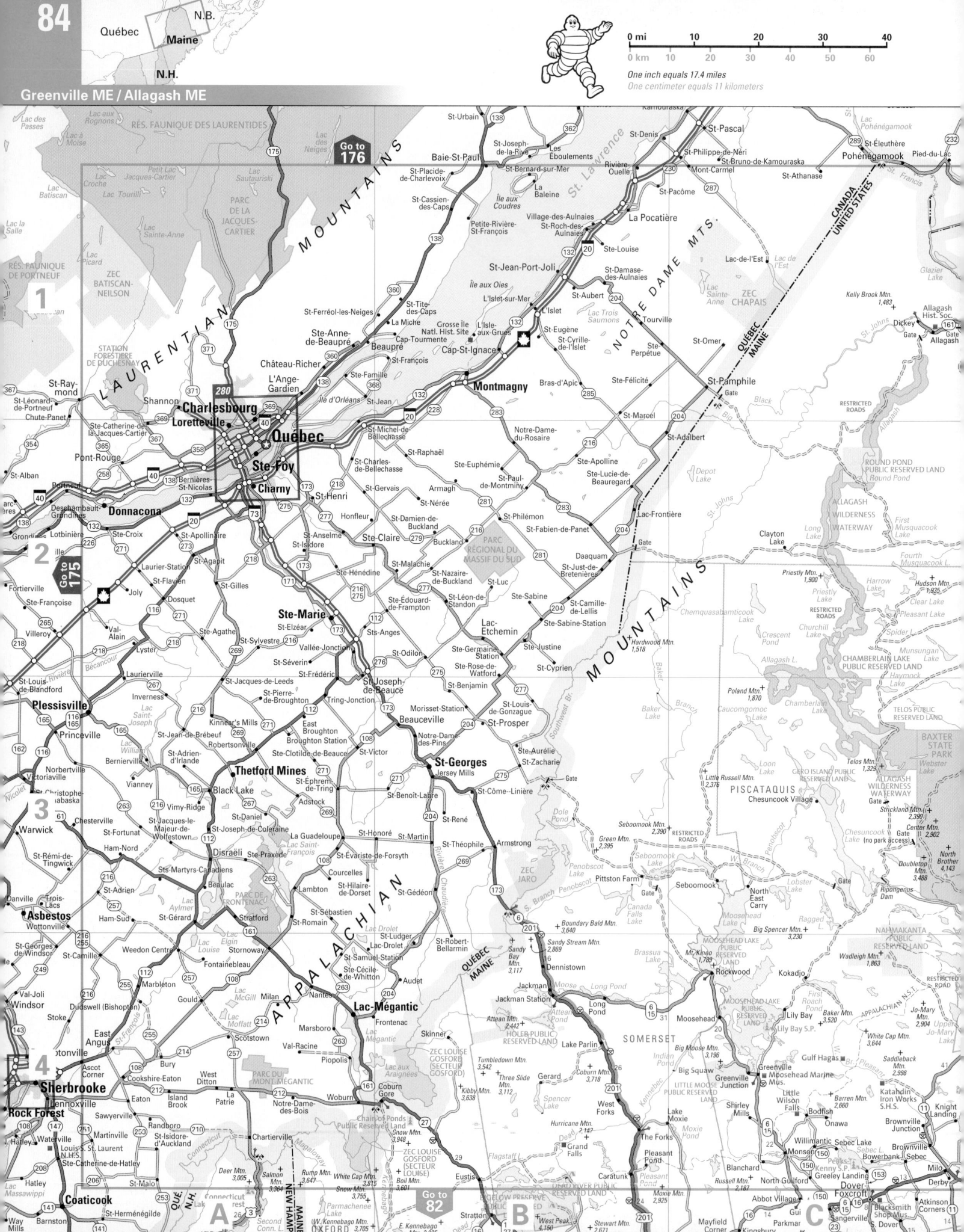

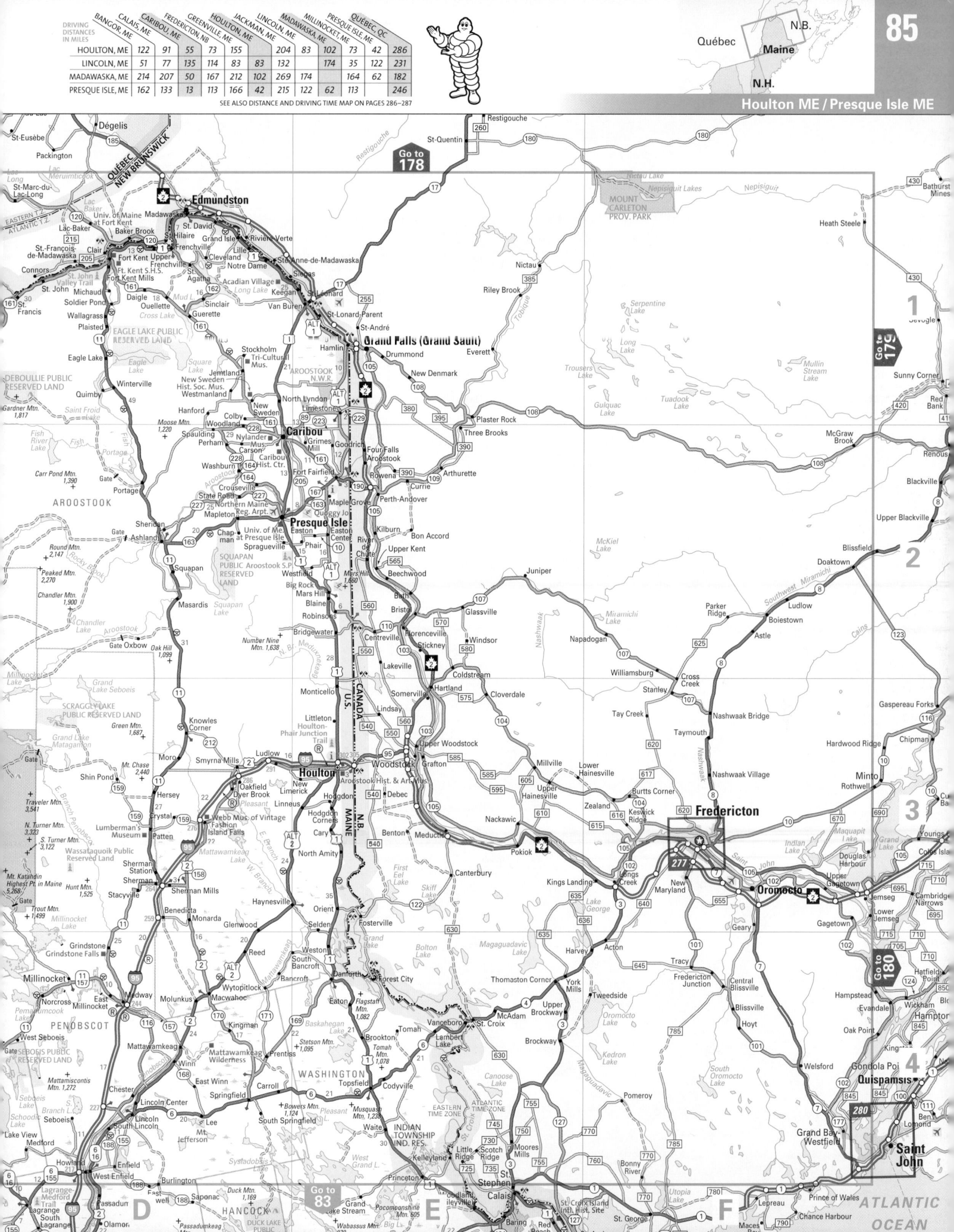

One inch equals 17.4 miles
One centimeter equals 11 kilometers

Go to 72
Go to 35
Go to 96

DRIVING DISTANCES IN MILES	AMES, IA	BURLINGTON, IA	CARROLL, IA	CEDAR RAPIDS, IA	CRESTON, IA	DAVENPORT, IA	DES MOINES, IA	IOWA CITY, IA	KIRKSVILLE, MO	MARYVILLE, MO	OMAHA, NE	OTTUMWA, IA
CEDAR RAPIDS, IA	108	106	173		211	87	129	28	170	266	266	111
DES MOINES, IA	34	157	90	129	81	171		113	145	146	316	86
IOWA CITY, IA	136	82	195	28	195	59	113		143	260	250	83
OMAHA, NE	171	328	97	266	98	308	136	250	275	112		221

SEE ALSO DISTANCE AND DRIVING TIME MAP ON PAGES 286-287

Go to 73

Go to 88

Go to 97

0 mi 10 20 30 40
0 km 10 20 30 40 50 60
One inch equals 17.4 miles
One centimeter equals 11 kilometers

One inch equals 17.4 miles
One centimeter equals 11 kilometers

DRIVING DISTANCES IN MILES	AKRON, OH	CLEVELAND, OH	COLUMBUS, OH	DETROIT, MI	ERIE, PA	FORT WAYNE, IN	LIMA, OH	MANSFIELD, OH	MUNCIE, IN	TOLEDO, OH	WHEELING, WV	YOUNGSTOWN, OH
CLEVELAND, OH	38		144	171	106	214	163	81	287	119	16	275
FORT WAYNE, IN	237	214	186	170	322		66	151	75	109	290	274
MANSFIELD, OH	66	81	67	156	179	151	93		209	105	141	112
TOLEDO, OH	142	119	148	60	227	109	83	105	180		261	179

SEE ALSO DISTANCE AND DRIVING TIME MAP ON PAGES 286–287

One inch equals 17.4 miles
One centimeter equals 11 kilometers

Go to 82

Go to 151

Go to 149

DRIVING DISTANCES IN MILES	ALBANY, NY	BOSTON, MA	HARTFORD, CT	MANCHESTER, NH	NEWBURGH, NY	NEW HAVEN, CT	NEW YORK, NY	ONEONTA, NY	PROVIDENCE, RI	PROVINCETOWN, MA	SPRINGFIELD, MA	WORCESTER, MA
ALBANY, NY		172	111	145	89	150	151	81	170	271	86	133
BOSTON, MA	172		102	54	201	139	215	251	52	117	95	46
HARTFORD, CT	111	102		131	99	39	115	190	73	200	25	62
NEW YORK, NY	151	215	115	245	56	78		193	177	292	141	176

SEE ALSO DISTANCE AND DRIVING TIME MAP ON PAGES 286–287

Illinois
Indiana
Missouri
Kentucky

0 mi　10　20　30　40
0 km　10　20　30　40　50　60
One inch equals 17.4 miles
One centimeter equals 11 kilometers

St. Louis

Springfield

Decatur

Alton

St. Charles

O'Fallon

St. Peters

Chesterfield

Ballwin

Wildwood

Clayton

Kirkwood

Mehlville

Oakville

Arnold

Columbia

Waterloo

Festus

De Soto

Union

Eureka

Pacific

Granite City

Collinsville

E. St. Louis

Cahokia

Belleville

Fairview Hts.

Edwardsville

Highland

Greenville

Vandalia

Effingham

Litchfield

Carlinville

Jacksonville

Chatham

Taylorville

Pana

Mattoon

Shelbyville

Monticello

Clinton

Lincoln

Beardstown

Jerseyville

Godfrey

Staunton

Salem

Centralia

Mt. Vernon

Nashville

Pinckneyville

Du Quoin

Benton

W. Frankfort

Herrin

Murphysboro

Harrisburg

Chester

Ste. Genevieve

Farmington

Park Hills

Go to 88

Go to 97

Go to 108

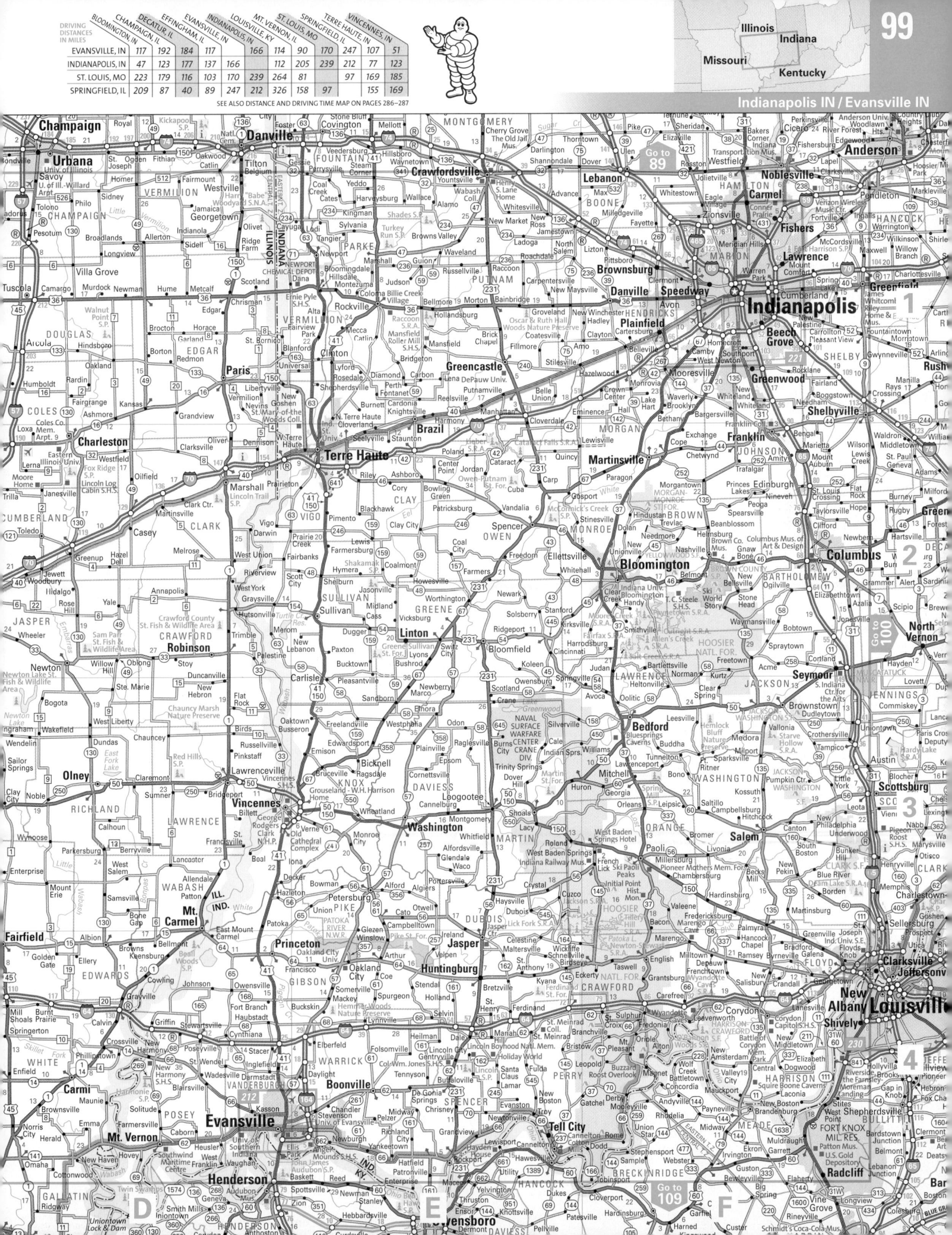

DRIVING DISTANCES IN MILES	BLOOMINGTON, IN	CHAMPAIGN, IL	DECATUR, IL	EFFINGHAM, IL	EVANSVILLE, IN	INDIANAPOLIS, IN	LOUISVILLE, KY	MT. VERNON, IL	ST. LOUIS, MO	SPRINGFIELD, IL	TERRE HAUTE, IN	VINCENNES, IN
EVANSVILLE, IN	117	192	184	117		166	114	90	170	247	107	51
INDIANAPOLIS, IN	47	123	177	137	166		112	205	239	212	72	123
ST. LOUIS, MO	223	179	116	103	170	239	264	81		97	169	185
SPRINGFIELD, IL	209	87	40	89	247	212	326	158	97		155	169

SEE ALSO DISTANCE AND DRIVING TIME MAP ON PAGES 286–287

0 mi   10   20   30   40
0 km   10   20   30   40   50   60

One inch equals 17.4 miles
One centimeter equals 11 kilometers

Pennsylvania
Ohio   Md.
           Delaware
W.Va.
     Virginia

0 mi   10   20   30   40
0 km   10   20   30   40   50   60

One inch equals 17.4 miles
One centimeter equals 11 kilometers

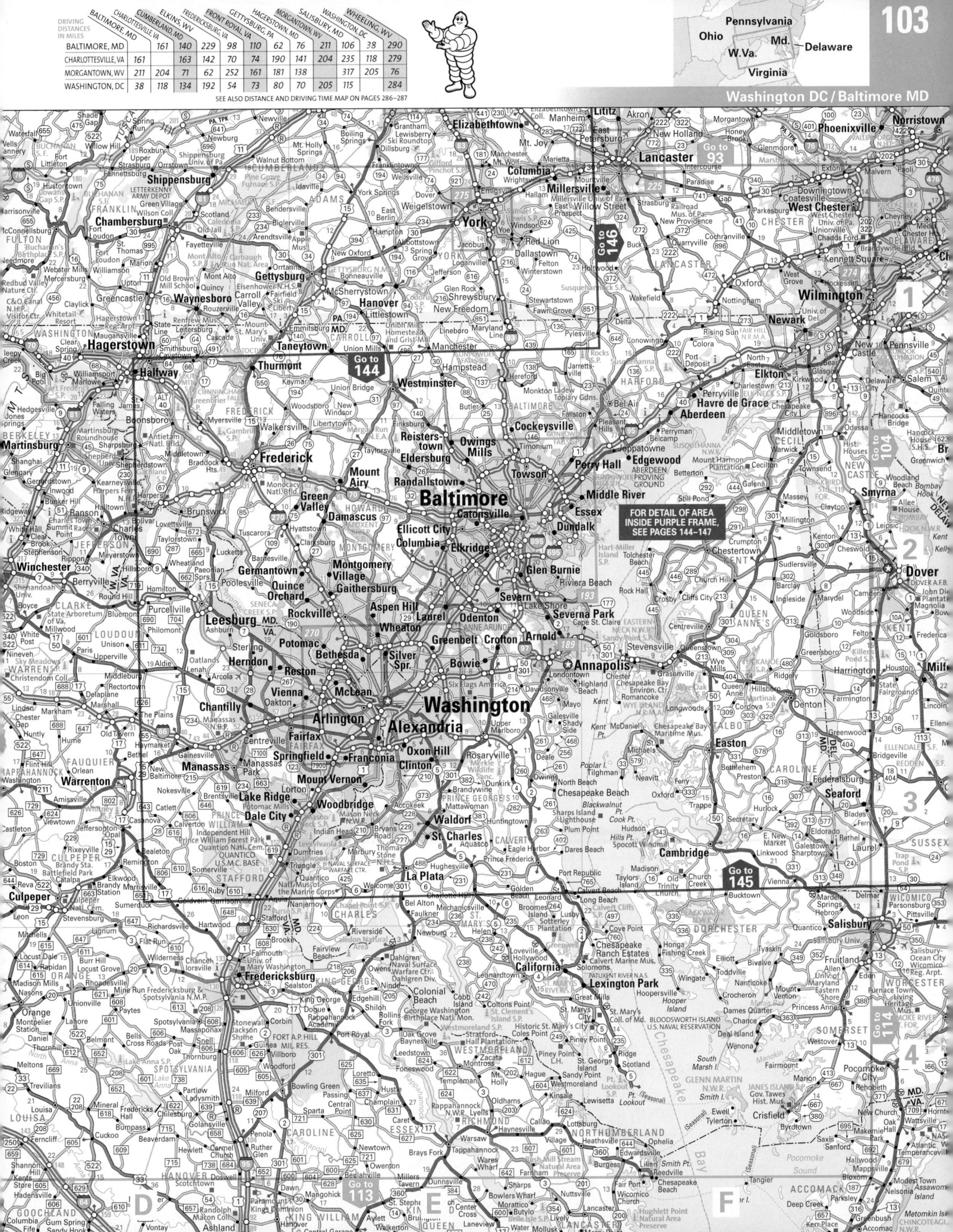

DRIVING DISTANCES IN MILES	BALTIMORE, MD	CHARLOTTESVILLE, VA	CUMBERLAND, WV	ELKINS, WV	FREDERICKSBURG, VA	FRONT ROYAL, VA	GETTYSBURG, PA	HAGERSTOWN, MD	MORGANTOWN, WV	SALISBURY, MD	WASHINGTON, DC	WHEELING, WV
BALTIMORE, MD		161	140	229	98	110	62	76	211	106	38	290
CHARLOTTESVILLE, VA	161		163	142	70	74	190	141	204	235	118	279
MORGANTOWN, WV	211	204	71	62	252	161	181	138		317	205	76
WASHINGTON, DC	38	118	134	192	54	73	80	70	205	115		284

SEE ALSO DISTANCE AND DRIVING TIME MAP ON PAGES 286–287

N.Y.
Pennsylvania New Jersey
Md. Delaware
Virginia

0 mi   10   20   30   40
0 km 10 20 30 40 50 60
One inch equals 17.4 miles
One centimeter equals 11 kilometers

1 2 3 4

A B C

Go to 93
Go to 93
Go to 146
Go to 144
Go to 103
Go to 144
Go to 145
Go to 114

Major cities and towns:

Washington, Baltimore, Philadelphia, Harrisburg, Allentown, Bethlehem, Reading, Lancaster, York, Trenton, Wilmington, Camden, Annapolis, Dover, Alexandria, Arlington, Frederick, Lebanon, Pottsville, Hazleton, Bloomsburg, Berwick, Easton, Phillipsburg, Norristown, King of Prussia, West Chester, Chester, Newark, Elkton, Havre de Grace, Aberdeen, Towson, Cockeysville, Westminster, Hanover, Gettysburg, Carlisle, Sunbury, Selinsgrove, Shamokin, Mount Carmel, Shenandoah, Tamaqua, Lehighton, Stroudsburg, E. Stroudsburg, Bangor, Quakertown, Doylestown, Lansdale, Levittown, Vineland, Bridgeton, Millville, Smyrna, Milford, Cape May, Wildwood, Lewes, Rehoboth Beach, Seaford, Georgetown, Denton, Easton, Chestertown, Centreville, Rockville, Bethesda, Silver Spr., Gaithersburg, Laurel, Bowie, Crofton, Severna Park, Glen Burnie, Dundalk, Essex, Middle River, Catonsville, Ellicott City, Columbia, Elkridge, Randallstown, Reisterstown, Owings Mills, Eldersburg, Mount Airy, Damascus, Germantown, Olney, Aspen Hill, Wheaton, Vienna, McLean, Fairfax, Springfield, Franconia, Woodbridge, Dale City, Manassas, Mount Vernon, Oxon Hill, Clinton, Waldorf

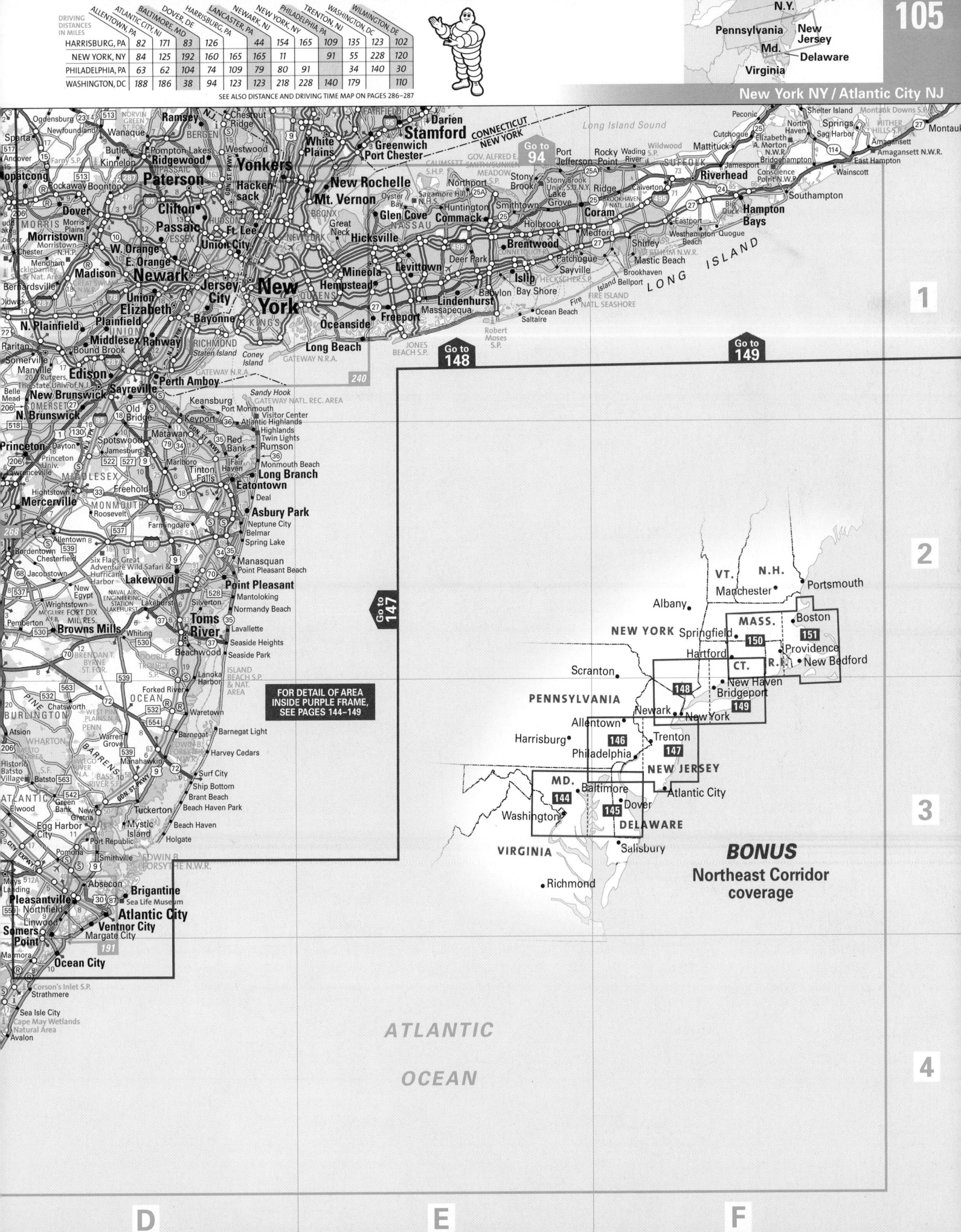

DRIVING
DISTANCES
IN MILES

	ALLENTOWN, PA	ATLANTIC CITY, NJ	BALTIMORE, MD	DOVER, DE	HARRISBURG, PA	LANCASTER, PA	NEWARK, NJ	NEW YORK, NY	PHILADELPHIA, PA	TRENTON, NJ	WASHINGTON, DC	WILMINGTON, DE
HARRISBURG, PA	82	171	83	126		44	154	165	109	135	123	102
NEW YORK, NY	84	125	192	160	165	165	11		91	55	228	120
PHILADELPHIA, PA	63	62	104	74	109	79	80	91		34	140	30
WASHINGTON, DC	188	186	38	94	123	123	218	228	140	179		110

SEE ALSO DISTANCE AND DRIVING TIME MAP ON PAGES 286-287

BONUS
Northeast Corridor
coverage

ATLANTIC

OCEAN

FOR DETAIL OF AREA
INSIDE PURPLE FRAME,
SEE PAGES 144-149

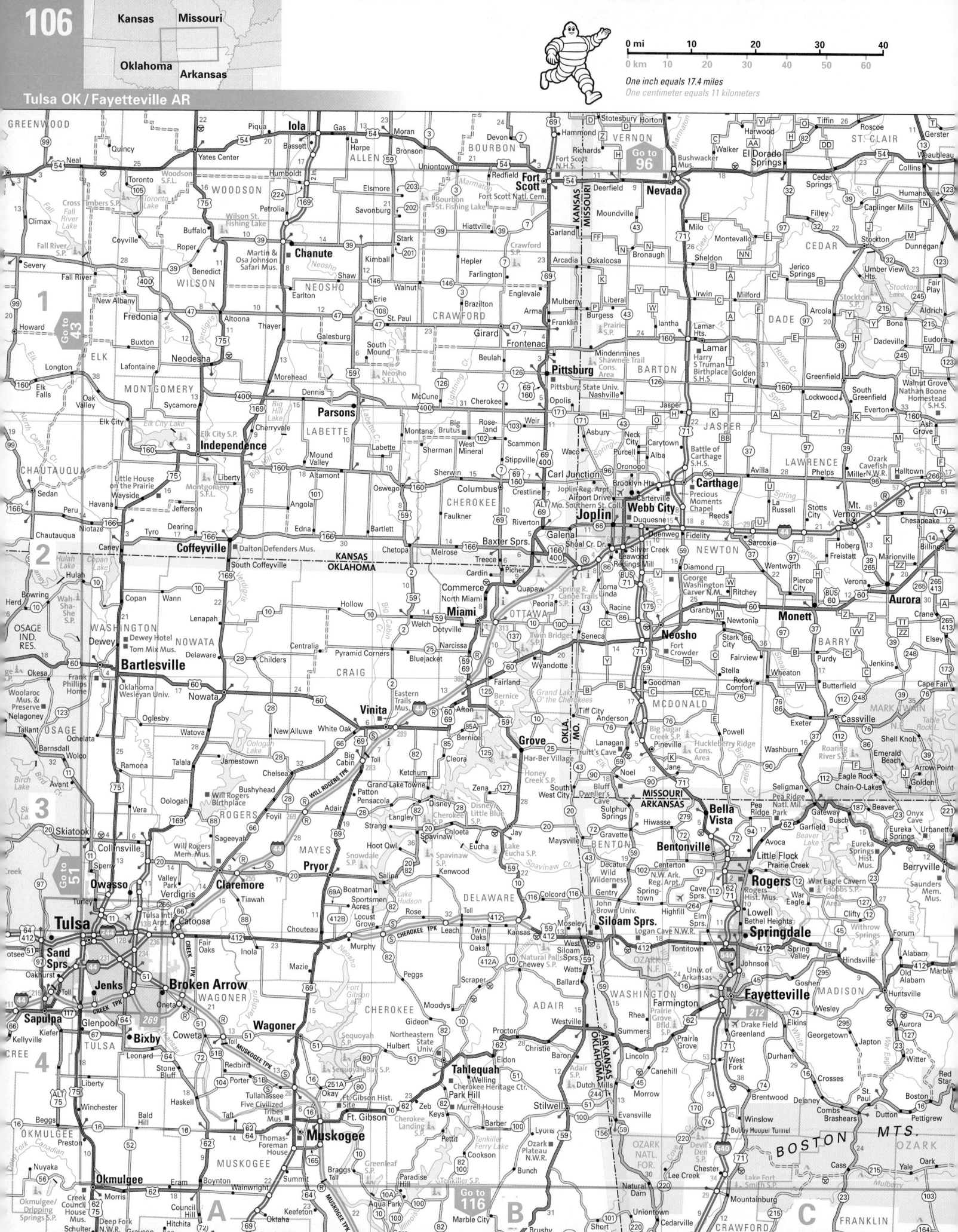

Go to 98

Go to 107

Go to 118

Go to 118

Illinois Ind.
Missouri Kentucky
Tennessee
Arkansas

One inch equals 17.4 miles
One centimeter equals 11 kilometers

One inch equals 17.4 miles
One centimeter equals 11 kilometers

DRIVING DISTANCES IN MILES	ASHEVILLE, NC	BECKLEY, WV	BRISTOL TN/VA	COOKEVILLE, TN	GATLINBURG, TN	HICKORY, NC	JOHNSON CITY, TN	KNOXVILLE, TN	LONDON, KY	MAMMOTH CAVE N.P., KY	PIKEVILLE, KY	RICHMOND, KY
BRISTOL, TN/VA	83	140		224	118	98	24	117	213	348	116	265
HICKORY, NC	78	196	98	291	147		98	185	280	415	214	332
KNOXVILLE, TN	109	256	117	107	40	185	107		100	234	202	151
LONDON, KY	205	287	213	129	136	280	203	100		136	121	53

SEE ALSO DISTANCE AND DRIVING TIME MAP ON PAGES 286–287

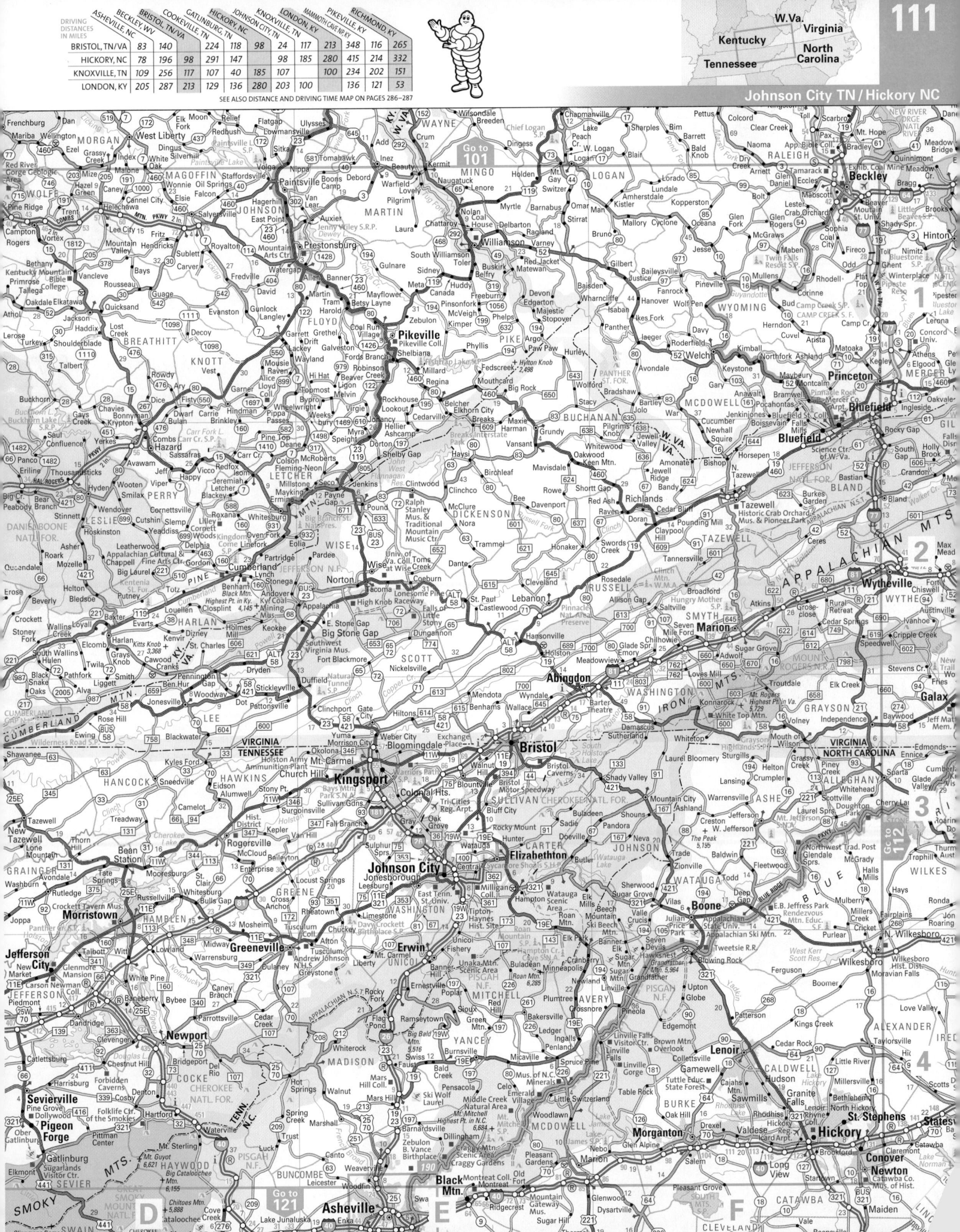

W.Va.
Virginia
North
Carolina

Greensboro NC / Roanoke VA

0 mi   10   20   30   40
0 km   10   20   30   40   50   60

One inch equals 17.4 miles
One centimeter equals 11 kilometers

DRIVING DISTANCES IN MILES	GREENSBORO, NC	DANVILLE, VA	GREENSBORO, NC	LYNCHBURG, VA	NORFOLK, VA	RALEIGH, NC	RICHMOND, VA	ROANOKE, VA	ROANOKE RAPIDS, NC	ROCKY MOUNT, NC	WILLIAMSBURG, VA	WINSTON-SALEM, NC	WYTHEVILLE, VA
GREENSBORO, NC	46		106	230	69	200	101	132	124	237	30	120
RALEIGH, NC	89	69	140	179		157	156	84	54	204	96	186
RICHMOND, VA	160	200	114	91	157		192	91	127	49	228	256
ROANOKE, VA	83	101	55	285	156	192		190	211	243	107	78

SEE ALSO DISTANCE AND DRIVING TIME MAP ON PAGES 286–287

Md.
Delaware
Virginia
North
Carolina

0 mi   10   20   30   40
0 km 10 20 30 40 50 60

One inch equals 17.4 miles
One centimeter equals 11 kilometers

FOR DETAIL OF AREA
INSIDE PURPLE FRAME,
SEE PAGES 144–145

Go to 104
Go to 144
Go to 145
Go to 103
Go to 113
Go to 115

ATLANTIC

OCEAN

DRIVING DISTANCES IN MILES	GREENVILLE, NC	MOREHEAD CITY, NC	NAGS HEAD, NC	NEW BERN, NC	NORFOLK, VA	OCEAN CITY, MD	RICHMOND, VA	SALISBURY, MD	VIRGINIA BEACH, VA	WASHINGTON, DC	WILLIAMSBURG, VA
MOREHEAD CITY, NC	150	82		184		185	326	241	321	206	352	221
NAGS HEAD, NC	59	135	184		149	82	214	179	209	94	284	131
NORFOLK, VA	50	130	185	82	151		138	91	133	18	196	43
WASHINGTON, DC	243	270	352	284	317	196	139	108	115	212		153

SEE ALSO DISTANCE AND DRIVING TIME MAP ON PAGES 286–287

DRIVING DISTANCES IN MILES	ARKADELPHIA, AR	FORT SMITH, AR	HENRYETTA, OK	HOT SPRINGS, AR	LITTLE ROCK, AR	MCALESTER, OK	MENA, AR	NEWPORT, AR	PARIS, TX	PINE BLUFF, AR	RUSSELLVILLE, AR	TEXARKANA, AR/TX
FORT SMITH, AR	152		100	126	165	114	81	220	214	210	87	180
HOT SPRINGS, AR	37	126	224		65	193	75	154	207	76	67	117
LITTLE ROCK, AR	72	165	263	65		278	141	89	242	45	81	153
TEXARKANA, AR/TX	83	180	227	117	153	188	99	241	92	163	180	

SEE ALSO DISTANCE AND DRIVING TIME MAP ON PAGES 286-287

Oklahoma   Arkansas

Texas

DRIVING DISTANCES IN MILES	BIRMINGHAM, AL	CLARKSDALE, MS	COLUMBIA, TN	COLUMBUS, MS	DECATUR, AL	FLORENCE, AL	GREENVILLE, AL	HUNTSVILLE, AL	JACKSON, TN	MEMPHIS, TN	OXFORD, MS	TUPELO, MS
BIRMINGHAM, AL		248	161	122	83	121	286	101	223	241	185	136
HUNTSVILLE, AL	101	260	79	163	25	65	318		205	216	196	148
MEMPHIS, TN	241	76	210	175	191	156	148	216	91		85	109
TUPELO, MS	136	113	159	66	123	92	172	148	107	109	50	

SEE ALSO DISTANCE AND DRIVING TIME MAP ON PAGES 286–287

Atlanta GA / Chattanooga TN

0 mi 10 20 30 40

0 km 10 20 30 40 50 60

One inch equals 17.4 miles
One centimeter equals 11 kilometers

Go to 111

Go to 112

Go to 121

Go to 130

Go to 131

N. CAROLINA
S. CAROLINA

North Carolina
South Carolina

Go to 117

Go to 126

Go to 133

DRIVING DISTANCES IN MILES	ALEXANDRIA, LA	EL DORADO, AR	GREENVILLE, AR	LONGVIEW, TX	LUFKIN, TX	MONROE, LA	NACOGDOCHES, TX	NATCHEZ, MS	NATCHITOCHES, LA	SHREVEPORT, LA	TEXARKANA, AR/TX	TYLER, TX
ALEXANDRIA, LA		147	276	179	160	96	167	76	55	121	190	213
MONROE, LA	96	86	267	170	223		203	95	100	103	172	204
SHREVEPORT, LA	121	96	165	68	121	103	101	198	73		69	102
TYLER, TX	213	196	77	42	82	204	76	288	164	102	118	

SEE ALSO DISTANCE AND DRIVING TIME MAP ON PAGES 286–287

Arkansas
Miss. Alabama
Louisiana

One inch equals 17.4 miles
One centimeter equals 11 kilometers

DRIVING DISTANCES IN MILES

	BIRMINGHAM, AL	EVERGREEN, AL	GREENVILLE, AL	HATTIESBURG, MS	JACKSON, MS	McCOMB, MS	MERIDIAN, MS	NATCHEZ, MS	SELMA, AL	TUSCALOOSA, AL	VICKSBURG, MS	WINONA, MS
HATTIESBURG, MS	239	184	215		90	75	89	142	193	183	132	180
JACKSON, MS	241	243	125	90		76	91	102	195	185	42	94
MERIDIAN, MS	149	152	216	89	91	167		194	104	94	133	113
TUSCALOOSA, AL	61	211	225	183	185	261	94	287	82		227	144

SEE ALSO DISTANCE AND DRIVING TIME MAP ON PAGES 286–287

SEE ALSO DISTANCE AND DRIVING TIME MAP ON PAGES 286–287

0 mi   10   20   30   40
0 km 10 20 30 40 50 60
One inch equals 17.4 miles
One centimeter equals 11 kilometers

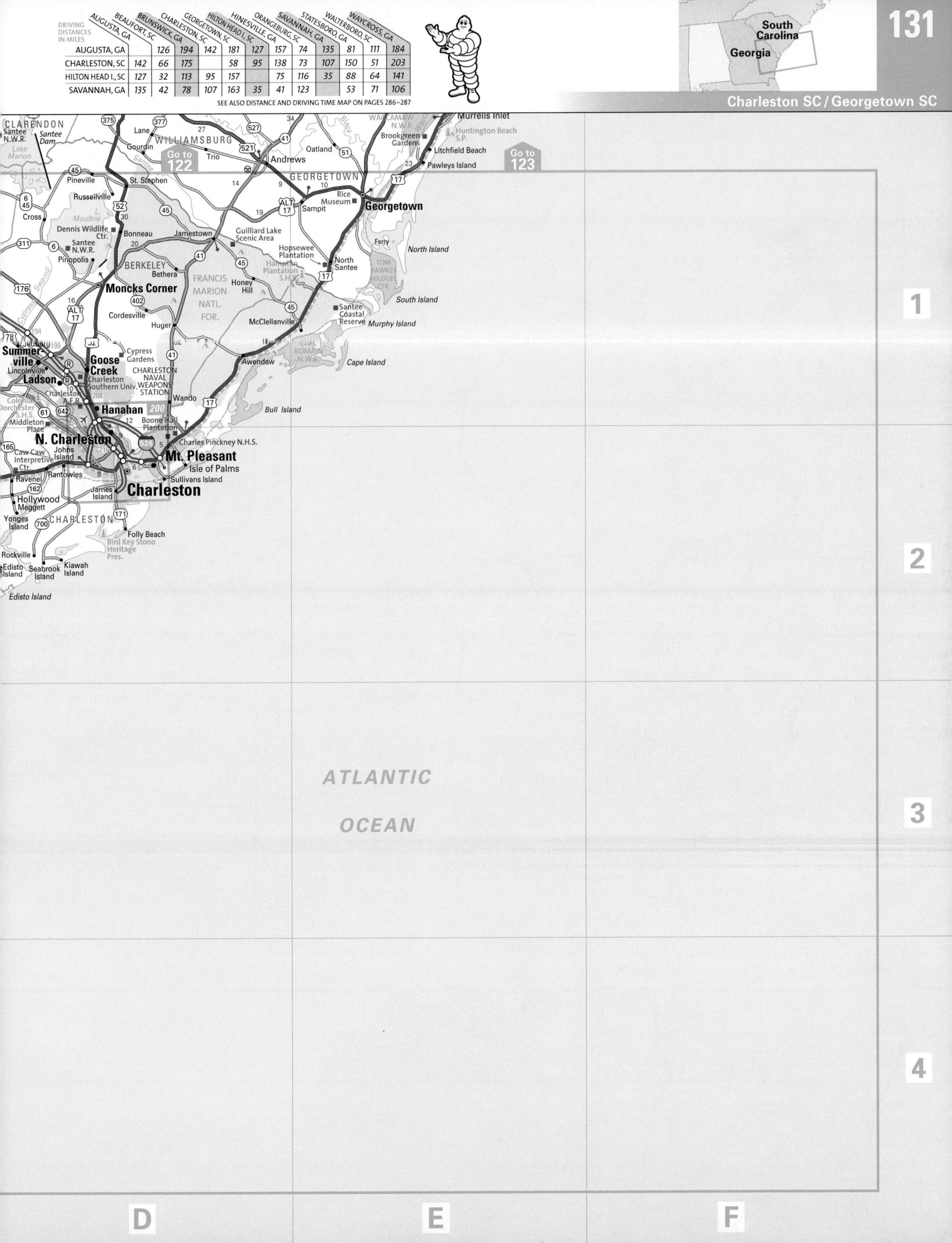

DRIVING DISTANCES IN MILES

	AUGUSTA, GA	BEAUFORT, SC	BRUNSWICK, GA	CHARLESTON, SC	GEORGETOWN, SC	HILTON HEAD I., SC	HINESVILLE, GA	ORANGEBURG, SC	SAVANNAH, GA	STATESBORO, GA	WALTERBORO, SC	WAYCROSS, GA
AUGUSTA, GA		126	194	142	181	127	157	74	135	81	111	184
CHARLESTON, SC	142	66	175		58	95	138	73	107	150	51	203
HILTON HEAD I., SC	127	32	113	95	157		75	116	35	88	64	141
SAVANNAH, GA	135	42	78	107	163	35	41	123		53	71	106

SEE ALSO DISTANCE AND DRIVING TIME MAP ON PAGES 286–287

Go to 122

Go to 123

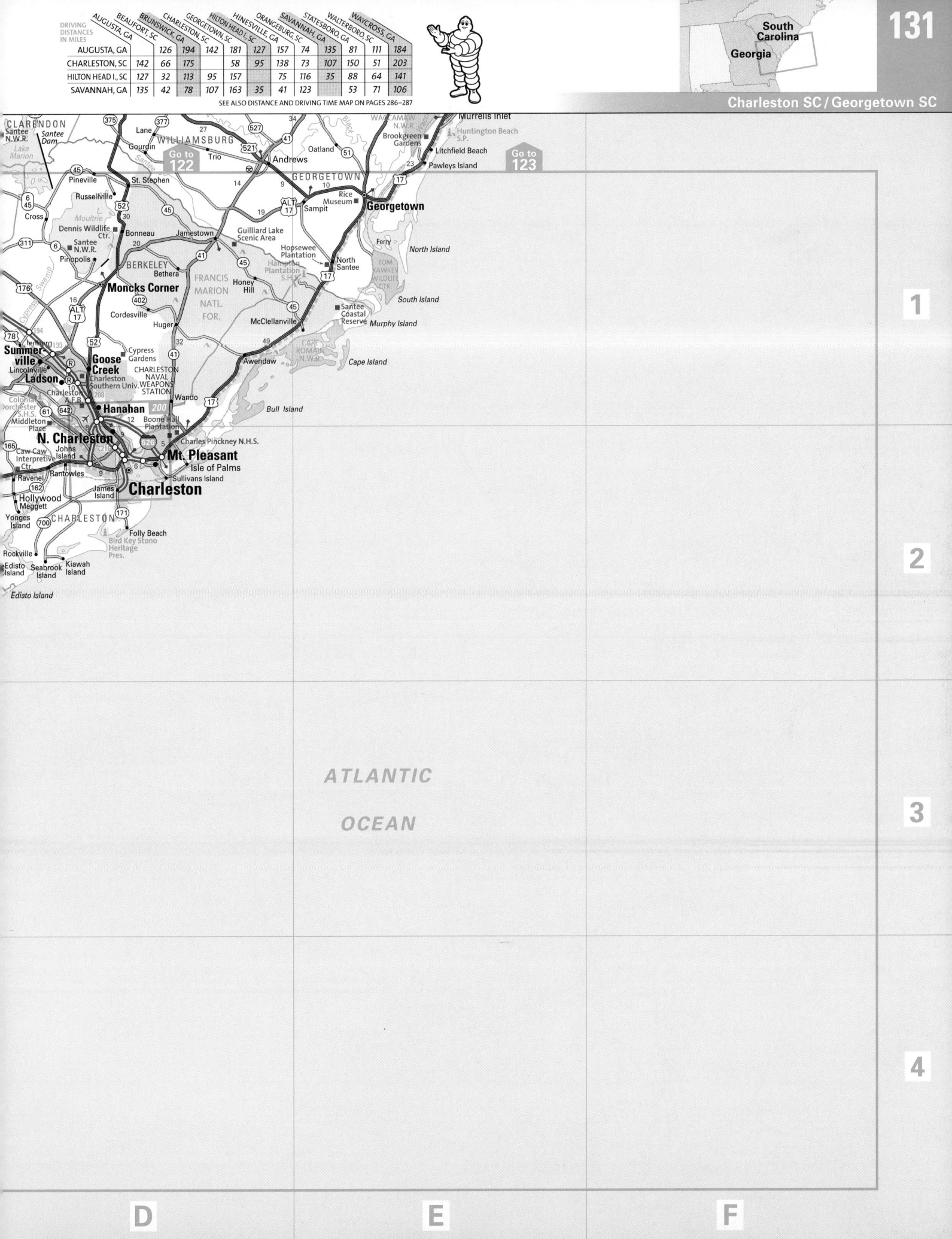

DRIVING DISTANCES IN MILES	AUGUSTA, GA	BEAUFORT, SC	BRUNSWICK, GA	CHARLESTON, SC	GEORGETOWN, SC	HILTON HEAD I., SC	HINESVILLE, GA	ORANGEBURG, SC	SAVANNAH, GA	STATESBORO, GA	WALTERBORO, SC	WAYCROSS, GA
AUGUSTA, GA		126	194	142	181	127	157	74	135	81	111	184
CHARLESTON, SC	142	66	175		58	95	138	73	107	150	51	203
HILTON HEAD I., SC	127	32	113	95	157		75	116	35	88	64	141
SAVANNAH, GA	135	42	78	107	163	35	41	123		53	71	106

SEE ALSO DISTANCE AND DRIVING TIME MAP ON PAGES 286–287

DRIVING DISTANCES IN MILES	ALEXANDRIA, LA	BEAUMONT, TX	DE RIDDER, LA	FREEPORT, TX	GALVESTON, TX	HOUSTON, TX	HUNTSVILLE, TX	LAFAYETTE, LA	LAKE CHARLES, LA	LUFKIN, TX	OPELOUSAS, LA	PORT ARTHUR, TX
BEAUMONT, TX	157		82	143	75	84	157	133	57	112	144	18
HOUSTON, TX	241	84	166	61	53		75	217	141	121	228	93
LAFAYETTE, LA	87	133	119	276	208	217	290		76	216	27	130
LAKE CHARLES, LA	100	57	49	200	132	141	214	76		140	87	54

SEE ALSO DISTANCE AND DRIVING TIME MAP ON PAGES 286–287

0 mi   10   20   30   40
0 km   10   20   30   40   50   60
One inch equals 17.4 miles
One centimeter equals 11 kilometers

Miss. Alabama
Louisiana Florida

DRIVING DISTANCES IN MILES	BATON ROUGE, LA	BILOXI, MS	GULFPORT, MS	GULF SHORES, AL	HAMMOND, LA	HATTIESBURG, MS	HOUMA, LA	McCOMB, MS	MOBILE, AL	NEW ORLEANS, LA	PASCAGOULA, MS	PENSACOLA, FL
BATON ROUGE, LA		151	140	254	51	174	101	102	205	91	170	264
BILOXI, MS	151		12	110	106	82	148	161	61	93	20	120
MOBILE, AL	205	61	75	48	159	97	201	215		146	41	58
NEW ORLEANS, LA	91	93	81	195	57	115	57	111	146		112	205

SEE ALSO DISTANCE AND DRIVING TIME MAP ON PAGES 286–287

One inch equals 17.4 miles
One centimeter equals 11 kilometers

GULF OF MEXICO

SEE ALSO DISTANCE AND DRIVING TIME MAP ON PAGES 286–287

Alabama Georgia

Florida

0 mi 10 20 30 40
0 km 10 20 30 40 50 60
One inch equals 17.4 miles
One centimeter equals 11 kilometers

Georgia
Florida

Go to 129

Go to 137

Go to 140

GULF OF MEXICO

GEORGIA
FLORIDA

A B C

1 2 3 4

DRIVING DISTANCES IN MILES	BRUNSWICK, GA	DAYTONA BEACH, FL	GAINESVILLE, FL	JACKSONVILLE, FL	LAKE CITY, FL	OCALA, FL	PERRY, FL	ST. AUGUSTINE, FL	STARKE, FL	TALLAHASSEE, FL	VALDOSTA, GA	WAYCROSS, GA
DAYTONA BEACH, FL	160		99	91	154	77	225	53	92	258	209	173
JACKSONVILLE, FL	69	91	70		62	101	133	41	45	166	117	78
OCALA, FL	171	77	40	101	80		120	81	57	186	137	170
TALLAHASSEE, FL	235	258	152	166	109	186	52	207	145		85	146

SEE ALSO DISTANCE AND DRIVING TIME MAP ON PAGES 286–287

Georgia

Florida

Go to 130

Go to 141

ATLANTIC OCEAN

Major locations shown on map: St. Simons Island, Brunswick, Jekyll Island, Kingsland, St. Marys, Fernandina Beach, Yulee, Amelia Island, Jacksonville, Atlantic Beach, Neptune Beach, Jacksonville Beach, Ponte Vedra Beach, Palm Valley, Orange Park, Fruit Cove, Middleburg, Green Cove Sprs., St. Augustine, St. Augustine Beach, St. Augustine Shores, Butler Beach, Crescent Beach, Palatka, Palm Coast, Beverly Beach, Flagler Beach, Bunnell, Ormond-by-the-Sea, Ormond Beach, Holly Hill, Daytona Beach, Daytona Beach Shores, S. Daytona, Port Orange, New Smyrna Beach, Edgewater, De Land, De Bary, Deltona

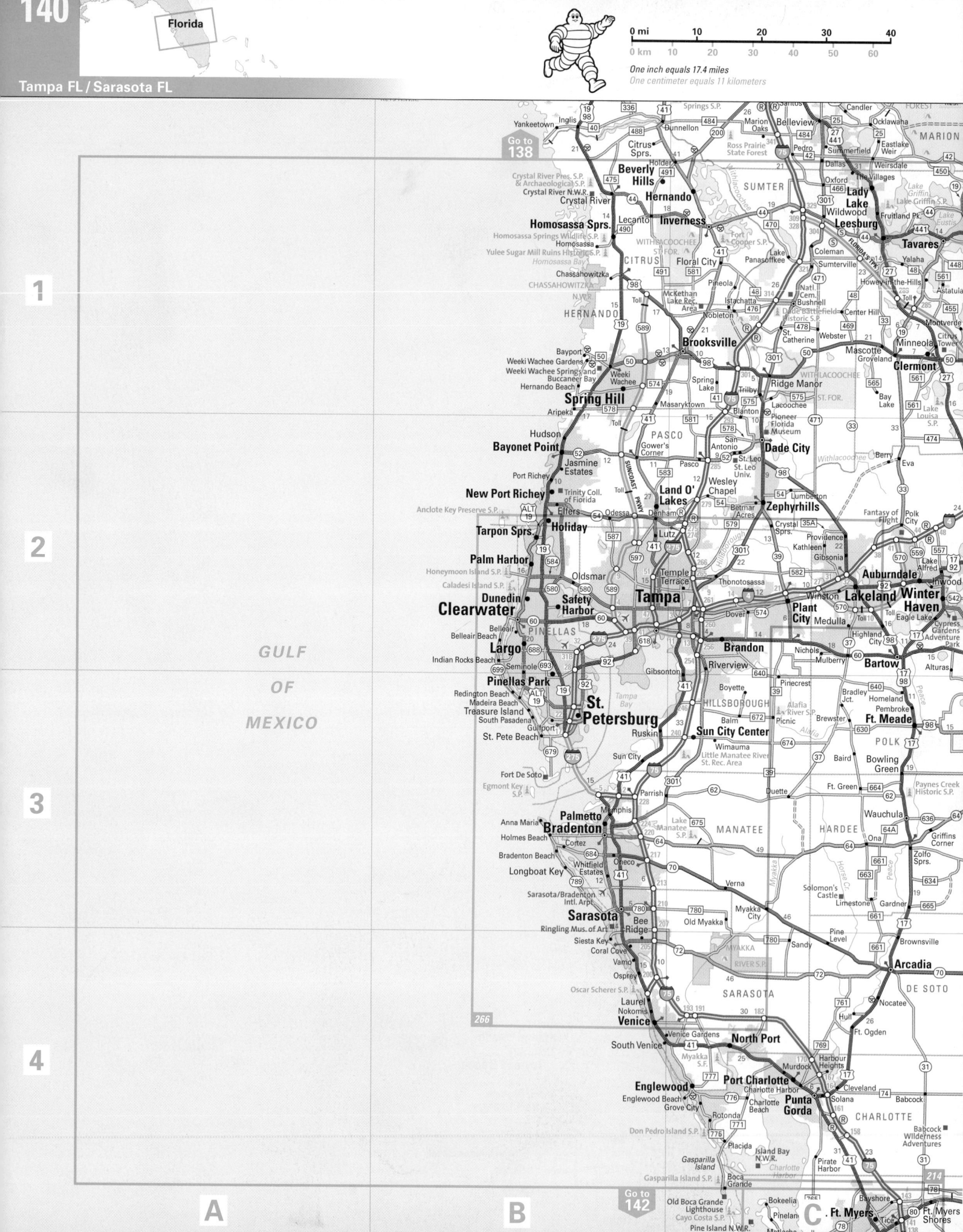

One inch equals 17.4 miles
One centimeter equals 11 kilometers

GULF

OF

MEXICO

Florida

DRIVING DISTANCES IN MILES	FORT MYERS, FL	FORT PIERCE, FL	LAKELAND, FL	MELBOURNE, FL	OKEECHOBEE, FL	ORLANDO, FL	PUNTA GORDA, FL	ST. PETERSBURG, FL	SARASOTA, FL	TAMPA, FL	TITUSVILLE, FL	W. PALM BEACH, FL
FORT PIERCE, FL	126		122	57	36	120	127	197	150	172	95	57
ORLANDO, FL	155	120	56	72	108		131	107	130	82	40	169
SARASOTA, FL	74	150	85	190	114	130	50	35		60	170	184
TAMPA, FL	123	172	37	142	162	82	99	25	60		121	223

SEE ALSO DISTANCE AND DRIVING TIME MAP ON PAGES 286–287

Go to 139

Go to 143

ATLANTIC OCEAN

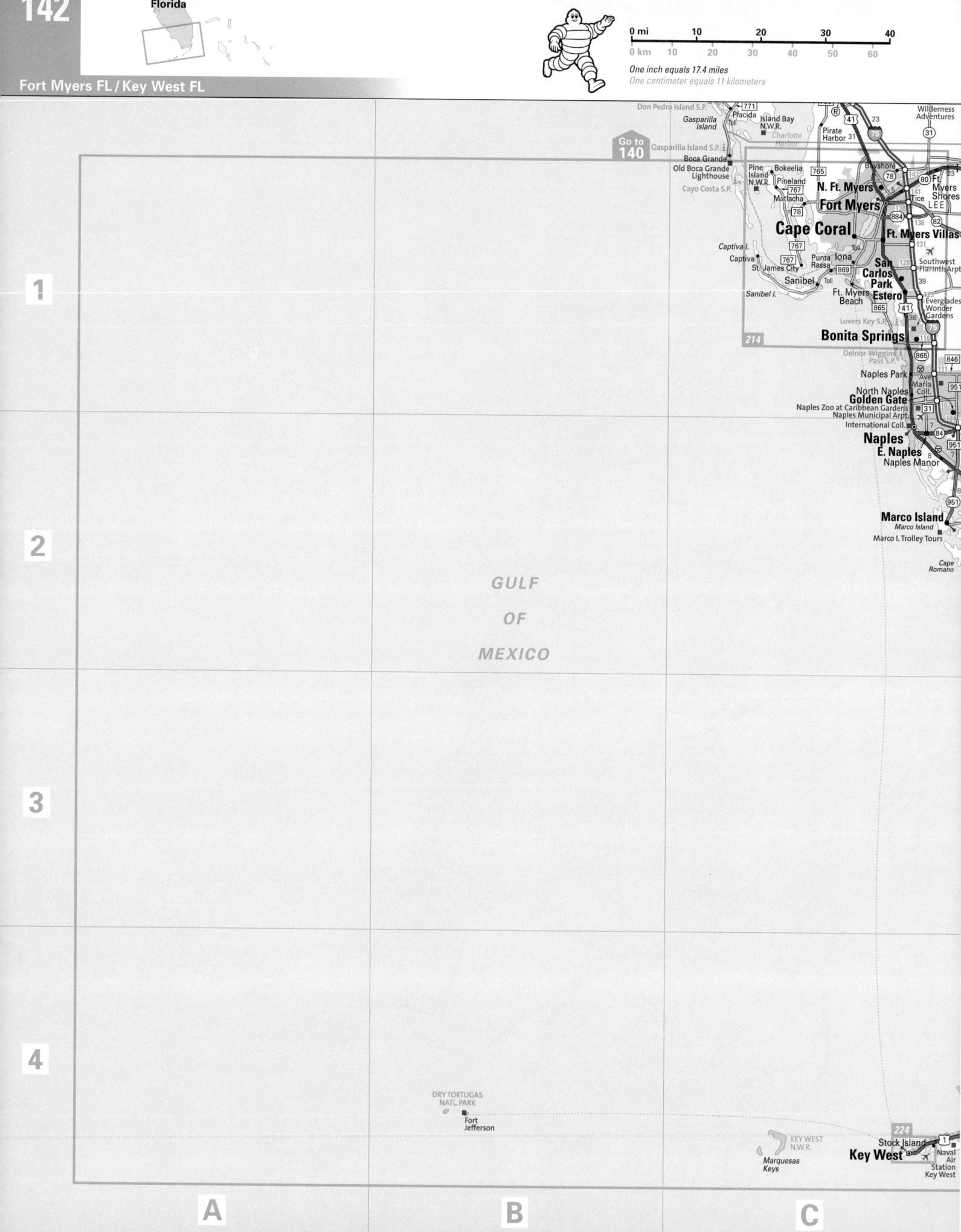

0 mi ..... 10 ..... 20 ..... 30 40
0 km ... 10 ... 20 ... 30 ... 40 ... 50 ... 60
One inch equals 17.4 miles
One centimeter equals 11 kilometers

Go to 140

Don Pedro Island S.P.
Gasparilla Island
Placida
Island Bay N.W.R.
Charlotte Harbor
Wilderness Adventures
Pirate Harbor
Gasparilla Island S.P.
Boca Grande
Old Boca Grande Lighthouse
Pine Island N.W.R.
Bokeelia
Pineland
Matlacha
Bayshore
N. Ft. Myers
Ft. Myers Shores
Tice
Fort Myers
LEE
Cayo Costa S.P.
Captiva I.
Captiva
Cape Coral
Ft. Myers Villas
St. James City
Punta Rassa
Iona
Southwest Fla. Intl. Arpt.
Sanibel
San Carlos Park
Sanibel I.
Ft. Myers Beach
Estero
Everglades Wonder Gardens
Lovers Key S.P.
Bonita Springs
214
Delnor-Wiggins Pass S.P.
Naples Park
Ave Maria Coll.
North Naples
Golden Gate
Naples Zoo at Caribbean Gardens
Naples Municipal Arpt.
International Coll.
Naples
E. Naples
Naples Manor
Marco Island
Marco Island
Marco I. Trolley Tours
Cape Romano

GULF

OF

MEXICO

DRY TORTUGAS NATL. PARK
Fort Jefferson

KEY WEST N.W.R.
Stock Island
224
Naval Air Station Key West
Key West
Marquesas Keys

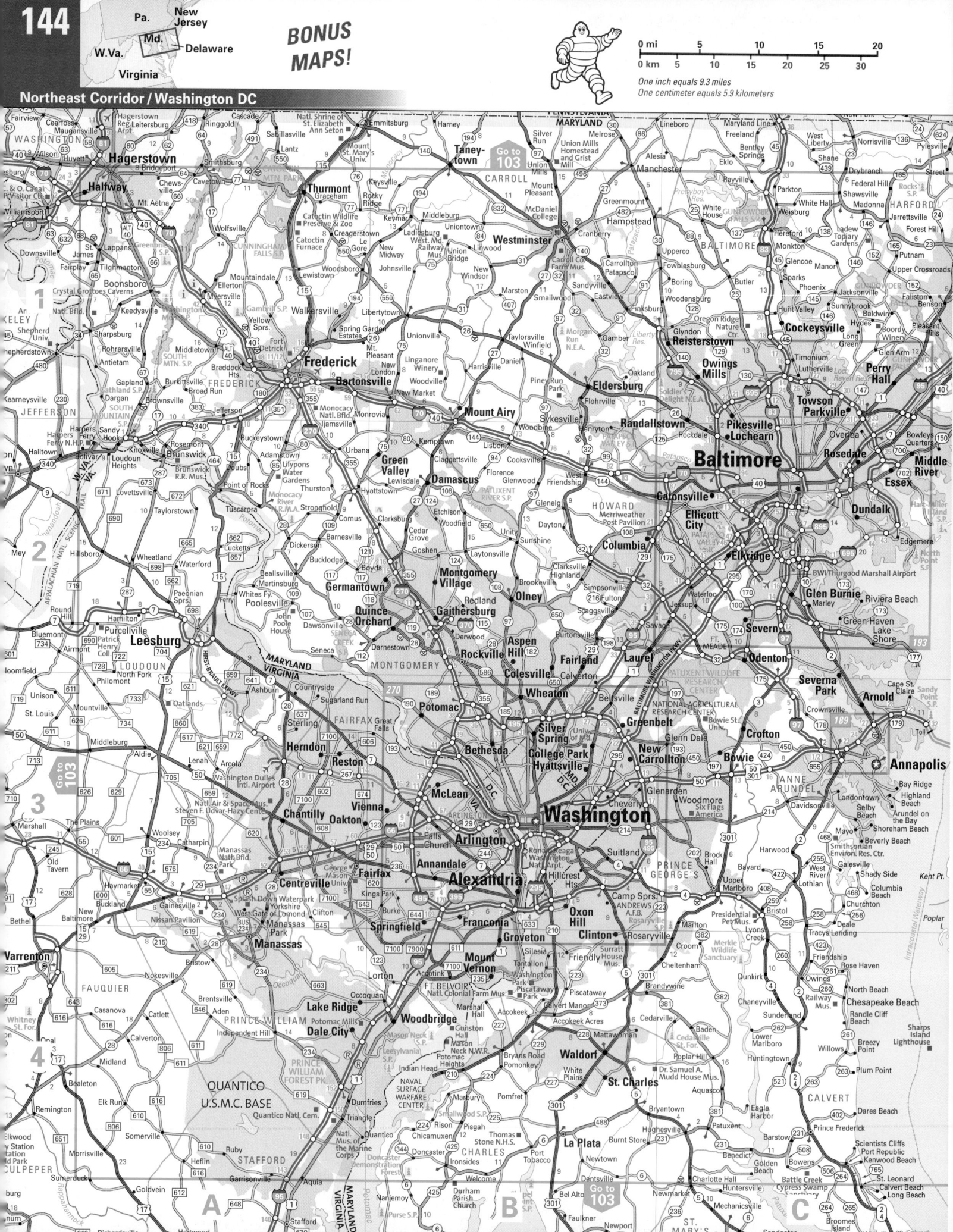

DRIVING DISTANCES IN MILES

	ANNAPOLIS, MD	BALTIMORE, MD	CAMBRIDGE, MD	DOVER, DE	ELKTON, MD	FREDERICK, MD	HAGERSTOWN, MD	LEESBURG, VA	MANASSAS, VA	REHOBOTH BEACH, DE	VINELAND, NJ	WASHINGTON, DC
BALTIMORE, MD	25		78	98	58	51	76	71	67	111	109	38
DOVER, DE	62	98	64		40	135	160	131	43	77	94	
FREDERICK, MD	73	51	128	135	106		28	25	61	161	158	44
WASHINGTON, DC	31	38	87	94	94	44	70	38	31	120	145	

SEE ALSO DISTANCE AND DRIVING TIME MAP ON PAGES 286–287

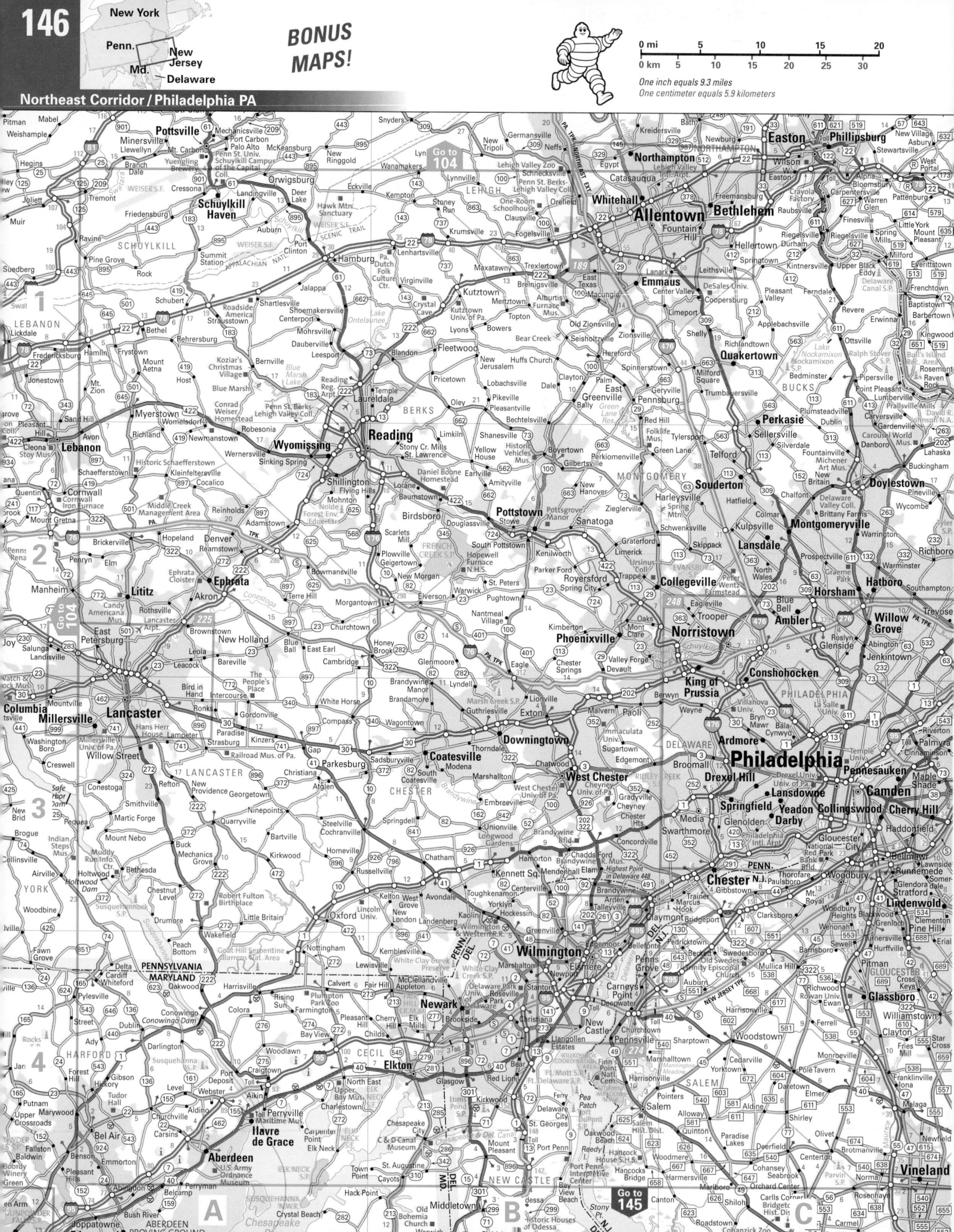

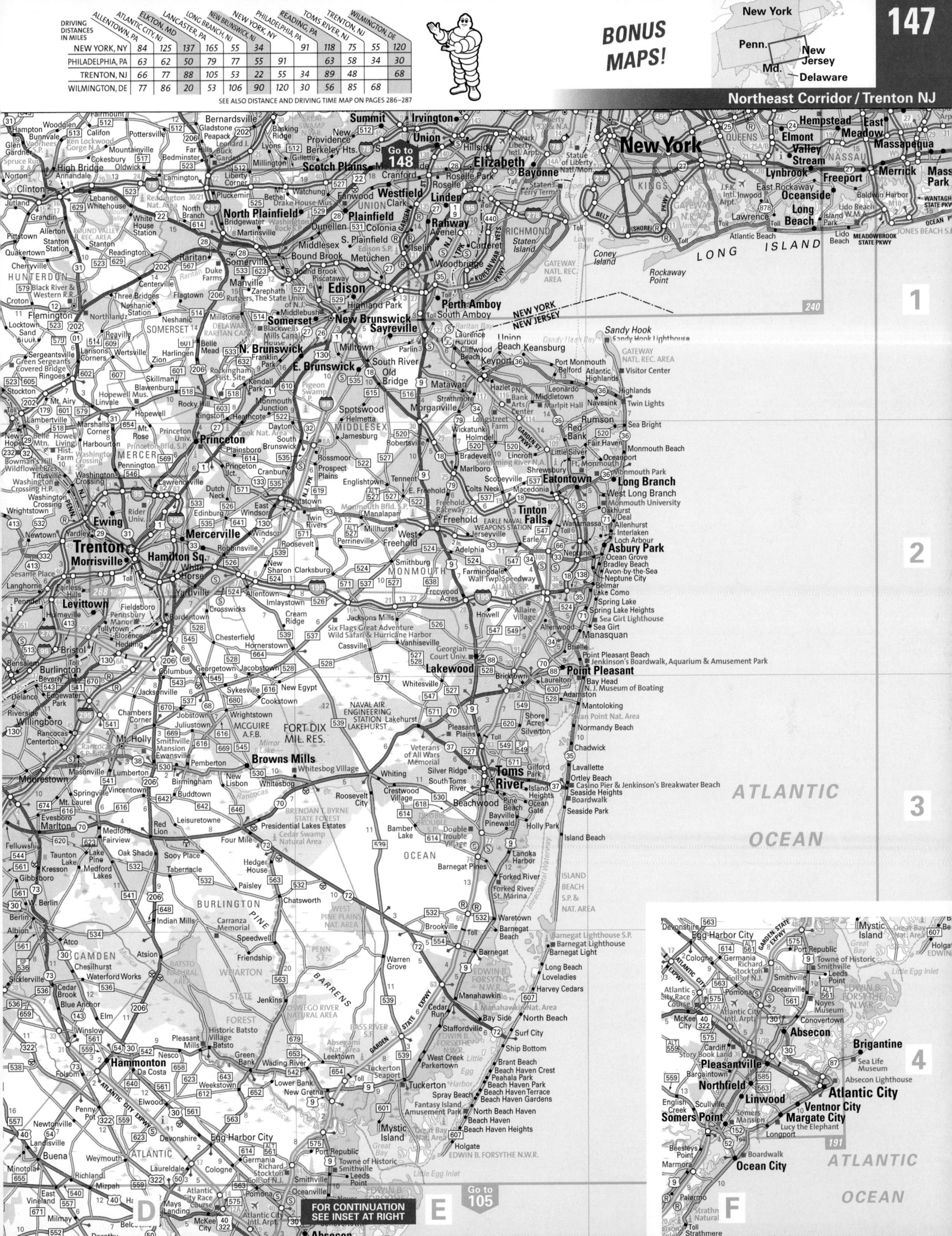

147

BONUS MAPS!

Northeast Corridor / Trenton NJ

New York
Penn.
New Jersey
Md.
Delaware

Go to 148

Go to 105

Go to 191

FOR CONTINUATION
SEE INSET AT RIGHT

DRIVING DISTANCES IN MILES	ALLENTOWN, PA	ATLANTIC CITY, NJ	ELKTON, MD	LANCASTER, PA	LONG BRANCH, NJ	NEW BRUNSWICK, NJ	NEW YORK, NY	PHILADELPHIA, PA	READING, PA	TOMS RIVER, NJ	TRENTON, NJ	WILMINGTON, DE
NEW YORK, NY	84	125	137	165	55	34		91	118	75	55	120
PHILADELPHIA, PA	63	62	50	79	55	91			63	58	34	30
TRENTON, NJ	66	77	88	105	53	22	55	34	89	48		68
WILMINGTON, DE	77	86	20	53	106	90	120	30	56	85	68	

SEE ALSO DISTANCE AND DRIVING TIME MAP ON PAGES 286-287

ATLANTIC OCEAN

LONG ISLAND

148

New York
Pa.
Rhode Island
Conn.
New Jersey

BONUS MAPS!

Northeast Corridor / New York NY

0 mi   5   10   15   20
0 km   5   10   15   20   25   30
One inch equals 9.3 miles
One centimeter equals 5.9 kilometers

Go to 94

Go to 94

Go to 147

NEW YORK
NEW JERSEY

DRIVING DISTANCES IN MILES	BRIDGEPORT, CT	DANBURY, CT	HARTFORD, CT	NEWARK, NJ	NEWBURGH, NY	NEW HAVEN, CT	NEW LONDON, CT	NEW YORK, NY	PATERSON, NJ	RIVERHEAD, NY	STAMFORD, CT	WATERBURY, CT
BRIDGEPORT, CT		31	56	69	73	19	64	60	71	115	21	33
NEWARK, NJ	69	79	125		66	88	134	11	18	88	48	108
NEW HAVEN, CT	19	35	39	88	78		46	78	89	133	40	30
NEW YORK, NY	60	69	115	11	56	78	124		16	78	38	99

SEE ALSO DISTANCE AND DRIVING TIME MAP ON PAGES 286–287

BONUS MAPS!

Massachusetts
Rhode Island
Connecticut

0 mi 5 10 15 20
0 km 5 10 15 20 25 30

One inch equals 9.3 miles
One centimeter equals 5.9 kilometers

Go to 94

Go to 95

1

Greenfield Gardner Fitchburg Leominster Chelmsford

Northampton Amherst Worcester Shrewsbury Marlborough Framingham Natick

2

Holyoke Chicopee Westfield West Springfield Springfield Aggawam Longmeadow Southbridge Webster Woonsocket Milford Franklin

Go to 94

MASS.
CONN.

3

Hartford West Hartford East Hartford Manchester Vernon Storrs Willimantic Putnam Danielson Central Falls Pawtucket Providence E. Providence Cranston Johnson

New Britain Newington Wethersfield West Warwick Warwick

4

Meriden Middletown Southington Colchester Norwich New London Groton Westerly Wakefield

North Haven New Haven

Go to 149

A   **B**   **C**

Block Island Sound

BONUS MAPS!

SEE ALSO DISTANCE AND DRIVING TIME MAP ON PAGES 286-287

DRIVING DISTANCES IN MILES	BOSTON, MA	GLOUCESTER, MA	HARTFORD, CT	HYANNIS, MA	NEW BEDFORD, MA	NEW LONDON, CT	NEWPORT, RI	PLYMOUTH, MA	PROVIDENCE, RI	PROVINCETOWN, MA	SPRINGFIELD, MA	WORCESTER, MA
BOSTON, MA		35	102	72	60	109	73	41	52	117	95	46
HARTFORD, CT	102	136		155	104	46	85	127	73	200	25	62
PROVIDENCE, RI	52	92	73	71	33	58	33	41		117	75	43
SPRINGFIELD, MA	95	129	25	148	127	71	111	120	75	193		55

FOR CONTINUATION
SEE INSET AT RIGHT

Go to
95

ATLANTIC
OCEAN

1

Massachusetts
Bay

ATLANTIC OCEAN

2

CAPE COD
NATL.
SEASHORE

Cape Cod

Cape Cod
Bay

3

Nantucket
Sound

Monomoy I.

MONOMOY
N.W.R.

Monomoy Pt.

4

Nantucket
Sound

Nantucket
N.W.R. Great Pt.

NANTUCKET

Nantucket
Island

F

Rhode Island Sound

Martha's
Vineyard

Muskeget Channel

D

E

0 mi   10   20   30   40
0 km   10   20   30   40   50   60
One inch equals 17.4 miles
One centimeter equals 11 kilometers

1

2

3

4

A   **B**   **C**

PACIFIC OCEAN

Kaua'i

Ni'ihau
(RESTRICTED
PUBLIC ACCESS)

FOR CONTINUATION
SEE MAP BELOW

FOR CONTINUATION
SEE MAP ABOVE

O'ahu

Honolulu

Moloka'i

Lāna'i

Maui

Kaho'olawe

PACIFIC OCEAN

FOR CONTINUATION
SEE MAP AT RIGHT

DRIVING DISTANCES IN MILES

	HĀNA	HILO	HONOLULU	HO'OLEHUA	KAHULUI	KAILUA	KAILUA-KONA	LAHAINA	LANAI CITY	LIHUE	WAIHAWĀ	WAIMEA
HILO	149*		217*	169*	121*	235*	88	142*	155*	319*	234*	54
HONOLULU	129*	217*		54*	101*	14	185*	92*	74*	102*	23	172*
KAHULUI	42	121*	101*		76*	119*	109*	23	57*	202*	118*	79*
LIHUE	230*	319*	102*	156*	202*	120*	285*	225*	176*		119*	174*

*DISTANCE INCLUDES AIR TRAVEL   SEE ALSO DISTANCE AND DRIVING TIME MAP ON PAGES 286–287

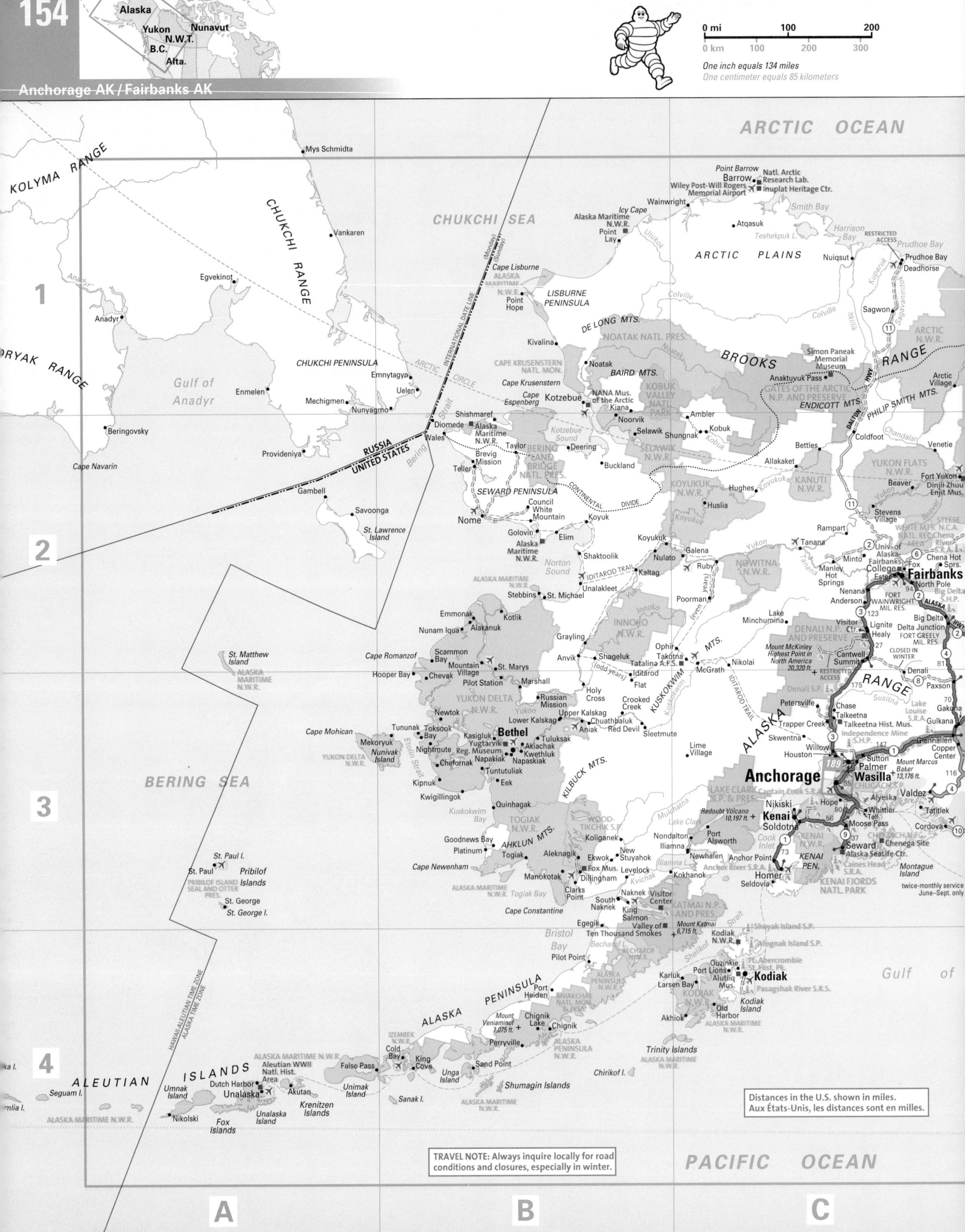

ARCTIC OCEAN

KOLYMA RANGE

CHUKCHI SEA

Mys Schmidta

Vankaren

CHUKCHI RANGE

CHUKCHI PENINSULA

Egvekinot

Anadyr

Gulf of Anadyr

KORYAK RANGE

Enmelen

Mechigmen

Nunyamgo

Uelen

Emnytagvy

Beringovsky

Cape Navarin

Providenya

RUSSIA
UNITED STATES

Gambell

Savoonga

St. Lawrence Island

BERING SEA

St. Matthew Island

ALASKA MARITIME N.W.R.

Cape Mohican

Nunivak Island

Mekoryuk

St. Paul I.

St. Paul

Pribilof Islands

PRIBILOF ISLAND SEAL AND OTTER PRES.

St. George

St. George I.

ALEUTIAN ISLANDS

Seguam I.

Umnak Island

Nikolski

Fox Islands

Dutch Harbor

Unalaska

Akutan

Krenitzen Islands

Unalaska Island

Unimak Island

False Pass

King Cove

Unga Island

Sand Point

Sanak I.

Shumagin Islands

Chirikof I.

ARCTIC OCEAN

ARCTIC PLAINS

Point Barrow
Barrow
Wiley Post-Will Rogers
Memorial Airport

Natl. Arctic
Research Lab.
Inupiat Heritage Ctr.

Wainwright

Atqasuk

Smith Bay

Harrison Bay

RESTRICTED ACCESS

Prudhoe Bay

Nuiqsut

Sagwon

Deadhorse

Icy Cape
Alaska Maritime N.W.R.
Point Lay

Teshekpuk L.

Colville

Cape Lisburne
N.W.R.
Point Hope

LISBURNE PENINSULA

DE LONG MTS.

BROOKS

RANGE

ARCTIC N.W.R.

NOATAK NATL. PRES.

Kivalina

Simon Paneak Memorial Museum

Anaktuvuk Pass

GATES OF THE ARCTIC N.P. AND PRESERVE

ENDICOTT MTS.

PHILIP SMITH MTS.

Arctic Village

CAPE KRUSENSTERN NATL. MON.

Noatak

BAIRD MTS.

NANA Mus. of the Arctic

DALTON HWY.

Coldfoot

Cape Krusenstern

Cape Espenberg

Kotzebue

Kiana

Noorvik

KOBUK VALLEY NATL PARK

Ambler

Shungnak

Kobuk

Bettles

Venetie

YUKON FLATS N.W.R.

Fort Yukon

Beaver

Dinjii Zhuu Enjit Mus.

Shishmaref

Diomede

Wales

SEWARD PENINSULA

Kotzebue Sound

Selawik

SELAWIK N.W.R.

KANUTI N.W.R.

KOYUKUK N.W.R.

Deering

Buckland

Alaska Maritime N.W.R.

Brevig Mission

Teller

BERING LAND BRIDGE NATL. PRES.

CONTINENTAL DIVIDE

Allakaket

Hughes

Huslia

Koyukuk

Koyuk

Rampart

Stevens Village

College

WHITE MTS. N.R.A.

STEESE NATL. REC. AREA

Chena Hot Sprs.

Council White Mountain

Golovin

Elim

Alaska Maritime N.W.R.

Norton Sound

Nome

Shaktoolik

Koyukuk

Nulato

Galena

NOWITNA N.W.R.

Tanana

Manley Hot Springs

Minto

Univ. of Alaska-Fairbanks

Fox

Fairbanks
North Pole

IDITAROD TRAIL

Unalakleet

Kaltag

Ruby

Poorman

Nenana

Anderson

FORT WAINWRIGHT MIL. RES.

ALASKA HWY.

Big Delta

Stebbins

St. Michael

Emmonak

Kotlik

Nunam Iqua

Alakanuk

INNOKO N.W.R.

Grayling

Ophir

Takotna

McGrath

Nikolai

Lignite Healy

DENALI N.P. AND PRESERVE

Delta Junction

FORT GREELY MIL. RES.

CLOSED IN WINTER

Visitor Ctr.

123

Cape Romanzof

Scammon Bay

Mountain Village

St. Marys

Anvik

Shageluk

Iditarod

Flat

Mount McKinley Highest Point in North America 20,320 ft.

Cantwell Summit

RESTRICTED ACCESS

Denali

Paxson

Hooper Bay

Chevak

Pilot Station

Marshall

Holy Cross

Crooked Creek

KUSKOKWIM

MTS.

IDITAROD TRAIL

Denali S.P.

Petersville

ALASKA

RANGE

Gakona

YUKON DELTA N.W.R.

Russian Mission

Upper Kalskag

Chuathbaluk

Red Devil

Sleetmute

Lime Village

Chase

Talkeetna

Talkeetna Hist. Mus.

Lake Louise S.R.A.

Gulkana

Newtok

Lower Kalskag

Aniak

Trapper Creek

Glennallen

Copper Center

Toksook Bay

Kasigluk

Bethel

Tuluksak

Skwentna

Independence Mine

Tununak

Yugtarvik Reg. Museum

Akiachak

Kwethluk

KILBUCK MTS.

Willow

Houston

Sutton

Palmer

Mount Marcus Baker 13,176 ft.

Nightmute

Napakiak

Napaskiak

Wasilla

CHUGACH

Kipnuk

Chefornak

Tuntutuliak

Eek

Anchorage

Captain Cook S.R.A.

Hope

Whittier

Valdez

Tatitlek

Kwigillingok

Quinhagak

TOGIAK N.W.R.

Kuskokwim Bay

WOOD-TIKCHIK S.P.

AHKLUN MTS.

Redoubt Volcano 10,197 ft.

LAKE CLARK N.P. & PRES.

Nondalton

Port Alsworth

Nikiski

Kenai

Soldotna

Toll

Moose Pass

Seward

KENAI FJORDS NATL. PARK

Chenega Site

Cordova

Goodnews Bay

Platinum

Togiak

Aleknagik

Koliganek

Ekwok

New Stuyahok

Iliamna

Newhalen

Kohanok

Anchor Point

Anchor River S.R.A.

KENAI PEN.

Homer

Seldovia

Caines Head S.R.A.

Alaska SeaLife Ctr.

Alyeska

Montague Island

Cape Newenham

Manokotak

Dillingham

Fox Mus.

Levelock

Cook Inlet

twice-monthly service June-Sept. only

Clarks Point

South Naknek

Naknek

King Salmon

Visitor Center

KATMAI N.P. AND PRES.

Mount Katmai 6,715 ft.

Shuyak Island S.P.

Afognak Island S.P.

Egegik

Valley of Ten Thousand Smokes

Bechanof L.

BECHAROF N.W.R.

Shelikof Strait

Kodiak N.W.R.

Pilot Point

Ouzinkie

Port Lions

Karluk

Kodiak

KODIAK N.W.R.

Alutiiq Mus.

Gulf of

Port Heiden

ANIAKCHAK NATL. MON. & PRES.

Larsen Bay

Akhiok

Old Harbor

Kodiak Island

FT. ABERCROMBIE ST. HIST. PK.

Pasagshak River S.R.S.

ALASKA

PENINSULA

Mount Veniaminof 7,075 ft.

Chignik Lake

Chignik

ALASKA PENINSULA N.W.R.

Trinity Islands

Alaska Maritime N.W.R.

IZEMBEK N.W.R.

Cold Bay

Perryville

Aleutian WWII Natl. Hist. Area

PACIFIC OCEAN

A   B   C

DRIVING DISTANCES IN MILES	ANCHORAGE, AK	DAWSON CREEK, BC	DENALI NP, AK	FAIRBANKS, AK	HOMER, AK	JUNEAU, AK	PRINCE GEORGE, BC	PRINCE RUPERT, BC	SKAGWAY, AK	TOK, AK	WHITEHORSE, YT	YELLOWKNIFE, NT
ANCHORAGE, AK		1516	275	378	225	841*	1679	1514	807	323	697	1844
DAWSON CREEK, BC	1516		1503	1400	1740	963*	224	625	862	1193	819	741
FAIRBANKS, AK	378	1400	103		603	726*	1564	1398	691	207	581	1729
WHITEHORSE, YT	697	819	684	581	921	211*	982	817	110	374		1147

*DISTANCE INCLUDES FERRY TRAVEL   SEE ALSO DISTANCE AND DRIVING TIME MAP ON PAGES 286–287

Distances in Canada shown in kilometers.
Au Canada, les distances sont en kilomètres.

The Alaska Marine Highway—with ferry service to
30 communities in Alaska, plus Bellingham WA and
Prince Rupert BC—is an All-American Road

Go to 158
Go to 164
Go to 156
Go to 157

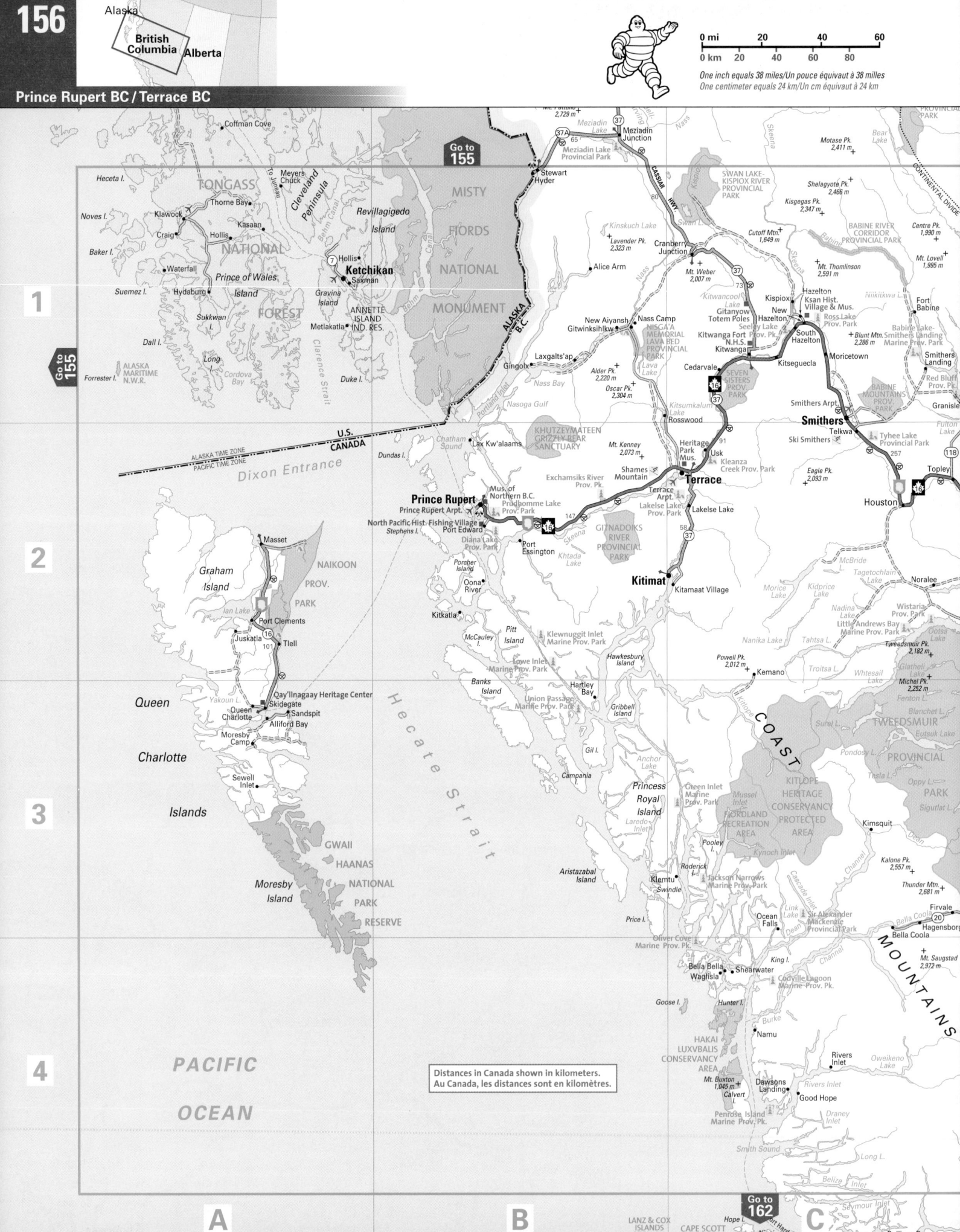

0 mi 20 40 60
0 km 20 40 60 80

One inch equals 38 miles/Un pouce équivaut à 38 milles
One centimeter equals 24 km/Un cm équivaut à 24 km

Distances in Canada shown in kilometers.
Au Canada, les distances sont en kilomètres.

Go to 155
Go to 155
Go to 162

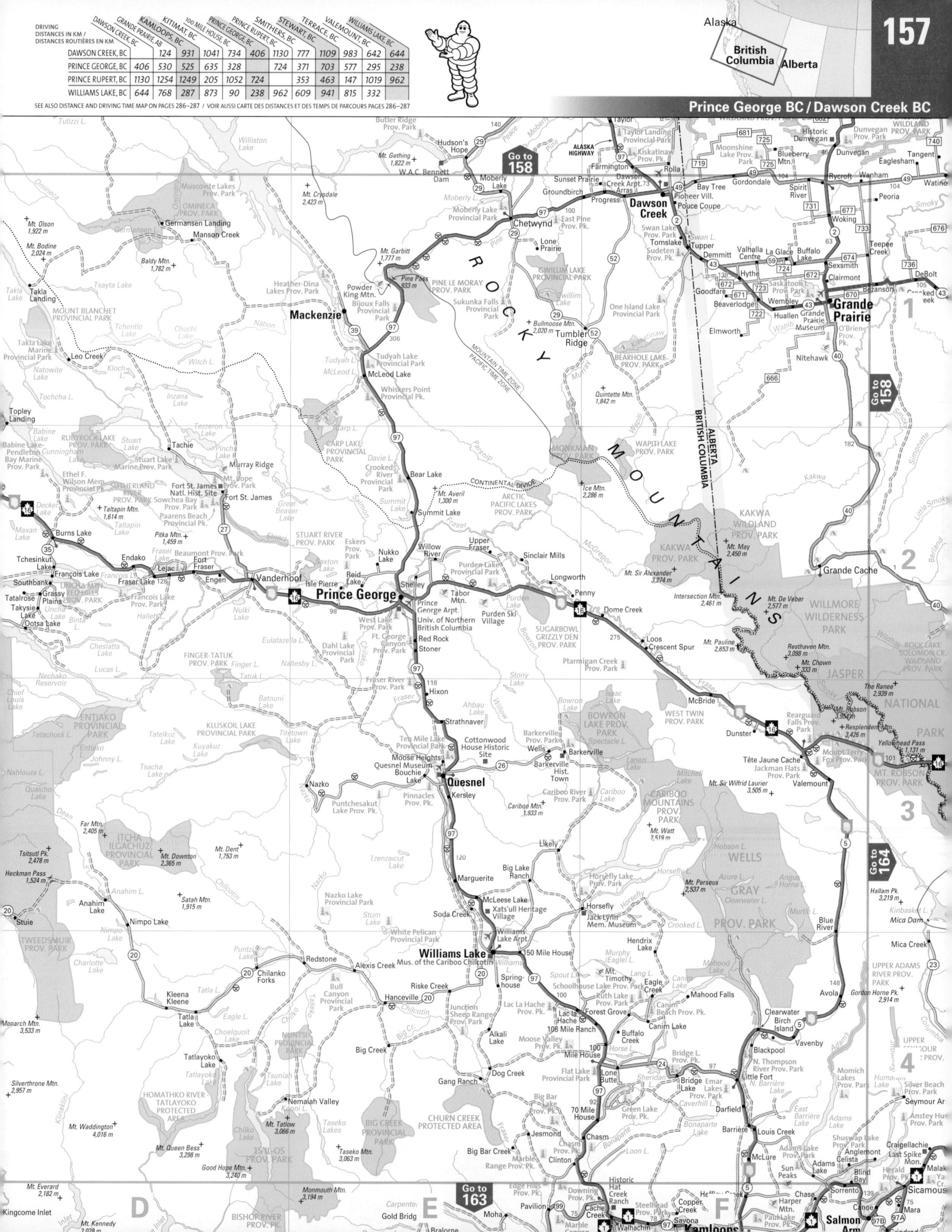

Go to 158

Go to 158

Go to 164

Go to 163

DRIVING DISTANCES IN KM / DISTANCES ROUTIÈRES EN KM	DAWSON CREEK, BC	GRANDE PRAIRIE, AB	KAMLOOPS, BC	KITIMAT, BC	100 MILE HOUSE, BC	PRINCE GEORGE, BC	PRINCE RUPERT, BC	SMITHERS, BC	STEWART, BC	TERRACE, BC	VALEMOUNT, BC	WILLIAMS LAKE, BC	
DAWSON CREEK, BC		124	931	1041	734	406	1130	777	1109	983	642	644	
PRINCE GEORGE, BC	406	530	525	635	328		724	371	703	577	295	238	
PRINCE RUPERT, BC	1130	1254	1249	205	1052	724		353	463	147	1019	962	
WILLIAMS LAKE, BC	644	768	287	873	90	238	962	609	941	815	332		

SEE ALSO DISTANCE AND DRIVING TIME MAP ON PAGES 286–287 / VOIR AUSSI CARTE DES DISTANCES ET DES TEMPS DE PARCOURS PAGES 286–287

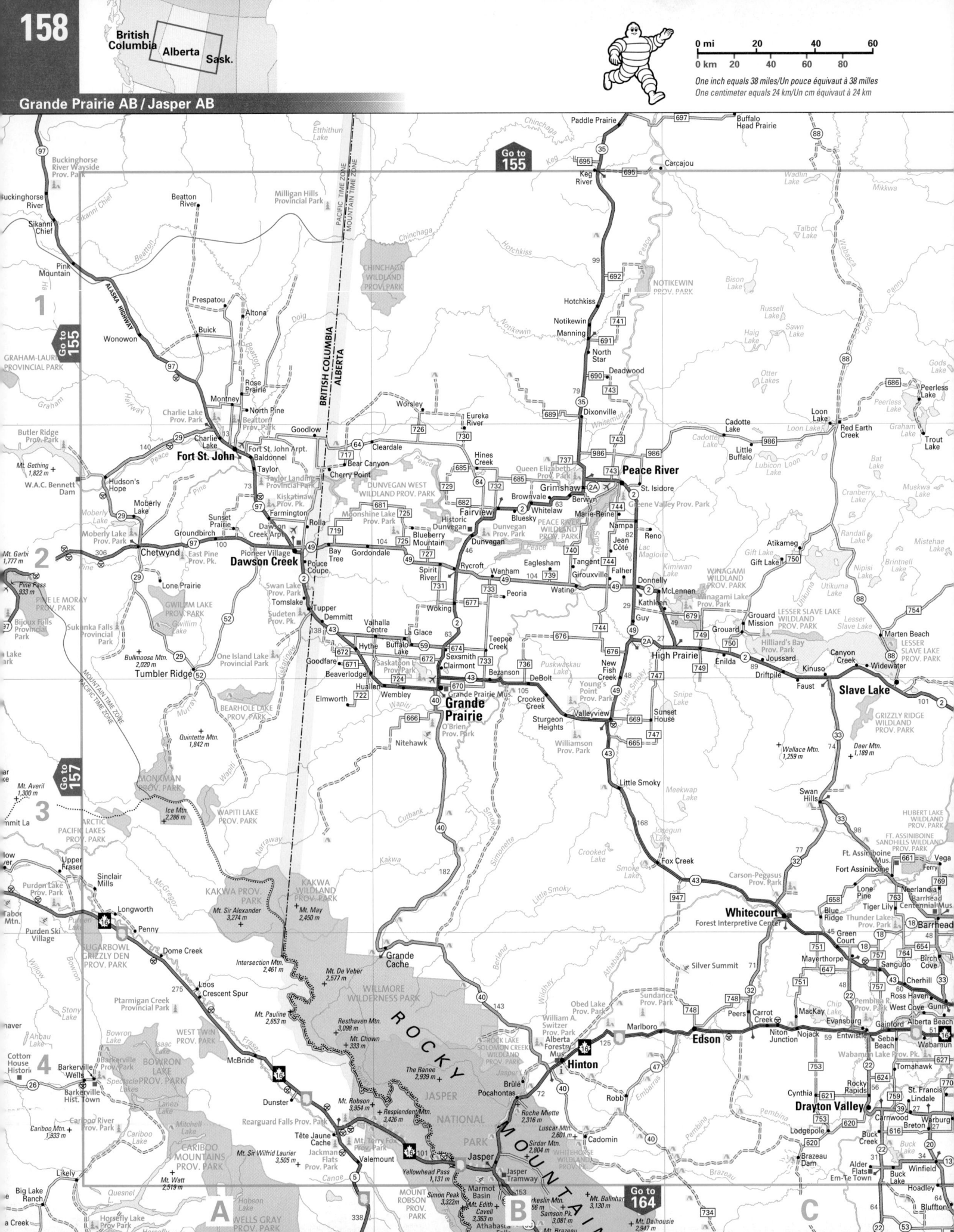

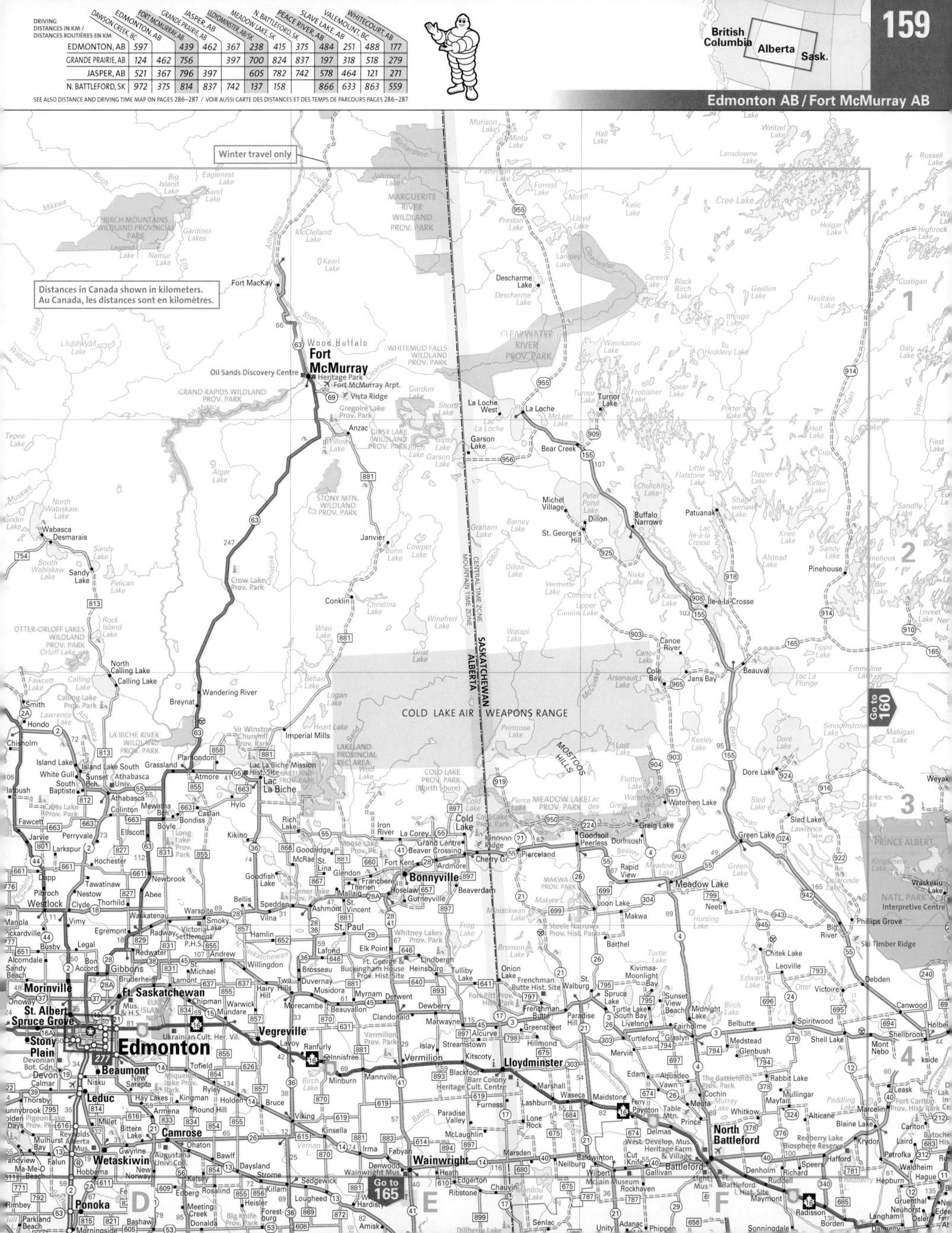

DRIVING
DISTANCES IN KM /
DISTANCES ROUTIÈRES EN KM

	DAWSON CREEK, BC	EDMONTON, AB	FORT McMURRAY, AB	GRANDE PRAIRIE, AB	JASPER, AB	LLOYDMINSTER, AB/SK	MEADOW LAKE, SK	N. BATTLEFORD, SK	PEACE RIVER, AB	SLAVE LAKE, AB	VALEMOUNT, BC	WHITECOURT, AB
EDMONTON, AB	597		439	462	367	238	415	375	484	251	488	177
GRANDE PRAIRIE, AB	124	462	756		397	700	824	837	197	318	518	279
JASPER, AB	521	367	796	397		605	782	742	578	464	121	271
N. BATTLEFORD, SK	972	375	814	837	742	137	158		866	633	863	559

SEE ALSO DISTANCE AND DRIVING TIME MAP ON PAGES 286–287 / VOIR AUSSI CARTE DES DISTANCES ET DES TEMPS DE PARCOURS PAGES 286–287

Winter travel only

Distances in Canada shown in kilometers.
Au Canada, les distances sont en kilomètres.

Go to 160

Go to 165

One inch equals 38 miles/Un pouce équivaut à 38 milles
One centimeter equals 24 km/Un cm équivaut à 24 km

Go to 159
Go to 165
Go to 166

DRIVING
DISTANCES IN KM /
DISTANCES ROUTIÈRES EN KM

	FLIN FLON, MB	GILLAM, MB	GRAND RAPIDS, MB	LA LOCHE, SK	LA RONGE, SK	LYNN LAKE, MB	MEADOW LAKE, SK	NIPAWIN, SK	N. BATTLEFORD, SK	PRINCE ALBERT, SK	THE PAS, MB	THOMPSON, MB
FLIN FLON, MB		676	402	889	613	703	633	388	571	375	141	380
MEADOW LAKE, SK	633	1309	867	305	496	1336		399	158	258	569	1013
PRINCE ALBERT, SK	375	1051	609	514	238	1078	258	141	196		311	781
THOMPSON, MB	380	296	328	1269	697	323	1013	640	977	781	470	

SEE ALSO DISTANCE AND DRIVING TIME MAP ON PAGES 286–287 / VOIR AUSSI CARTE DES DISTANCES ET DES TEMPS DE PARCOURS PAGES 286–287

Alberta Sask. Manitoba
Ontario

Distances in Canada shown in kilometers.
Au Canada, les distances sont en kilomètres.

Go to 167

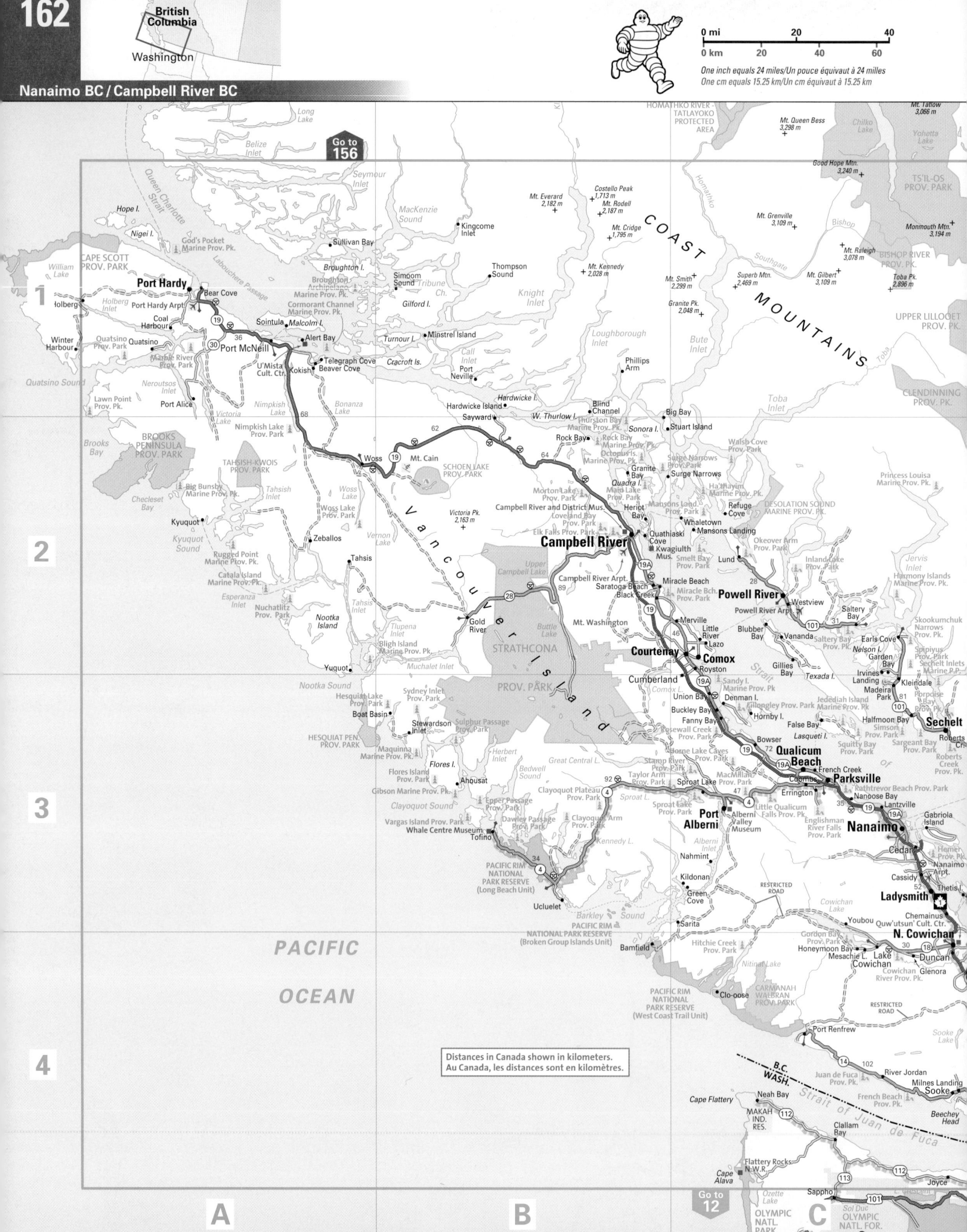

0 mi 20 40
0 km 20 40 60
One inch equals 24 miles/Un pouce équivaut à 24 milles
One cm equals 15.25 km/Un cm équivaut à 15.25 km

Go to
156

COAST

MOUNTAINS

Long Lake

Belize Inlet

Seymour Inlet

HOMATHKO RIVER - TATLAYOKO PROTECTED AREA

Mt. Tatlow 3,066 m

Mt. Queen Bess 3,298 m

Chilko Lake

Yoholla Lake

Mt. Everard 2,182 m

Costello Peak 1,713 m
Mt. Rodell 2,187 m

Good Hope Mtn. 3,240 m

TS'IL-OS PROV. PARK

Queen Charlotte Strait

Hope I.

Nigei I.

God's Pocket Marine Prov. Pk.

MacKenzie Sound

Kingcome Inlet

Mt. Cridge 1,795 m

Mt. Grenville 3,109 m

Monmouth Mtn. 3,194 m

Sullivan Bay

Labouchere Passage

Broughton I.

Simoom Sound Tribune Ch.

Thompson Sound

Mt. Kennedy 2,028 m

Granite Pk. 2,048 m

Mt. Smith 2,299 m

Bishop

Mt. Raleigh 3,078 m

BISHOP RIVER PROV. PK.

CAPE SCOTT PROV. PARK

William Lake

Holberg

Port Hardy

Bear Cove

Holberg Inlet

Port Hardy Arpt.

Broughton Archipelago

Gilford I.

Knight Inlet

Mt. Gilbert 3,109 m

Toba Pk. 2,896 m

1

Winter Harbour

Quatsino Prov. Park

Quatsino

Coal Harbour

Sointula

Malcolm I.

Cormorant Channel Marine Prov. Pk.

Loughborough Inlet

Phillips Arm

Bute Inlet

UPPER LILLOOET PROV. PK.

Alert Bay

Turnour I.

Minstrel Island

Marble River Prov. Park

Port McNeill

Neroutsos Inlet

U'Mista Cult. Ctr.

Kokish

Telegraph Cove

Beaver Cove

Cracroft Is.

Call Inlet

Port Neville

CLENDINNING PROV. PK.

Quatsino Sound

Lawn Point Prov. Pk.

Port Alice

Victoria Lake

Nimpkish Lake

Bonanza Lake

Hardwicke I.

Hardwicke Island

Blind Channel

Big Bay

Toba Inlet

BROOKS PENINSULA PROV. PARK

Brooks Bay

Big Bunsby Marine Prov. Pk.

68

Nimpkish Lake Prov. Park

Sayward

Thurston Bay Marine Prov. Pk.

W. Thurlow I.

Stuart Island

Princess Louisa Marine Prov. Pk.

Checleset Bay

TAHSISH-KWOIS PROV. PARK

Tahsish Inlet

Woss

62

Mt. Cain

SCHOEN LAKE PROV. PARK

64

Rock Bay

Rock Bay Marine Prov. Pk.

Octopus I.

Sonora I.

Surge Narrows

Walsh Cove Prov. Park

Kyuquot

Woss Lake

Woss Lake Prov. Park

Victoria Pk. 2,163 m

Granite Bay

Quadra I.

Surge Narrows

Ha'thayim Marine Prov. Pk.

Refuge Cove

DESOLATION SOUND MARINE PROV. PK.

2

Kyuquot Sound

Rugged Point Marine Prov. Pk.

Zeballos

Vernon Lake

Main Lake Prov. Park

Mansons Land.

Whaletown

Mansons Landing

Okeover Arm Prov. Pk.

Jervis Inlet

Catala Island Marine Prov. Pk.

Tahsis

Morton Lake Prov. Park

Campbell River and District Mus.

Loveland Bay Prov. Park

Elk Falls Prov. Park

Heriot Bay

Quathiaski Cove

Kwagiulth Mus.

Lund

Inland Lake Prov. Park

Harmony Islands Marine Prov. Pk.

Esperanza Inlet

Nuchatlitz Prov. Park

Nootka Island

Campbell River

19A

Smelt Bay Prov. Park

Powell River

Westview

Texada I.

Skookumchuck Narrows Prov. Pk.

Upper Campbell Lake

28

Campbell River Arpt.

Saratoga Beach

Black Creek

Miracle Beach

Miracle Bch. Prov. Park

28

Powell River Arpt.

101

31

Saltery Bay

Earls Cove

Garden Bay

Nootka Sound

Gold River

Buttle Lake

Mt. Washington

19

Merville

Little River

Lazo

46

Blubber Bay

Vananda

Saltery Bay Prov. Park

Nelson I.

Sechelt Inlets Marine P.P.

Irvines Landing

Madeira Park

81

STRATHCONA

Courtenay

Comox

Gillies Bay

Spipiyus Prov. Pk.

Hesquiat Lake Prov. Park

Boat Basin

Sydney Inlet Prov. Park

Sulphur Passage Prov. Park

PROV. PARK

Royston

Cumberland

Comox L.

19A

Sandy I. Marine Prov. Pk

Denman I.

Fillongley Prov. Park

Hornby I.

Jedediah Island Marine Prov. Pk

Halfmoon Bay

Simson Prov. Pk

Kleindale

Porpoise Bay Prov. Pk.

Sechelt

HESQUIAT PEN. PROV. PARK

Stewardson Inlet

Herbert Inlet

Union Bay

Buckley Bay

Fanny Bay

False Bay

Lasqueti I.

Squitty Bay Prov. Park

Sargeant Bay Prov. Pk.

Roberts Creek Prov. Pk.

Maquinna Marine Prov. Pk.

Flores I.

Bedwell Sound

Rosewall Creek Prov. Park

Bowser

101

Roberts Creek

3

Flores Island Prov. Park

Ahousat

Gibson Marine Prov. Pk.

Clayoquot Sound

Epper Passage Prov. Park

Dawley Passage Prov. Park

Great Central L.

Clayoquot Plateau Prov. Park

Clayoquot Arm Prov. Pk.

92

Horne Lake Caves Prov. Park

Stamp River Prov. Park

Taylor Arm Prov. Park

Sproat Lake

Qualicum Beach

19

72

Coombs

19A

French Creek

Parksville

MacMillan Prov. Park

47

Errington

Little Qualicum Falls Prov. Park

Rathtrevor Beach Prov. Park

Nanoose Bay

35

Gabriola Island

Vargas Island Prov. Park

Whale Centre Museum

Tofino

4

Kennedy L.

Port Alberni

Alberni Valley Museum

Sproat Lake Prov. Park

Englishman River Falls Prov. Park

19

Nanaimo

19A

Cedar

Nahmint

Alberni Inlet

Lantzville

Hemer Prov. Pk.

Nanaimo Arpt.

PACIFIC RIM NATIONAL PARK RESERVE (Long Beach Unit)

4

Kildonan

Green Cove

Cassidy

52

Thetis I.

Ucluelet

Barkley Sound

Sarita

Youbou

Quw'utsun' Cult. Ctr.

Ladysmith

Chemainus

Thetis I.

PACIFIC RIM NATIONAL PARK RESERVE (Broken Group Islands Unit)

Bamfield

Hitchie Creek Prov. Park

Gordon Bay Prov. Park

Honeymoon Bay

Mesachie L.

Lake Cowichan

Cowichan Lake

Cowichan River Prov. Park

Glenora

30

N. Cowichan

Duncan

4

PACIFIC

OCEAN

Nitinat Lake

Clo-oose

CARMANAH WALBRAN PROV. PARK

PACIFIC RIM NATIONAL PARK RESERVE (West Coast Trail Unit)

RESTRICTED ROAD

Port Renfrew

14

102

Juan de Fuca Prov. Park

River Jordan

Sooke Lake

Sooke

Distances in Canada shown in kilometers.
Au Canada, les distances sont en kilomètres.

B.C.
WASH.

Strait of Juan de Fuca

French Beach Prov. Park

Beechey Head

Cape Flattery

Neah Bay

MAKAH IND. RES.

112

Clallam Bay

Milnes Landing

Flattery Rocks N.W.R.

Cape Alava

Ozette Lake

113

Sappho

101

Joyce

Go to
12

Sol Duc

OLYMPIC NATL. FOR.

Forks

OLYMPIC NATL. PARK

A   B   C

DRIVING DISTANCES IN KM / DISTANCES ROUTIÈRES EN KM	CAMPBELL RIVER, BC	KAMLOOPS, BC	KELOWNA, BC	MERRITT, BC	NANAIMO, BC	OSOYOOS, BC	PORT ALBERNI, BC	PORT HARDY, BC	SALMON ARM, BC	VANCOUVER, BC	VICTORIA, BC	WHISTLER, BC
KAMLOOPS, BC	512		163	87	363	231	441	750	108	355	393	475
NANAIMO, BC	153	363	403	279		404	82	391	471	23	113	104
VANCOUVER, BC	172	355	395	271	23	396	101	410	463		69	123
VICTORIA, BC	266	393	433	309	113	434	195	504	501	69		192

SEE ALSO DISTANCE AND DRIVING TIME MAP ON PAGES 286–287 / VOIR AUSSI CARTE DES DISTANCES ET DES TEMPS DE PARCOURS PAGES 286–287

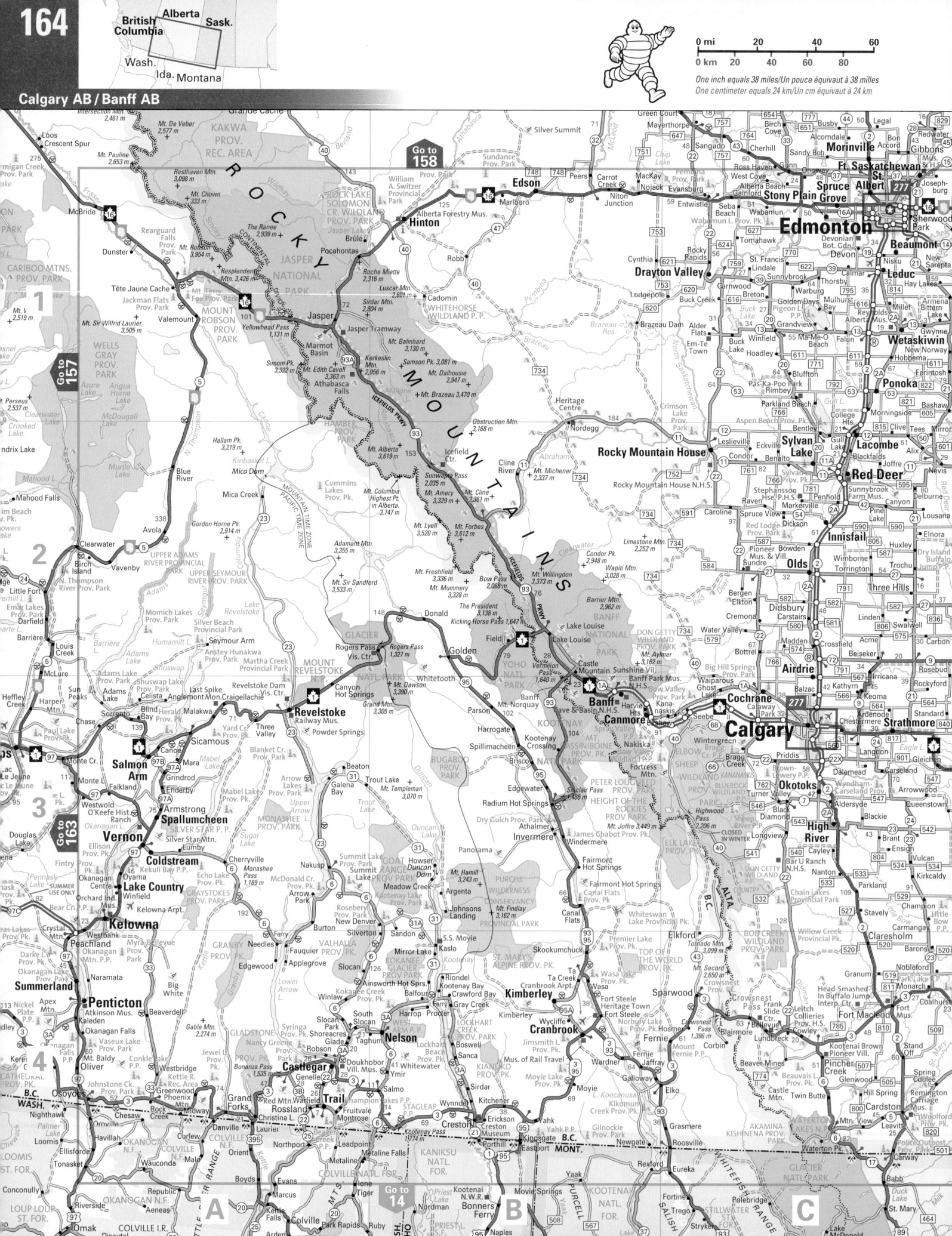

Go to
158

Go to
157

Go to
163

Go to
14

One inch equals 38 miles/Un pouce équivaut à 38 milles
One centimeter equals 24 km/Un cm équivaut à 24 km

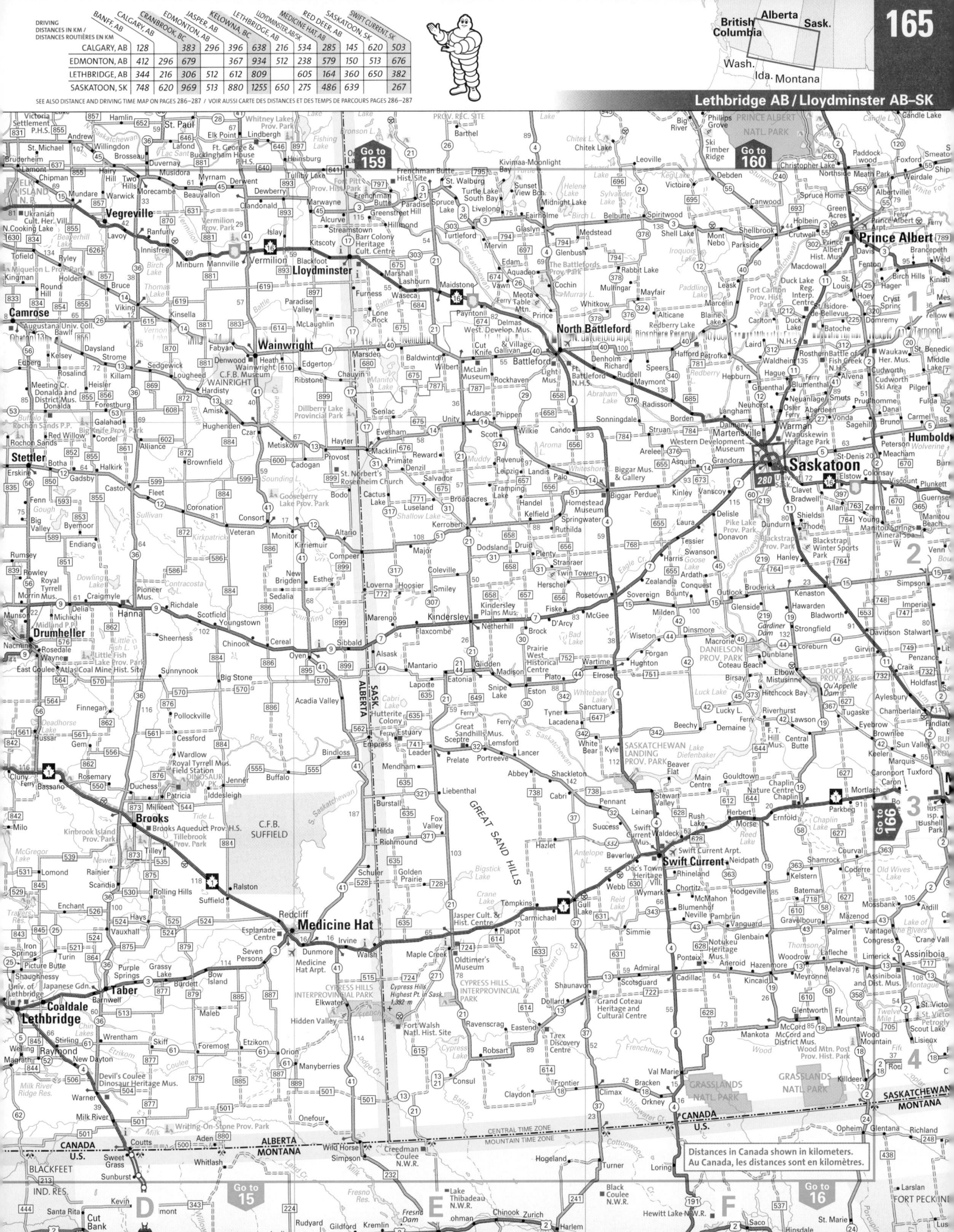

Go to 159
Go to 160
Go to 166
Go to 15
Go to 16

Distances in Canada shown in kilometres.
Au Canada, les distances sont en kilomètres.

Sask.
Manitoba
Ontario
Montana
N.D.
Minn.

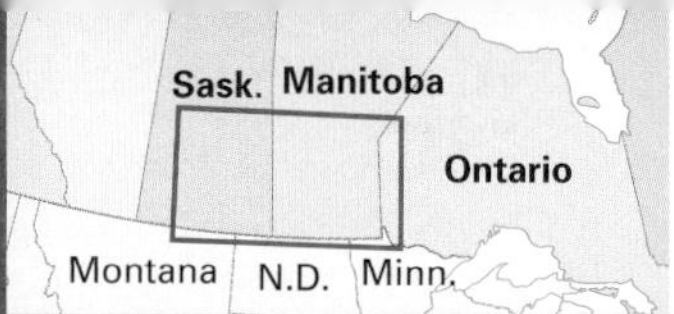

0 mi 20 40 60
0 km 20 40 60 80
One inch equals 38 miles/Un pouce équivaut à 38 milles
One centimeter equals 24 km/Un cm équivaut à 24 km

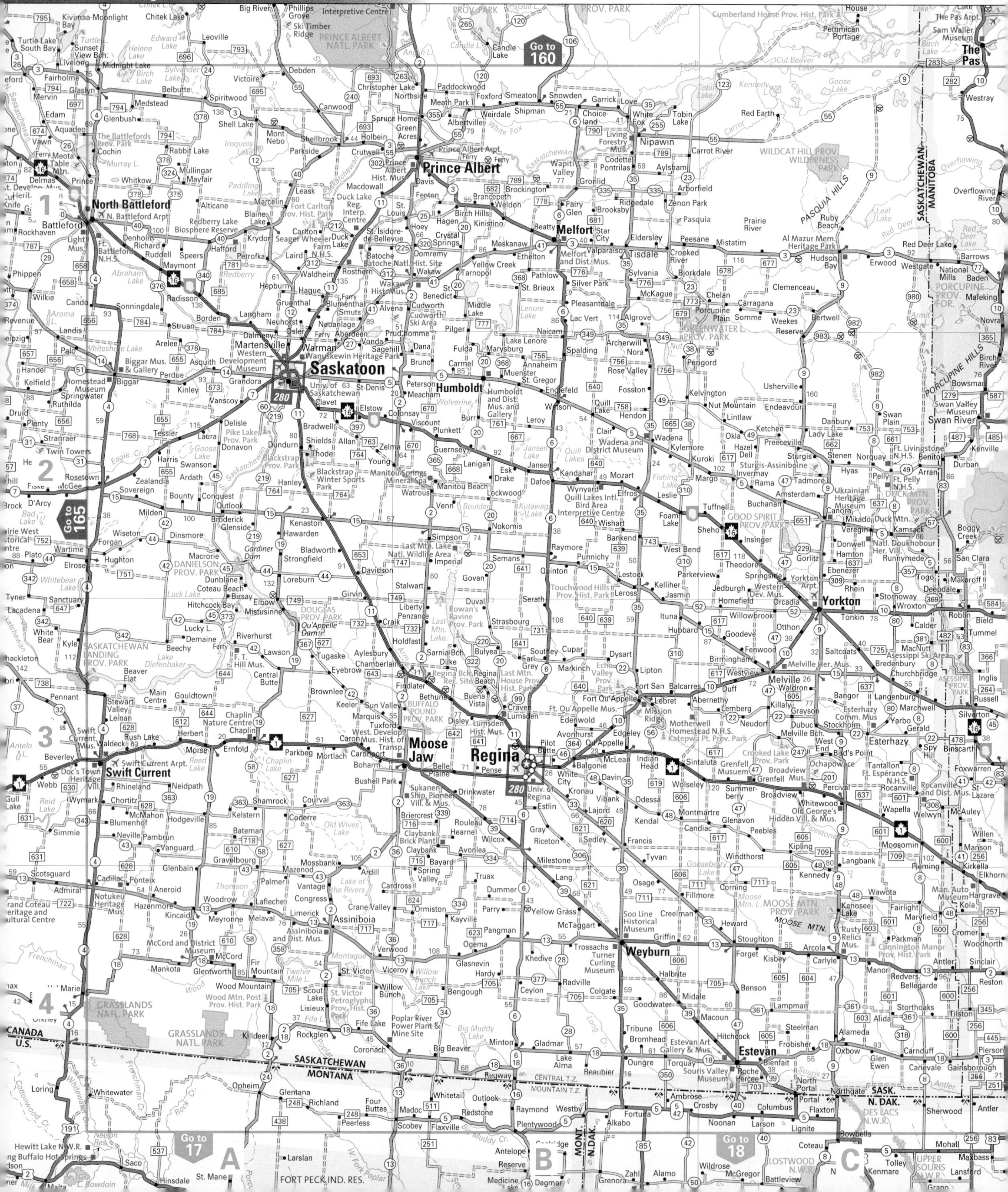

Go to 160
Go to 165
Go to 17
Go to 18
Saskatoon
Regina
Prince Albert
North Battleford
Battleford
Moose Jaw
Swift Current
Yorkton
Melfort
Humboldt
Weyburn
Estevan
Melville
Tisdale
Nipawin
The Pas
Swan River
Prince Albert Natl. Park
Grasslands Natl. Park
Saskatchewan
Manitoba
Montana
N. Dak.
Canada
U.S.
Central T.Z.
Mountain T.Z.
1
2
3
4
A
B
C

DRIVING
DISTANCES IN KM /
DISTANCES ROUTIÈRES EN KM

	BRANDON, MB	DAUPHIN, MB	GRAND RAPIDS, MB	MOOSE JAW, SK	PORTAGE LA PRAIRIE, MB	PRINCE ALBERT, SK	REGINA, SK	SASKATOON, SK	SWIFT CURRENT, SK	THE PAS, MB	WINNIPEG, MB	YORKTON, SK
BRANDON, MB		166	525	448	134	745	377	639	618	570	216	270
REGINA, SK	377	366	787	68	511	368		261	241	557	593	195
SASKATOON, SK	639	502	689	224	691	141	261		267	578	773	331
WINNIPEG, MB	216	322	430	664	82	819	593	773	834	611		442

SEE ALSO DISTANCE AND DRIVING TIME MAP ON PAGES 286–287 / VOIR AUSSI CARTE DES DISTANCES ET DES TEMPS DE PARCOURS PAGES 286–287

Distances in Canada shown in kilometers.
Au Canada, les distances sont en kilomètres.

Go to 161

Go to 168

Go to 19

168

Manitoba
Ontario
N.D. Minn.
Mich.

Kenora ON / Fort Frances ON

One inch equals 38 miles/Un pouce équivaut à 38 milles
One centimeter equals 24 km/Un cm équivaut à 24 km

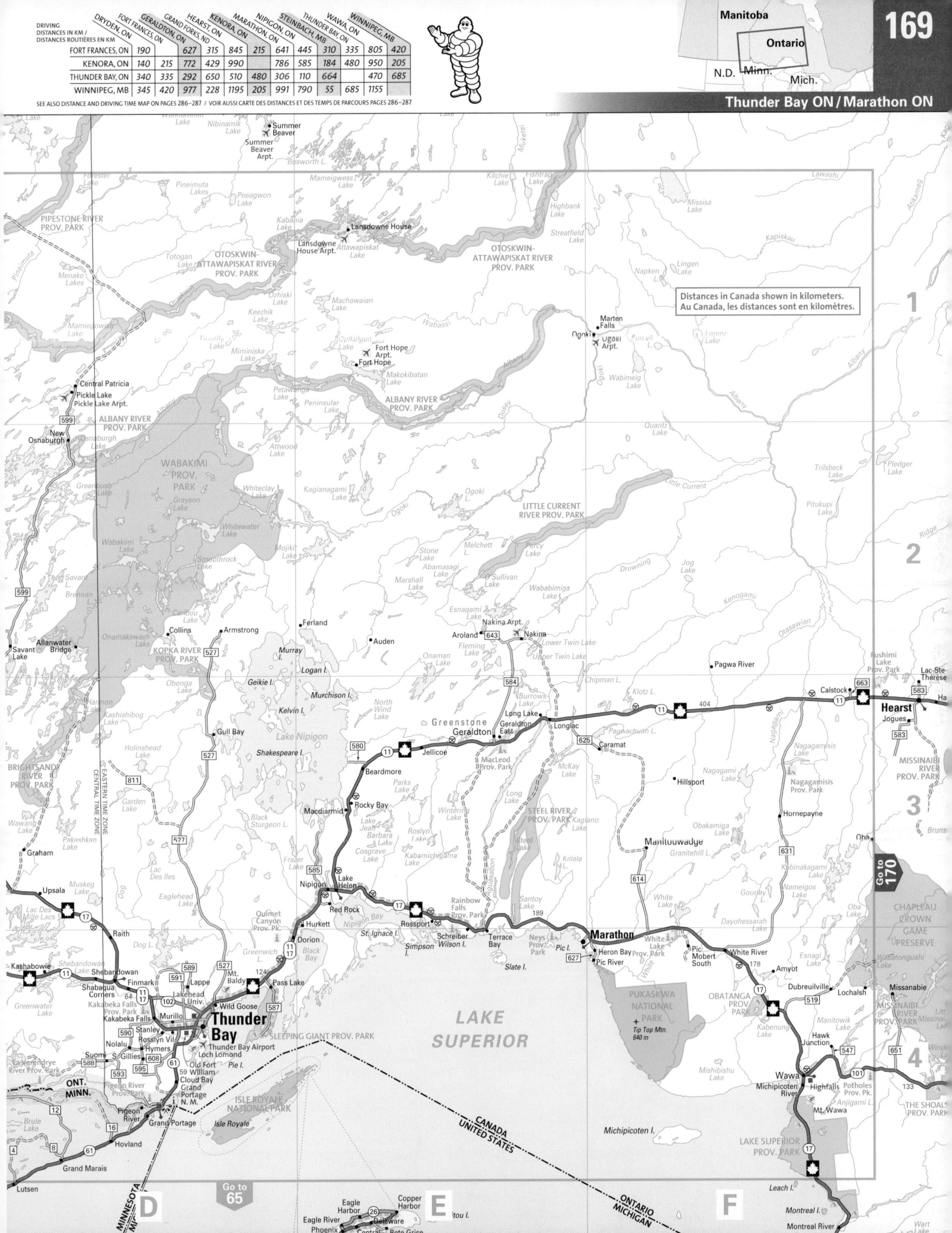

DRIVING
DISTANCES IN KM /
DISTANCES ROUTIÈRES EN KM

	DRYDEN, ON	FORT FRANCES, ON	GERALDTON, ON	GRAND FORKS, ND	HEARST, ON	KENORA, ON	MARATHON, ON	NIPIGON, ON	STEINBACH, MB	THUNDER BAY, ON	WAWA, ON	WINNIPEG, MB
FORT FRANCES, ON	190		627	315	845	215	641	445	310	335	805	420
KENORA, ON	140	215	772	429	990		786	585	184	480	950	205
THUNDER BAY, ON	340	335	292	650	510	480	306	110	664		470	685
WINNIPEG, MB	345	420	977	228	1195	205	991	790	55	685	1155	

SEE ALSO DISTANCE AND DRIVING TIME MAP ON PAGES 286–287 / VOIR AUSSI CARTE DES DISTANCES ET DES TEMPS DE PARCOURS PAGES 286–287

Distances in Canada shown in kilometers.
Au Canada, les distances sont en kilomètres.

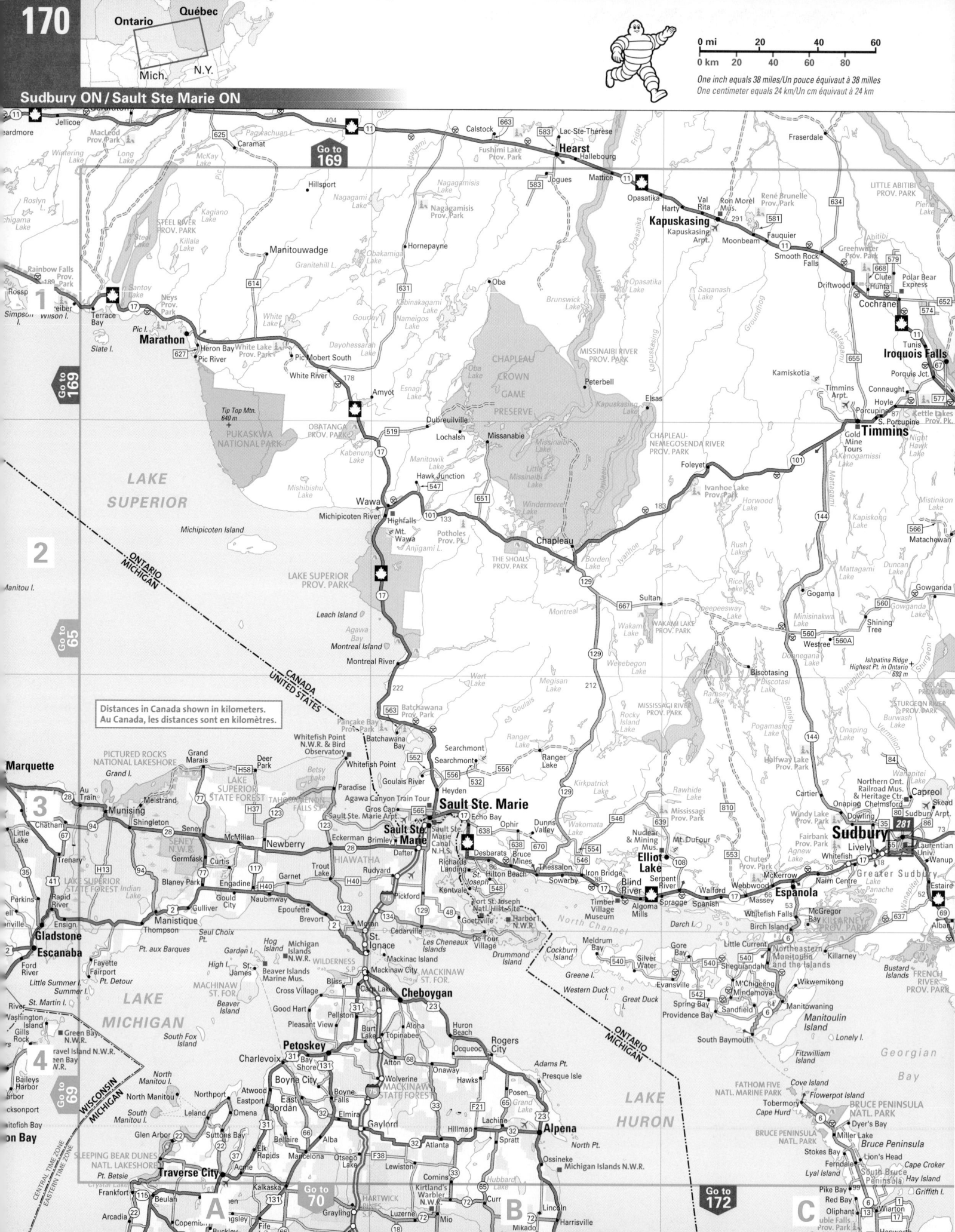

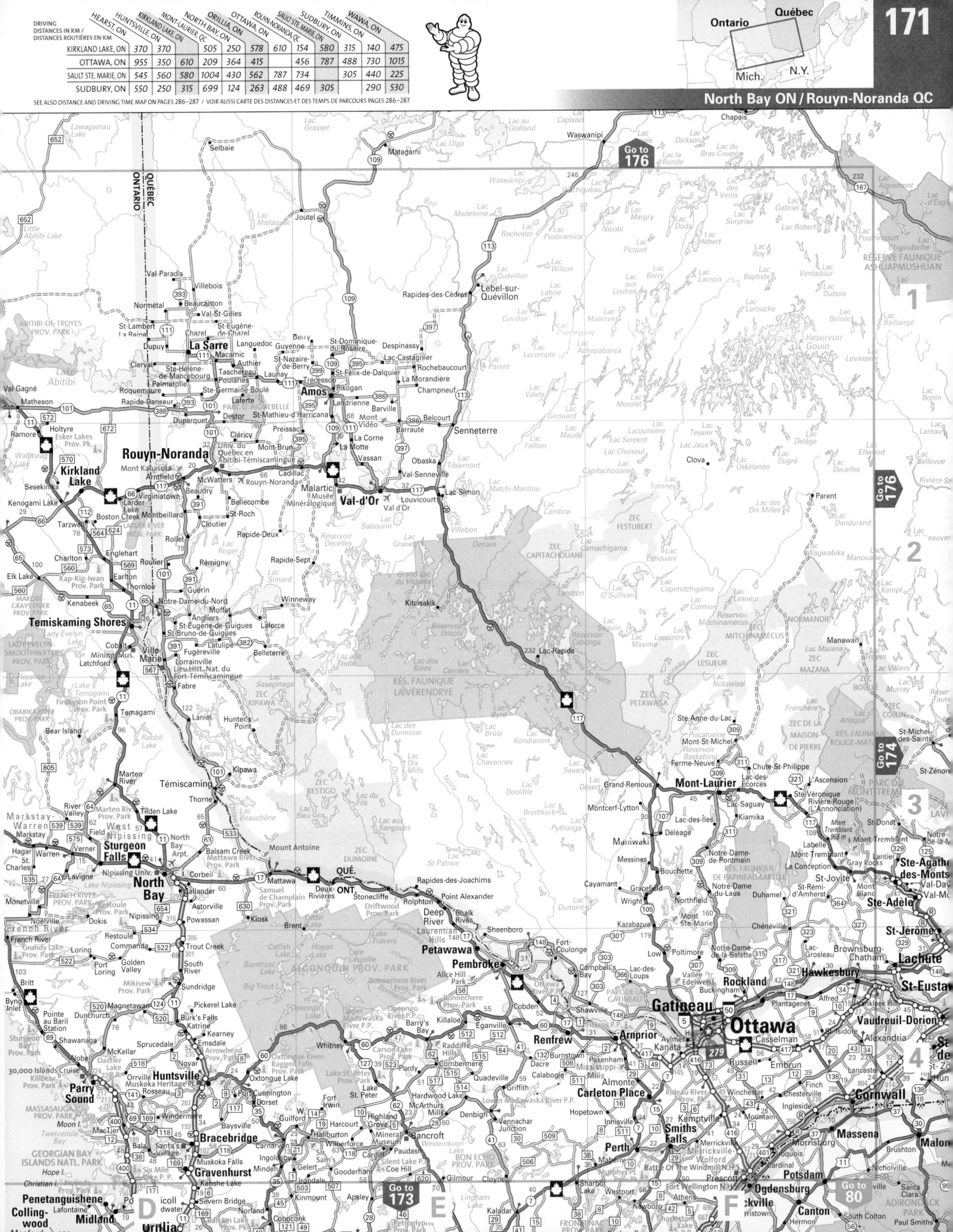

DRIVING
DISTANCES IN KM /
DISTANCES ROUTIÈRES EN KM

	HUNTSVILLE, ON	KIRKLAND LAKE, ON	MONT-LAURIER, QC	NORTH BAY, ON	ORILLIA, ON	OTTAWA, ON	ROUYN-NORANDA QC	SAULT STE. MARIE, ON	SUDBURY, ON	TIMMINS, ON	WAWA, ON
KIRKLAND LAKE, ON	370	370		505	250	578	610	154	580	315	140	475
OTTAWA, ON	955	350	610	209	364		415	456	787	488	730	1015
SAULT STE. MARIE, ON	545	560	580	1004	430	562	787	734		305	440	225
SUDBURY, ON	550	250	315	699	124	263	488	469	305		290	530

SEE ALSO DISTANCE AND DRIVING TIME MAP ON PAGES 286-287 / VOIR AUSSI CARTE DES DISTANCES ET DES TEMPS DE PARCOURS PAGES 286-287

172

Ontario
Mich. N.Y.
Pa.
Ohio

London ON / Windsor ON

0 mi · 20 · 40
0 km · 20 · 40 · 60

One inch equals 24 miles/Un pouce équivaut à 24 milles
One cm equals 15.25 km/Un cm équivaut à 15.25 km

Distances in Canada shown in kilometers.
Au Canada, les distances sont en kilomètres.

Go to 170
Go to 76
Go to 90
Go to 91
Go to 212

DRIVING DISTANCES IN KM / DISTANCES ROUTIÈRES EN KM	BARRIE, ON	HAMILTON, ON	KINGSTON, ON	KITCHENER, ON	LONDON, ON	NIAGARA FALLS, ON	ORILLIA, ON	OWEN SOUND, ON	PETERBOROUGH, ON	SARNIA, ON	TORONTO, ON	WINDSOR, ON
KINGSTON, ON	350	330		430	430	390	317	430	180	530	260	620
NIAGARA FALLS, ON	200	68	390	130	190		237	260	260	290	130	380
TORONTO, ON	90	70	260	105	185	130	127	190	135	280		370
WINDSOR, ON	430	310	620	285	190	380	467	390	490	160	370	

SEE ALSO DISTANCE AND DRIVING TIME MAP ON PAGES 286–287 / VOIR AUSSI CARTE DES DISTANCES ET DES TEMPS DE PARCOURS PAGES 286–287

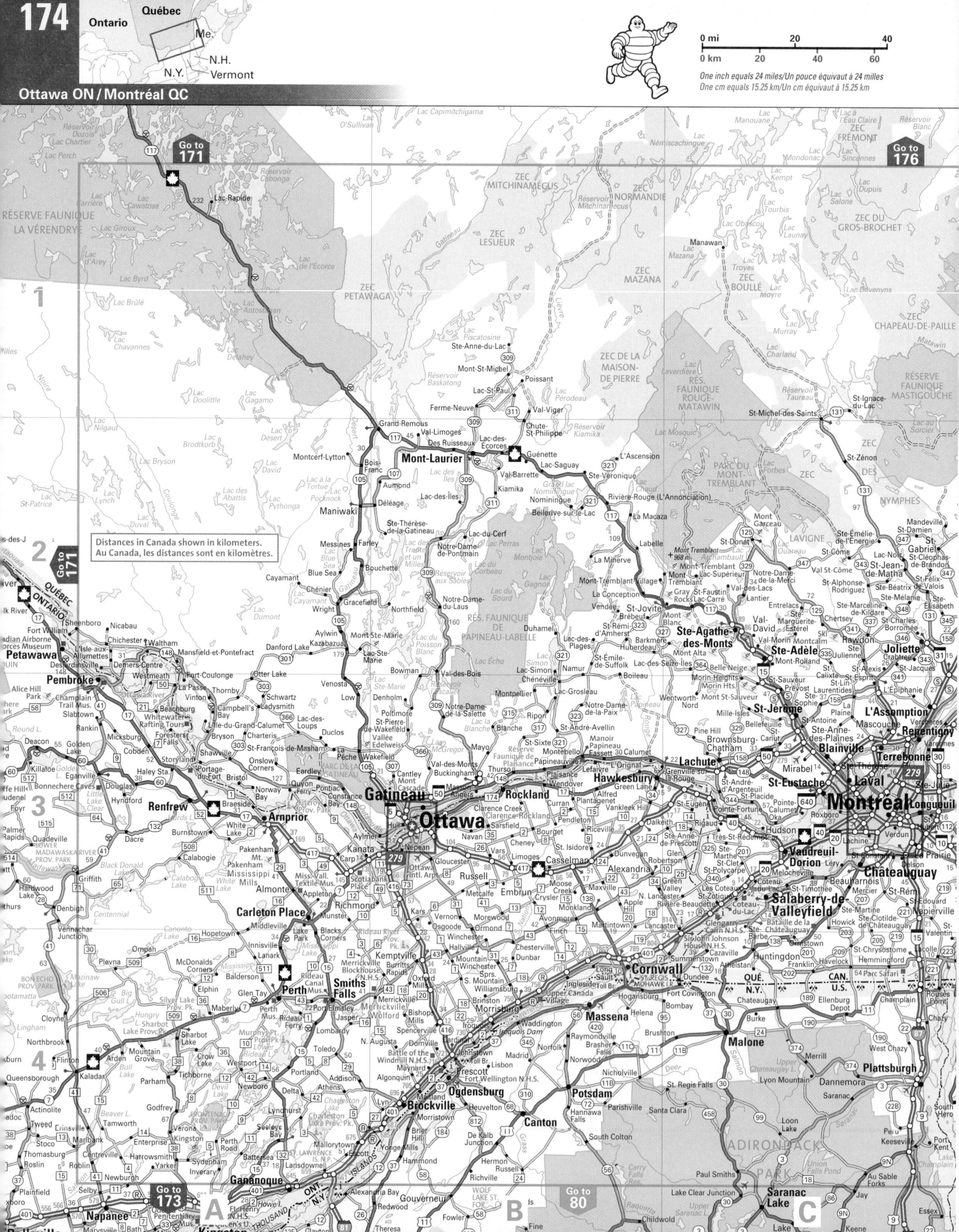

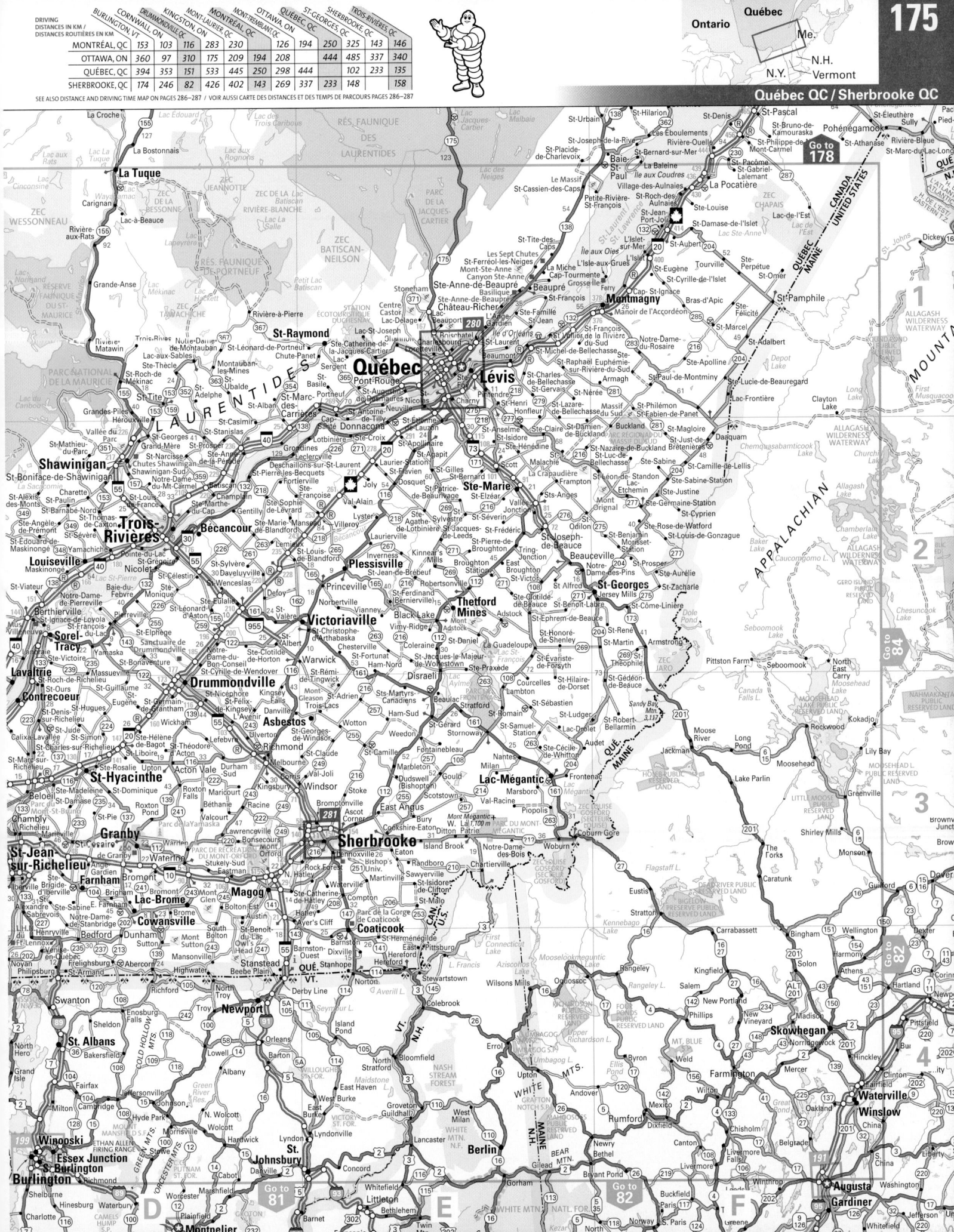

	BURLINGTON, VT	CORNWALL, ON	DRUMMONDVILLE, QC	KINGSTON, ON	MONT-LAURIER, QC	MONTRÉAL, QC	MONT-TREMBLANT, QC	OTTAWA, QC	QUÉBEC, QC	ST-GEORGES, QC	SHERBROOKE, QC	TROIS-RIVIÈRES, QC
MONTRÉAL, QC	153	103	116	283	230		126	194	250	325	143	146
OTTAWA, ON	360	97	310	175	209	194	208		444	485	337	340
QUÉBEC, QC	394	353	151	533	445	250	298	444		102	233	135
SHERBROOKE, QC	174	246	82	426	402	143	269	337	233	148		158

Québec
Ontario

Me.

N.H.
N.Y.
Vermont

Go to 178

Go to 84

Go to 82

Go to 81

Go to 82

Québec
P.E.I.
N.B.
Maine

0 mi   20   40   60
0 km   20   40   60   80
One inch equals 38 miles/Un pouce équivaut à 38 milles
One centimeter equals 24 km/Un cm équivaut à 24 km

Distances in Canada shown in kilometers.
Au Canada, les distances sont en kilomètres.

1
2
3 Go to 171
4 Go to 174

Lac Nemiscau
Lac Jolliet
Lac Tésécau
Lac le Gardeur
Lac Legoff
Lac Rocher
RÉSERVE FAUNIQUE ASSINICA
Lac la Chevardière
Lac Assinica
Lac Omo
Lac Opataca
Lac Lemieux
Lac Troïlus
Lac Buells
Lac à l'Eau Froide
RÉSERVE FAUNIQUE DES LACS-ALBANEL-MISTASSINI-ET-WACONICHI
Lac Mistassini
Mistissini
Lac Heidi
Lac File Axe
Lac du Sauvage
Lac Waconichi
167
Lac Eva
Lac Margonne
Lac Laganière
Lac Cauvet
Lac Péribonka
Lac du Grand Détour
Mont de la Sentinelle Solitaire 530 m
Mont Opémisca 538 m
Mont Springer 556 m
Chibougamau
113
12
Lac Opémisca
France
Lac des Cygnes
Lac du Goéland
246
Waswanipi
Chapais
Chibougamau
167
Lac Dickson
Lac du Bras Coupé
Lac Chibougamau
Lac Rivard
Lebel-sur-Quévillon
113
Lac Charron
232
Lac Aigremont
Lac d'Eglis
ZEC DE LA RIVIÈRE-AUX-RATS
ZEC DES PASSES
ZEC ONATCHIWAY-EST
Notre-Dame-de-Lorette
Girardville
St-Stanislas
St-Thomas-Didyme d'Argentenay
St-Eugène
Dolbeau-Mistassini
St-Ludger-de-Milot
St-Edmond-les-Plaines
Albanel
Normandin
169
373
37
Ste-Jeanne-d'Arc
St-Augustin
Ste-Monique
L'Ascension-de-Notre-Seigneur
ZEC DU LAC-DE-LA-BOITEUSE
St-Méthode
169
Lamarche (Notre-Dame-du-Rosaire)
Zoo sauvage de St-Félicien
PARC DE POINTE-TAILLON
St-David-de-Falardeau
St- Félicien
41
St-Henri-de-Taillon
Delisle
St-Nazaire
St-Honoré
Univ. du Québec à Chicoutimi
PARC DES MONTS-VALIN
St-Prime
Mashteuiatsh
Alma
18
172
Ste-Hedwidge
Roberval
St-Gédéon
16
St-Bruno
St-Ambroise
St-Fulgence
Saguenay
PARC DU SAGUENAY
Val-Jalbert
19
11
170
49
Chicoutimi
172
Chambord
Métabetchouan-Lac-à-la-Croix
Hébertville
Jonquière
St-François-de-Sales
St-André-du-Lac-St-Jean
Mont Lac-Vert
Laterrière
70
La Baie
L'Anse-St-Jean
Lac-Bouchette
169
175
Rivière-Éternité
Ferland
Mont Édouard
Sacré-Coeur
145
Lac-des-Commissaires
127
Boilleau
Mont-Apica
Lac Hal Ha!
381
Sagard
Baie-des-Rochers
Port-aux-Quilles
155
ZEC BORGIA
ZEC MARS-MOULIN
PARC DES HAUTES-GORGES-DE-LA-RIVIÈRE-MALBAIE
170
St-Siméon
82
78
ZEC KISKISSINK
RÉS. FAUNIQUE DES LAURENTIDES
Clova
Parent
La Croche
Lac-Edouard
175
PARC DES GRANDS-JARDINS
Clermont
La Malbaie
La Bostonnais
Notre-Dame-des-Monts
362
138
132
La Tuque
Carignan
Lac-à-Beauce
123
Baie-St-Paul
St-Placide-de-Charlevoix
Rivière-Ouelle
Mont-Carmel
Rivière-aux-Rats
92
Petite-Rivière-St-François
Île aux Coudres
La Pocatière
St-Roch-des-Aulnaies
Grande-Anse
STATION ÉCOTOURISTIQUE DUCHESNAY
138
L'Islet-sur-Mer
Rivière-à-Pierre
Mt. Ste-Anne
St-Ferréol-les-Neiges
St-Tite-des-Caps
414
155
St-Raymond
365
Château-Richer
Beaupré
285
St-Jean
Montmagny
Trois-Rives
Ste-Anne
Donnacona
40
70
Québec
280
Lévis
204
Shawinigan
Grand-Mère
138
132
20
116
73
Ste-Marie
204
Mont-Laurier
Maniwaki
117
309
311
Shawinigan

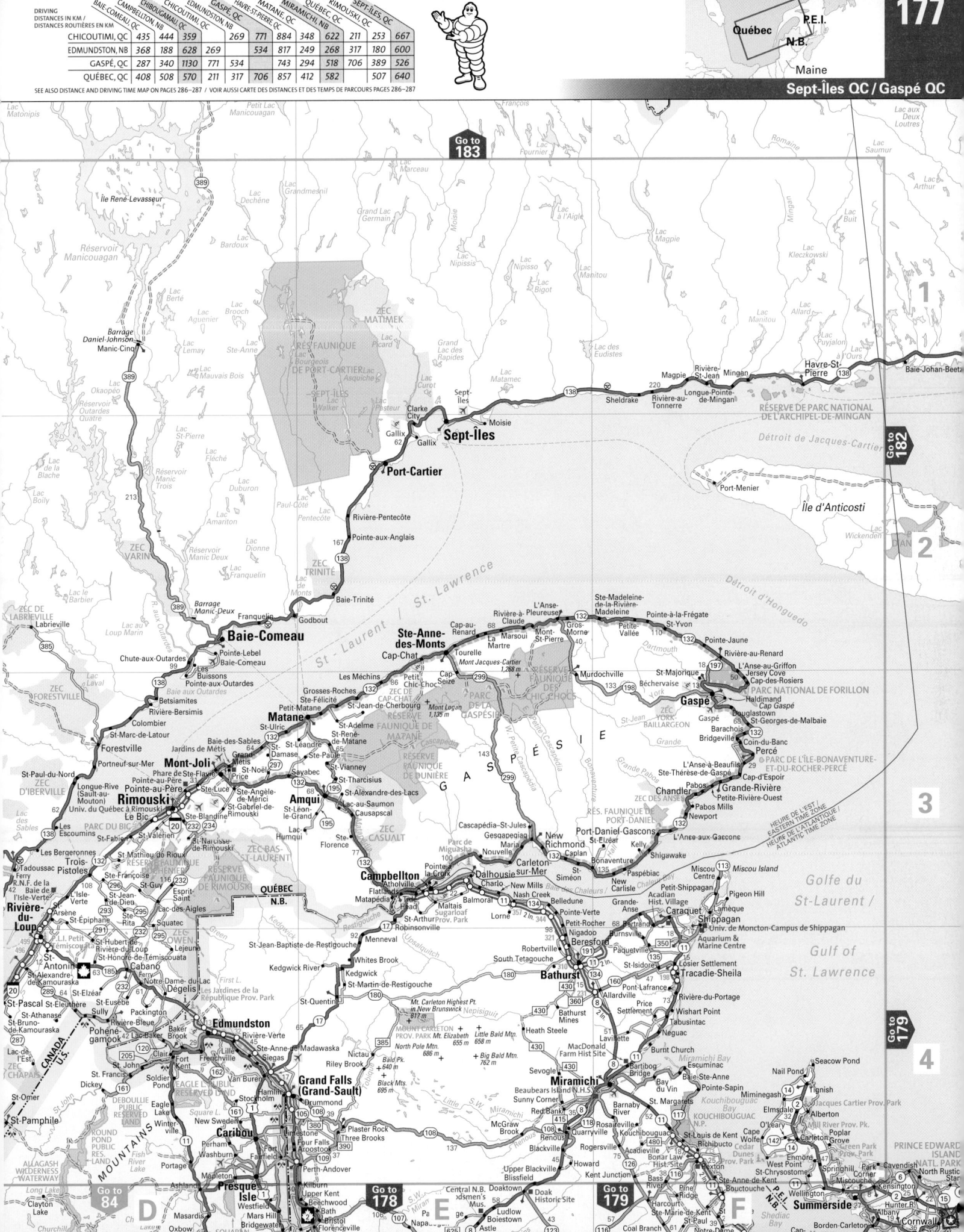

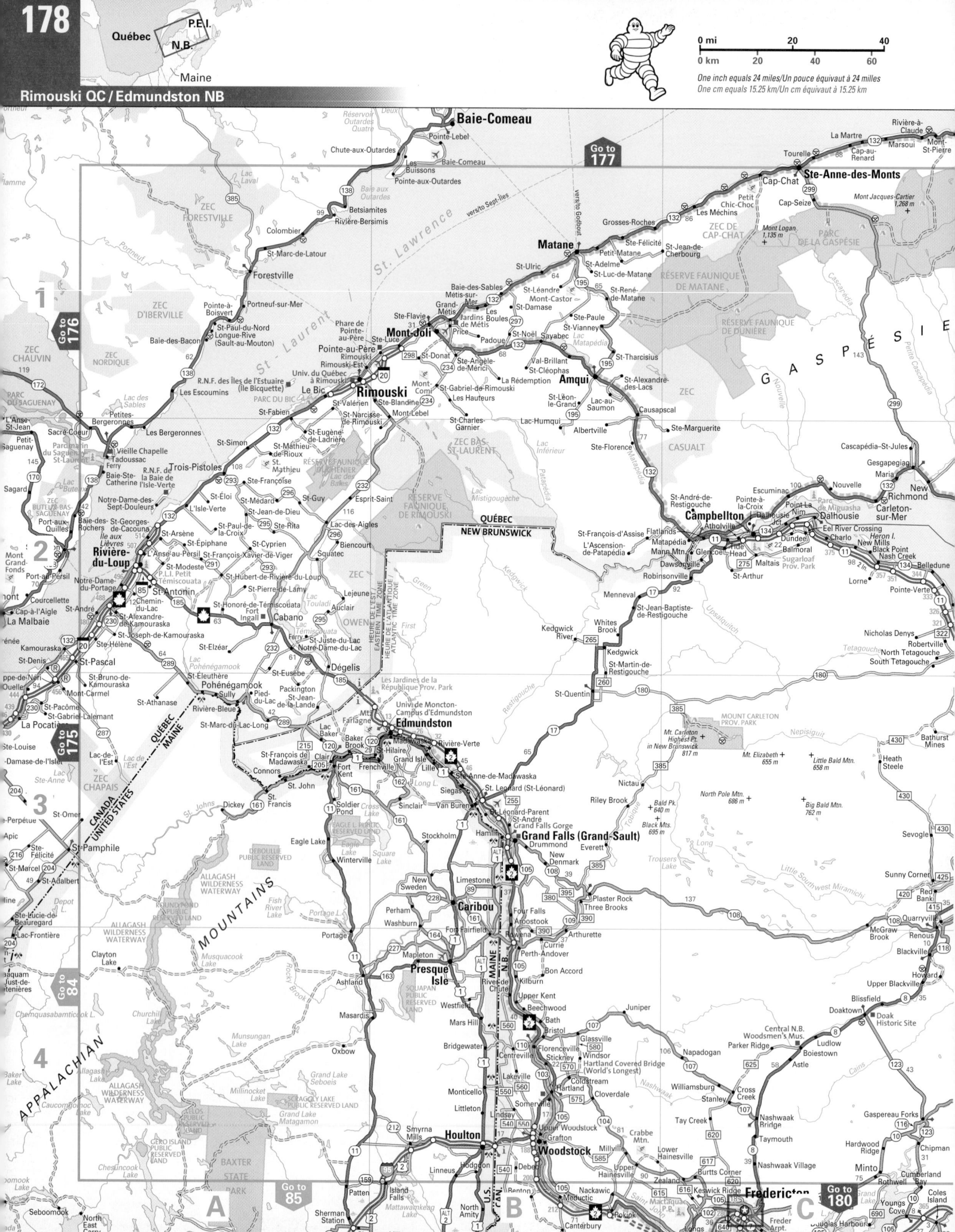

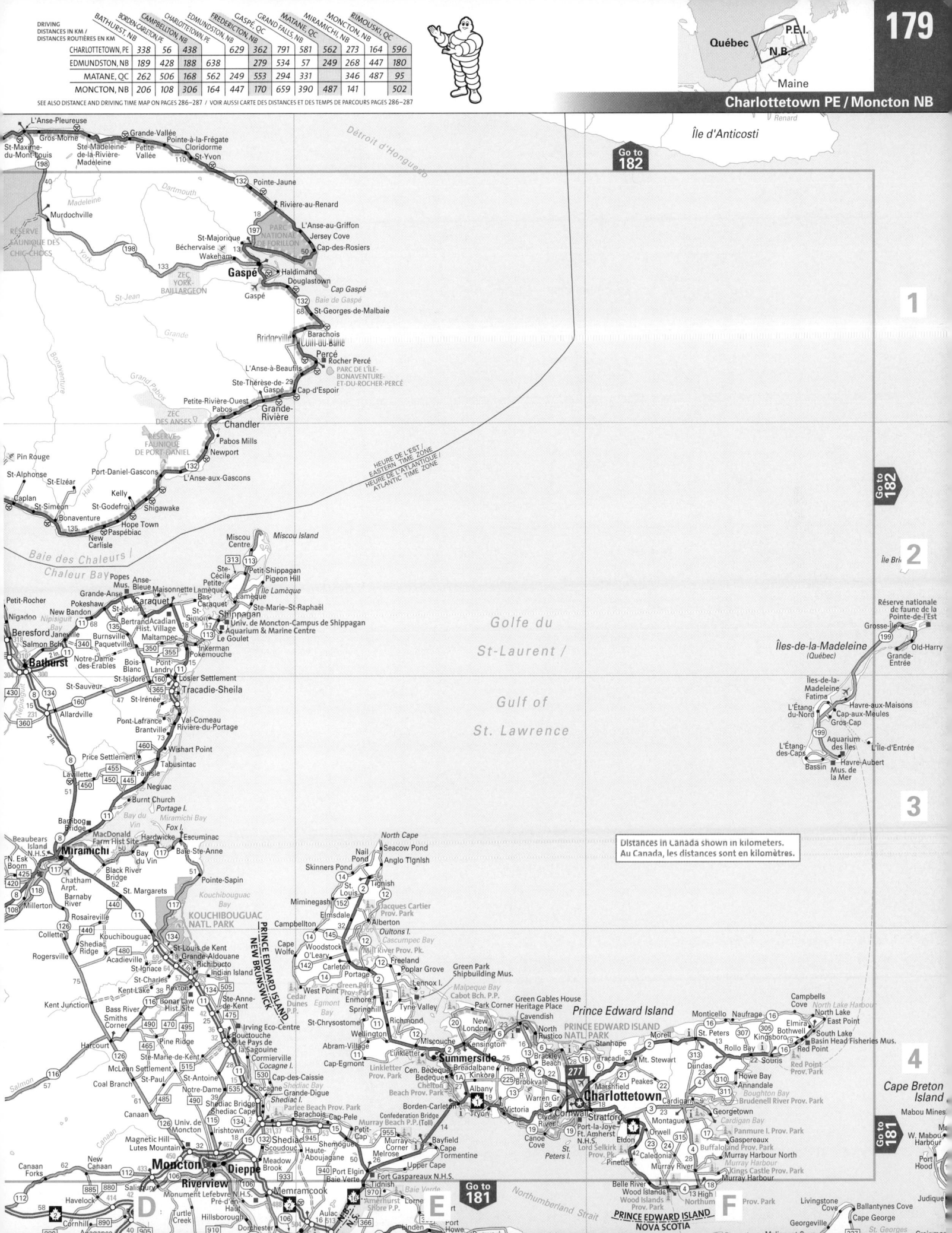

179

Charlottetown PE / Moncton NB

DRIVING DISTANCES IN KM / DISTANCES ROUTIÈRES EN KM

	BATHURST, NB	BORDEN-CARLETON, PE	CAMPBELLTON, NB	CHARLOTTETOWN, PE	EDMUNDSTON, NB	FREDERICTON, NB	GASPÉ, QC	GRAND FALLS, NB	MATANE, QC	MIRAMICHI, NB	MONCTON, NB	RIMOUSKI, QC
CHARLOTTETOWN, PE	338	56	438			629	362	791	581	562	273	164	596
EDMUNDSTON, NB	189	428	188	638			279	534	57	249	268	447	180
MATANE, QC	262	506	168	562	249		553	294	331		346	487	95
MONCTON, NB	206	108	306	164	447	170	659	390	487	141			502

SEE ALSO DISTANCE AND DRIVING TIME MAP ON PAGES 286–287 / VOIR AUSSI CARTE DES DISTANCES ET DES TEMPS DE PARCOURS PAGES 286–287

Distances in Canada shown in kilometers.
Au Canada, les distances sont en kilomètres.

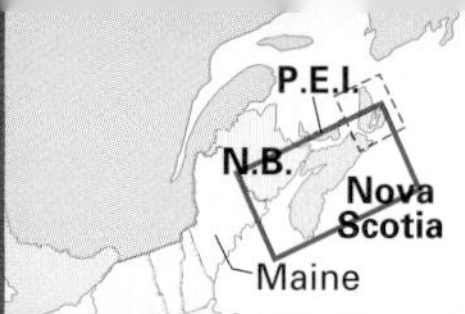

P.E.I.

N.B.

Nova Scotia

Maine

0 mi 20 40

0 km 20 40 60

One inch equals 24 miles/Un pouce équivaut à 24 milles
One cm equals 15.25 km/Un cm équivaut à 15.25 km

Go to 178

Go to 179

Go to 85

Go to 83

NEW BRUNSWICK
NOVA SCOTIA

PRINCE EDWARD ISLAND
NEW BRUNSWICK

U.S. CANADA

Bay of Fundy

Gulf of Maine

Chignecto Bay

Minas Basin

EASTERN TIME ZONE
ATLANTIC TIME ZONE

to Bar Harbor, Maine

to Portland, Maine

1 **2** **3** **4**

A **B** **C**

DRIVING DISTANCES IN KM /
DISTANCES ROUTIÈRES EN KM

	CHARLOTTETOWN PE	CHETICAMP NS	DIGBY NS	FREDERICTON NB	HALIFAX NS	MONCTON NB	PORT HAWKESBURY NS	SAINT JOHN NB	ST. STEPHEN NB	SYDNEY NS	TRURO NS	YARMOUTH NS
HALIFAX, NS	322	425	235	462		260	265	410	515	415	89	339
MONCTON, NB	164	481	231	170	260		374	150	278	497	182	599
SAINT JOHN, NB	350	640	72	114	410	150		497	119	647	321	176
SYDNEY, NS	374	173	623	689	415	497	123	647	766		326	727

SEE ALSO DISTANCE AND DRIVING TIME MAP ON PAGES 286–287 • VOIR AUSSI CARTE DES DISTANCES ET DES TEMPS DE PARCOURS PAGES 286–287

P.E.I.
N.B.
Nova Scotia
Maine

Cape Breton Island
FOR CONTINUATION SEE INSET LOWER RIGHT

Go to 182

Distances in Canada shown in kilometers.
Au Canada, les distances sont en kilomètres.

ATLANTIC OCEAN

Cape Breton Island

FORTRESS OF LOUISBOURG N.H.S.

ATLANTIC OCEAN

Nfld. & Lab.

Québec

P.E.I

Nova Scotia

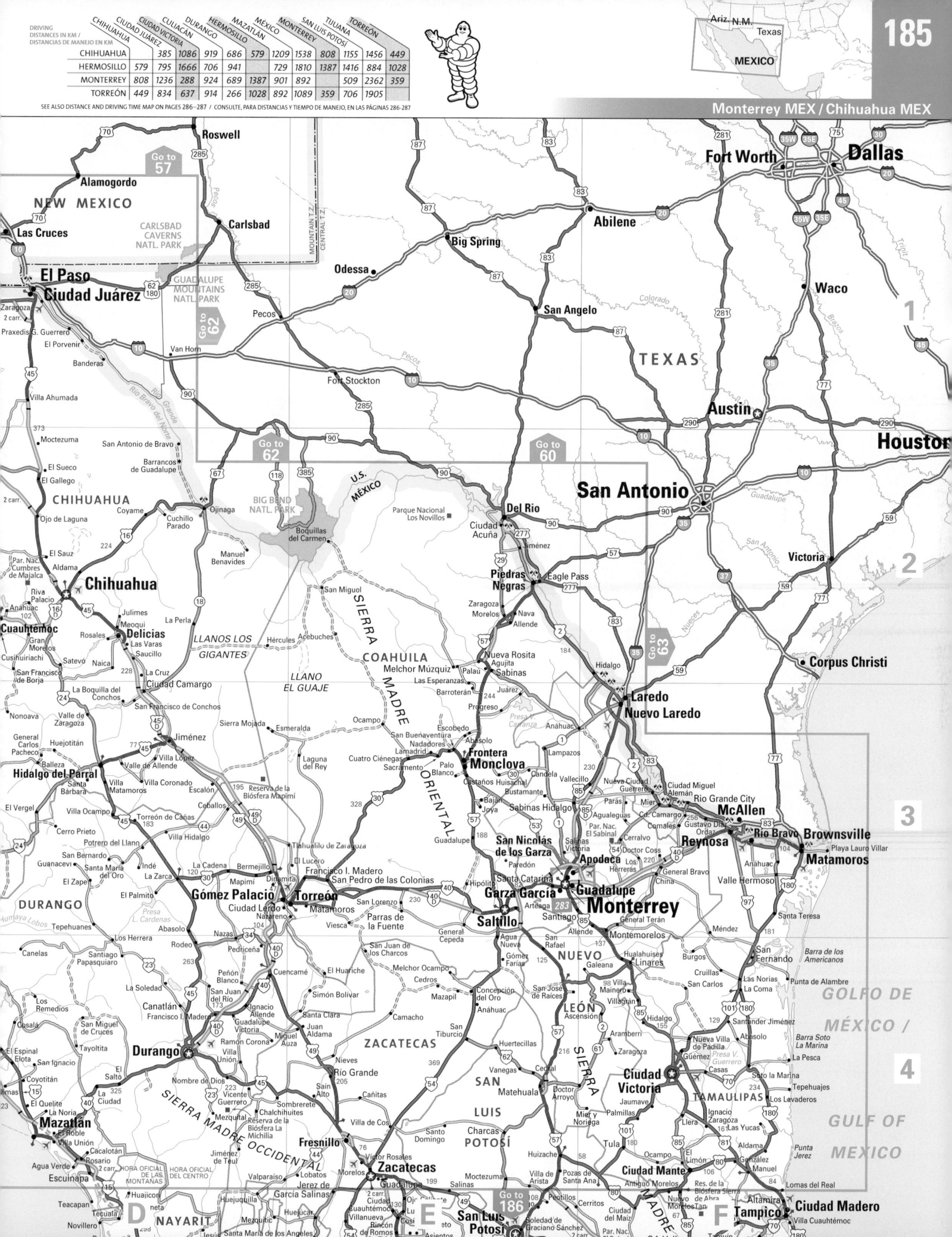

DRIVING DISTANCES IN KM / DISTANCIAS DE MANEJO EN KM

	CHIHUAHUA	CIUDAD JUÁREZ	CULIACÁN	CIUDAD VICTORIA	DURANGO	HERMOSILLO	MAZATLÁN	MÉXICO	MONTERREY	SAN LUIS POTOSÍ	TIJUANA	TORREÓN
CHIHUAHUA		385	1086	919	686	579	1209	1538	808	1155	1456	449
HERMOSILLO	579	795	1666	706	941		729	1810	1387	1416	884	1028
MONTERREY	808	1236	288	924	689	1387	901	892		509	2362	359
TORREÓN	449	834	637	914	266	1028	892	1089	359	706	1905	

SEE ALSO DISTANCE AND DRIVING TIME MAP ON PAGES 286-287 / CONSULTE, PARA DISTANCIAS Y TIEMPO DE MANEJO, EN LAS PÁGINAS 286-287

MEXICO · Puerto Rico

DRIVING DISTANCES IN KM / DISTANCIAS DE MANEJO EN KM	ACAPULCO	CANCÚN	CIUDAD VICTORIA	DURANGO	GUADALAJARA	MAZATLÁN	MÉRIDA	MÉXICO	PUEBLA	SAN LUIS POTOSÍ	TUXTLA GUTIÉRREZ	VERACRUZ
GUADALAJARA	897	2275	774	599		523	1904	578	691	336	1510	943
MÉRIDA	1777	321	1725	2182	1904	2408		1326	1282	1707	786	995
MÉXICO	422	1736	682	856	578	1081	1326		133	381	932	365
SAN LUIS POTOSÍ	834	2161	438	475	336	687	1707	381	496		1313	747

SEE ALSO DISTANCE AND DRIVING TIME MAP ON PAGES 286–287 / CONSULTE, PARA DISTANCIAS Y TIEMPO DE MANEJO, EN LAS PÁGINAS 286–287

PUERTO RICO

Distances in Puerto Rico shown in kilometers.
Distancias en Puerto Rico constan en kilómetros.

OCÉANO ATLÁNTICO / ATLANTIC OCEAN

MAR CARIBE / CARIBBEAN SEA

HORA OFICIAL DEL ATLÁNTICO / ATLANTIC TIME ZONE

GOLFO DE MÉXICO / GULF OF MEXICO

PENÍNSULA DE YUCATÁN

YUCATÁN

QUINTANA ROO

CAMPECHE

TABASCO

VERACRUZ

OAXACA

CHIAPAS

ISTMO DE TEHUANTEPEC

SIERRA MADRE DE CHIAPAS

MAR CARIBE / CARIBBEAN SEA

Golfo de Honduras / Gulf of Honduras

Golfo de Tehuantepec

MÉXICO / GUATEMALA

GUATEMALA / HONDURAS

GUATEMALA / HONDURAS

Figures after entries indicate population, page number, and grid reference.

UNITED STATES

A

Abbeville AL, 2987 ...128 B4
Abbeville GA, 2298 ...129 E3
Abbeville LA, 11887 ...133 F3
Abbeville MS, 423 ...118 C3
Abbeville SC, 5840 ...121 E3
Abbeville Co. SC, 26167 ...121 E3
Abbotsford WI, 1956 ...68 A4
Abbottstown PA, 905 ...103 E1
Abercrombie ND, 296 ...19 F4
Aberdeen ID, 1840 ...31 F1
Aberdeen MD, 13842 ...145 D1
Aberdeen MS, 6415 ...119 D4
Aberdeen NC, 3400 ...122 C1
Aberdeen OH, 1603 ...100 C3
Aberdeen SD, 24658 ...27 E2
Aberdeen WA, 16461 ...12 B4
Abernathy TX, 2839 ...58 A1
Abilene KS, 6543 ...43 E2
Abilene TX, 115930 ...58 C3
Abingdon IL, 3612 ...88 A3
Abingdon MD, 950 ...145 D1
Abingdon VA, 7780 ...111 E3
Abington MA, 14605 ...151 D2
Abita Sprs. LA, 1957 ...134 B2
Absarokee MT, 1234 ...24 A1
Absecon NJ, 7638 ...147 F4
Acadia Par. LA, 58861 ...133 E2
Accokeek MD, 7349 ...144 B4
Accokeek Acres MD, 1500 ...144 B4
Accomac VA, 547 ...114 C3
Accomack Co. VA, 38305 ...114 C3
Accord MA, 2300 ...151 D2
Accord NY, 562 ...94 A3
Achille OK, 506 ...59 F1
Achilles VA, 650 ...113 F2
Ackerman MS, 1696 ...126 C1
Ackley IA, 1809 ...73 D4
Acme MI, 650 ...69 F4
Acomita NM, 288 ...48 B3
Acton CA, 2390 ...52 C2
Acton MA, 2700 ...150 C1
Acushnet MA, 3171 ...151 D3
Acworth GA, 13422 ...120 C3
Ada MN, 1657 ...19 F3
Ada OH, 5582 ...90 B3
Ada OK, 15691 ...51 F4
Ada Co. ID, 300904 ...22 B4
Adair IA, 839 ...86 B2
Adair OK, 704 ...106 A3
Adair Co. IA, 8243 ...86 B2
Adair Co. KY, 17244 ...110 B2
Adair Co. MO, 24977 ...87 D4
Adair Co. OK, 21038 ...106 A4
Adairsville GA, 2542 ...120 B3
Adair Vil. OR, 536 ...20 B3
Adairville KY, 920 ...109 F3
Adams MA, 5784 ...94 C1
Adams MN, 800 ...73 D2
Adams NE, 489 ...35 F4
Adams NY, 1624 ...79 E2
Adams OR, 297 ...21 F1
Adams TN, 566 ...109 E3
Adams WI, 1914 ...74 A1
Adams Ctr. NY, 1500 ...79 E2
Adams Co. CO, 348618 ...41 F1
Adams Co. ID, 3476 ...22 B2

Adams Co. IL, 68277 ...87 F4
Adams Co. IN, 33625 ...90 A3
Adams Co. IA, 4482 ...86 B3
Adams Co. MS, 34340 ...126 A4
Adams Co. NE, 31151 ...35 D4
Adams Co. ND, 2593 ...26 A1
Adams Co. OH, 27330 ...100 C3
Adams Co. PA, 91292 ...103 E1
Adams Co. WA, 16428 ...13 F4
Adams Co. WI, 18643 ...74 A2
Adamston NJ, 4900 ...147 E3
Adamstown MD, 650 ...144 A2
Adamstown PA, 1203 ...146 A2
Adamsville AL, 4965 ...119 F4
Adamsville RI, 550 ...151 D4
Adamsville TN, 1983 ...119 D1
Addis LA, 2238 ...134 A2
Addison AL, 723 ...119 E3
Addison IL, 35914 ...203 C4
Addison ME, 300 ...83 D2
Addison MI, 627 ...90 B1
Addison NY, 1797 ...93 D1
Addison TX, 14166 ...207 D1
Addison Co. VT, 35974 ...81 D3
Adel GA, 5307 ...137 F1
Adel IA, 3435 ...86 C2
Adelanto CA, 18130 ...53 D2
Adelphi MD, 14998 ...270 E1
Adelphia NJ, 900 ...147 E2
Adena OH, 815 ...91 F4
Adrian GA, 579 ...129 F2
Adrian MI, 21574 ...90 B1
Adrian MN, 1234 ...72 A2
Adrian MO, 1780 ...96 B4
Advance IN, 562 ...99 E1
Advance MO, 1244 ...108 B2
Adwolf VA, 1457 ...111 F3
Afton IA, 917 ...86 C3
Afton MN, 2826 ...66 C3
Afton NY, 836 ...93 F1
Afton OK, 1118 ...106 B3
Afton WY, 1911 ...31 F1
Agawam MA, 28144 ...150 B2
Agency IA, 622 ...87 E3
Agency MO, 599 ...96 B1
Agoura Hills CA, 20537 ...228 C2
Agua Dulce TX, 737 ...63 E2
Agua Fria NM, 2051 ...49 D2
Aguilar CO, 593 ...41 E4
Ahoskie NC, 4523 ...113 F3
Ahsahka ID, 600 ...14 B4
Ahuimanu HI, 8506 ...152 A3
Aiken SC, 25337 ...121 F4
Aiken Co. SC, 142552 ...122 A4
Ainsworth IA, 524 ...87 F2
Ainsworth NE, 1862 ...34 C1
Airmont NY, 7799 ...148 B3
Airport Drive MO, 622 ...106 B2
Airway Hts. WA, 4500 ...13 F3
Aitkin MN, 1984 ...64 B4
Aitkin Co. MN, 15301 ...64 B4
Ajo AZ, 3705 ...54 C3
Ak-Chin AZ, 669 ...54 C2
Akiachak AK, 585 ...154 B3
Akins OK, 449 ...116 B1

Akron NY, 3085 ...78 B3
Akron OH, 217074 ...91 E3
Akron PA, 4046 ...146 A2
Akutan AK, 713 ...154 A4
Alabaster AL, 22619 ...127 E1

Alachua FL, 6098 ...138 C3
Alachua Co. FL, 217955 ...138 C3
Alakanuk AK, 652 ...154 B2
Alamance Co. NC, 130800 ...112 C4
Alameda CA, 72259 ...259 C3
Alameda NM, 4200 ...48 C1
Alameda Co. CA, 1443741 ...36 B4
Alamo CA, 15626 ...259 D2
Alamo GA, 1943 ...129 E3
Alamo NM, 1183 ...48 B4
Alamo TN, 2392 ...108 C4
Alamo TX, 14760 ...63 E4
Alamogordo NM, 35582 ...56 C2
Alamo Hts. TX, 7319 ...257 E2
Alamosa CO, 7960 ...41 D4
Alamosa Co. CO, 14966 ...41 D4
Alanson MI, 785 ...70 C3
Alapaha GA, 682 ...129 E4
Alba MO, 588 ...106 B2
Albany CA, 16444 ...259 C3
Albany GA, 76939 ...129 D4
Albany IL, 895 ...88 A1
Albany IN, 2368 ...90 A4
Albany KY, 2220 ...110 B3
Albany LA, 865 ...134 B2
Albany MN, 1796 ...66 B2
Albany MO, 1937 ...86 B4
Albany NY, 95658 ...94 B1
Albany OH, 808 ...101 E2
Albany OR, 40852 ...20 B3
Albany TX, 1921 ...58 C2
Albany Co. NY, 294565 ...94 B1
Albany Co. WY, 32014 ...33 E2
Albemarle NC, 15680 ...122 B1
Albemarle Co. VA, 79236 ...102 C4
Albert City IA, 709 ...72 B4
Albert Lea MN, 18356 ...72 C2
Alberton MT, 374 ...15 D4
Albertville AL, 17247 ...120 A3
Albertville MN, 3621 ...66 C3
Albia IA, 3706 ...87 E2
Albin VA, 700 ...102 C3
Albion ID, 262 ...31 D2
Albion IL, 1933 ...99 D4
Albion IN, 2284 ...90 A3
Albion IA, 592 ...87 D1

Albion MI, 9144 ...76 A4
Albion NE, 1797 ...35 E3
Albion NY, 7438 ...78 B3
Albion PA, 1607 ...91 F1
Albion WA, 616 ...14 A4
Albuquerque NM, 448607 ...48 C3
Alburg VT, 488 ...81 D1
Alburnett IA, 559 ...87 E1
Alburtis PA, 2117 ...146 B1
Alcalde NM, 377 ...49 D2
Alcester SD, 880 ...35 F1
Alcoa TN, 7734 ...110 C4
Alcona Co. MI, 11719 ...71 D4
Alcorn MS, 1200 ...126 A3
Alcorn Co. MS, 34558 ...119 D2
Alda NE, 652 ...35 D4
Aldan PA, 4313 ...248 B4
Alden IA, 904 ...72 C4
Alden MN, 621 ...72 C2
Alden NY, 2666 ...78 B3
Alderson WV, 1091 ...112 A1
Alderwood Manor WA, 15329 ...262 B2
Aledo IL, 3613 ...87 F2
Aledo TX, 1726 ...59 E2
Alex OK, 635 ...51 E3
Alexander AR, 614 ...117 E2
Alexander ND, 217 ...17 F2
Alexander City AL, 15008 ...128 A1
Alexander Co. IL, 9590 ...108 C4
Alexander Co. NC, 33603 ...112 A4
Alexandria AL, 3692 ...120 A4

Alexandria IN, 6260 ...89 F4
Alexandria KY, 8286 ...100 B3
Alexandria LA, 46342 ...125 E4
Alexandria MN, 8820 ...66 B2
Alexandria SD, 563 ...27 E4
Alexandria TN, 814 ...110 A4
Alexandria VA, 128283 ...144 B3
Alexandria Bay NY, 1088 ...79 E1
Alexis IL, 863 ...88 A3
Alfalfa Co. OK, 6105 ...51 D1
Alford FL, 466 ...136 C1
Alfred ME, 700 ...82 B4
Alfred NY, 3954 ...92 C1
Alger OH, 888 ...90 B3
Alger Co. MI, 9862 ...69 E1
Algodones NM, 688 ...48 C3
Algoma MS, 508 ...118 C3
Algoma WI, 3357 ...69 D4
Algona IA, 5741 ...72 B3
Algona WA, 2460 ...262 B5
Algonac MI, 4613 ...76 C4
Algonquin IL, 23276 ...88 C1
Alhambra CA, 85804 ...228 C2
Alhambra IL, 630 ...98 B3
Alice TX, 19104 ...63 E2
Aliceville AL, 2567 ...127 E1
Ali Chuk AZ, 450 ...54 B3
Aliquippa PA, 11734 ...91 F3
Aliso Viejo CA, 40596 ...229 G6

Allamuchy NJ, 3125 ...94 A3
Allardt TN, 642 ...110 B3
Allegan MI, 4998 ...75 F4
Allegan Co. MI, 105665 ...75 F4
Allegany NY, 1883 ...92 C1
Allegany Co. MD, 74930 ...102 C1
Allegany Co. NY, 49927 ...78 C4
Alleghany Co. NC, 10677 ...111 F3
Alleghany Co. VA, 17215 ...102 A4
Allegheny Co. PA, 1281666 ...92 A4
Allen NE, 419 ...35 F2
Allen OK, 951 ...51 F4
Allen SD, 419 ...26 B4
Allen TX, 43554 ...59 F2
Allen Co. IN, 331849 ...90 A3
Allen Co. KS, 14385 ...96 A4
Allen Co. KY, 17800 ...109 F2
Allen Co. OH, 108473 ...90 B3
Allendale IL, 11555 ...75 F3
Allendale NJ, 6699 ...148 B3
Allendale SC, 4052 ...130 B3
Allendale Co. SC, 11211 ...130 B3
Allenhurst GA, 788 ...130 B3
Allenhurst NJ, 496 ...147 F2
Allen Par. LA, 25440 ...133 D1
Allen Park MI, 29376 ...210 B4
Allenspark CO ...41 D1
Allenton RI, 1400 ...150 C4
Allentown NJ, 1882 ...147 E2
Allentown PA, 106632 ...146 B1
Allenwood NJ, 935 ...147 F3

Albany / Schenectady / Troy NY

Place	Grid	Place	Grid
Albany	D3	Maywood	D2
Alplaus	C1	McCormack Corners	C2
Best	E3	McKownville	C3
Bethlehem Ctr.	D3	Meadowdale	C3
Boght Corners	E1	Menands	D2
Calico Colony	D1	Mohawk View	D2
Clifton Gardens	D1	New Salem	C3
Clifton Park	D1	New Scotland	C3
Clifton Park Ctr.	D1	Newtonville	E2
Clinton Park	E3	Niskayuna	D2
Cohoes	D2	Normanville	D3
Colonie	D2	N. Bethlehem	D3
Crescent	D1	Rensselaer	D3
Defreestville	E3	Rexford	D1
Delmar	D3	Roessleville	D2
Dunnsville	C2	Rotterdam	C2
Dunsbach Ferry	E1	Schenectady	C1
E. Greenbush	E3	Scotia	C1
Elsmere	D3	Sherwood Park	E3
Ft. Hunter	C2	Slingerlands	D3
Glenmont	D3	Snyders Corners	E3
Glenridge	C1	Speigletown	E1
Grant Hollow	E1	Sycaway	E2
Green Island	E2	Troy	E2
Guilderland	C2	Unionville	D3
Guilderland Ctr.	C2	Verdoy	D2
Halfmoon	E1	Vischer Ferry	D1
Hartmans Corners	C2	Voorheesville	C3
Hawthorne Hill	E2	Waterford	E1
Latham	E2	Watervliet	E2
Loudonville	D2	W. Hill	C1
Luther	E3	Westmere	D2
Maple Wood	D2	Wynantskill	E2

Akron OH

Place	Grid	Place	Grid
Akron	A1	Montrose	A1
Barberton	A2	Munroe Falls	B1
Copley	A1	Norton	A2
Cuyahoga Falls	B1	Portage Lakes	A2
Fairlawn	A1	Silver Lake	B1
Ghent	A1	Stow	B1
Lakemore	B2	Tallmadge	B1
Mogadore	B2		

Entries in **bold black** indicate counties or parishes. Entries in ***bold color*** indicate cities with detailed inset maps.

Allerton–Annville   189

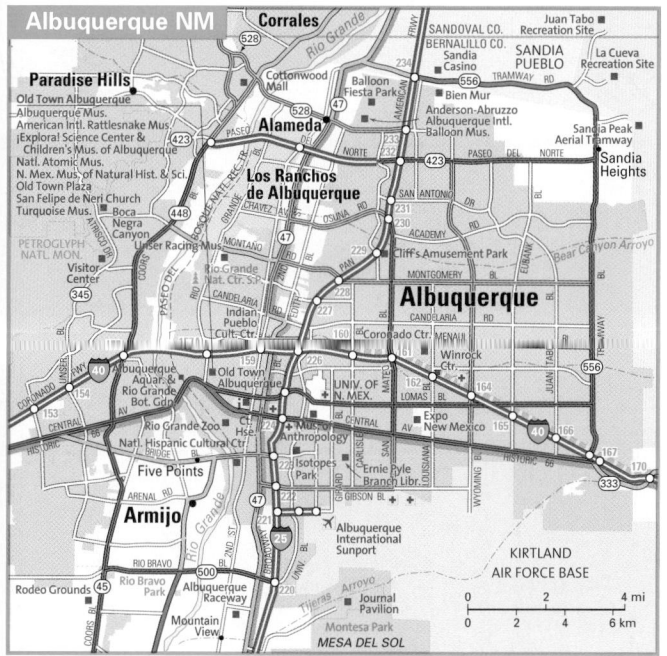

Albuquerque NM

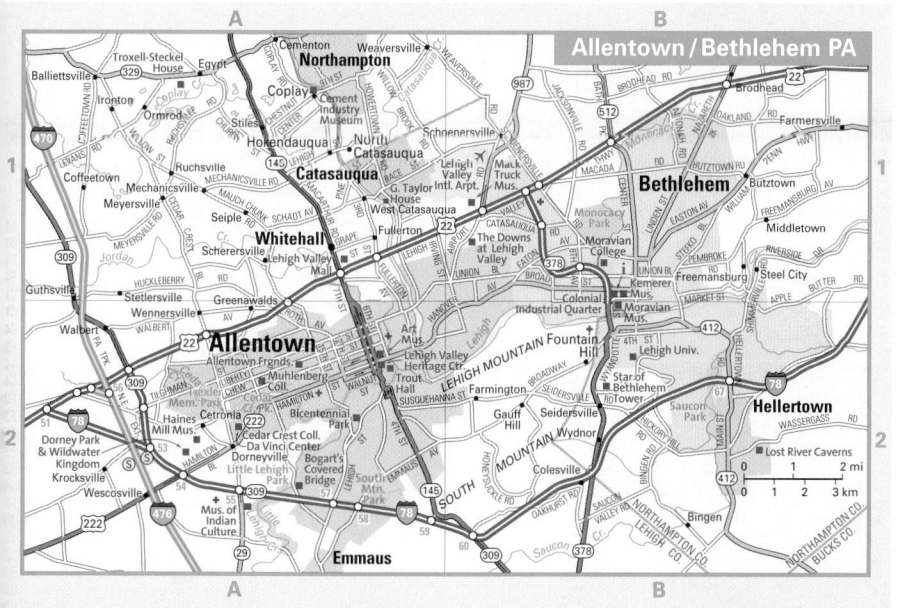

Allentown / Bethlehem PA

Amarillo TX

Anchorage AK

Annapolis MD

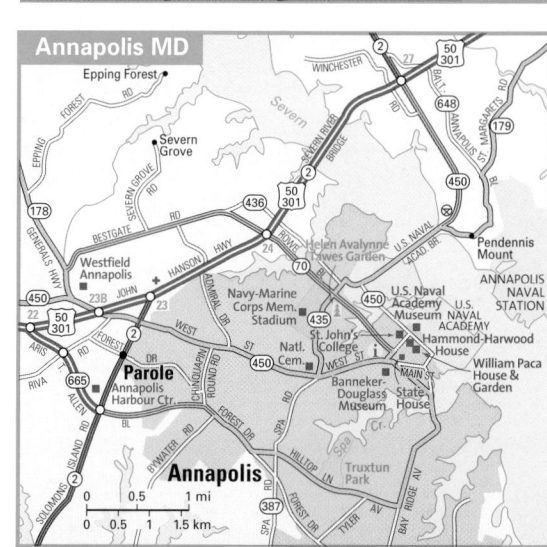

190   Anoka–Arbyrd

Figures after entries indicate population, page number, and grid reference.

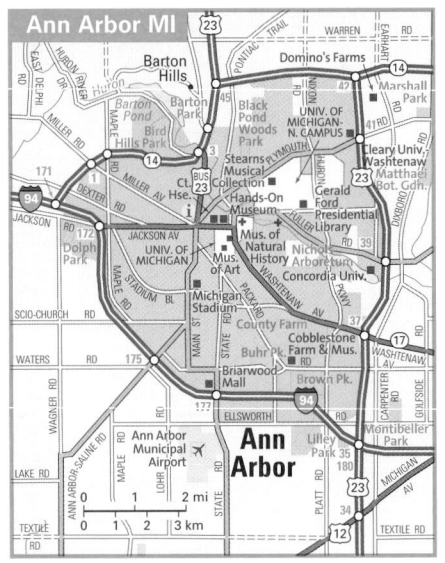

Ann Arbor MI

Atlanta GA

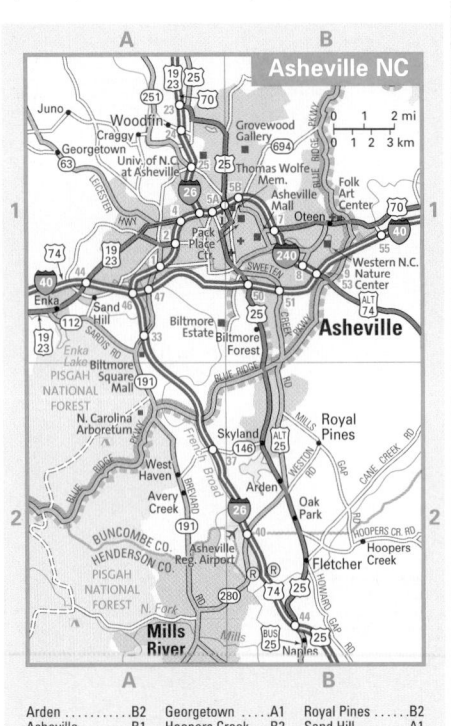

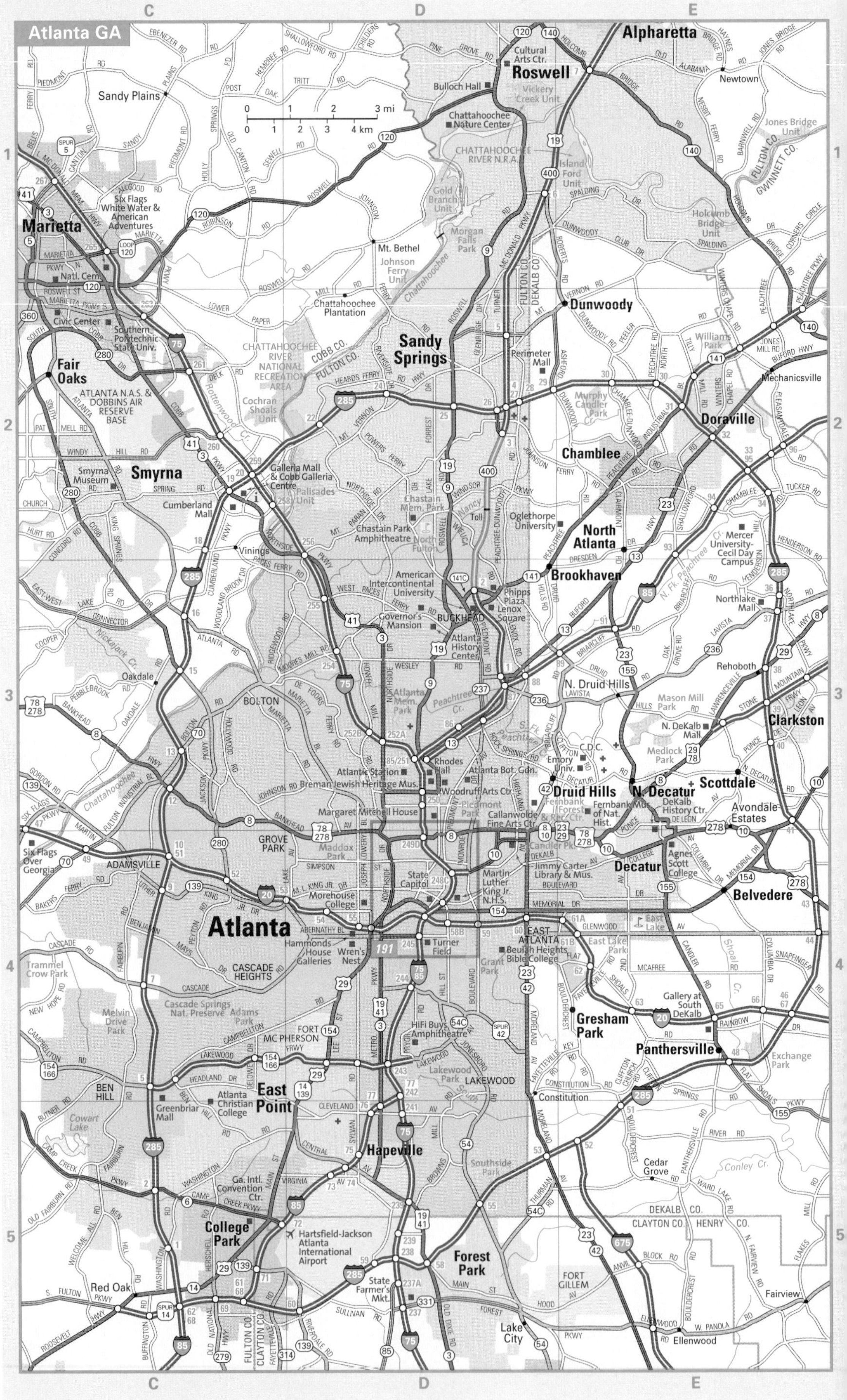

Asheville NC

Mills River

Entries in **bold black** indicate counties or parishes. Entries in **bold color** indicate cities with detailed inset maps.

Arcade–Augusta **191**

Downtown Atlanta GA

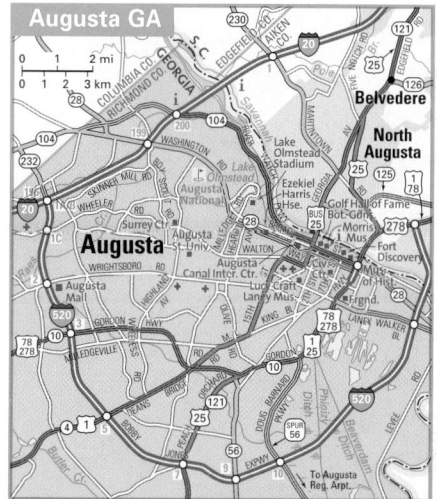

Atlantic City NJ

Augusta GA

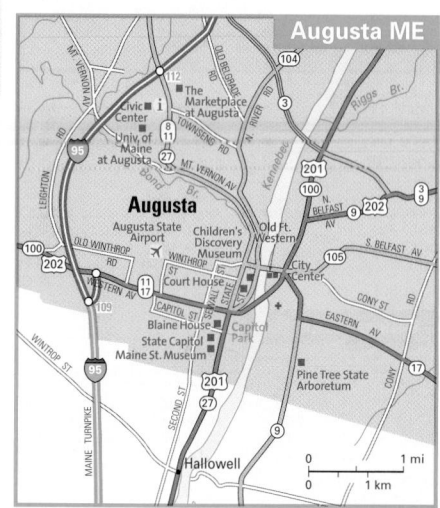

Augusta ME

POINTS OF INTEREST

APEX Mus. B1
Atlanta Civic Center B1
Atlanta Cyclorama B2
Atlanta Heritage Row A2
Atlanta Historic Center Downtown ..B1
Big Bethel African Meth. Episcopal Church ..B1
Boisfeuillet Jones Atlanta Civic Center ..B1
Bus Station A1
Children's Mus. of Atlanta A1
City Hall A2
Civic Center Auditorium B1

Clark Atlanta Univ. A2
CNN Center A1
Ebenezer Baptist Church B1
Federal Reserve Bank Monetary Mus. ..A1
Fox Theatre B1
Georgia Aquarium A1
Georgia Dome A1
Georgia Institute of Technology ..A1
Georgia State Univ. B2
Georgia World Congress Center ..A1
Grant Field A1
The King Center B1

Martin Luther King, Jr. Natl. Hist. Site ..B1
Morris Brown Coll. A1
Museum of Design B1
Peachtree Center A1
Philips Arena A1
The Rialto A1
Spelman Coll. A2
State Capitol B2
Turner Field A2
Underground Atlanta A2
World of Coca-Cola A1, B2
Zoo Atlanta B2

192 Augusta County–Belmont

Figures after entries indicate population, page number, and grid reference.

Augusta Co. VA, 65615...102 B4
Aulander NC, 888...113 A3
Ault CO, 1432...33 E4
Aumsville OR, 3003...20 B2
Aurelia IA, 1062...72 A4
Aurora CO, 276393...41 E1
Aurora IL, 142990...88 C1
Aurora IN, 3965...100 B3
Aurora MN, 1850...64 C3
Aurora MO, 7014...106 C2
Aurora NE, 4225...35 E4
Aurora NY, 720...79 D4
Aurora NC, 583...115 D3
Aurora OH, 13556...91 E4
Aurora OR, 655...20 C2
Aurora SD, 500...27 F3
Aurora TX, 853...59 D4
Aurora UT, 947...39 E2
Aurora Co. SD, 3058...27 D4

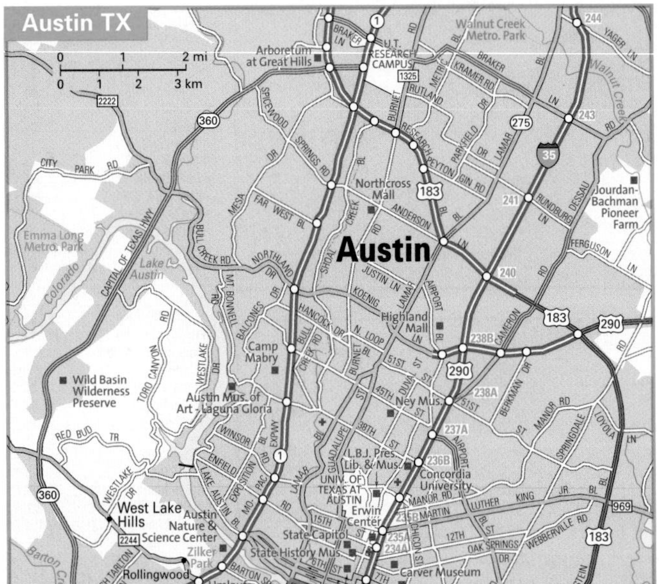

Au Sable MI, 1533...76 C1
Au Sable Forks NY, 670...81 D2
Austin AR, 605...117 F2
Austin IN, 4724...99 F3
Austin MN, 23314...73 D2
Austin NV, 600...37 F1
Austin PA, 623...92 C2
Austin TX, 656562...61 E1
Austin Co. TX, 23590...61 E2
Austintown OH, 31627...91 F3

Avon IN, 6248...99 F1
Avon MN, 1242...66 C2
Avon NY, 2977...78 C3
Avon OH, 11446...91 D2
Avon PA, 2856...146 A2
Avon SD, 561...35 E1
Avon NC, 550...115 F3
Avon-by-the-Sea NJ, 2244...147 F2
Avondale AZ, 35883...54 C1
Avondale CO, 754...41 E3
Avondale LA, 5441...134 B3
Avondale MO, 529...224 C2
Avondale PA, 1108...146 B3
Avondale Estates GA, 2609...190 B3
Aventura FL, 25267...143 F2
Averill Park NY, 1517...94 B1
Avery CA, 672...37 D3
Avery Creek NC, 1405...121 E1
Avilla IN, 2049...90 A2
Avis PA, 1492...93 D2

Aviston IL, 1231...98 B3
Avoca IA, 1610...86 A2
Avoca NY, 1008...78 C4
Avoca PA, 2851...261 C2
Avoca WI, 608...74 A3
Avon AL, 466...137 D1
Avon CO, 5561...40 C1
Avon CT, 1500...94 C3
Avon IL, 915...88 A3

Avoyelles Par. LA, 41481...125 F4
Awendaw SC, 1195...131 D1
Axtell KS, 445...43 F1
Axtell NE, 696...35 D4
Ayden NC, 4622...115 D3
Ayer MA, 2960...95 D1
Aynor SC, 587...122 C3
Azalea Park FL, 11073...246 D2
Azle TX, 9600...59 E2
Aztec NM, 6378...48 B1
Azusa CA, 44712...228 E2

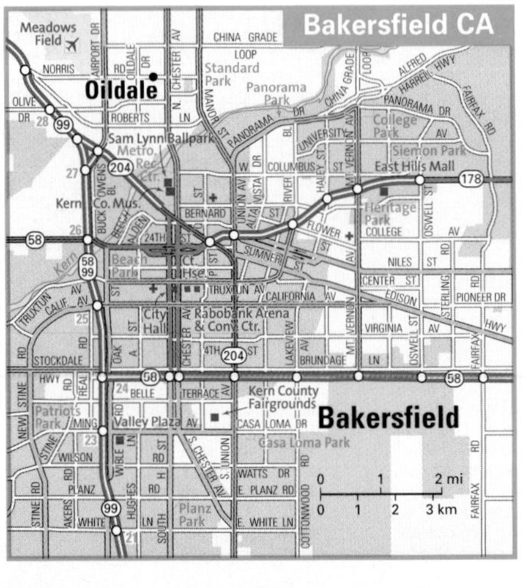

B
Babbie AL, 627...128 A4
Babbitt MN, 1670...64 C3
Babson Park FL, 1182...141 D4
Babylon NY, 12615...148 C4
Baca Co. CO, 4517...42 A4
Bacon Co. GA, 10103...129 F4
Baconton GA, 804...129 D4
Bad Axe MI, 3462...76 C2
Baden PA, 4377...92 A3
Badger IA, 610...72 C4
Badin NC, 1154...122 B1
Bagdad AZ, 1578...46 C4
Bagdad FL, 1490...135 F2
Baggs WY, 348...32 C3
Bagley MN, 1235...64 A3
Bahama NC, 550...112 C4
Bailey NC, 670...113 D4
Bailey Co. TX, 6594...49 F4
Baileys Crossroads VA, 23166...270 B4
Bailey's Prairie TX, 694...132 A4
Baileyton AL, 684...119 F3
Baileyton TN, 504...111 D3
Bainbridge GA, 11722...137 D1
Bainbridge IN, 743...99 E1
Bainbridge NY, 1365...79 E4

Bainbridge OH, 1012...101 D2
Bainbridge Island WA, 20308...12 C3
Baird TX, 1623...58 C3
Baiting Hollow NY, 1449...149 E3
Baker LA, 13793...134 A2
Baker MT, 1695...17 F4
Baker City OR, 9860...21 F2
Baker Co. FL, 22259...138 C2
Baker Co. GA, 4074...128 C4
Baker Co. OR, 16741...21 E2
Bakersfield CA, 247057...45 D4
Bakersville NC, 357...111 E4
Bala-Cynwyd PA, 10300...146 C3
Balaton MN, 637...72 A1
Balch Sprs. TX, 19375...207 E3
Balcones Hts. TX, 3016...257 E2
Bald Knob AR, 3210...117 F1
Baldwin FL, 1634...139 D2
Baldwin GA, 2425...121 D3
Baldwin IL, 3627...98 B4
Baldwin LA, 2497...133 F3
Baldwin MD, 850...144 C1
Baldwin MI, 1107...75 F2
Baldwin WI, 19999...250 D3
Baldwin City KS, 3400...96 A3
Baldwin Co. AL, 140415...135 E1
Baldwin Co. GA, 44700...129 E1
Baldwin Harbor NY, 8147...147 F1
Baldwin Park CA, 75837...228 E2
Baldwinsville NY, 7053...79 D3
Baldwinville MA, 1852...95 D1
Baldwyn MS, 3321...119 D3
Balfour NC, 1200...121 E1
Bal Harbour FL, 3305...233 B3
Ball LA, 3681...125 E4
Ballantine MT, 346...24 C1
Ballentine SC, 850...122 A3
Ball Ground GA, 730...120 C3
Ballinger TX, 4243...58 C4
Ballouville CT, 950...150 B3
Ballston Spa NY, 5556...80 C4
Ballville OH, 3255...90 C2
Ballwin MO, 31283...98 A3
Bally PA, 1062...146 B1
Balmorhea TX, 527...62 B2
Balmville NY, 3339...148 B1
Balsam Lake WI, 950...67 E4
Baltic CT, 1500...149 F1
Baltic OH, 743...91 E4
Baltic SD, 811...27 F4
Baltimore MD, 651154...144 C2
Baltimore OH, 2881...101 D1
Baltimore Co. MD, 754292...144 A1
Baltimore Highlands MD, 15724...193 C4
Bamberg SC, 3733...130 C1
Bamberg Co. SC, 16658...130 B1
Bancroft ID, 382...31 E1
Bancroft IA, 808...72 B3
Bancroft KY, 536...230 F1
Bancroft MI, 616...76 B3
Bancroft NE, 520...35 F2
Bancroft WV, 367...101 E3
Bandera TX, 957...61 D2
Bandera Co. TX, 17645...60 C2
Bandon OR, 2833...28 A1
Bangor ME, 31473...83 D1
Bangor MI, 1933...75 E4
Bangor PA, 5319...93 F3
Bangor WI, 1400...73 F2
Bangs TX, 1620...59 D4
Banks OR, 1286...20 B1

Barnhart MO, 6108...98 A4
Barnsboro NJ, 2500...146 C4
Barnsdall OK, 1325...51 F1
Barnstable MA, 47821...151 F3
Barnstable Co. MA, 222230...151 E4
Barnum MN, 525...64 C4
Bar Nunn WY, 936...33 D1
Barnwell SC, 5035...130 B1
Barnwell Co. SC, 23478...130 B1
Baroda MI, 858...89 E1
Barrackville WV, 1288...102 A1
Barre MA, 1150...150 B1
Barre VT, 9291...81 E2
Barre Plains MA, 1200...150 B1
Barren Co. KY, 38033...110 A2
Barrett NJ, 2872...132 B3
Barrington IL, 10168...203 B2
Barrington NH, 600...81 F4
Barrington NY, 7084...248 D4
Barrington RI, 16819...151 D3
Barrington Hills IL, 3915...203 A3
Barron WI, 3248...67 E3
Barron Co. WI, 44963...67 E3
Barrow AK, 4581...154 C1
Barrow Co. GA, 46144...121 D3
Barry IL, 1368...97 F1
Barry Co. MI, 56755...75 F4
Barry Co. MO, 34010...106 C2
Barstow CA, 21119...53 D1
Barstow MD, 750...144 C4
Bartelso IL, 823...98 B3
Bartholomew Co. IN, 71435...99 F2
Bartlesville OK, 34748...51 F1
Bartlett IL, 36706...203 A3
Bartlett NE, 128...35 D2
Bartlett NH, 550...81 F2
Bartlett TN, 40543...118 B4
Bartlett TX, 1675...61 E1
Barton VT, 742...81 E1
Barton Co. KS, 28205...43 D3
Barton Co. MO, 12541...106 B1
Bartonsville MD, 12529...144 A1
Bartonville IL, 6310...88 B3
Bartow FL, 15340...140 C2
Bartow GA, 76019...120 B3
Barview OR, 1872...20 A4
Basalt CO, 2681...40 C2
Basalt ID, 419...23 E4
Basehor KS, 2238...96 B2
Basile LA, 1660...133 E2
Basin MT, 255...15 E4
Basin WY, 1238...24 C2
Basin City WA, 968...13 E4
Baskin LA, 550...125 F4
Basking Ridge NJ, 3600...148 A4
Bassett NE, 743...35 D1
Bassett VA, 1338...112 B2
Bass Harbor ME, 600...83 D2
Bass Lake IN, 1249...89 E2
Bastrop LA, 12988...125 F2
Bastrop TX, 5340...61 E2
Bastrop Co. TX, 57733...61 E2
Basye VA, 986...102 C3
Batavia IL, 23866...88 C1
Batavia IA, 500...87 E3
Batavia NY, 16256...78 B3
Batavia OH, 2833...100 B2
Batesburg-Leesville SC, 5517...122 A4
Bates Co. MO, 16653...96 B4
Batesville AR, 9445...107 F4
Batesville IN, 6033...100 A2
Batesville MS, 7113...118 B3
Batesville TX, 1298...60 C3
Bath ME, 9266...82 C3
Bath MI, 1200...76 A3
Bath NY, 5641...78 C4
Bath PA, 2678...93 F3
Bath Co. KY, 11085...100 C4
Bath Co. VA, 5048...102 B4
Baton Rouge LA, 227818...134 A2
Battle Creek IA, 743...72 A4
Battle Creek MI, 53364...75 F4
Battle Creek NE, 1158...35 E2
Battlefield MO, 2385...107 D2
Battle Ground IN, 1323...89 E4
Battle Ground WA, 9296...20 C1
Battle Lake MN, 686...19 F4
Battle Mtn. NV, 2871...30 C4
Baudette MN, 1104...64 A1
Baumstown PA, 1000...146 B2
Bauxite AR, 432...117 E2
Bawcomville LA, 7616...125 E2
Baxley GA, 4150...129 F3
Baxter IA, 1052...87 D1
Baxter MN, 5555...64 A4
Baxter TN, 1279...110 A4
Baxter Co. AR, 38386...107 E4
Baxter Estates NY, 1006...241 G2
Baxter Sprs. KS, 4602...106 B1
Bay AR, 1800...108 A4
Bayard IA, 536...86 B1
Bayard NM, 2534...55 F2
Bayboro NC, 741...115 D3
Bay City MI, 36817...76 B3
Bay City OR, 1149...20 B1
Bay City TX, 18667...61 F3
Bay Co. FL, 168852...136 C2
Bay Co. MI, 110157...76 B3
Bayfield CO, 1549...40 C4
Bayfield WI, 611...65 D2

Bayfield Co. WI, 15013...65 D3
Bay Harbor Islands FL, 5146...233 B3
Bay Head NJ, 1238...147 E3
Bay Hill FL, 5177...246 B3
Baylor Co. TX, 4093...59 D1
Bay Minette AL, 7820...135 E1
Bayonet Pt. FL, 23577...140 B2
Bayonne NJ, 61842...148 B4
Bay Pt. CA, 21534...259 D1
Bayport MN, 3162...67 D4
Bayport NY, 8662...149 D4
Bay Ridge MD, 2300...144 C3
Bay St. Louis MS, 8209...134 C2
Bayshore FL, 750...142 C1
Bay Shore NY, 23852...149 D4
Bayshore Gardens FL, 17350...266 B5
Bay Side NJ, 1800...147 E4
Bayside WI, 4518...234 D1
Bay Sprs. MS, 2097...126 C3
Baytown TX, 66430...132 B3
Bay View OH, 692...91 D2
Bay Vil. OH, 16087...204 D2
Bayville NJ, 4700...147 E3
Bayville NY, 7135...148 C3
Beach ND, 1116...17 F4
Beach City OH, 1137...91 E3
Beach City TX, 1645...132 B4
Beach Haven NJ, 1278...147 E4
Beach Haven Gardens NJ, 1200...147 E4
Beach Haven Terrace NJ, 1100...147 E4
Beachwood NJ, 10375...147 E3
Beachwood OH, 12186...204 G2
Beacon IA, 518...87 D2
Beacon NY, 13808...148 B1
Beacon Falls CT, 1500...149 D1
Beadle Co. SD, 17023...27 D3
Bealeton VA, 2100...103 D3
Beals ME, 750...83 F2
Bean Sta. TN, 2634...111 D3
Bear DE, 17593...145 E1
Bear Creek AL, 1053...119 E3
Bearden AR, 1125...117 E4
Bear Lake Co. ID, 6411...31 F3
Bear River City UT, 750...31 E3
Beasley TX, 590...132 A4
Beatrice AL, 412...127 F4
Beatrice NE, 12496...35 F4
Beatty NV, 1154...45 F2
Beattyville KY, 1193...110 C1
Beatyestown NJ, 3223...94 A4
Beaufort NC, 3771...115 E4
Beaufort SC, 12950...130 C2
Beaufort Co. NC, 44958...113 F4
Beaufort Co. SC, 120937...130 C3
Beaumont CA, 11384...53 D2
Beaumont MS, 977...135 D1
Beaumont TX, 113866...132 C3
Beaumont Place TX, 4500...220 D2
Beauregard Par. LA, 32986...133 D2
Beaver OK, 1570...50 C1
Beaver PA, 4775...91 F4
Beaver UT, 2454...39 D3
Beaver WV, 1378...111 F1
Beaver City NE, 641...42 C1
Beaver Co. OK, 5857...50 C1
Beaver Co. PA, 181412...91 F3
Beaver Co. UT, 6005...39 D3
Beavercreek OH, 37984...100 C1
Beaver Crossing NE, 457...35 E4
Beaver Dam KY, 3033...109 E1
Beaver Dam WI, 15169...74 B2
Beaver Falls PA, 9920...91 F3
Beaverhead Co. MT, 9202...23 D1
Beaver Meadows PA, 968...93 E3
Beaver Sprs. PA, 634...93 D3
Beaverton MI, 1106...76 A2
Beaverton OR, 76129...20 C2
Beavertown PA, 870...93 D3
Bechtelsville PA, 931...146 B1
Beckemeyer IL, 1043...98 B3
Becker MN, 2673...66 C3
Becker Co. MN, 30000...19 F3
Beckett NJ, 4726...146 C4
Beckley WV, 17254...111 F1
Beckville TX, 752...124 C3
Bedford IN, 13768...99 F3
Bedford IA, 1620...86 B3
Bedford KY, 677...100 A3
Bedford MA, 12595...151 D1
Bedford NH, 1300...95 D1
Bedford NY, 1724...148 C2
Bedford OH, 14214...204 F3
Bedford PA, 3141...92 C4
Bedford TX, 47152...207 B2
Bedford VA, 6299...112 B1
Bedford Co. PA, 49984...92 C4
Bedford Co. TN, 37586...120 A1
Bedford Co. VA, 60371...112 B1
Bedford Hills NY, 5500...148 C2
Bedford Park IL, 574...203 D5

Beebe AR, 4930...117 F2
Bee Cave TX, 656...61 E1
Beech Bottom WV, 606...91 F4
Beech Creek PA, 717...93 D3
Beecher IL, 2033...89 D2
Beecher City IL, 972...99 D1
Beech Grove IN, 14880...99 F1
Beechwood Vil. KY, 1173...230 E1
Beemer NE, 773...35 F2
Bee Ridge FL, 8744...140 B4
Beersheba Sprs. TN, 553...120 A1
Beesleys Pt. NJ, 1400...147 F4
Beeville TX, 13129...61 E4
Beggs OK, 1364...51 F2
Bel Air MD, 10080...145 D1
Belcamp MD, 1900...145 D1
Belchertown MA, 2626...150 A1
Belcourt ND, 2440...18 C1
Belding MI, 5877...75 F3
Belen NM, 6901...48 C4
Belfair WA, 700...12 C3
Belfast ME, 6381...82 C2
Belfast NY, 800...78 B4
Belfield ND, 866...18 A4
Belford NJ, 1340...147 E1
Belfry MT, 219...24 C2
Belgium WI, 1678...75 D2
Belgrade MN, 750...66 B3
Belgrade MT, 5728...23 F1
Belgrade Lakes ME, 350...82 B2
Belhaven NC, 1968...115 E3
Belinda City TN, 2100...109 F4
Belington WV, 1788...102 A2
Belknap Co. NH, 56325...81 F3
Bell CA, 36664...228 D3
Bellair FL, 16539...222 C4
Bellaire MI, 1164...69 F4
Bellaire OH, 4892...101 F1
Bellaire TX, 15642...132 A3
Bellamy AL, 600...127 E2
Bella Vista AR, 16582...106 C3
Bella Vista CA, 550...28 C4
Bella Villa MO, 687...256 D3
Bellbrook OH, 7009...100 C1
Bell Buckle TN, 391...119 F1
Bell Co. KY, 30060...110 C3
Bell Co. TX, 237974...61 E1
Belle MO, 1344...97 F4
Belle WV, 1259...101 F4
Belleair FL, 4067...140 B2
Belleair Beach FL, 1751...140 B2
Belleair Bluffs FL, 2243...266 A3
Belle Chasse LA, 9848...134 B3
Bellefontaine OH, 13069...90 C4
Bellefontaine Neighbors MO, 11271...256 C1
Bellefonte DE, 1237...146 C3
Bellefonte KY, 837...101 D3
Bellefonte PA, 6395...92 C3
Belle Fourche SD, 4565...25 F1
Belle Glade FL, 14906...143 E1
Belle Haven CA, 480...114 B3
Belle Isle FL, 5531...141 D1
Bellemeade KY, 871...230 F2
Belle Plaine IA, 2878...87 E2
Belle Plaine KS, 1708...43 E3
Belle Plaine MN, 3789...66 C4
Belle Rose LA, 1944...134 A3
Bellerose NY, 1173...241 G3
Bellerose Terrace NY, 2157...241 G3
Belle Terre NY, 832...149 D3
Belle Vernon PA, 1211...92 A4
Belleview FL, 3478...139 D4
Belleville IL, 41410...98 B3
Belleville KS, 2239...43 E1
Belleville MI, 3997...90 C1
Belleville NJ, 35928...148 A3
Belleville PA, 1386...92 C3
Belleville WI, 1908...74 B3
Bellevue ID, 1876...22 C4
Bellevue IA, 1887...88 B1
Bellevue KY, 6480...204 B3
Bellevue MI, 1365...76 A4
Bellevue NE, 44382...86 A1
Bellevue OH, 8193...91 D2
Bellevue PA, 8770...92 A4
Bellevue WA, 109569...12 C3
Bellevue WI, 11828...74 C1
Bellflower CA, 72878...228 D3
Bell Gardens CA, 44054...228 D3
Bellingham MA, 4497...150 C2
Bellingham WA, 67171...12 C1
Bellmawr NJ, 11262...146 C3
Bellmead TX, 9214...59 E4
Bellows Falls VT, 3165...81 E4
Bellport NY, 2363...149 D3
Bells TN, 2171...108 C4
Bells TX, 1190...59 F1
Bellview FL, 21201...247 A1
Bellville OH, 1773...91 D4
Bellville TX, 3794...61 F2
Bellwood IL, 20535...203 D5
Bellwood NE, 446...35 E3
Bellwood PA, 2016...92 C3
Bellwood VA, 5974...270 B?
Belmar NJ, 6045...147 F2
Belmond IA, 2560...72 C3
Belmont CA, 25123...259 C4
Belmont MA, 24194...151 D1

[Map inset: Austin TX]

[Map inset: Bakersfield CA]

Entries in **bold black** indicate counties or parishes. Entries in **bold color** indicate cities with detailed inset maps.

193

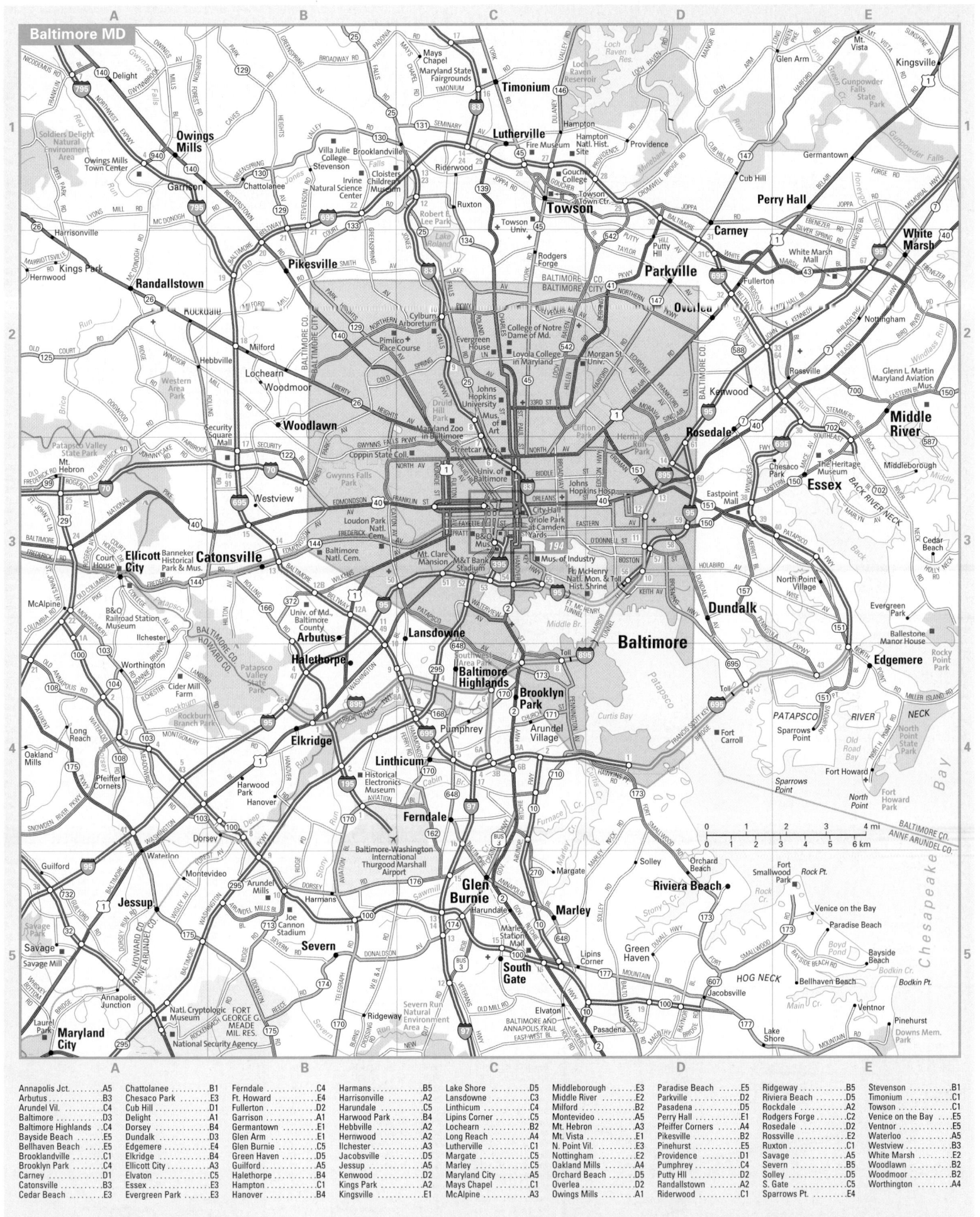

Baltimore MD

194 Belmont–Blair County

Figures after entries indicate population, page number, and grid reference.

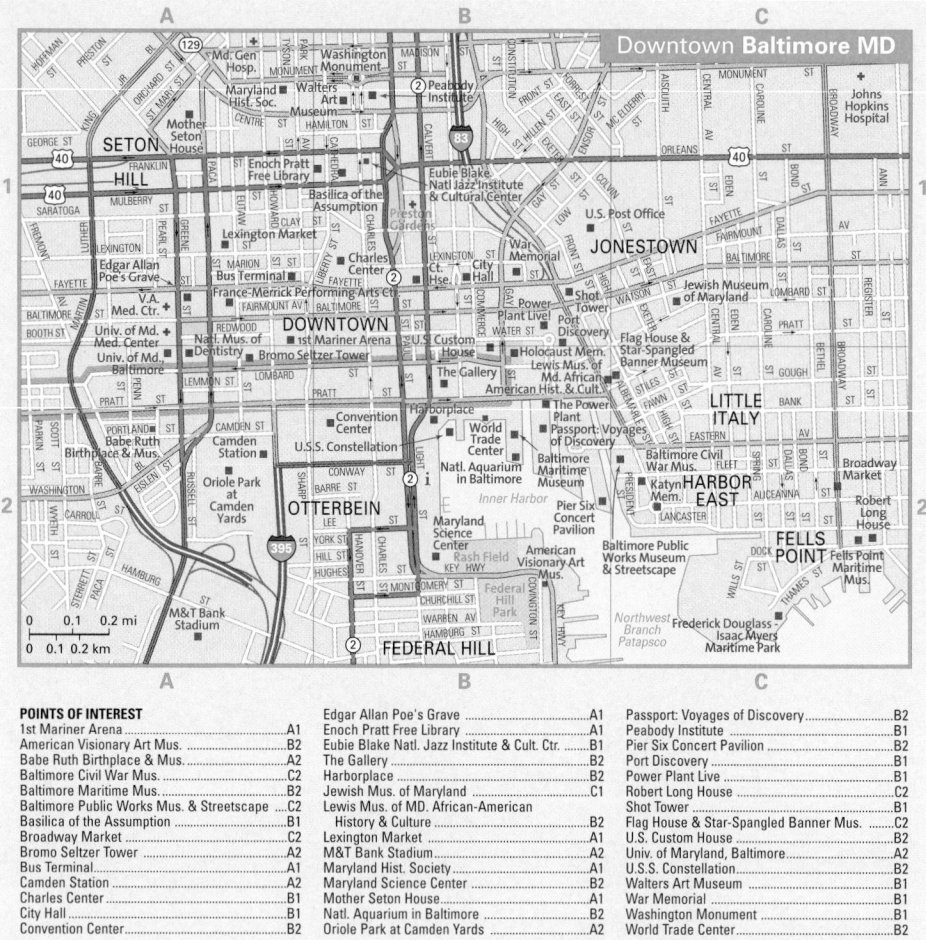

Downtown **Baltimore MD**

POINTS OF INTEREST

1st Mariner Arena	A1	Edgar Allan Poe's Grave	A1	Passport: Voyages of Discovery	B2

1st Mariner Arena A1
American Visionary Art Mus. B2
Babe Ruth Birthplace & Mus. A2
Baltimore Civil War Mus. C2
Baltimore Maritime Mus. B2
Baltimore Public Works Mus. & Streetscape C2
Basilica of the Assumption B1
Broadway Market C2
Bromo Seltzer Tower A2
Bus Terminal A1
Camden Station A2
Charles Center B1
City Hall B1
Convention Center B2

Edgar Allan Poe's Grave A1
Enoch Pratt Free Library A1
Eubie Blake Natl. Jazz Institute & Cult. Ctr. B1
The Gallery B2
Harborplace B2
Jewish Mus. of Maryland C1
Lewis Mus. of MD. African-American
    History & Culture B2
Lexington Market A1
M&T Bank Stadium A2
Maryland Hist. Society A1
Maryland Science Center B2
Mother Seton House A1
Natl. Aquarium in Baltimore B2
Oriole Park at Camden Yards A2

Passport: Voyages of Discovery B2
Peabody Institute B1
Pier Six Concert Pavilion B1
Port Discovery B1
Power Plant Live B1
Robert Long House C2
Shot Tower B1
Flag House & Star-Spangled Banner Mus. C2
U.S. Custom House B2
Univ. of Maryland, Baltimore A2
U.S.S. Constellation B2
Walters Art Museum B1
War Memorial B1
Washington Monument B1
World Trade Center B2

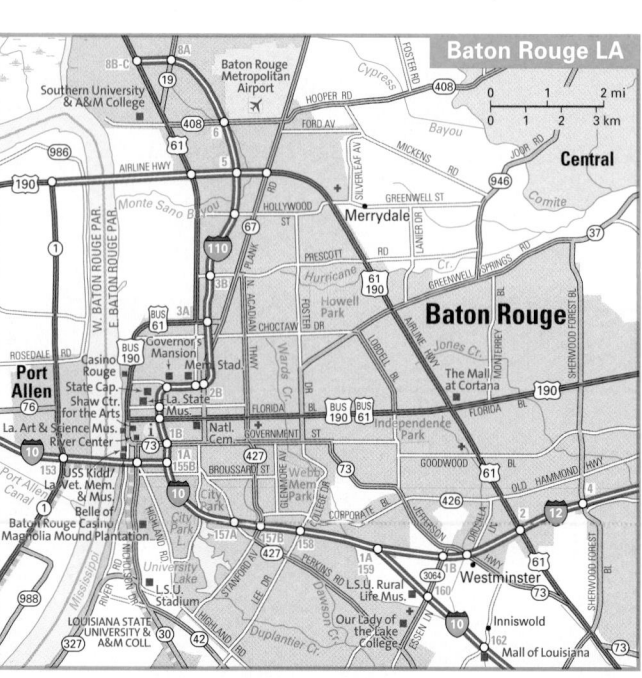

Baton Rouge LA

Port Allen

Baton Rouge

Central

Merrydale

Westminster

Inniswold

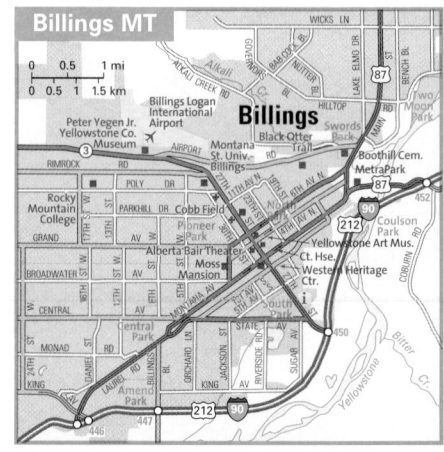

Billings MT

Billings

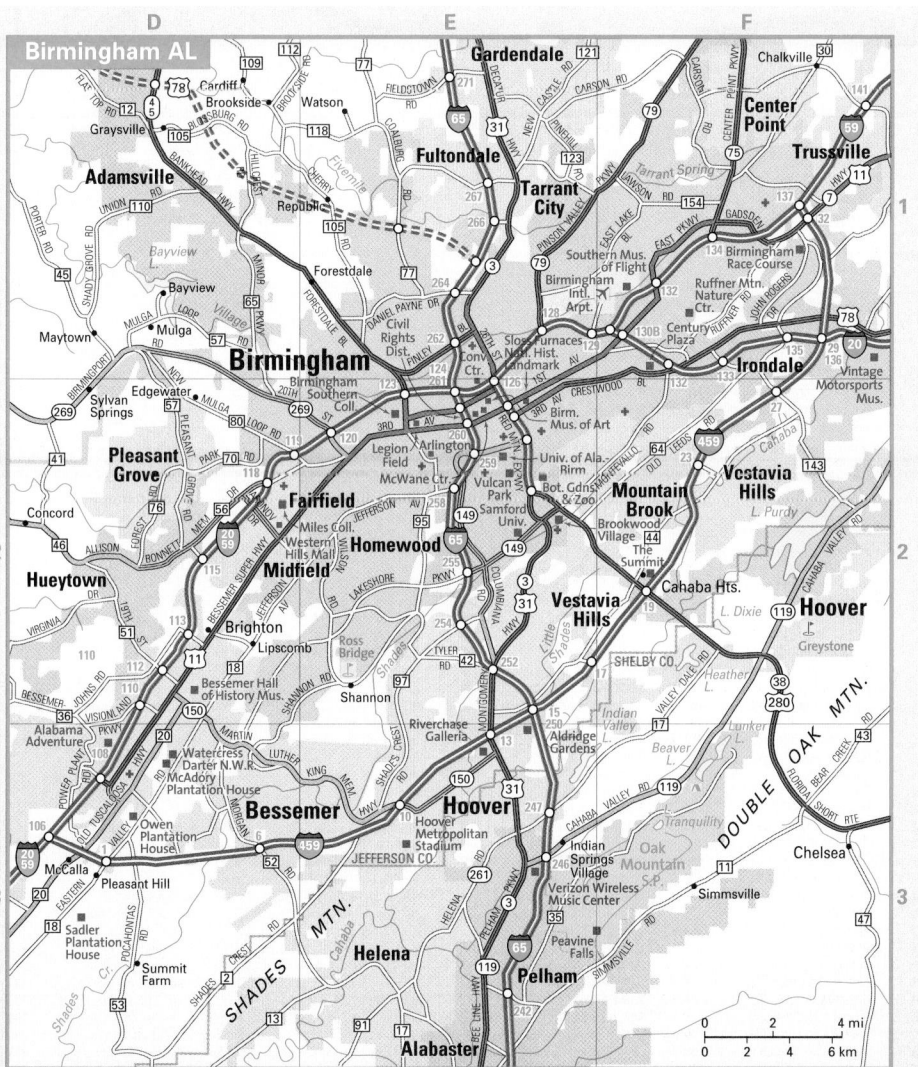

Entries in **bold black** indicate counties or parishes. Entries in *bold color* indicate cities with detailed inset maps.

Blairs–Bowdoin Center **195**

Bowdoinham ME, 600 ...82 B3
Bowdon GA, 1959 ...120 B4
Bowen IL, 535 ...87 F4
Bowie AZ, 550 ...55 E3
Bowie MD, 50269 ...144 C3
Bowie TX, 5219 ...59 E1
Bowie Co. TX, 89306 ...116 B4
Bowleys Quarters MD, 6314 ...144 C2
Bowling Green FL, 2892 ...140 C3
Bowling Green KY, 49296 ...109 F2
Bowling Green MO, 3260 ...97 E2
Bowling Green OH, 29636 ...90 C2
Bowling Green VA, 936 ...103 D4
Bowman GA, 898 ...121 E3
Bowman ND, 1600 ...25 F1
Bowman SC, 1198 ...130 C1
Bowman Co. ND, 3242 ...25 F1
Bow Mar CO, 847 ...209 B4
Boxborough MA, 1400 ...150 C1
Box Butte Co. NE, 12158 ...34 A2
Box Elder MT, 794 ...16 B2
Box Elder SD, 2841 ...26 A3
Box Elder Co. UT, 42745 ...31 D3
Boxford MA, 2340 ...151 E1
Boyce LA, 1190 ...125 E4
Boyce VA, 426 ...103 D2
Boyceville WI, 1043 ...67 E3
Boyd TX, 1099 ...59 D4
Boyd WI, 680 ...67 F4
Boyd Co. KY, 49752 ...101 D4
Boyd Co. NE, 2438 ...35 D1
Boyden IA, 672 ...35 F1
Boydton VA, 454 ...113 D3
Boyertown PA, 3940 ...146 B2
Boyette FL, 5895 ...140 C3
Boykins VA, 620 ...113 E3
Boyle MS, 720 ...118 A4
Boyle Co. KY, 27697 ...110 B1
Boyne City MI, 3503 ...70 B3
Boynton Beach FL, 60389 ...143 F1
Boys Town NE, 818 ...245 A2
Bozeman MT, 27509 ...23 F1
Braceville IL, 792 ...88 C2
Bracken Co. KY, 8279 ...100 C3
Brackettville TX, 1876 ...60 B3
Bradbury CA, 855 ...228 E2
Braddock PA, 2912 ...250 C2
Braddock Hts. MD, 4627 ...144 A1
Braddock Hills PA, 1998 ...250 C2
Bradenton FL, 49504 ...140 B3
Bradenton Beach FL, 1482 ...140 B3
Bradford AR, 800 ...117 F1
Bradford IL, 805 ...88 B1
Bradford NH, 600 ...81 E4
Bradford OH, 1859 ...90 B4
Bradford PA, 9175 ...92 B1
Bradford RI, 1497 ...150 C4
Bradford TN, 1113 ...108 C4
Bradford VT, 815 ...81 E3
Bradford Co. FL, 26088 ...138 C3
Bradford Co. PA, 62761 ...93 E2
Bradfordville FL, 1100 ...137 E2
Bradford Woods PA, 1149 ...92 A3
Bradley AR, 563 ...125 D1

Brandon FL, 77895 ...140 C2
Brandon MS, 16436 ...126 B3
Brandon SD, 5693 ...27 F4
Brandon VT, 1684 ...81 D3
Brandon WI, 912 ...74 C2
Brandywine MD, 1410 ...144 B4
Brandywine Manor PA, 1200 ...146 B2
Branford CT, 5735 ...149 D2
Branford FL, 695 ...138 B3
Branson MO, 6050 ...107 D3
Brant Beach NJ, 800 ...147 E4
Brantley AL, 920 ...128 A4
Brantley Co. GA, 14629 ...129 F4
Brant Rock MA, 5100 ...151 E2
Braselton GA, 1206 ...121 D3
Brasher Falls NY, 1140 ...80 B1
Bratenahl OH, 1337 ...204 F1
Brattleboro VT, 8289 ...94 C1
Brawley CA, 22052 ...53 E4
Braxton Co. WV, 14702 ...101 F4
Bray OK, 1035 ...51 E4
Braymer MO, 910 ...96 C1
Brazil IN, 8188 ...99 E1
Brazoria TX, 2787 ...132 A4
Brazoria Co. TX, 241767 ...132 A4
Brazos Co. TX, 152415 ...61 F1
Breathitt Co. KY, 16100 ...111 D1
Breaux Bridge LA, 7281 ...133 F2

Brent AL, 4024 ...127 F1
Brent FL, 22257 ...135 F2
Brentsville VA, 650 ...144 A4
Brentwood CA, 23302 ...36 B3
Brentwood MO, 7693 ...256 B2
Brentwood NY, 53917 ...149 D4
Brentwood PA, 10466 ...250 B3
Brentwood TN, 23445 ...109 E4
Brevard NC, 6789 ...121 E1
Brevard Co. FL, 476230 ...141 E2
Brewer ME, 8987 ...83 D1
Brewerton NY, 3453 ...79 D3
Brewster MA, 2212 ...151 F3
Brewster MN, 502 ...72 A4
Brewster NE, 29 ...34 C2
Brewster NY, 2162 ...148 C2
Brewster OH, 2324 ...91 E3
Brewster Co. TX, 8866 ...62 C3
Brewster Hill NY, 2226 ...148 C1
Brewton AL, 5498 ...135 F1
Briar TX, 5350 ...59 E2
Briarcliff TX, 895 ...61 D1
Briarcliffe Acres SC, 470 ...123 E2
Briarcliff Manor NY, 7696 ...148 B2
Briar Creek PA, 651 ...93 E3
Briarwood KY, 554 ...230 F1

Bridgeton NJ, 22771 ...145 F1
Bridgetown OH, 12569 ...204 A2
Bridgeview IL, 15335 ...203 D5
Bridgeville DE, 1436 ...145 E4
Bridgeville PA, 5341 ...250 A3
Bridgewater MA, 6664 ...151 E2
Bridgewater NJ, 3200 ...147 D1
Bridgewater NY, 579 ...79 E3
Bridgewater SD, 607 ...27 E4
Bridgewater VA, 5203 ...102 C4
Bridgman MI, 2428 ...89 E1
Bridgton ME, 1200 ...82 B2
Brielle NJ, 4893 ...147 E2
Brier WA, 6383 ...262 B2
Brigantine NJ, 12594 ...147 F4
Brigham City UT, 17411 ...31 E3
Bright IN, 5405 ...100 B3
Brighton AL, 3640 ...195 D2
Brighton CO, 20905 ...41 E1
Brighton IL, 2196 ...98 A3
Brighton IA, 687 ...87 E2
Brighton MI, 6701 ...76 B4
Brighton NY, 35584 ...78 C3
Brighton TN, 1719 ...118 B1
Brightwaters NY, 3248 ...149 D4
Brightwood VA, 500 ...102 C3
Brilliant AL, 762 ...119 E3
Brilliant OH, 1600 ...91 F4
Brillion WI, 2937 ...74 C1

Bronson FL, 964 ...138 C4
Bronson MI, 2421 ...90 A1
Bronte TX, 1076 ...58 C4
Bronwood GA, 513 ...128 C3
Bronx Co. NY, 1332650 ...148 B3
Brook IN, 1062 ...89 D3
Brookdale CA, 4724 ...122 A4
Brooke Co. WV, 25447 ...91 F4
Brookfield CT, 2700 ...148 C1
Brookfield IL, 19085 ...203 C5
Brookfield MA, 1200 ...150 B1
Brookfield MO, 4769 ...97 D1
Brookfield OH, 1288 ...276 C1
Brookfield WI, 38649 ...234 B2
Brookfield Ctr. CT, 1800 ...148 C1
Brookhaven MS, 9861 ...126 B4
Brookhaven PA, 7985 ...248 A4
Brookings OR, 5447 ...28 A1
Brookings SD, 18504 ...27 F3
Brookings Co. SD, 28220 ...27 F3
Brookland AR, 1332 ...108 A4
Brooklandville MD, 2200 ...193 C1
Brooklawn NJ, 2354 ...248 C4
Brooklet GA, 1113 ...130 B2
Brookline MA, 57107 ...151 D1
Brookline NH, 650 ...95 D1
Brooklyn CT, 1100 ...150 B3

Brown Co. SD, 35460 ...27 E1
Brown Co. TX, 37674 ...59 D3
Brown Co. WI, 226778 ...74 C1
Brown Deer WI, 12170 ...234 C1
Brownfield TX, 9488 ...58 A2
Browning MT, 1065 ...15 E2
Brownsboro TX, 796 ...59 E4
Brownsburg IN, 14520 ...99 F1
Browns Mills NJ, 11257 ...147 D3
Brownstown IL, 705 ...98 C2
Brownstown IN, 2978 ...99 F3
Browns Valley MN, 690 ...27 F1
Brownsville CA, 1069 ...36 C1
Brownsville KY, 921 ...109 F2
Brownsville MN, 517 ...73 F2
Brownsville OR, 1449 ...20 B3
Brownsville PA, 2804 ...102 B3
Brownsville TN, 10748 ...118 C4
Brownsville TX, 139722 ...63 F4
Brownsville WI, 570 ...74 C2
Brownton MN, 807 ...66 C4
Brownville NY, 1022 ...79 E2
Brownville Jct. ME, 750 ...84 C1
Brownwood TX, 18813 ...59 D4
Broxton GA, 1428 ...129 E4
Broyhill Park VA, 17000 ...270 B4
Bruce MS, 2097 ...118 C3
Bruce SD, 272 ...27 F3

Buckley IL, 593 ...89 D4
Buckley WA, 4145 ...12 C3
Bucklin KS, 725 ...42 C4
Bucklin MO, 524 ...97 D1
Buckner KY, 4000 ...100 A4
Buckner MO, 2725 ...96 C2
Bucks Co. PA, 597635 ...146 C3
Bucksport ME, 2970 ...83 D1
Bucksport SC, 1117 ...123 E2
Bucoda WA, 628 ...12 C4
Bucyrus OH, 13224 ...90 C3
Buda IL, 592 ...88 B2
Buda TX, 2404 ...61 E2
Budd Lake NJ, 8100 ...147 D1
Bude MS, 1037 ...126 A4
Buellton CA, 3828 ...52 A2
Buena WA, 950 ...13 D4
Buena NJ, 3873 ...147 D4
Buena Park CA, 78282 ...228 E3
Buena Ventura Lakes FL, 14100 ...206 C5
Buena Vista CO, 2195 ...41 D2
Buena Vista GA, 1664 ...128 C2
Buena Vista MI, 7845 ...76 B2
Buena Vista VA, 6349 ...112 C1
Buffalo IN, 672 ...89 E3
Buffalo IA, 1321 ...87 F2
Buffalo KY, 475 ...110 A1

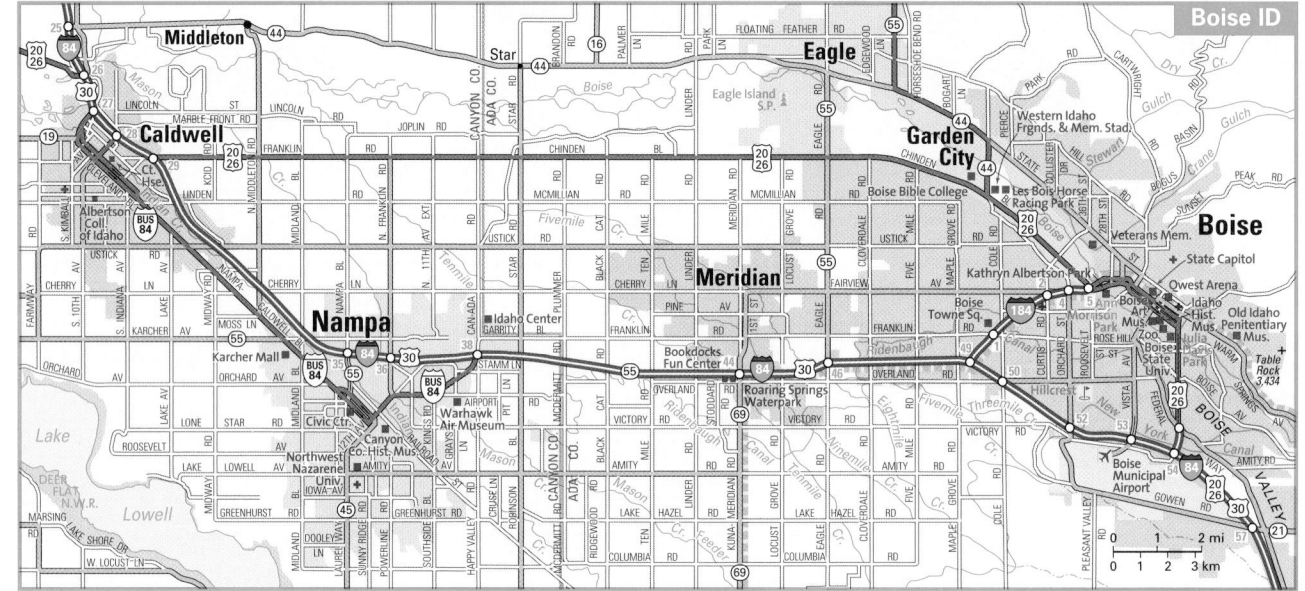

Boise ID

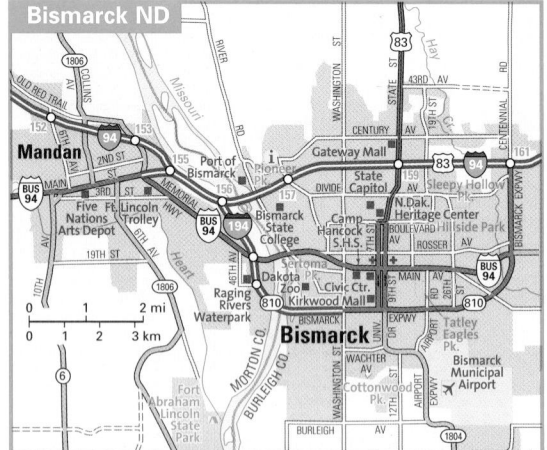

Bismarck ND

Bradley IL, 12784 ...89 D3
Bradley ME, 650 ...83 D1
Bradley WV, 2371 ...101 F4
Bradley Beach NJ, 4793 ...147 F2
Bradley Co. AR, 12600 ...117 E4
Bradley Co. TN, 87965 ...120 C4
Bradley Jct. FL, 850 ...140 C3
Bradshaw OH, 1171 ...90 C2
Brady TX, 5523 ...58 C4
Braham MN, 1276 ...66 C2
Braidwood IL, 5203 ...88 C2
Brainerd MN, 13178 ...64 B4
Braintree MA, 33698 ...151 D2
Bramwell WV, 426 ...111 F1
Branch Co. MI, 45787 ...90 A1
Branchland WV, 825 ...101 F4
Branchville NJ, 845 ...94 A4
Branchville SC, 1083 ...130 C1
Brandenburg KY, 2049 ...99 F4

Breckenridge CO, 2408 ...41 D1
Breckenridge MI, 1339 ...76 A2
Breckenridge MN, 3559 ...27 F1
Breckenridge TX, 5868 ...59 D2
Breckenridge Hills MO, 4817 ...256 B2
Breckinridge Co. KY, 18648 ...99 F4
Brecksville OH, 13382 ...204 F3
Breese IL, 4048 ...98 B3
Breezy Pt. MN, 800 ...64 B4
Breezy Pt. NY, 2700 ...144 A4
Breinigsville PA, 1700 ...146 B1
Bremen GA, 4579 ...120 B4
Bremen IN, 4588 ...89 F2
Bremen KY, 365 ...109 E1
Bremen OH, 1265 ...101 D1
Bremer Co. IA, 23325 ...73 D4
Bremerton WA, 37259 ...12 C3
Bremond TX, 876 ...59 F4
Brenham TX, 13507 ...61 F2

Briceville TN, 650 ...110 C4
Brickerville PA, 1287 ...146 A3
Bridge City LA, 8323 ...239 B2
Bridge City TX, 8651 ...132 C4
Bridgehampton NY, 1381 ...149 F3
Bridgeport AL, 2728 ...120 A2
Bridgeport CA, 200 ...37 E3
Bridgeport CT, 139529 ...149 D2
Bridgeport IL, 2168 ...99 D3
Bridgeport MI, 7849 ...76 B3
Bridgeport NE, 1594 ...34 A3
Bridgeport NY, 1665 ...79 E3
Bridgeport PA, 4371 ...248 A1
Bridgeport TX, 4309 ...59 E2
Bridgeport WV, 2059 ...102 A3
Bridgeport WV, 7306 ...102 A2
Bridger MT, 745 ...24 B2
Bridgeton MO, 15550 ...256 B1

Brimfield IL, 933 ...88 B3
Brinckerhoff NY, 2734 ...148 B1
Brinkley AR, 3940 ...117 F2
Brinnon WA, 803 ...12 C3
Brisbane CA, 3597 ...259 B3
Bristol CT, 60062 ...149 D1
Bristol FL, 845 ...137 D2
Bristol IN, 1382 ...89 F1
Bristol NH, 1670 ...81 F3
Bristol PA, 9923 ...147 D2
Bristol RI, 22469 ...151 D3
Bristol SD, 377 ...27 E2
Bristol TN, 24821 ...111 E3
Bristol VT, 1800 ...81 D2
Bristol VA, 17367 ...111 E3
Bristol WI, 1800 ...74 C4
Bristol Co. MA, 534678 ...151 D2
Bristol Co. RI, 50648 ...151 D3
Bristow OK, 4325 ...51 F2
Britt IA, 2052 ...72 C4
Britton MI, 699 ...90 B1
Britton SD, 1328 ...27 E1
Broadalbin NY, 1411 ...80 C4
Broad Brook CT, 3469 ...150 A3
Broadmoor CA, 4026 ...259 B3
Broadus MT, 451 ...25 E2
Broadview IL, 8264 ...203 C4
Broadview Hts. OH, 15967 ...204 F4
Broadwater Co. MT, 4385 ...15 F4
Broadway NC, 1015 ...123 D1
Broadway VA, 2192 ...102 C3
Brock Hall MD, 1200 ...144 C3
Brockport NY, 8103 ...78 C3
Brockton MA, 94304 ...151 D2
Brockton MT, 245 ...17 E2
Brockway PA, 2139 ...92 B3
Brocton NY, 1547 ...78 A4

Brooklyn IL, 676 ...256 C2
Brooklyn IN, 1545 ...99 F1
Brooklyn IA, 1367 ...87 E1
Brooklyn MI, 1197 ...90 B1
Brooklyn OH, 11586 ...204 E2
Brooklyn WI, 916 ...74 B3
Brooklyn Ctr. MN, 29172 ...235 B1
Brooklyn Park MD, 10938 ...193 C4
Brooklyn Hts. OH, 1558 ...204 F2
Brooklyn Park MN, 67388 ...235 A1
Brookneal VA, 1259 ...112 C2
Brook Park OH, 21218 ...204 E3
Brookport IL, 1054 ...108 C2
Brooks GA, 553 ...128 C1
Brooks ME, 550 ...82 C2
Brooks Co. GA, 16450 ...137 F1
Brooks Co. TX, 7976 ...63 E3
Brookshire TX, 3450 ...61 F2
Brookside DE, 14806 ...146 B4
Brookside OH, 644 ...91 F4
Brookston IN, 1717 ...89 E3
Brooksville FL, 7264 ...140 B2
Brooksville KY, 589 ...100 C3
Brooksville MS, 1182 ...127 D1
Brookville IN, 2596 ...100 A2
Brookville OH, 5289 ...100 B1
Brookville PA, 4230 ...92 B3
Brookwood AL, 1483 ...127 F1
Broomall PA, 11046 ...248 A3
Broome Co. NY, 200536 ...93 F1
Broomfield CO, 38272 ...41 E1
Broomfield Co. CO, 38272 ...41 E1
Brooten MN, 649 ...66 B3
Broussard LA, 5874 ...133 F3
Broward Co. FL, 1623010 ...143 E3
Browerville MN, 735 ...66 B2
Brown City MI, 1334 ...76 C3
Brown Co. IL, 6950 ...87 F4
Brown Co. IN, 14957 ...99 F2
Brown Co. KS, 10724 ...96 A1
Brown Co. MN, 26911 ...72 B1
Brown Co. NE, 3525 ...34 C1
Brown Co. OH, 44285 ...100 C2

Bruce WI, 787 ...67 F3
Bruceton TN, 1554 ...109 D4
Bruceville-Eddy TX, 1490 ...59 E4
Brule Co. SD, 5364 ...27 D4
Brundidge AL, 2341 ...128 B4
Brunson SC, 589 ...130 B1
Brunswick GA, 15600 ...139 D1
Brunswick ME, 14816 ...82 B3
Brunswick MD, 4894 ...144 A2
Brunswick MO, 925 ...97 D2
Brunswick OH, 33388 ...91 E2
Brunswick Co. NC, 73143 ...123 E3
Brunswick Co. VA, 18419 ...113 D3
Brush CO, 5117 ...33 F4
Brush Prairie WA, 2384 ...20 C1
Brushy OK, 787 ...116 B1
Brusly LA, 2020 ...134 A2
Bryan OH, 8333 ...90 B2
Bryan TX, 65660 ...61 F1
Bryan Co. GA, 23417 ...130 B3
Bryan Co. OK, 36534 ...59 F1
Bryans Road MD, 4912 ...144 B4
Bryant AR, 9764 ...117 E2
Bryant SD, 396 ...27 E3
Bryant Pond ME, 2600 ...82 B2
Bryn Athyn PA, 1351 ...248 D1
Bryn Mawr PA, 4382 ...146 C3
Bryson TX, 528 ...59 D2
Bryson City NC, 1411 ...121 D1

Buffalo MN, 10097 ...66 C3
Buffalo MO, 2781 ...107 D1
Buffalo NY, 292648 ...78 B3
Buffalo ND, 209 ...19 E4
Buffalo OK, 1200 ...50 C1
Buffalo SC, 1426 ...121 F2
Buffalo SD, 380 ...25 F1
Buffalo TX, 1804 ...59 F4
Buffalo WY, 3900 ...25 D3
Buffalo WV, 1040 ...101 E3
Buffalo WI, 1040 ...73 E1
Buffalo Ctr. IA, 963 ...72 C3
Buffalo Co. NE, 42259 ...35 D4
Buffalo Co. SD, 2032 ...27 D3
Buffalo Co. WI, 13804 ...73 E1
Buffalo Grove IL, 42909 ...203 C1
Buffalo Lake MN, 768 ...66 B4
Buford GA, 10668 ...120 C3
Buhl ID, 3985 ...30 C1
Buhl MN, 983 ...64 C3
Buhler KS, 1358 ...43 E3
Buies Creek NC, 2215 ...123 D1
Bullard TX, 1150 ...124 A3
Bullhead SD, 308 ...26 C1
Bullhead City AZ, 39540 ...46 A4
Bullitt Co. KY, 61236 ...99 F4
Bulloch Co. GA, 55883 ...130 B2
Bullock Co. AL, 11714 ...128 B3
Bulls Gap TN, 714 ...111 D3
Bull Shoals AR, 2000 ...107 E3
Bull Valley IL, 726 ...74 C4
Bulverde TX, 3761 ...61 D2
Buna TX, 2269 ...132 C2
Buncombe Co. NC, 206330 ...111 E4
Bunker Hill IL, 1801 ...98 B2
Bunker Hill IN, 987 ...89 F3
Bunker Hill OR, 1462 ...20 A4
Bunker Hill Village TX, 3654 ...220 B2
Bunkerville NV, 1014 ...46 B1
Bunkie LA, 4662 ...133 E2
Bunnell FL, 2122 ...139 E4
Buras LA, 3358 ...134 C4
Burbank CA, 100316 ...228 D1
Burbank IL, 27902 ...203 D5
Burbank WA, 3303 ...13 E4
Burden KS, 564 ...43 F4

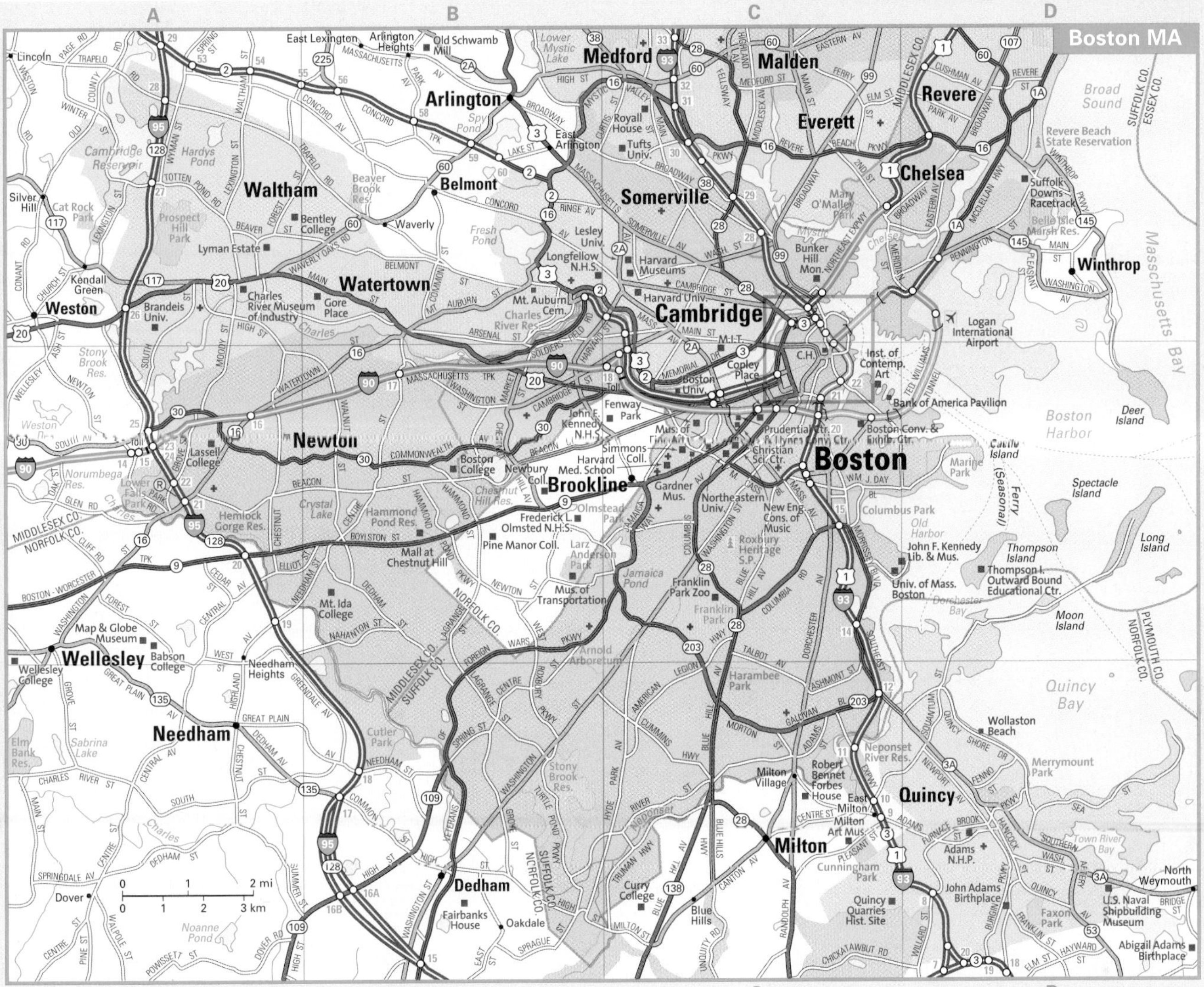

Entries in **bold black** indicate counties or parishes. Entries in **bold color** indicate cities with detailed inset maps.

BUREAU COUNTY–BUTTE COUNTY 197

Boston MA

Downtown Boston MA

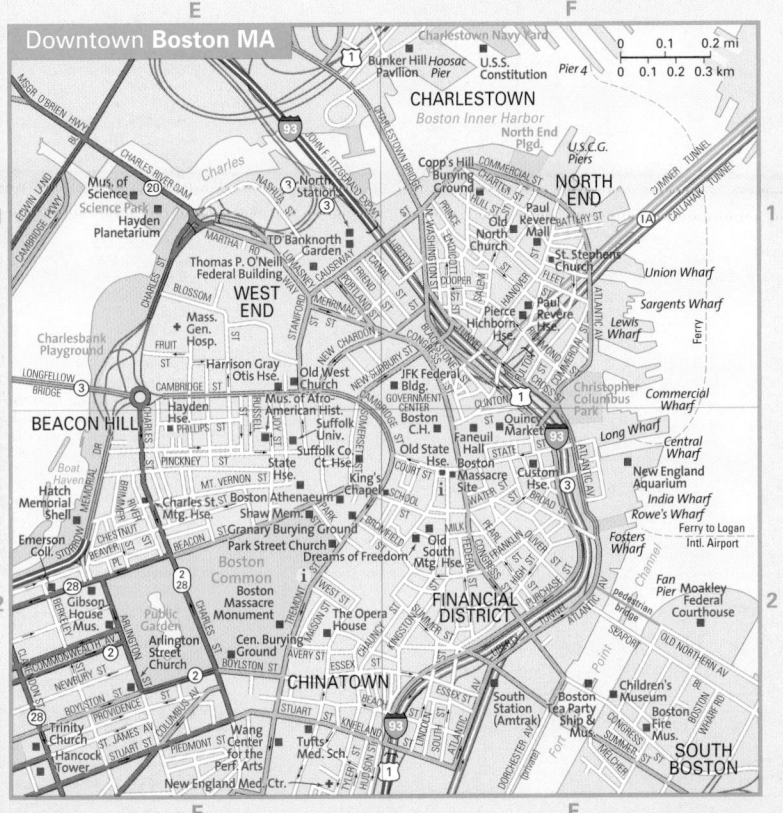

POINTS OF INTEREST

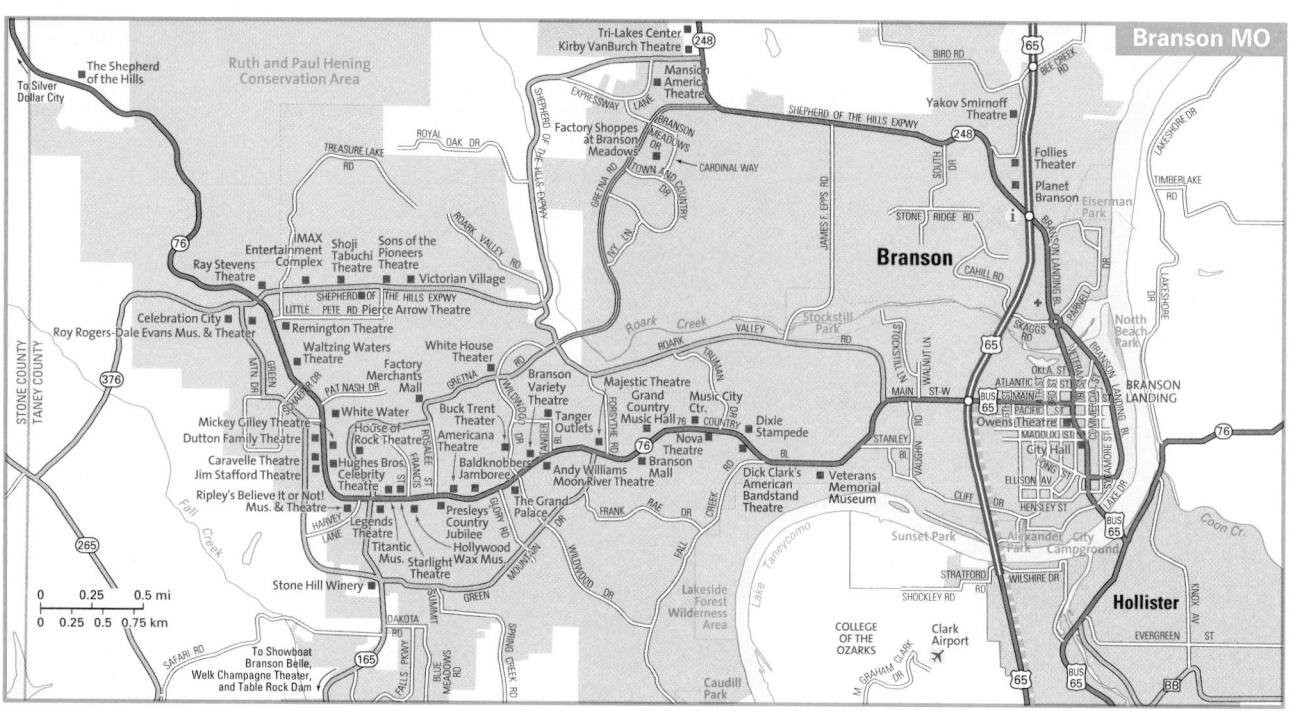

Branson MO

Buffalo / Niagara Falls NY

Place	Grid
Amherst	C2
Beach Ridge	C1
Bergholtz	B1
Bowmansville	B2
Buffalo	B2
Cheektowaga	C3
Colonial Vil.	B1
Crystal Beach	A3
Depew	C3
E. Amherst	C2
Ft. Erie	A3
Getzville	C2
Glenwood	A1
Grandyle Vil.	B1
Kenmore	B2
Lackawanna	B3
Lewiston	A1
Lockport	C1
Niagara Falls, NY	A1
Niagara Falls, ON	A2
Niagara-on-the-Lake	A1
N. Tonawanda	B1
Pekin	C1
Pendleton	C1
Pendleton Ctr.	C1
Port Colborne	A3
Queenston	A1
Ridgeway	A3
St. Davids	A1
St. Johnsburg	B1
Sanborn	B1
Sandy Beach	B1
Shawnee	B1
Sherkston	A3
Sloan	C3
Snyder, NY	C2
Snyder, ON	A2
S. Lockport	C1
Spring Brook	C3
Stevensville	A2
Swormville	C2
Tonawanda	B2
Wendelville	C1
W. Seneca	C3
Williamsville	C2

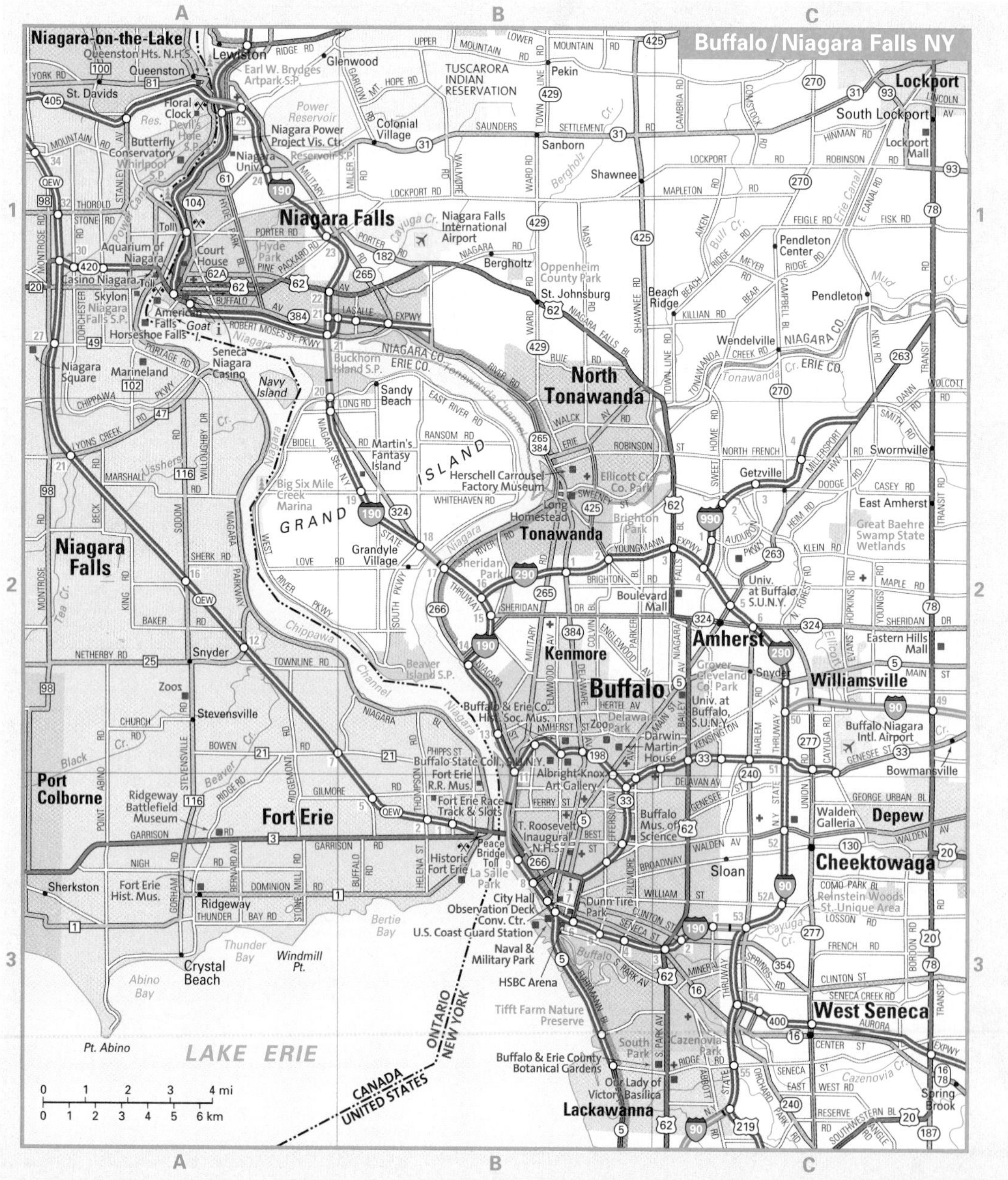

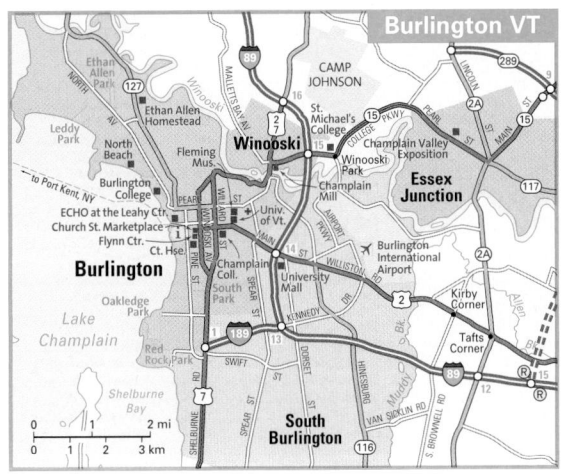

Burlington VT

Carson City NV

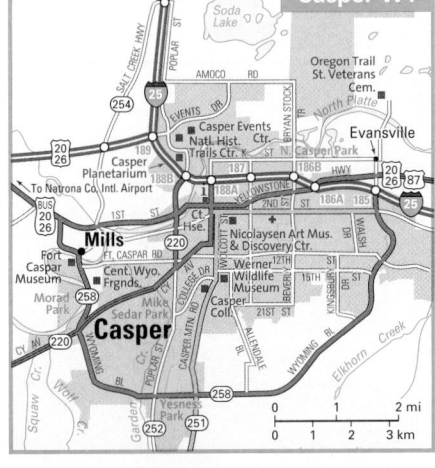

Casper WY

Canton OH

Cairo	B1
Canton	B1
Crystal Sprs.	A1
Fairhope	B1

Green	A1
Hills and Dales	A1
Louisville	B1
Massillon	A2

McDonaldsville	A1
Meyers Lake	B2
Middlebranch	B1
N. Canton	B1

Perry Hts.	A2
Reedurban	A2
Richville	A2
Waco	B2

Cattaraugus Co. NY, 83955 ....78 A4
Cavalier ND, 1537 ....19 E1
Cavalier Co. ND, 4831 ....19 D1
Cave City AR, 1946 ....107 F4
Cave City KY, 1880 ....110 A2
Cave Creek AZ, 3728 ....54 C1
Cave Jct. OR, 1363 ....28 B2
Cave Spr. GA, 975 ....120 B3
Cave Spr. VA, 24941 ....112 B2
Cave Sprs. AR, 1103 ....106 C3
Cavetown MD, 1486 ....144 A1
Cawker City KS, 521 ....43 D1
Cawood KY, 800 ....111 D2
Cayce SC, 12150 ....122 A3
Cayucos CA, 2943 ....44 B4
Cayuga IN, 1109 ....99 E1
Cayuga NY, 509 ....79 D3
Cayuga Co. NY, 81963 ....79 D4
Cayuga Hts. NY, 3273 ....79 D4
Cazenovia NY, 2614 ....79 E3
Cecil PA, 2585 ....92 A4
Cecil Co. MD, 85951 ....145 E1
Cecilia KY, 600 ....110 A1
Cecilia LA, 1505 ....133 F2
Cecilton MD, 474 ....145 E1
Cedar Bluff AL, 1467 ....120 A3
Cedar Bluff VA, 1085 ....111 F2
Cedar Bluffs NE, 615 ....35 F3
Cedar Brook NJ, 1100 ....147 D4
Cedarburg WI, 10908 ....74 C3
Cedar City UT, 20527 ....39 D4
Cedar Co. IA, 18187 ....87 F1
Cedar Co. MO, 13733 ....106 C1
Cedar Co. NE, 9615 ....35 E1
Cedar Creek NE, 396 ....35 F3
Cedar Crest NM, 1060 ....48 C3
Cedaredge CO, 1854 ....40 B2
Cedar Falls IA, 36145 ....73 D4
Cedar Fort UT, 341 ....31 E4
Cedar Grove FL, 5367 ....136 C2
Cedar Grove MD, 950 ....144 B2
Cedar Grove NJ, 12300 ....148 A3
Cedar Grove NM, 599 ....48 C3
Cedar Grove WV, 862 ....101 F4
Cedar Grove WI, 1887 ....75 D2
Cedar Hill MO, 1703 ....98 A4
Cedar Hill TX, 32093 ....207 C3
Cedar Hills OR, 8949 ....251 C2
Cedarhurst NY, 6164 ....241 G5
Cedar Key FL, 790 ....138 B4
Cedar Lake IN, 9279 ....89 D2
Cedar Park TX, 26049 ....61 E1
Cedar Pt. NC, 929 ....115 D4
Cedar Rapids IA, 120758 ....87 E1
Cedar Rapids NE, 407 ....35 E3
Cedar Sprs. MI, 3112 ....75 F3
Cedartown GA, 9470 ....120 B3
Cedar Vale KS, 723 ....51 F1
Cedarville AR, 1133 ....116 C1
Cedarville IL, 719 ....74 B4
Cedarville NJ, 793 ....145 F2
Cedarville OH, 3828 ....100 C1
Celebration FL, 2736 ....141 D1
Celeste TX, 817 ....59 F2
Celina OH, 10303 ....90 B4
Celina TN, 1379 ....110 A3
Celina TX, 1861 ....59 F2
Celoron NY, 1295 ....92 B1
Cement OK, 530 ....51 E3
Cement City MI, 452 ....90 B1
Centennial CO, 102821 ....209 C4
Center CO, 2392 ....41 D4
Center MO, 644 ....97 F1
Center NE, 90 ....35 E1
Center ND, 678 ....18 B3
Center TX, 5678 ....124 C3
Center Barnstead NH, 500 ....81 F4
Centerbrook CT, 950 ....149 E2
Center Brunswick NY, 900 ....94 B1
Centerburg OH, 1432 ....91 D4
Center City MN, 582 ....67 D3
Centereach NY, 27285 ....149 D3
Centerfield UT, 1048 ....39 E2
Center Harbor NH, 600 ....81 F3
Center Hill FL, 910 ....140 C1
Center Line MI, 8531 ....210 C2
Center Moriches NY, 6655 ....149 D4
Center Ossipee NH, 650 ....81 F3
Center Pt. AL, 22784 ....119 F4
Center Pt. IA, 2007 ....87 E1
Center Pt. TX, 750 ....61 D2
Centerport NY, 5446 ....148 C3
Centerton AR, 2146 ....106 C3
Centerton NJ, 2000 ....147 D3
Centertown KY, 416 ....109 E1
Center Valley PA, 1600 ....146 C1
Centerville GA, 4278 ....129 D2
Centerville IN, 2427 ....100 B1
Centerville IA, 5924 ....87 D3
Centerville LA, 800 ....133 F3
Centerville MA, 9200 ....151 F3
Centerville MO, 171 ....108 A1
Centerville OH, 23024 ....100 B1
Centerville PA, 3390 ....92 A4
Centerville SC, 5181 ....121 E3
Centerville SD, 910 ....35 F1
Centerville TN, 3793 ....109 E4
Centerville TX, 903 ....124 A4
Centerville UT, 14585 ....31 E4
Central AZ, 425 ....55 E2
Central SC, 3522 ....121 E2
Central TN, 2717 ....111 E3
Central Bridge NY, 900 ....79 F4
Central City AR, 531 ....116 C1
Central City CO, 515 ....41 D1
Central City IL, 1371 ....98 C3
Central City IA, 1157 ....87 F1
Central City KY, 5893 ....109 E1
Central City NE, 2998 ....35 E3
Central City PA, 1258 ....92 B4
Central Falls RI, 18928 ....150 C3
Central High OK, 954 ....51 E4
Centralia IL, 14136 ....98 C3
Centralia KS, 534 ....43 F1
Centralia MO, 3774 ....97 E2
Centralia WA, 14742 ....12 B4
Central Islip NY, 31950 ....149 D4
Central Lake MI, 990 ....69 F3
Central Park WA, 2558 ....12 B4
Central Pt. OR, 12493 ....28 B2
Central Square NY, 1646 ....79 D3
Central Valley NY, 1857 ....148 B2
Central Vil. CT, 1400 ....150 B3
Central Vil. MA, 600 ....151 D4
Centre AL, 3216 ....120 A3
Centre Co. PA, 135758 ....92 C3
Centre Hall PA, 1079 ....92 C3
Centreville AL, 2466 ....127 F1
Centreville IL, 5951 ....98 A3
Centreville MD, 1970 ....145 D3
Centreville MI, 1579 ....89 F1
Centreville MS, 1680 ....134 A1
Centreville VA, 48661 ....144 A3
Centuria WI, 865 ....67 E3
Century FL, 1714 ....135 F1
Ceres CA, 34609 ....36 C4
Ceresco NE, 920 ....35 F3
Cerritos CA, 51488 ....228 E4
Cerro Gordo IL, 1436 ....98 C1
Cerro Gordo Co. IA, 46447 ....73 D3
Chackbay LA, 4018 ....134 A3
Chadbourn NC, 2129 ....123 D3
Chadron NE, 5634 ....34 A1
Chaffee MO, 3044 ....108 B2
Chaffee Co. CO, 16242 ....41 D2
Chaffinville MA, 3100 ....150 B1
Chagrin Falls OH, 4024 ....91 E2
Chalco NE, 10736 ....35 F3
Chalfant PA, 870 ....250 D2
Chalfont PA, 3900 ....146 C2
Chalkville AL, 3829 ....195 F1
Challenge CA, 1069 ....36 C1
Challis ID, 909 ....23 D3
Chalmers IN, 513 ....89 E3
Chalmette LA, 32069 ....134 B3
Chama NM, 1199 ....48 C1
Chamberino NM, 425 ....56 C3
Chamberlain SD, 2338 ....27 D4
Chamberlayne Farms VA, 4700 ....254 B1
Chambersburg PA, 17862 ....103 D1
Chambers Co. AL, 36583 ....128 B1
Chambers Co. TX, 26031 ....132 B3
Chamblee GA, 9552 ....120 C4
Chamisal NM, 301 ....49 D2
Champaign IL, 67518 ....88 C4
Champaign Co. IL, 179669 ....89 D4
Champaign Co. OH, 38890 ....90 C4
Champion OH, 4727 ....91 F2
Champlain NY, 1173 ....81 D1
Chancellor SD, 328 ....27 F4
Chandler AZ, 176581 ....54 C2
Chandler IN, 3094 ....99 E4
Chandler OK, 2842 ....51 F2
Chandler TX, 2099 ....124 A2
Chandler Hts. AZ, 950 ....54 C2
Chandlerville IL, 704 ....88 A4
Chanhassen MN, 20321 ....66 C4
Channahon IL, 7344 ....88 C2
Channel Lake IL, 1785 ....74 C4
Channelview TX, 29685 ....132 B3
Channing TX, 356 ....50 A2
Chantilly VA, 41041 ....144 A3
Chanute KS, 9411 ....106 A1
Chaparral NM, 6117 ....56 C3
Chapel Hill NC, 48715 ....112 C4
Chapel Hill TN, 943 ....119 F1
Chapin IL, 592 ....98 A1
Chapin SC, 628 ....122 A3
Chaplin KY, 500 ....100 A4
Chapman KS, 1241 ....43 F2
Chapmanville WV, 1211 ....101 E4
Chappaqua NY, 9468 ....148 B2
Chappell NE, 983 ....34 A3
Chardon OH, 5156 ....91 E2
Charenton LA, 1944 ....133 F3
Chariton IA, 4321 ....87 D3
Chariton Co. MO, 8438 ....97 D1
Charlack MO, 1431 ....256 B2
Charleroi PA, 4120 ....92 A4
Charles City IA, 7812 ....73 D3
Charles City VA, 175 ....113 E1
Charles City Co. VA, 6926 ....113 E1
Charles Co. MD, 120546 ....144 B4
Charles Mix Co. SD, 9350 ....27 D4
Charleston AR, 2965 ....116 C1
Charleston IL, 21039 ....99 D2
Charleston ME, 300 ....82 C1
Charleston MS, 2198 ....118 B3
Charleston MO, 5947 ....108 C2
Charleston SC, 96650 ....131 D2
Charleston TN, 630 ....120 C1
Charleston UT, 378 ....31 F4
Charleston WV, 53421 ....101 E4
Charleston Co. SC, 309969 ....131 D2
Charlestown IN, 5993 ....100 A3
Charlestown MD, 1019 ....145 D1
Charlestown NH, 1145 ....81 E4
Charlestown RI, 950 ....150 C4
Charles Town WV, 2907 ....103 D2
Charlevoix MI, 2994 ....69 F3
Charlevoix Co. MI, 26090 ....70 B3
Charlo MT, 439 ....15 D3
Charlotte MI, 8389 ....76 A4
Charlotte NC, 540828 ....122 A1
Charlotte TN, 1153 ....109 E4
Charlotte TX, 1637 ....61 D3
Charlotte Beach FL, 1600 ....140 C4
Charlotte Co. FL, 141627 ....140 C4
Charlotte Co. VA, 12472 ....113 D2
Charlotte C.H. VA, 404 ....113 D2
Charlotte Hall MD, 1214 ....144 C4
Charlotte Harbor FL, 3647 ....140 C4
Charlottesville VA, 45049 ....102 C4
Charlton MA, 1100 ....150 B2
Charlton NY, 700 ....94 B1
Charlton City MA, 1400 ....150 B2
Charlton Co. GA, 10282 ....138 C1
Charlton Depot MA, 1200 ....150 B2
Charter Oak CA, 9027 ....229 F2
Charter Oak IA, 530 ....86 A1
Chartley MA, 1600 ....151 D2
Chase KS, 490 ....43 D3
Chase City VA, 2457 ....113 D2
Chase Co. KS, 3030 ....43 F3
Chase Co. NE, 4068 ....34 B4
Chaska MN, 17449 ....66 C4
Chassahowitzka FL, 700 ....140 B1
Chassell MI, 800 ....65 F4
Chateaugay NY, 798 ....80 C1
Chatfield MN, 2394 ....73 E2
Chatham IL, 8583 ....98 B1
Chatham LA, 623 ....125 E2
Chatham MA, 1667 ....151 F3
Chatham NJ, 8460 ....148 A4
Chatham NY, 1758 ....94 B2
Chatham VA, 1338 ....112 C2
Chatham Co. GA, 232048 ....130 B3
Chatham Co. NC, 49329 ....112 C4
Chatom AL, 1193 ....127 D4
Chatsworth GA, 3531 ....120 C2
Chatsworth IL, 1265 ....88 C3
Chattahoochee FL, 3287 ....137 D1
Chattahoochee Co. GA, 14882 ....128 C2
Chattanooga OK, 432 ....51 D4
Chattanooga TN, 155554 ....120 B2
Chattaroy WV, 1136 ....111 E1
Chattooga Co. GA, 25470 ....120 B3
Chatwood PA, 3600 ....146 B3
Chaumont NY, 592 ....79 D1
Chauncey OH, 1067 ....101 E2
Chautauqua Co. KS, 4359 ....43 F4
Chautauqua Co. NY, 139750 ....78 A4
Chauvin LA, 3229 ....134 B4
Chaves Co. NM, 61382 ....57 E2
Chazy NY, 600 ....81 D1
Cheatham Co. TN, 35912 ....109 E3
Cheat Neck WV, 950 ....102 B1
Chebanse IL, 1148 ....89 D3
Cheboygan MI, 5295 ....70 C2
Cheboygan Co. MI, 26448 ....70 C3
Checotah OK, 3481 ....116 A1
Cheektowaga NY, 79988 ....78 B3
Chefornak AK, 394 ....154 B3
Chehalis WA, 7057 ....12 B4
Chelan WA, 3522 ....13 E3
Chelan Co. WA, 66616 ....13 D2
Chelmsford MA, 32400 ....95 E1
Chelsea AL, 2949 ....127 F1
Chelsea MA, 35080 ....151 D1
Chelsea MI, 4398 ....76 B4
Chelsea NY, 2300 ....148 B1
Chelsea OK, 2136 ....106 A3
Chelsea VT, 275 ....81 E3
Cheltenham MD, 650 ....144 C4
Cheltenham PA, 5500 ....248 C2
Chelyan WV, 1400 ....101 F4
Chemung Co. NY, 91070 ....93 E1
Chenango Bridge NY, 4100 ....93 E1
Chenango Co. NY, 51401 ....79 E4
Chenequa WI, 583 ....74 C3
Cheney KS, 1783 ....43 E4
Cheney WA, 8832 ....13 F3
Cheneyville LA, 901 ....133 E1
Chenoa IL, 1845 ....88 C3
Chenoweth OR, 3412 ....21 D1
Chepachet RI, 900 ....150 C3
Cheraw SC, 5524 ....122 C2
Cheriton VA, 499 ....114 B3
Cherokee AL, 1237 ....119 D2
Cherokee IA, 5369 ....72 A4
Cherokee KS, 722 ....106 B1
Cherokee OK, 1630 ....51 D1
Cherokee Co. AL, 23988 ....120 A3
Cherokee Co. GA, 141903 ....120 C3
Cherokee Co. IA, 13035 ....72 A3
Cherokee Co. KS, 22605 ....106 B2
Cherokee Co. NC, 24298 ....121 D1
Cherokee Co. OK, 42521 ....106 B4
Cherokee Co. SC, 52537 ....121 F2
Cherokee Co. TX, 46659 ....124 A3
Cherokee Forest SC, 8000 ....217 A1
Cherokee Vil. AR, 4648 ....107 F3
Cherry Co. NE, 6148 ....34 B1
Cherry Creek NY, 551 ....78 A4
Cherryfield ME, 375 ....83 E2
Cherry Grove OH, 4555 ....204 C3
Cherry Hill NJ, 69965 ....146 C3
Cherry Hills Vil. CO, 5958 ....209 C4
Cherryvale KS, 2386 ....106 A2
Cherryvale SC, 2461 ....122 B4
Cherry Valley AR, 704 ....118 A1
Cherry Valley NY, 592 ....79 F4
Cherryville NC, 5361 ....122 A1
Chesaning MI, 2548 ....76 B3
Chesapeake OH, 842 ....101 D3
Chesapeake VA, 199184 ....113 F3
Chesapeake WV, 1643 ....101 F4
Chesapeake Beach MD, 3180 ....144 C4
Chesapeake City MD, 787 ....145 E1
Chesapeake Ranch Estates MD, 11503 ....103 F4
Cheshire CT, 5789 ....149 D1
Cheshire MA, 1200 ....94 C1
Cheshire Co. NH, 73825 ....81 E4
Chesilhurst NJ, 1520 ....147 D4
Chesnee SC, 1003 ....121 F1
Chester CA, 2316 ....29 D4
Chester CT, 1546 ....149 E2
Chester IL, 5185 ....98 B4
Chester MD, 3723 ....145 D3
Chester MA, 800 ....94 C2
Chester MT, 871 ....15 F2
Chester NH, 550 ....81 F4
Chester NJ, 1635 ....94 A4
Chester NY, 3445 ....148 A2
Chester PA, 36854 ....146 C3
Chester SC, 6476 ....122 A2
Chester VT, 999 ....81 E4
Chester VA, 17890 ....113 E1
Chester WV, 2592 ....91 F3
Chester Co. PA, 433501 ....146 B3
Chester Co. SC, 34068 ....122 A2
Chester Co. TN, 15540 ....119 D1
Chester Depot VT, 850 ....81 E4
Chesterfield IN, 2969 ....89 F4
Chesterfield MO, 46802 ....98 A3
Chesterfield SC, 1318 ....122 B2
Chesterfield VA, 3558 ....113 E1
Chesterfield Co. SC, 42768 ....122 B2
Chesterfield Co. VA, 259903 ....113 E1
Chester Hts. PA, 2481 ....146 B3
Chester Hill PA, 918 ....92 C3
Chesterland OH, 2646 ....91 E2
Chesterton IN, 10488 ....89 E2
Chestertown MD, 4746 ....145 D2
Chestnut Mtn. GA, 650 ....121 D3
Chestnut Ridge NY, 7829 ....148 B3
Cheswick PA, 1899 ....250 D1
Cheswold DE, 313 ....145 E2
Chetek WI, 2180 ....67 E3
Chetopa KS, 1281 ....106 B2
Chevak AK, 765 ....154 B3
Cheverly MD, 6433 ....144 B3
Cheviot OH, 9015 ....100 B2
Chevy Chase MD, 2726 ....270 C2
Chevy Chase View MD, 863 ....270 C1
Chewelah WA, 2186 ....13 F2
Cheyenne OK, 778 ....50 C3
Cheyenne WY, 53011 ....33 E3
Cheyenne Co. CO, 2231 ....42 A2
Cheyenne Co. KS, 3165 ....42 B1
Cheyenne Co. NE, 9830 ....34 A3
Cheyenne Wells CO, 1010 ....42 A2
Cheyney PA, 1600 ....146 B3
Chicago IL, 2896016 ....89 D1
Chicago Hts. IL, 32776 ....89 D2
Chicago Ridge IL, 14127 ....203 D5
Chichester NH, 500 ....81 F4
Chickamauga GA, 2245 ....120 B2
Chickasaw AL, 6364 ....135 E1
Chickasaw Co. IA, 13095 ....73 E3
Chickasaw Co. MS, 19440 ....118 C4
Chickasha OK, 15850 ....51 E3
Chico CA, 59954 ....36 B1
Chico TX, 947 ....59 E2
Chicopee MA, 54653 ....150 A2
Chicora PA, 1021 ....92 A3
Chicot Co. AR, 14117 ....125 F1
Chiefland FL, 1993 ....138 B4
Chilchinbito AZ, 462 ....47 F1
Chilcoot CA, 387 ....37 D1
Childersburg AL, 4927 ....128 A1
Childress TX, 6778 ....50 C4
Childress Co. TX, 7688 ....50 C4
Chilhowie VA, 1827 ....111 F2
Chillicothe IL, 5996 ....88 B3
Chillicothe MO, 8968 ....96 C1
Chillicothe OH, 21796 ....101 D2
Chillicothe TX, 798 ....50 C4
Chillum MD, 34252 ....270 D2
Chiloquin OR, 716 ....28 C1
Chilton WI, 3708 ....74 C1
Chilton Co. AL, 39593 ....127 F2
Chimayo NM, 2924 ....49 D2
China TX, 1112 ....132 C3
China Grove NC, 3616 ....122 B1
China Grove TX, 1247 ....61 D3
Chinchilla PA, 2300 ....261 E1
Chincoteague VA, 4317 ....114 C2
Chinle AZ, 5366 ....47 F2
Chino CA, 67168 ....229 G3
Chino Hills CA, 66787 ....229 G3
Chinook MT, 1386 ....16 B2
Chinook WA, 457 ....20 B1
Chino Valley AZ, 7835 ....47 D4
Chipita Park CO, 1709 ....205 C1
Chipley FL, 3592 ....136 C1
Chippewa Co. MI, 38543 ....70 B1
Chippewa Co. MN, 13088 ....66 A3
Chippewa Co. WI, 55195 ....67 F3
Chippewa Falls WI, 12925 ....67 F4

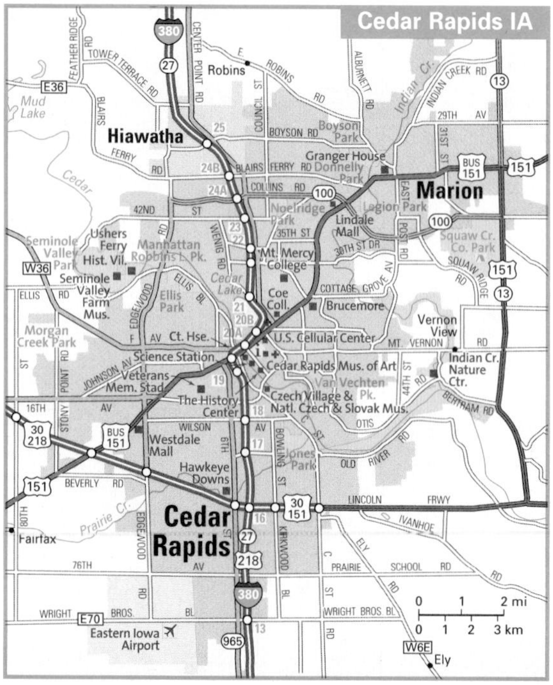
Cedar Rapids IA
Hiawatha
Marion
Cedar Rapids
Robins
Eastern Iowa Airport
Fairfax
Ely
Indian Cr. Nature Ctr.
Cedar Rapids Mus. of Art
Brucemore
Lindale Mall
Westdale Mall
Czech Village & Natl. Czech & Slovak Mus.
U.S. Cellular Center
Science Station
Ushers Ferry Hist. Vil.
0 1 2 mi
0 1 2 3 km

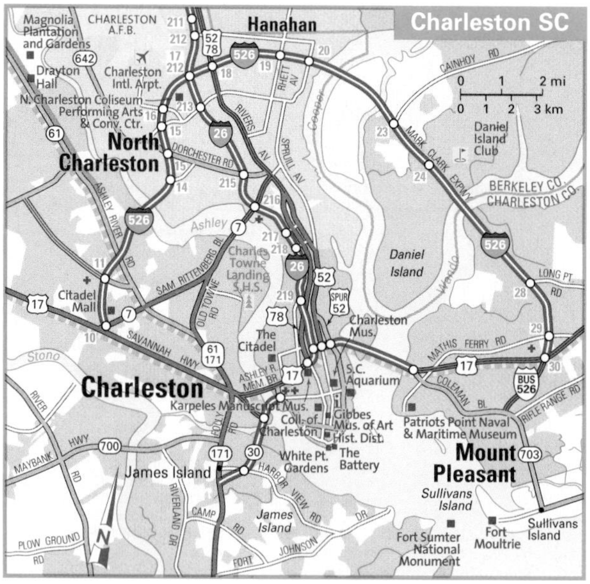
Charleston SC
Hanahan
North Charleston
Charleston
Mount Pleasant
James Island
Daniel Island
Sullivans Island
Magnolia Plantation and Gardens
Drayton Hall
Charleston Intl. Arpt.
N. Charleston Coliseum Performing Arts & Conv. Ctr.
Charles Towne Landing S.H.S.
Citadel Mall
The Citadel
S.C. Aquarium
Charleston Mus.
Karpeles Manuscript Mus.
Gibbes Mus. of Art
Patriots Point Naval & Maritime Museum
Fort Sumter National Monument
Fort Moultrie
White Pt. Gardens
The Battery
Daniel Island Club
BERKELEY CO.
CHARLESTON CO.
0 1 2 mi
0 1 2 3 km

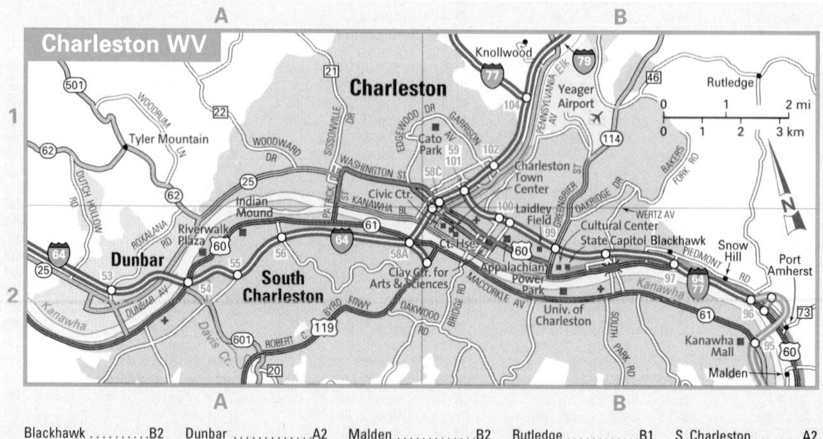
Charleston WV
Charleston
South Charleston
Dunbar
Knollwood
Rutledge
Yeager Airport
Tyler Mountain
Charleston Town Center
Cultural Center
State Capitol
Blackhawk
Snow Hill
Port Amherst
Kanawha Mall
Malden
Univ. of Charleston
Clay Ctr. for Arts & Sciences
Appalachian Power Park
Civic Ctr.
Laidley Field
Riverwalk Plaza
Indian Mound
Cato Park
0 1 2 mi
0 1 2 3 km

Blackhawk B2
Charleston A1
Dunbar A2
Knollwood B1
Malden B2
Port Amherst B2
Rutledge B1
Snow Hill B2
S. Charleston A2
Tyler Mtn. A1

Entries in **bold black** indicate counties or parishes. Entries in **bold color** indicate cities with detailed inset maps.

Charlotte NC

Charlottesville VA

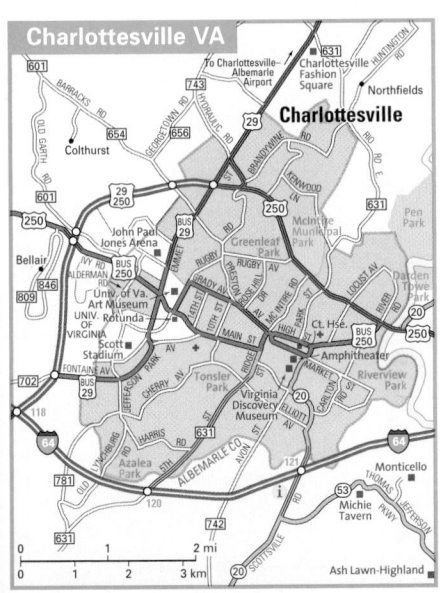

Chattanooga TN

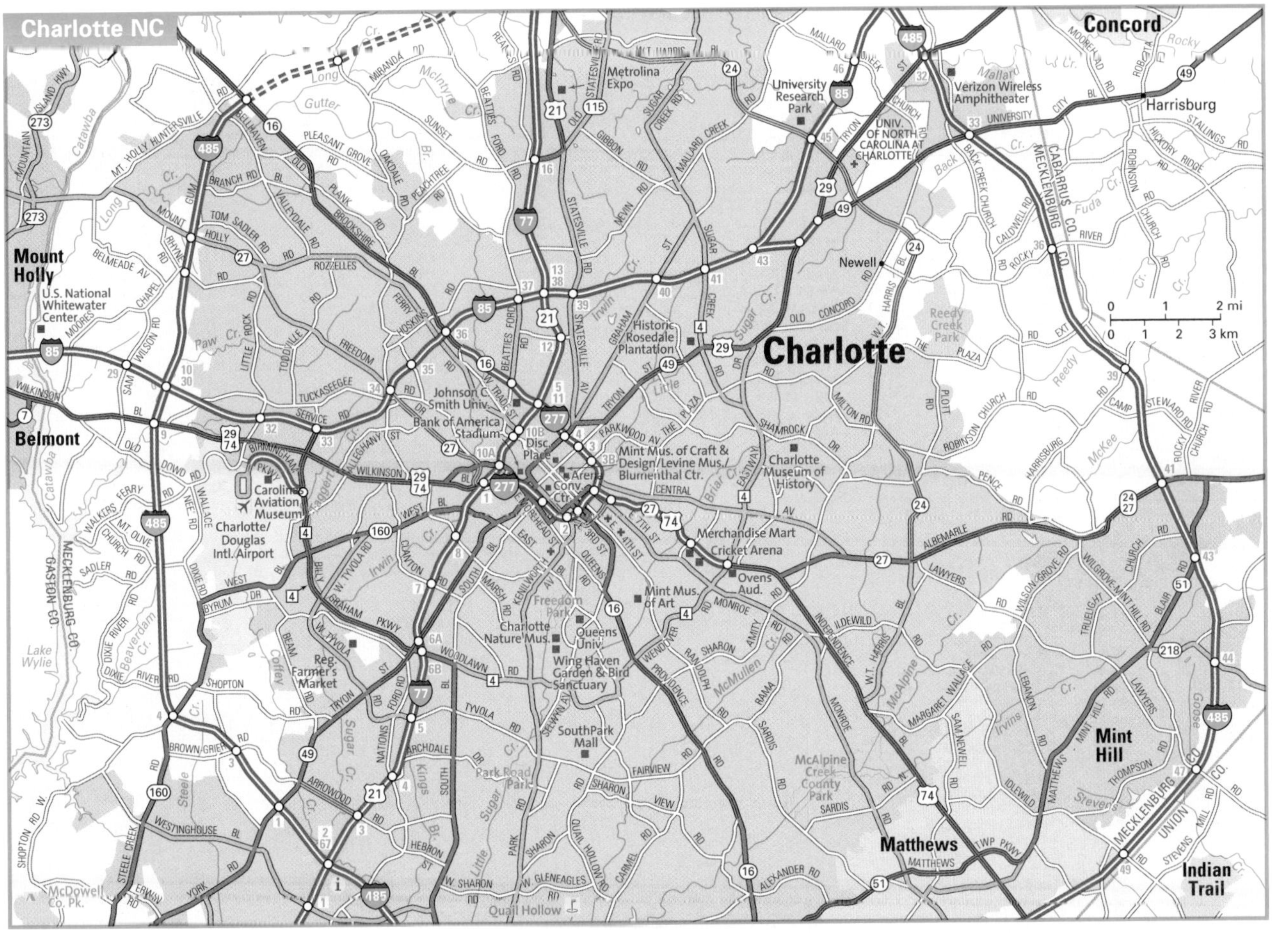

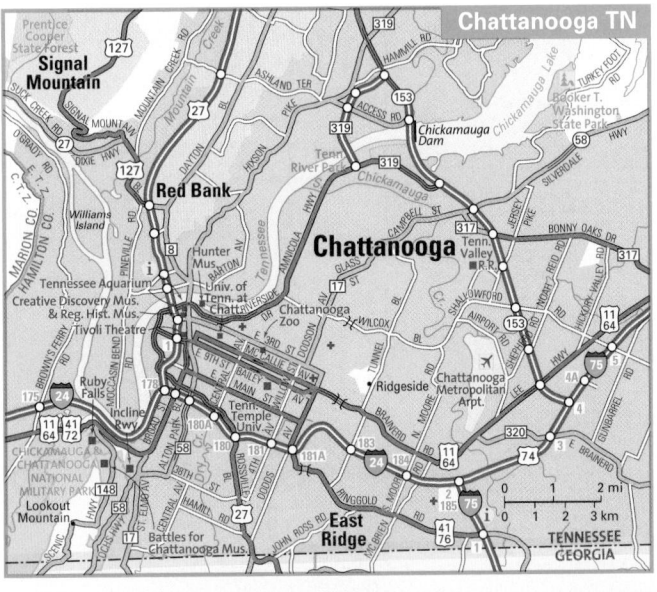

Figures after entries indicate population, page number, and grid reference.

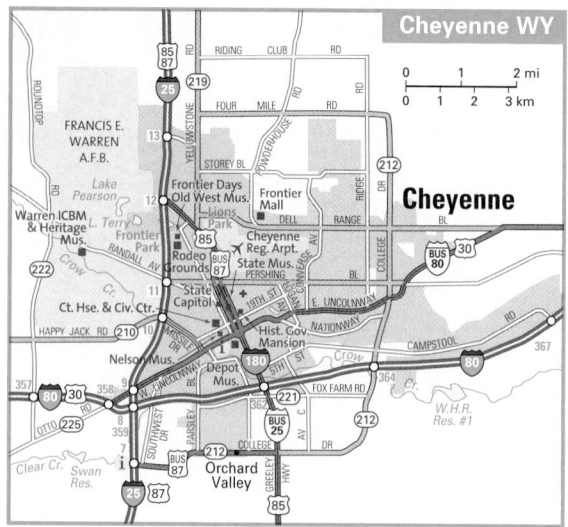

Cheyenne WY

0 1 2 mi
0 1 2 3 km

Cheyenne

CHICAGO MAP INDEX

POINTS OF INTEREST

Downtown Chicago IL

0 0.25 0.5 mi
0 0.25 0.5 0.75 km

Entries in **bold black** indicate counties or parishes. Entries in **bold color** indicate cities with detailed inset maps.

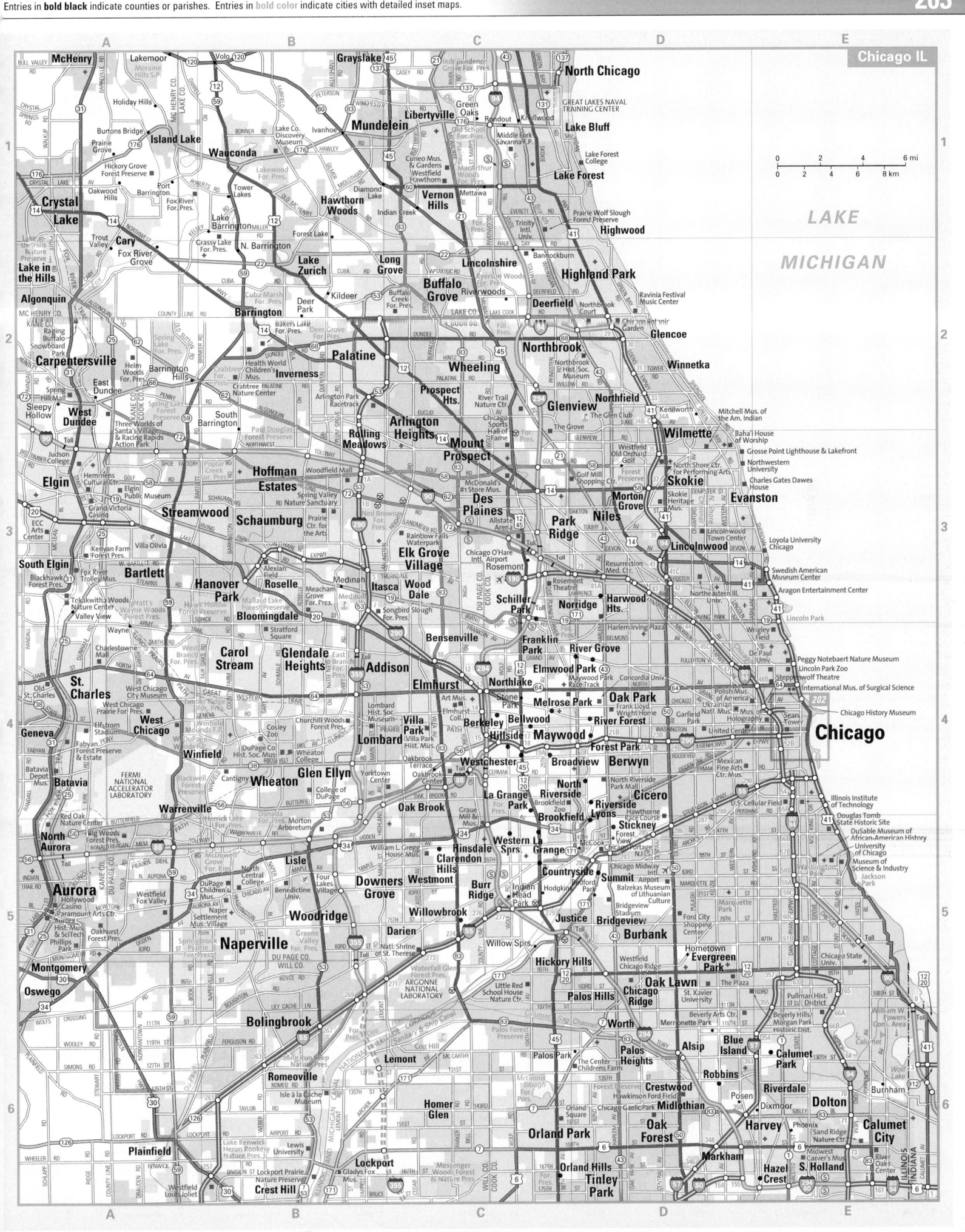

Chicago IL

LAKE

MICHIGAN

204 **Columbiaville–Comstock**

Figures after entries indicate population, page number, and grid reference.

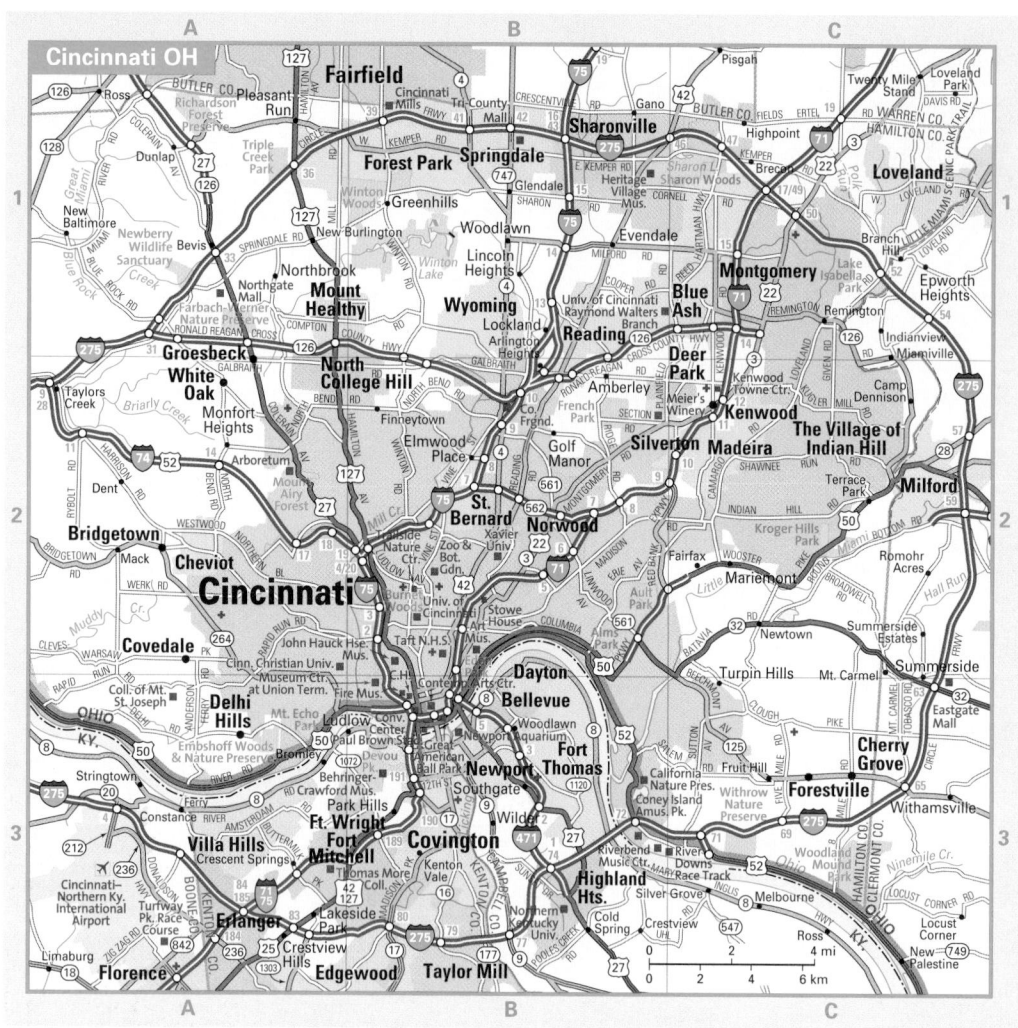

Cincinnati OH

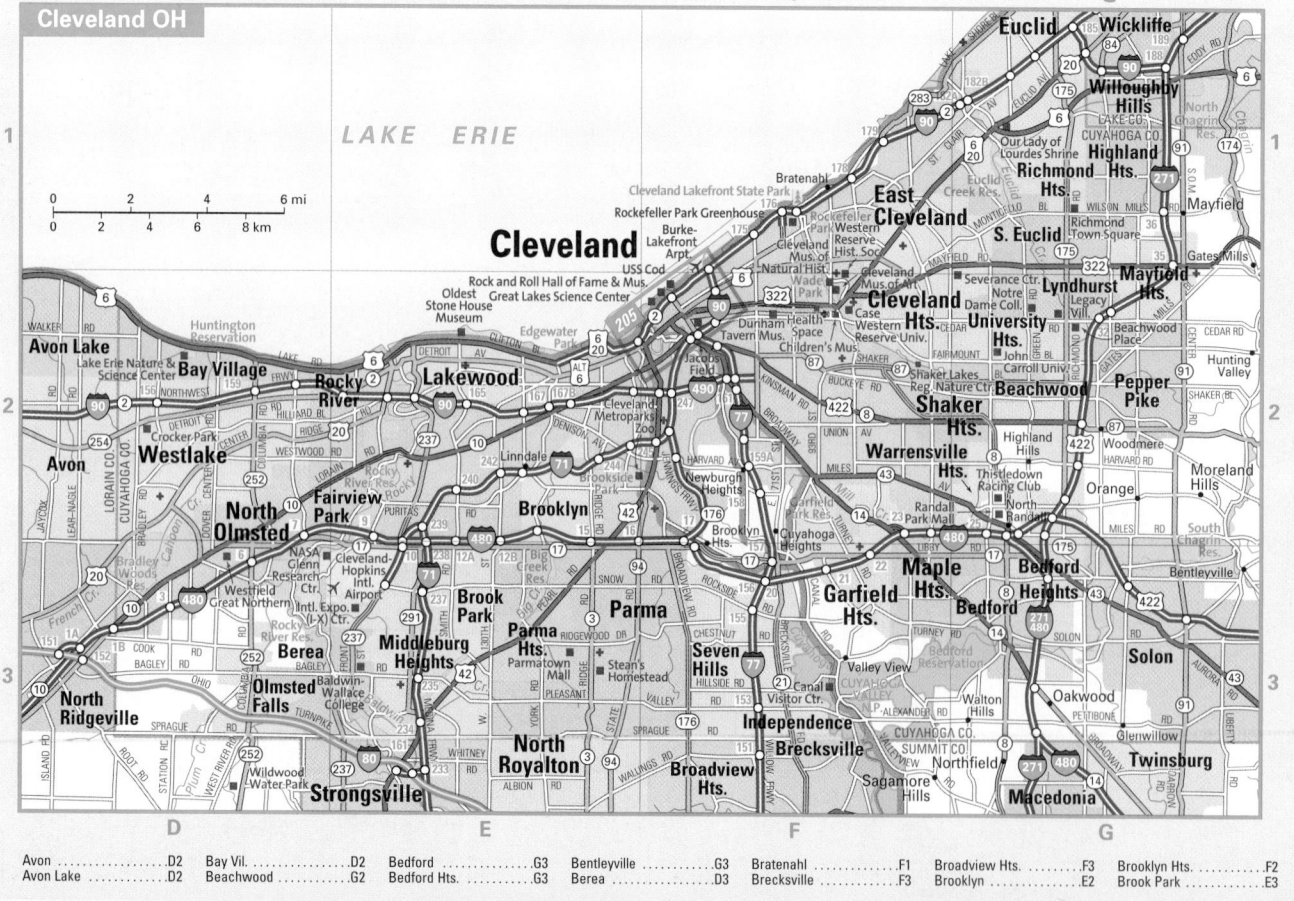

Cleveland OH

Entries in **bold black** indicate counties or parishes. Entries in ***bold color*** indicate cities with detailed inset maps.

Columbia SC

Colorado Springs CO

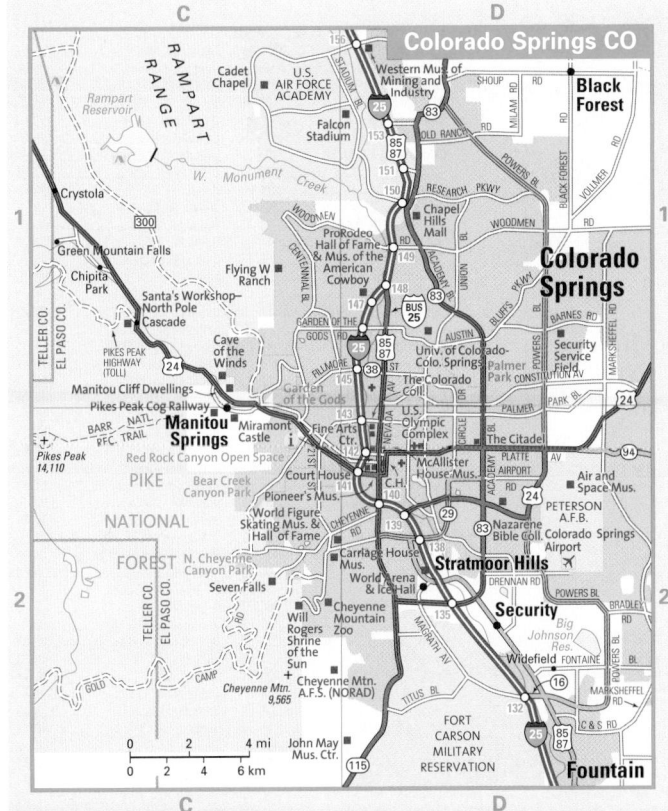

Downtown Cleveland OH

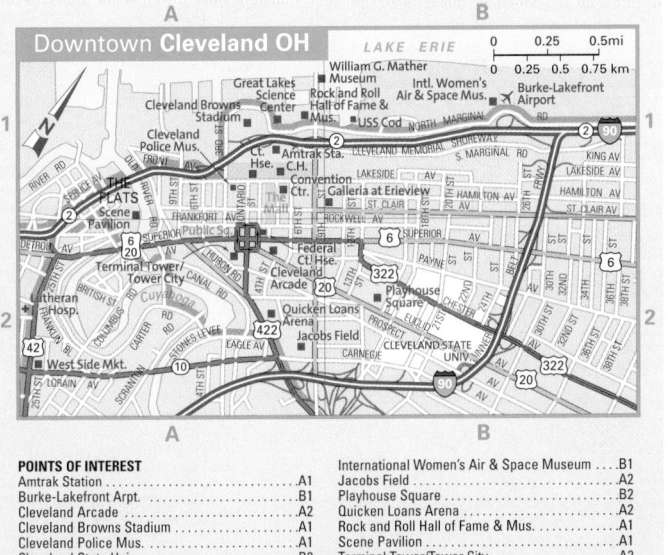

POINTS OF INTEREST

Columbus GA

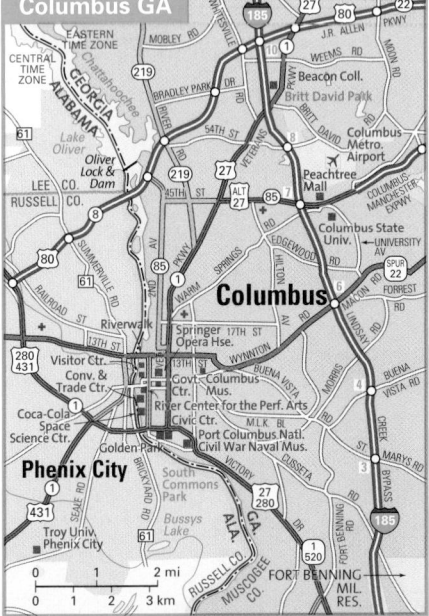

206 Crescent–Decatur

Figures after entries indicate population, page number, and grid reference.

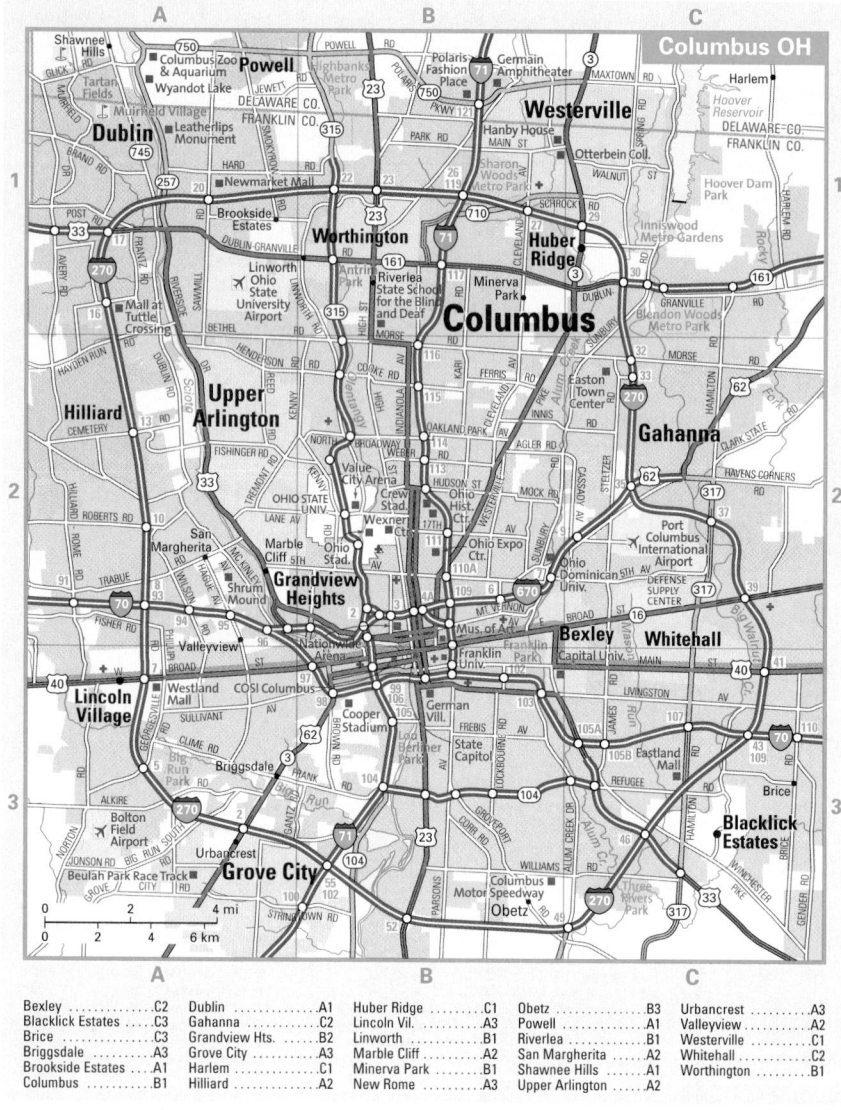

Columbus OH

Map legend / place index:

Crescent OK, 1281 ... 51 E2
Crescent Beach FL, 985 ... 139 E3
Crescent City CA, 4006 ... 28 A2
Crescent City FL, 1776 ... 139 D4
Crescent City IL, 631 ... 89 D3
Crescent Sprs. KY, 3931 ... 204 A3
Cresco IA, 3905 ... 73 E2
Cresson PA, 1631 ... 92 B4
Cressona PA, 1635 ... 146 A1
Crested Butte CO, 1529 ... 40 C2
Crest Hill IL, 13329 ... 89 D2

Crestline CA, 10218 ... 53 D2
Crestline OH, 5088 ... 91 D3
Creston IA, 7597 ... 86 B3
Creston OH, 2161 ... 91 E3
Crestview FL, 14766 ... 136 B1
Crestview KY, 471 ... 204 B1
Crestview Hills KY, 2889 ... 204 A3
Crestwood IL, 11251 ... 203 D6
Crestwood KY, 1999 ... 100 A4
Crestwood MO, 11863 ... 256 B3
Crestwood Vil. NJ, 8392 ... 147 E3

Creswell OR, 3579 ... 20 B4
Crete IL, 7346 ... 89 D2
Crete NE, 6028 ... 35 F4
Creve Coeur MO, 16500 ... 256 A2
Crewe VA, 2378 ... 113 D2
Cricket NC, 2053 ... 111 F4
Cridersville OH, 1817 ... 90 B3
Crimora VA, 1796 ... 102 C4
Cripple Creek CO, 1115 ... 41 E2
Crisfield MD, 2723 ... 103 F4
Crittenden KY, 2401 ... 100 B3
Crittenden Co. AR, 50866 ... 118 B1
Crittenden Co. KY, 9384 ... 109 E2
Crivitz WI, 988 ... 68 C3
Crocker MO, 1033 ... 97 E4
Crockett CA, 3194 ... 259 C1
Crockett TX, 7141 ... 124 A4
Crockett Co. TN, 14532 ... 108 C4
Crockett Co. TX, 4099 ... 60 C4
Crofton KY, 838 ... 109 E2
Crofton MD, 20091 ... 144 C2
Crofton NE, 754 ... 27 E3
Croghan NY, 665 ... 79 E2
Crompond NY, 2050 ... 148 B2
Cromwell CT, 750 ... 149 E1
Crook Co. OR, 19182 ... 21 D3
Crook Co. WY, 5887 ... 25 F3
Crooked Lake Park FL, 1682 ... 141 D3
Crooks SD, 859 ... 27 F4
Crookston MN, 8192 ... 19 F3
Crooksville OH, 2483 ... 101 E1
Crosby MN, 2299 ... 64 B4
Crosby ND, 1089 ... 18 A1
Crosby TX, 1714 ... 132 B3
Crosby Co. TX, 7072 ... 58 A1
Crosbyton TX, 1874 ... 58 A1
Cross City FL, 1775 ... 137 F3
Cross Co. AR, 19526 ... 118 A1
Crossett AR, 6097 ... 125 F1
Cross Hill SC, 601 ... 121 F3
Cross Keys NJ, 3600 ... 146 C4
Crosslake MN, 1893 ... 64 B4
Cross Plains TN, 1381 ... 109 D3
Cross Plains TX, 1068 ... 59 D3
Cross Plains WI, 3084 ... 74 B3
Cross Roads TX, 603 ... 59 F2
Crossville AL, 1431 ... 120 B3

Crossville IL, 782 ... 99 D4
Crossville TN, 8981 ... 110 B4
Crosswicks NJ, 900 ... 147 D2
Croswell MI, 2467 ... 76 C3
Crothersville IN, 1570 ... 99 F3
Croton Falls NY, 1200 ... 148 C2
Croton-on-Hudson NY, 7606 ... 148 B2
Crow Agency MT, 1552 ... 24 C1
Crowder MS, 766 ... 118 B3
Crowder OK, 436 ... 116 A1
Crowell TX, 1141 ... 58 C1
Crowley LA, 14225 ... 133 E2
Crowley TX, 7467 ... 59 E2
Crowley Co. CO, 5518 ... 41 F3
Crown Hts. NY, 2992 ... 148 B1
Crown Pt. IN, 19806 ... 89 D2
Crown Pt. LA, 650 ... 134 B3
Crownpoint NM, 2630 ... 48 B2
Crown Pt. NY, 650 ... 81 D3
Crownsville MD, 1670 ... 144 C3

Crow Wing Co. MN, 55099 ... 66 C1
Croydon PA, 9993 ... 248 E1
Crozet VA, 2820 ... 102 C4
Cruger MS, 449 ... 126 B1
Crump TN, 1521 ... 119 D1
Crystal MN, 22698 ... 235 B2
Crystal NM, 347 ... 48 A1
Crystal Beach FL, 4000 ... 266 A1
Crystal City MO, 4247 ... 98 A4
Crystal City TX, 7190 ... 60 C4
Crystal Falls MI, 1791 ... 68 C2
Crystal Lake CT, 1459 ... 150 A3
Crystal Lake IL, 38000 ... 88 C1
Crystal Lakes OH, 1411 ... 100 C1
Crystal River FL, 3485 ... 140 B1
Crystal Sprs. FL, 1175 ... 140 C2
Crystal Sprs. MS, 5873 ... 126 B3
Cuba IL, 1418 ... 88 A4
Cuba MO, 3230 ... 97 F4
Cuba NM, 590 ... 48 C2
Cuba NY, 1633 ... 92 C1
Cuba City WI, 2156 ... 74 A4
Cudahy CA, 24208 ... 228 D3
Cudahy WI, 18429 ... 75 D3
Cuddebackville NY, 750 ... 148 A1
Cudjoe FL, 1695 ... 143 D4
Cuero TX, 6571 ... 61 E3
Culberson Co. TX, 2975 ... 57 E4
Culdesac ID, 378 ... 14 B4
Cullen LA, 1296 ... 125 D1
Cullman AL, 13995 ... 119 F3
Cullman Co. AL, 77483 ... 119 F3
Culloden WV, 2940 ... 101 E3
Cullowhee NC, 3579 ... 121 D1
Culpeper VA, 9664 ... 103 D3
Culpeper Co. VA, 34262 ... 103 D3
Culver IN, 1539 ... 89 E2
Culver OR, 802 ... 21 D3
Culver City CA, 38816 ... 228 C3
Cumberland IN, 5500 ... 99 F1
Cumberland KY, 2611 ... 111 D2
Cumberland MD, 21518 ... 102 C1
Cumberland NC, 4400 ... 123 D2
Cumberland VA, 125 ... 113 D1
Cumberland WI, 2280 ... 67 E3
Cumberland Ctr. ME, 2596 ... 82 B3
Cumberland Co. IL, 11253 ... 99 D2
Cumberland Co. KY, 7147 ... 110 C2
Cumberland Co. ME, 265612 ... 82 B3
Cumberland Co. NJ, 146438 ... 145 F2
Cumberland Co. NC, 302963 ... 123 D2
Cumberland Co. PA, 213674 ... 103 D1
Cumberland Co. TN, 46802 ... 110 B4
Cumberland Co. VA, 9017 ... 113 D1
Cumberland Foreside ME, 500 ... 82 B3
Cumberland Hill RI, 7738 ... 150 C2
Cumby TX, 616 ... 124 A1
Cuming Co. NE, 10203 ... 35 F2
Cumming GA, 4220 ... 120 C3
Cunningham KS, 514 ... 43 D4
Cupertino CA, 50546 ... 36 B4
Curlew FL, 5900 ... 266 A1
Currituck NC, 125 ... 115 E1
Currituck Co. NC, 18190 ... 115 E1
Curry Co. NM, 45044 ... 49 F4
Curry Co. OR, 21137 ... 28 A2
Curtis NE, 832 ... 34 C4
Curwensville PA, 2650 ... 92 B3
Cushing OK, 8371 ... 51 F2
Cushing TX, 637 ... 124 B3
Cusseta GA, 1196 ... 128 C3
Custer SD, 1860 ... 25 F4
Custer Co. CO, 3503 ... 41 E3
Custer Co. ID, 4342 ... 23 D3
Custer Co. MT, 11696 ... 17 E1
Custer Co. NE, 11793 ... 34 C3
Custer Co. OK, 26142 ... 51 D2
Custer Co. SD, 7275 ... 25 F4
Cut and Shoot TX, 1158 ... 132 A2
Cut Bank MT, 3105 ... 15 E1
Cutchogue NY, 2849 ... 149 E3
Cuthbert GA, 3731 ... 128 C3

Cutler CA, 4491 ... 45 D3
Cutler Ridge FL, 24781 ... 143 E3
Cutlerville MI, 15114 ... 75 F3
Cut Off LA, 5635 ... 134 B3
Cutten CA, 2933 ... 28 A4
Cuyahoga Co. OH, 1393978 ... 91 E2
Cuyahoga Falls OH, 49374 ... 91 E3
Cuyahoga Hts. OH, 599 ... 204 E2
Cygnet OH, 564 ... 90 C2
Cynthiana IN, 693 ... 99 D4
Cynthiana KY, 6258 ... 100 B4
Cypress CA, 46229 ... 228 E4
Cypress Quarters FL, 1150 ... 141 E4
Cyril OK, 1168 ... 51 E3

D

Dacono CO, 3015 ... 41 E1
Dacula GA, 3848 ... 121 D3
Dade City FL, 6188 ... 140 C2
Dade Co. GA, 15154 ... 120 B2
Dade Co. MO, 7923 ... 106 C1
Dadeville AL, 3212 ... 128 B2
Daggett CA, 600 ... 53 D1
Daggett Co. UT, 921 ... 32 A1
Dagsboro DE, 519 ... 145 F4
Dahlgren IL, 997 ... 103 E4
Dahlonega GA, 3638 ... 120 C3
Daingerfield TX, 2517 ... 124 B1
Daisetta TX, 1034 ... 132 B2
Dakota City IA, 911 ... 72 C4
Dakota City NE, 1821 ... 35 F2
Dakota Co. MN, 355904 ... 67 D4
Dakota Co. NE, 20253 ... 35 F2
Dale IN, 1568 ... 99 E4
Dale City VA, 55971 ... 144 A4
Dale Co. AL, 49129 ... 128 B4
Daleville AL, 4653 ... 128 B4
Daleville IN, 1658 ... 89 F4
Daleville VA, 1454 ... 112 B1
Dalhart TX, 7237 ... 50 A2
Dallam Co. TX, 6222 ... 50 A2
Dallas GA, 5056 ... 120 B4
Dallas NC, 3402 ... 122 A1
Dallas OR, 12459 ... 20 B2
Dallas PA, 2557 ... 93 E2
Dallas TX, 1188580 ... 59 F2
Dallas City IL, 1055 ... 87 F3
Dallas Co. AL, 46365 ... 127 F3
Dallas Co. AR, 9210 ... 117 E4
Dallas Co. IA, 40750 ... 86 C2
Dallas Co. MO, 15661 ... 107 D1
Dallas Co. TX, 2218899 ... 59 F2
Dallastown PA, 4087 ... 103 E1
Dalton GA, 27912 ... 120 B2
Dalton MA, 4100 ... 94 C1
Dalton OH, 1605 ... 91 E4
Dalton PA, 1294 ... 93 F2
Dalton City IL, 581 ... 98 C1
Dalton Gardens ID, 2846 ... 14 B3
Dalworthington Gardens TX, 2186 ... 207 B3
Daly City CA, 103621 ... 36 B4
Dalzell SC, 2260 ... 122 B3
Damariscotta ME, 1751 ... 82 C3
Damascus MD, 11430 ... 144 B2
Damascus VA, 981 ... 111 F3
Damon TX, 535 ... 132 A4
Dana IN, 662 ... 99 E1
Dana Pt. CA, 35110 ... 52 C3
Danboro PA, 1500 ... 146 C2
Danbury CT, 74848 ... 148 C2
Danbury NC, 108 ... 112 B3
Danbury TX, 1611 ... 132 A4
Dandridge TN, 2078 ... 111 D4
Dane WI, 662 ... 74 B3
Dane Co. WI, 426526 ... 74 B3
Danforth IL, 587 ... 89 D3
Dania Beach FL, 20061 ... 143 F2
Daniel MD, 650 ... 144 B1
Daniels Co. MT, 2017 ... 17 E1
Danielson CT, 4265 ... 150 B3
Danielsville GA, 457 ... 121 D3
Dannemora NY, 4129 ... 80 C1
Dansville NY, 4832 ... 78 C4

Dante VA, 650 ... 111 E2
Danube MN, 529 ... 66 B4
Danvers IL, 1183 ... 88 B4
Danvers MA, 25212 ... 151 F1
Danville AR, 2392 ... 117 D2
Danville CA, 41715 ... 259 E4
Danville IL, 33904 ... 89 D4
Danville IN, 6418 ... 99 F1
Danville IA, 914 ... 87 F3
Danville KY, 15477 ... 110 B1
Danville NH, 1300 ... 95 E1
Danville OH, 1104 ... 91 D4
Danville PA, 4897 ... 93 E3
Danville VT, 475 ... 81 E2
Danville VA, 48411 ... 112 C3
Danville WV, 550 ... 101 E4
Daphne AL, 16581 ... 135 E2
Darby MT, 710 ... 23 D1
Darby PA, 10299 ... 146 C3
Dardanelle AR, 4228 ... 117 D1
Dardenne Prairie MO, 4384 ... 98 A3
Dare Co. NC, 29967 ... 115 F2
Dares Beach MD, 1400 ... 144 C4
Darien CT, 19607 ... 148 C3
Darien GA, 1719 ... 130 B4
Darien IL, 22860 ... 203 C5
Darien WI, 1572 ... 74 C4
Darke Co. OH, 53309 ... 100 B1
Darlington IN, 854 ... 89 E4
Darlington SC, 6720 ... 122 C3
Darlington WI, 2418 ... 74 A4
Darlington Co. SC, 67394 ... 122 B3
Darmstadt IN, 1313 ... 99 D4
Darnestown MD, 6378 ... 144 B2
Darrington WA, 1136 ... 12 C2
Dasher GA, 834 ... 137 F1
Dassel MN, 1233 ... 66 C3
Dauphin PA, 773 ... 93 D4
Dauphin Co. PA, 251798 ... 93 D4
Dauphin Island AL, 1371 ... 135 E4
Davenport FL, 1924 ... 141 D2
Davenport IA, 98359 ... 88 A2
Davenport ND, 261 ... 19 E4
Davenport OK, 881 ... 51 F2
Davenport WA, 1730 ... 13 F3
David City NE, 2597 ... 35 F3
Davidson NC, 7139 ... 122 A1
Davidson Co. NC, 147246 ... 112 B4
Davidson Co. TN, 569891 ... 109 F4
Davidsville PA, 1119 ... 92 B4
Davie FL, 75720 ... 143 E2
Davie Co. NC, 34585 ... 112 A4
Daviess Co. IN, 29820 ... 99 E3
Daviess Co. KY, 91545 ... 109 E1
Daviess Co. MO, 8016 ... 96 C1
Davis CA, 60308 ... 36 C3
Davis OK, 2610 ... 51 F4
Davis WV, 624 ... 102 B2
Davisboro GA, 1544 ... 129 F1
Davis Co. IA, 8541 ... 87 E3
Davis Co. UT, 238994 ... 31 E3
Davison MI, 5536 ... 76 B3
Davison Co. SD, 18741 ... 27 E4
Davy WV, 373 ... 111 F1
Dawes Co. NE, 9060 ... 34 A1
Dawson GA, 5058 ... 128 C3
Dawson MN, 1539 ... 27 F2
Dawson TX, 852 ... 59 F3
Dawson Co. GA, 15999 ... 120 C3
Dawson Co. MT, 9059 ... 17 F1
Dawson Co. NE, 24365 ... 35 D4
Dawson Co. TX, 14985 ... 58 A2
Dawson Sprs. KY, 2980 ... 109 E2
Dawsonville GA, 619 ... 120 C3
Day Co. SD, 6267 ... 27 E2
Dayton ID, 444 ... 31 E2
Dayton IN, 1120 ... 89 E4
Dayton IA, 884 ... 72 C4
Dayton KY, 5966 ... 204 B2
Dayton MN, 4699 ... 235 A1
Dayton NV, 5907 ... 37 D2
Dayton NJ, 6235 ... 147 D1
Dayton OH, 166179 ... 100 B1
Dayton OR, 2119 ... 20 B2
Dayton TN, 6180 ... 120 B1
Dayton TX, 5709 ... 132 B3
Dayton VA, 1344 ... 102 C3
Dayton WA, 2655 ... 13 F4
Dayton WY, 678 ... 24 C2
Daytona Beach FL, 64112 ... 139 E4
Daytona Beach Shores FL, 4299 ... 139 E4
Dayville CT, 1600 ... 150 B3
Deadwood SD, 1380 ... 25 F3
Deaf Smith Co. TX, 18561 ... 49 F3
Deal NJ, 1070 ... 147 F2
Deale MD, 4796 ... 144 C3
Deal Island MD, 578 ... 103 F4
Dearborn MI, 97775 ... 76 C4
Dearborn MO, 529 ... 96 B1
Dearborn Co. IN, 46109 ... 100 B3
Dearborn Hts. MI, 58264 ... 210 B3
Dearing KS, 415 ... 106 A2
DeArmanville AL, 700 ... 120 A4
Deary ID, 552 ... 14 B4
Deaver WY, 177 ... 24 B2
De Baca Co. NM, 2240 ... 49 E4
De Bary FL, 15559 ... 141 D1
De Beque CO, 451 ... 40 B2
Decatur AL, 53929 ... 119 F2
Decatur AR, 1314 ... 106 B3
Decatur GA, 18147 ... 120 C4

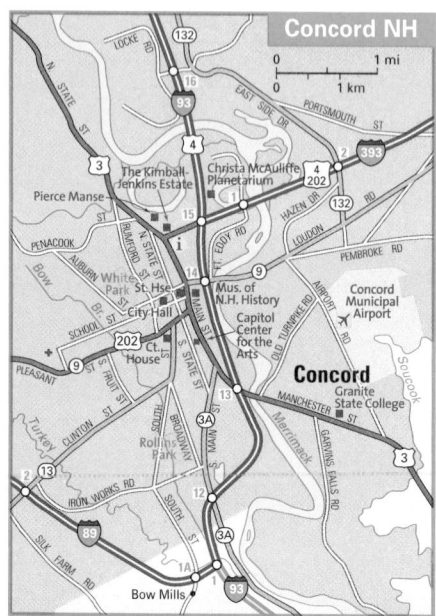

Concord NH

Crescent City FL, 1776 ... 139 D4

Corpus Christi TX

Entries in **bold black** indicate counties or parishes. Entries in **bold color** indicate cities with detailed inset maps.

Decatur–Des Peres 207

Addison D1	Cedar Hill C3	De Soto D3	Ft. Worth A2	Hutchins E3
Arlington C3	Cockrell Hill D2	Duncanville D3	Garland E1	Irving C2
Avondale A1	Colleyville B1	Edgecliff A3	Grand Prairie C3	Keller B1
Balch Sprs. E3	Coppell C1	Euless C2	Grapevine C1	Kennedale B3
Bedford B2	Crowley A3	Everman B3	Haltom City B2	Lakeview A1
Benbrook A3	Dallas D2	Farmers Branch D1	Haslet A1	Lake Worth A2
Blue Mound A2	Dalworthington	Flower Mound C1	Highland Park D2	Lancaster D3
Carrollton D1	Gardens B3	Forest Hill B3	Hurst B2	Lewisville C1

Mansfield B3	Richland Hills B2	Southlake B1	Wilmer E3
Mesquite E2	River Oaks A2	Trophy Club B1	Wylie E1
Murphy E1	Roanoke A1	University Park D2	
Newark A1	Rowlett E1	Watauga B2	
N. Richland Hills B2	Sachse E1	Westlake B1	
Pantego B3	Saginaw A2	Westover Hills A2	
Plano D1	Sansom Park A2	Westworth A2	
Richardson E1	Seagoville E3	White Settlement A2	

Dallas / Fort Worth TX

Downtown Dallas TX

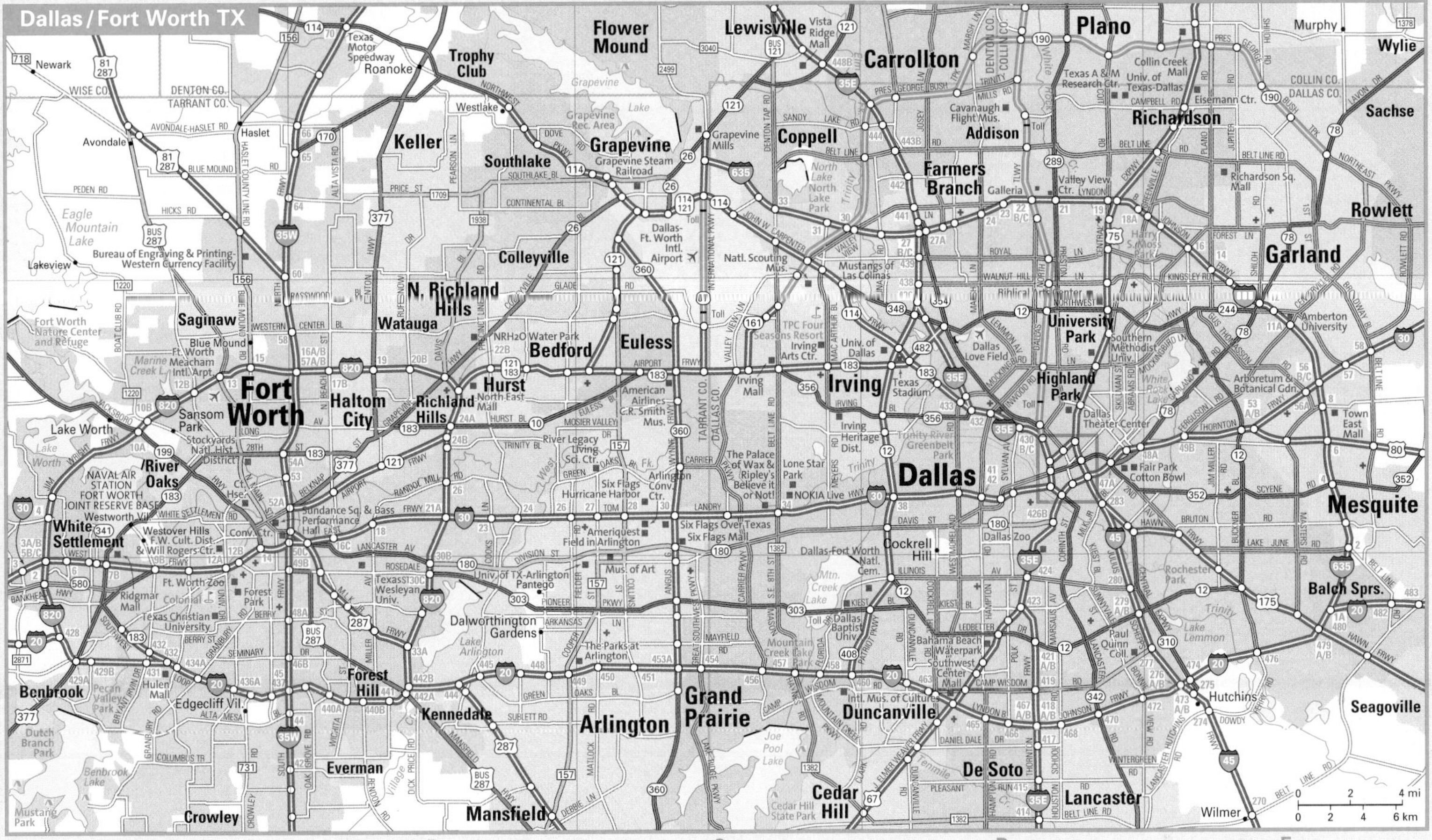

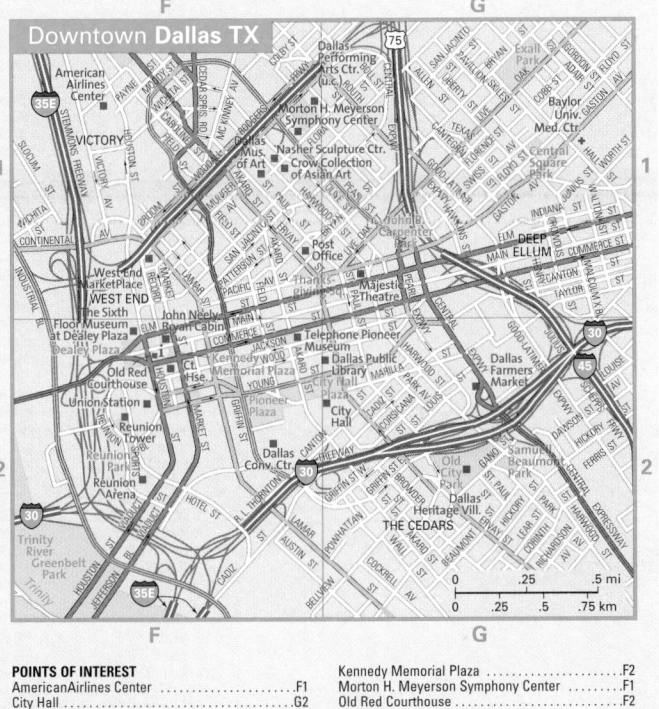

POINTS OF INTEREST

AmericanAirlines Center F1	Kennedy Memorial Plaza F2
City Hall G2	Morton H. Meyerson Symphony Center F1
Court House F2	Old Red Courthouse F2
Dallas Convention Center F2	Post Office F2
Dallas Memorial Auditorium F2	Reunion Arena F2
Dallas Mus. of Art F1	Reunion Tower F2
Dallas Public Library G2	The Sixth Floor Mus. at Dealey Plaza F2
Dallas Theater Center G1	Telephone Pioneer Mus. F1
Farmers Market G2	Union Station F2
	West End MarketPlace F1

208 Des Plaines–Duck Hill

Figures after entries indicate population, page number, and grid reference.

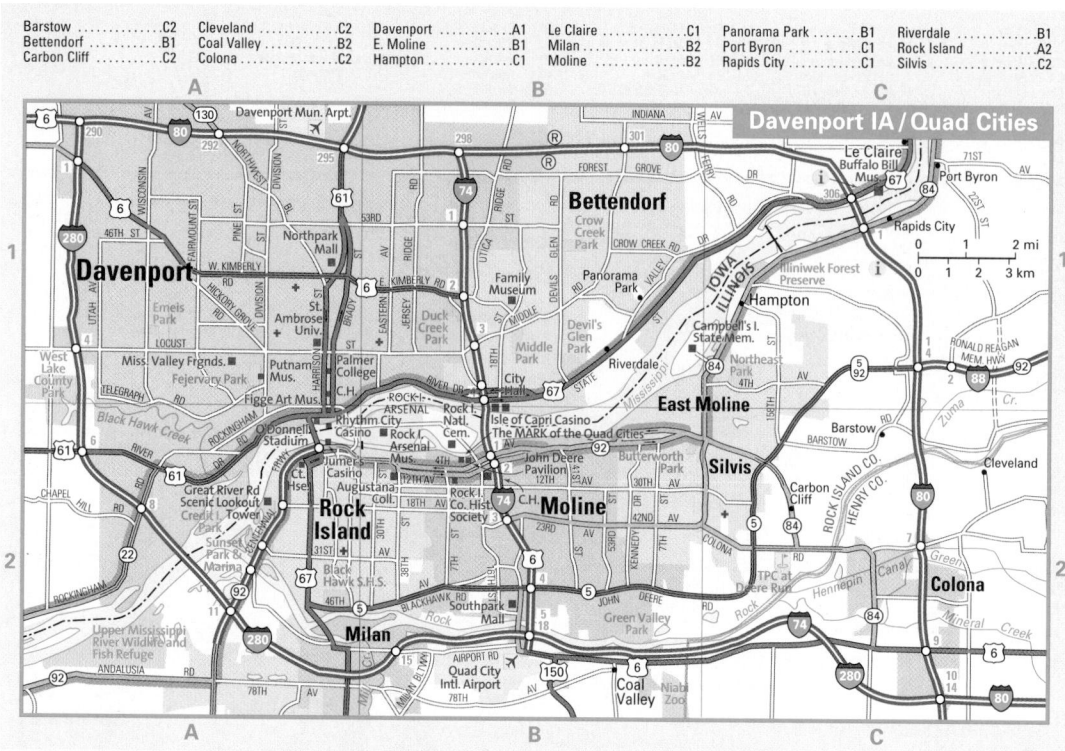

Davenport IA / Quad Cities

Barstow C2	Cleveland C2	Davenport A1	Le Claire C1	Panorama Park B1	Riverdale B1
Bettendorf B1	Coal Valley B2	E. Moline B1	Milan B2	Port Byron C1	Rock Island A2
Carbon Cliff C2	Colona C2	Hampton C1	Moline B2	Rapids City C1	Silvis C2

Dilworth MN, 3001 ....19 F4
Dimmit Co. TX, 10248 ....60 C4
Dimmitt TX, 4375 ....50 A4
Dimondale MI, 1342 ....76 A4
Dinosaur CO, 319 ....32 B4
Dinuba CA, 18844 ....45 D3
Dinwiddie VA, 350 ....113 E2
Dinwiddie Co. VA, 24533 ....113 E2
District Hts. MD, 5958 ....271 F2
Divernon IL, 1201 ....98 B1
Divide Co. ND, 2283 ....17 C1
Dixfield ME, 1137 ....82 B2
Dixie Co. FL, 13827 ....137 F3
Dixmoor IL, 3934 ....203 E6
Dixon CA, 16103 ....36 B3
Dixon IL, 15941 ....88 B1
Dixon KY, 632 ....109 E1
Dixon MO, 1570 ....97 E4
Dixon MT, 216 ....15 D3
Dixon Co. NE, 6339 ....35 F1
D'Lo MS, 394 ....126 B3
Dobbins Hts. NC, 936 ....122 C2
Dobbs Ferry NY, 10622 ....148 B3
Dobson NC, 1457 ....112 A3
Dock Jct. GA, 6951 ....139 D1
Doctor Phillips FL, 9548 ....246 B3
Doctors Inlet FL, 1400 ....139 D2
Doddridge Co. WV, 7403 ....102 A2
Dodge NE, 700 ....35 F2
Dodge Ctr. MN, 2226 ....73 D1
Dodge City AL, 612 ....119 F3
Dodge City KS, 25176 ....42 C4
Dodge Co. GA, 19171 ....129 E3
Dodge Co. MN, 17731 ....73 D1
Dodge Co. NE, 36160 ....35 F3
Dodge Co. WI, 85897 ....74 C3
Dodgeville WI, 4220 ....74 A3
Doerun GA, 828 ....129 D4
Doland SD, 297 ....27 E2
Dolan Sprs. AZ, 1867 ....46 B3
Dolgeville NY, 2166 ....79 F3
Dollar Bay MI, 950 ....65 F3
Dolores CO, 857 ....40 B4
Dolores Co. CO, 1844 ....40 B4
Dolton IL, 25614 ....203 E6
Doña Ana NM, 1379 ....56 B3
Dona Ana Co. NM, 174682 ....56 B3
Donald OR, 608 ....20 B2
Donaldsonville LA, 7605 ....134 A2
Donalsonville GA, 2796 ....137 D1
Dongola IL, 806 ....108 C1
Doniphan MO, 1932 ....108 A3
Doniphan NE, 763 ....35 E4
Doniphan Co. KS, 8249 ....96 B1
Donna TX, 14768 ....63 E4
Donnellson IA, 963 ....87 F2
Donora PA, 5653 ....92 A4
Doolittle MO, 644 ....97 E4
Dooly Co. GA, 11525 ....129 D3
Doon IA, 533 ....27 F4
Door Co. WI, 27961 ....69 D4
Dora AL, 2413 ....119 F4
Doraville GA, 9862 ....120 C4
Dorchester NE, 615 ....35 F4
Dorchester WI, 827 ....68 A3

Dorchester Co. MD, 30674 ....103 F4
Dorchester Co. SC, 96413 ....130 C1
Dormont PA, 9305 ....250 B3
Dorr MI, 2800 ....75 F4
Dorris CA, 886 ....28 C2
Dorset VT, 400 ....81 D4
Dorsey MD, 1000 ....193 B4
Dortches NC, 809 ....113 D4
Dos Palos CA, 4581 ....45 D1
Dothan AL, 57737 ....128 A4
Double Sprs. AL, 1003 ....119 E3
Doubs MD, 750 ....144 A2
Dougherty Co. GA, 96065 ....128 C4
Douglas AL, 530 ....120 A3
Douglas AZ, 14312 ....55 E4
Douglas GA, 10639 ....129 E4
Douglas MA, 800 ....150 C2
Douglas WY, 5288 ....33 E4
Douglas Co. CO, 175766 ....41 E2
Douglas Co. GA, 92174 ....120 C4
Douglas Co. IL, 19922 ....99 D3
Douglas Co. KS, 99962 ....96 A3
Douglas Co. MN, 32821 ....66 B2
Douglas Co. MO, 13084 ....107 E2
Douglas Co. NE, 463585 ....35 F3
Douglas Co. NV, 41259 ....37 D2
Douglas Co. OR, 100399 ....20 A2
Douglas Co. SD, 3458 ....27 E4
Douglas Co. WA, 32603 ....13 E3
Douglas Co. WI, 43287 ....64 C4
Douglass KS, 1813 ....43 F4
Douglass Hills KY, 5718 ....230 F2
Douglassville PA, 1300 ....146 B2
Douglasville GA, 20065 ....120 C4
Dousman WI, 1584 ....74 C3
Dove Creek CO, 698 ....40 A4
Dover AR, 1329 ....117 D1
Dover DE, 32135 ....145 E2
Dover FL, 2798 ....140 C2
Dover ID, 342 ....14 B2
Dover MA, 2216 ....151 D1
Dover NH, 26884 ....82 A4
Dover NJ, 18188 ....148 A3
Dover OH, 12210 ....91 E4
Dover TN, 1442 ....109 D3
Dover-Foxcroft ME, 2592 ....82 C1
Dover Plains NY, 1996 ....94 B3
Dowagiac MI, 6147 ....89 F1
Dow City IA, 503 ....86 A1
Dowling Park FL, 650 ....137 F2
Downers Grove IL, 48724 ....89 D1
Downey CA, 107323 ....52 C2
Downey ID, 613 ....31 E2
Downieville CA, 80 ....36 C1
Downingtown PA, 7589 ....146 B3
Downs IL, 776 ....88 C4
Downs KS, 1038 ....43 D1
Dows IA, 675 ....72 C4
Doyle TN, 525 ....110 A4
Doylestown OH, 2799 ....91 E3
Doylestown PA, 8227 ....146 C2
Doyline LA, 841 ....125 D2
Drain OR, 1021 ....20 B4
Drake ND, 322 ....18 C2
Drakesboro KY, 627 ....109 E2
Drakes Branch VA, 504 ....113 D2
Draper UT, 25220 ....31 E4
Dravosburg PA, 2015 ....250 C3
Drayton ND, 913 ....19 E2
Dresden OH, 1423 ....91 D4
Dresden TN, 2855 ....109 D3
Dresser WI, 732 ....67 D3
Drew MS, 2434 ....118 A4
Drew Co. AR, 18723 ....117 F4
Drexel MO, 1090 ....96 B3
Drexel NC, 1938 ....111 F4
Drexel OH, 2057 ....208 D1
Drexel Hill PA, 29364 ....146 C3
Driggs ID, 1100 ....23 F4
Dripping Sprs. TX, 1548 ....61 D2
Driscoll TX, 825 ....63 F2
Druid Hills GA, 12741 ....190 D3
Drummond MT, 318 ....15 E4
Drumright OK, 2905 ....51 F2
Dryden ME, 1100 ....82 B2
Dryden MI, 815 ....76 C3
Dryden NY, 1832 ....79 D4
Dryden VA, 1253 ....111 D2
Dry Mills ME, 700 ....82 B3
Dry Prong LA, 421 ....125 E4
Dry Ridge KY, 1995 ....100 B3
Duarte CA, 21486 ....228 E2
Dubach LA, 800 ....125 E2
Dublin CA, 29973 ....259 E3
Dublin GA, 15857 ....129 E2
Dublin IN, 697 ....100 A1
Dublin MD, 650 ....146 C2
Dublin OH, 31392 ....90 C4
Dublin PA, 2083 ....146 C2
Dublin TX, 3754 ....59 D3
Dublin VA, 2288 ....112 A2
DuBois ID, 647 ....23 E4
DuBois PA, 8123 ....92 B3
Dubois WY, 962 ....24 B4
Dubois Co. IN, 39674 ....99 E3
Duboistown PA, 1280 ....93 D2
Dubuque IA, 57686 ....73 F4
Dubuque Co. IA, 89143 ....73 F4
Duchesne UT, 1408 ....32 A4
Duchesne Co. UT, 14371 ....39 F1
Duck Hill MS, 746 ....118 B4

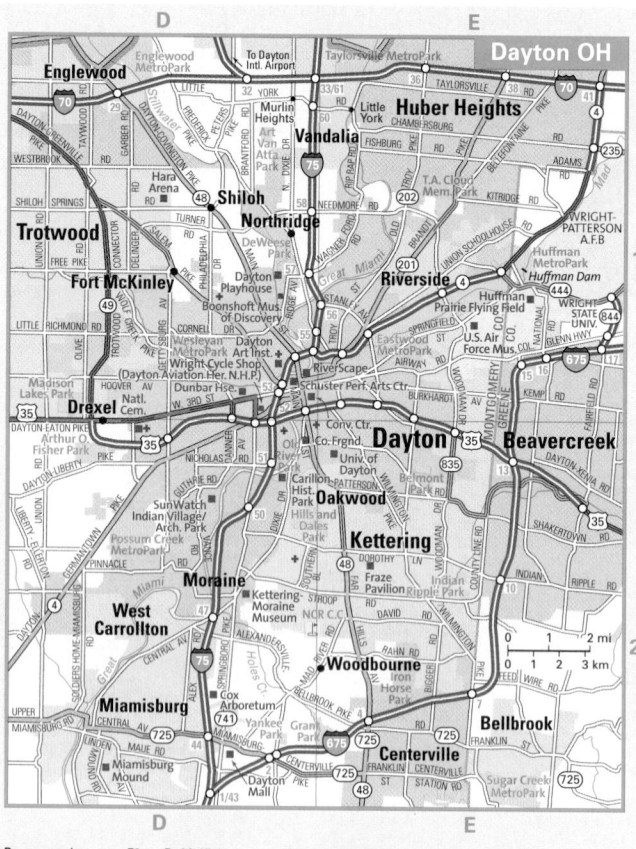

Dayton OH

Beavercreek E2	Ft. McKinley D1	Murlin Hts. D1	Vandalia E1
Bellbrook E2	Huber Hts. E1	Northridge D1	W. Carrollton D2
Centerville E2	Kettering E2	Oakwood E2	Woodbourne E2
Dayton E2	Little York D1	Riverside E1	
Drexel D1	Miamisburg D2	Shiloh D1	
Englewood D1	Moraine D2	Trotwood D1	

Des Plaines IL, 58720 ....89 D1
Destin FL, 11119 ....136 B2
Destrehan LA, 11260 ....134 B3
Detroit MI, 951270 ....76 C4
Detroit TX, 776 ....116 A4
Detroit Beach MI, 2289 ....90 C1
Detroit Lakes MN, 7348 ....19 F4
Deuel Co. NE, 2098 ....34 A3
Deuel Co. SD, 4498 ....27 F2
De Valls Bluff AR, 783 ....117 F2
Deville LA, 1007 ....125 E4
Devils Lake ND, 7222 ....19 D2
Devine TX, 4140 ....61 D3

Devola OH, 2771 ....101 F2
Devon PA, 5067 ....248 A2
Dewar OK, 919 ....116 A1
Dewey OK, 3179 ....51 F1
Dewey Beach DE, 301 ....145 F4
Dewey Co. OK, 4743 ....51 D2
Dewey Co. SD, 5972 ....26 C2
Deweyville TX, 1190 ....132 C2
Deweyville UT, 278 ....31 E3
De Witt AR, 3552 ....117 F3
De Witt IA, 5049 ....88 A1
De Witt MI, 4702 ....76 A3

De Witt NE, 572 ....35 F4
De Witt NY, 8200 ....79 D3
De Witt Co. IL, 16798 ....88 B4
DeWitt Co. TX, 20013 ....61 E3
Dexter GA, 509 ....129 E2
Dexter IA, 689 ....86 C2
Dexter ME, 2201 ....82 C1
Dexter MI, 2338 ....76 B4
Dexter MO, 7356 ....108 B3
Dexter NM, 1235 ....57 E2
Dexter NY, 1120 ....79 E1
Diablo CA, 988 ....259 E3

Diamond IL, 1393 ....88 C2
Diamond MO, 807 ....106 C2
Diamond Bar CA, 56287 ....229 F3
Diamond City AR, 730 ....107 D3
Diamondhead MS, 5912 ....134 C2
Diamond Hill RI, 1100 ....150 C2
Diamond Sprs. CA, 4888 ....36 C2
Diamondville WY, 716 ....31 F2
Diaz AR, 1284 ....107 F4
D'Iberville MS, 7608 ....135 D2
Dickens TX, 332 ....58 B1
Dickens Co. TX, 2762 ....58 B1
Dickenson Co. VA, 16395 ....111 D2
Dickey Co. ND, 5757 ....27 D1
Dickeyville WI, 1043 ....73 F4
Dickinson ND, 16010 ....18 A4
Dickinson TX, 17093 ....132 B4
Dickinson Co. IA, 16424 ....72 B3
Dickinson Co. KS, 19344 ....43 E2
Dickinson Co. MI, 27472 ....69 D2

Dickson OK, 1139 ....51 F4
Dickson TN, 12244 ....109 E4
Dickson City PA, 6205 ....93 E2
Dickson Co. TN, 43156 ....109 E4
Dierks AR, 1230 ....116 C3
Dieterich IL, 591 ....98 C2
Dighton KS, 1261 ....42 C3
Dighton MA, 1200 ....151 D3
Dike IA, 944 ....73 D4
Dilkon AZ, 1265 ....47 F3
Dill City OK, 526 ....51 D3
Dillingham AK, 2466 ....154 B3
Dillon CO, 802 ....41 D1
Dillon MT, 3752 ....23 E2
Dillon SC, 6316 ....122 C3
Dillon Co. SC, 30722 ....122 C3
Dillonvale OH, 781 ....91 F4
Dillsboro IN, 1436 ....100 A2
Dillsburg PA, 2063 ....93 D4
Dillwyn VA, 447 ....113 D1

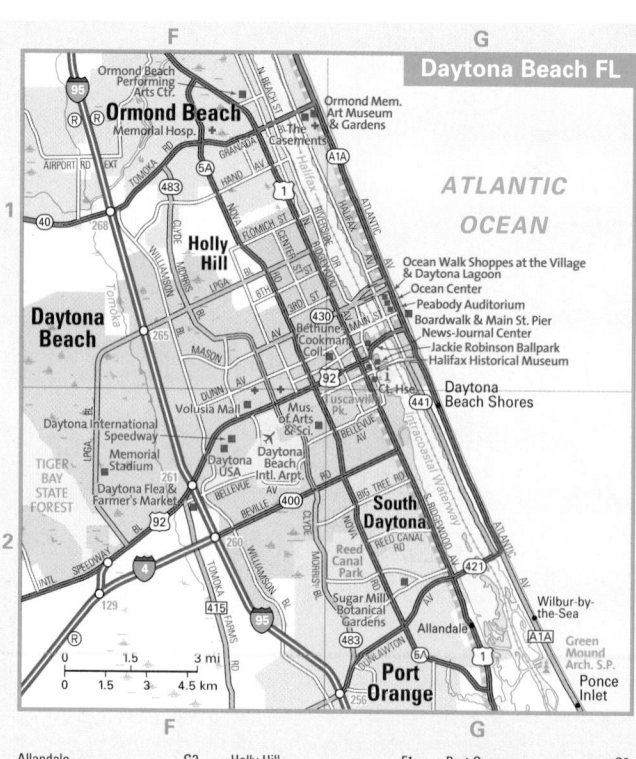

Daytona Beach FL

Allandale G2	Holly Hill F1	Port Orange G2
Daytona Beach F1	Ormond Beach F1	S. Daytona F1
Daytona Beach Shores G2	Ponce Inlet G2	Wilbur-by-the-Sea G2

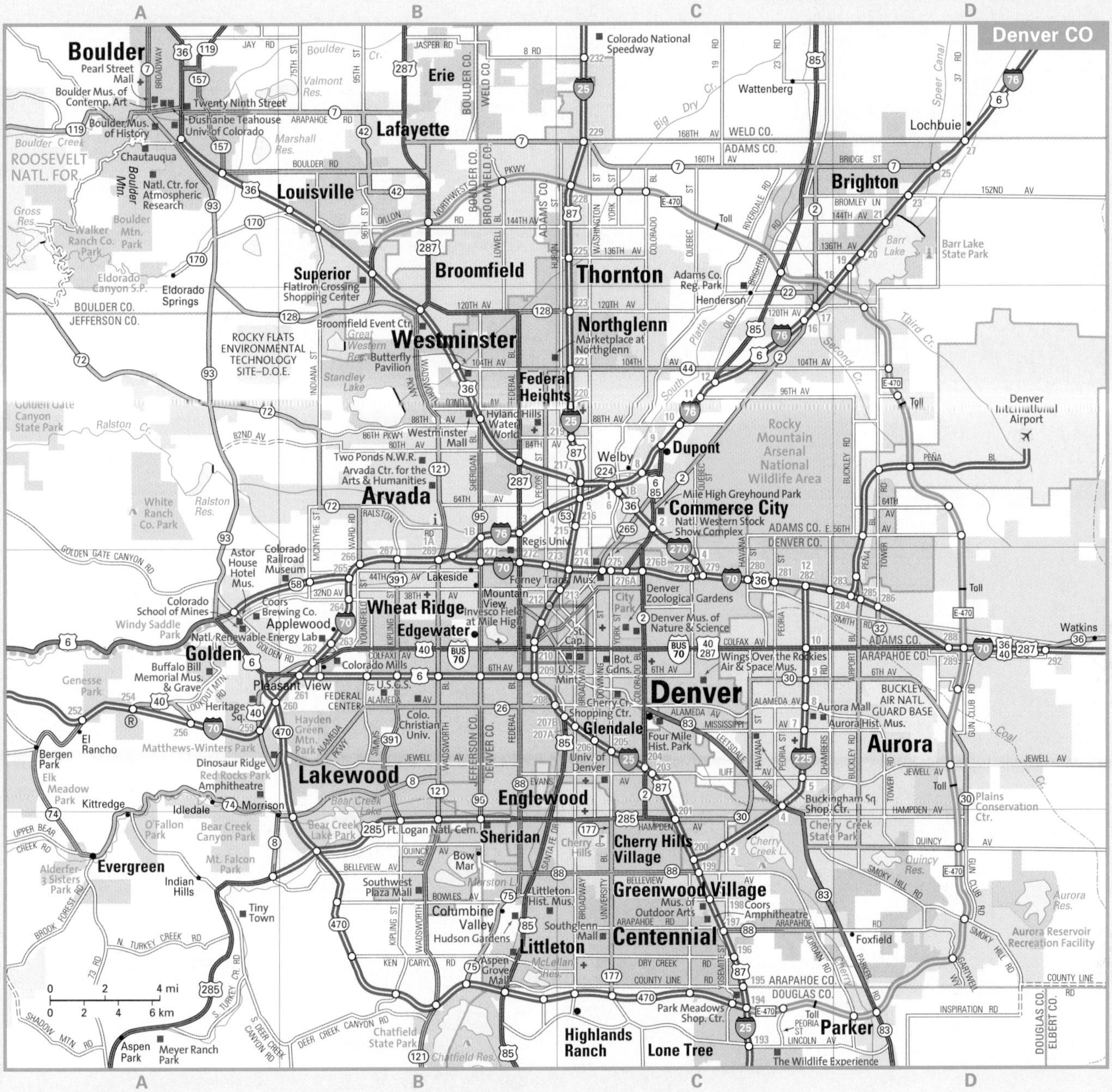

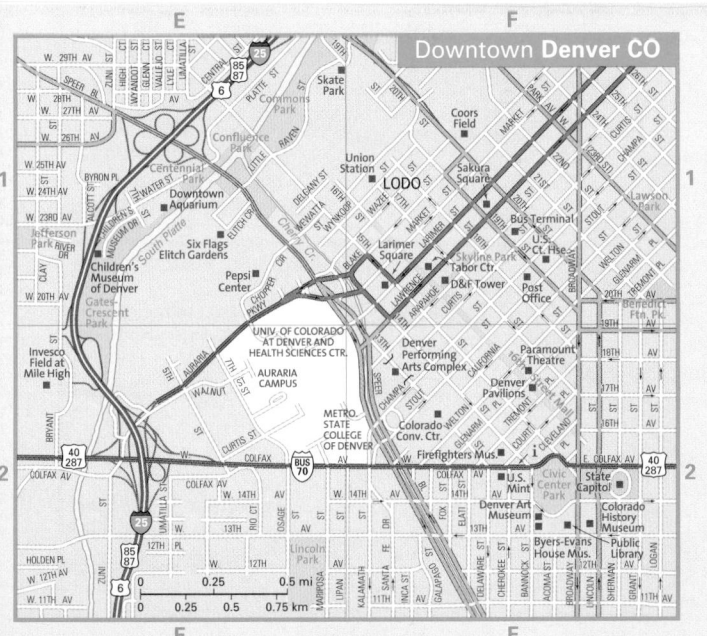

Denver CO

Downtown Denver CO

POINTS OF INTEREST

210

Figures after entries indicate population, page number, and grid reference.

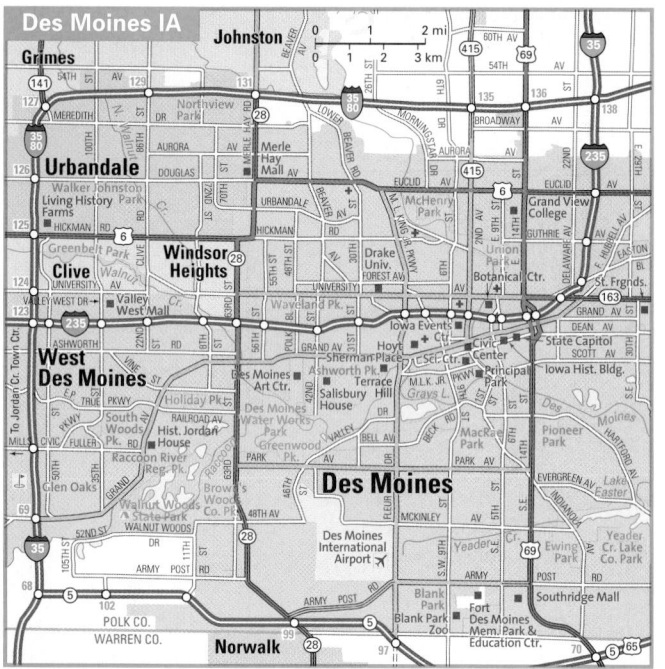

Des Moines IA

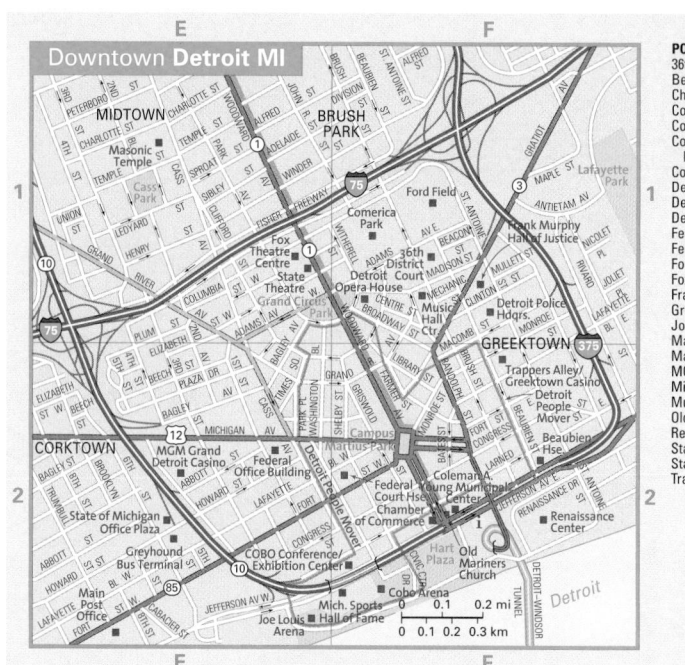

Downtown Detroit MI

Detroit MI

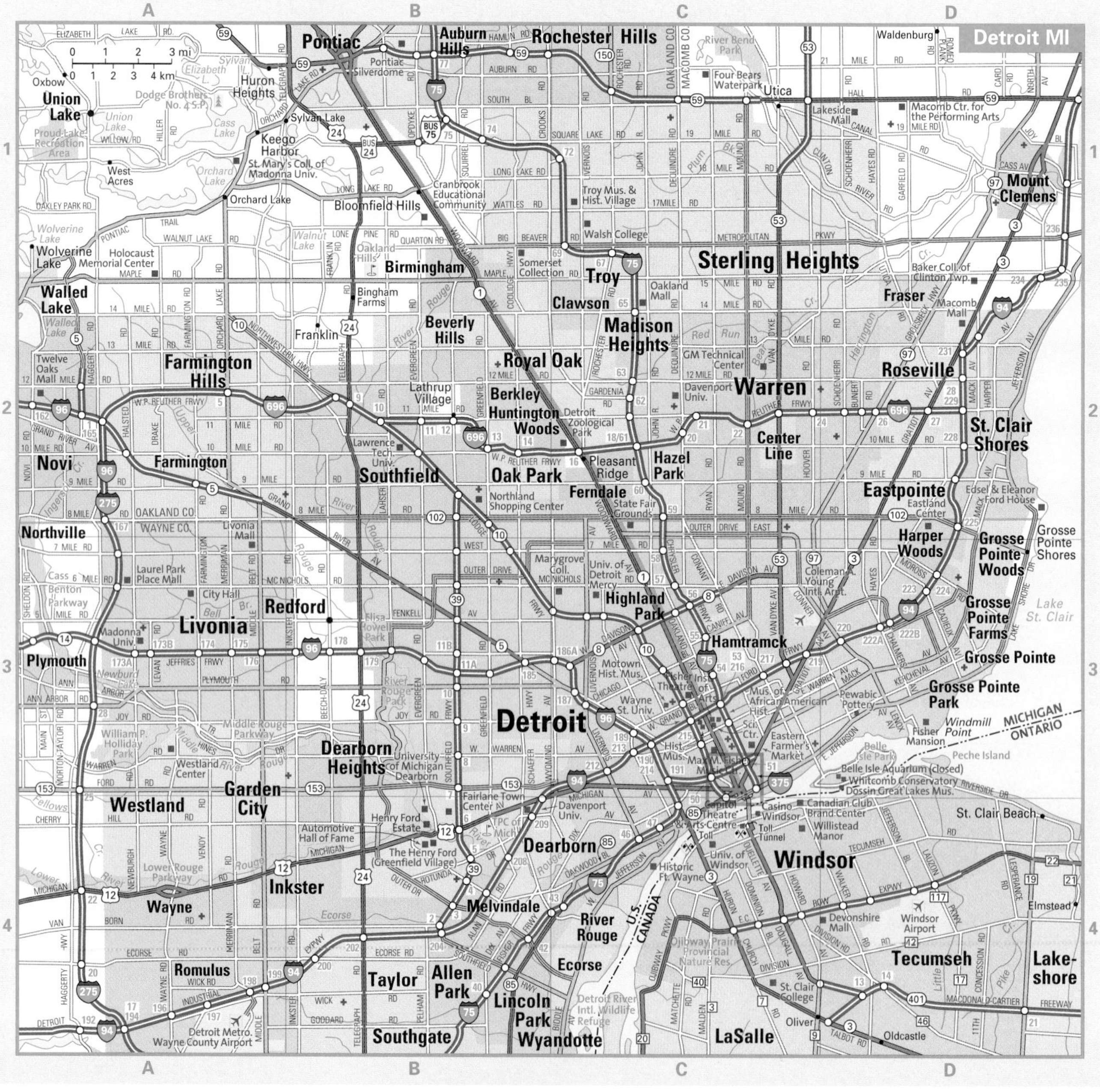

Entries in **bold black** indicate counties or parishes. Entries in **bold color** indicate cities with detailed inset maps.

Durand–Elizabeth Lake 211

Durand WI, 1968 67 E4
Durango CO, 13922 40 B4
Durant IA, 1677 87 F2
Durant MS, 2932 126 B1
Durant OK, 13549 59 F1
Durham CA, 5220 36 B1
Durham CT, 2773 149 E1
Durham NH, 9024 82 A4
Durham NC, 187035 112 C4
Durham OR, 1382 251 C3
Durham Co. NC, 223314 112 C4

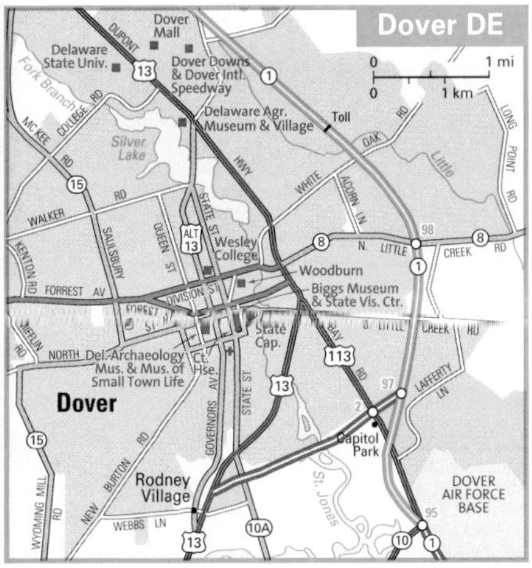

Dover DE
Dover Mall
Delaware State Univ.
Dover Downs & Dover Intl. Speedway
Delaware Agr. Museum & Village
Silver Lake
Wesley College
Woodburn
Biggs Museum & State Vis. Ctr.
Legislative Hall
State Cap.
Del. Archaeology Mus. & Mus. of Small Town Life
Old State House
Dover
Capitol Park
Rodney Village
St. Jones
DOVER AIR FORCE BASE
0 1 mi
0 1 km

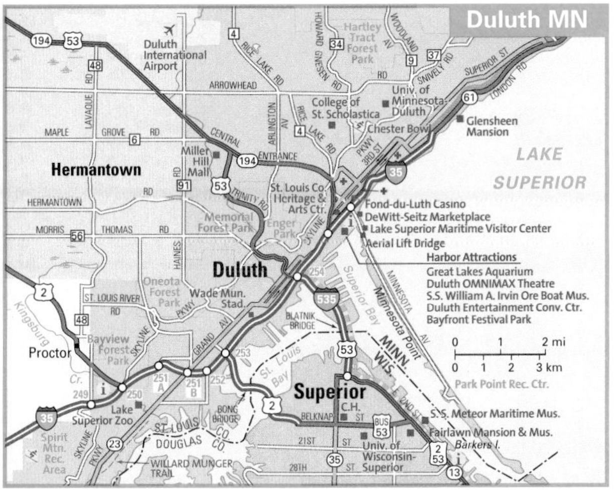

Duluth MN
Duluth International Airport
Hartley Tract Forest Park
Univ. of Minnesota-Duluth
College of St. Scholastica
Glensheen Mansion
Chester Bowl
Miller Hill Mall
Hermantown
LAKE SUPERIOR
St. Louis Co. Heritage & Arts Ctr.
Fond-du-Luth Casino
DeWitt-Seitz Marketplace
Lake Superior Maritime Visitor Center
Aerial Lift Bridge
Harbor Attractions
Great Lakes Aquarium
Duluth OMNIMAX Theatre
S.S. William A. Irvin Ore Boat Mus.
Duluth Entertainment Conv. Ctr.
Bayfront Festival Park
Duluth
Memorial Forest Park
Enger Park
Oneota Forest Park
Wade Mun. Stad.
Bayview Forest Park
Proctor
Lake Superior Zoo
Spirit Mtn. Rec. Area
Willard Munger Trail
Superior
S.S. Meteor Maritime Mus.
Fairlawn Mansion & Mus.
Barkers I.
Univ. of Wisconsin-Superior
Minnesota Point
Superior Bay
St. Louis Bay
MINN. WIS.
Park Point Rec. Ctr.
0 1 2 mi
0 1 2 3 km

Duryea PA, 4634 93 F2
Dushore PA, 663 93 E2
Duson LA, 1672 133 E2
Dustin OK, 452 51 F3
Dutchess Co. NY, 280150 148 C1
Dutch Neck NJ, 4400 147 D2
Dutton MT, 389 15 F2
Duval Co. FL, 778879 139 D2
Duval Co. TX, 13120 63 E2
Duvall WA, 4616 12 C3
Duxbury MA, 1426 151 E2
Duxbury VT, 325 81 E2
Dwaar Kill NY, 1400 148 A1
Dwarf KY, 550 111 D1
Dwight IL, 4363 88 C3
Dyer AR, 585 116 C1
Dyer IN, 13895 89 D2
Dyer TN, 2406 108 C4
Dyer Co. TN, 37279 108 C4
Dyersburg TN, 17452 108 C4
Dyersville IA, 4035 73 F4
Dyess AR, 515 118 B1
Dysart IA, 1303 87 E1

E

Eads CO, 747 42 A3
Eagan MN, 63557 235 D4
Eagar AZ, 4033 48 A4
Eagle CO, 3032 40 C1
Eagle ID, 11085 22 B4
Eagle NE, 1105 35 F4
Eagle WI, 1707 74 C3
Eagle Bend MN, 595 66 B1
Eagle Butte SD, 619 26 B2
Eagle Co. CO, 41659 40 C1
Eagle Grove IA, 3712 72 C4
Eagle Lake FL, 2496 140 C2
Eagle Lake ME, 600 85 D1
Eagle Lake MN, 1787 72 C1
Eagle Lake TX, 3664 61 F2
Eagle Mtn. UT, 2157 31 E4
Eagle Nest NM, 306 49 D1
Eagle Pass TX, 22413 60 B4
Eagle Pt. OR, 4797 28 C2
Eagle River MI, 20 65 F3
Eagle River WI, 1443 68 B2
Eagleton Vil. TN, 4883 110 C4
Eagleville PA, 4458 146 C2
Eagleville TN, 464 109 F4
Earle AR, 3036 118 A1
Earlham IA, 1298 86 C2
Earlimart CA, 6583 45 D4
Earlington KY, 1649 109 E2
Earlsboro OK, 633 51 F3
Earlville IL, 1778 88 C2
Earlville IA, 900 73 F4
Earlville NY, 791 79 E4
Earlville PA, 800 146 B2
Early IA, 605 72 A4
Early TX, 2588 59 D4
Early Co. GA, 12354 128 C4
Earlysville VA, 750 102 C4
Earth TX, 1109 50 A4
Easley SC, 17754 121 E2
E. Alton IL, 6830 98 A3
E. Arcadia NC, 524 123 E3
E. Arlington VT, 750 81 D4
E. Atlantic Beach NY, 2257 241 G5
E. Aurora NY, 6673 78 B4
E. Bank WV, 933 101 F4
E. Barre VT, 2136 81 E2
E. Barrington NH, 400 81 F4
E. Baton Rouge Par. LA, 412852 134 A1
E. Bend NC, 659 112 A3
E. Berlin PA, 1365 103 E1
E. Bernard TX, 1729 61 F2
E. Bernstadt KY, 774 110 C2
E. Bethel MN, 10941 67 D3
E. Blackstone MA, 1600 150 C2
E. Brady PA, 1038 92 A3
E. Brewster MA, 850 151 F3
E. Brewton AL, 2496 135 F1
E. Bridgewater MA, 4000 151 D2
E. Brookfield MA, 1410 150 B2
E. Brooklyn CT, 1473 150 B3
E. Brunswick NJ, 46756 147 E1
E. Butler PA, 679 92 A3
E. Camden AR, 902 117 E4
E. Canton OH, 1629 91 E3
E. Carbon UT, 1393 39 F1
E. Carroll Par. LA, 9421 126 A2
Eastchester NY, 18564 148 B3
E. Chicago IN, 32414 89 D2
E. Cleveland OH, 27217 91 E2
E. Dennis MA, 3299 151 F3
E. Douglas MA, 2319 150 C2
E. Dublin GA, 2484 129 E2
E. Dubuque IL, 1995 73 F4
E. Dundee IL, 2955 203 A2
E. Ellijay GA, 707 120 C2
E. End AR, 5623 117 E2
E. Falmouth MA, 6615 151 E4
E. Feliciana Par. LA, 21360 134 A1
E. Flat Rock NC, 4151 121 E1
E. Freehold NJ, 4936 147 E2
E. Freetown MA, 1200 151 D3
E. Gaffney SC, 3349 121 F1
E. Galesburg IL, 839 88 A3
Eastgate WA, 4558 262 B3
E. Glacier Park MT, 396 15 D2
E. Glastonbury CT, 1400 149 E1
E. Glenville NY, 6064 94 B1
E. Grand Forks MN, 7501 19 E2
E. Grand Rapids MI, 10764 215 B2
E. Greenbush NY, 4085 188 E3
E. Greenville PA, 3103 146 B1
E. Greenwich RI, 4300 150 C3
E. Gull Lake MN, 978 64 A4
E. Haddam CT, 550 149 E1
Eastham MA, 1100 151 F3
E. Hampton CT, 2254 149 E1
Easthampton MA, 15994 150 A1
E. Hampton NY, 1334 149 F3
E. Hanover NJ, 9900 148 A3
E. Hardwick VT, 300 81 E2
E. Hartford CT, 49575 150 A3
E. Harwich MA, 4744 151 F3
E. Haven CT, 28189 149 D2
E. Helena MT, 1642 15 E4
E. Highland Park VA, 12488 254 B1
E. Holden ME, 475 83 D1
E. Hope ID, 200 14 B2
E. Ithaca NY, 2192 79 D4
E. Jordan MI, 2507 69 F3
Eastlake OH, 20255 91 E2
Eastland TX, 3769 59 D3
Eastland Co. TX, 18297 59 D3
E. Lansdowne PA, 2586 248 B3
E. Lansing MI, 46525 76 A4
E. Lebanon ME, 650 82 A4
E. Liverpool OH, 13089 91 F3
E. Longmeadow MA, 14100 150 A2
E. Los Angeles CA, 124283 228 D3
Eastman GA, 5440 129 E3
E. Marion MA, 550 151 E3
E. Marion NY, 756 149 E2
E. McKeesport PA, 2343 250 D3
E. Meadow NY, 37461 148 C4
E. Middlebury VT, 650 81 D3
E. Middletown NY, 5000 148 A1
E. Millcreek UT, 21385 257 B2
E. Millinocket ME, 1701 85 D4
E. Moline IL, 20333 88 A2
E. Montpelier VT, 450 81 E2
E. Moriches NY, 4550 149 E4
E. Mtn. TX, 580 124 B2
E. Naples FL, 23000 142 C2
E. Nassau NY, 571 94 B1
E. Newark NJ, 2377 240 B3
E. Newnan GA, 1305 128 C1
E. Northport ME, 350 82 C2
E. Northport NY, 20845 148 C3
E. Olympia WA, 900 12 C4
Easton CA, 1966 44 C3
Easton CT, 750 148 C2
Easton ME, 475 85 E2
Easton MD, 11708 145 D3
Easton PA, 26263 93 F3
Easton TX, 524 124 B2
E. Orange NJ, 69824 148 A4
E. Orleans MA, 1800 151 F3
Eastover NC, 1376 123 D1
Eastover SC, 830 122 B4
E. Palatka FL, 1707 139 D3
E. Palestine OH, 4917 91 F3
E. Palo Alto CA, 29506 259 D5
E. Patchogue NY, 20824 149 D4
E. Peoria IL, 22638 88 B3
E. Petersburg PA, 4450 146 A2
E. Pittsburgh PA, 2017 250 D2
Eastpoint FL, 2158 137 D3
E. Point GA, 39595 120 C4
Eastpointe MI, 34077 210 D2
Eastport ME, 1640 83 F1
Eastport NY, 1454 149 E3
E. Poultney VT, 400 81 D3
E. Prairie MO, 3227 108 C2
E. Prospect PA, 678 103 E1
E. Providence RI, 48688 150 C3
E. Quincy CA, 2398 36 C1
E. Quogue NY, 4265 149 E3
E. Randolph NY, 630 92 B1
E. Ridge TN, 20640 120 B2
E. Rochester NY, 6650 254 G2
E. Rockaway NY, 10414 147 F1
E. Rockingham NC, 3885 122 C2
E. Rutherford NJ, 8716 240 C2
E. St. Louis IL, 31542 98 A3
E. Sandwich MA, 3720 151 E3
E. Setauket NY, 15931 149 D3
E. Shoreham NY, 5809 149 D3
Eastsound WA, 750 12 C1
E. Spencer NC, 1755 112 A4
E. Stroudsburg PA, 9888 93 F3
E. Swanzey NH, 475 95 D1
E. Syracuse NY, 3178 265 B2
E. Tawakoni TX, 775 59 F2
E. Tawas MI, 2951 76 B1
E. Texas PA, 6000 146 B1
E. Thermopolis WY, 274 24 C4
E. Troy WI, 3564 74 C4
E. Vassalboro ME, 300 82 C2
Eastview MD, 650 144 B1
Eastview TN, 618 119 D2
E. Village CT, 1500 149 D2
Eastville VA, 203 114 B3
E. Wareham MA, 1700 151 E3
E. Washington PA, 1930 92 A4
E. Wenatchee WA, 5757 13 D3
E. Wilton ME, 550 82 B2
E. Winthrop ME, 650 82 B2
Eastwood LA, 3374 125 D2
E. York PA, 8782 275 F1
Eaton CO, 2690 33 E4
Eaton IN, 1603 90 A4
Eaton OH, 8133 100 B1
Eaton Co. MI, 103655 76 A4
Eaton Estates OH, 1409 91 D2
Eaton Park FL, 3000 266 E2
Eaton Rapids MI, 5330 76 A4
Eatons Neck NY, 1388 148 C3
Eatonton GA, 6764 129 E1
Eatontown NJ, 14008 147 E2
Eatonville FL, 2432 246 C1
Eatonville WA, 2012 12 C4
Eau Claire MI, 656 89 F1
Eau Claire WI, 61704 67 F4
Eau Claire Co. WI, 93142 67 F4
Ebensburg PA, 3091 92 B4
Eccles WV, 700 111 F1
Echo OR, 650 21 E1
Echols Co. GA, 3754 138 B1
Eclectic AL, 1037 128 A2
Economy PA, 9363 92 A3
Ecorse MI, 11229 210 C4
Ecru MS, 947 118 C3
Ector TX, 600 59 F1
Ector Co. TX, 121123 57 F3
Edcouch TX, 3342 63 E4
Eddington ME, 700 83 D1
Eddy Co. NM, 51658 57 E3
Eddy Co. ND, 2757 19 D3
Eddystone PA, 2442 248 A4
Eddyville IA, 1064 87 D2
Eddyville KY, 2350 109 D2
Eden ID, 411 31 D1
Eden MD, 793 103 F4
Eden NY, 3579 78 A4
Eden NC, 15908 112 B3
Eden TX, 2561 58 C4
Eden WI, 687 74 C2
Eden WY, 388 32 A2
Eden Prairie MN, 54901 235 A4
Edenton NC, 5394 113 F4
Eden Valley MN, 866 66 B3
Edenville NY, 650 148 A2
Edgar NE, 539 35 E4
Edgar WI, 1386 68 A4
Edgar Co. IL, 19704 99 D1
Edgard LA, 2637 134 B3
Edgartown MA, 1100 151 E4
Edgecliff Vil. TX, 2550 207 A3
Edgecombe Co. NC, 55606 113 E4
Edgefield SC, 4449 121 F4
Edgefield Co. SC, 24595 121 F4
Edgeley ND, 637 19 D4
Edgemere MD, 9248 144 C2
Edgemont SD, 867 25 F4
Edgemoor DE, 5992 146 B4
Edgerton KS, 1440 96 B3
Edgerton MN, 1033 27 F4
Edgerton MO, 533 96 B2
Edgerton OH, 2117 90 A2
Edgerton WI, 4933 74 B3
Edgerton WY, 169 25 D4
Edgewater AL, 730 195 D2
Edgewater CO, 5445 209 B3
Edgewater FL, 18668 139 E4
Edgewater NJ, 7677 240 D2
Edgewater Park NJ, 8400 147 D3
Edgewood FL, 1901 246 C3
Edgewood IN, 1988 89 F4
Edgewood IA, 923 73 F4
Edgewood KY, 9400 204 B3
Edgewood MD, 23378 145 D1
Edgewood NM, 1893 48 C3
Edgewood OH, 4762 91 F1
Edgewood PA, 3311 250 C2
Edgewood TX, 1348 124 A2
Edgewood WA, 9089 262 B5
Edina MN, 47425 67 D4
Edina MO, 1233 87 F4
Edinboro PA, 6950 92 A1
Edinburg IL, 1135 98 B1
Edinburg NJ, 900 147 D2
Edinburg ND, 252 19 E2
Edinburg TX, 48465 63 E4
Edinburg VA, 813 102 C3
Edinburgh IN, 4505 99 F2
Edison GA, 1340 128 C4
Edison NJ, 97687 147 E1
Edisto Beach SC, 641 130 C2
Edmond OK, 68315 51 E2
Edmonds WA, 39515 12 C3
Edmondson AR, 513 118 B1
Edmonson Co. KY, 11644 109 F2
Edmonston MD, 959 270 E2
Edmonton KY, 1586 110 A2
Edmore MI, 1244 76 A2
Edmore ND, 256 19 D2
Edmunds Co. SD, 4367 27 D2
Edmundson MO, 840 256 B1
Edna KS, 423 106 A2
Edna TX, 5899 61 F3
Edon OH, 898 90 A2
Edwards CO, 8257 40 C1
Edwards MS, 1347 126 A2
Edwardsburg MI, 1147 89 F1
Edwards Co. IL, 6971 99 D4
Edwards Co. KS, 3449 43 D4
Edwards Co. TX, 2162 60 B2
Edwardsville IL, 21491 98 B3
Edwardsville KS, 4146 96 B2
Edwardsville PA, 4984 261 A1
Effingham IL, 12384 98 C2
Effingham KS, 588 96 A1
Effingham Co. GA, 37535 130 B2
Effingham Co. IL, 34264 98 C2
Effort PA, 900 93 F3
Egan SD, 265 27 F3
Egg Harbor City NJ, 4545 147 D4
Egypt PA, 2700 189 A1
Ehrenberg AZ, 1357 53 F3
Ehrhardt SC, 614 130 C1
Ekalaka MT, 410 25 F1
Elaine AR, 865 118 A3
Elam PA, 2000 146 B3
Elba AL, 4185 128 A4
Elba NY, 696 78 B3
Elberfeld IN, 636 99 E4
Elberta AL, 552 135 F2
Elberta MI, 457 69 E4
Elberta UT, 278 39 E1
Elbert Co. CO, 19872 41 E2
Elbert Co. GA, 20511 121 E3
Elberton GA, 4743 121 E3
Elbow Lake MN, 1275 27 F1
Elbridge NY, 1103 79 D3
Elburn IL, 2756 88 C1
El Cajon CA, 94869 53 D4
El Campo TX, 10945 61 F3
El Cenizo TX, 3545 63 D2
El Centro CA, 37835 53 E4
El Cerrito CA, 4590 229 H4
El Cerrito CA, 23171 259 B2
Eldersburg MD, 27741 144 B1
Eldon IA, 998 87 E3
Eldon MO, 4895 97 E4
Eldon OK, 991 106 B4
Eldora IA, 3035 73 D4
El Dorado AR, 21930 125 E1
Eldorado IL, 4534 109 D1
El Dorado KS, 12057 43 F4
Eldorado OK, 527 50 C4
Eldorado TX, 1951 60 B1
El Dorado Co. CA, 156299 36 C2
Eldorado Sprs. CO, 557 209 A1
El Dorado Sprs. MO, 3775 96 C4
Eldred PA, 858 92 C1
Eldridge IA, 4159 88 A2
Eleanor WV, 1345 101 E3
Electra TX, 3168 59 D1
Electric City WA, 922 13 E2
Eleele HI, 2040 152 B1
Elephant Butte NM, 1390 56 B2
Eleva WI, 635 67 F4
Elfers FL, 13161 140 B2
Elfrida AZ, 475 55 E4
Elgin AZ, 309 55 D4
Elgin IL, 94487 88 C1
Elgin IA, 676 73 E3
Elgin MN, 826 73 E1
Elgin NE, 735 35 E2
Elgin ND, 659 18 B4
Elgin OK, 1210 51 D4
Elgin OR, 1654 21 F1
Elgin SC, 806 122 A3
Elgin SC, 2426 122 B2
Elgin TX, 5700 61 E1
El Granada CA, 5724 259 B5
Elida OH, 1917 90 B3
Elihu KY, 650 110 B2
Elizabeth CO, 1434 41 E2
Elizabeth IL, 682 74 A4
Elizabeth LA, 574 133 E1
Elizabeth NJ, 120568 148 A4
Elizabeth PA, 1609 92 A4
Elizabeth WV, 994 101 F2
Elizabeth City NC, 17188 113 F3
Elizabeth Lake CA, 750 52 C2

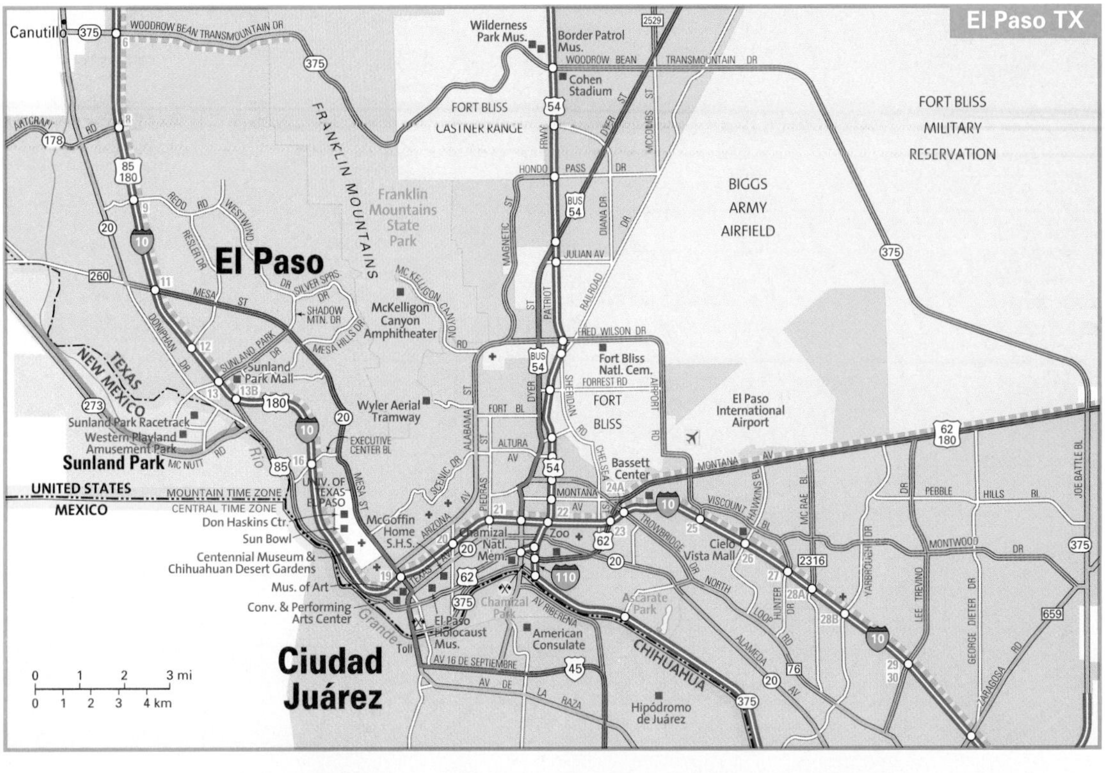

El Paso TX
Canutillo
Wilderness Park Mus.
Border Patrol Mus.
Cohen Stadium
FORT BLISS CASTNER RANGE
FRANKLIN MOUNTAINS
Franklin Mountains State Park
FORT BLISS MILITARY RESERVATION
BIGGS ARMY AIRFIELD
El Paso
McKelligon Canyon Amphitheater
Sunland Park Mall
TEXAS
NEW MEXICO
Sunland Park Racetrack
Western Playland Amusement Park
Sunland Park
Wyler Aerial Tramway
Fort Bliss Natl. Cem.
FORT BLISS
El Paso International Airport
Bassett Center
UNITED STATES
MEXICO
MOUNTAIN TIME ZONE
CENTRAL TIME ZONE
Don Haskins Ctr.
Sun Bowl
UNIV. OF TEXAS EL PASO
McGoffin Home S.H.S.
Centennial Museum & Chihuahuan Desert Gardens
Mus. of Art
Conv. & Performing Arts Center
Chamizal Natl. Mem.
Zoo
Cielo Vista Mall
Chamizal Park
El Paso Holocaust Mus.
American Consulate
Ascarate Park
Rio Grande
Ciudad Juárez
Hipódromo de Juárez
0 1 2 3 mi
0 1 2 3 4 km

212 Elizabethton–Ewa Beach

Figures after entries indicate population, page number, and grid reference.

Elizabethton TN, 13372......111 E3
Elizabethtown IL, 348......109 D1
Elizabethtown KY, 22542......110 A1
Elizabethtown NY, 750......81 D2
Elizabethtown PA, 11887......93 E4
Elizabethville PA, 1344......93 D4
El Jebel CO, 4488......40 C2
Elkader IA, 1465......73 F3
Elk City OK, 10510......50 C3
Elk Co. KS, 3261......43 F4
Elk Co. PA, 35112......92 B2
Elk Grove CA, 75175......36 C3
Elkhart IN, 51874......89 F2
Elkhart KS, 2233......50 A1
Elkhart TX, 1215......124 A4
Elkhart Co. IN, 182791......89 F2
Elkhorn CA, 1591......236 E2
Elk Horn IA, 649......86 B2
Elkhorn NE, 6062......35 F3
Elkhorn WI, 7305......74 C4
Elkhorn City KY, 1060......111 E1

Elkin NC, 4109......112 A3
Elkins AR, 1251......106 C4
Elkins WV, 7032......102 A3
Elkland PA, 1786......93 D1
Elk Mound WI, 785......67 E4
Elko NV, 16708......30 B4
Elk Pt. SD, 1714......35 F1
Elk Rapids MI, 1642......69 F4
Elkridge MD, 22042......144 C2
Elk Ridge UT, 1838......39 E1
Elk River MN, 16447......66 C3
Elk Run Hts. IA, 1052......73 E4
Elkton KY, 1984......109 E2
Elkton MD, 11893......145 E1
Elkton MI, 863......76 C2
Elkton OR, 470......27 A3
Elkton TN, 510......119 F2
Elkton VA, 2042......102 C3
Elkview WV, 1182......101 F3
El Lago TX, 3075......132 B3
Ellaville GA, 1609......129 D3

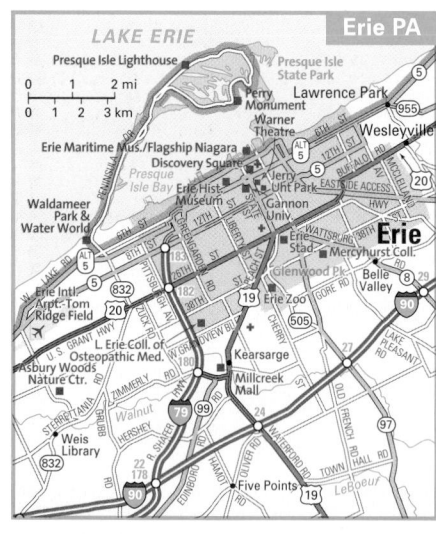

Erie PA

Ellenboro NC, 479......121 F1
Ellenboro WV, 373......101 F2
Ellendale DE, 327......145 E3
Ellendale MN, 590......72 C2
Ellendale ND, 1559......27 D1
Ellensburg WA, 15414......13 D4
Ellenton FL, 3142......266 B4
Ellenville NY, 4130......94 A3
Ellerbe NC, 1021......122 C2
Ellerslie MD, 600......102 C1
Ellettsville IN, 5078......99 F2
Ellicott NY, 2200......78 B4
Ellicott City MD, 56397......144 C2
Ellijay GA, 1584......120 C2
Ellington CT, 1300......150 A3
Ellington MO, 1045......108 A2
Ellinwood KS, 2164......43 D3
Elliott Co. KY, 6748......101 D4
Ellis KS, 1873......42 C2
Ellis Co. KS, 27507......43 D2
Ellis Co. OK, 4075......50 C2
Ellis Co. TX, 111360......59 F3
Ellisport WA, 1200......262 A4
Ellisville MS, 3465......126 C4
Ellisville MO, 9104......256 A4
Elloree SC, 742......122 B4
Ellsworth IA, 531......72 C4
Ellsworth KS, 2965......43 E2
Ellsworth ME, 6456......83 D2
Ellsworth MI, 483......69 F3
Ellsworth MN, 540......27 F4
Ellsworth PA, 1083......92 A4
Ellsworth WI, 2909......67 E4
Ellsworth Co. KS, 6525......43 E3
Ellwood City PA, 8688......91 F3
Elma IA, 598......73 D3
Elma NY, 2491......78 B3
Elma WA, 3049......12 B4
Elm City NC, 1113......113 D4
Elm Creek NE, 894......35 D4
Elmendorf TX, 664......61 D3
Elmer NJ, 1384......145 F1
Elm Grove WI, 6249......234 B2
Elmhurst IL, 42762......89 D1
El Mirage AZ, 7609......249 A1
Elmira NY, 30940......93 D1
Elmira Hts. NY, 4170......93 D1
Elm Mott TX, 1200......59 E4
Elmo UT, 368......39 F2
Elmont NY, 32657......148 C4
Elmont VA, 500......113 E1
El Monte CA, 115965......228 E2
Elmore MN, 735......72 C2
Elmore OH, 1426......90 C2

Elmore City OK, 756......51 E4
Elmore Co. AL, 56045......59 F3
Elmore Co. ID, 29130......22 B4
Elm Sprs. AR, 1044......106 C3
Elmvale CT, 1300......150 B3
Elmwood IL, 1945......88 A3
Elmwood NE, 668......35 F4
Elmwood WI, 841......67 E4
Elmwood Park IL, 25405......203 D4
Elmwood Park NJ, 18925......240 C1
Elmwood Place OH, 2681......204 B3
Elnora IN, 721......99 E3
Elnora NY, 2700......94 B3
Elon NC, 6738......112 C4
Eloy AZ, 10375......54 C2
El Paso IL, 2695......88 B3
El Paso Co. CO, 516929......41 E2
El Paso Co. TX, 679622......56 C4
El Portal FL, 2505......233 B4
El Prado NM, 400......49 D1
El Reno OK, 16212......51 E3
El Rio CA, 6193......52 B2
El Rito NM, 425......48 C2
El Sobrante CA, 12260......259 C1
Elton LA, 1261......133 E2
Elvaton MD, 3500......193 C5
Elverson PA, 959......146 B2
Elwood IL, 1620......89 D2
Elwood IN, 9737......89 F4
Elwood KS, 1145......96 B1
Elwood NE, 761......34 C4
Elwood NJ, 1392......147 E4
Elwood UT, 678......31 E3
Ely IA, 1149......87 E1
Ely MN, 3724......64 C2
Ely NV, 4041......38 B2
Elyria OH, 55953......91 D2
Elysburg PA, 2067......93 E3
Elysian MN, 486......72 C1
Emanuel Co. GA, 21837......129 F3
Emerado ND, 510......19 E2
Emerald Isle NC, 3488......115 D4
Emerson GA, 1092......120 C3
Emerson NE, 817......35 F2
Emerson NJ, 7197......148 B3
Emery SD, 439......27 E4
Emery UT, 308......39 E2
Emery Co. UT, 10860......39 F2
Emery Mills ME, 350......82 A4
Emeryville CA, 6882......259 C2
Emigsville PA, 2467......103 E1
Emily MN, 847......64 B4
Eminence KY, 2231......100 A4
Eminence MO, 548......107 F2
Emlenton PA, 784......92 A2
Emmaus PA, 11313......146 B1
Emmet Co. IA, 11027......72 B3
Emmet Co. MI, 31437......70 B3
Emmetsburg IA, 3958......72 B3
Emmett ID, 5490......22 B4
Emmitsburg MD, 2290......103 D1
Emmonak AK, 767......154 B2
Emmons Co. ND, 4331......18 C4
Emmorton MD, 4000......145 D1
Emory TX, 1021......124 A4
Emory VA, 2266......111 F2
Empire CO, 355......41 D1
Empire LA, 2211......134 C4
Empire NV, 499......29 E4
Empire City OK, 734......51 E4
Emporia KS, 26760......43 F3
Emporia VA, 5665......113 E3
Emporium PA, 2526......92 C2
Emsworth PA, 2598......250 A1
Encampment WY, 443......33 D3
Encinal TX, 629......60 C4
Encinitas CA, 58014......53 D4
Enderlin ND, 947......19 E4
Endicott NY, 13038......93 E1
Endicott WA, 621......13 F4
Endwell NY, 11706......93 E1
Energy IL, 1175......108 C1
Enfield CT, 8125......150 A2
Enfield IL, 625......99 D4
Enfield NH, 1698......81 E3
Enfield NC, 2347......113 E4
Enfield Ctr. NH, 600......81 E3
England AR, 2972......117 E2
Englewood CO, 31727......41 E1
Englewood FL, 16196......140 C4
Englewood NJ, 26203......148 B3
Englewood OH, 12235......100 B1
Englewood TN, 1590......120 C1
Englewood Beach FL, 1000......140 C4
Englewood Cliffs NJ, 5322......240 D1
English IN, 673......99 F4
Englishtown NJ, 1764......147 E2
Enhaut PA, 2809......218 C2
Enid OK, 47045......51 E1
Enigma GA, 869......129 E4
Enka NC, 1500......121 E1

Ennis MT, 840......23 E2
Ennis TX, 18513......59 F3
Enoch UT, 3467......39 D4
Enochville NC, 2851......122 B1
Enola PA, 5627......218 A1
Enon OH, 2638......100 C1
Enoree SC, 700......121 F2
Enosburg Falls VT, 1473......81 D1
Ensley FL, 18752......135 F2
Ensor NY, 500......109 E1
Enterprise AL, 21178......128 B4
Enterprise KS, 836......43 F2
Enterprise MS, 474......127 D3
Enterprise OR, 1895......22 A2
Enterprise UT, 1285......38 C4
Enterprise WV, 939......102 A2
Entiat WA, 957......13 D3
Enumclaw WA, 11116......12 C3
Ephraim UT, 4505......39 E2
Ephrata PA, 13213......146 A2
Ephrata WA, 6808......13 E3
Epping NH, 1673......81 F4
Epps LA, 1153......125 F2
Epworth IA, 1428......73 F4
Epworth Hts. OH, 3300......204 C1
Equality IL, 721......109 D1
Erath LA, 2187......133 F3
Erath Co. TX, 33001......59 D3
Erda UT, 2473......31 E4
Erick OK, 1023......50 C3
Erie CO, 6291......209 B1
Erie IL, 1589......88 A2
Erie KS, 1211......106 A1
Erie PA, 103717......92 A1
Erie Co. NY, 950265......78 B4
Erie Co. OH, 79551......91 D2
Erie Co. PA, 280843......92 A1
Erin TN, 1490......109 E3
Erlanger KY, 16676......100 B2
Erwin NC, 4537......123 D1
Erwin TN, 5610......111 E4
Erwinville LA, 700......134 A2
Escalante UT, 818......39 E4
Escalon CA, 5963......36 C4

Escambia Co. AL, 38440......136 A1
Escambia Co. FL, 294410......135 F1
Escanaba MI, 13140......69 D2
Escatawpa MS, 3566......195 C1
Escobares TX, 1954......63 D4
Escondido CA, 133559......53 D4
Esko MN, 1300......64 C4
Eskridge KS, 589......43 F2
Esmeralda Co. NV, 971......37 E4
Espanola NM, 9688......49 D2
Espanong NJ, 2700......148 A3
Esparto CA, 1858......36 B2
Espy PA, 1428......93 E3
Essex CT, 2573......149 E2
Essex IA, 886......86 A3
Essex MD, 39078......144 C2
Essex MA, 1426......151 F1
Essex Co. MA, 723419......151 F1
Essex Co. NJ, 793633......148 A3
Essex Co. NY, 38851......80 C3
Essex Co. VT, 6459......81 F1
Essex Co. VA, 9989......113 E2
Essex Fells NJ, 2162......240 A3
Essex Jct. VT, 8591......81 D2
Essexville MI, 3766......76 B2
Estacada OR, 2371......20 C2
Estancia NM, 1584......49 D4
Estelle LA, 15880......239 C2
Estelline SD, 675......27 F3
Estell Manor NJ, 1585......104 C3
Ester AK, 1680......154 C2
Estero FL, 9503......142 C1
Estherville IA, 6656......72 B2
Estherwood LA, 807......133 E2
Estill SC, 2425......130 B2
Estill Co. KY, 15307......110 C1
Estill Sprs. TN, 2152......120 A1
Estral Beach MI, 486......90 C1
Ethan SD, 330......27 E4
Ethel MS, 452......126 C1
Ethete WY, 1455......32 B1
Ethridge TN, 536......119 E1
Etna CA, 781......28 C1

Etna PA, 3924......250 C1
Etna Green IN, 663......89 F2
Etowah NC, 2766......121 E1
Etowah TN, 3663......120 C1
Etowah Co. AL, 103459......120 A3
Ettrick VA, 5627......113 E2
Ettrick WI, 521......73 F1
Eubank KY, 358......110 B1
Euclid OH, 52717......91 E2
Eudora AR, 2819......126 A1
Eudora KS, 4307......96 B3
Eufaula AL, 13908......128 B3
Eufaula OK, 2639......116 A1
Eugene OR, 137893......20 B2
Euharlee GA, 3208......120 B3
Euless TX, 46005......207 C2
Eunice LA, 11499......133 E2
Eunice NM, 2562......57 F3
Eupora MS, 2326......118 C4
Eureka CA, 26128......28 A4
Eureka IL, 4871......88 B3
Eureka KS, 2914......43 F4
Eureka MO, 7676......98 A3
Eureka MT, 1017......14 C1
Eureka NV, 550......38 A1
Eureka SD, 1101......27 D1
Eureka UT, 766......39 E1
Eureka Co. NV, 1651......30 B4
Eureka Mill SC, 1737......122 A4
Eureka Sprs. AR, 2278......106 C2
Eustace TX, 798......59 F3
Eustis FL, 15106......140 C1
Eustis NE, 464......34 C4
Eutaw AL, 1878......127 E2
Eutawville SC, 315......122 A4
Eva AL, 491......119 F3
Evadale TX, 1430......132 C2
Evangeline Par. LA, 35434......133 E1
Evans CO, 9514......33 E4
Evans GA, 17727......121 F4
Evans WV, 750......101 F3
Evans City PA, 2009......92 A3
Evans Co. GA, 10495......130 B3
Evansdale IA, 4526......73 E4
Evans Mills NY, 619......79 E1
Evanston IL, 74239......203 D2
Evanston WY, 11507......31 F4
Evansville IN, 121582......99 D4
Evansville MN, 566......66 A2
Evansville WI, 4039......74 B4
Evansville WY, 2255......33 D1
Evaro MT, 329......15 D4
Evart MI, 1738......75 F1
Evarts KY, 1101......111 D2
Eveleth MN, 3865......64 C3
Evendale OH, 3090......204 B2
Evening Shade AR, 465......107 F4
Everett MA, 38037......197 C1
Everett PA, 1905......102 C1
Everett WA, 91488......12 C2
Everglades City FL, 479......143 D2
Evergreen AL, 3630......127 F4
Evergreen CO, 9216......41 D1
Evergreen MT, 6215......15 D2
Evergreen Park IL, 20821......203 D5
Everly IA, 647......72 A3
Everman TX, 5836......207 B3
Everson PA, 842......92 A4
Everson WA, 2035......12 C1
Evesboro NJ, 2400......147 D3
Ewa Beach HI, 14650......152 A3

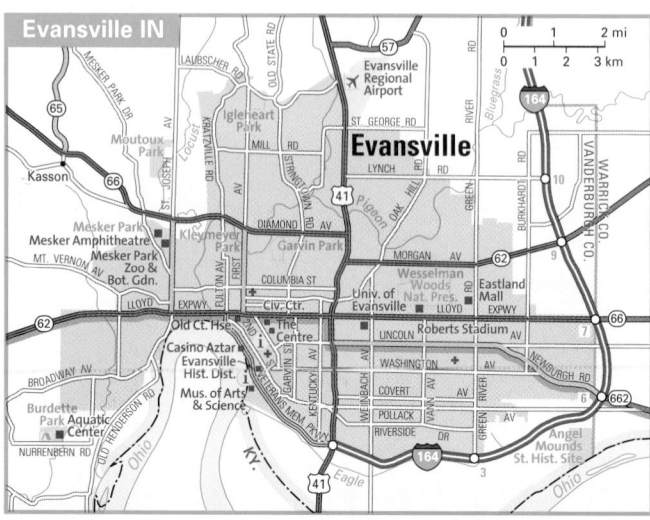

Eugene OR

Evansville IN

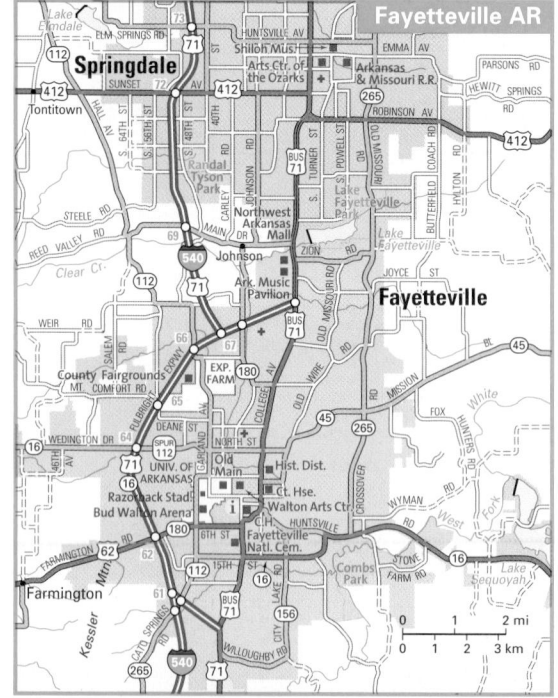

Fargo ND

Fayetteville AR

Entries in **bold black** indicate counties or parishes. Entries in **bold color** indicate cities with detailed inset maps.

Ewa Villages–Fogelsville 213

Fayetteville NC

Flagstaff AZ

Flint MI

Fort Collins CO

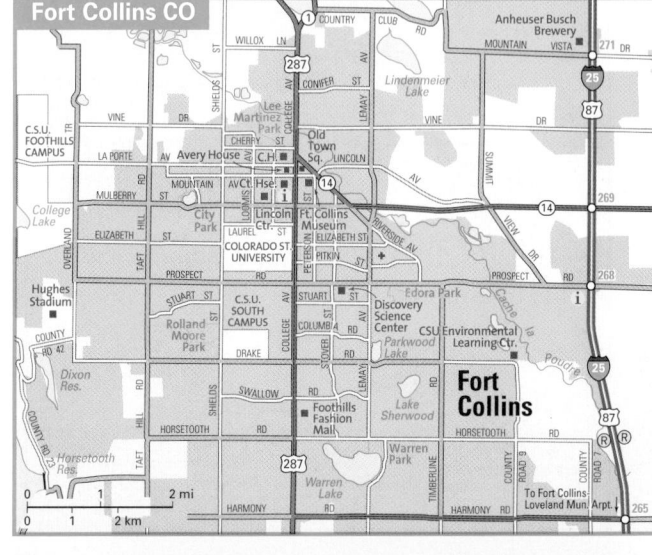

214 Folcroft–Franklin County

Figures after entries indicate population, page number, and grid reference.

Folcroft PA, 6978 ..... 248 B4	Ford City PA, 3451 ..... 92 A3	**Forest Co. PA,** 4946 ..... 92 B2	Forest View IL, 778 ..... 203 D5	Ft. Lupton CO, 6787 ..... 41 E1	Ft. Yukon AK, 595 ..... 154 C2	Framingham MA, 66910 ..... 150 C1
Foley AL, 7590 ..... 135 C2	**Ford Co. IL,** 14241 ..... 88 C4	**Forest Co. WI,** 10024 ..... 68 C2	Forestville CA, 2370 ..... 36 A3	Ft. Madison IA, 10715 ..... 87 F3	Fossil OR, 469 ..... 21 E2	Francesville IN, 905 ..... 89 C3
Foley MN, 2154 ..... 66 C2	**Ford Co. KS,** 32458 ..... 42 C4	Forestdale AL, 10509 ..... 195 E1	Forestville MD, 12707 ..... 271 F4	Ft. McKinley OH, 3989 ..... 208 D1	Fosston MN, 1575 ..... 19 F3	Francis UT, 698 ..... 31 F4
Folkston GA, 2178 ..... 139 D1	Fordland MO, 684 ..... 107 D2	Forestdale MA, 3992 ..... 151 E3	Forestville NY, 770 ..... 78 A4	Ft. Meade FL, 5691 ..... 140 C3	Foster Ctr. RI, 500 ..... 150 C3	Francisco IN, 543 ..... 99 E4
Follansbee WV, 3115 ..... 91 F4	Fordoche LA, 933 ..... 133 F2	Forest Dale VT, 800 ..... 81 D3	Forestville OH, 10978 ..... 100 B2	Ft. Mill SC, 7587 ..... 122 A2	Foster City CA, 28803 ..... 259 C4	Francis Creek WI, 681 ..... 75 D1
Folly Beach SC, 2116 ..... 131 D2	Fords NJ, 15032 ..... 240 A6	Forest Grove OR, 17708 ..... 20 B2	Forgan OK, 532 ..... 50 C1	Ft. Mitchell KY, 8089 ..... 204 A3	**Foster Co. ND,** 3759 ..... 19 D3	Franconia VA, 31907 ..... 144 B3
Folsom CA, 51884 ..... 36 C3	Fords Prairie WA, 1961 ..... 12 B4	Forest Grove PA, 3800 ..... 250 A1	Forked River NJ, 4914 ..... 147 E3	Ft. Montgomery NY, 1418 ..... 148 B3	Fostoria MI, 600 ..... 76 C3	Frankenmuth MI, 4838 ..... 76 B3
Folsom LA, 525 ..... 134 B2	Fordsville KY, 531 ..... 109 F1	Forest Hts. MD, 2585 ..... 270 D5	Forkland AL, 629 ..... 127 E2	Ft. Morgan CO, 11034 ..... 33 F4	Fostoria OH, 13931 ..... 90 C3	Frankford DE, 714 ..... 145 F4
Folsom NJ, 1972 ..... 147 D4	Fordville ND, 266 ..... 19 E2	Forest Hill LA, 456 ..... 133 E1	Forks WA, 3120 ..... 12 A2	*Ft. Myers FL, 48208* *142 C1*	Fouke AR, 814 ..... 124 C1	Frankford IL, 10391 ..... 89 E4
Folsom PA, 8072 ..... 248 A4	Fordyce AR, 4799 ..... 117 E4	Forest Hill TX, 12949 ..... 59 E2	Forman ND, 506 ..... 27 E1	Ft. Myers Beach FL, 6561 ..... 142 C1	Fountain CO, 15197 ..... 41 E2	Frankfort IN, 16662 ..... 89 C4
Fonda IA, 648 ..... 72 B4	Foreman AR, 1125 ..... 116 C4	Forest Hills FL, 989 ..... 139 D4	Forney TX, 5588 ..... 59 F2	Ft. Myers Shores FL, 5793 ..... 142 C1	Fountain NC, 533 ..... 113 E4	Frankfort KS, 855 ..... 43 F1
Fonda NY, 810 ..... 79 F3	Forest MS, 5987 ..... 126 C2	Forest Hills NY, 494 ..... 230 F2	Forrest IL, 1225 ..... 88 C3	Ft. Myers Villas FL, 11346 ..... 142 C1	Fountain City IN, 735 ..... 100 B1	*Frankfort KY, 27741* *100 B4*
Fond du Lac Co. WI, 97296 ..... 74 C2	Forest OH, 1488 ..... 90 C3	Forest Hills PA, 6831 ..... 250 C2	Forreston IL, 1469 ..... 88 B1	Ft. Payne AL, 12938 ..... 120 A1	Fountain Green UT, 945 ..... 39 E1	Frankfort NY, 2537 ..... 79 E3
Fontana CA, 128929 ..... 229 H2	Forest VA, 8006 ..... 112 C1	Forest Lake IL, 1530 ..... 203 B1	Forest City AR, 14774 ..... 118 A3	**Forrest Co. MS,** 72604 ..... 126 C4	Fountain Co. IN, 17954 ..... 89 D4	Frankfort OH, 1011 ..... 101 D2
Fontana WI, 1754 ..... 74 C3	Forest Acres SC, 10558 ..... 205 F1	Forest Lake MN, 15098 ..... 67 D3	Forsyth GA, 3776 ..... 129 D1	Ft. Pierce FL, 37516 ..... 141 E3	Fountain Hills AZ, 20235 ..... 54 C1	Franklin GA, 902 ..... 128 C1
Fontanelle IA, 692 ..... 86 B2	Forestbrook SC, 3391 ..... 123 D4	Forest Park FL, 12612 ..... 246 B1	Forsyth IL, 2434 ..... 98 C1	Ft. Pierre SD, 1991 ..... 26 C3	**Fountain Co. IN,** 17954 ..... 89 D4	Franklin ID, 641 ..... 31 E2
Foothill Farms CA, 17426 ..... 255 C1	Forest City IA, 4362 ..... 72 C3	Forest Park GA, 21447 ..... 190 D5	Forsyth MO, 1686 ..... 107 D3	Ft. Pillow TN, 650 ..... 108 B4	Fountain Inn SC, 6017 ..... 121 F2	Franklin IN, 19463 ..... 99 F2
Footville WI, 788 ..... 74 B4	Forest City NC, 7549 ..... 121 F1	Forest Park IL, 15688 ..... 203 D4	Forsyth MT, 1944 ..... 25 D1	Ft. Plain NY, 2288 ..... 79 F3	Fountain Lake AR, 409 ..... 117 D2	Franklin KY, 7996 ..... 109 F3
Ford City CA, 3512 ..... 52 B1	Forest City PA, 1855 ..... 93 F2	Forest Park OK, 1066 ..... 244 E2	**Forsyth Co. GA,** 98407 ..... 120 C3	Ft. Recovery OH, 1273 ..... 90 A4	Fountain Valley CA, 54978 ..... 228 E5	Franklin LA, 7660 ..... 133 F3

Fort Myers FL

Bayshore B1	Flamingo Bay A1	N. Ft. Myers B1	Sanibel A2
Bokeelia A1	Ft. Myers B1	Pine Island Ctr. A1	Tice B1
Bonita Sprs. B2	Ft. Myers Beach B2	Pineland A1	Truckland B2
Cape Coral A1	Ft. Myers Shores B1	Punta Rassa A2	
Captiva A2	Ft. Myers Villas B1	St. James City A2	
Estero B2	Matlacha A1	San Carlos Park B2	

Frankfort KY

Fresno CA

Fort Wayne IN

Forsyth Co. NC, 306067 ..... 112 A4	Ft. Salonga NY, 9634 ..... 148 C3	Four Corners OR, 13922 ..... 20 B2	Franklin LA, 8354 ..... 133 F3
Ft. Ann NY, 471 ..... 81 D4	Ft. Scott KS, 8297 ..... 106 B1	Four Corners TX, 2954 ..... 220 A3	Franklin ME, 300 ..... 83 D2
Ft. Ashby WV, 1354 ..... 102 C2	Ft. Shaw MT, 274 ..... 15 F3	Four Mile NJ, 900 ..... 147 D3	Franklin MA, 29560 ..... 150 C2
Ft. Atkinson WI, 11621 ..... 74 B3	Ft. Shawnee OH, 3855 ..... 90 B3	Four Oaks NC, 1424 ..... 123 D1	Franklin MI, 2937 ..... 210 B2
Ft. Belknap Agency MT, 1262 ..... 16 C2	Ft. Smith AR, 80268 ..... 116 C3	Four Seasons MO, 1493 ..... 97 D4	Franklin MN, 498 ..... 66 B4
Ft. Bend Co. TX, 354452 ..... 132 A4	Ft. Stockton TX, 7846 ..... 62 C2	Fowlblesburg MD, 600 ..... 144 C1	Franklin NE, 1026 ..... 43 D1
Ft. Benton MT, 1594 ..... 15 F2	Ft. Sumner NM, 1249 ..... 49 E4	Fowler CA, 3979 ..... 44 C3	Franklin NH, 8405 ..... 81 F4
Ft. Bragg CA, 7026 ..... 36 A1	Ft. Thomas KY, 16495 ..... 204 B3	Fowler CO, 1206 ..... 41 F3	Franklin NJ, 5160 ..... 148 A2
Ft. Branch IN, 2320 ..... 99 D4	Ft. Thompson SD, 1375 ..... 27 D3	Fowler IN, 2415 ..... 89 D3	Franklin OH, 11396 ..... 100 B1
Ft. Bridger WY, 400 ..... 32 A3	Ft. Totten ND, 952 ..... 19 D2	Fowler KS, 567 ..... 42 C4	Franklin PA, 7212 ..... 92 A2
Ft. Calhoun NE, 856 ..... 35 F3	Ft. Towson OK, 611 ..... 116 A3	Fowler MI, 1136 ..... 76 B3	Franklin TN, 41842 ..... 109 F4
Ft. Chiswell VA, 911 ..... 112 A4	Fortuna CA, 10497 ..... 28 A4	Fowlerville MI, 2972 ..... 76 B4	Franklin TX, 1470 ..... 59 F4
Ft. Cobb OK, 667 ..... 51 D3	Ft. Valley GA, 8005 ..... 129 D2	Foxboro MA, 5509 ..... 151 D2	Franklin VA, 8346 ..... 113 F3
Ft. Collins CO, 118652 ..... *33 E4*	Fortville IN, 3444 ..... 99 F1	Fox Chapel PA, 5436 ..... 250 C1	Franklin WV, 797 ..... 102 B3
Ft. Covington NY, 700 ..... 80 C1	Ft. Walton Beach FL, 19973 ..... 136 B2	Fox Chase KY, 476 ..... 100 A4	Franklin WI, 29494 ..... 74 C3
Ft. Davis TX, 1050 ..... 62 B2	Ft. Washakie WY, 1477 ..... 32 B1	Foxfield CO, 746 ..... 209 D4	**Franklin Co. AL,** 31223 ..... 119 E3
Ft. Defiance AZ, 4061 ..... 48 A2	Ft. Washington MD, 3680 ..... 248 C5	Foxfire NC, 474 ..... 122 C1	**Franklin Co. AR,** 17771 ..... 116 C3
Ft. Deposit AL, 1270 ..... 128 A3	Ft. Wingate NM, 550 ..... 48 A3	Fox Island WA, 2803 ..... 262 A6	**Franklin Co. FL,** 11057 ..... 137 D3
Ft. Dodge IA, 25136 ..... 72 C4	Ft. Worth TX, 534694 ..... 59 E2	Fox Lake IL, 9178 ..... 74 C3	**Franklin Co. GA,** 20285 ..... 121 D3
Ft. Dodge KS, 550 ..... 42 C4	Ft. Wright KY, 5681 ..... 204 B3	Fox Lake WI, 1454 ..... 74 B2	**Franklin Co. ID,** 11329 ..... 31 F2
Ft. Duchesne UT, 621 ..... 32 A4	Ft. Yates ND, 228 ..... 26 C1	Fox Pt. WI, 7012 ..... 234 D1	**Franklin Co. IL,** 39018 ..... 98 C4
Ft. Edward NY, 3141 ..... 81 D4	Forty Fort PA, 4579 ..... 261 B1	Fox River Grove IL, 4862 ..... 88 C1	**Franklin Co. IN,** 22151 ..... 100 B2
Ft. Fairfield ME, 1600 ..... 85 E2			
Ft. Gaines GA, 1110 ..... 128 C4			
Ft. Garland CO, 432 ..... 41 D4			
Ft. Gates TX, 800 ..... 59 E4			
Ft. Gay WV, 819 ..... 101 D4			
Ft. Gibson OK, 4054 ..... 106 A4			
Ft. Grant AZ, 800 ..... 55 D4			
Ft. Hall ID, 3193 ..... 31 E1			
Ft. Hancock TX, 1713 ..... 56 C4			
Ft. Johnson NY, 491 ..... 79 F3			
Ft. Jones CA, 660 ..... 28 B3			
Ft. Kent ME, 1978 ..... 248 C1			
Ft. Kent Mills ME, 325 ..... 85 D1			
Ft. Laramie WY, 243 ..... 33 E2			
Ft. Lauderdale FL, 152397 ..... 143 F2			
Ft. Lawn SC, 864 ..... 122 A1			
Ft. Lee NJ, 35461 ..... 148 B3			
Ft. Loramie OH, 1344 ..... 90 B4			

Grand Rapids MI

Ada B2
Cascade B2
Comstock Park A1
E. Grand Rapids ..B2
Grand Rapids B1
Grandville A1
Jenison A2
Kentwood B2
Marne A1
Tallmadge A1
Walker A2
Wyoming A2

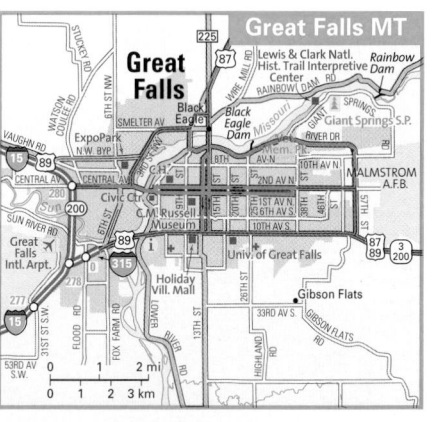

Great Falls MT

216 Glen Ellen–Grayson

Figures after entries indicate population, page number, and grid reference.

Green Bay WI

Greensboro / Winston-Salem NC

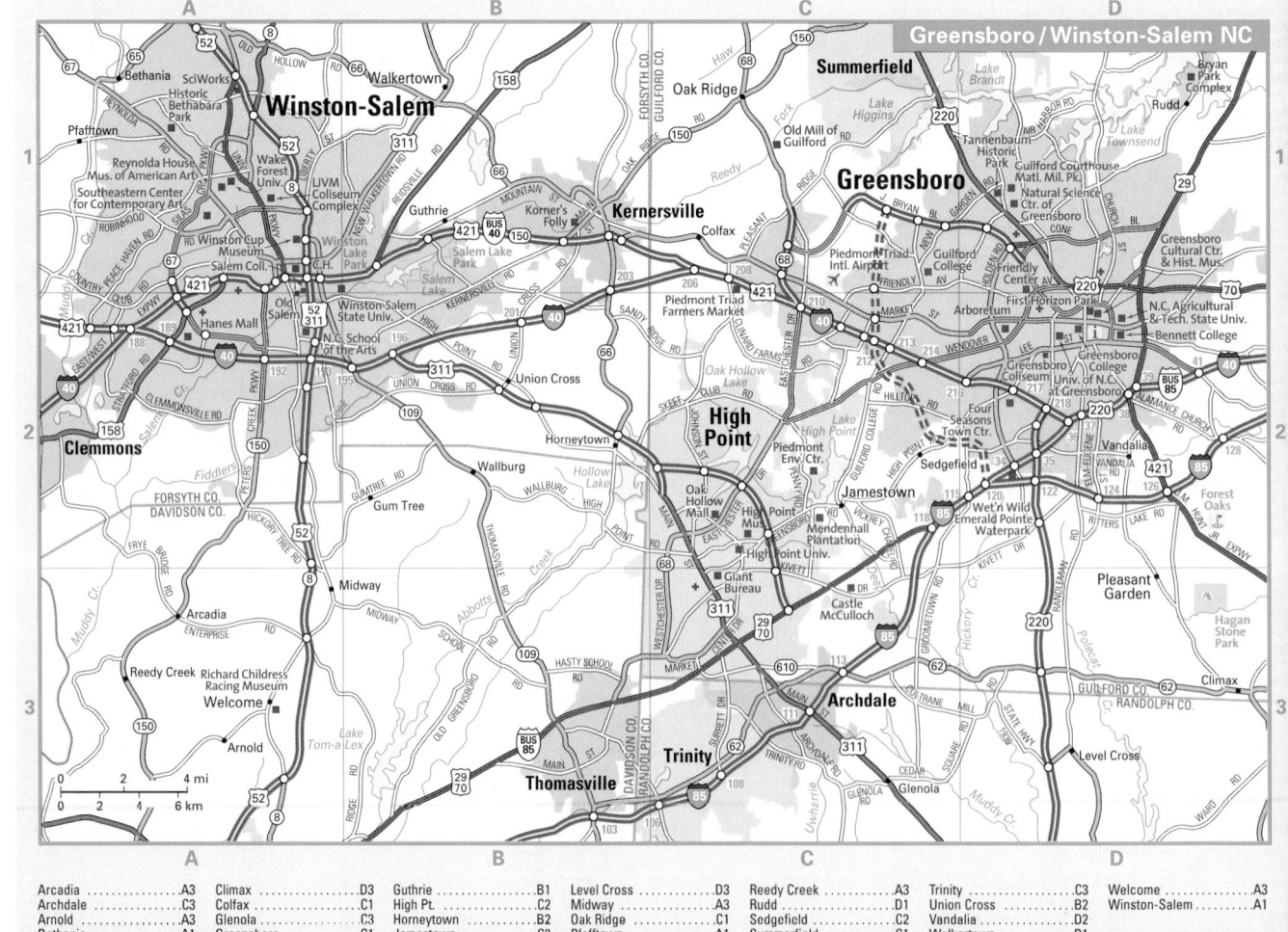

Entries in **bold black** indicate counties or parishes. Entries in bold color indicate cities with detailed inset maps.
Grayson–Harrington 217

Grayson KY, 3877 101 D4
Grayson LA, 531 125 E3
Grayson Co. KY, 24053 109 F1
Grayson Co. TX, 110595 59 F1
Grayson Co. VA, 17917 111 F3
Gray Summit MO, 2640 98 A3
Graysville AL, 2344 119 F4
Graysville TN, 1411 120 B1
Grayville IL, 1725 99 D4
Greasewood AZ, 581 47 F3
Great Barrington MA, 2459 94 B2
Great Bend KS, 15345 43 D3
Great Bend NY, 801 79 E1
Great Bend PA, 700 93 F1
Great Falls MT, 56690 15 F3
Great Falls SC, 2194 122 A2
Great Falls VA, 8549 144 B3
Great Meadows NJ, 1264 94 A4
Great Mills MD, 2600 103 E4
Great Neck NY, 9538 148 B4
Great Neck Estates NY, 2756 241 G3
Great Neck Gardens NY, 1089 241 G2
Great Neck Plaza NY, 6433 241 G2
Great River NY, 1546 149 D4
Greece NY, 14614 78 C3
Greeley CO, 76930 33 E4
Greeley NE, 531 35 D3
Greeley Co. KS, 1534 42 B3
Greeley Co. NE, 2714 35 D3
Greeleyville SC, 452 122 B4
Green OH, 22817 91 E3
Green OR, 6174 28 B1
Greenacres CA, 7400 45 D4
Greenacres FL, 27569 143 F1
Greenback TN, 954 110 C4
Green Bay WI, 102313 68 C4
Greenbelt MD, 21456 144 B3
Greenbrier AR, 3042 117 E1
Greenbrier TN, 4940 109 F3
Greenbrier Co. WV, 34453 102 A4
Greenbush MA, 550 151 E2
Greenbush MN, 784 19 F1
Greencastle IN, 9880 99 E1
Greencastle PA, 3722 103 D1
Green City MO, 688 87 D4
Green Co. KY, 11518 110 A1
Green Co. WI, 33647 74 B4
Green Cove Sprs. FL, 5378 139 D3
Green Creek NJ, 1300 104 C4
Greendale IN, 4296 100 B2
Greendale MO, 722 256 B2
Greendale WI, 14405 234 C3
Greene IA, 1099 73 D3
Greene ME, 950 82 B2
Greene NY, 1701 79 E4
Greene Co. AL, 9974 127 E2
Greene Co. AR, 37331 108 A3
Greene Co. GA, 14406 121 E4
Greene Co. IL, 14761 98 A2
Greene Co. IN, 33157 99 E2
Greene Co. IA, 10366 86 B1
Greene Co. MS, 13299 127 D4
Greene Co. MO, 240391 107 D1
Greene Co. NY, 48195 94 A2
Greene Co. NC, 18974 115 C3
Greene Co. OH, 147886 100 C1
Greene Co. PA, 40672 102 A1
Greene Co. TN, 62909 111 D3
Greene Co. VA, 15244 102 C4
Greenevers NC, 560 123 E2
Greeneville TN, 15198 111 D4
Greenfield CA, 12583 44 B3
Greenfield IL, 1179 98 A2
Greenfield IN, 14600 99 F1
Greenfield IA, 2129 86 B2
Greenfield MA, 13716 94 C1
Greenfield MO, 1358 106 C1
Greenfield NH, 375 95 D1
Greenfield OH, 4906 100 C2
Greenfield TN, 2208 108 C4
Greenfield WI, 35476 234 C3
Green Forest AR, 2717 107 D3
Green Harbor MA, 2397 151 E2
Green Haven MD, 17415 144 C2
Green Haven NY, 3000 148 C1
Green Hill TN, 7068 109 F3
Greenhills OH, 4103 204 B1
Green Island NY, 2278 188 E2
Green Lake WI, 1100 74 B2
Green Lake Co. WI, 19105 74 B2
Greenland AR, 907 106 C4
Greenland NH, 1100 82 A4
Green Lane PA, 584 146 B2
Greenleaf ID, 862 22 A4
Greenlee Co. AZ, 8547 55 E2
Greenmount MD, 600 144 B1
Green Mtn. Falls CO, 773 205 C1
Green Oaks IL, 3572 203 C1
Green Park MO, 2666 256 B3
Green Pond NJ, 1400 148 A3
Greenport NY, 2048 149 E3
Green River UT, 973 39 F2
Green River WY, 11808 32 A3
Greensboro AL, 2731 127 E2
Greensboro FL, 619 137 D2
Greensboro GA, 3238 121 D4
Greensboro MD, 1632 145 E3
Greensboro NC, 223891 112 B4
Greensboro Bend VT, 350 81 E2
Greensburg IN, 10260 100 A2
Greensburg KS, 1574 43 D4
Greensburg KY, 2396 110 A2
Greensburg LA, 631 134 B1
Greensburg PA, 15889 92 A4
Green Sprs. OH, 1247 90 C2
Greensville Co. VA, 11560 113 E2
Greentown IN, 2546 89 F4
Greentown OH, 3154 91 E3
Green Tree PA, 4719 250 B2
Greenup IL, 1532 99 D2
Greenup KY, 1198 101 D3
Greenup Co. KY, 36891 101 D3
Green Valley AZ, 17283 55 D3
Green Valley CA, 600 52 C2
Green Valley IL, 728 88 B4
Green Valley MD, 12262 144 B2
Greenview IL, 862 88 B4
Green Vil. PA, 1100 103 D1
Greenville AL, 7228 128 A3
Greenville CA, 1160 36 C1
Greenville DE, 2332 146 B3
Greenville FL, 837 137 F2
Greenville GA, 946 128 C1
Greenville IL, 6955 98 B3
Greenville IN, 591 99 F4
Greenville KY, 4398 109 E2
Greenville ME, 1319 84 C4
Greenville MI, 7935 75 F3
Greenville MS, 41633 126 A1
Greenville MO, 451 108 A2
Greenville NH, 1131 95 D1
Greenville NY, 493 94 B2
Greenville NC, 60476 115 D2
Greenville OH, 13294 90 A4
Greenville PA, 6380 91 F2
Greenville RI, 8626 150 C3
Greenville SC, 56002 121 E2
Greenville TX, 23960 59 F2
Greenville VA, 886 102 B4
Greenville WI, 950 74 C1
Greenville Co. SC, 379616 121 E2
Greenville Jct. ME, 850 84 C4
Greenwich CT, 61101 148 C3
Greenwich NY, 1902 81 D4
Greenwich OH, 1525 91 D3
Greenwood AR, 7112 116 C1
Greenwood DE, 837 145 E3
Greenwood FL, 735 137 D1
Greenwood IN, 36037 99 F1
Greenwood LA, 2458 124 C2
Greenwood MS, 18425 118 B4
Greenwood MO, 5352 96 D3
Greenwood NE, 544 35 F3
Greenwood SC, 22071 121 F3
Greenwood WI, 1079 68 A4
Greenwood Co. KS, 7673 43 F3
Greenwood Co. SC, 66271 121 F3
Greenwood Lake NY, 3411 148 A2
Greenwood Vil. CO, 11035 209 C4
Greer SC, 16843 121 E2
Greer Co. OK, 6061 50 C3
Greers Ferry AR, 930 117 E1
Gregg Co. TX, 111379 124 B2
Gregory SD, 1342 35 D1
Gregory TX, 2318 63 F2
Gregory Co. SD, 4792 35 D1
Greilickville MI, 1415 69 F4
Grenada MS, 14879 118 B4
Grenada Co. MS, 23263 118 B4
Gresham OR, 90205 20 C2
Gresham WI, 575 68 C4
Gresham Park GA, 9215 190 E4
Gretna FL, 1709 137 D2
Gretna LA, 17423 134 B3
Gretna NE, 2355 35 F3
Gretna VA, 1257 112 C2
Greybull WY, 1815 24 C3
Gridley CA, 5382 36 B2
Gridley IL, 1411 88 C3
Gridley KS, 372 96 A4
Griffin GA, 23451 129 D1
Griffith IN, 17334 89 D2
Grifton NC, 2073 115 D3
Griggs Co. ND, 2754 19 D3
Griggsville IL, 1258 98 A1
Grimes AL, 459 128 B4
Grimes IA, 5098 86 C2
Grimes Co. TX, 23552 132 A2
Grinnell IA, 9105 87 D1
Griswold IA, 1039 86 B2
Groesbeck OH, 7202 204 A2
Groesbeck TX, 4291 59 F4
Groom TX, 587 50 B3
Grosse Pointe MI, 5670 210 D3
Grosse Pointe Farms MI, 9764 210 D3
Grosse Pointe Park MI, 12443 210 D3
Grosse Pointe Shores MI, 2823 210 D3
Grosse Pointe Woods MI, 17080 76 C4
Grosse Tete LA, 670 133 F2
Grosvenor Dale CT, 700 150 B2
Groton CT, 10010 149 F2
Groton MA, 1113 95 D1
Groton NY, 2470 79 D4
Groton SD, 1356 27 E2
Groton VT, 450 81 E2
Groton Long Pt. CT, 667 149 F2
Grottoes VA, 2114 102 C4
Grove OK, 5131 106 B3
Grove City FL, 2092 140 C4
Grove City MN, 608 66 B3
Grove City OH, 27075 101 D1
Grove City PA, 8024 92 A2
Grove Hill AL, 1438 127 E4
Groveland CA, 3388 37 D4
Groveland FL, 2360 140 C1
Groveland MA, 2800 95 E1
Groveport OH, 3865 101 D1
Grover NC, 698 122 A1
Grover Beach CA, [illegible] 52 A1
Groves TX, 15733 132 C3
Groveton NH, 1197 81 F2
Groveton TX, 1107 132 B1
Groveton VA, 21296 144 B4
Grovetown GA, 6089 121 F4
Grubbs AR, 438 107 F4
Gruetli-Laager TN, 1867 120 A1
Grundy VA, 1105 111 E2
Grundy Ctr. IA, 2596 73 D4
Grundy Co. IL, 37535 88 C2
Grundy Co. IA, 12369 73 D4
Grundy Co. MO, 10432 86 C4
Grundy Co. TN, 14332 120 A1
Gruver TX, 1162 50 B2
Guadalupe AZ, 5228 249 C3
Guadalupe CA, 5659 52 A1
Guadalupe Co. NM, 4680 49 E4
Guadalupe Co. TX, 89023 61 E3
Guerneville CA, 2441 36 A3
Guernsey WY, 1147 33 E2
Guernsey Co. OH, 40792 91 E4
Gueydan LA, 1598 133 E3
Guilderland NY, 1700 188 C2
Guildhall VT, 400 81 F2
Guilford CT, 2603 149 E2
Guilford ME, 945 82 C1
Guilford MD, 12918 193 A5
Guilford Co. NC, 421048 112 B4
Guin AL, 2389 119 E4
Gulf Breeze FL, 5665 135 F2
Gulf Co. FL, 13332 137 D3
Gulfport FL, 12527 140 B3
Gulfport MS, 71127 135 D2
Gulf Shores AL, 5044 135 E2
Gulf Stream FL, 716 143 F1
Gun Barrel City TX, 5145 59 F3
Gunnison CO, 5409 40 C3
Gunnison MS, 633 118 A4
Gunnison UT, 2394 39 E2
Gunnison Co. CO, 13956 40 C2
Gunter TX, 1230 59 F1
Guntersville AL, 7395 120 A3
Guntown MS, 1183 119 D3
Gurdon AR, 2276 117 D4
Gurley AL, 876 119 F2
Gurn Spr. NY, 600 80 C4
Gustavus AK, 429 155 D4
Gustine CA, 4698 36 C4
Guthrie KY, 1469 109 E3
Guthrie OK, 9925 51 E2
Guthrie TX, 10 58 C1
Guthrie Ctr. IA, 1668 86 B2
Guthrie Co. IA, 11353 86 B2
Guthriesville PA, 1800 146 B3
Guttenberg IA, 1987 73 F4
Guttenberg NJ, 10807 240 D2
Guymon OK, 10472 50 B1
Guys TN, 483 119 D2
Guyton GA, 917 130 B2
Gwinn MI, 1965 69 D1
Gwinner ND, 717 27 E1
Gwinnett Co. GA, 588448 121 D4
Gwynn VA, 600 113 F1
Gypsum CO, 3654 40 C1
Gypsum KS, 414 43 E2

H

Haakon Co. SD, 2196 26 B3
Habersham Co. GA, 35902 121 D2
Hacienda Hts. CA, 53122 228 E3
Hackberry LA, 1699 133 D3
Hackensack NJ, 42677 148 B3
Hackett AR, 694 116 C1
Hackettstown NJ, 10403 94 A4
Hackleburg AL, 1527 119 E3
Haddam CT, 650 149 E1
Haddonfield NJ, 11659 146 C3
Haddon Hts. NJ, 7547 248 D4
Hadley MA, 1200 150 A1
Hadley NY, 2240 80 C4
Hagaman NY, 1357 80 C4
Hagan GA, 898 129 F3
Hagerhill KY, 900 111 D1
Hagerman ID, 656 30 C1
Hagerman NM, 1168 57 E2
Hagerstown IN, 1768 100 A1
Hagerstown MD, 36687 144 A1
Hahira GA, 1626 137 F1
Hahnville LA, 2792 134 B3
Haiku HI, 6578 153 D1
Hailey ID, 6200 22 C4
Haileyville OK, 891 116 A2
Haines AK, 1811 155 D3
Haines OR, 426 21 F2
Haines City FL, 13174 141 D2
Halaula HI, 495 153 E2
Halawa HI, 13891 152 C3
Hale Ctr. TX, 2263 58 A1
Hale Co. AL, 17185 127 E2
Hale Co. TX, 36602 58 A1
Haledon NJ, 8252 148 B3
Haleiwa HI, 2225 152 A2
Hales Corners WI, 7765 74 C3
Haleyville AL, 4182 119 E3
Halfmoon NY, 2300 188 E1
Half Moon NC, 6645 115 D4
Half Moon Bay CA, 11842 36 B4
Halfway MD, 10065 144 A1
Halfway OR, 337 22 A2
Halifax MA, 1000 151 D2
Halifax NC, 344 113 E3
Halifax PA, 875 93 D4
Halifax VA, 1389 112 C2
Halifax Co. NC, 57370 113 E4
Halifax Co. VA, 37355 112 C2
Haliimaile HI, 895 153 D1
Hallam PA, 1532 103 E1
Hallandale Beach FL, 34282 143 F2
Hall Co. GA, 139277 121 D3
Hall Co. NE, 53534 35 D4
Hall Co. TX, 3782 50 B4
Hallettsville TX, 2345 61 F3
Halliday ND, 227 18 A3
Hallock MN, 1196 19 E1
Hallowell ME, 2467 82 C2
Halls TN, 2311 108 C4
Hallsburg TX, 518 59 F4
Halls Crossroads TN, 2100 110 C4
Halls Gap KY, 450 110 B1
Hallstead PA, 1216 93 F1
Hallsville MO, 978 97 E2
Hallsville TX, 2772 124 B2
Halsey OR, 724 20 B3
Halstad MN, [illegible]
Halstead KS, 1873 43 E3
Haltom City TX, 39018 207 B2
Hamblen Co. TN, 58128 111 D3
Hamburg AR, 3039 125 F1
Hamburg IA, 1240 86 A3
Hamburg MN, 538 66 C4
Hamburg NJ, 3105 148 A2
Hamburg NY, 10116 78 B4
Hamburg PA, 4114 146 A1
Hamden CT, 56913 149 D2
Hamden OH, 871 101 D2
Hamel IL, 570 98 B3
Hamilton AL, 6786 119 D3
Hamilton GA, 307 128 C2
Hamilton IL, 3029 87 F4
Hamilton IN, 1233 90 A2
Hamilton MI, 1300 75 F4
Hamilton MO, 1813 96 C1
Hamilton MT, 3705 23 D1
Hamilton NY, 3509 79 E3
Hamilton NC, 516 113 E4
Hamilton OH, 60690 100 B2
Hamilton RI, 2500 150 C4
Hamilton TX, 2977 59 E4
Hamilton VA, 562 144 A2
Hamilton City CA, 1903 36 B1
Hamilton Co. FL, 13327 138 C2
Hamilton Co. IL, 8621 98 C4
Hamilton Co. IN, 182740 99 F1
Hamilton Co. IA, 16438 72 C4
Hamilton Co. KS, 2670 42 A3
Hamilton Co. NE, 9403 35 E4
Hamilton Co. NY, 5379 79 F2
Hamilton Co. OH, 845303 100 B2
Hamilton Co. TN, 307896 120 B1
Hamilton Co. TX, 8229 59 D4
Hamilton Square NJ, 26419 147 D2
Ham Lake MN, 12710 67 D3
Hamler OH, 650 90 B2
Hamlet IN, 820 89 E2
Hamlet NC, 6018 122 C2
Hamlin TX, 2248 58 C2
Hamlin WV, 1119 101 E4
Hamlin Co. SD, 5540 27 E3
Hammon OK, 469 50 C3
Hammond IL, 518 98 C1
Hammond IN, 83048 89 D2
Hammond LA, 17639 134 B2
Hammond WI, 1153 67 E4
Hammondsport NY, 731 78 C4
Hammondville AL, 486 120 A2
Hammonton NJ, 12604 147 D4
Hamorton PA, 1400 146 B3
Hampden ME, 4126 83 D1
Hampden Co. MA, 456228 150 A2
Hampden Sydney VA, 1264 113 D2
Hampshire IL, 2900 88 C1
Hampshire Co. MA, 152251 94 C2
Hampshire Co. WV, 20203 102 C2
Hampstead MD, 5060 144 B1
Hampstead NH, 1100 95 E1
Hampton AR, 1579 117 E4
Hampton FL, 431 138 C3
Hampton GA, 3857 129 D1
Hampton IL, 1626 208 C1
Hampton IA, 4218 73 D4
Hampton MD, 5004 193 C1
Hampton NE, 439 35 E4
Hampton NH, 9126 95 E1
Hampton NJ, 1546 104 C1
Hampton PA, 633 103 E1
Hampton SC, 2837 130 B2
Hampton TN, 1300 111 E3
Hampton VA, 146437 113 F2
Hampton Bays NY, 12236 149 E3
Hampton Beach NH, 1800 95 E1
Hampton Co. SC, 21386 130 B2
Hampton Park NY, 950 149 E3
Hamtramck MI, 22976 210 C3
Hana HI, 709 153 E1
Hanahan SC, 12937 131 D1
Hanamaulu HI, 3272 152 B1
Hanapepe HI, 2153 152 B1
Hanceville AL, 2951 119 F3
Hancock MD, 1725 102 C1
Hancock MI, 4323 65 F3
Hancock MN, 717 66 A3
Hancock NH, 375 81 E4
Hancock NY, 1189 93 F1
Hancock Co. GA, 10076 129 E1
Hancock Co. IL, 20121 87 F4
Hancock Co. IN, 55391 100 A1
Hancock Co. IA, 12100 72 C3
Hancock Co. KY, 8392 109 F1
Hancock Co. ME, 51791 83 D1
Hancock Co. MS, 42967 134 C2
Hancock Co. OH, 71295 90 B3
Hancock Co. TN, 6786 111 D3
Hancock Co. WV, 32667 91 F4
Hand Co. SD, 3741 27 D3
Hanford CA, 41686 45 D3
Hankinson ND, 1058 27 F1
Hanley Hills MO, 2124 256 B2
Hanna WY, 873 33 D2
Hanna City IL, 1013 88 B3
Hannibal MO, 17757 97 F1
Hannibal NY, 542 79 D3
Hanover CT, 700 149 F1
Hanover IL, 836 74 A4
Hanover IN, 2834 100 A3
Hanover KS, 653 43 F1
Hanover MA, 2200 151 E2
Hanover MN, [illegible]
Hanover NH, 8162 81 E3
Hanover NJ, 11500 148 A3
Hanover OH, 885 91 D4
Hanover PA, 14535 103 E1
Hanover VA, 225 113 E1
Hanover Co. VA, 86320 103 D4
Hanover Park IL, 38278 203 B3
Hansen ID, 970 30 C1
Hansford Co. TX, 5369 50 B2
Hanson KY, 625 109 E1
Hanson MA, 2044 151 D2
Hanson Co. SD, 3139 27 E4
Hapeville GA, 6180 190 D5
Happy TX, 647 50 A4
Happy Camp CA, 800 28 B2
Happy Valley OR, 4519 251 D2
Harahan LA, 9885 239 B2
Haralson Co. GA, 25690 120 B4
Harbert MI, 1619 89 E1
Harbeson DE, 375 145 F4
Harbor OR, 2622 28 A2
Harbor Beach MI, 1837 76 C2
Harbor Bluffs FL, 2807 266 A2
Harbor Hills NY, 563 241 G2
Harbor Hills OH, 1303 101 D1
Harbor Sprs. MI, 1567 70 B3
Harbour Hts. FL, 2873 140 C4
Hardee Co. FL, 26938 140 C3
Hardeeville SC, 1793 130 B3
Hardeman Co. TN, 28105 118 C1
Hardeman Co. TX, 4724 50 C4
Hardin IL, 959 98 A2
Hardin KY, 564 109 D2
Hardin MO, 614 96 C2
Hardin MT, 3384 24 C1
Hardin TX, 755 132 B2
Hardin Co. IL, 4800 109 D1
Hardin Co. IA, 18812 73 D4
Hardin Co. KY, 94174 110 A1
Hardin Co. OH, 31945 90 C3
Hardin Co. TN, 25578 119 D1
Hardin Co. TX, 48073 132 C2
Harding Co. NM, 810 49 E2
Harding Co. SD, 1353 25 F1
Hardinsburg KY, 2345 109 F1
Hardwick GA, 5135 129 E1
Hardwick VT, 1100 81 E2
Hardy AR, 578 107 F3
Hardy Co. WV, 12669 102 C2
Harewood Park MD, 3400 145 D1
Harford Co. MD, 218590 144 C1
Hargill TX, 900 63 E4
Harker Hts. TX, 17308 59 E4
Harkers Island NC, 1525 115 E4
Harlan IA, 5282 86 A2
Harlan KY, 2081 111 D2
Harlan Co. KY, 33202 111 D2
Harlan Co. NE, 3786 35 D4
Harlem FL, 2730 141 D4
Harlem GA, 1814 129 F1
Harlem MT, 848 16 C2
Harleysville PA, 8795 146 C2
Harleyville SC, 594 130 C1
Harlingen TX, 57564 63 F4
Harlowton MT, 1062 16 B4
Harmon Co. OK, 3283 50 C4
Harmony IN, 589 99 E1
Harmony MN, 1080 73 E2
Harmony NC, 526 112 A4
Harmony PA, 937 92 A3
Harmony RI, 850 150 C3
Harnett Co. NC, 91025 123 D1
Harney Co. OR, 7609 21 E4
Harold KY, 1400 111 E1
Harper KS, 1567 43 E4
Harper TX, 1006 60 C1
Harper Co. KS, 6536 43 E4
Harper Co. OK, 3562 50 C1
Harpersville AL, 1620 128 A1
Harper Woods MI, 14254 210 D2
Harrah OK, 4719 51 E3
Harrah WA, 542 13 D4
Harriman NY, 2252 148 B2
Harriman TN, 6744 110 B4
Harrington DE, 3174 145 E3

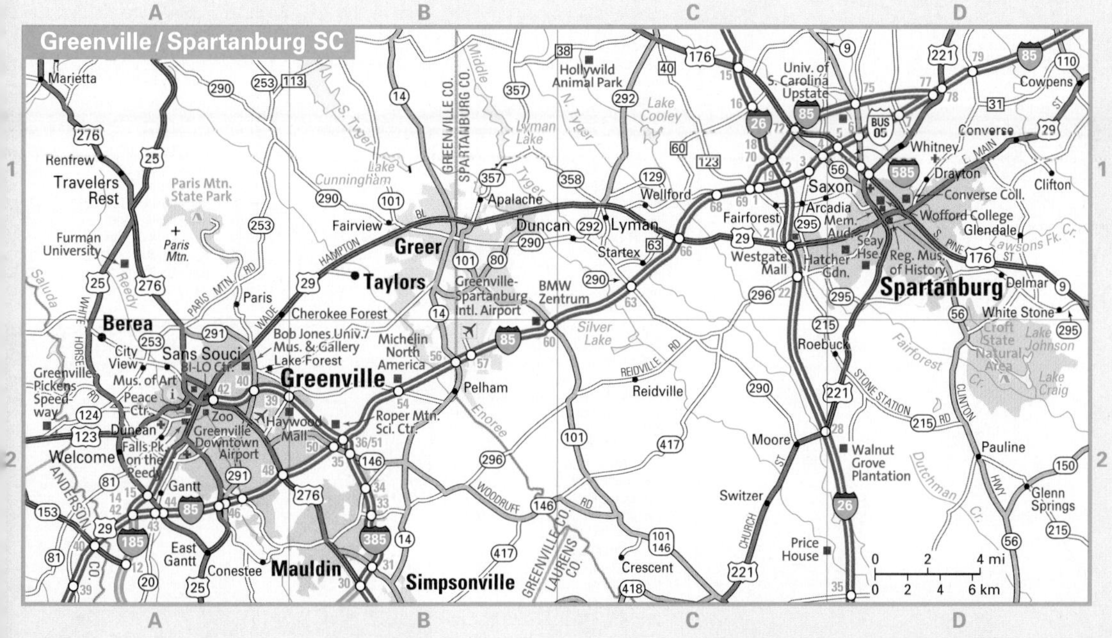

Apalache B1
Arcadia C1
Berea A2
Cherokee Forest A1
City View A2
Clifton D1
Conestee A2
Converse D1
Cowpens D1
Crescent C2
Delmar D1
Drayton D1
Duncan C1
Dunean A2
E. Gantt A2
Fairforest C1
Fairview B1
Gantt A2
Glendale D1
Glenn Sprs. D2
Greenville A2
Greer B1
Lake Forest A2
Lyman C1
Marietta A1
Mauldin B2
Moore C2
Paris A1
Pauline D2
Pelham B2
Reidville C2
Renfrew A1
Roebuck D2
Sans Souci A2
Saxon C1
Simpsonville B2
Spartanburg D1
Startex C1
Switzer C2
Taylors B1
Travelers Rest A1
Welcome A2
Wellford C1
White Stone D1
Whitney D1

218 Harrington–Henry County

Figures after entries indicate population, page number, and grid reference.

Harrington ME, 425 ....**83** E2	Harrisburg NE, 75 ....**33** F3	Harris Co. GA, 23695 ....**128** C2	Harrison ME, 375 ....**82** B2
Harrington WA, 426 ....**13** F3	Harrisburg NC, 4493 ....**122** B1	Harris Co. TX, 3400578 ....**132** A3	Harrison MN, 2108 ....**76** A1
Harris MN, 1121 ....**67** D3	Harrisburg OR, 2795 ....**20** B3	Harrison AR, 12152 ....**107** D3	Harrison NE, 279 ....**33** F1
Harrisburg AR, 2192 ....**118** A1	Harrisburg PA, 48950 ....**93** D4	Harrison GA, 509 ....**129** F2	Harrison NJ, 14424 ....**148** B4
Harrisburg IL, 9860 ....**109** D1	Harrisburg SD, 958 ....**27** F4	Harrison ID, 267 ....**14** B3	Harrison NY, 24154 ....**148** C3

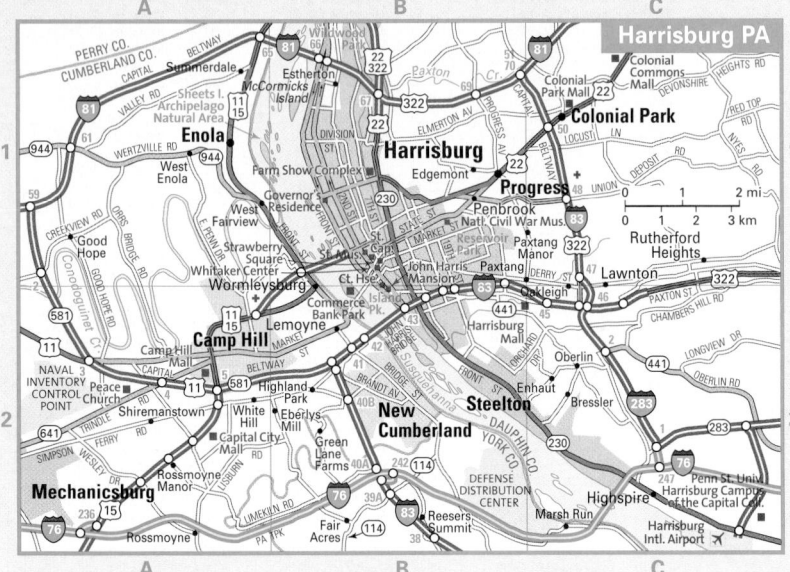

Bressler C2	Fair Acres B2	Marsh Run C2	Penbrook B1	Summerdale A1
Camp Hill A2	Good Hope A1	Mechanicsburg ...A2	Progress B1	W. Enola A1
Colonial Park C1	Green Lane Farms ..B2	New Cumberland ...B2	Reesers Summit ...C2	W. Fairview A1
Eberlys Mill B2	Harrisburg B1	Oakleigh C2	Rossmoyne A2	White Hill A2
Edgemont B1	Highland Park B2	Oberlin C2	Rossmoyne Manor ..A2	Wormleysburg B2
Enhaut C2	Highspire C2	Paxtang B1	Rutherford Hts. ...C1	
Enola A1	Lawnton C1	Paxtang Manor C1	Shiremanstown A2	
Estherton A1	Lemoyne B1	Paxtonia C1	Steelton B2	

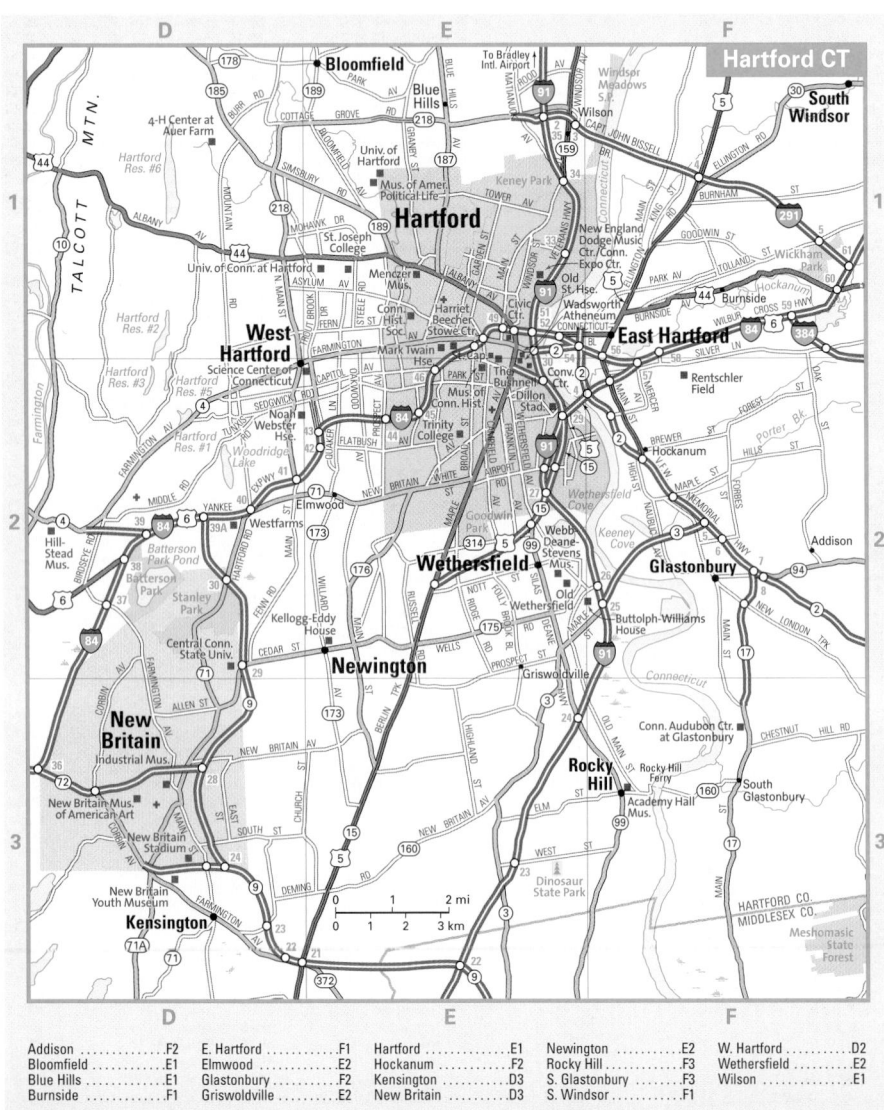

Addison F2	E. Hartford F1	Hartford E1	Newington E2	W. Hartford D2
Bloomfield E1	Elmwood E2	Hockanum F1	Rocky Hill F3	Wethersfield E2
Blue Hills E1	Glastonbury F2	Kensington D3	S. Glastonbury ...F3	Wilson E1
Burnside F1	Griswoldville E2	New Britain D3	S. Windsor F1	

Harrison OH, 7487 ....**100** B2	Haviland KS, 612 ....**43** D4	Heber AZ, 2722 ....**47** E4	Heber CA, 2988 ....**53** E4
Harrison TN, 7630 ....**120** B1	Havre MT, 9621 ....**16** B2	Heber City UT, 7291 ....**31** F4	
Harrisonburg LA, 746 ....**125** F3	Havre de Grace MD, 11331 .....**145** D1	Heber Sprs. AR, 6432 ....**117** E1	
Harrisonburg VA, 40468 ......**102** A3	Hawaiian Gardens CA, 14779 ...**228** E4	Hebron CT, 1200 ....**149** E1	
Harrison Co. IN, 34325 ....**99** F4	**Hawaii Co. HI, 148677** **153** E2	Hebron IN, 3596 ....**89** E2	
Harrison Co. IA, 15666 ....**86** A3	Hawarden IA, 2478 ....**35** F1	Hebron KY, 1300 ....**100** B2	
Harrison Co. KY, 17983 ......**100** B3	Hawesville KY, 971 ....**99** E4	Hebron MD, 807 ....**145** F3	
Harrison Co. MS, 189601 ...**134** C2	Hawkins TX, 1331 ....**124** B2	Hebron NE, 1565 ....**43** E1	
Harrison Co. MO, 8850 ....**86** C4	**Hawkins Co. TN, 53563** **111** D3	Hebron ND, 803 ....**18** B4	
Harrison Co. OH, 15856 ....**91** E4	Hawkinsville GA, 3280 ....**129** E3	Hebron OH, 2034 ....**101** D1	
Harrison Co. TX, 62110 ......**124** B2	Hawley MN, 1882 ....**19** F4	Hebron Estates KY, 1104 .....**100** A4	
Harrison Co. WV, 68652 .....**102** A2	Hawley PA, 1303 ....**93** F2	Hecla SD, 314 ....**27** E1	
Harrisonville MO, 8946 ....**96** B3	Hawley TX, 646 ....**58** C2	Hector AR, 506 ....**117** D1	
Harristown IL, 1338 ....**98** C1	Hawleyville CT, 800 ....**148** C1	Hector MN, 1166 ....**66** C3	
Harrisville MD, 600 ....**146** A4	Haw River NC, 1908 ....**112** C4	Hedrick IA, 837 ....**87** E2	
Harrisville MI, 514 ....**71** D4	Hawthorn PA, 587 ....**92** B3	Hedwig Vil. TX, 2334 ....**220** B2	
Harrisville NH, 400 ....**95** D1	Hawthorne CA, 84112 ....**228** C3	Heeia HI, 4944 ....**152** A3	
Harrisville NY, 653 ....**79** E1	Hawthorne FL, 1415 ....**138** C3	Heflin AL, 3002 ....**120** A4	
Harrisville PA, 883 ....**92** A3	Hawthorne NV, 3311 ....**37** E3	Heidelberg MS, 840 ....**127** D3	
Harrisville RI, 1561 ....**150** C2	Hawthorne NJ, 18218 ....**148** B3	Heidelberg PA, 1225 ....**250** A3	
Harrisville UT, 3645 ....**31** E3	Hawthorne NY, 5083 ....**148** B3	Heilwood PA, 786 ....**92** B3	
Harrisville WV, 1842 ....**101** F2	Haxtun CO, 982 ....**34** A2	Helena AL, 10296 ....**127** F1	
Harrodsburg KY, 8014 ....**110** B1	Hayden AL, 470 ....**119** F4	Helena AR, 6323 ....**118** A4	
Harrogate TN, 4052 ....**110** C3	Hayden AZ, 892 ....**55** D2	Helena GA, 2307 ....**129** E3	
Harrold SD, 209 ....**27** D3	Hayden CO, 1634 ....**32** C4	Helena MS, 778 ....**195** C1	
Hart MI, 1950 ....**75** E2	Hayden ID, 9159 ....**14** B3	*Helena MT, 25780* **15** E4	
Hart TX, 1198 ....**50** A4	Hayden Lake ID, 494 ....**14** B3	Helenwood TN, 846 ....**110** B3	
Hart Co. GA, 22997 ....**121** E3	Hayes LA, 750 ....**133** E2	Hellertown PA, 5606 ....**146** C1	
Hart Co. KY, 17445 ....**110** A2	Hayes Ctr. NE, 240 ....**34** B4	Helmetta NJ, 1825 ....**147** E1	
Hartford AL, 2369 ....**136** C1	**Hayes Co. NE, 1068** **34** B4	Helotes TX, 4285 ....**61** D2	
Hartford AR, 772 ....**116** C2	Hayesville NC, 297 ....**121** D2	Helper UT, 2025 ....**39** F1	
Hartford CT, 121578 ....**150** A3	Hayesville OR, 18222 ....**20** B2	Hemet CA, 58812 ....**53** D3	
Hartford IL, 1545 ....**98** A3	Hayfield MN, 1325 ....**73** D2	Hemingford NE, 993 ....**34** A2	
Hartford IA, 759 ....**86** C2	Hayfork CA, 2315 ....**28** B4	Hemingway SC, 573 ....**122** C4	
Hartford KS, 500 ....**43** F3	Haymarket VA, 879 ....**144** A3	Hemlock MI, 1585 ....**76** B3	
Hartford KY, 2571 ....**109** E1	Haynesville LA, 2519 ....**125** D1	Hemlock WI, 919 ....**74** A4	
Hartford MI, 2476 ....**89** F1	Haynesville VA, 550 ....**103** E4	Hemphill TX, 1106 ....**124** C4	
Hartford SD, 1844 ....**27** F4	Hayneville AL, 1177 ....**128** A3	**Hemphill Co. TX, 3351** **50** C2	
Hartford WV, 519 ....**101** E2	Hays KS, 20013 ....**43** D2	Hempstead NY, 56554 ....**148** C4	
Hartford WI, 10905 ....**74** B4	Hays MT, 702 ....**16** C2	Hempstead TX, 4691 ....**61** F2	
Hartford City IN, 6928 ....**90** A4	Hays NC, 1731 ....**112** A3	**Hempstead Co. AR, 23587** ...**116** C4	
Hartford Co. CT, 857183 .....**150** A3	**Hays Co. TX, 97589** **61** D2	Henagar AL, 2400 ....**120** A2	
Hartington NE, 1640 ....**35** E1	Hay Sprs. NE, 652 ....**34** A1	Henderson KY, 27373 ....**109** D1	
Hartland ME, 872 ....**82** C1	Hayti MO, 3207 ....**108** B3	Henderson LA, 1531 ....**133** E2	
Hartland VT, 500 ....**81** E3	Hayti SD, 367 ....**27** F3	Henderson MN, 910 ....**66** C4	
Hartland WI, 7905 ....**74** B4	Hayti Hts. MO, 771 ....**108** B3	Henderson NE, 986 ....**35** E4	
Hartley IA, 1733 ....**72** A3	Hayward CA, 140030 ....**36** B4	Henderson NV, 175381 ....**46** B2	
Hartley Co. TX, 5537 ....**50** A2	Hayward WI, 2129 ....**67** F2	Henderson NC, 16095 ....**113** D3	
Hartly DE, 78 ....**145** E2	**Haywood Co. NC, 54033** **111** D4	Henderson TN, 5670 ....**119** D1	
Hartman AR, 596 ....**116** C1	**Haywood Co. TN, 19797** **108** C4	Henderson TX, 11273 ....**124** B3	
Harts WV, 2361 ....**101** E4	Hazard KY, 4806 ....**111** D2	**Henderson Co. IL, 8213** **87** D4	
Hartselle AL, 12019 ....**119** F3	Hazardville CT, 4900 ....**150** A3	**Henderson Co. KY, 44829** **109** D1	
Hartshorne OK, 2102 ....**116** A2	Hazel KY, 440 ....**109** D3	**Henderson Co. NC, 89173** ...**121** E1	
Hartsville SC, 7556 ....**122** B3	Hazel Crest IL, 14816 ....**203** E6	**Henderson Co. TN, 25522** ...**109** D4	
Hartsville TN, 7354 ....**109** F3	Hazel Green AL, 3805 ....**119** F2	**Henderson Co. TX, 73277** ...**124** A2	
Hartville MO, 607 ....**107** D2	Hazel Green WI, 1183 ....**74** A4	Hendersonville NC, 10420 ...**121** E1	
Hartville OH, 2174 ....**91** E3	Hazel Park MI, 18963 ....**210** C2	Hendersonville TN, 40620 ...**109** E3	
Hartwell GA, 4188 ....**121** E4	Hazelton ID, 687 ....**31** D1	Hendricks MN, 725 ....**27** F3	
Harvard IL, 7996 ....**74** C4	Hazelton KS, 237 ....**43** D4	**Hendricks Co. IN, 104093** **99** F1	
Harvard MA, 800 ....**150** C1	Hazelton ND, 237 ....**18** C4	Hendron KY, 4239 ....**108** C2	
Harvard NE, 998 ....**35** E4	Hazelwood MO, 26206 ....**256** B1	**Hendry Co. FL, 36210** **143** D1	
Harvest AL, 3054 ....**119** F2	Hazelwood NC, 4500 ....**111** D4	Henefer UT, 684 ....**31** F3	
Harvey IL, 30000 ....**203** E6	Hazen AR, 1637 ....**117** F2	Henlopen Acres DE, 139 .....**145** F4	
Harvey LA, 22226 ....**239** C2	Hazen ND, 2457 ....**18** B3	Hennepin IL, 707 ....**88** B2	
Harvey MI, 1321 ....**69** D2	Hazleton IA, 950 ....**73** E4	**Hennepin Co. MN, 1116200** ..**66** C4	
Harvey ND, 1989 ....**18** C3	Hazleton PA, 23329 ....**93** E3	Hennessey OK, 2058 ....**51** E2	
Harvey Co. KS, 32869 ....**43** E3	Hazleton WI, 4400 ....**126** B3	Henniker NH, 1627 ....**81** F4	
Harveysburg OH, 563 ....**100** C2	Hazlehurst GA, 3787 ....**129** E3	Henning MN, 719 ....**64** A4	
Harveys Lake PA, 2888 ....**93** E2	Hazlehurst MS, 4400 ....**126** B3	Henning TN, 990 ....**108** B4	
Harwich MA, 1832 ....**151** F3	Hazleton IA, 950 ....**73** E4	Henrico Co. VA, 262300 .....**113** E1	
Harwich Port MA, 1809 .....**151** F3	Hazleton PA, 23329 ....**93** E3	Henrietta NY, 6600 ....**78** C3	
Harwinton CT, 3242 ....**94** C3	Hazlettville DE, 450 ....**145** E2	Henrietta TX, 3264 ....**59** D1	
Harwood ND, 607 ....**19** F4	Headland AL, 3523 ....**128** C4	Henry IL, 2540 ....**88** B3	
Harwood Hts. IL, 8297 ......**203** E5	Head of the Harbor NY, 1447 .**149** D3	Henry SD, 268 ....**27** E2	
Hasbrouck Hts. NJ, 11662 ...**240** C1	Healdsburg CA, 10722 ....**36** B3	Henry TN, 520 ....**109** D3	
Haskell AR, 2645 ....**117** E3	Healdton OK, 2786 ....**51** E4	**Henry Co. AL, 16310** **128** B4	
Haskell OK, 1765 ....**106** C1	Healy AK, 1000 ....**154** C2	**Henry Co. GA, 119341** **129** D1	
Haskell TX, 3106 ....**58** C1	**Heard Co. GA, 11012** **128** C1	**Henry Co. IL, 51020** **88** A2	
Haskell Co. KS, 4307 ....**42** B4	Hearne TX, 4690 ....**61** F1	**Henry Co. IN, 48508** **100** A1	
Haskell Co. OK, 11792 ....**116** B1	Heart Butte MT, 698 ....**15** E2	**Henry Co. IA, 20336** **87** F3	
Haskell Co. TX, 6093 ....**58** C2	Heath OH, 8527 ....**101** D1	**Henry Co. KY, 15060** **100** A3	
Haskins OH, 638 ....**90** C2	Heathcote NJ, 4755 ....**147** D1	**Henry Co. MO, 21997** **96** C4	
Haslet TX, 1134 ....**207** A1	Heath Sprs. SC, 864 ....**122** B2	**Henry Co. OH, 29210** **90** B2	
Haslett MI, 11283 ....**76** A4	Heathsville VA, 301 ....**103** E4	**Henry Co. TN, 31115** **109** D3	
Hastings FL, 521 ....**139** D2	Heavener OK, 3201 ....**116** B2		
Hastings MI, 7095 ....**75** F4	Hebbronville TX, 4498 ....**63** D4		
Hastings MN, 18204 ....**67** D4	Hebbville MD, 10900 ....**193** A2		
Hastings NE, 24064 ....**35** D4			
Hatboro PA, 7393 ....**146** C2			
Hatch NM, 1673 ....**56** B2			
Hatfield AR, 402 ....**116** C3			
Hatfield IN, 1000 ....**99** E4			
Hatfield MA, 1298 ....**150** A1			
Hatfield PA, 2605 ....**146** C2			
Hatley MS, 476 ....**119** D4			
Hatteras NC, 515 ....**113** F3			
Hattiesburg MS, 44779 ......**126** C4			
Hatton ND, 707 ....**19** E3			
Haubstadt IN, 1529 ....**99** D4			
Haughton LA, 2792 ....**125** D2			
Hauppauge NY, 20100 ....**149** D3			
Hauser ID, 668 ....**14** B3			
Haula HI, 3651 ....**152** A2			
Havana FL, 1713 ....**137** D2			
Havana IL, 3577 ....**88** A4			
Havelock NC, 22442 ....**115** D4			
Haven KS, 1175 ....**43** E3			
Haverhill FL, 1454 ....**143** F1			
Haverhill MA, 58969 ....**95** E1			
Haverhill NH, 500 ....**81** E4			
Haverstraw NY, 10117 ....**148** B3			
Havertown PA, 22300 ....**248** B3			

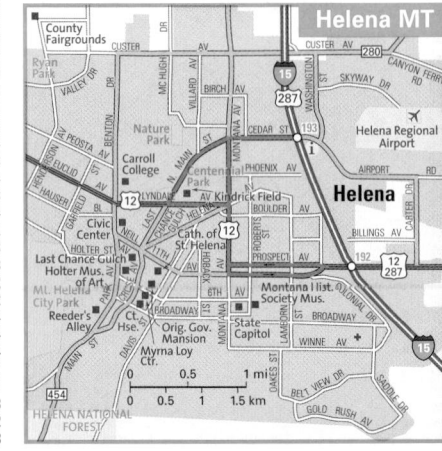

Henry County–Hopkins County 219

Entries in **bold black** indicate counties or parishes. Entries in **bold color** indicate cities with detailed inset maps.

Henry Co. VA, 57930 ... 112 B2
Henryetta OK, 6096 ... 51 F3
Henryville IN, 1545 ... 100 A3
Hephzibah GA, 3880 ... 129 F1
Heppner OR, 1395 ... 21 E2
Herculaneum MO, 2805 ... 98 A4
Hercules CA, 19488 ... 259 C1
Hereford PA, 1400 ... 146 B1
Hereford TX, 14597 ... 50 A4
Herington KS, 2563 ... 43 F3
Herkimer NY, 7498 ... 79 F3
Herkimer Co. NY, 64427 ... 79 F2
Hermann MO, 2674 ... 97 F3
Hermantown MN, 7448 ... 64 C4
Herminie PA, 856 ... 92 A4
Hermiston OR, 13154 ... 21 E1
Hermitage AR, 769 ... 117 E4
Hermitage MO, 406 ... 97 D4
Hermitage PA, 16157 ... 91 F2
Hermon ME, 750 ... 83 D1
Hermosa CO, 700 ... 40 B4
Hermosa SD, 315 ... 26 A4
Hermosa Beach CA, 18566 ... 228 C4
Hernandez NM, 600 ... 48 C2
Hernando FL, 8253 ... 140 C1
Hernando MS, 6812 ... 118 B2
Hernando Beach FL, 2185 ... 140 B1
Hernando Co. FL, 130802 ... 140 B1
Herndon VA, 21655 ... 144 A3
Heron Lake MN, 768 ... 72 A2
Herreid SD, 482 ... 26 C1
Herricks NY, 4076 ... 241 G3
Herriman UT, 1523 ... 31 E4
Herrin IL, 11298 ... 108 C1
Herscher IL, 1523 ... 89 D3
Hershey NE, 572 ... 34 B3
Hershey PA, 12771 ... 93 E4
Hertford NC, 2070 ... 113 F3
Hertford Co. NC, 22601 ... 113 F3
Hesperia CA, 62582 ... 53 D2
Hesperia MI, 954 ... 75 E2
Hessmer LA, 642 ... 133 F1
Hesston KS, 3509 ... 43 E3
Hettinger ND, 1307 ... 26 A1
Hettinger Co. ND, 2715 ... 18 A4
Heuvelton NY, 804 ... 80 B2
Hewitt TX, 11085 ... 59 E4
Hewitt WI, 670 ... 68 A4
Hewlett NY, 7060 ... 241 G4
Hewlett Harbor NY, 1271 ... 241 G5
Hewlett Neck NY, 504 ... 241 G5
Heyburn ID, 2899 ... 31 D1
Heyworth IL, 2431 ... 88 C4
Hialeah FL, 226419 ... 143 E2
Hialeah Gardens FL, 19297 ... 143 E2
Hiawassee GA, 808 ... 121 D2
Hiawatha IA, 6480 ... 87 E1
Hiawatha KS, 3417 ... 96 A1
Hibbing MN, 17071 ... 64 B3
Hickman KY, 2560 ... 108 C3
Hickman NE, 1084 ... 35 F4
Hickman Co. KY, 5262 ... 108 C3
Hickman Co. TN, 22295 ... 109 E4
Hickory MS, 499 ... 126 C2
Hickory NC, 37222 ... 111 F4
Hickory Co. MO, 8940 ... 97 D4
Hickory Flat MS, 565 ... 118 C2
Hickory Hills IL, 13926 ... 203 D5
Hickory Withe TN, 2574 ... 118 C1
Hicksville NY, 41260 ... 148 C4
Hicksville OH, 3649 ... 90 A2
Hico TX, 1341 ... 59 E3
Hidalgo TX, 7322 ... 63 E4
Hidalgo Co. NM, 5932 ... 55 F4
Hidalgo Co. TX, 569463 ... 63 E3
Hidden Hills CA, 1875 ... 228 A2
Hiddenite NC, 650 ... 112 A4
Hideaway TX, 2672 ... 124 A2
Higbee MO, 623 ... 97 E2
Higganum CT, 1671 ... 149 E1
Higginsville MO, 4682 ... 96 C2
High Bridge NJ, 3776 ... 104 C1
Highgate Ctr. VT, 600 ... 81 D1
Highgrove CA, 3445 ... 229 J3
Highland AR, 986 ... 107 F3
Highland CA, 44605 ... 229 K2
Highland IL, 8438 ... 98 B3
Highland IN, 23546 ... 89 D2
Highland KS, 976 ... 96 A1
Highland MD, 800 ... 144 B2
Highland NY, 5060 ... 94 B3
Highland UT, 8172 ... 31 F4
Highland WI, 855 ... 74 A3
Highland Beach FL, 3775 ... 143 F1
Highland City FL, 2051 ... 140 C2
Highland Co. OH, 40875 ... 100 C2
Highland Co. VA, 2536 ... 102 B4
Highland Falls NY, 3678 ... 148 B2
Highland Hts. KY, 6554 ... 204 B3
Highland Hts. OH, 8082 ... 204 G1
Highland Hills OH, 1618 ... 204 G2
Highland Lakes NJ, 5051 ... 148 A2
Highland Mills NY, 3468 ... 148 B2
Highland Park IL, 31365 ... 89 D1
Highland Park MI, 16746 ... 210 C3
Highland Park NJ, 13999 ... 147 E1
Highland Park PA, 4900 ... 218 B2
Highland Park TX, 8842 ... 207 D2
Highlands NJ, 5097 ... 147 F1
Highlands NC, 909 ... 121 D2
Highlands TX, 7089 ... 132 B3
Highlands Co. FL, 87366 ... 141 D4
Highland Sprs. VA, 15137 ... 254 C2
Highlands Ranch CO, 70931 ... 209 C4
Highlandville MO, 872 ... 107 D2
Highmore SD, 851 ... 27 D3
High Pt. FL, 5800 ... 266 B2
High Pt. NC, 85839 ... 112 B4
High Ridge MO, 4236 ... 98 A3
High Rolls NM, 425 ... 56 C2
High Shoals NC, 729 ... 122 A1
Highspire PA, 2720 ... 218 C2
High Sprs. FL, 3863 ... 138 C3
Hightstown NJ, 5216 ... 147 D2
Hightsville NC, 759 ... 275 A1
Highwood IL, 4143 ... 203 D1
Higley AZ, 425 ... 249 D3
Hiland Park FL, 999 ... 136 C2
Hilbert WI, 1089 ... 74 C1
Hilda SC, 436 ... 130 B1
Hildale UT, 1895 ... 46 C1
Hillandale MD, 3054 ... 270 E1
Hillburn NY, 881 ... 148 B2
Hill City KS, 1604 ... 42 C2
Hill City MN, 479 ... 64 B4
Hill City SD, 780 ... 25 F4
Hill Country Vil. TX, 1028 ... 257 E1
Hill Co. MT, 16673 ... 16 A1
Hill Co. TX, 32321 ... 59 E3
Hillcrest IL, 1158 ... 88 B1
Hillcrest NY, 7106 ... 148 B2
Hillcrest TX, 722 ... 132 B4
Hillcrest Hts. MD, 16359 ... 144 B3
Hilliard FL, 2702 ... 139 D1
Hilliard OH, 24230 ... 101 D1
Hillman MI, 685 ... 70 C3
Hills IA, 679 ... 87 F2
Hills MN, 565 ... 27 F4
Hillsboro AL, 608 ... 119 E2
Hillsboro IL, 4359 ... 98 B2
Hillsboro IN, 489 ... 89 E4
Hillsboro KS, 2854 ... 43 E3
Hillsboro MO, 1675 ... 98 A4
Hillsboro ND, 1563 ... 19 E3
Hillsboro OH, 6368 ... 100 C2
Hillsboro OR, 70186 ... 20 B2
Hillsboro TX, 8232 ... 59 E3
Hillsboro WI, 1302 ... 74 A2
Hillsboro Beach FL, 2163 ... 143 F1
Hillsborough CA, 10825 ... 259 B4
Hillsborough NH, 1842 ... 81 E4
Hillsborough NC, 5446 ... 112 C4
Hillsborough Co. FL, 998948 ... 140 C3
Hillsborough Co. NH, 380841 ... 81 F4
Hillsdale IL, 588 ... 88 A2
Hillsdale MI, 8233 ... 90 B1
Hillsdale MO, 1477 ... 256 B2
Hillsdale NJ, 10087 ... 148 B3
Hillsdale Co. MI, 46527 ... 90 B1
Hillside IL, 8155 ... 203 C4
Hillside NJ, 21747 ... 148 A4
Hillside Lake NY, 2022 ... 148 B1
Hillsville VA, 2607 ... 112 A2
Hilltop MN, 766 ... 235 C1
Hillview KY, 7037 ... 100 A4
Hilmar CA, 4807 ... 36 C4
Hilo HI, 40759 ... 153 F3
Hilshire Vil. TX, 720 ... 220 B2
Hilton NY, 5856 ... 78 C3
Hilton Head Island SC, 33862 ... 130 C3
Hinckley IL, 1994 ... 88 C1
Hinckley MN, 1291 ... 67 D2
Hinckley UT, 698 ... 39 D2
Hindman KY, 787 ... 111 D1
Hinds Co. MS, 250800 ... 126 B3
Hines OR, 1623 ... 21 E4
Hinesburg VT, 900 ... 81 D2
Hinesville GA, 30392 ... 130 B3
Hingham MA, 5352 ... 151 D1
Hinsdale IL, 17349 ... 203 C5
Hinsdale MA, 750 ... 94 C1
Hinsdale NH, 1713 ... 94 C1
Hinsdale Co. CO, 790 ... 40 C4
Hinson FL, 750 ... 137 E2
Hinton IA, 808 ... 35 F1
Hinton OK, 2175 ... 51 D3
Hinton WV, 2880 ... 112 A1
Hiram GA, 1361 ... 120 C4
Hiram OH, 1242 ... 91 E2
Hitchcock TX, 6386 ... 132 B4
Hitchcock Co. NE, 3111 ... 34 B4
Hitchins KY, 475 ... 101 D4
Hobart IN, 25363 ... 89 D2
Hobart OK, 3997 ... 51 D3
Hobart WA, 6251 ... 12 C3
Hobbs NM, 28657 ... 57 F2
Hobe Sound FL, 11376 ... 141 F4
Hoboken NJ, 38577 ... 148 B4
Hobson MT, 244 ... 16 B4
Hockessin DE, 12902 ... 146 B3
Hocking Co. OH, 28241 ... 101 D1
Hockley Co. TX, 22716 ... 58 A1
Hodge LA, 492 ... 125 E3
Hodgeman Co. KS, 2085 ... 42 C3
Hodgenville KY, 2874 ... 110 A1
Hodgkins IL, 2134 ... 203 C5
Hoffman MN, 672 ... 66 A2
Hoffman NC, 624 ... 122 C2
Hoffman Estates IL, 49495 ... 203 B3
Hogansville GA, 2774 ... 128 C1
Hohenwald TN, 3754 ... 119 E1
Hoisington KS, 2975 ... 43 D3
Hokah MN, 614 ... 73 F2
Hoke Co. NC, 33646 ... 123 D2
Hokendauqua PA, 3411 ... 189 A1
Hokes Bluff AL, 4149 ... 120 A3
Holbrook AZ, 4917 ... 47 F3
Holbrook MA, 10785 ... 151 D2
Holbrook NY, 27512 ... 149 D4
Holcomb KS, 2026 ... 42 B3
Holcomb MO, 696 ... 108 B3
Holden MA, 4200 ... 150 B1
Holden MO, 2510 ... 96 C3
Holden UT, 400 ... 39 E2
Holden WV, 1105 ... 111 E1
Holden Beach NC, 787 ... 123 E4
Holdenville OK, 4732 ... 51 F3
Holdingford MN, 736 ... 66 B2
Holdrege NE, 5636 ... 35 D4
Holgate OH, 1194 ... 90 B2
Holiday FL, 21904 ... 140 B2
Holiday Hills IL, 831 ... 203 A1
Holiday Lakes TX, 1095 ... 132 A4
Holladay UT, 14561 ... 257 B2
Holland AR, 577 ... 117 E1
Holland IN, 695 ... 99 E4
Holland MA, 1444 ... 150 B2
Holland MI, 35048 ... 75 E4
Holland NY, 1261 ... 78 B4
Holland OH, 1306 ... 90 C2
Holland TX, 1102 ... 61 E1
Hollandale MS, 3437 ... 126 A1
Holley FL, 650 ... 135 F2
Holley NY, 1802 ... 78 B3
Holliday TX, 1632 ... 59 D1
Hollidaysburg PA, [illegible] ... [illegible] D1
Hollins VA, 14309 ... 112 B1
Hollis NH, 550 ... 95 D1
Hollis OK, 2264 ... 50 C4
Hollis Ctr. ME, 450 ... 82 B3
Hollister CA, 34413 ... 44 B2
Hollister MO, 3867 ... 107 D3
Hollister NC, 600 ... 113 D3
Holliston MA, 3400 ... 150 C2
Hollow Creek KY, 815 ... 230 E3
Hollow Rock TN, 963 ... 109 D4
Holly CO, 1048 ... 42 A3
Holly MI, 6135 ... 76 B4
Holly Grove AR, 722 ... 117 F2
Holly Hill FL, 12119 ... 139 E4
Holly Hill SC, 1281 ... 130 C1
Holly Park NJ, 2200 ... 147 E3
Holly Pond AL, 645 ... 119 F3
Holly Ridge NC, 831 ... 115 C4
Holly Sprs. GA, 3195 ... 120 C3
Holly Sprs. MS, 7957 ... 118 C2
Holly Sprs. NC, 9192 ... 112 C4
Hollyvilla KY, 481 ... 100 A4
Hollywood AL, 950 ... 120 A2
Hollywood FL, 139357 ... 143 F2
Hollywood MD, 650 ... 103 E4
Hollywood SC, 3946 ... 131 D2
Hollywood Park TX, 2983 ... 61 D2
Holmdel NJ, 1200 ... 147 E2
Holmen WI, 6200 ... 73 F1
Holmes Beach FL, 4966 ... 140 B3
Holmes Co. FL, 18564 ... 136 C1
Holmes Co. MS, 21609 ... 126 B1
Holmes Co. OH, 38943 ... 91 D4
Holstein IA, 1470 ... 72 A4
Holt AL, 4103 ... 127 E1
Holt MI, 11315 ... 76 A4
Holt Co. MO, 5351 ... 86 A4
Holt Co. NE, 11551 ... 35 D1
Holton KS, 3353 ... 96 A2
Holts Summit MO, 2935 ... 97 E3
Holtville CA, 5612 ... 53 E4
Holualoa HI, 6107 ... 153 E3
Holyoke CO, 2261 ... 34 A4
Holyoke MA, 39838 ... 150 A2
Holyrood KS, 464 ... 43 D3
Homecroft IN, 751 ... 99 F1
Homedale ID, 2528 ... 22 A4
Home Gardens CA, 9461 ... 229 H4
Homeland CA, 3710 ... 229 K4
Homeland GA, 765 ... 139 D1
Homeland Park SC, 6337 ... 121 E3
Homer AK, 3946 ... 154 C3
Homer GA, 950 ... 121 D3
Homer IL, 1200 ... 99 D1
Homer LA, 3788 ... 125 D2
Homer MI, 1851 ... 90 A1
Homer NE, 590 ... 35 F2
Homer NY, 3368 ... 79 D4
Homer City PA, 1844 ... 92 B4
Homer Glen IL, 22899 ... 203 C6
Homerville GA, 2803 ... 138 C1
Homestead FL, 31909 ... 143 E3
Homestead PA, 3569 ... 250 C2
Homestead Valley CA, 10691 ... 259 A2
Hometown IL, 4467 ... 203 D5
Hometown PA, 1399 ... 93 E3
Hometown WV, 750 ... 101 E3
Homewood AL, 25043 ... 119 F4
Hominy OK, 2584 ... 51 F1
Homosassa FL, 2294 ... 140 B1
Homosassa Sprs. FL, 12458 ... 140 B1
Honaker VA, 945 ... 111 E2
Honalo HI, 1987 ... 153 E3
Honaunau HI, 2414 ... 153 E3
Hondo TX, [illegible] ... [illegible]
Honea Path SC, 3504 ... 121 E3
Honeoye NY, 800 ... 78 C4
Honeoye Falls NY, 2595 ... 78 C3
Honesdale PA, 4874 ... 93 F2
Honey Brook PA, 1287 ... 146 B2
Honey Grove TX, 1746 ... 59 F1
Honeyville UT, 1214 ... 31 E3
Honokaa HI, 2233 ... 153 E2
Honokowai HI, 6788 ... 153 D1
Honolulu HI, 371657 ... 152 A3
Honolulu Co. HI, 876156 ... 152 A3
Honomu HI, 541 ... 153 F3
Hood Co. TX, 41100 ... 59 E3
Hood River OR, 5831 ... 21 D1
Hood River Co. OR, 20411 ... 20 C2
Hooker OK, 1788 ... 50 B1
Hooker Co. NE, 783 ... 34 B2
Hooks TX, 2973 ... 116 C4
Hooksett NH, 3609 ... 81 F4
Hoonah AK, 860 ... 155 D4
Hooper NE, 827 ... 35 F3
Hooper UT, 4026 ... 244 A2
Hooper Bay AK, 1014 ... 154 B3
Hoopeston IL, 5965 ... 89 D4
Hoople ND, 292 ... 19 E2
Hoosick Falls NY, 3436 ... 94 B1
Hoover AL, 62742 ... 127 F1
Hooverson Hts. WV, 2909 ... 91 F4
Hooversville PA, 779 ... 92 B4
Hopatcong NJ, 15888 ... 148 A3
Hope AR, 10616 ... 117 D4
Hope IN, 2140 ... 99 F2
Hope ND, 303 ... 19 E3
Hope RI, 1900 ... 150 C3
Hopedale IL, 929 ... 88 B4
Hopedale MA, 4158 ... 150 C2
Hopedale OH, 984 ... 91 F4
Hope Mills NC, 11237 ... 123 D2
Hope Valley RI, 1649 ... 150 C4
Hopewell NJ, 2035 ... 147 D1
Hopewell TN, 1815 ... 120 B1
Hopewell VA, 22354 ... 113 E1
Hopewell Jct. NY, 2610 ... 148 B1
Hopkins MI, 592 ... 75 F4
Hopkins MN, 17145 ... 235 A3
Hopkins MO, 579 ... 86 B4
Hopkins Co. KY, 46519 ... 109 E2

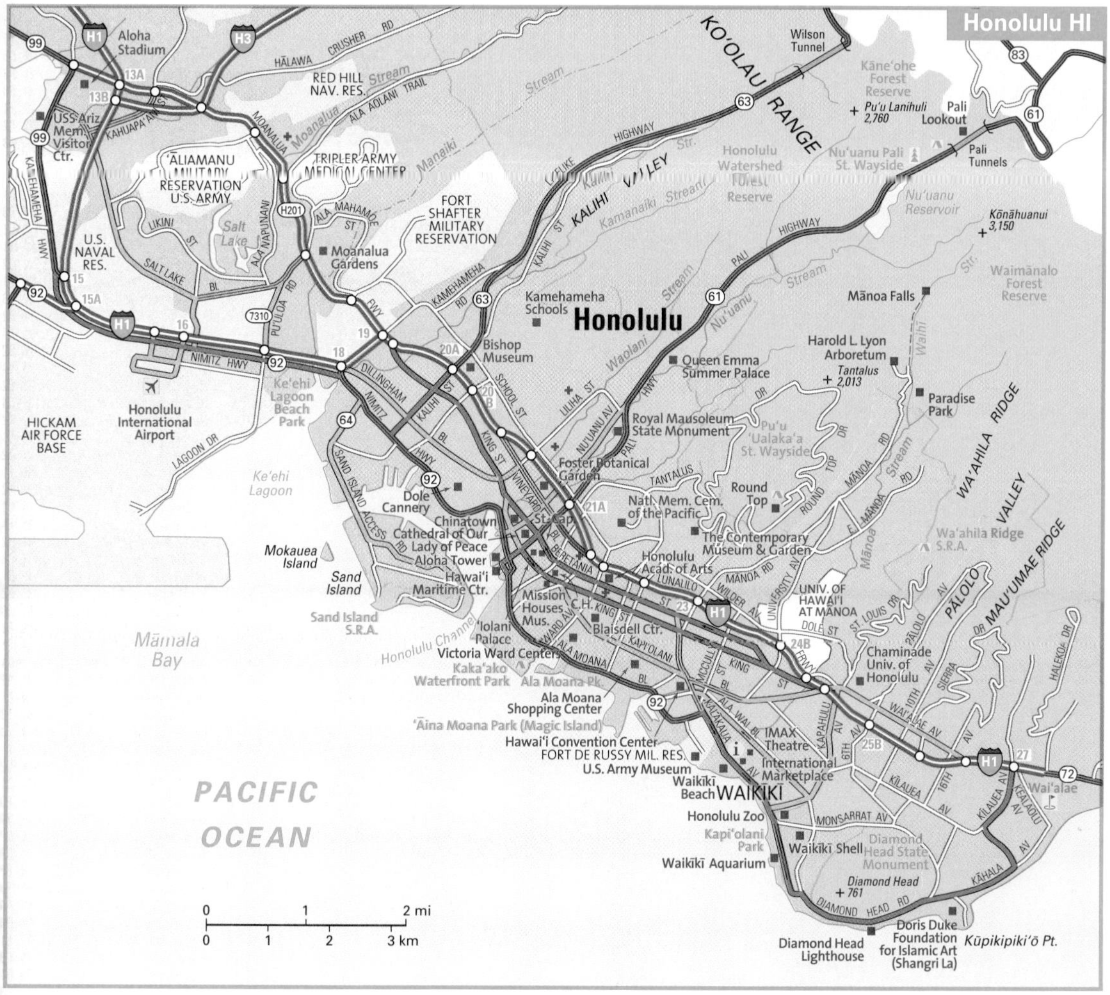
Honolulu HI
Honolulu
Aloha Stadium
RED HILL NAV. RES.
KO'OLAU RANGE
Wilson Tunnel
Kāne'ohe Forest Reserve
Pu'u Lanihuli 2,760
Pali Lookout
Pali Tunnels
Nu'uanu Pali St. Wayside
USS Arizona Mem. Visitor Ctr.
'ALIAMANU MILITARY RESERVATION U.S. ARMY
TRIPLER ARMY MEDICAL CENTER
FORT SHAFTER MILITARY RESERVATION
U.S. NAVAL RES.
Moanalua Gardens
KALIHI VALLEY
Honolulu Watershed Forest Reserve
Nu'uanu Reservoir
Kōnāhuanui 3,150
Waimānalo Forest Reserve
Kamehameha Schools
Bishop Museum
Mānoa Falls
Harold L. Lyon Arboretum
Tantalus 2,013
Queen Emma Summer Palace
Paradise Park
HICKAM AIR FORCE BASE
Honolulu International Airport
Ke'ehi Lagoon Beach Park
Ke'ehi Lagoon
Royal Mausoleum State Monument
Pu'u 'Ualaka'a St. Wayside
Foster Botanical Garden
Round Top
Natl. Mem. Cem. of the Pacific
WA'AHILA RIDGE
Dole Cannery
Chinatown
Cathedral of Our Lady of Peace
Aloha Tower
Hawai'i Maritime Ctr.
The Contemporary Museum & Garden
Wa'ahila Ridge S.R.A.
Mokauea Island
Sand Island
Sand Island S.R.A.
Honolulu Acad. of Arts
UNIV. OF HAWAI'I AT MĀNOA
PALOLO
MAU'UMAE RIDGE
Mission Houses Mus.
'Iolani Palace
Blaisdell Ctr.
Māmala Bay
Honolulu Channel
Victoria Ward Centers
Kaka'ako Waterfront Park
Ala Moana Pk.
Ala Moana Shopping Center
'Āina Moana Park (Magic Island)
Chaminade Univ. of Honolulu
Hawai'i Convention Center
FORT DE RUSSY MIL. RES.
U.S. Army Museum
IMAX Theatre
International Marketplace
Waikīkī Beach
WAIKĪKĪ
Honolulu Zoo
Kapi'olani Park
Waikīkī Shell
Waikīkī Aquarium
Diamond Head State Monument
Diamond Head 761
PACIFIC OCEAN
Wai'alae
Doris Duke Foundation for Islamic Art (Shangri La)
Diamond Head Lighthouse
Kūpikipiki'ō Pt.
0 1 2 mi
0 1 2 3 km

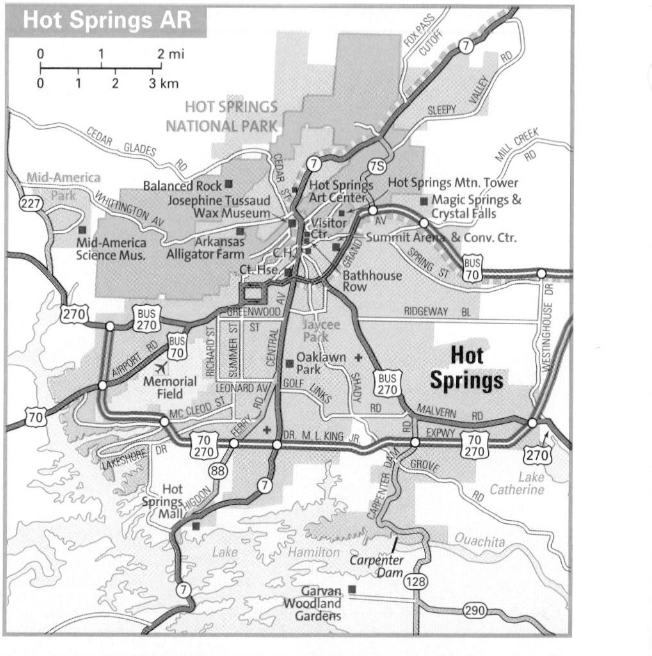
Hot Springs AR
0 1 2 mi
0 1 2 3 km
HOT SPRINGS NATIONAL PARK
FOX PASS CUTOFF
SLEEPY VALLEY
MILL CREEK RD
CEDAR GLADES RD
Mid-America Park
Balanced Rock
Josephine Tussaud Wax Museum
Hot Springs Art Center
Hot Springs Mtn. Tower
Magic Springs & Crystal Falls
Visitor Ctr.
Summit Arena & Conv. Ctr.
Mid-America Science Mus.
Arkansas Alligator Farm
Ct. Hse.
Bathhouse Row
RIDGEWAY BL
Jaycee Park
Oaklawn Park
Memorial Field
Hot Springs
MALVERN RD
EXPWY
Lake Catherine
Ouachita
Lake Hamilton
Carpenter Dam
Hot Springs Mall
Garvan Woodland Gardens

220 Hopkins County–Humboldt County

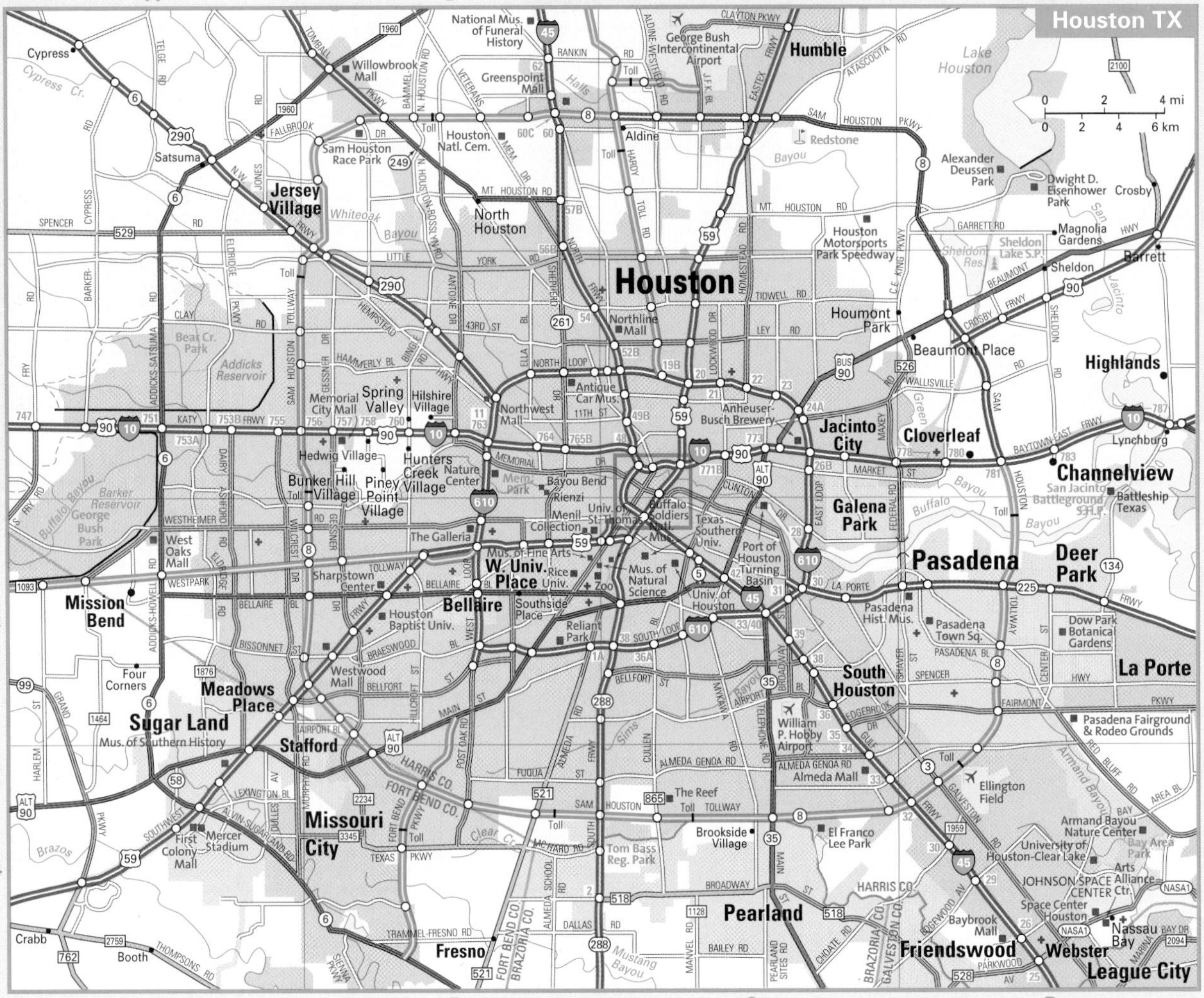

Figures after entries indicate population, page number, and grid reference.

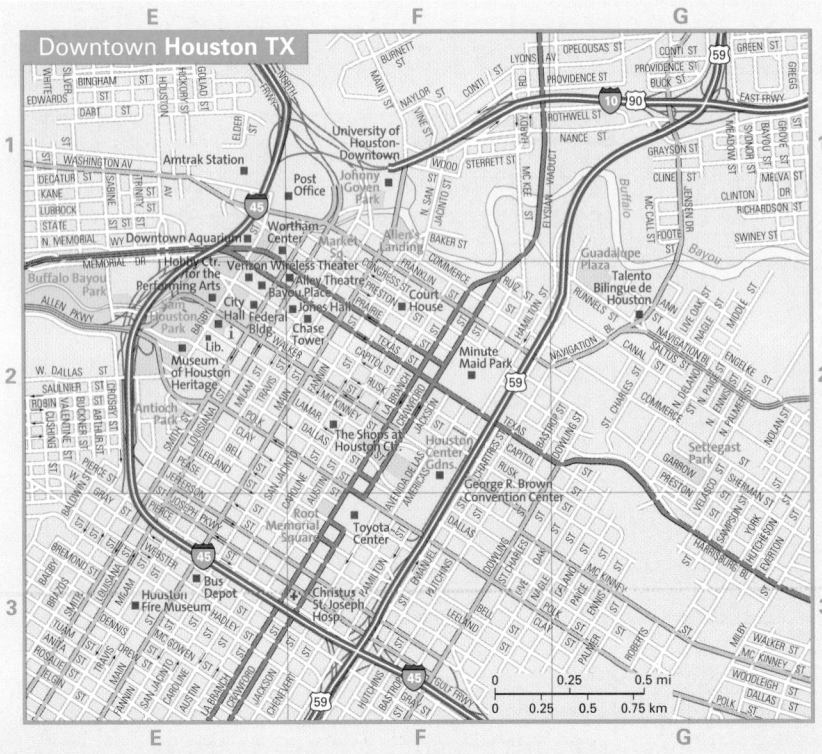

Houston TX

Downtown Houston TX

POINTS OF INTEREST

Entries in **bold black** indicate counties or parishes. Entries in **bold color** indicate cities with detailed inset maps.

Humeston–Indian Shores **221**

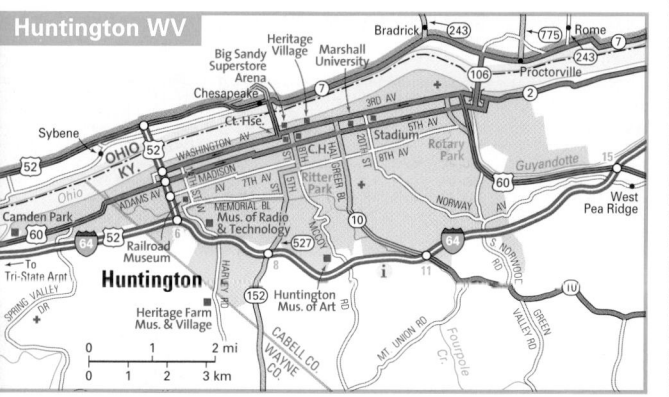

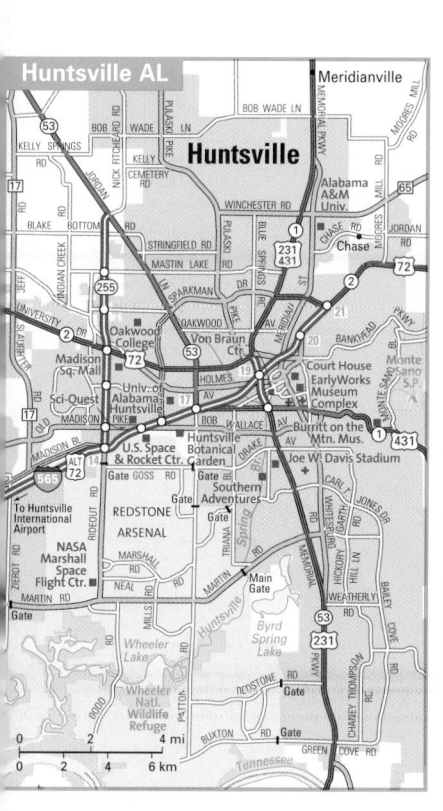

Indianapolis IN

	A	B	C	D

POINTS OF INTEREST

American Legion National Headquarters ..A1
Bus Terminal A2
Canal Walk District A1
Circle Centre A2
City Market B2
Conseco Fieldhouse B2
Eiteljorg Mus. A2
Federal Court House A2
Federal Post Office A2
Indiana Convention Center A2
Indiana State Mus. A2
Indiana Univ./Purdue Univ. Indianapolis ..A1
Indiana War Memorial A1

James Whitcomb Riley Home B1
Madame Walker Theatre Center A1
Massachusetts Avenue Arts District B1
Morris-Butler House B1
Murat Center B1
NCAA Hall of Champions A2
President Benjamin Harrison Home B1
RCA Dome A2
Scottish Rite Cathedral A1
Soldiers & Sailors Monument A2
State Capitol A2
Union Station A2
Victory Field A2
Zoo A2

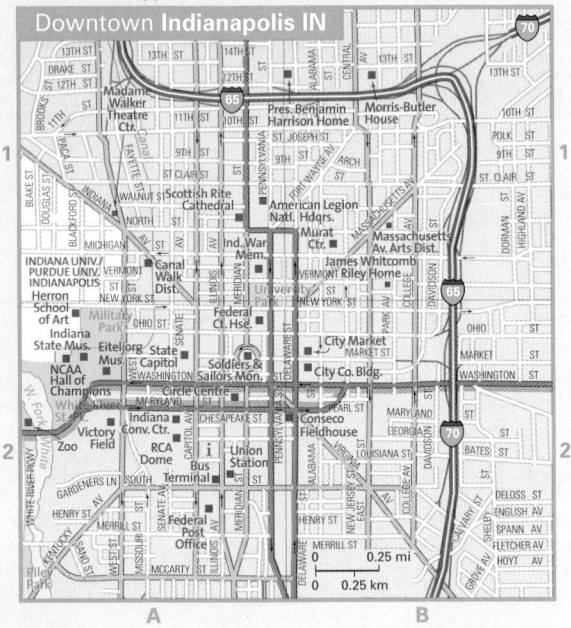

Downtown **Indianapolis IN**

Indian Sprs. NV, 1302 ....46 A1
Indian Sprs. Vil. AL, 2225 .....127 F1
Indiantown FL, 5588 ....141 E4
Indian Trail NC, 11905 ....122 B2
Indian Wells CA, 3816 ....53 E3
Indio CA, 49116 ....53 E3
Indrio FL, 550 ....141 E4
Industry CA, 777 ....228 E3
Industry PA, 1921 ....91 E3
Inez KY, 466 ....101 D4
Inez TX, 1787 ....61 F1
Ingalls IN, 1168 ....99 F1
Ingham Co. MI, 279320 ....76 A4
Ingleside TX, 9388 ....63 F2

Ingleside on the Bay TX, 659 ...63 F2
Inglewood CA, 112580 ....52 C2
Inglis FL, 1491 ....138 C4
Ingold NC, 484 ....123 C2
Ingram PA, 3712 ....250 A2
Ingram TX, 1740 ....60 C2
Inkom ID, 738 ....31 E1
Inkster MI, 30115 ....210 B4
Inman GA, 650 ....128 C1
Inman KS, 1142 ....43 E3
Inman SC, 1884 ....121 F2
Inola OK, 1589 ....106 A4
Intercession City FL, 900 .....141 D2
Interlachen FL, 1475 ....139 D3

Interlaken NJ, 900 ....147 F2
Interlaken NY, 674 ....79 D4
Interlochen MI, 600 ....69 F4
International Falls MN, 6703 ...64 B2
Inver Grove Hts. MN, 29751 ...235 D4
Inverness CA, 1421 ....36 A3
Inverness FL, 6789 ....140 C1
Inverness IL, 6749 ....203 B2
Inverness MS, 1153 ....126 B1
Inwood FL, 6925 ....140 C2
Inwood IA, 875 ....27 F4
Inwood NY, 9325 ....147 F1
Inwood WV, 2084 ....103 D2
Inyo Co. CA, 17945 ....37 E4

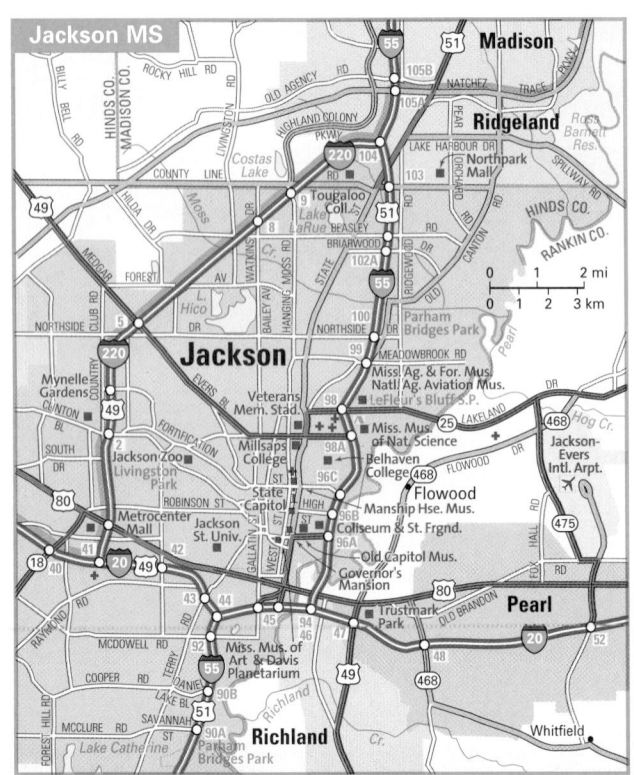

Jackson MS

Inyokern CA, 984 ....45 E4
Iola KS, 6302 ....96 A4
Iola WI, 1298 ....68 B4
Iona ID, 1201 ....23 E4
Ione CA, 7129 ....36 C3
Ione OR, 321 ....21 E2
Ione WA, 447 ....13 F1
Ionia MI, 10569 ....76 A3
Ionia Co. MI, 61518 ....75 F3
Iosco Co. MI, 27339 ....76 B1
Iota LA, 1376 ....133 E2
Iowa LA, 2663 ....133 D2
Iowa City IA, 62220 ....87 F2
Iowa Colony TX, 804 ....132 A4
Iowa Co. IA, 15671 ....87 E2
Iowa Co. WI, 22780 ....74 A3
Iowa Falls IA, 5193 ....73 D4
Iowa Park TX, 6431 ....59 D1
Ipswich MA, 4161 ....151 F1
Ipswich SD, 943 ....27 D3
Iraan TX, 1238 ....60 A1
Iredell Co. NC, 122660 ......112 A4
Irene SD, 432 ....35 E1
Ireton IA, 585 ....35 F1
Irion Co. TX, 1771 ....58 B4
Irmo SC, 11039 ....122 A3
Iron City TN, 368 ....119 C1
Iron Co. MI, 13138 ....68 C1
Iron Co. MO, 10697 ....108 A1
Iron Co. UT, 33779 ....39 D4
Iron Co. WI, 6861 ....68 A1
Irondale AL, 9813 ....119 F3
Irondequoit NY, 52354 ....78 C3
Iron Gate VA, 412 ....112 B1
Iron Mtn. MI, 8154 ....68 C2
Iron Mtn. Lake MO, 693 ....108 A1
Iron Ridge WI, 998 ....74 C3
Iron River MI, 3386 ....68 C2
Ironton MN, 498 ....64 B4
Ironton MO, 1471 ....108 A1

Ironton OH, 11211 ....101 D3
Ironwood MI, 6293 ....65 E4
Iroquois SD, 278 ....27 E3
Iroquois Co. IL, 31334 ....89 D3
Irrigon OR, 1702 ....21 E1
Irvine CA, 143072 ....52 C3
Irvine KY, 2843 ....110 C1
Irving IL, 2484 ....98 B2
Irving TX, 191615 ....59 F2
Irvington IL, 736 ....98 C3
Irvington KY, 1257 ....99 F4
Irvington NE, 950 ....245 A1
Irvington NJ, 60695 ....148 A4
Irvington NY, 6631 ....148 B3
Irvington VA, 673 ....113 F1
Irvona PA, 680 ....92 B3
Irwin PA, 4366 ....92 A4
Irwindale CA, 1446 ....228 E2
Irwinton GA, 587 ....129 E2
Irwin Co. GA, 9931 ....129 E4
Isabel SD, 239 ....26 B2
Isabella CA, 1246 ....45 D3
Isabella Co. MI, 63351 ......76 A2
Isanti MN, 2324 ....67 D3
Isanti Co. MN, 31287 ....67 D3
Iselin NJ, 16698 ....147 E1
Ishpeming MI, 6686 ....65 F4
Islamorada FL, 6846 ....143 E4
Island KY, 435 ....109 D1
Island City OR, 916 ....21 F2
Island Co. WA, 71558 ....12 C2
Island Falls ME, 450 ....85 D3
Island Hts. NJ, 1751 ....147 E3
Island Lake IL, 8153 ....74 C4
Island Park ID, 215 ....23 E3
Island Park NY, 4732 ....147 F1
Island Pond VT, 849 ....81 E1
Isla Vista CA, 18344 ....52 A2
Isle MN, 707 ....67 D2
Isle of Hope GA, 2605 ....130 C3

Isle of Palms SC, 4583 ......131 D2
Isle of Wight VA, 100 ....113 F2
Isle of Wight Co. VA, 29728 ..113 F2
Isleta NM, 496 ....48 C3
Isleton CA, 828 ....36 C3
Islip NY, 20575 ....149 D4
Isola MS, 768 ....126 B1
Issaquah WA, 11212 ....12 C3
Issaquena Co. MS, 2274 .....126 A2
Italy TX, 1993 ....59 F3
Itasca IL, 8302 ....203 B3
Itasca TX, 1503 ....59 F3
Itasca Co. MN, 43992 ....64 B3
Itawamba Co. MS, 22770 ....119 D3
Ithaca MI, 3098 ....76 A3
Ithaca NY, 29287 ....79 D3
Itta Bena MS, 2208 ....118 B4
Iuka IL, 598 ....98 C3
Iuka MS, 3059 ....119 D2
Iva SC, 1156 ....121 E3
Ivanhoe CA, 4474 ....45 D3
Ivanhoe MN, 679 ....27 F3
Ivanhoe VA, 500 ....112 A2
Ivey GA, 1100 ....129 E1
Ivins UT, 4450 ....38 C4
Ixonia WI, 642 ....74 C3
Izard Co. AR, 13249 ....107 D3

J

Jacinto City TX, 10302 ....220 C2
Jack Co. TX, 8763 ....59 D2
Jackman ME, 700 ....84 B4
Jackman Sta. ME, 750 ....84 B4
Jackpot NV, 1100 ....30 C2
Jacksboro TN, 1887 ....110 C3
Jacksboro TX, 4732 ....59 D2
Jackson Par. LA, 15397 ......125 E2
Jackson AL, 5419 ....127 E4
Jacksons Gap AL, 761 ....128 C3
Jackson CA, 3989 ....36 C3
Jackson GA, 3934 ....129 D1
Jackson KY, 2490 ....111 D1

Jackson LA, 4130 ....134 A1
Jackson MI, 36316 ....76 A4
Jackson MN, 3501 ....72 B2
Jackson MS, *184256* 126 B3
Jackson MO, 11947 ....108 B1
Jackson NC, 695 ....113 E3
Jackson OH, 6184 ....101 D2
Jackson SC, 1625 ....130 A4
Jackson TN, 59643 ....119 D1
Jackson WI, 4938 ....74 C3
Jackson WY, 8647 ....23 D1
Jackson Ctr. OH, 1369 ....90 B4
Jackson Co. AL, 53926 ......120 A2
Jackson Co. CO, 1577 ....33 D4
Jackson Co. FL, 46755 ......137 D3
Jackson Co. GA, 41589 ......121 D3
Jackson Co. IL, 59612 ......98 B4
Jackson Co. IN, 41335 ......99 F3
Jackson Co. IA, 20296 ......87 F1
Jackson Co. KS, 12657 ......96 A2
Jackson Co. KY, 13495 ......110 C1
Jackson Co. MI, 158422 .....76 A4
Jackson Co. MN, 11268 ......72 B2
Jackson Co. MS, 131420 .....135 D2
Jackson Co. MO, 654880 .....96 C3
Jackson Co. NC, 33121 ......121 D1
Jackson Co. OH, 33121 ......101 D3
Jackson Co. OK, 28439 ......50 C4
Jackson Co. OR, 181269 .....28 B4
Jackson Co. SD, 2930 ....26 B4
Jackson Co. TN, 10984 ......110 A3
Jackson Co. TX, 14391 ......61 E3
Jackson Co. WV, 28000 ......101 E3
Jackson Co. WI, 19100 ......67 F4
Jacksons Gap AL, 761 ....128 C3
Jacksonville AL, 8404 ....120 A4
Jacksonville AR, 29916 ......117 E2
Jacksonville FL, *735617* 139 D2

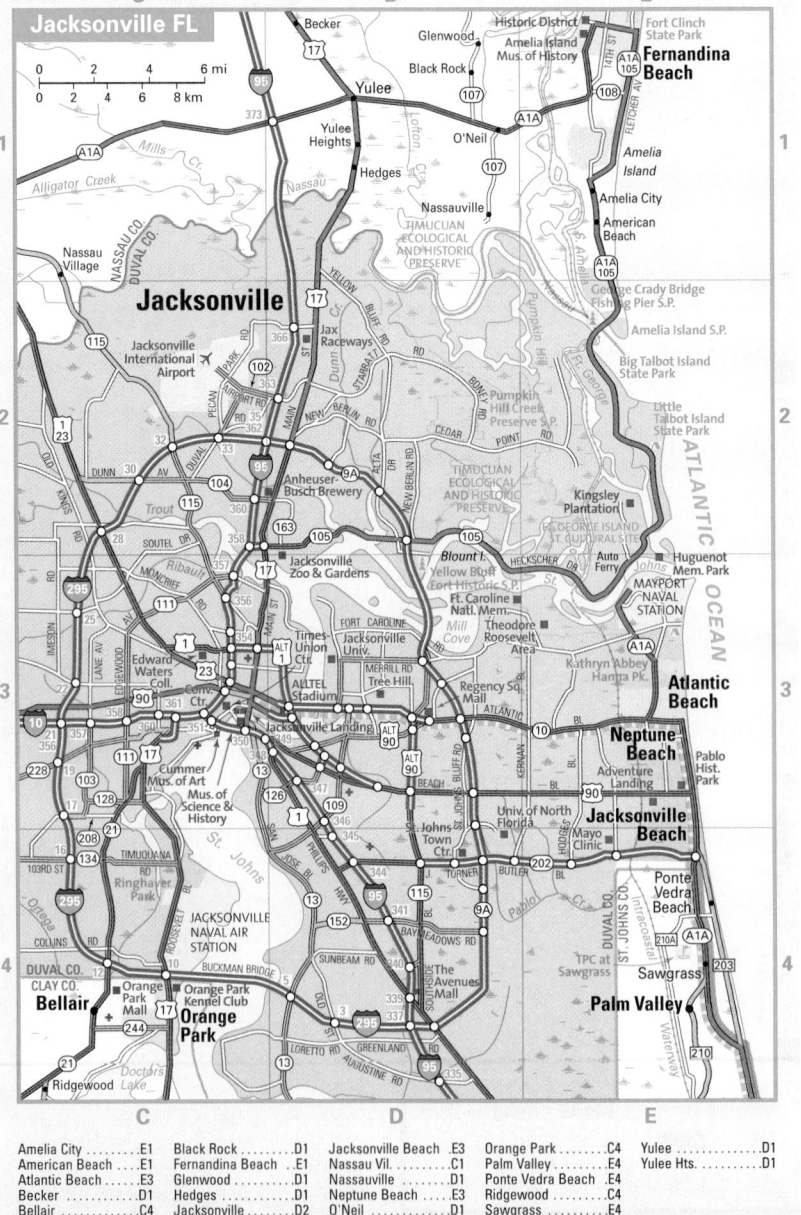

Jacksonville FL

Amelia City E1
American Beach E1
Atlantic Beach E3
Becker D1
Bellair C4

Black Rock D1
Fernandina Beach E1
Glenwood D1
Hedges D1
Jacksonville D2

Jacksonville Beach ...E3
Nassau Vil. C1
Nassauville C1
Neptune Beach E3
O'Neil D1

Orange Park C4
Palm Valley E4
Ponte Vedra Beach ...E4
Ridgewood C4
Sawgrass E4

Yulee D1
Yulee Hts. D1

Entries in **bold black** indicate counties or parishes. Entries in **bold color** indicate cities with detailed inset maps.

Jacksonville–Keystone Heights 223

Jacksonville IL, *18940* 98 A1
Jacksonville MD, *900* 144 C1
Jacksonville NC, *66715* 115 D4
Jacksonville OR, *2235* 28 B2
Jacksonville PA, *675* 92 B4
Jacksonville TX, *13868* 124 A3
Jacksonville VT, *237* 94 C1
Jacksonville Beach FL, *20990* 139 D2
Jacobstown NJ, *950* 147 D2
Jacobus PA, *1203* 103 E1
Jaffrey NH, *2802* 95 D1
Jal NM, *1996* 57 F3
Jamaica Beach TX, *1075* 132 B4
Jamesburg NJ, *6025* 147 E2
James City NC, *5420* 115 D3
James City Co. VA, *48102* 113 F1
Jamesport MO, *505* 96 C1
Jamesport NY, *1526* 149 E3
Jamestown CA, *3017* 37 D3
Jamestown IN, *886* 99 E1
Jamestown KS, *399* 43 E1
Jamestown KY, *1624* 110 B2
Jamestown MI, *750* 75 F3
Jamestown NY, *31730* 92 B1
Jamestown NC, *3088* 112 B4
Jamestown ND, *15527* 19 D4
Jamestown OH, *1917* 100 C1
Jamestown PA, [illegible] 91 F3
Jamestown RI, *5622* 150 C4
Jamestown TN, *1839* 110 B3
James Town WY, *552* 32 A3
Jamesville NC, *502* 113 F4
Jamul CA, *5920* 53 D4
Jane Lew WV, *406* 102 A2
Janesville CA, *550* 29 D4
Janesville IA, *829* 73 D4
Janesville MN, *2109* 72 C1
Janesville WI, *59498* 74 B4
Jarales NM, *1434* 48 C4
Jarratt VA, *589* 113 E2
Jarrell TX, *1384* 61 E1
Jarrettsville MD, *2756* 144 C1
Jasmine Estates FL, *18213* 140 B2
Jasonville IN, *2490* 99 E2
Jasper AL, *14052* 119 E4
Jasper AR, *498* 107 D4
Jasper FL, *1780* 138 B2
Jasper GA, *2167* 120 C3
Jasper IN, *12100* 99 E4
Jasper MN, *597* 27 F4
Jasper MO, *1011* 106 C1
Jasper OR, *700* 20 B4
Jasper TN, *3214* 120 A2
Jasper TX, *8247* 132 C1
Jasper Co. GA, *11426* 129 D1
Jasper Co. IL, *10117* 99 D2
Jasper Co. IN, *30043* 89 E3
Jasper Co. IA, *37213* 87 D2
Jasper Co. MS, *18149* 126 C3
Jasper Co. MO, *104686* 106 C2
Jasper Co. SC, *20678* 130 C3
Jasper Co. TX, *35604* 132 C1
Jay FL, *579* 135 F1
Jay ME, *325* 82 B2
Jay OK, *2482* 106 B3
Jay Co. IN, *21806* 90 A4
Jayton TX, *513* 58 B2
Jeanerette LA, *5997* 133 F3
Jean Lafitte LA, *2137* 134 B3
Jeannette PA, *10654* 92 A4
Jeddito AZ, *390* 47 F2
Jeff Davis Co. GA, *12684* 129 F3
Jeff Davis Co. TX, *2207* 62 B2
Jefferson GA, *3825* 121 D3
Jefferson IA, *4626* 86 B1
Jefferson LA, *11843* 239 B1
Jefferson MA, *1600* 150 B1
Jefferson NC, *1422* 111 F3
Jefferson OH, *3572* 91 F1
Jefferson OR, *2487* 20 B3
Jefferson PA, *631* 103 E1
Jefferson SC, [illegible] 122 D2
Jefferson SD, *586* 35 F1
Jefferson TX, *2024* 124 C2
Jefferson WI, *7338* 74 B3
Jefferson City MO, *39636* 97 E3
Jefferson City MT, *295* 15 E4
Jefferson City TN, *7760* 111 D4
Jefferson Co. AL, *662047* 119 F4
Jefferson Co. AR, *84278* 117 F3
Jefferson Co. CO, *525507* 41 E1
Jefferson Co. FL, *12902* 137 E2
Jefferson Co. GA, *17266* 129 F1
Jefferson Co. ID, *19155* 23 E4
Jefferson Co. IL, *40045* 98 C4
Jefferson Co. IN, *31705* 100 A3
Jefferson Co. IA, *16181* 87 E3
Jefferson Co. KS, *18426* 96 A2
Jefferson Co. KY, *693604* 100 A4
Jefferson Co. MS, *9740* 126 A3
Jefferson Co. MO, *198099* 98 A4
Jefferson Co. MT, *10049* 23 E1
Jefferson Co. NE, *8333* 35 F4
Jefferson Co. NY, *111738* 79 E2
Jefferson Co. OH, *73894* 91 F4
Jefferson Co. OK, *6818* 59 E1
Jefferson Co. OR, *19009* 20 C3
Jefferson Co. PA, *45932* 92 B2
Jefferson Co. TN, *44294* 111 D4
Jefferson Co. TX, *252051* 132 C3
Jefferson Co. WA, *25953* 12 B3
Jefferson Co. WV, *42190* 103 D2
Jefferson Co. WI, *74021* 74 C3
Jefferson Davis Co. MS, *13962* 126 B4
Jefferson Davis Par. LA, *31435* 133 E2
Jefferson Hts. NY, *1104* 94 B2
Jefferson Hills PA, *9666* 92 A4
Jefferson Par. LA, *455466* 134 B3
Jeffersontown KY, *26633* 100 A4
Jefferson Valley NY, *14891* 148 B2
Jeffersonville GA, *1209* 129 E2
Jeffersonville IN, *27362* 100 A4
Jeffersonville KY, *1804* 100 C4
Jeffersonville OH, *1288* 100 C1
Jeffersonville PA, *10200* 248 A1
Jeffersonville VT, *568* 81 D1
Jellico TN, *2448* 110 C3
Jemez Pueblo NM, *1953* 48 C3
Jemez Sprs. NM, *375* 48 C2
Jemison AL, *2248* 127 F1
Jena LA, *2971* 125 E4
Jenison MI, *17211* 75 F3
Jenkins KY, *2401* 111 E2
Jenkins Co. GA, *8575* 129 F2
Jenkintown PA, *4478* 146 C2
Jenks OK, [illegible] 51 F3
Jennerstown PA, *714* 92 B4
Jennings FL, *833* 137 F2
Jennings LA, *10986* 133 E2
Jennings MO, *15469* 256 B1
Jennings Co. IN, *27554* 100 A3
Jenny Lind AR, *650* 116 C1
Jensen Beach FL, *11100* 141 E4
Jerauld Co. SD, *2295* 27 D3
Jericho NY, *13045* 148 C4
Jericho VT, *1457* 81 D2
Jermyn PA, *2287* 93 F2
Jerome AZ, *329* 47 D4
Jerome ID, *7780* 30 C1
Jerome PA, *1068* 92 B4
Jerome Co. ID, *18342* 31 D1
Jersey City NJ, *240055* 148 B4
Jersey Co. IL, *21668* 98 A2
Jersey Shore PA, *4482* 93 D2
Jersey Vil. TX, *6880* 132 A3
Jerseyville IL, *7984* 98 A2
Jerseyville NJ, *1000* 147 E2
Jerusalem RI, *800* 150 C4
Jessamine Co. KY, *39041* 100 B4
Jessup MD, *7865* 144 C2
Jessup PA, *4718* 93 F2
Jesup GA, *9279* 130 A4
Jesup IA, *2212* 73 E4
Jetmore KS, *903* 42 C3
Jewell IA, *1239* 72 C4
Jewell KS, *483* 43 E1
Jewell Co. KS, *3791* 43 E1
Jewett OH, *784* 91 F4
Jewett TX, *861* 59 F4
Jewett City (Griswold) CT, *3053* 149 F1
Jim Hogg Co. TX, *5281* 63 E3
Jim Thorpe PA, *4804* 93 F3
Jim Wells Co. TX, *39326* 63 E2
Joanna SC, *1609* 121 F3
Joaquin TX, *925* 124 C3
Jo Daviess Co. IL, *22289* 74 A4
John Day OR, *1821* 21 F3
Johns Island SC, *650* 131 D2
Johnson AR, *2319* 106 C4
Johnson VT, *1420* 81 E2
Johnsonburg PA, *3003* 92 B2
Johnson City KS, *1528* 42 B4
Johnson City NY, *15535* 93 E1
Johnson City OR, *634* 251 D3
Johnson City TN, *55469* 111 E3
Johnson City TX, *1191* 61 D1
Johnson Co. AR, *22781* 117 D1
Johnson Co. GA, *8560* 129 F2
Johnson Co. IL, *12878* 108 C1
Johnson Co. IN, *115209* 99 F2
Johnson Co. IA, *111006* 87 F2
Johnson Co. KS, *451086* 96 B3
Johnson Co. KY, *23445* 111 D1
Johnson Co. MO, *48258* 96 C3
Johnson Co. NE, *4488* 35 F4
Johnson Co. TN, *17499* 111 F3
Johnson Co. TX, *126811* 59 E3
Johnson Co. WY, *7075* 25 D4
Johnson Creek WI, *1581* 74 C3
Johnsonville SC, *1418* 122 C4
Johnston IA, *8649* 86 C2
Johnston SC, *2336* 121 F4
Johnston City IL, *3557* 108 C1
Johnston Co. NC, *121965* 113 D4
Johnston Co. OK, *10513* 51 F4
Johnstown CO, *3827* 33 E4
Johnstown NY, *8511* 79 F3
Johnstown OH, *3440* 91 D4
Johnstown PA, *23906* 92 B4
Joiner AR, *540* 118 B1
Joliet IL, *106221* 89 D2
Joliet MT, *575* 24 B2
Jollyville TX, *15813* 61 E1
Jones OK, *2517* 51 E3
Jonesboro AR, *55515* 108 A4
Jonesboro GA, *3829* 120 C4
Jonesboro IL, *1853* 108 C1
Jonesboro IN, *1887* 89 F4
Jonesboro LA, *3914* 125 E3
Jonesborough TN, *4168* 111 E3
Jonesburg MO, *695* 97 F3
Jones Co. GA, *23639* 129 D1
Jones Co. IA, *20221* 87 F1
Jones Co. MS, *64958* 126 C4
Jones Co. NC, *10381* 115 D3
Jones Co. SD, *1193* 26 C4
Jones Co. TX, *20785* 58 C2
Jones Creek TX, *2130* 132 A4
Jonesport ME, *650* 83 E2
Jonestown MS, *1701* 118 A3
Jonestown PA, *1028* 93 E4
Jonestown TX, *1681* 61 E1
Jonesville LA, *2469* 125 F4
Jonesville MI, *2337* 90 B1
Jonesville NC, *2259* 112 A3
Jonesville SC, *982* 121 F2
Jonesville VT, *375* 81 D2
Jonesville VA, *995* 111 D3
Joplin MO, *45504* 106 B2
Joplin MT, *210* 15 F2
Joppatowne MD, *11391* 145 D1
Jordan MN, *3833* 66 C4
Jordan MT, *364* 17 D3
Jordan NY, *1314* 79 D3
Joseph OR, *1054* 22 A2
Joseph City AZ, *1000* 47 F3
Josephine TX, *594* 59 F2
Josephine Co. OR, *75726* 28 B2
Joshua TX, *4528* 59 E3
Joshua Tree CA, *4207* 53 E2
Jourdanton TX, *3732* 61 D3
Juab Co. UT, *8238* 39 D1
Judith Basin Co. MT, *2329* 16 A3
Judsonia AR, *1982* 117 F1
Julesburg CO, *1467* 34 A3
Juliaetta ID, *609* 14 B4
Julian CA, *1621* 53 D4
Julian NC, *600* 112 B4
Jumpertown MS, *404* 119 D2
Junction TX, *2618* 60 C1
Junction UT, *177* 39 E3
Junction City AR, *721* 125 E1
Junction City KS, *18886* 43 F2
Junction City KY, *2184* 110 B1
Junction City LA, *652* 125 E1
Junction City OH, *818* 101 E1
Junction City OR, *4721* 20 B3
Juneau AK, *30711* 155 E4
Juneau WI, *2485* 74 C2
Juneau Co. WI, *24316* 74 A1
Juniata NE, *693* 35 D4
Juniata Co. PA, *22821* 93 D3
Junior WV, *450* 102 A2
Juno Beach FL, *3262* 141 F4
Jupiter FL, *39328* 141 F4
Jupiter Island FL, *620* 141 F4
Justice IL, *12193* 203 D5
Justin TX, *1891* 59 E2
Justus PA, *950* 261 E1

K

Kaaawa HI, *1324* 152 A2
Kaanapali HI, *1375* 153 D1
Kadoka SD, *706* 26 B4
Kahaluu HI, *2935* 152 A3
Kahoka MO, *2241* 87 E4
Kahuku HI, *2097* 152 A2
Kahului HI, *20146* 153 D1
Kaibab AZ, *275* 47 D1
Kaibito AZ, *1607* 47 E1
Kailua HI, *36513* 152 B3
Kailua-Kona HI, *9870* 153 E3
Kake AK, *710* 155 E4
Kalaheo HI, *3913* 152 B1
Kalama WA, *1783* 20 C1
Kalamazoo MI, *77145* 75 F4
Kalamazoo Co. MI, *238603* 75 F4
Kalaoa HI, *6794* 153 E3
Kalaupapa HI, 152 C3
Kalawao Co. HI, *147* 152 C3
Kaleva MI, *509* 75 F1
Kalida OH, *1031* 90 B3
Kalihiwai HI, *717* 152 B1
Kalispell MT, *14223* 15 D2
Kalkaska MI, *2226* 69 F4
Kalkaska Co. MI, *16571* 70 B4
Kalona IA, *2293* 87 E2
Kamas UT, *1274* 31 F4
Kamiah ID, *1160* 22 B1
Kanab UT, *3564* 47 D1
Kanabec Co. MN, *14996* 67 D2
Kanarraville UT, *311* 39 D4
Kanawha IA, *739* 72 C3
Kanawha WV, *500* 101 F2
Kanawha Co. WV, *200073* 101 F4
Kandiyohi MN, *555* 66 B3
Kandiyohi Co. MN, *41203* 66 B3
Kane PA, *4126* 92 B2
Kane Co. IL, *404119* 88 C1
Kane Co. UT, *6046* 39 E4
Kaneohe HI, *34970* 152 A3
Kankakee IL, *27491* 89 D3
Kankakee Co. IL, *103833* 89 D2
Kannapolis NC, *36910* 122 B1
Kanopolis KS, *543* 43 E2
Kanosh UT, *485* 39 D2
Kansas IL, *842* 99 D1
Kansas OK, *685* 106 B3
Kansas City KS, *146866* 96 B2
Kansas City MO, *441545* 96 B2
Kapaa HI, *9472* 152 B1
Kapaau HI, *1159* 153 E2
Kaplan LA, *5177* 133 E3
Karlstad MN, *794* 19 F2
Karnak IL, *619* 108 C2
Karnes City TX, *3457* 61 E3
Karnes Co. TX, *15446* 61 E3
Karns TN, *1500* 110 C4
Kasigluk AK, *543* 154 B3
Kasota MN, *680* 72 C1
Kasson IN, *1500* 99 D4
Kasson MN, *4398* 73 D1
Kathleen FL, *3280* 140 C2
Kathleen GA, *650* 129 D2
Katonah NY, *3600* 148 C2
Katy TX, *11775* 132 A3
Kauai Co. HI, *58463* 152 B1
Kaufman TX, *6490* 59 F2
Kaufman Co. TX, *71313* 59 F3
Kaukauna WI, *12983* 74 C1
Kaumakani HI, *607* 152 B1
Kaunakakai HI, *2726* 152 C3
Kawkawlin MI, *1600* 76 B2
Kaycee WY, *249* 25 D4
Kay Co. OK, *48080* 51 E1
Kayenta AZ, *4922* 47 F1
Kaysville UT, *20351* 31 E3
Keaau HI, *2010* 153 F3
Kealakekua HI, *1645* 153 E3
Keams Canyon AZ, *260* 47 F2
Keansburg NJ, *10732* 147 E1
Kearney MO, *5472* 96 B2
Kearney NE, *27431* 35 D4
Kearney Co. NE, *6882* 35 D4
Kearneysville WV, *650* 103 D2
Kearns UT, *33659* 257 A2
Kearny AZ, *2249* 55 D2
Kearny NJ, *40513* 148 B4
Kearny Co. KS, *4531* 42 B3
Keauhou HI, *2414* 153 E3
Keavy KY, *450* 110 C2
Kechi KS, *1038* 43 E4
Keedysville MD, *482* 144 A1
Keegan ME, *550* 85 E1
Keego Harbor MI, *2769* 210 A1
Keene NH, *22563* 95 D1
Keene TX, *5003* 59 E3
Keener NC, *508* 123 E2
Keenesburg CO, *855* 41 E1
Keeseville NY, *1850* 81 D2
Keewatin MN, *1164* 64 B3
Keiser AR, *808* 108 B4
Keith Co. NE, *8875* 34 B3
Keithsburg IL, *714* 87 F3
Keizer OR, *32203* 20 B2
Kekaha HI, *3175* 152 B1
Keller TX, *27345* 59 E2
Kellogg ID, *2395* 14 B3
Kellogg IA, *606* 87 D1
Kellyville OK, *906* 51 F2
Kelseyville CA, *2928* 36 B2
Kelso MO, *527* 108 B2
Kelso WA, *11895* 20 B1
Kemah TX, *2330* 132 B3
Kemblesville PA, *1000* 146 B4
Kemmerer WY, *2651* 31 F2
Kemp TX, [illegible] 59 F3
Kemper Co. MS, *10453* 127 D2
Kempner TX, *1004* 59 E4
Kenai AK, *6942* 154 C3
Kenansville NC, *1149* 123 E2
Kenbridge VA, *1253* 113 D2
Kendall FL, *75226* 143 E2
Kendall NY, *750* 78 B3
Kendall Co. IL, *54544* 88 C2
Kendall Co. TX, *23743* 61 D2
Kendall Park NJ, *9006* 147 D1
Kendallville IN, *9616* 90 A2
Kendrick FL, *600* 138 C4
Kendrick ID, *369* 14 B4
Kenedy TX, *3487* 61 E3
Kenedy Co. TX, *414* 63 F3
Kenefick TX, *667* 132 B3
Kenesaw NE, *873* 35 D4
Kenilworth IL, *2494* 203 D2
Kenilworth NJ, *7675* 240 A4
Kenilworth PA, *1576* 146 B2
Kenly NC, *1569* 123 E1
Kenmare ND, *1081* 18 B1
Kenmore NY, *16426* 78 A3
Kenmore WA, *18678* 262 B2
Kennebec SD, *286* 26 C4
Kennebec Co. ME, *117114* 82 B2
Kennebunk ME, *4804* 82 B4
Kennebunkport ME, *1376* 82 B4
Kennedale TX, *5850* 207 B3
Kennedy AL, *541* 119 D4
Kenner LA, *70517* 134 B3
Kennesaw GA, *21675* 120 C3
Kenneth City FL, *4400* 266 A3
Kennett MO, *11260* 108 B3
Kennett Square PA, *5273* 146 B3
Kennewick WA, *54693* 21 E1
Keno OR, *650* 28 C2
Kenosha WI, *90352* 75 D4
Kenosha Co. WI, *149577* 74 C4
Kenova WV, *3485* 101 D4
Kensett AR, *1791* 117 F1
Kensington CA, *4936* 259 C2
Kensington CT, *8541* 149 E1
Kensington KS, *529* 43 D1
Kensington MD, *1873* 270 C1
Kensington NY, *1209* 241 G2
Kensington Park FL, *3720* 266 C5
Kent CT, *650* 94 B3
Kent OH, *27906* 91 E3
Kent WA, *79524* 12 C3
Kent City MI, *1061* 75 F3
Kent Co. DE, *126697* 145 E3
Kent Co. MD, *19197* 145 D2
Kent Co. MI, *574335* 75 F3
Kent Co. RI, *167090* 150 C3
Kent Co. TX, *859* 58 B2
Kentfield CA, *6351* 259 A1
Kentland IN, *1822* 89 D3
Kenton DE, *237* 145 E2
Kenton KY, *375* 100 B3
Kenton OH, *8336* 90 C3
Kenton TN, *1306* 108 C3
Kenton Co. KY, *151464* 100 B2
Kentwood LA, *2205* 134 B1
Kentwood MI, *45255* 75 F3
Kenvil NJ, *12569* 148 A3
Kenwood MD, *9800* 193 D2
Kenwood OH, *7423* 204 C2
Kenwood Beach MD, *600* 144 C4
Kenyon MN, *1661* 73 D1
Keokuk IA, [illegible] 87 F4
Keokuk Co. IA, *11400* 87 E2
Keosauqua IA, *1066* 87 E3
Keota IA, *1025* 87 E2
Keota OK, *517* 116 B1
Kerens TX, *1681* 59 F3
Kerhonkson NY, *1732* 94 A3
Kerkhoven MN, *759* 66 B3
Kerman CA, *8551* 44 C3
Kermit TX, *5714* 57 F3
Kern Co. CA, *661645* 45 D4
Kernersville NC, *17126* 112 B4
Kernville CA, *1736* 45 E4
Kerr Co. TX, *43653* 60 C2
Kerrville TX, *20425* 60 C2
Kersey CO, *1389* 33 E4
Kershaw SC, *1645* 122 B2
Kershaw Co. SC, *52647* 122 B3
Keshena WI, *1394* 68 C4
Ketchikan AK, *7922* 155 F4
Ketchum ID, *3003* 22 C4
Kettering OH, *57502* 100 B1
Kettle Falls WA, *1527* 13 F1
Kettleman City CA, *1499* 44 C3
Kevil KY, *574* 108 C2
Kewanee IL, *12944* 88 A2
Kewanna IN, *614* 89 E3
Kewaskum WI, *3274* 74 C2
Kewaunee WI, *2806* 75 D1
Kewaunee Co. WI, *20187* 69 D4
Keweenaw Co. MI, *2301* 65 F3
Keya Paha Co. NE, *983* 35 D1
Key Biscayne FL, *10507* 143 F2
Key Colony Beach FL, *788* 143 D4
Keyes CA, *4575* 36 C4
Key Largo FL, *11886* 143 E3
Keyport NJ, *7568* 147 E1
Keys OK, *458* 106 B4
Keyser WV, *5303* 102 C2
Keystone CO, *825* 41 D1
Keystone IA, *687* 87 E1
Keystone SD, *311* 25 F4
Keystone WV, *453* 111 F1
Keystone Hts. FL, *1349* 139 D3

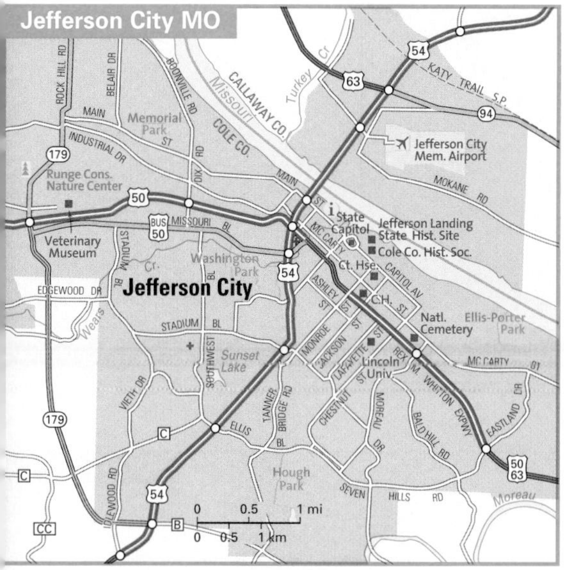
Jefferson City MO
Jefferson City
Jefferson City Mem. Airport
State Capitol
Jefferson Landing State Hist. Site
Cole Co. Hist. Soc.
Runge Cons. Nature Center
Veterinary Museum
Natl. Cemetery
Lincoln Univ.
Hough Park
CALLAWAY CO.
COLE CO.
Missouri
KATY TRAIL S.P.
0 0.5 1 mi
0 0.5 1 km

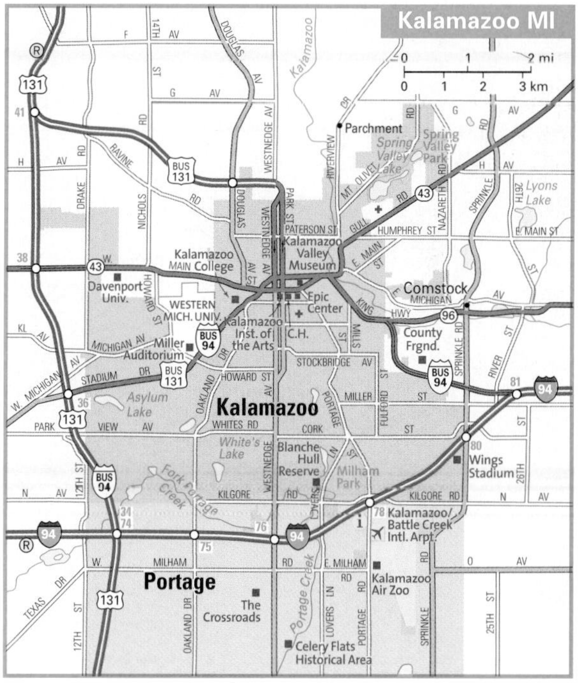
Kalamazoo MI
Kalamazoo
Portage
Comstock
Parchment
Kalamazoo Valley Museum
Kalamazoo College
Western Mich. Univ.
Kalamazoo Inst. of the Arts
Miller Auditorium
Kalamazoo/Battle Creek Intl. Arpt.
Kalamazoo Air Zoo
Celery Flats Historical Area
The Crossroads
Wings Stadium
County Frgnd.
0 1 2 mi
0 1 2 3 km

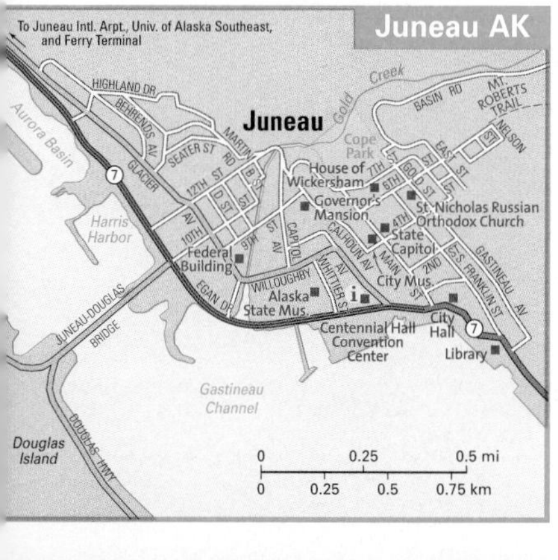
Juneau AK
To Juneau Intl. Arpt., Univ. of Alaska Southeast, and Ferry Terminal
Juneau
House of Wickersham
Governor's Mansion
St. Nicholas Russian Orthodox Church
State Capitol
Federal Building
Alaska State Mus.
City Mus.
Centennial Hall Convention Center
City Hall
Library
Gastineau Channel
Douglas Island
Harris Harbor
Aurora Basin
0 0.25 0.5 mi
0 0.25 0.5 0.75 km

Kansas City MO / KS
A
B
C
D
1
2
3
4
0 1 2 3 mi
0 1 2 3 4 km
Smithville
Kansas City International Airport
Ferrelview
Farley
Tiffany Springs City Park
Zona Rosa
Metro North Mall
Shoal Creek Living History Museum
Hodge City Park
Jesse James Bank Mus.
William Jewell College
Rush Creek Cons. Area
Clay Co. Hist. Mus.
Walnut Woods Cons. Area
Liberty
Platte Woods
Lake Waukomis
Weatherby Lake
Waldron
Missouri
Maple Woods Natural Area
Gladstone
Pleasant Valley
Glenaire
Line Cr. Pk. Arch. Reserve
Oakview
Oakwood Park
Oakwood
Oaks
Claycomo
Houston Lake
Riss Lake
Park Univ.
Parkville
Lakeside Speedway
LEAVENWORTH CO.
WYANDOTTE CO.
Northmoor
Riverside
Searcy Creek Pkwy.
Worlds of Fun and Oceans of Fun
River Bend
La Benite County Park
Birmingham
Hidden Valley Park
Randolph
Avondale
Ameristar Casino
River Bluff County Reserve
The Woodlands Race Track
Wyandotte Co. Pk.
Wyandotte County L.
Argosy Casino
North Kansas City
Harrah's North Kansas City Casino
Kansas City
Community America Ballpark
Village West
Indian Springs Shopping Ctr. & Children's Mus. of K.C.
Charles B. Wheeler Downtown Airport
Isle of Capri Casino
Harry S Truman Presidential Mus. & Library
Sugar Creek
Harry S Truman N.H.S.
Independence Mus.
Kansas Speedway
Wyandotte Co. Frgnds.
Historic Huron Indian Cemetery
Kessler Park
Kansas City Museum
1859 Jail, Marshal's Home & Mus.
Natl. Frontier Trails Center
Little Blue Trace County Park
Grinter Place St. Hist. Site
Edwardsville
Kemper Arena
Crown Ctr.
T.H. Benton Home & Studio S.H.S.
World Hdqrs. Complex Community of Christ
Bingham-Waggoner Estate
Independence
Kauffman Stadium
Arrowhead Stadium
Shawnee Indian Mission S.H.S.
Country Club Plaza
Nelson-Atkins Mus. of Art
Roeland Park
Mission
Univ. of Mo.-K.C.
Westwood
Independence Center
Lake Quivira
Quivira Lake
Shawnee
Shawnee Town
Merriam
Fairway
John Wornall House Mus.
Rockhurst Univ.
Blue Ridge Mall
Little Blue Trace County Park
Johnson Co. Mus.
Mission Center Mall
Mission Hills
Starlight Theatre
Swope Park
Kansas City Zoo
Lakewood Lakes
Blue Springs Lake
Fleming Park
Shawnee Mission Park
Prairie Village
Raytown
Alexander Majors House
K.C. Intl. Drag Strip
Lake Jacomo
Missouri Town 1855
Oak Park Mall
Legler Barn Mus.
Ward Parkway Centre
Metcalf South Shop. Ctr.
Benjamin Ranch on the Santa Fe Trail
Bannister Mall
Unity Lakes
Unity Village
Lenexa
Overland
Park
Regents Ctr.
Olathe
Johnson Co. Comm. Coll. Carlsen Ctr. & Nerman Mus. of Art
Overland Park Conv. Center
Town Center Plaza
Blue River Parkway
Longview Lake Park
Lees Summit

Key West FL
Man of War Harbor
to Ft. Myers Beach
to Dry Tortugas N.P.
Fleming Key
U.S. NAVAL RESERVATION
Dredgers Key
U.S. NAVAL HOUSING
Salt Pond Keys
Stock Island
Wisteria Island
U.S. COAST GUARD
Turning Basin
NAVAL AIR STATION KEY WEST TRUMBO POINT ANNEX
Flagler Station Over-Sea Railway Historeum
U.S. NAVAL RES.
Sunset Key
Mallory Square
Key West Bight
Garrison Bight
Curry Mansion
Audubon Hse. & Tropical Gardens
City Cemetery
Little White House Mus.
Ships Basin
Hemingway Home & Mus.
USS Maine Monument
Key West International Airport
Fort Zachary Taylor Hist. S.P.
Smathers Beach
East Martello Tower & Museum
NAVAL AIR STATION KEY WEST HARRY S TRUMAN ANNEX
Key West
Hawk Channel
Whitehead Spit
Key West Lighthouse Mus.
Southernmost Point
West Martello Tower
0 0.5 1 mi
0 0.5 1 1.5 km

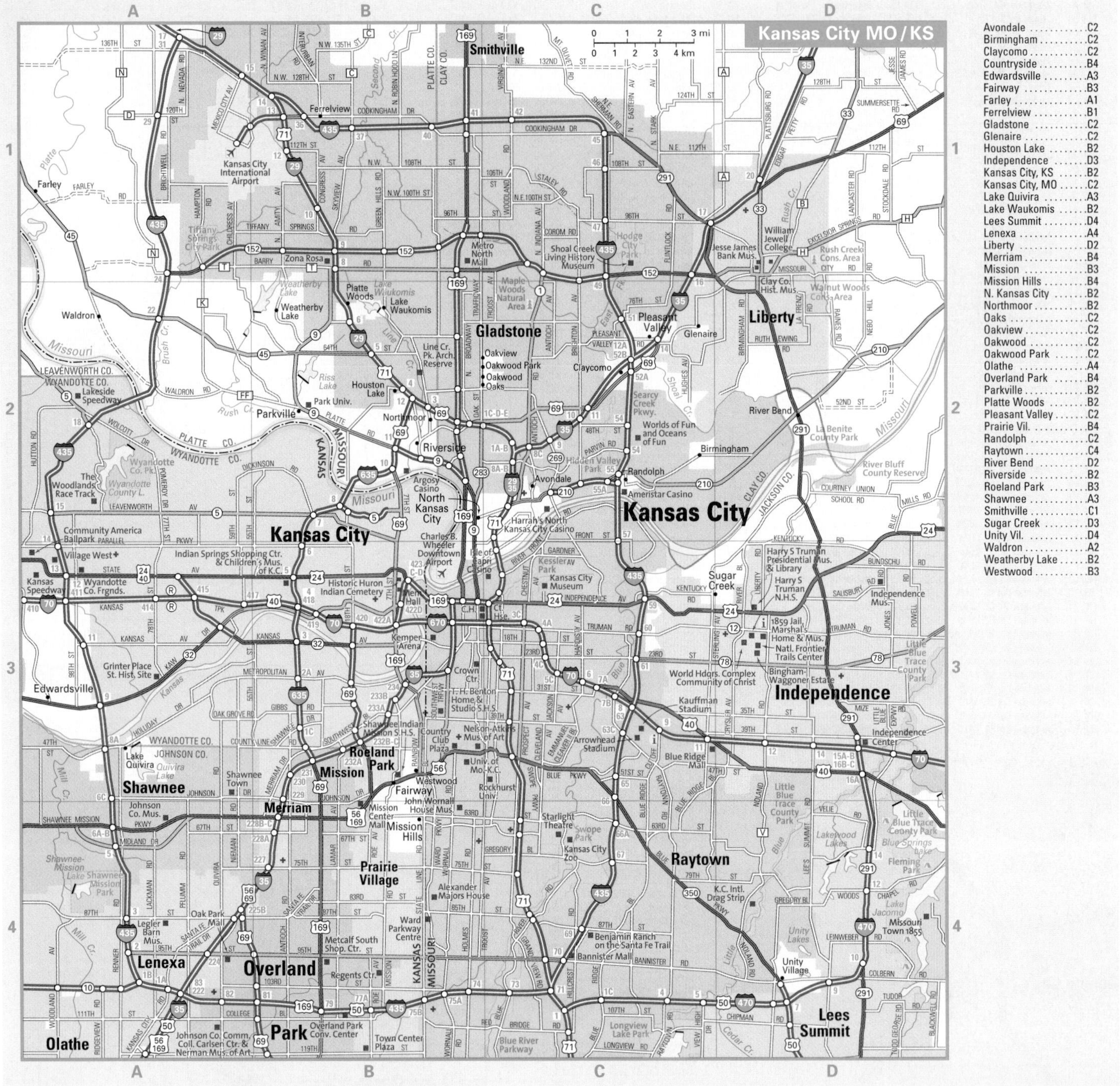

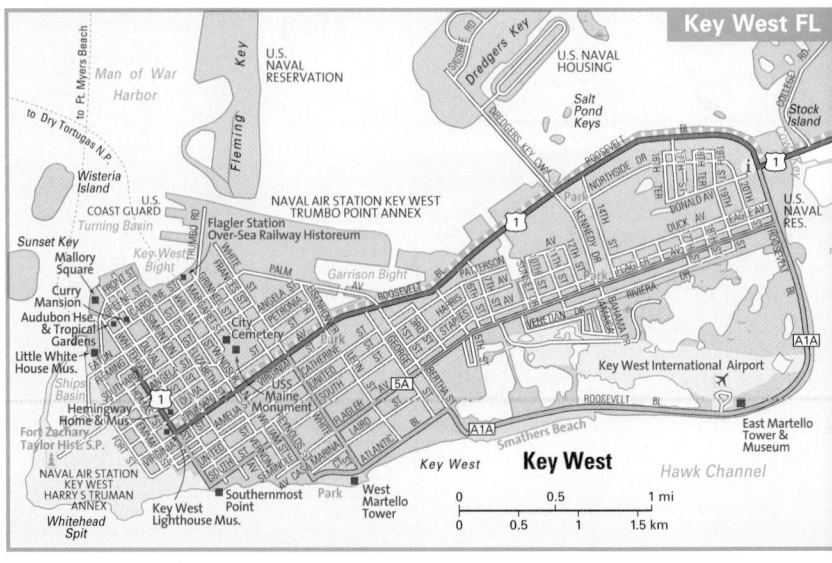

Entries in **bold black** indicate counties or parishes. Entries in **bold color** indicate cities with detailed inset maps.

Kingston–Lake Forest Park 225

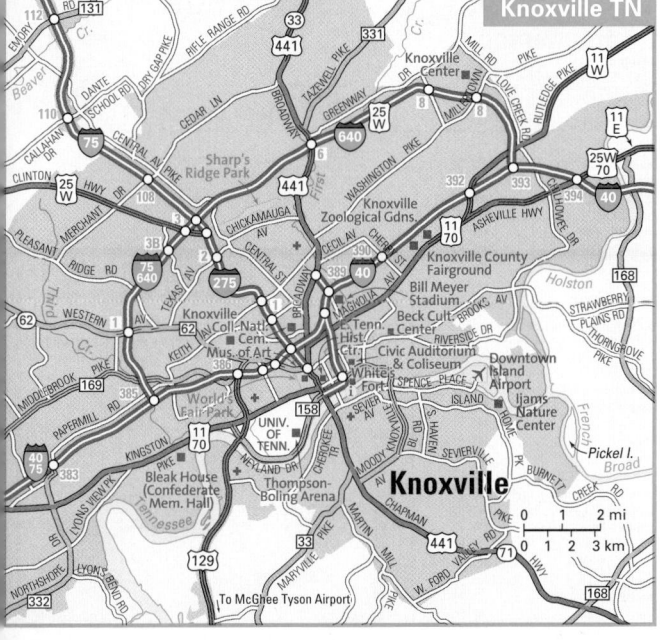

Knoxville TN

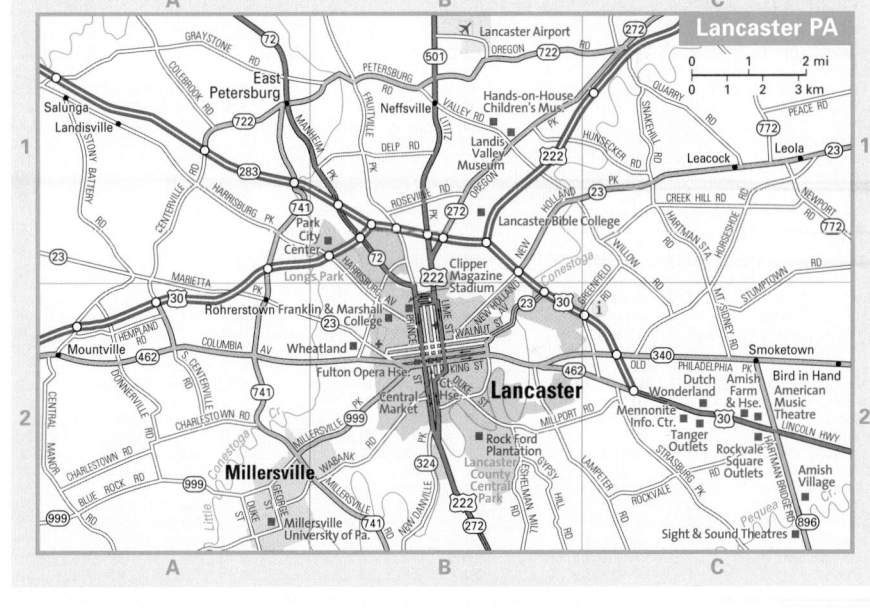

Lancaster PA

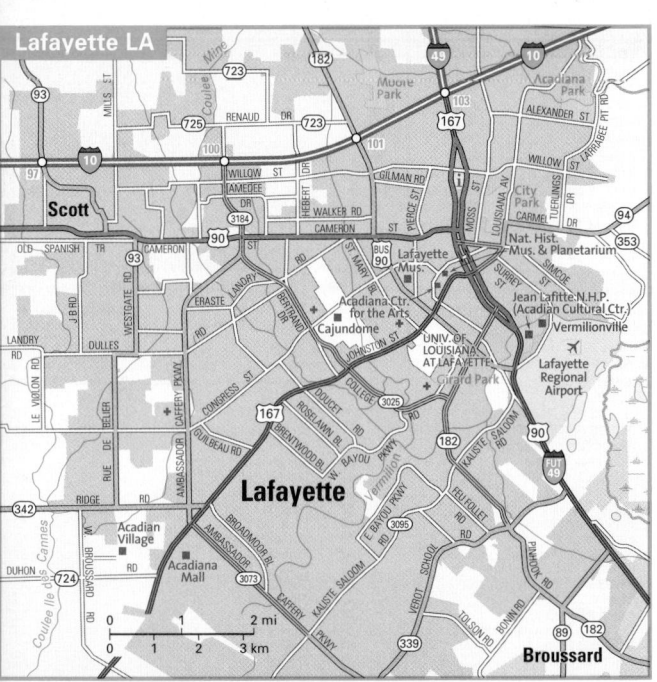

Lafayette LA

Lansing MI

226 Lake Geneva–Lawnside
Figures after entries indicate population, page number, and grid reference

Lake Geneva WI, 7148 74 C4
Lake George NY, 985 80 E4
Lake Grove NY, 10250 149 D3
Lake Hamilton AR, 1609 117 D3
Lake Hamilton FL, 1304 141 D2
Lake Havasu City AZ, 41938 46 B4
Lakehead CA, 549 28 C4
Lake Helen FL, 2743 139 E4
Lakehills TX, 4668 61 D2
Lakehurst NJ, 2522 147 E3
Lake in the Hills IL, 23152 203 A2
Lake Isabella CA, 3315 45 E4
Lake Isabella MI, 1243 76 A2
Lake Jackson TX, 26386 132 A4
Lake Junaluska NC, 2675 121 E1
Lakeland FL, 78452 140 C2
Lakeland GA, 2730 137 F1
Lakeland MN, 1917 67 D4
Lakeland NY, 2852 265 A1
Lakeland TN, 6862 118 B1
Lakeland Vil. CA, 5626 229 J5
Lake Linden MI, 1081 65 F3
Lake Lotawana MO, 1872 96 C3
Lake Lure NC, 1027 121 F1
Lake Luzerne NY, 2240 80 C4
Lake Mary FL, 11458 141 D1
Lake Michigan Beach MI, 1509 89 E1
Lake Mills IA, 2140 72 C2
Lake Mills WI, 4843 74 B3
Lake Mohawk NJ, 1500 148 A3
Lakemont PA, 1600 92 C4
Lake Montezuma AZ, 3344 47 D4
Lakemoor IL, 2788 203 A1
Lakemore OH, 2561 188 B2
Lake Nebagamon WI, 1015 64 C4
Lake Norden SD, 432 27 F3
Lake Odessa MI, 2272 75 F3
Lake of the Woods IL, 3026 88 C4
Lake of the Woods Co. MN, 4522 64 A1
Lake Orion MI, 2715 76 C4
Lake Oswego OR, 35278 20 C2
Lake Ozark MO, 1489 97 D4
Lake Panasoffkee FL, 3413 140 C1
Lake Park FL, 8721 141 F4
Lake Park GA, 549 137 F1
Lake Park IA, 1023 72 A2
Lake Park MN, 782 19 F4
Lake Peekskill NY, 3800 148 B2
Lake Placid FL, 1668 141 D3
Lake Placid NY, 2638 80 C2
Lake Pleasant NY, 100 79 F2
Lake Pocotopaug CT, 3169 149 E1
Lakeport CA, 4820 36 A2
Lakeport MI, 700 76 C3
Lakeport TX, 861 124 B2
Lake Preston SD, 737 27 E3
Lake Providence LA, 5104 126 A2
Lake Quivira KS, 932 224 A3
Lake Ridge VA, 30404 144 A4
Lake St. Croix Beach MN, 1140 67 D4
Lake St. Louis MO, 10169 98 A3
Lakeshire MO, 1375 256 B3
Lake Shore MD, 13065 144 C2
Lake Shore MN, 966 64 A4
Lakeside CA, 19560 53 D4
Lakeside CT, 1300 149 D1
Lakeside MT, 1679 15 D2
Lakeside OR, 1371 20 A4
Lakeside VA, 11157 113 E1
Lakeside City TX, 984 59 D1
Lakeside Park KY, 2869 204 A3
Lakesite TN, 1845 120 B1
Lakes of the Four Seasons IN, 7291 89 D2
Lake Sta. IN, 13948 89 D2
Lake Stevens WA, 6361 12 C2
Lake Success NY, 2797 241 G3
Lake Summerset IL, 2061 74 B4
Lake Tanglewood TX, 825 50 A3
Lake Tapawingo MO, 843 96 C2
Laketon IN, 700 89 F3
Lake View AL, 1357 127 F1
Lakeview AR, 763 107 E3
Lake View AR, 531 118 A3
Lakeview CA, 1619 229 K4
Lake View IA, 1278 72 B4
Lakeview MI, 1112 75 F2
Lake View NY, 2100 78 A4
Lakeview NY, 5607 241 G4
Lakeview OH, 1074 90 B4
Lakeview OR, 2474 29 D2
Lake View SC, 789 122 C3
Lake Villa IL, 5864 74 C4
Lake Vil. AR, 2823 125 F1
Lake Vil. IN, 855 89 D3
Lakeville CT, 900 94 B2
Lakeville IN, 567 89 F2
Lakeville MA, 2233 151 D3
Lakeville MN, 43128 67 D4
Lake Waccamaw NC, 1411 123 D3
Lake Wales FL, 10194 141 D2
Lake Waukomis MO, 917 224 B2
Lakeway TX, 8002 61 E1
Lake Winnebago MO, 902 96 B3
Lakewood CA, 79345 228 D4
Lakewood CO, 144126 41 E1
Lakewood IL, 2337 88 C1
Lakewood NJ, 36065 147 E2
Lakewood NY, 3258 92 B1
Lakewood OH, 56646 91 E2
Lakewood TN, 2341 109 F3
Lakewood WA, 58211 12 C3

Lakewood Club MI, 1006 75 E2
Lakewood Park FL, 10458 141 E3
Lakewood Park ND, 425 19 D2
Lake Worth FL, 35133 143 F1
Lake Worth TX, 4618 207 A2
Lake Wylie SC, 3061 122 A1
Lake Zurich IL, 18104 89 D1
Lakin KS, 2316 42 B3
Lakota ND, 781 19 D2
La Luz NM, 1615 56 C2
Lamar AR, 1415 117 D1
Lamar CO, 8869 42 A3
Lamar MO, 4425 106 C1
Lamar SC, 1015 122 B3
Lamar Co. AL, 15904 119 D4
Lamar Co. GA, 15912 129 D1
Lamar Co. MS, 39070 126 C4
Lamar Co. TX, 48499 116 A4
La Marque TX, 13682 132 B4
Lamb Co. TX, 14709 50 A4
Lambert MS, 1967 118 B3
Lamberton MN, 859 72 A1
Lambertville MI, 9299 90 C1
Lambertville NJ, 3868 147 D2
Lame Deer MT, 2018 25 D1
La Mesa CA, 54749 53 D4
La Mesa NM, 800 56 C3
Lamesa TX, 9952 58 A2
La Mirada CA, 46783 228 E3
La Moille IL, 773 88 B2
Lamoille Co. VT, 23233 81 E1
Lamoni IA, 2444 86 C3
Lamont CA, 13296 45 D4
Lamont IA, 503 73 E4
Lamont OK, 465 51 E1
La Monte MO, 1064 97 D3
LaMoure ND, 944 19 D4
LaMoure Co. ND, 4701 19 D4
Lampasas TX, 6786 59 D4
Lampasas Co. TX, 17762 59 D4
Lampeter PA, 1300 146 A3
Lanai City HI, 3164 152 C4
Lanare CA, 540 44 C3
Lanark IL, 1584 88 B1
Lanark PA, 1500 146 C1
Lanark Vil. FL, 550 137 D3
Lancaster CA, 118718 52 C2
Lancaster KY, 3734 110 B1
Lancaster MA, 1700 150 C1
Lancaster MO, 737 87 D4
Lancaster NH, 1695 81 F2
Lancaster NY, 11188 78 B3
Lancaster OH, 35335 101 D1
Lancaster PA, 56348 146 A3
Lancaster SC, 8177 122 B2
Lancaster TX, 25894 59 F2
Lancaster VA, 100 113 F1
Lancaster WI, 4070 73 F3
Lancaster Co. NE, 250291 35 F3
Lancaster Co. PA, 470658 146 A3
Lancaster Co. SC, 61351 122 B2
Lancaster Co. VA, 11567 113 F1
Lander WY, 6867 32 B1
Lander Co. NV, 5794 30 A4
Landfall MN, 700 235 E3
Landis NC, 2996 122 B1
Landisville PA, 4771 225 A1
Land O' Lakes FL, 20971 140 B2
Landover MD, 22900 270 E3
Landover Hills MD, 1534 271 F2
Landrum SC, 2472 121 F1
Lane SC, 585 122 C4
Lane Co. KS, 2155 42 C3
Lane Co. OR, 322959 20 C4
Lanesboro MN, 788 73 E2
Lanesboro PA, 588 93 F1
Lanesborough MA, 850 94 C1
Lanesville CT, 3100 148 C1

Lanesville IN, 614 99 F4
Lanett AL, 7897 128 B2
Langdon ND, 2101 19 D1
Langdon Place KY, 974 230 F1
Langford SD, 290 27 E1
Langhorne PA, 1981 147 D2
Langlade Co. WI, 20740 68 B3
Langley OK, 669 106 B3
Langley VA, 3500 270 B2
Langley WA, 959 12 C2
Langley Park MD, 16214 270 D2
Langston OK, 1670 51 E2
Lanham MD, 18190 271 F2
Lanier Co. GA, 7241 137 F1
Lannon WI, 1009 234 A1
Lanoka Harbor NJ, 3800 147 E3
Lansdale PA, 16071 146 C2
Lansdowne MD, 15724 193 C3
Lansdowne PA, 11044 146 C3
L'Anse MI, 2107 65 F4
Lansford ND, 253 18 B2
Lansford PA, 4230 93 E3
Lansing IA, 1012 73 F2
Lansing KS, 9199 96 B2
Lansing MI, 119128 76 A4
Lansing NY, 3417 79 D4
Lantana FL, 9437 143 F1
Laona WI, 700 68 C3
La Palma CA, 15408 228 E4
La Paz IN, 489 89 F2
La Paz Co. AZ, 19715 54 A1
Lapeer MI, 9072 76 C3

Lapeer Co. MI, 87904 76 C3
Lapel IN, 1855 89 F4
La Pine OR, 5799 21 D4
Laplace LA, 27684 134 B3
La Plata MD, 6551 144 B4
La Plata MO, 1486 97 E1
La Plata Co. CO, 43941 40 B4
Laporte CO, 2691 33 E4
La Porte IN, 21621 89 E2
Laporte PA, 290 93 E2
La Porte TX, 31880 132 B3
La Porte City IA, 2275 73 E4
LaPorte Co. IN, 110106 89 E2
La Prairie MN, 605 64 B3
La Pryor TX, 1491 60 C3
La Puente CA, 41063 228 E3
Lapwai ID, 1134 14 B4
La Quinta CA, 23694 53 E3
Laramie WY, 27204 33 E3
Laramie Co. WY, 81607 33 E3
Larchmont NY, 6485 241 F1
Larchwood IA, 788 27 F4
Laredo TX, 176576 63 D2
Largo FL, 69371 140 B2
Largo MD, 8408 271 F3
Larimer Co. CO, 251494 33 E4
Larimore ND, 1433 19 E2
Larkspur CA, 12014 259 A1
Larksville PA, 4694 261 A1
Larned KS, 4236 43 D3
Larose LA, 7306 134 B3
La Rue OH, 775 90 C4
Larue Co. KY, 13373 110 A1
La Sal UT, 339 40 A3
La Salle CO, 1849 33 E4
La Salle IL, 9796 88 B2
La Salle Co. IL, 111509 88 C2
La Salle Co. TX, 5866 60 C4
La Salle Par. LA, 14282 125 E3
Las Animas CO, 2758 41 F3
Las Animas Co. CO, 15207 41 F4
Lasara TX, 1024 63 E4
Las Cruces NM, 74267 56 C3
Las Lomas CA, 3078 236 E2
Lassen Co. CA, 33828 29 D4
Las Vegas NV, 478434 46 A2
Las Vegas NM, 14565 49 D3
Latah Co. ID, 34935 14 B4
Latham NY, 10100 188 E2
Lathrop CA, 10445 36 C4
Lathrop MO, 2092 96 B1
Lathrup Vil. MI, 4236 210 B2
Latimer IA, 535 72 C4
Latimer MS, 4288 135 D2
Latimer Co. OK, 10692 116 B2
Laton CA, 1236 44 C3
Latrobe PA, 8994 92 A4
Latta OK, 800 51 F4
Latta SC, 1410 122 C3
Lattingtown NY, 1860 148 C3
Lauderdale MN, 2364 235 C2
Lauderdale-by-the-Sea FL, 2563 233 C2
Lauderdale Co. AL, 87966 119 E2
Lauderdale Co. MS, 78161 127 D3
Lauderdale Co. TN, 27101 108 B4
Lauderdale Lakes FL, 31705 233 B2

Lauderhill FL, 57585 233 B2
Laughlin NV, 7076 46 B3
La Union NM, 850 56 C3
Laura KY, 600 111 E1
Laurel DE, 3668 145 E4
Laurel FL, 8393 140 B4
Laurel IN, 579 100 A1
Laurel MD, 19960 144 B2
Laurel MS, 18393 126 C4
Laurel MT, 6255 24 B1
Laurel NE, 986 35 F2
Laurel NY, 1188 149 E3
Laurel VA, 14875 113 E1
Laurel Bay SC, 6625 130 C2
Laurel Co. KY, 52715 110 C2
Laureldale NJ, 800 147 D4
Laureldale PA, 3759 146 B1
Laurel Hill FL, 549 136 B1
Laurel Hill NC, 1400 122 C2
Laurel Park NC, 1835 121 E1
Laurel Run PA, 723 261 B2
Laurence Harbor NJ, 6227 147 E1
Laurens IA, 1476 72 B3
Laurens SC, 9916 121 F3
Laurens Co. GA, 44874 129 E3
Laurens Co. SC, 69567 121 F3
Laurie MO, 663 97 D4
Laurinburg NC, 15874 122 C2
Laurium MI, 2126 65 F3
Lavaca AR, 1825 116 C1
Lavaca Co. TX, 19210 61 E3
Lava Hot Sprs. ID, 521 31 E1
LaVale MD, 4613 102 C1
Lavalette WV, 850 101 D4
Lavallette NJ, 2665 147 E3
Laveen AZ, 850 54 C2
La Vergne TN, 18687 109 F4
La Verkin UT, 3392 39 D4
La Verne CA, 31638 229 F2
Laverne OK, 1097 50 C1
La Vernia TX, 931 61 D3
La Veta CO, 924 41 E4
La Villa TX, 1305 63 E4
Lavina MT, 209 24 B1
La Vista NE, 11699 35 F3
Lavonia GA, 1827 121 E3
Lawai HI, 1984 152 B1
Lawndale CA, 31711 228 C3
Lawndale NC, 642 121 F1
Lawnside NJ, 2692 146 C3

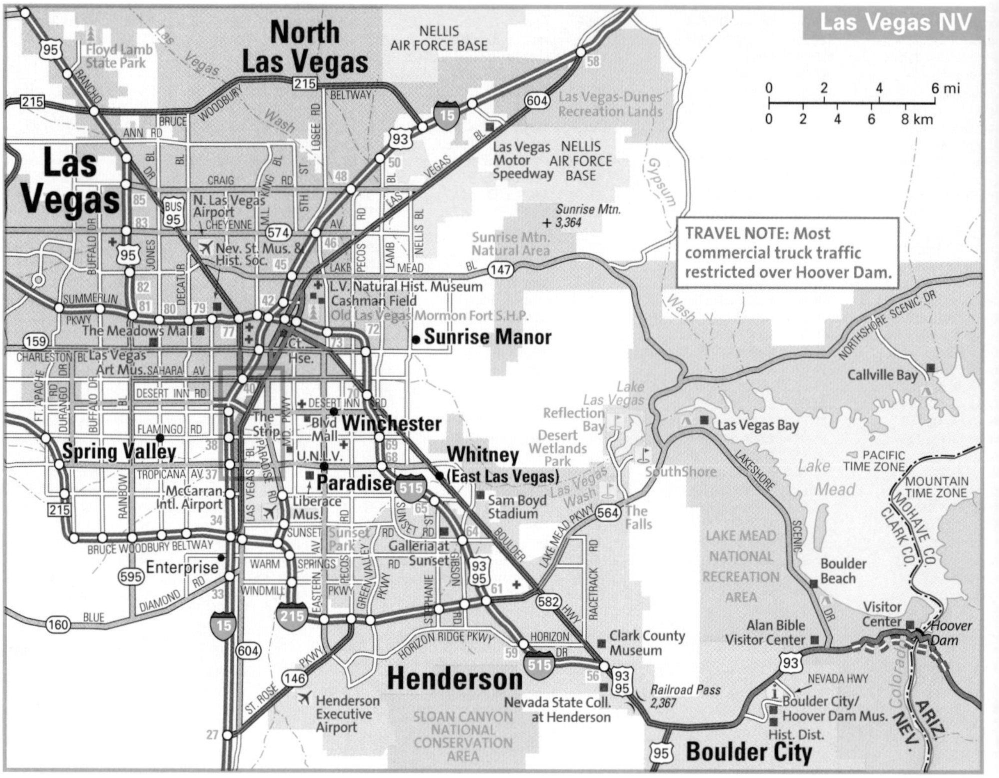
Las Vegas NV
North Las Vegas
NELLIS AIR FORCE BASE
Las Vegas
Floyd Lamb State Park
Las Vegas Motor Speedway
Las Vegas-Dunes Recreation Lands
Sunrise Mtn. + 3,364
Sunrise Mtn. Natural Area
TRAVEL NOTE: Most commercial truck traffic restricted over Hoover Dam.
N. Las Vegas Airport
Nev. St. Mus. & Hist. Soc.
L.V. Natural Hist. Museum
Cashman Field
Old Las Vegas Mormon Fort S.H.P.
Sunrise Manor
The Meadows Mall
Las Vegas Art Mus.
Winchester
Spring Valley
Whitney (East Las Vegas)
Paradise
McCarran Intl. Airport
Liberace Mus.
Sam Boyd Stadium
Galleria at Sunset
Enterprise
Henderson
Henderson Executive Airport
Clark County Museum
Nevada State Coll. at Henderson
SLOAN CANYON NATIONAL CONSERVATION AREA
Boulder City
Railroad Pass 2,367
Boulder City/ Hoover Dam Mus.
Hist. Dist.
Alan Bible Visitor Center
Visitor Center
Hoover Dam
Boulder Beach
LAKE MEAD NATIONAL RECREATION AREA
Lake Mead
Las Vegas Bay
Callville Bay
Reflection Bay
Desert Wetlands Park
The Falls
PACIFIC TIME ZONE
MOUNTAIN TIME ZONE
ARIZ.
NEV.
0 2 4 6 mi
0 2 4 6 8 km

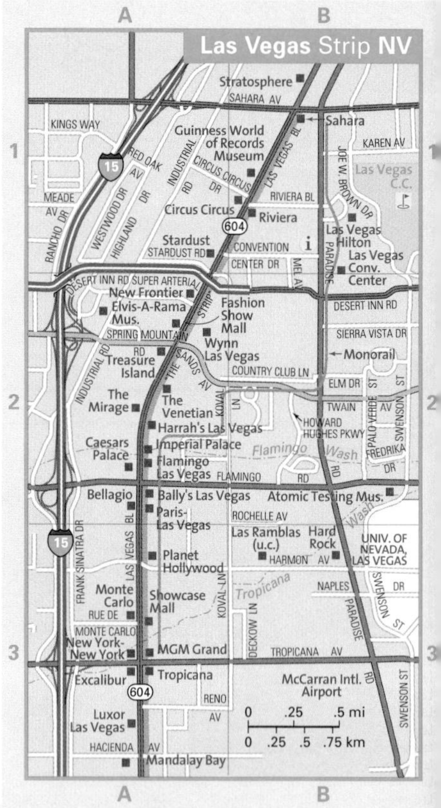
Las Vegas Strip NV
A B
1 2 3
Stratosphere
Sahara
Guinness World of Records Museum
Riviera
Circus Circus
Las Vegas Hilton
Las Vegas Conv. Center
Stardust
Fashion Show Mall
New Frontier
Elvis-A-Rama Mus.
Treasure Island
Wynn Las Vegas
The Mirage
The Venetian
Harrah's Las Vegas
Caesars Palace
Imperial Palace
Flamingo Las Vegas
Bellagio
Bally's Las Vegas
Atomic Testing Mus.
Paris-Las Vegas
Las Ramblas (u.c.)
Hard Rock
UNIV. OF NEVADA, LAS VEGAS
Planet Hollywood
Monte Carlo
Showcase Mall
New York-New York
MGM Grand
Tropicana
Excalibur
Luxor Las Vegas
Mandalay Bay
McCarran Intl. Airport
Monorail
0 .25 .5 mi
0 .25 .5 .75 km

POINTS OF INTEREST

Atomic Testing Museum B2
Bally's Las Vegas A2
Bellagio A2
Caesars Palace A2
Circus Circus B1
Elvis-A-Rama Museum A2
Excalibur A3
Flamingo Las Vegas A2
Guinness World of Records Mus. B1
Hard Rock B3
Harrah's Las Vegas A2
Imperial Palace A2
Las Vegas Convention Center B1
Las Vegas Hilton B1
Luxor Las Vegas A3
Mandalay Bay A3
McCarran Intl. Arpt. B3
MGM Grand A3
The Mirage A2
Monte Carlo A3
New Frontier A2
New York-New York A3
Paris-Las Vegas A2
Planet Hollywood A3
Riviera B1
Sahara B1
Stardust A1
Stratosphere B1
Treasure Island A2
Tropicana A3
Univ. of Nevada, Las Vegas B3
The Venetian A2
Wynn Las Vegas A2

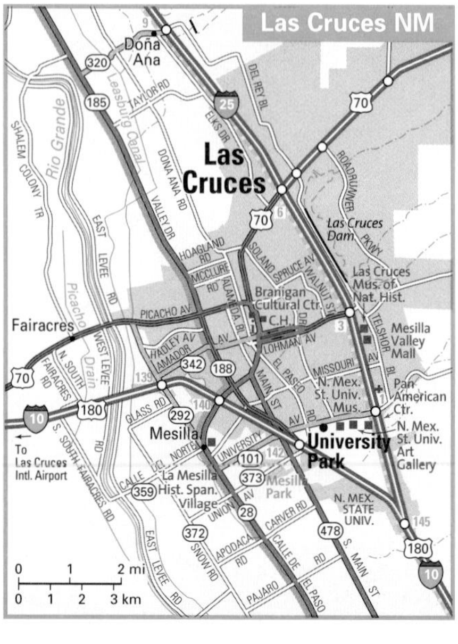
Las Cruces NM
Doña Ana
Las Cruces
Las Cruces Dam
Fairacres
Branigan Cultural Ctr.
Las Cruces Mus. of Nat. Hist.
Mesilla Valley Mall
N. Mex. St. Univ. Mus.
Pan American Ctr.
N. Mex. St. Univ. Art Gallery
Mesilla
University Park
La Mesilla Hist. Span. Village
N. MEX. STATE UNIV.
To Las Cruces Intl. Airport
Rio Grande
0 1 2 mi
0 1 2 3 km

Entries in **bold black** indicate counties or parishes. Entries in **bold color** indicate cities with detailed inset maps.

Lawnton–Lexington 227

Becknerville C3
Boonesboro C3
Clays Ferry C3
Clintonville C1
Colby C2
E. Hickman B3
Faywood A1
Ford C3
Ft. Garrett A2
Georgetown A1
Hootentown C3
Hutchison C1
Keene A3
Lexington B1
Lisletown C3
Locust Grove C3
Midway A1
New Zion B1
Nicholasville A3
Nugent Crossroads ..A1
Old Pine Grove C2
Paris C1
Pinckard A3
Pine Grove C2
Pisgah A2
Troy A3
Wallace A1
Wyandotte C2

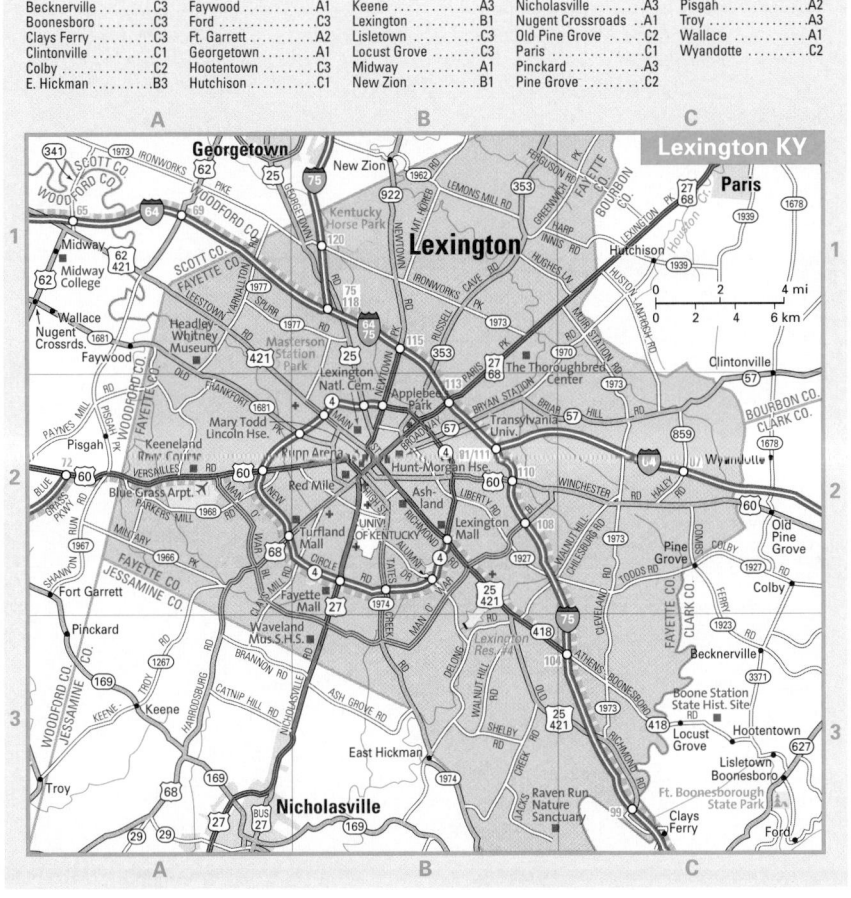

Lexington KY

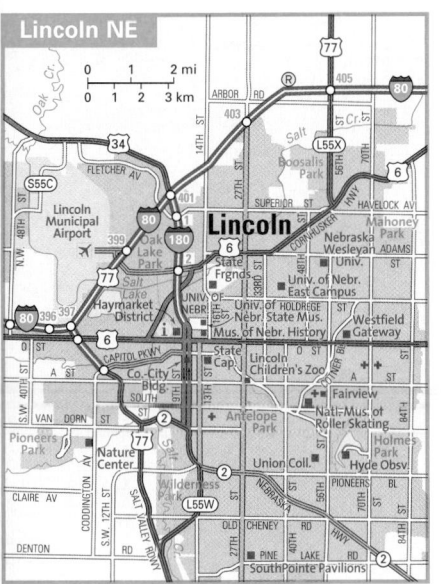

Lincoln NE

Little Rock AR

TRAVEL NOTE: California has started numbering freeway exits using a mileage-based numbering system (shown here). Full implementation is expected to take several years.

Entries in **bold black** indicate counties or parishes. Entries in **bold color** indicate cities with detailed inset maps.

229

Los Angeles CA

POINTS OF INTEREST

Angels Flight	A1
Bradbury Building	A1
Bus Terminal	B2
Cathedral of Our Lady of the Angels	A1
Chinese American Museum	B1
City Hall	B1
Convention Center	A2
Court House	A1
Dodger Stadium	B1
El Pueblo de Los Angeles Hist. Monument	B1
Japanese American Natl. Mus.	B1
Library	A1
Mt. St. Mary's College	A2
Museum of Contemporary Art	A1
Museum of Neon Art	A2
Music Center	A1
Olvera Street	A1
STAPLES Center	A2
Union Station	B1

Downtown Los Angeles CA

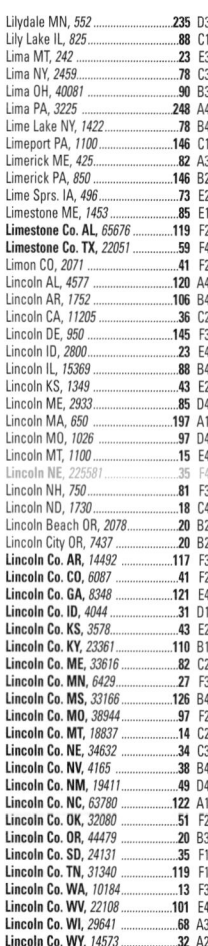

Lexington IL, 1912	88 C3	Lilydale MN, 552	235 D3
Lexington KY, 260512	100 B4	Lily Lake IL, 825	88 C1
Lexington MA, 30355	151 D1	Lima MT, 242	23 E3
Lexington MN, 2214	235 C1	Lima NY, 2459	78 C3
Lexington MO, 4453	96 C2	Lima OH, 40081	90 B3
Lexington MS, 2025	126 C1	Lima PA, 3225	248 A4
Lexington NC, 19953	112 B4	Lime Lake NY, 1422	78 A4
Lexington NE, 10011	34 C4	Limeport PA, 1100	146 C1
Lexington OH, 4165	91 D3	Limerick ME, 425	82 A3
Lexington OK, 2086	51 E3	Limerick PA, 850	146 B2
Lexington SC, 9793	122 A4	Lime Sprs. IA, 496	73 E2
Lexington TN, 7393	109 D4	Limestone ME, 1453	85 E1
Lexington TX, 1178	61 E1	Limestone Co. AL, 65676	119 F2
Lexington Co. SC, 216014	122 A4	Limestone Co. TX, 22051	59 F4
Lexington Park MD, 11021	103 F4	Limon CO, 2071	41 F2
Libby MT, 2626	14 C2	Lincoln AL, 4577	120 A4
Liberal KS, 19666	50 B1	Lincoln AR, 1752	106 B4
Liberal MO, 779	106 B1	Lincoln CA, 11205	36 C2
Liberty IL, 519	97 F1	Lincoln DE, 950	145 F3
Liberty IN, 2061	100 B1	Lincoln ID, 2800	23 E4
Liberty KY, 1850	110 B1	Lincoln IL, 15369	88 B4
Liberty ME, 300	82 C2	Lincoln KS, 1349	43 E2
Liberty MS, 633	134 A1	Lincoln ME, 2933	85 D4
Liberty MO, 26232	96 B2	Lincoln MA, 650	197 A1
Liberty NY, 3975	94 A3	Lincoln MO, 1026	97 D4
Liberty NC, 2661	112 B4	Lincoln MT, 1100	15 E4
Liberty PA, 2670	250 C3	Lincoln NH, 750	81 E3
Liberty SC, 3009	121 E2	Lincoln ND, 1730	18 C4
Liberty TN, 367	110 A4	Lincoln Beach OR, 2078	20 B2
Liberty TX, 8033	132 B3	Lincoln City OR, 7437	20 B2
Liberty Ctr. OH, 1109	90 B2	**Lincoln Co. AR,** 14492	117 F3
Liberty City TX, 1935	124 B2	**Lincoln Co. CO,** 6087	41 F2
Liberty Corner NJ, 1700	147 D1	**Lincoln Co. GA,** 8348	121 E4
Liberty Co. FL, 7021	137 D2	**Lincoln Co. ID,** 4044	31 D1
Liberty Co. GA, 61610	130 B3	**Lincoln Co. KS,** 3578	43 E2
Liberty Co. MT, 2158	15 F1	**Lincoln Co. KY,** 23361	110 B1
Liberty Co. TX, 70154	132 B2	**Lincoln Co. ME,** 33616	82 C2
Liberty Hill TX, 1409	61 E1	**Lincoln Co. MN,** 6429	27 F3
Liberty Lake WA, 3076	14 B3	**Lincoln Co. MS,** 33166	126 B4
Libertyville IL, 20742	74 C4	**Lincoln Co. MO,** 38944	97 F2
Licking MO, 1471	107 E1	**Lincoln Co. MT,** 18837	14 C2
Licking Co. OH, 145491	101 D4	**Lincoln Co. NE,** 34632	34 C3
Lidgerwood ND, 738	27 E1	**Lincoln Co. NV,** 4165	38 B4
Lido Beach NY, 2825	147 F1	**Lincoln Co. NM,** 19411	49 D4
Lighthouse Pt. FL, 10767	143 F1	**Lincoln Co. NC,** 63780	122 A1
Ligonier IN, 4357	89 F2	**Lincoln Co. OK,** 32080	51 E2
Ligonier PA, 1695	92 B4	**Lincoln Co. OR,** 44479	20 B2
Lihue HI, 5674	152 B1	**Lincoln Co. SD,** 24131	35 F1
Lilbourn MO, 1303	108 B3	**Lincoln Co. TN,** 31340	119 F1
Lillington NC, 2915	123 D1	**Lincoln Co. WA,** 10184	13 F3
Lilly PA, 948	92 B4	**Lincoln Co. WV,** 22108	101 E4
Lily KY, 1200	110 C2	**Lincoln Co. WI,** 29641	68 A3
		Lincoln Co. WY, 14573	32 A2
		Lincolndale NY, 2018	148 C1

Lincoln Hts. OH, 4113	204 B1	Lionville PA, 6298	146 B3
Lincolnia VA, 15788	270 B4	Lipscomb AL, 2458	195 C3
Lincoln Par. LA, 42509	125 E2	Lipscomb TX, 44	50 C2
Lincoln Park CO, 3904	41 E3	**Lipscomb Co. TX,** 3057	50 C2
Lincoln Park MI, 40008	90 C1	Lisbon IA, 1898	87 F1
Lincoln Park NJ, 10930	148 A3	Lisbon ME, 1800	82 B3
Lincolnshire IL, 6108	203 C2	Lisbon NH, 1070	81 E2
Lincolnton GA, 1595	121 E4	Lisbon OH, 2788	91 F3
Lincolnton NC, 9965	122 A1	Lisbon OH, 2292	19 E4
Lincoln Vil. OH, 9482	206 A3	Lisbon Falls ME, 4420	82 B3
Lincolnville SC, 904	131 D1	Lisle IL, 21182	203 B5
Lincolnville Ctr. ME, 325	82 C2	Lisman AL, 653	127 D3
Lincolnwood IL, 12359	203 D3	Litchfield CT, 1328	94 C3
Lincroft NJ, 6255	147 E2	Litchfield IL, 6815	98 B4
Lind WA, 582	13 F4	Litchfield ME, 425	82 B2
Linda CA, 13474	36 C2	Litchfield MI, 1458	90 A1
Lindale GA, 4088	120 B3	Litchfield MN, 6562	66 C3
Lindale TX, 2954	124 A2	**Litchfield Co. CT,** 182193	94 B3
Lindcove CA, 650	45 D3	Litchfield Park AZ, 3810	249 A3
Linden GA, 2424	127 E3	Lithia Sprs. GA, 2072	120 C4
Linden IN, 700	89 E4	Lithia Sprs. GA, 2187	120 C4
Linden MI, 2861	76 B3	Lithopolis OH, 600	101 D1
Linden NJ, 39334	147 E1	Lititz PA, 9029	146 A2
Linden TN, 1015	119 E1	Little Canada MN, 9771	235 D2
Linden TX, 2256	124 C1	Little Chute WI, 10476	74 C1
Linden WI, 615	74 A3	Little Compton RI, 400	151 D4
Lindenhurst IL, 12539	74 C4	Little Creek DE, 195	145 E2
Lindenhurst NY, 27819	148 C4	Little Cypress TX, 3646	132 C2
Lindenwold NJ, 17414	146 C3	Little Eagle SD, 370	26 C1
Lindon UT, 8363	31 F4	Little Elm TX, 3646	59 F2
Lindsay CA, 10297	45 D3	Little Falls MN, 7719	66 C2
Lindsay OK, 2889	51 E4	Little Falls NJ, 10855	148 A3
Lindsay TX, 788	59 E1	Little Falls NY, 5188	79 F3
Lindsborg KS, 3321	43 E3	Little Ferry NJ, 10800	240 C2
Lindstrom MN, 3015	67 D3	Littlefield TX, 6507	58 A1
Linesville PA, 1155	91 F2	Little Flock AR, 2585	106 C3
Lineville AL, 2401	128 B1	Littlefork MN, 680	64 B2
Lingle WY, 510	33 F2	Little Heaven DE, 1400	145 E3
Linglestown PA, 6414	93 D4	Little River KS, 536	43 E3
Linn KS, 425	43 F1	Little River SC, 7027	123 D4
Linn MO, 1354	97 E3	Little River-Academy TX, 1645	61 E1
Linn TX, 958	63 E3	**Little River Co. AR,** 13628	116 C4
Linn Co. IA, 191701	87 E1	Littlerock CA, 1402	52 C2
Linn Co. KS, 9570	96 B4	Little Silver NJ, 6170	147 E2
Linn Co. MO, 13754	97 D1	Littlestown PA, 3947	103 E1
Linn Co. OR, 103069	20 C3	Littleton CO, 40340	41 E1
Linneus MO, 369	97 D1	Littleton NH, 4431	81 F2
Linn Valley KS, 562	96 B4	Little Valley NY, 1130	92 B1
Lino Lakes MN, 16791	235 D2	Littleville AL, 978	119 E2
Linthicum MD, 7539	193 C4	Live Oak CA, 6229	36 C2
Linton IN, 5774	99 E2	Live Oak CA, 16628	236 D1
Linton ND, 1321	26 C1	Live Oak FL, 6480	138 B2
Linwood IN, 700	89 F4	Live Oak TX, 9156	61 D2
Linwood KS, 374	96 B2	**Live Oak Co. TX,** 12309	61 D4
Linwood MI, 1200	76 B2	Livermore CA, 73345	36 B4
Linwood NJ, 7172	147 F4		

Livermore KY, 1482	109 E1		
Livermore Falls ME, 1626	82 B2		
Liverpool NY, 2505	265 A1		
Liverpool PA, 876	93 D4		
Livingston AL, 3297	127 D2		
Livingston CA, 10473	36 C3		
Livingston IL, 825	98 B2		
Livingston LA, 1342	134 C4		
Livingston MT, 6851	24 A2		
Livingston NJ, 27391	148 A4		
Livingston TN, 3498	110 A3		
Livingston TX, 5433	132 B1		
Livingston Co. IL, 39678	88 C3		
Livingston Co. KY, 9804	109 D2		
Livingston Co. MI, 156951	76 B3		
Livingston Co. MO, 14558	96 C1		
Livingston Co. NY, 64328	78 C4		
Livingston Manor NY, 1355	94 A3		
Livingston Par. LA, 91814	134 B2		
Livonia LA, 1339	133 F2		
Livonia MI, 100545	76 B4		
Livonia NY, 1373	78 C3		
Llangollen Estates DE, 5600	145 E2		
Llano TX, 3325	61 D1		
Llano Co. TX, 17044	61 D1		
Lloyd Harbor NY, 3675	148 C3		
Loa UT, 525	39 E3		
Loami IL, 804	98 B1		
Lobelville TN, 915	109 E4		
Lochbuie CO, 2049	209 D1		
Lochearn MD, 25269	144 C2		
Lockeford CA, 3179	36 C3		
Lockesburg AR, 711	116 C4		
Lockhart AL, 548	136 B1		
Lockhart FL, 12944	246 B1		
Lockhart TX, 11615	61 E2		
Lock Haven PA, 9149	93 D3		
Lockland OH, 3707	204 B1		
Lockney TX, 2056	50 B4		
Lockport IL, 15191	89 D2		
Lockport LA, 2624	134 B3		
Lockport NY, 22279	78 B3		
Lockwood MO, 989	106 C1		
Locust NC, 2416	122 B1		
Locust Fork AL, 1016	119 F3		
Locust Grove GA, 2322	129 D1		
Locust Grove OK, 1366	106 B3		
Locust Valley NY, 3521	148 C3		
Lodge Grass MT, 510	24 C2		
Lodgepole NE, 214	16 C2		
Lodi CA, 56999	36 C3		
Lodi NJ, 23971	240 C1		
Lodi OH, 3061	91 D3		
Lodi WI, 2882	74 B3		

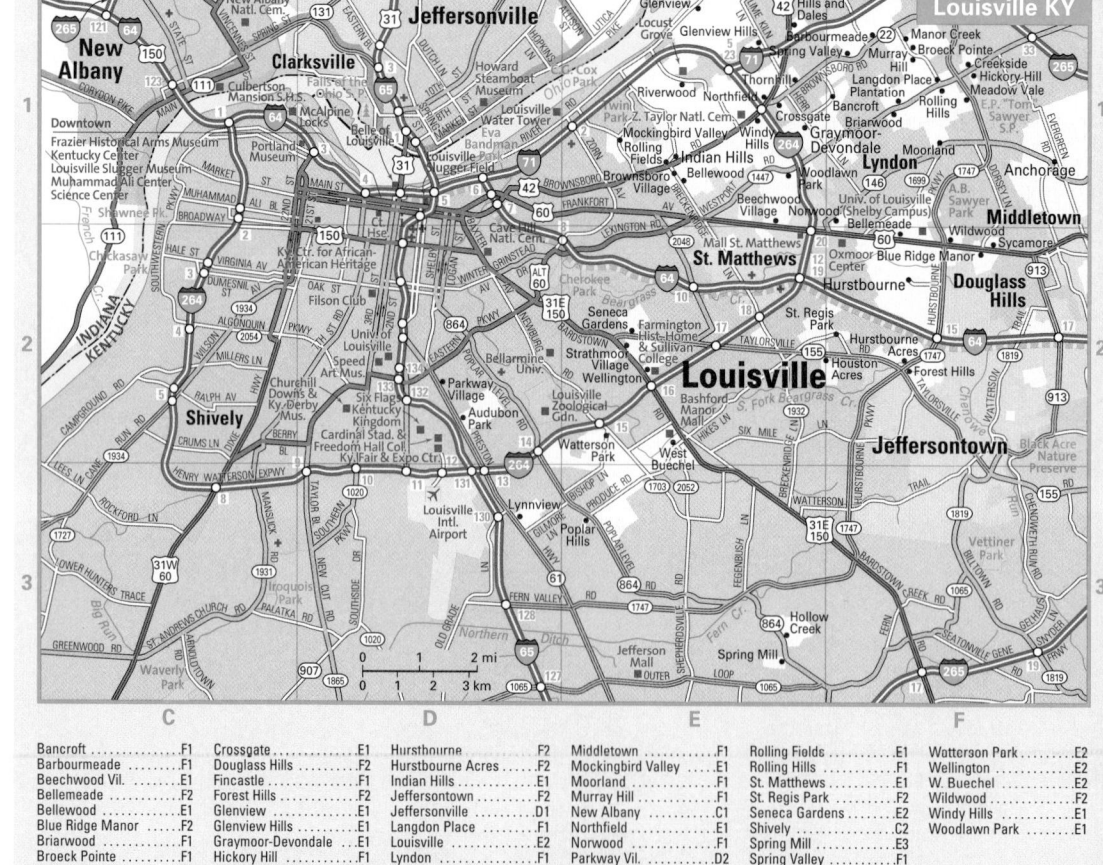

Louisville KY

Bancroft	F1	Crossgate	E1
Barbourmeade	F1	Douglass Hills	F2
Beechwood Vil.	E1	Fincastle	F2
Bellemeade	E1	Forest Hills	F2
Bellewood	E1	Glenview	E1
Blue Ridge Manor	E2	Glenview Hills	E1
Briarwood	E1	Graymoor-Devondale	E1
Broeck Pointe	E1	Hickory Hill	F2
Brownsboro Vil.	E1	Hills and Dales	E1
Clarksville	D1	Hollow Creek	E3
Creekside	F1	Houston Acres	F2

Hurstbourne	F2	Middletown	E1
Hurstbourne Acres	F2	Mockingbird Valley	E1
Indian Hills	E1	Moorland	E1
Jeffersontown	F2	Murray Hill	E1
Jeffersonville	D1	New Albany	C1
Langdon Place	F1	Northfield	E1
Louisville	E2	Norwood	C1
Lyndon	F1	Parkway Vil.	E2
Lynnview	D3	Plantation	E1
Manor Creek	F1	Poplar Hills	E3
Meadow Vale	F1	Riverwood	E1

Rolling Fields	E1	Watterson Park	E2
Rolling Hills	E1	Wellington	E2
St. Matthews	E1	W. Buechel	F2
St. Regis Park	E2	Wildwood	F2
Seneca Gardens	E2	Windy Hills	E1
Shively	C2	Woodlawn Park	E1
Spring Mill	C3		
Spring Valley	F1		
Strathmoor Vil.	E2		
Sycamore	F2		
Thornhill	E1		

Entries in **bold black** indicate counties or parishes. Entries in *bold color* indicate cities with detailed inset maps.

Logan IA, 1545 ....86 A2
Logan KS, 603 ....42 C1
Logan NM, 1094 ....49 F3
Logan OH, 6704 ....101 D1
Logan UT, 42670 ....31 E2
Logan WV, 1630 ....101 E4
Logan Co. AR, 22486 ....116 C1
Logan Co. CO, 20504 ....34 A4
Logan Co. IL, 31183 ....98 B1
Logan Co. KS, 3046 ....42 B2
Logan Co. KY, 26573 ....109 F2
Logan Co. NE, 774 ....34 C3
Logan Co. ND, 2308 ....18 C4
Logan Co. OH, 46005 ....90 B4
Logan Co. OK, 33924 ....51 E2
Logan Co. WV, 37710 ....101 E4

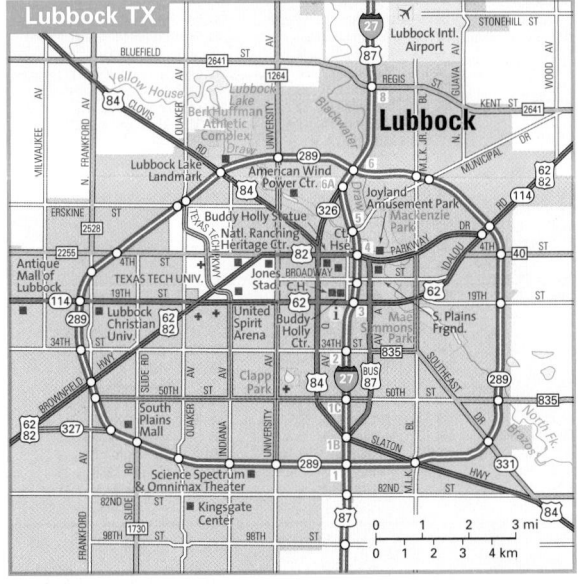

Lubbock TX

Logandale NV, 800 ....46 B1
Logansport IN, 19684 ....89 E3
Logansport LA, 1630 ....124 C3
Loganville GA, 5435 ....121 D4
Loganville PA, 908 ....103 E1
Log Cabin TX, 733 ....59 F3
Loleta CA, 600 ....28 A4
Lolita TX, 548 ....61 F3
Lolo MT, 3388 ....15 D4
Loma Linda CA, 18681 ....229 J3
Loma Linda MO, 507 ....106 B2
Loma Rica CA, 2075 ....36 C2
Lombard IL, 42322 ....203 B4
Lometa TX, 782 ....59 D4
Lomira WI, 2233 ....74 C2
Lomita CA, 20046 ....228 C4
Lompoc CA, 41103 ....52 C1
Lonaconing MD, 1205 ....102 C1
London AR, 925 ....117 D1
London KY, 5692 ....110 C2
London OH, 8771 ....100 C1
Londonderry NH, 11417 ....95 E1
Londonderry VT, 300 ....81 D4
Londontown MD, 7595 ....144 C4
Lone Grove OK, 4631 ....51 E4
Lone Jack MO, 528 ....96 C3

Lone Oak KY, 454 ....108 C2
Lone Oak TX, 521 ....59 F2
Lone Pine CA, 1655 ....45 E3
Lone Rock WI, 929 ....74 A3
Lone Star LA, 1400 ....239 A2
Lone Star TX, 1631 ....124 B1
Lone Tree CO, 4873 ....209 G4
Lone Tree IA, 1151 ....87 F2
Long Beach CA, 461522 ....228 D4
Long Beach IN, 1559 ....89 E1
Long Beach MS, 17320 ....135 D2
Long Beach MD, 2487 ....103 E4
Long Beach NY, 35462 ....147 F1
Long Beach WA, 1283 ....12 B4
Longboat Key FL, 7603 ....140 B3

Long Branch NJ, 31340 ....147 F2
Long Co. GA, 10304 ....130 B3
Long Creek IL, 1364 ....98 C1
Long Green MD, 1000 ....144 C1
Long Grove IL, 6735 ....203 C2
Long Grove IA, 597 ....88 A1
Long Lake MN, 1842 ....66 C4
Longmeadow MA, 15633 ....150 A2
Longmont CO, 71093 ....41 E1
Long Pond MA, 1500 ....151 E3
Longport NJ, 1054 ....147 F4
Long Prairie MN, 3040 ....66 B2
Longton KS, 394 ....43 F4
Long Valley NJ, 1818 ....94 A4
Long View NC, 4722 ....111 F4
Longview TX, 73344 ....124 B2
Longview WA, 34660 ....20 B4
Longwood FL, 13745 ....141 D1
Lonoke AR, 4287 ....117 F2
Lonoke Co. AR, 52828 ....117 F2
Lonsdale MN, 1491 ....67 D4
Loogootee IN, 2741 ....99 E3
Lookout Mtn. GA, 1617 ....120 B2
Lookout Mtn. TN, 2000 ....120 B2
Loomis CA, 6200 ....36 C1
Loomis NE, 397 ....35 D4
Lorain OH, 68652 ....91 D2

Lorain Co. OH, 284664 ....91 D2
Loraine TX, 656 ....58 B3
Lorane PA, 2994 ....146 B2
Lordsburg NM, 3379 ....55 F3
Lordstown OH, 3633 ....91 F2
Loreauville LA, 938 ....133 F3
Lorena TX, 1433 ....59 E4
Lorenzo TX, 1372 ....58 A1
Loretto KY, 623 ....110 A1
Loretto MN, 570 ....66 C3
Loretto PA, 1190 ....92 B4
Loretto TN, 1665 ....119 E2
Loris SC, 2079 ....123 D3
Lorton VA, 17786 ....144 B4
Los Alamitos CA, 11536 ....228 E4
Los Alamos CA, 1372 ....52 A1

Los Alamos NM, 11909 ....48 C2
Los Alamos Co. NM, 18343 ....48 C2
Los Altos CA, 27693 ....36 B4
Los Altos Hills CA, 7902 ....259 C6
Los Angeles CA, 3694820 ....52 C2
Los Angeles Co. CA, 9519338 ....52 C2
Los Banos CA, 25869 ....44 B2
Los Chavez NM, 5033 ....48 C4
Los Fresnos TX, 4512 ....63 F4
Los Gatos CA, 28592 ....36 B4
Los Indios TX, 1149 ....63 F4
Los Lunas NM, 10034 ....48 C4
Los Molinos CA, 1952 ....36 B1
Los Olivos CA, 950 ....52 A2
Los Osos CA, 14351 ....44 B4
Los Padillas NM, 1800 ....48 C3
Los Ranchos de Albuquerque NM, 5092 ....48 C3
Lost Creek WV, 467 ....102 A2
Lost Hills CA, 1938 ....44 C4
Lost Nation IA, 497 ....87 F1
Lott TX, 724 ....59 F4
Loudon TN, 4476 ....110 C4
Loudon Co. TN, 39086 ....110 C4
Loudonville NY, 10800 ....94 B1
Loudonville OH, 2906 ....91 D3
Loudoun Co. VA, 169599 ....144 A2

Loughman FL, 1385 ....141 D2
Louisa KY, 2018 ....101 D4
Louisa VA, 1401 ....103 D4
Louisa Co. IA, 12183 ....87 F2
Louisa Co. VA, 25627 ....103 D4
Louisburg KS, 2576 ....96 B3
Louisburg NC, 3111 ....113 D4
Louise TX, 977 ....61 F3
Louisiana MO, 3863 ....97 F2
Louisville AL, 612 ....128 B3
Louisville CO, 18937 ....41 E1
Louisville GA, 2712 ....129 F1
Louisville IL, 1242 ....98 C3
Louisville KY, 529548 ....100 A4
Louisville MS, 7006 ....126 C1
Louisville NE, 1035 ....35 F3
Louisville OH, 8904 ....91 E3
Louisville TN, 2001 ....110 C4
Loup City NE, 996 ....35 D3
Loup Co. NE, 712 ....35 D2
Lovelady TX, 608 ....132 A1
Loveland CO, 50608 ....33 E4
Loveland OH, 11677 ....100 B2
Loveland Park OH, 1799 ....204 C1
Lovell WY, 2281 ....24 C2
Loves Park IL, 20044 ....74 B4
Lovettsville VA, 853 ....144 A2
Loveville MD, 650 ....103 E4
Lovilia IA, 583 ....87 D3
Loving NM, 1326 ....57 E3
Loving Co. TX, 67 ....57 E3

Lovingston VA, 475 ....112 C1
Lovington IL, 1222 ....98 C1
Lovington NM, 9471 ....57 F2
Lowden IA, 794 ....87 F1
Lowell AR, 5013 ....106 C3
Lowell IN, 7505 ....89 D2
Lowell MA, 105167 ....95 E1
Lowell MI, 4013 ....75 F3
Lowell NC, 2662 ....122 A1
Lowell OH, 628 ....101 F1
Lowell OR, 857 ....20 C4
Lowellville OH, 1281 ....91 F3
Lower Brule SD, 599 ....27 D3
Lower Lake CA, 1755 ....36 B2
Lowesville NC, 1440 ....122 A1
Low Moor VA, 367 ....112 B1
Lowndes Co. AL, 13473 ....127 E1
Lowndes Co. GA, 92115 ....137 F1
Lowndes Co. MS, 61586 ....127 D1
Lowry City MO, 728 ....96 C4
Lowville NY, 3476 ....79 E2
Loxley AL, 1348 ....135 E2
Loyal WI, 1308 ....68 A4
Loyalhanna PA, 3415 ....92 B4
Loyall KY, 766 ....111 D2
Loyalton CA, 862 ....37 D1
Lubbock TX, 199564 ....58 A1
Lubbock Co. TX, 242628 ....58 A1
Lubec ME, 650 ....83 F1
Lubeck WV, 1303 ....101 E2
Lucama NC, 847 ....113 D1
Lucas KS, 436 ....43 D2
Lucas OH, 620 ....91 D3
Lucas TX, 2890 ....59 F2
Lucas Co. IA, 9422 ....87 D3
Lucas Co. OH, 455054 ....90 C2
Lucasville OH, 1588 ....101 D3
Luce Co. MI, 7024 ....69 F1

Lucedale MS, 2458 ....135 D1
Lucerne CA, 2870 ....36 B2
Lucerne WY, 525 ....24 C4
Lucernemines PA, 951 ....92 B4
Luck WI, 1210 ....67 E3
Luckoy OH, 998 ....90 C2
Ludington MI, 8357 ....75 E1
Ludingtonville NY, 1000 ....148 C1
Ludlow KY, 4409 ....204 A3
Ludlow MA, 7400 ....150 A2
Ludlow VT, 958 ....81 E4
Ludowici GA, 1440 ....130 B4
Lufkin TX, 32709 ....124 B4
Lugoff SC, 6278 ....122 B3
Lukachukai AZ, 1565 ....48 A1
Lula GA, 1438 ....121 D3
Luling LA, 11512 ....239 D3
Luling TX, 5080 ....61 E2
Lumber City GA, 1247 ....129 F3
Lumberport WV, 937 ....102 A2
Lumberton MS, 2228 ....134 C1
Lumberton NJ, 2500 ....147 D3
Lumberton NC, 20795 ....123 D2
Lumberton TX, 8731 ....132 C2
Lumpkin GA, 1369 ....128 C3
Lumpkin Co. GA, 21016 ....120 C3
Luna Co. NM, 25016 ....56 A3
Luna Pier MI, 1483 ....90 C1
Lunenburg MA, 1695 ....95 D1
Lunenburg VT, 325 ....81 F2
Lunenburg VA, 40 ....113 D2
Lunenburg Co. VA, 13146 ....113 D2
Lupton AZ, 375 ....48 A3
Luray VA, 4871 ....102 C4
Lusby MD, 1666 ....103 F3
Lusk WY, 1447 ....33 E1
Lutcher LA, 3735 ....134 B3
Luther OK, 612 ....51 E2
Luthersville GA, 783 ....128 C1
Luttrell TN, 915 ....110 C4
Lutz FL, 7081 ....140 B2
Luverne AL, 2635 ....128 A4

Luverne MN, 4617 ....27 F4
Luxemburg WI, 1935 ....69 D4
Luxora AR, 1317 ....108 A1
Luzerne PA, 2952 ....261 B1
Luzerne Co. PA, 319250 ....93 E3
Lycoming Co. PA, 120044 ....93 D2
Lydia LA, 1079 ....133 F3
Lydick IN, 1300 ....89 E2
Lyerly GA, 488 ....120 B3
Lyford TX, 1973 ....63 F4
Lykens PA, 1937 ....93 E4
Lyle MN, 566 ....73 D2
Lyle WA, 530 ....21 D1
Lyman NE, 421 ....33 F2
Lyman SC, 2659 ....121 F2
Lyman WA, 409 ....12 C2
Lyman WY, 1938 ....32 A3
Lyman Co. SD, 3895 ....26 C4
Lynbrook NY, 19911 ....147 F1
Lynch KY, 900 ....111 D2
Lynchburg MS, 2959 ....118 B2
Lynchburg OH, 1350 ....100 C2
Lynchburg SC, 588 ....122 B3
Lynchburg TN, 5740 ....119 F1
Lynchburg VA, 65269 ....112 C1
Lynch Hts. DE, 550 ....145 E1
Lynch Sta. VA, 500 ....112 C2
Lyndell PA, 1000 ....146 B3
Lynden WA, 9020 ....12 C1
Lyndhurst NJ, 19383 ....240 C2
Lyndhurst OH, 15279 ....204 G2
Lyndhurst VA, 1527 ....102 C4

Lyndon KS, 1038 ....96 A3
Lyndon KY, 10167 ....230 F1
Lyndon NY, 4600 ....265 B2
Lyndon VT, 375 ....81 E2
Lyndon Ctr. VT, 1200 ....81 E2
Lyndonville NY, 862 ....78 B3
Lyndonville VT, 1227 ....81 E2
Lynn AL, 597 ....119 E3
Lynn IN, 1143 ....90 A4
Lynn MA, 89050 ....151 D1
Lynn Co. TX, 6550 ....58 A2
Lynn Haven FL, 12451 ....136 C2
Lynnview KY, 965 ....230 D3
Lynnville IN, 781 ....99 E4
Lynnwood WA, 33847 ....12 C3
Lynwood CA, 69845 ....228 D3
Lyon MS, 418 ....118 A3
Lyon Co. IA, 11763 ....27 F4
Lyon Co. KS, 35935 ....43 F3
Lyon Co. KY, 8080 ....109 D2
Lyon Co. MN, 25425 ....72 A1
Lyon Co. NV, 34501 ....37 E2
Lyons CO, 1585 ....33 E4
Lyons GA, 4169 ....129 F3
Lyons IL, 10255 ....203 D5
Lyons IN, 748 ....99 E3
Lyons KS, 3732 ....43 E3
Lyons MI, 726 ....76 A3
Lyons NE, 963 ....35 F2
Lyons NY, 3695 ....79 D3
Lyons OH, 559 ....90 B2

Lyons OR, 1008 ....20 C3
Lyons Falls NY, 591 ....79 E2
Lyons Plain CT, 2100 ....148 C1
Lytle TX, 2383 ....61 D3

M
Mabank TX, 2151 ....59 F3
Mabel MN, 766 ....73 E2
Maben MS, 803 ....118 C4
Mableton GA, 29733 ....120 C4
Mabscott WV, 1403 ....111 F1
Mabton WA, 1891 ....21 E1
Macclenny FL, 4459 ....138 C2
Macedon NY, 1496 ....78 C3
Macedonia OH, 9224 ....91 E2
Machesney Park IL, 20759 ....74 B4
Machias ME, 1376 ....83 E1
Machias NY, 1422 ....78 B4
Mack OH, 8900 ....204 B3
Mackay ID, 566 ....23 D4
Mackinac Co. MI, 11943 ....70 B1
Mackinac Island MI, 523 ....70 C1
Mackinaw IL, 1452 ....88 B4
Mackinaw City MI, 859 ....70 C2
Macksville KS, 514 ....43 D3
Macomb IL, 18558 ....88 A3
Macomb Co. MI, 788149 ....76 C3
Macon GA, 97255 ....129 D2
Macon IL, 1213 ....98 C1
Macon MS, 2461 ....127 D1
Macon MO, 5538 ....97 D1

Fitchburg A2		Shorewood Hills A2	
Madison A1	McFarland B2	Sun Prairie B1	
Maple Bluff B1	Middleton A1	Waunakee A1	
	Monona B2		

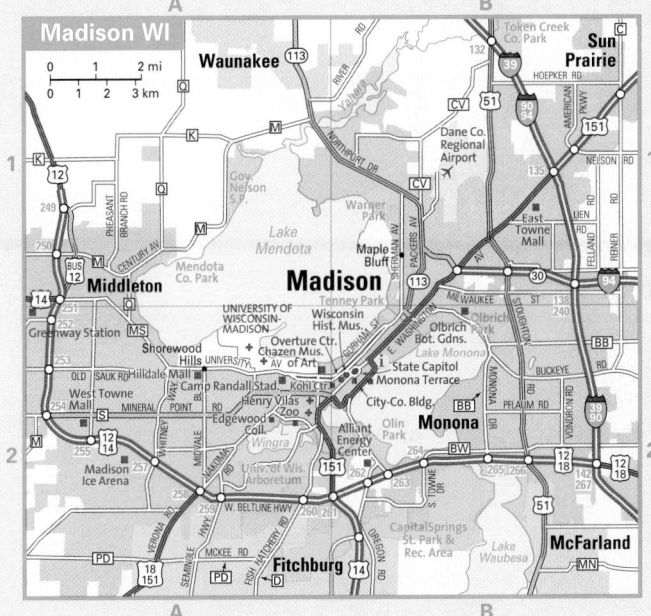

Madison WI

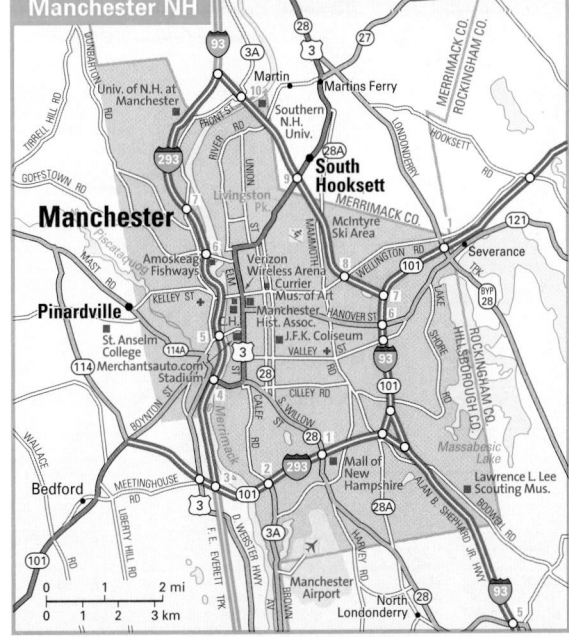

Manchester NH

Macon GA

232   **Macon County–Many Farms**

Figures after entries indicate population, page number, and grid reference.

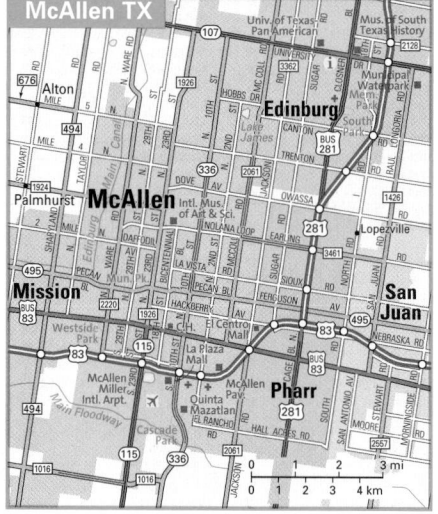

McAllen TX

Melbourne / Titusville FL

Memphis TN

Entries in **bold black** indicate counties or parishes. Entries in *bold color* indicate cities with detailed inset maps.

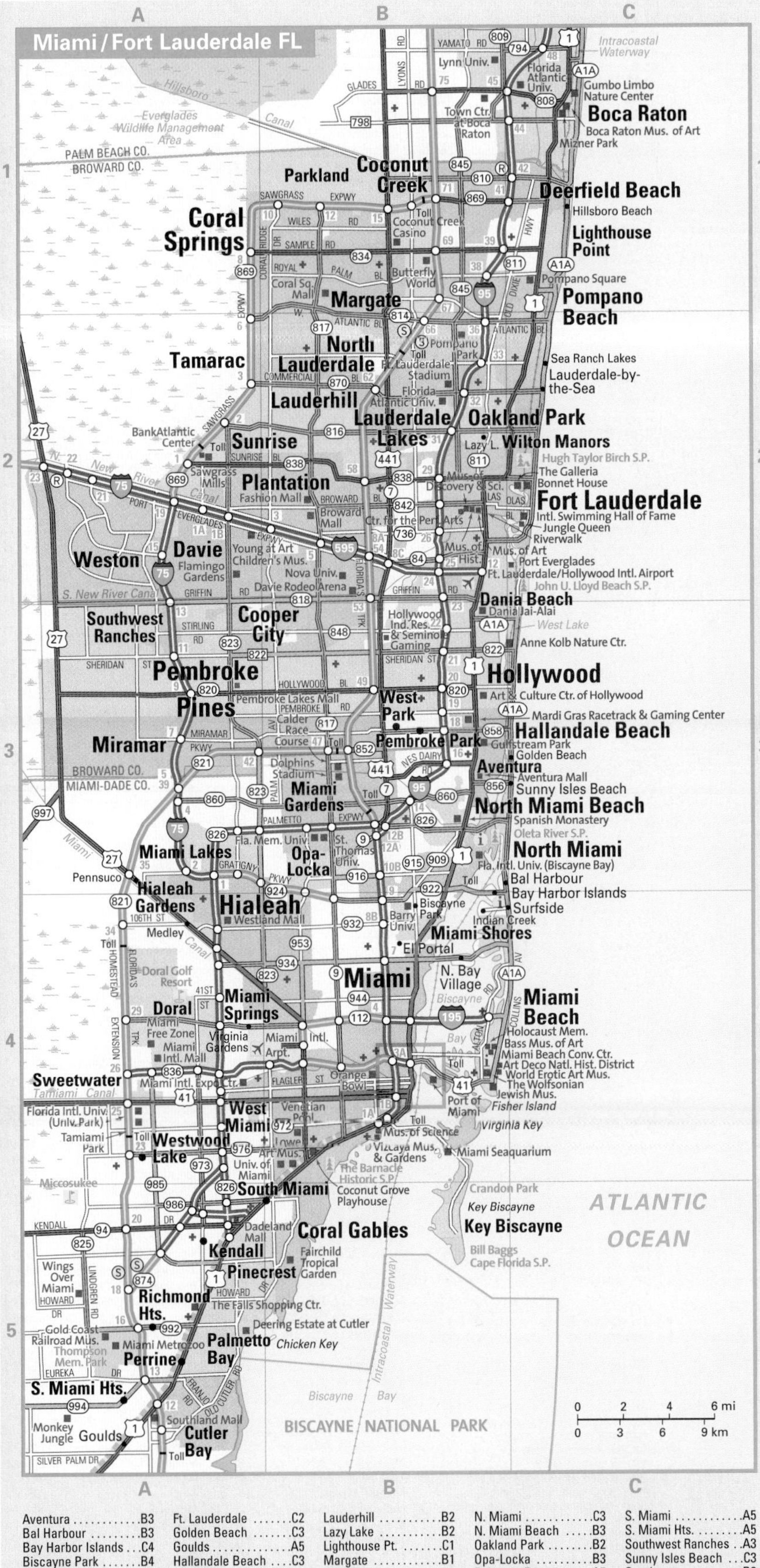

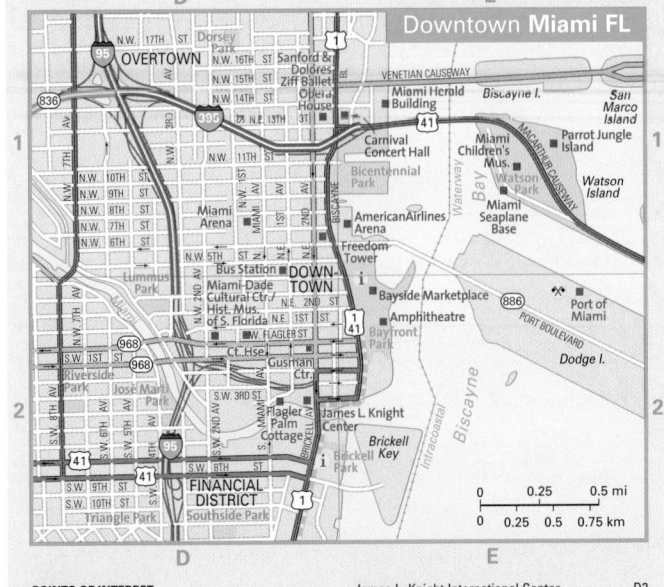

Miami / Fort Lauderdale FL

Downtown Miami FL

Aventura B3	Ft. Lauderdale C2	Lauderhill B2	N. Miami C3	S. Miami A5
Bal Harbour B3	Golden Beach C3	Lazy Lake B2	N. Miami Beach B3	S. Miami Hts. A5
Bay Harbor Islands B3	Goulds A5	Lighthouse Pt. C1	Oakland Park B2	Southwest Ranches A3
Biscayne Park B4	Hallandale Beach B3	Margate B1	Opa-Locka B3	Sunny Isles Beach C3
Boca Raton C1	Hialeah A4	Medley A4	Palmetto Bay B5	Sunrise A2
Coconut Creek B1	Hialeah Gardens A4	Miami B4	Parkland B1	Surfside C4
Cooper City A3	Hillsboro Beach C1	Miami Beach C4	Pembroke Park B3	Sweetwater A4
Coral Gables B5	Hollywood B3	Miami Gardens B3	Pembroke Pines A3	Tamarac A2
Coral Sprs. A1	Indian Creek C4	Miami Lakes A3	Perrine A5	Virginia Gardens A4
Cutler Ridge A5	Kendall A5	Miami Shores B4	Pinecrest A5	W. Miami A4
Dania Beach B3	Key Biscayne B5	Miami Sprs. A4	Plantation A2	Weston A3
Davie A2	Lauderdale-	N. Bay Vil. B4	Pompano Beach C1	West Park B3
Deerfield Beach C1	by-the-Sea C2	N. Lauderdale B2	Richmond Hts. A5	Westwood Lake A4
El Portal B4	Lauderdale Lakes B2	N. Miami C3	Rockdale A5	Wilton Manors B2

POINTS OF INTEREST

AmericanAirlines Arena E1	James L. Knight International Center D2	
Amphitheatre E2	Miami Arena D1	
Bayside Marketplace E1	Miami-Dade Cultural Center/Hist. Mus. of	
Bus Station D1	Southern Florida D2	
Court House D2	Miami Herald Building E1	
Flagler Palm Cottage D2	Miami Seaplane Base E1	
Freedom Tower E1	Omni International Mall D1	
Gusman Center D2	Parrot Jungle Island E1	
	Port of Miami E1	

234 MARYSVALE–MEDINA COUNTY

Figures after entries indicate population, page number, and grid reference.

Marysvale UT, 381 .... 39 E3
Marysville CA, 12268 .... 36 C2
Marysville KS, 3271 .... 43 F1
Marysville MI, 9684 .... 76 C3
Marysville OH, 15942 .... 90 C4
Marysville PA, 2306 .... 93 D4
Marysville WA, 25315 .... 12 C2
Maryville IL, 4651 .... 256 D1
Maryville MO, 10581 .... 86 B4
Maryville TN, 23120 .... 110 C4
Marywood MD, 6000 .... 145 D1
Masaryktown FL, 920 .... 140 B1
Mascot TN, 2119 .... 110 C4
Mascotte FL, 2687 .... 140 C1
Mascoutah IL, 5659 .... 98 B3
Mashpee MA, 901 .... 151 E4

Mason MI, 6714 .... 76 A4
Mason NV, 500 .... 37 C2
Mason NH, 550 .... 95 D1
Mason OH, 22016 .... 100 B2
Mason TX, 2134 .... 60 C1
Mason TN, 1089 .... 118 C4
Mason WV, 1064 .... 101 C2
Masonboro NC, 11812 .... 123 D4
Mason City IL, 2558 .... 88 B4
Mason City IA, 29172 .... 73 D3
Mason Co. IL, 16038 .... 88 A4
Mason Co. KY, 16800 .... 100 C3
Mason Co. MI, 28274 .... 75 E1
Mason Co. TX, 3738 .... 60 C1
Mason Co. WA, 49405 .... 12 B3
Mason Co. WV, 25957 .... 101 C2

Masontown PA, 3611 .... 102 B1
Masontown WV, 647 .... 102 B1
Masonville KY, 1075 .... 109 E1
Masonville NY, 7300 .... 147 D3
Massac Co. IL, 15161 .... 108 C2
Massapequa NY, 22652 .... 148 C4
Massapequa Park NY, 17499 .... 148 C4
Massena NY, 11209 .... 80 D1
Massillon OH, 31325 .... 91 E3
Mastic NY, 15436 .... 149 D4
Mastic Beach NY, 11543 .... 149 D4
Masury OH, 2618 .... 91 F2
Matador TX, 740 .... 58 B1
Matagorda Co. TX, 37957 .... 132 A4
Matamoras PA, 2312 .... 94 A3
Matawan NJ, 8910 .... 147 E1

Matewan WV, 498 .... 111 E1
Matherville IL, 772 .... 88 B1
Mathews LA, 2003 .... 134 B3
Mathews VA, 850 .... 113 F1
Mathews Co. VA, 9207 .... 113 F1
Mathis TX, 5034 .... 61 E4
Mathiston MS, 720 .... 118 C4
Matlacha FL, 735 .... 142 C1
Mattapoisett MA, 2966 .... 151 E3
Mattawa WA, 2609 .... 13 E4
Mattawamkeag ME, 400 .... 85 D4
Mattawan MI, 2536 .... 89 F1
Mattawoman MD, 3100 .... 144 B4
Matteson IL, 12928 .... 89 D2
Matthews IN, 595 .... 89 F4
Matthews MO, 605 .... 108 B2

Matthews NC, 22127 .... 122 B1
Mattituck NY, 4198 .... 149 E3
Mattoon IL, 18291 .... 98 C2
Mattydale NY, 6367 .... 79 D3
Matunuck RI, 750 .... 150 C4
Maud OH, 4800 .... 100 B2
Maud OK, 1136 .... 51 F3
Maud TX, 1028 .... 124 C1
Maugansville MD, 2295 .... 103 D1
Maui Co. HI, 128094 .... 153 D1
Mauldin SC, 15224 .... 121 F2
Maumee OH, 15237 .... 90 C2
Maumelle AR, 10557 .... 117 C2
Maunawili HI, 4869 .... 152 B3
Maupin OR, 411 .... 21 D2
Maurertown VA, 550 .... 102 C3

Maurice LA, 642 .... 133 F2
Mauriceville TX, 2743 .... 132 C4
Maury City TN, 704 .... 108 C4
Maury Co. TN, 69498 .... 109 E4
Mauston WI, 3740 .... 74 A2
Mavisdale VA, 550 .... 111 E2
Max Meadows VA, 512 .... 112 A2
Max ND, 278 .... 18 B3
Maxton NC, 2551 .... 123 C3
Maxwell CA, 900 .... 36 B2
Maxwell IA, 807 .... 86 C1
Maxwell NM, 274 .... 49 E1
Maybee MI, 505 .... 90 C1
Mayberry WV, 550 .... 111 F1
Maybrook NY, 3084 .... 148 B1

Mayer AZ, 1408 .... 47 D4
Mayer MN, 554 .... 66 C4
Mayes Co. OK, 38369 .... 106 A3
Mayesville SC, 1001 .... 122 B3
Mayfield KY, 10349 .... 108 C3
Mayfield NY, 800 .... 81 D4
Mayfield OH, 3435 .... 204 G1
Mayfield PA, 1756 .... 93 F2
Mayfield UT, 420 .... 39 E2
Mayfield Hts. OH, 19386 .... 91 E2
Mayflower AR, 1631 .... 117 C2
Maynard IA, 900 .... 73 E4
Maynard MA, 10433 .... 150 C1
Maynardville TN, 1782 .... 110 A4
Mayo FL, 988 .... 137 F3
Mayo MD, 3153 .... 144 C3
Mayo SC, 746 .... 121 F1
Mayodan NC, 2417 .... 112 B3
Maypearl TX, 746 .... 59 F3
Mays Chapel MD, 11427 .... 193 C3
Mays Landing NJ, 2321 .... 105 D3
Maysville GA, 1247 .... 121 D3
Maysville KY, 8993 .... 100 C3
Maysville MO, 1212 .... 96 B1
Maysville NC, 1002 .... 115 D4
Maysville OK, 1313 .... 51 E4
Maytown AL, 435 .... 195 D1
Mayville MI, 1055 .... 76 C3
Mayville NY, 1756 .... 78 A4
Mayville ND, 1953 .... 19 E3
Mayville WI, 4902 .... 74 C2
Maywood CA, 28083 .... 228 D3
Maywood IL, 26987 .... 203 C4
Maywood NJ, 9523 .... 240 C1
Maywood NE, 4200 .... 188 D2
Maywood Park OR, 777 .... 251 D2
Mazeppa MN, 778 .... 73 D1
Mazomanie WI, 1485 .... 74 A3
Mazon IL, 904 .... 88 C2
McAdoo PA, 2274 .... 93 E3
McAfee NJ, 2600 .... 148 A2
McAlester OK, 17783 .... 116 A2
McAllen TX, 106414 .... 63 E4
McArthur OH, 1888 .... 101 D2
McBain MI, 584 .... 75 F1
McBee SC, 714 .... 122 B3
McCall ID, 2084 .... 22 B2
McCamey TX, 1805 .... 58 A4
McCammon ID, 805 .... 31 E1
McCandless PA, 29022 .... 92 A4
McCaysville GA, 1071 .... 120 C2
McClain Co. OK, 27740 .... 51 E3
McCleary WA, 1454 .... 12 B4
McClellandville DE, 2400 .... 146 B4
McClellanville SC, 459 .... 131 E1
McCloud CA, 1343 .... 28 C3
McClure OH, 761 .... 90 B2
McClure PA, 975 .... 93 D3
McClusky ND, 415 .... 18 C3
McColl SC, 2498 .... 122 C4
McComb MS, 13337 .... 126 B4
McComb OH, 1676 .... 90 B3
McConnellsburg PA, 1073 .... 103 D1
McConnelsville OH, 1676 .... 101 E1
McCook NE, 7994 .... 42 C1
McCook Co. SD, 5832 .... 27 E4
McCordsville IN, 1134 .... 99 F1
McCormack Corners NY, 2300 .... 188 C3
McCormick SC, 1489 .... 121 F4
McCormick Co. SC, 9958 .... 121 F4
McCracken Co. KY, 65514 .... 108 C3
McCreary Co. KY, 17080 .... 110 C2
McCrory AR, 1517 .... 117 F1
McCulloch Co. TX, 8205 .... 58 C4
McCune KS, 406 .... 106 B1
McCurtain OK, 466 .... 116 B1
McCurtain Co. OK, 34402 .... 116 B3
McDermitt NV, 269 .... 30 A2
McDonald OH, 3481 .... 276 B3
McDonald PA, 2281 .... 92 A4
McDonald Co. MO, 21681 .... 106 C3
McDonough GA, 8493 .... 120 C4
McDonough Co. IL, 32913 .... 88 A3
McDowell Co. NC, 42151 .... 111 F4
McDowell Co. WV, 27329 .... 111 F1
McDuffie Co. GA, 21231 .... 129 F1
McEwen TN, 1702 .... 109 E4
McFarland CA, 9618 .... 45 D4
McFarland WI, 6416 .... 74 B3
McGaheysville VA, 500 .... 102 C4
McGehee AR, 4570 .... 117 F4
McGill NV, 1054 .... 38 B2
McGrath AK, 401 .... 154 D2
McGraw NY, 1000 .... 79 E4

McGregor IA, 871 .... 73 F3
McGregor TX, 4727 .... 59 E4
McHenry IL, 21501 .... 74 C4
McHenry KY, 417 .... 109 E1
McHenry Co. IL, 260077 .... 74 C4
McHenry Co. ND, 5987 .... 18 C2
Maverick Co. TX, 47297 .... 60 B3
McIntosh FL, 453 .... 138 C2
McIntosh MN, 638 .... 19 F3
McIntosh SD, 217 .... 26 B1
McIntosh Co. GA, 10847 .... 130 B4
McIntosh Co. ND, 3390 .... 27 D1
McIntosh Co. OK, 19456 .... 116 A1
McIntyre GA, 718 .... 129 C3
McKean Co. PA, 45936 .... 92 B1
McKee KY, 878 .... 110 C1
McKee City NJ, 2800 .... 147 E4
McKeesport PA, 24040 .... 92 A4
McKees Rocks PA, 6622 .... 250 B1
McKenna WA, 800 .... 12 C4
McKenney VA, 441 .... 113 E2
McKenzie AL, 644 .... 127 F4
McKenzie TN, 5295 .... 109 D4
McKenzie Co. ND, 5737 .... 17 F2
McKinley Co. NM, 74798 .... 48 A2
McKinleyville CA, 13599 .... 28 A4
McKinney TX, 54369 .... 59 F2
McKownville NY, 2600 .... 188 D3
McLain MS, 603 .... 135 D1
McLaughlin SD, 775 .... 26 B1
McLean IL, 808 .... 88 B4
McLean TX, 830 .... 50 A4
McLean VA, 38929 .... 144 B3
McLean Co. IL, 150433 .... 88 C4
McLean Co. KY, 9938 .... 109 E1
McLean Co. ND, 9311 .... 18 B3
McLeansboro IL, 2945 .... 98 C4
McLennan Co. TX, 213517 .... 59 E4
McLeod Co. MN, 34898 .... 66 C4
McLoud OK, 3548 .... 51 F3
McLouth KS, 868 .... 96 A2
McMechen WV, 1937 .... 101 F1
McMinn Co. TN, 49015 .... 120 C1
McMinnville OR, 26499 .... 20 B2
McMinnville TN, 12749 .... 110 A4
McMullen Co. TX, 851 .... 61 D4
McMurray PA, 4726 .... 92 A4
McNairy Co. TN, 24653 .... 119 D1
McNary AZ, 349 .... 47 F4
McNeil AR, 662 .... 125 D1
McPherson KS, 13770 .... 43 E3
McPherson Co. KS, 29554 .... 43 E3
McPherson Co. NE, 533 .... 34 B3
McPherson Co. SD, 2904 .... 27 D1
McQueeney TX, 2527 .... 61 D2
McRae AR, 661 .... 117 F1
McRae GA, 2682 .... 129 E3
McRoberts KY, 921 .... 111 E2
McVeigh KY, 550 .... 111 E1
McVille ND, 470 .... 19 E3
Mead CO, 2017 .... 33 E4
Mead NE, 564 .... 35 F3
Mead WA, 2100 .... 14 A3
Meade KS, 1672 .... 42 C4
Meade Co. KS, 4631 .... 42 C4
Meade Co. KY, 26349 .... 99 F4
Meade Co. SD, 24253 .... 26 A3
Meadow TX, 658 .... 58 A1
Meadowlakes TX, 1293 .... 61 D1
Meadows Place TX, 4912 .... 132 A4
Meadow Vale KY, 765 .... 230 F1
Meadow Valley CA, 575 .... 36 C1
Meadowview VA, 2266 .... 111 F2
Meadville MS, 519 .... 126 A4
Meadville PA, 13685 .... 92 A2
Meagher Co. MT, 1932 .... 15 F4
Mebane NC, 7284 .... 112 C4
Mecca CA, 5402 .... 53 E4
Mechanic Falls ME, 2450 .... 82 B2
Mechanicsburg OH, 1744 .... 90 C4
Mechanicsburg PA, 9042 .... 93 D4
Mechanicsville IA, 1173 .... 87 F3
Mechanicsville MD, 750 .... 103 D3
Mechanicsville VA, 44113 .... 113 E1
Mechanicville NY, 5019 .... 94 B1
Mecklenburg Co. NC, 695454 .... 122 B1
Mecklenburg Co. VA, 32380 .... 113 D2
Mecosta Co. MI, 40553 .... 75 F3
Medanales NM, 450 .... 49 D2
Medaryville IN, 565 .... 89 E3
Medfield MA, 6670 .... 151 D2
Medford MA, 55765 .... 151 D1
Medford MN, 984 .... 73 D1
Medford NJ, 20123 .... 147 D3
Medford NY, 21985 .... 149 D4
Medford OK, 1172 .... 51 E1
Medford OR, 63154 .... 28 B2
Medford WI, 4350 .... 68 A3
Medford Lakes NJ, 4173 .... 147 D3
Media PA, 5533 .... 146 C3
Mediapolis IA, 1644 .... 87 F3
Medical Lake WA, 3758 .... 14 A3
Medicine Bow WY, 274 .... 33 F3
Medicine Lake MT, 269 .... 17 F2
Medina MN, 4005 .... 66 C3
Medina NY, 6415 .... 78 B3
Medina ND, 335 .... 19 D3
Medina OH, 25139 .... 91 E3
Medina TN, 969 .... 108 C4
Medina WA, 3011 .... 262 B3
Medina Co. OH, 151095 .... 91 E3
Medina Co. TX, 39304 .... 60 C2

Milwaukee WI

Bayside D1
Brookfield B2
Brown Deer C1
Butler B1
Cudahy D3
Elm Grove B2
Fox Pt. D1
Glendale C1
Greendale C3
Greenfield C3
Hales Corners B3
Lannon A1
Menomonee Falls B1
Milwaukee C2
New Berlin B3
Pewaukee (city) A2
Pewaukee (village) A2
River Hills C1
St. Francis D3
Shorewood D2
Sussex A1
Waukesha A2
Wauwatosa C2
W. Allis C3
W. Milwaukee C3
Whitefish Bay D1

Downtown Milwaukee WI

POINTS OF INTEREST

Amtrak Station F2
Betty Brinn Children's Mus. G2
Bradley Center F1
Broadway Theatre Center F2
City Hall F1
Court House E1
Cudahy Gardens G2
Discovery World at Wisconsin Pier G2
The Eisner American Mus. of Advertising & Design F2
Federal Plaza F2
Grain Exchange F2
Haggerty Mus. of Art E2
Helfaer Theatre E2
Hist. Third Ward F2
IMAX E1
Intercity Bus Depot E2
Maier Festival Park G2
Marcus Ctr. for the Performing Arts F1
Marquette Univ. E2
Midwest Airlines Center F2
Milwaukee Art Mus. & War Memorial Center G1
Milwaukee County Hist. Center F1
Milwaukee Institute of Art & Design F2
Milwaukee Public Mkt. F2
Milwaukee Public Mus. F1
Milwaukee School of Engineering F1
Milwaukee Theatre F1
Municipal Pier G2
Pabst Theater F1
Post Office F1
Potawatomi Bingo & Casino E2
St. Joan of Arc Chapel E2
The Shops of Grand Avenue F2
State Office Building F1
U.S. Cellular Arena F1
Wisconsin Conservatory of Music G1

Entries in **bold black** indicate counties or parishes. Entries in **bold color** indicate cities with detailed inset maps.

Minneapolis/St Paul MN

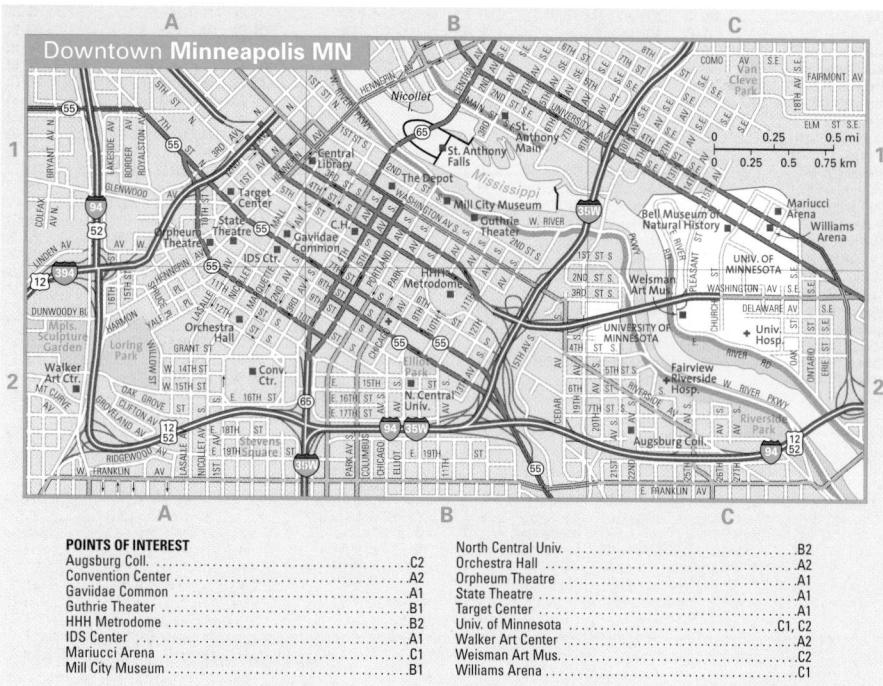

Downtown Minneapolis MN

POINTS OF INTEREST

Augsburg Coll.	C2
Convention Center	A2
Gavidae Common	A1
Guthrie Theater	B1
HHH Metrodome	B2
IDS Center	A1
Mariucci Arena	C1
Mill City Museum	B1
North Central Univ.	B2
Orchestra Hall	A2
Orpheum Theatre	A1
State Theatre	A1
Target Center	A1
Univ. of Minnesota	C1, C2
Walker Art Center	A2
Weisman Art Mus.	C2
Williams Arena	C1

Monterey Bay CA

Missoula MT

Mobile AL

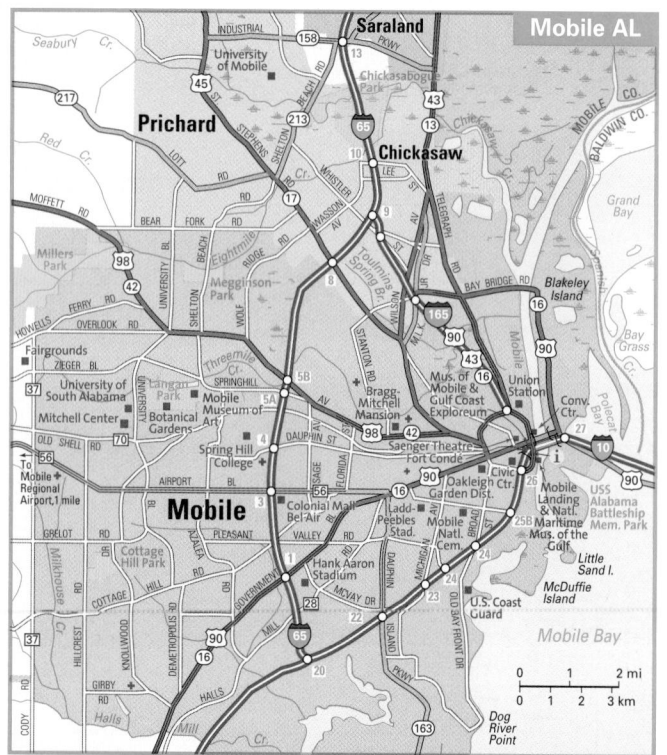

Montgomery AL

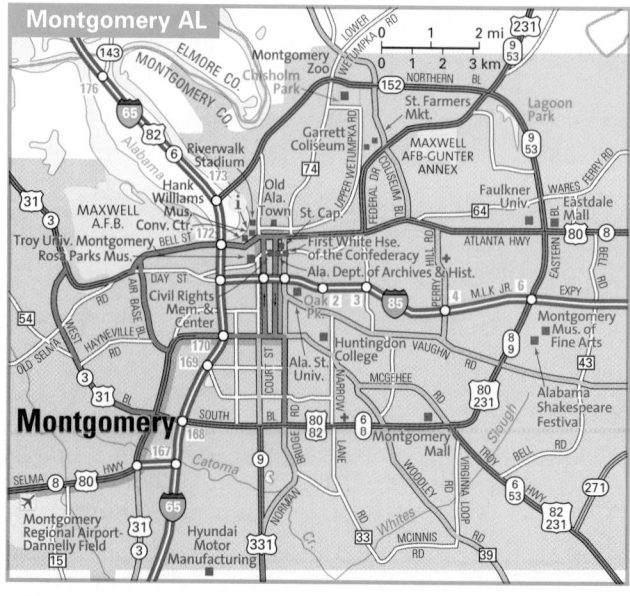

Entries in **bold black** indicate counties or parishes.   Entries in ***bold color*** indicate cities with detailed inset maps.

Miles City–Montegut   **237**

Miles City MT, 8487 ....17 E4	Mililani Town HI, 28608 ....152 A3	**Miller Co. MO,** 23564 ....97 E4	Milton NH, 950 ....81 F4	Minoa NY, 3348 ....79 E3
Milford CT, 52305 ....149 D2	**Millard Co. UT,** 12405 ....39 D2	Miller Place NY, 10580 ....149 D3	Milton NY, 1251 ....148 B1	Minocqua WI, 750 ....68 B2
Milford DE, 6732 ....145 F3	Millbourne PA, 943 ....248 B3	Millersburg IN, 868 ....89 F2	Milton PA, 6650 ....93 D3	Minong WI, 531 ....67 E2
Milford IL, 1369 ....89 D3	Millbrae CA, 20718 ....259 B4	Millersburg KY, 842 ....100 B4	Milton VT, 1537 ....45 D1	Minonk IL, 2168 ....88 C2
Milford IN, 1550 ....89 F2	Millbrook AL, 10386 ....128 C4	Millersburg OH, 3326 ....91 F1	Milton WV, 5795 ....262 B5	Minooka IL, 3971 ....88 C2
Milford IA, 2474 ....72 A4	Millbrook NY, 1429 ....94 B3	Millersburg OR, 651 ....20 B3	Milton WV, 5132 ....74 B4	Minot ME, 400 ....82 B3
Milford KS, 502 ....43 F2	Millburn NJ, 19765 ....240 A3	Millers Creek NC, 2071 .....111 F3	Milton MA, 1100 ....151 E2	Minot ND, 36567 ....18 B2
Milford ME, 2197 ....83 D1	Millbury MA, 4700 ....150 C2	Millers Falls MA, 1072 ....94 C1	Milton WV, 2206 ....101 E3	Minot MA, 1100 ....151 E2
Milford MD, 26527 ....193 B2	Millbury OH, 1161 ....90 C2	Millerstown PA, 679 ....93 D4	Milton WV, 5132 ....74 B4	Minster OH, 2794 ....90 B4
Milford MI, 24230 ....150 C2	Mill City OR, 1537 ....20 C4	Millerston PA, 679 ....93 D4	Milton-Freewater OR, 6470 ...21 F1	Mint Hill NC, 14922 ....122 B1
Milford MI, 6272 ....76 B4	Mill City WV, 300 ....29 F4	Millersville PA, 7774 ....93 E4	Miltonvale KS, 523 ....43 E2	Minto ND, 655 ....19 E2
Milford NE, 2070 ....35 F4	Mill Creek WA, 11525 ....12 C3	Millersville TN, 5308 ....109 F3		Minturn CO, 1068 ....41 D1
Milford NH, 8293 ....95 D1	Mill Creek WV, 662 ....102 A3	Millerton NY, 925 ....94 B2	Mims FL, 9147 ....141 E1	Mio MI, 2016 ....70 C4
Milford NJ, 1195 ....146 C1	Milledgeville GA, 18757 .....129 E1	Mill Hall PA, 1568 ....93 D3	Mina NV, 275 ....37 F3	Mira Loma CA, 17617 ....229 H3
Milford NY, 511 ....79 F4	Milledgeville IL, 1016 ....88 B1	Millican OR, ...20 C4	Minatare NE, 810 ....33 F2	Miramar FL, 72739 ....143 E2
Milford OH, 6284 ....100 B2	**Mille Lacs Co. MN,** 22330 ...66 C2	Milliken CO, 2888 ....33 E4	Minco OK, 1672 ....51 E3	Miramar Beach FL, 2435 ...136 B2
Milford PA, 1104 ....94 A3	Millen GA, 3492 ....129 F2	Millington MI, 1137 ....76 B3	Minden IA, 564 ....86 A2	Misenheimer NC, 750 ....122 B1
Milford TX, 685 ....59 F3	Miller MO, 754 ....106 C2	Millington NJ, 3500 ....148 A4	Minden LA, 13027 ....125 D2	Mishawaka IN, 46557 ....89 F2
Milford UT, 1451 ....39 D3	Miller SD, 1530 ....27 D3	Millington TN, 10433 ....118 B1	Minden NE, 2964 ....35 D4	Mishicot WI, 1422 ....75 D1
Milford Ctr. OH, 626 ....90 C4	**Miller Co. AR,** 40443 ....124 C1	Millinocket ME, 5190 ....85 D1	Minden NV, 2836 ....37 D2	Missaukee Co. MI, 14478 ...75 F1
Milford Square PA, 1100 .....146 C1	**Miller Co. GA,** 6383 ....128 C4	Millis MA, 4607 ....150 C2	Minden City MI, ...76 C3	Mission KS, 9727 ....224 B3
		Millport AL, 963 ....101 D1	Mineola NY, 19234 ....148 C4	Mission OR, 1019 ....21 F1
		Millport NY, 250 ....93 D4	Mineola TX, 4550 ....124 B2	Mission SD, 904 ....26 C4
		Milltown IN, 837 ....100 A4	Miner MO, 1056 ....108 B2	Mission TX, 45408 ....63 E4
		Mill Neck NY, 825 ....148 C3	Mineral VA, 424 ....103 D4	Mission Bend TX, 30831 ....220 A4
		Millry AL, 615 ....127 D4	Mineral City OH, 841 ....91 E4	Mission Hills KS, 3593 ....224 B4
		Millsboro DE, 2360 ....145 F4	**Mills Co. IA,** 14547 ....86 A3	Mineral Co. CO, 831 ....40 C4	Mission Viejo CA, 93102 ....229 G5
		Mills Co. TX, 5151 ....59 D4	**Mineral Co. MT,** 3884 ....14 C3	**Mississippi Co. AR,** 51979 ...108 B4
		Millstadt IL, 2794 ....98 A3	**Mineral Co. NV,** 5071 ....37 E3	**Mississippi Co. MO,** 13427 ...108 C2
		Millstone KY, 650 ....111 E2	**Mineral Co. WV,** 27078 ......102 C2	Mississippi State MS, 3500 ...119 D4
		Milltown NJ, 932 ....99 F4	Mineral Pt. WI, 2617 ....74 A3	Missoula MT, 57053 ....15 D4
		Milltown NJ, 7000 ....147 E1	Mineral Ridge OH, 3900 .....276 B2	**Missoula Co. MT,** 95802 ......15 D4
		Milltown WI, 888 ....67 E3	Mineral Sprs. AR, 1264 ......116 C4	Missouri City TX, 52913 .....132 A3
		Millvale PA, 4028 ....250 B1	Mineral Sprs. NC, 1370 .....122 B2	Missouri Valley IA, 2992 ......86 A2
		Mill Valley CA, 13600 ....36 B4	Mineral Wells TX, 16946 .....59 E2	Mitchell IN, 4567 ....99 F3
		Millville CA, 610 ....28 C4	Mineral Wells WV, 1860 ....101 E2	**Mitchell Co. GA,** 23932 .....137 E1
		Millville DE, 259 ....145 F4	Miner Co. SD, 2884 ....27 E3	Mitchell NE, 1831 ....33 F2
		Millville NJ, 26847 ....145 F1	Minersville PA, 4552 ....93 E3	**Mitchell Co. IA,** 10874 ....73 D2
		Millville OH, 817 ....100 B2	Minersville UT, 817 ....39 D3	**Mitchell Co. KS,** 6932 ....43 E2
		Millville PA, 991 ....93 D3	Minerva OH, 3934 ....91 F3	**Mitchell Co. NC,** 15687 ......111 E4
		Millville UT, 1507 ....31 E3	Minerva Park OH, 1288 ....206 B1	**Mitchell Co. TX,** 9698 ....58 B3
		Millwood NY, 2300 ....148 B2	Minetto NY, 1086 ....79 D2	Mitchellville IA, 2236 ....86 C3
		Millwood WA, 1649 ....14 A3	Mineville NY, 1747 ....81 D2	Mitchellville MD, 497 ....117 F4
		Milner GA, 522 ....129 D1	Mingo IA, 839 ....86 C2	Mitchellville IA, 1715 ....87 D2
		Milnor ND, 711 ....27 E1	Mingo WV, 28253 ....101 E4	Mi-Wuk Vil. CA, 1485 ....37 D3
		Milo IA, 839 ....86 C2	Mingo Jct. OH, 3631 ....91 F4	Moab UT, 4779 ....40 A3
		Milo ME, 1898 ....84 C4	Minidoka Co. ID, 20174 ....31 D1	Moapa NV, 928 ....46 B1
		Milpitas CA, 62698 ....36 B4	Minier IL, 1244 ....88 B4	Moberly MO, 11945 ....97 D3
		Milroy IN, 800 ....100 A2	Minneapolis KS, 2046 ....43 E2	Mobile AL, 198915 ....135 E1
		Milroy PA, 1386 ....93 D3	Minneapolis MN, 382618 .....67 D4	**Mobile Co. AL,** 399843 .....135 E1
		Milton DE, 1657 ....145 F3	Minneola FL, 5435 ....140 C1	Mobridge SD, 3574 ....26 C2
		Milton FL, 7045 ....135 F1	Minneola KS, 717 ....42 C4	Mocksville NC, 4178 ....112 A4
		Milton IN, 611 ....100 A1	Minneota MN, 1449 ....27 F3	Moclips WA, 615 ....12 B3
		Milton IA, 550 ....87 D3	Minnesota Lake MN, 681 .....72 C2	Modena NY, 1100 ....148 B1
		Milton KY, 525 ....100 A3	Minnetonka MN, 51301 .....235 A3	Modena PA, 610 ....146 B3
		Milton MA, 26062 ....151 D1	Minnewaukan ND, 318 ....19 D2		

Modesto CA, 188856 ....36 C4	Monroe MI, 22076 ....90 C1	
Modoc Co. CA, 9449 ....29 D3	Monroe NY, 7780 ....148 B1	
Moenkopi AZ, 901 ....47 E2	Monroe NC, 26228 ....122 B2	
Moffat Co. CO, 13184 ....32 B4	Monroe OH, 7133 ....100 B2	
Mogadore OH, 3893 ....188 D2	Monroe OR, 607 ....20 B3	
Mohall ND, 812 ....18 B1	Monroe UT, 1845 ....39 E3	
Mohave Co. AZ, 155032 ....46 B3	Monroe VA, 1200 ....112 C1	
Mohave Valley AZ, 13694 .....46 B3	Monroe WA, 13795 ....13 D3	
Mohawk MI, 750 ....65 D2	Monroe WI, 10843 ....74 B4	
Mohawk NY, 2660 ....79 F3	Monroe City IN, 548 ....99 E3	
Mohegan CT, 3500 ....149 E1	Monroe City MO, 2588 ....97 E1	
Mohegan Lake NY, 5700 .....148 A2	**Monroe Co. AL,** 24324 ....127 F4	
Mohnton PA, 2963 ....146 A2	**Monroe Co. AR,** 10254 ....118 A2	
Mohrsville PA, 800 ....146 A1	**Monroe Co. FL,** 79589 ....143 D3	
Mojave CA, 3836 ....52 C1	**Monroe Co. GA,** 21757 ......129 D1	
Mokelumne Hill CA, 774 ....36 C3	**Monroe Co. IL,** 27619 ....98 A3	
Mokuleia HI, 1839 ....152 A2	**Monroe Co. IN,** 120563 ....99 F2	
Molalla OR, 5647 ....20 C2	**Monroe Co. IA,** 8016 ....87 D3	
Molena GA, 475 ....128 C1	**Monroe Co. KY,** 11756 ....110 A2	
Moline IL, 43768 ....88 A1	**Monroe Co. MI,** 145945 ....90 C1	
Moline KS, 457 ....43 F4	**Monroe Co. MS,** 38014 ......119 D4	
Moline Acres MO, 2662 ......256 C1	**Monroe Co. MO,** 9311 ....97 E2	
Molino FL, 1312 ....135 F1	**Monroe Co. NY,** 735343 ....78 C3	
Momence IL, 3171 ....89 D2	**Monroe Co. OH,** 15180 ....101 F1	
Mona UT, 1057 ....39 E1	**Monroe Co. PA,** 138687 ....93 F3	
Monaca PA, 6286 ....91 F3	**Monroe Co. TN,** 38961 ....120 C1	
Monahans TX, 6821 ....57 F4	**Monroe Co. WV,** 14583 ......112 A1	
Monarch Mills SC, 1930 .....121 F2	**Monroe Co. WI,** 40899 ....73 F1	
Moncks Corner SC, 5952 ...131 D1	Monroeville AL, 6862 ....127 F4	
Mondovi WI, 2634 ....67 E4	Monroeville IN, 1236 ....90 A3	
Monee IL, 2924 ....89 D2	Monroeville OH, 1433 ....91 D2	
Monett MO, 7396 ....106 C2	Monroeville PA, 29349 ....92 A4	
Monette AR, 1179 ....108 A4	Monrovia CA, 36929 ....228 E2	
Monfort Hts. OH, 3880 ....204 A2	Monrovia IN, 628 ....99 F1	
Moniteau Co. MO, 14827 ....97 D3	Monsey NY, 14504 ....148 B2	
Monmouth IL, 9841 ....88 A3	Monson MA, 2103 ....150 A2	
Monmouth ME, 500 ....82 B2	Montague CA, 1456 ....28 C3	
Monmouth Co. NJ, 615301 ...147 E2	Montague MA, 800 ....94 C1	
Monmouth OR, 7741 ....20 B2	Montague MI, 2407 ....75 E2	
Monmouth Beach NJ, 3595 ...147 F2	Montague TX, 225 ....59 E1	
Monmouth Jct. NJ, 2721 ......147 D1	**Montague Co. TX,** 19117 ......59 E1	
Mono Co. CA, 12853 ....37 E4	Mont Alto PA, 1357 ....103 D1	
Monon IN, 1733 ....89 E3	Montana City MT, 2094 ....15 E4	
Monona IA, 1550 ....73 F3	Montara CA, 2950 ....259 A4	
Monona WI, 8018 ....74 B3	Montauk NY, 3851 ....149 F3	
Monona Co. IA, 10020 ....86 A1	Mont Belvieu TX, 2324 ....132 B3	
Monongah WV, 939 ....102 A2	Montcalm WV, 885 ....111 F1	
Monongahela PA, 4761 ....92 A4	**Montcalm Co. MI,** 61266 ....75 F2	
Monongalia Co. WV, 81866 ...102 A1	Montclair CA, 33049 ....229 G2	
Monponsett MA, 1700 ....151 E2	Montclair NJ, 38977 ....148 A3	
Monroe CT, 3000 ....149 D2	Mont Clare PA, 1040 ....146 B2	
Monroe GA, 11407 ....121 D4	Monteagle TN, 1238 ....120 A1	
Monroe IN, 734 ....90 A3	Monte Alto TX, 1611 ....63 E4	
Monroe IA, 1808 ....87 D2	Montebello CA, 62150 ....228 D3	
Monroe LA, 53107 ....125 E2	Montecito CA, 10000 ....52 B2	
	Montegut LA, 1803 ....134 B4	

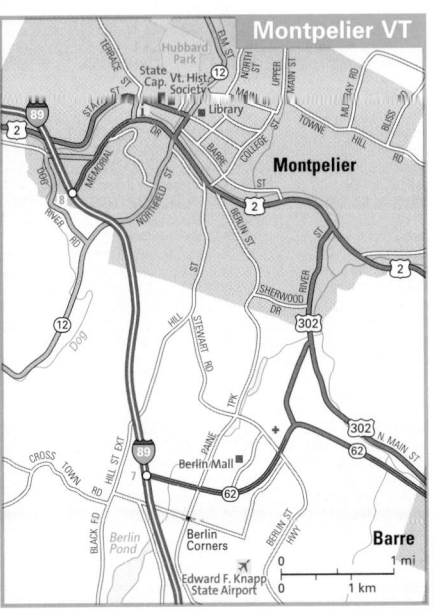

Montpelier VT

Montpelier

Barre

Berlin Mall

Berlin Corners

Berlin Pond

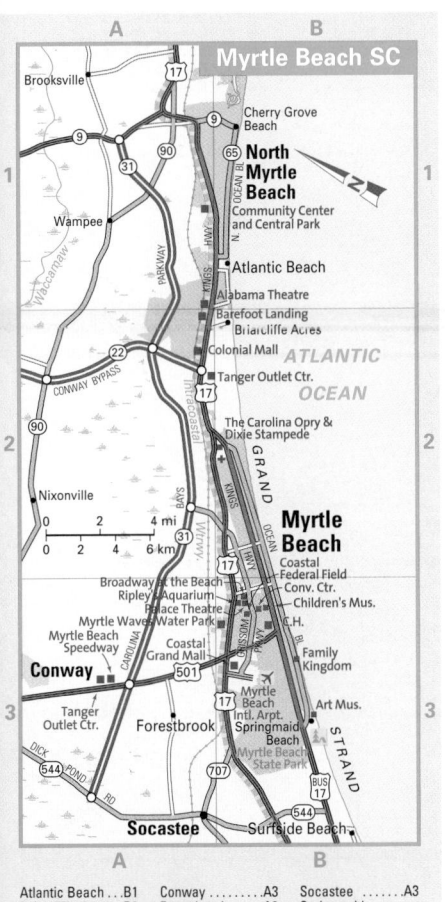

Myrtle Beach SC

North Myrtle Beach

Atlantic Beach

ATLANTIC OCEAN

Myrtle Beach

Conway

Socastee

Surfside Beach

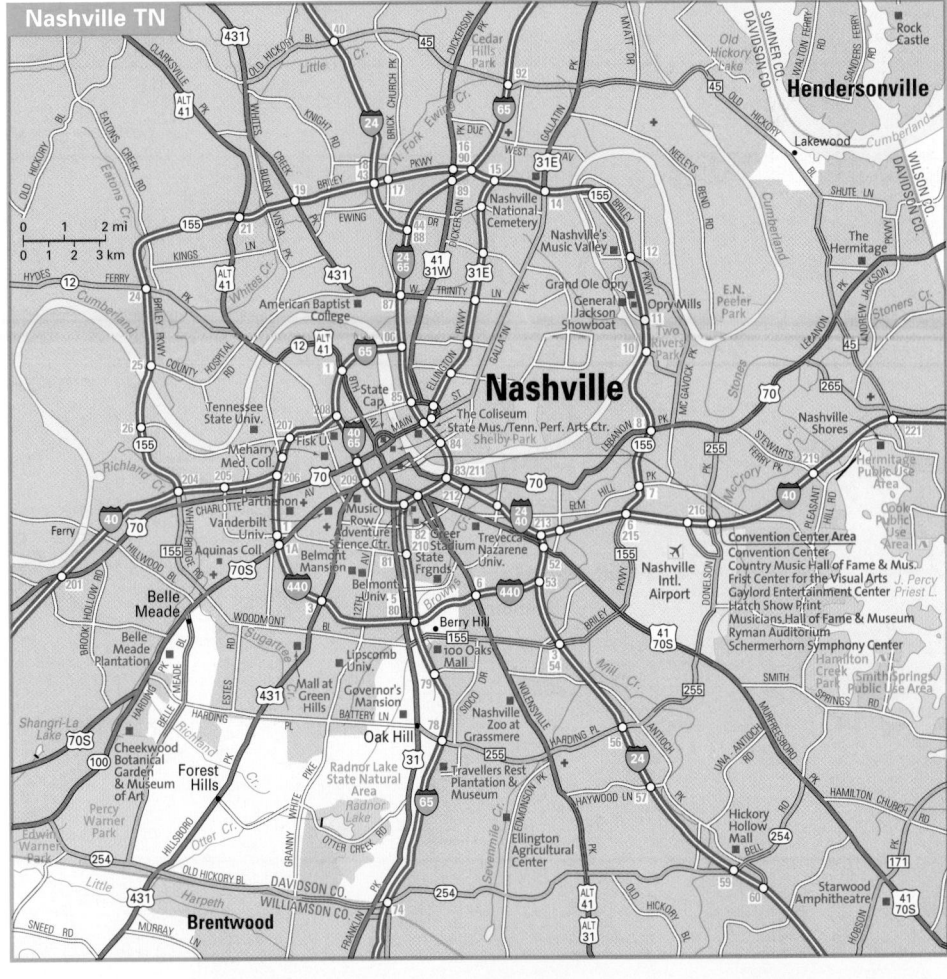

Nashville TN

Nashville

Hendersonville

Brentwood

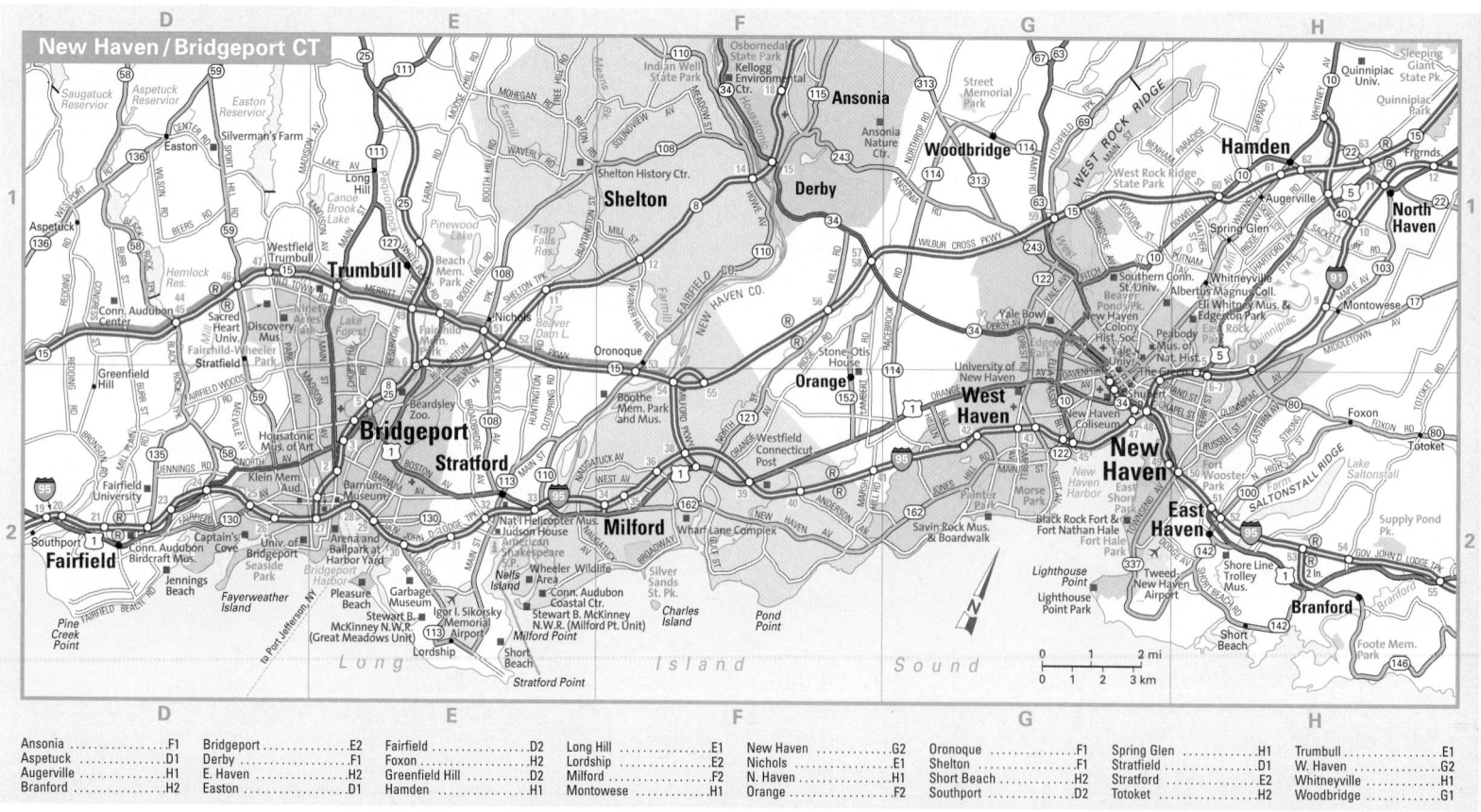

Entries in **bold black** indicate counties or parishes. Entries in **bold color** indicate cities with detailed inset maps.

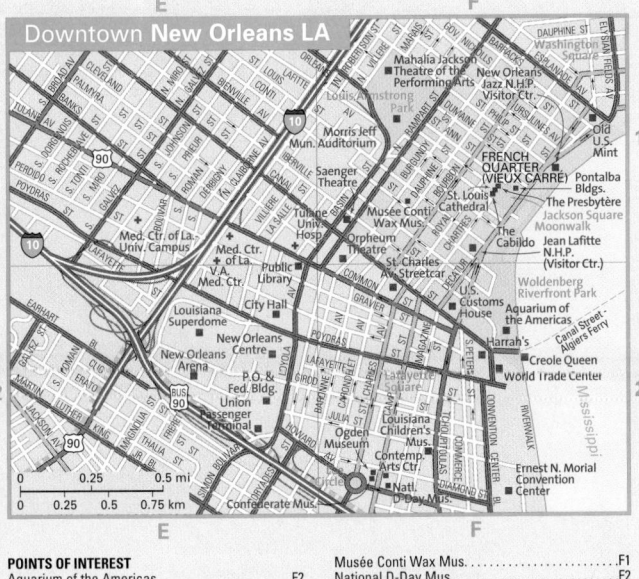

Downtown New Orleans LA

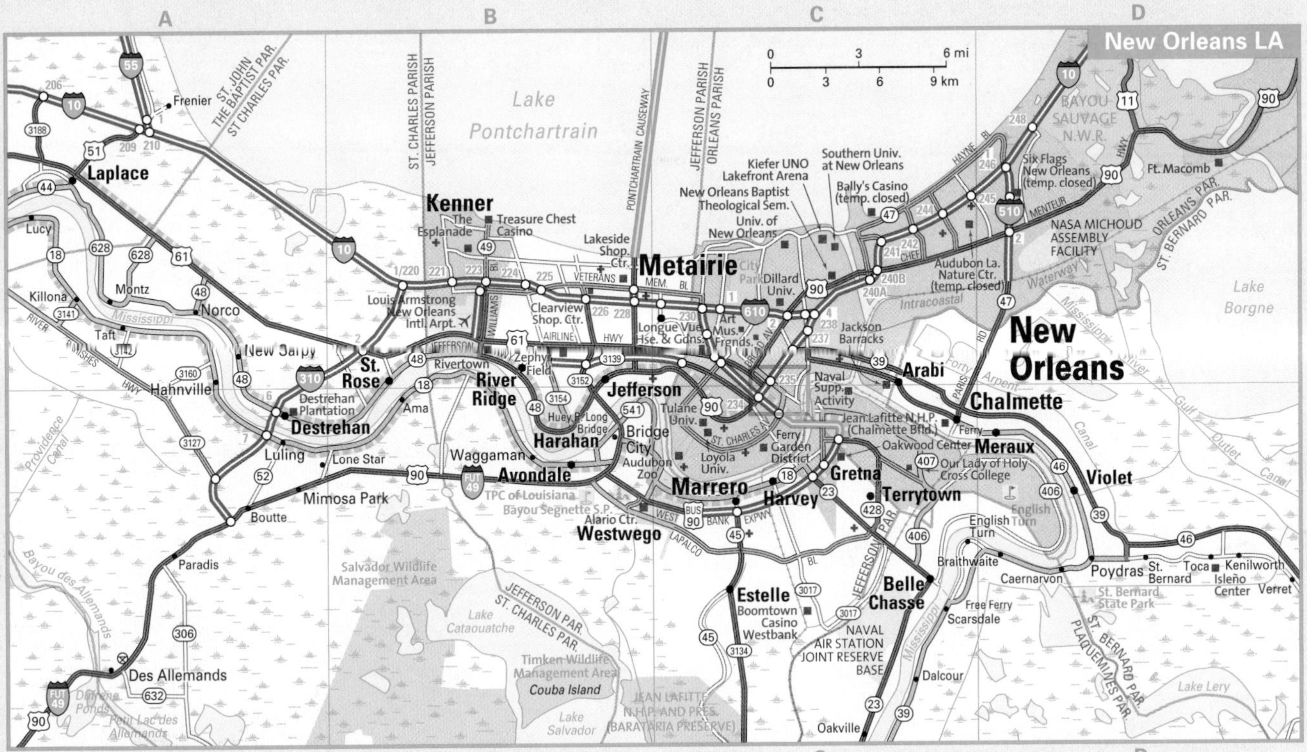

POINTS OF INTEREST

Aquarium of the Americas	F2
The Cabildo	F1
City Hall	E2
Confederate Mus.	F2
Creole Queen	F2
Ernest N. Morial Convention Center	F2
French Quarter (Vieux Carré)	F1
Harrah's	F2
Jackson Square	F1
Jean Lafitte Natl. Hist. Park (Visitor Center)	F1
Louisiana Children's Mus.	F2
Louisiana Superdome	E2
Mahalia Jackson Theatre for the Perf. Arts	F1
Morris Jeff Municipal Auditorium	F1
Musée Conti Wax Mus.	F1
National D-Day Mus.	F2
New Orleans Arena	E2
New Orleans Centre	E2
Old U.S. Mint	F1
Pontalba Buildings	F1
Post Office & Federal Building	E2
The Presbytère	F1
Public Library	E2
St. Charles Avenue Streetcar	F1
St. Louis Cathedral	F1
Union Passenger Terminal	E2
U.S. Customs House	F2
Woldenberg Riverfront Park	F2
World Trade Center	F2

Newport RI

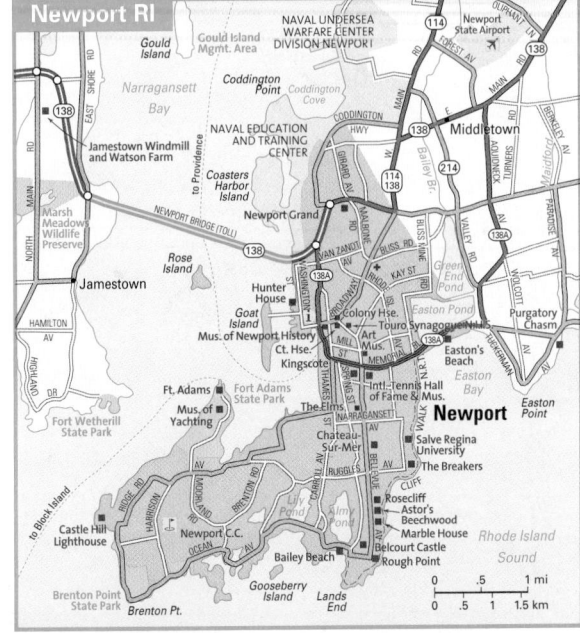

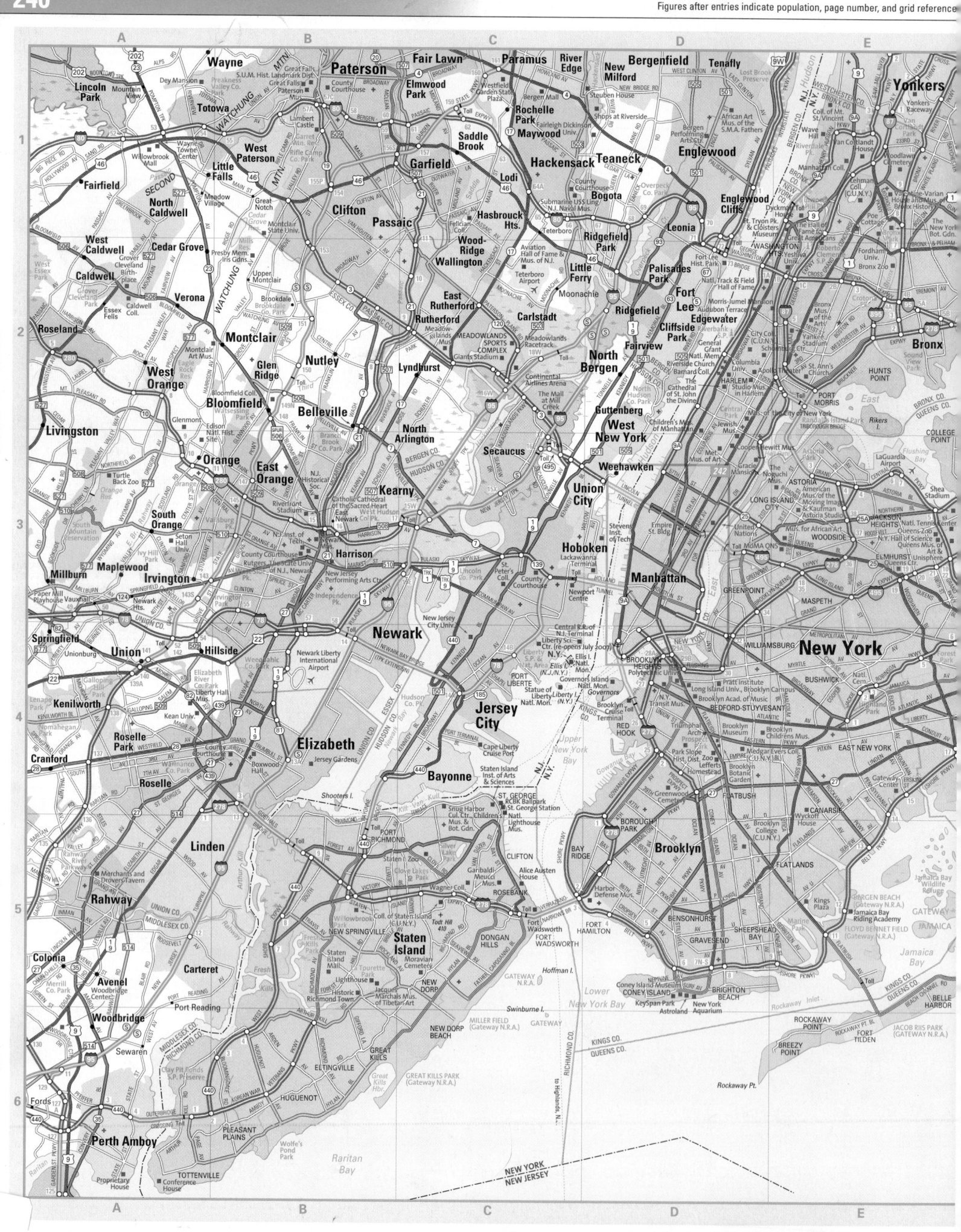

Entries in **bold black** indicate counties or parishes. Entries in **bold color** indicate cities with detailed inset maps.

Mukilteo–New Castle **241**

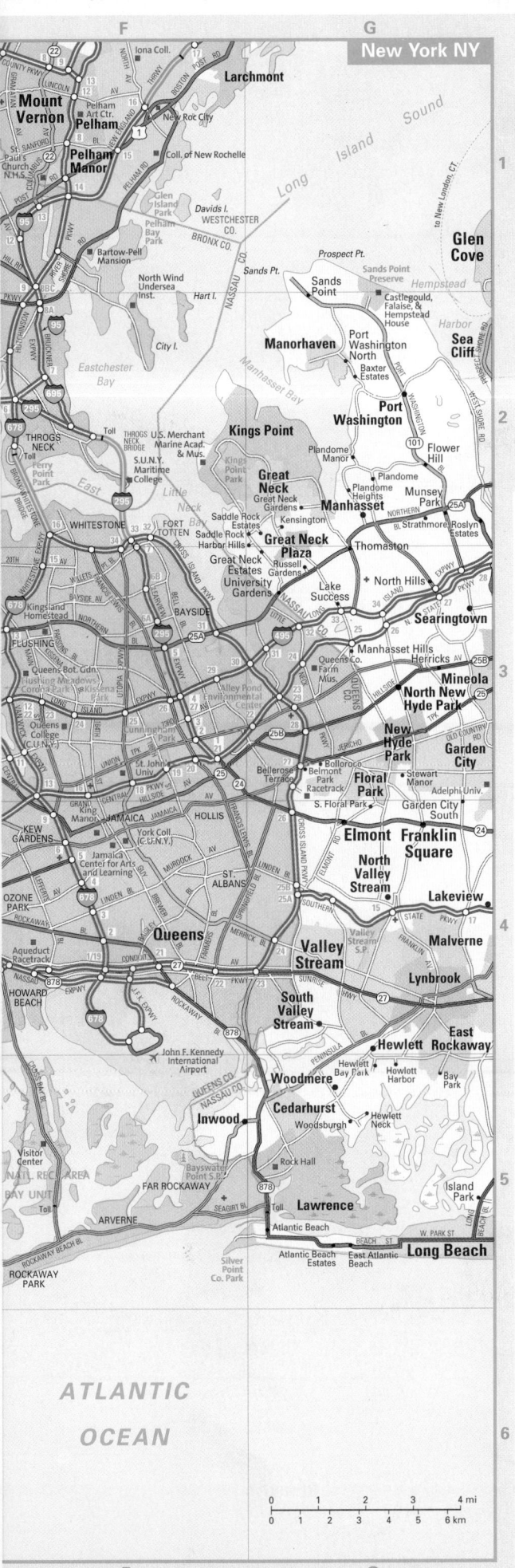

New York NY

POINTS OF INTEREST

Manhattan **New York NY**

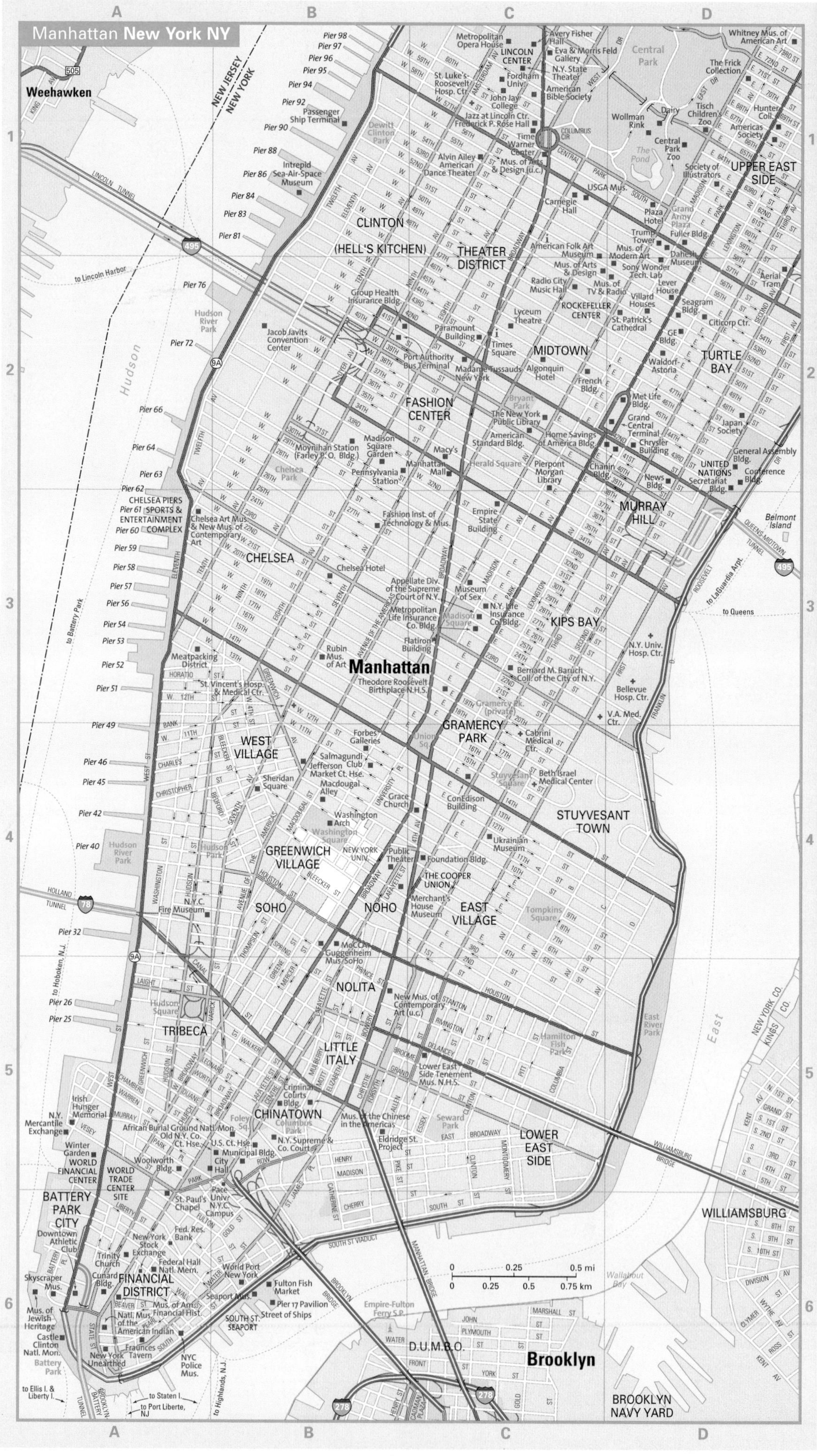

Entries in **bold black** indicate counties or parishes. Entries in **bold color** indicate cities with detailed inset maps.

New Llano LA, 2415 — 133 D1
New London CT, 25671 — 149 F2
New London IA, 1937 — 87 D3
New London MN, 1066 — 66 B3
New London MO, 1001 — 97 F1
New London NH, 1000 — 81 E4
New London OH, 2696 — 91 D3
New London PA, 1100 — 146 B3
New London TX, 987 — 124 B3
New London WI, 7085 — 74 C1
New London Co. CT, 259088 — 150 B4
New Lothrop MI, 603 — 76 B3
New Madison OH, 817 — 100 B1
New Madrid MO, 3334 — 108 B3
New Madrid Co. MO, 19760 — 108 B3
Newman CA, 7093 — 36 C4
Newman IL, 956 — 99 D1
Newman Grove NE, 797 — 35 E2
Newmanstown PA, 1536 — 146 A2
New Market AL, 1864 — 119 F2
New Market IA, 459 — 99 F1
New Market TN, 1234 — 111 D4
New Market VA, 1637 — 102 C3
New Martinsville WV, 5984 — 101 F1
New Matamoras OH, 957 — 101 F1
New Meadows ID, 533 — 22 B2
New Miami OH, 2469 — 100 B1
New Middletown OH, 1682 — 91 F1
New Milford CT, 6633 — 148 C1
New Milford NJ, 16400 — 240 D1
New Milford PA, 850 — 148 A2
New Milford PA, 878 — 93 F1
New Millford IL, 541 — 88 B1

Newnan GA, 16242 — 128 C1
New Orleans LA, 484674 — 134 B3
New Oxford PA, 1696 — 103 E1
New Palestine IN, 1264 — 99 F1
New Paltz NY, 6034 — 94 B3
New Paris IN, 1006 — 89 F2
New Paris OH, 1623 — 100 B1
New Pekin IN, 1334 — 99 F3
New Philadelphia OH, 17056 — 91 E4
New Philadelphia PA, 1149 — 93 E3
New Plymouth ID, 1400 — 22 A4
Newport AR, 7811 — 117 F1
Newport DE, 1122 — 146 B4
Newport IN, 578 — 99 E1
Newport KY, 17048 — 100 B2
Newport ME, 1754 — 82 C1
Newport MN, 3715 — 235 D3
Newport NH, 4008 — 81 E4
Newport NY, 640 — 79 F3
Newport NC, 3349 — 115 D4
Newport OH, 1100 — 101 F2
Newport OR, 9532 — 20 B3
Newport RI, 26475 — 151 D4
Newport TN, 7242 — 111 D4
Newport VT, 5005 — 81 E1
Newport WA, 1921 — 14 B2
Newport Beach CA, 70032 — 52 C4
Newport Co. RI, 85433 — 151 D4
Newport News VA, 180150 — 113 F2
New Port Richey FL, 16117 — 140 B2
New Prague MN, 4559 — 66 C4
New Preston CT, 1110 — 148 C1

New Providence NJ, 11907 — 148 A4
New Richland MN, 1197 — 72 C2
New Richmond OH, 2219 — 100 B3
New Richmond WI, 6310 — 67 E3
New River AZ, 10740 — 54 C1
New Roads LA, 4966 — 133 F1
New Rochelle NY, 72182 — 148 B3
New Rockford ND, 1463 — 19 D3
New Salem ND, 938 — 18 B4
New Salem PA, 808 — 102 B1
New Salem PA, 648 — 275 E2
New Sarpy LA, 1568 — 239 A1
New Sharon IA, 1301 — 87 D2
New Site AL, 848 — 128 B1
New Smyrna Beach FL, 20048 — 139 E4
New Stanton PA, 1906 — 92 A4
New Straitsville OH, 774 — 101 E1
New Strawn KS, 425 — 96 A4
New Stuyahok AK, 471 — 154 B3
New Summerfield TX, 998 — 124 B4
New Tazewell TN, 2871 — 111 D3
Newton AL, 1708 — 128 B4
Newton GA, 847 — 128 C4
Newton IL, 3069 — 99 D2
Newton IA, 15579 — 87 D2
Newton KS, 17190 — 43 E3
Newton MA, 83829 — 151 D1
Newton MS, 3699 — 126 C2
Newton NC, 12560 — 111 F4
Newton NJ, 8244 — 94 A4
Newton TX, 2459 — 132 C1
Newton UT, 699 — 31 E2
Newton Co. AR, 8608 — 107 D4

Newton Co. GA, 62001 — 121 D4
Newton Co. IN, 14566 — 89 D3
Newton Co. MS, 21838 — 126 C2
Newton Co. MO, 52636 — 106 C2
Newton Co. TX, 15072 — 133 D1
Newton Falls OH, 5002 — 91 F2
Newton Grove NC, 606 — 123 D1
Newtonville NY, 800 — 147 D4
Newtonville NY, 2100 — 188 E2
Newtown CT, 1843 — 149 F3
New Town ND, 1367 — 18 A2
Newtown OH, 2420 — 204 C2
Newtown PA, 2312 — 147 D2
New Ulm MN, 13594 — 72 B1
New Underwood SD, 616 — 26 A1
New Vernon NJ, 1200 — 148 A4
New Vienna OH, 1294 — 100 C2
Newville PA, 1367 — 93 D4
New Washington IN, 547 — 100 A3
New Washington OH, 987 — 91 D3
New Washoe City NV, 2900 — 37 D2
New Waterford OH, 1391 — 91 F3
New Waverly TX, 950 — 132 A4
New Whiteland IN, 4579 — 99 F1
New Wilmington PA, 2452 — 91 F3
New Windsor IL, 720 — 88 A2
New Windsor MD, 1303 — 144 B1
New Windsor NY, 9077 — 148 B1
New York NY, 8008278 — 148 B4
New York Co. NY, 1537195 — 148 B4
New York Mills MN, 1158 — 64 A4
Nezperce ID, 523 — 22 B1
Nez Perce Co. ID, 37410 — 22 B1

Niagara WI, 1880 — 68 C2
Niagara Co. NY, 219846 — 78 B3
Niagara Falls NY, 55593 — 78 A3
Niantic CT, 3085 — 149 F2
Niantic IL, 738 — 98 C1
Nibley UT, 2045 — 31 E3
Nice CA, 2509 — 36 B2
Niceville FL, 11684 — 136 B2
Nicholas Co. KY, 6813 — 100 C4
Nicholas Co. WV, 26562 — 101 E4
Nicholasville KY, 19680 — 100 B4
Nicholls GA, 1008 — 129 F4
Nichols NY, 574 — 93 E1
Nichols Hills OK, 4056 — 244 D2
Nicholson GA, 1247 — 121 D3
Nicholson MS, 1400 — 134 C2
Nicholson PA, 713 — 93 E1
Nickelsville VA, 448 — 111 E2
Nickerson KS, 1194 — 43 E3
Nickerson NE, 431 — 35 F3
Nicksville AZ, 425 — 55 E4
Nicollet MN, 889 — 72 C1
Nicollet Co. MN, 29771 — 72 B1
Nicoma Park OK, 2415 — 244 D2
Niederwald TX, 584 — 61 E2
Nikiski AK, 4327 — 154 C3
Niland CA, 1143 — 53 E3
Niles IL, 30068 — 203 D3
Niles MI, 12204 — 89 F1
Niles OH, 20932 — 91 F2
Ninety Six SC, 1936 — 121 F3
Ninnekah OK, 994 — 51 E3
Niobrara Co. WY, 2407 — 33 E1
Niota TN, 781 — 120 B1

Nipomo CA, 12626 — 52 A1
Niskayuna NY, 4892 — 188 D2
Nisland SD, 204 — 25 F3
Nissequogue NY, 1543 — 149 D3
Nisswa MN, 1953 — 64 A4
Nitro WV, 6824 — 101 E3
Niwot CO, 4160 — 33 D4
Nixa MO, 12124 — 107 D2
Nixon NV, 418 — 37 D1
Nixon TX, 2186 — 61 E4
Noank CT, 1830 — 149 F2
Noatak AK, 428 — 154 B1
Noble OK, 5260 — 51 E3
Noble Co. IN, 46275 — 89 F2
Noble Co. OH, 14058 — 101 F1
Noble Co. OK, 11411 — 51 E3
Nobles Co. MN, 20832 — 72 A2
Noblesville IN, 28590 — 89 F4
Nocatee FL, 700 — 140 C4
Nocona TX, 3198 — 59 E1
Nodaway Co. MO, 21912 — 106 B1
Noel MO, 1480 — 106 B3
Nogales AZ, 20878 — 55 D4
Nokesville VA, 1236 — 144 A4
Nokomis FL, 3334 — 140 B4
Nokomis IL, 2389 — 98 C2
Nolan Co. TX, 15802 — 59 B3
Nolanville TX, 2150 — 59 E4
Nolensville TN, 3099 — 109 F4
Nome AK, 3505 — 154 B2
Nome TX, 515 — 132 C3
Nooksack WA, 851 — 12 C1

Noonday TX, 515 — 124 A3
Noorvik AK, 634 — 154 B2
Nora Sprs. IA, 1532 — 73 D3
Norborne MO, 805 — 96 C2
Norco CA, 24157 — 53 D2
Norco LA, 3579 — 134 B3
Norcross GA, 8410 — 121 D3
Norfolk CT, 1000 — 94 C1
Norfolk MA, 1900 — 151 D1
Norfolk NE, 23516 — 35 E2
Norfolk NY, 1334 — 80 B1
Norfolk Co. MA, 650308 — 151 D1
Norfork AR, 484 — 107 E3
Norlina NC, 1107 — 113 D3
Normal IL, 45386 — 88 C4
Norman AR, 423 — 116 C3
Norman OK, 95694 — 51 E3
Norman Co. MN, 7442 — 19 F3
Normandy MO, 5153 — 256 D2
Normandy Park WA, 6392 — 262 B4
Normangee TX, 719 — 59 F4
Norman Park GA, 849 — 129 D4
Normans MD, 650 — 145 D3
Norphlet AR, 822 — 125 E1
Norridge IL, 14582 — 203 D3
Norridgewock ME, 1557 — 82 C1
Norris SC, 847 — 121 F1
Norris TN, 1446 — 110 C4
Norris City IL, 1057 — 99 D4
Norristown PA, 31282 — 146 C2
North SC, 813 — 122 A4
N. Acton MA, 3000 — 150 C1
N. Adams MA, 14681 — 94 C1

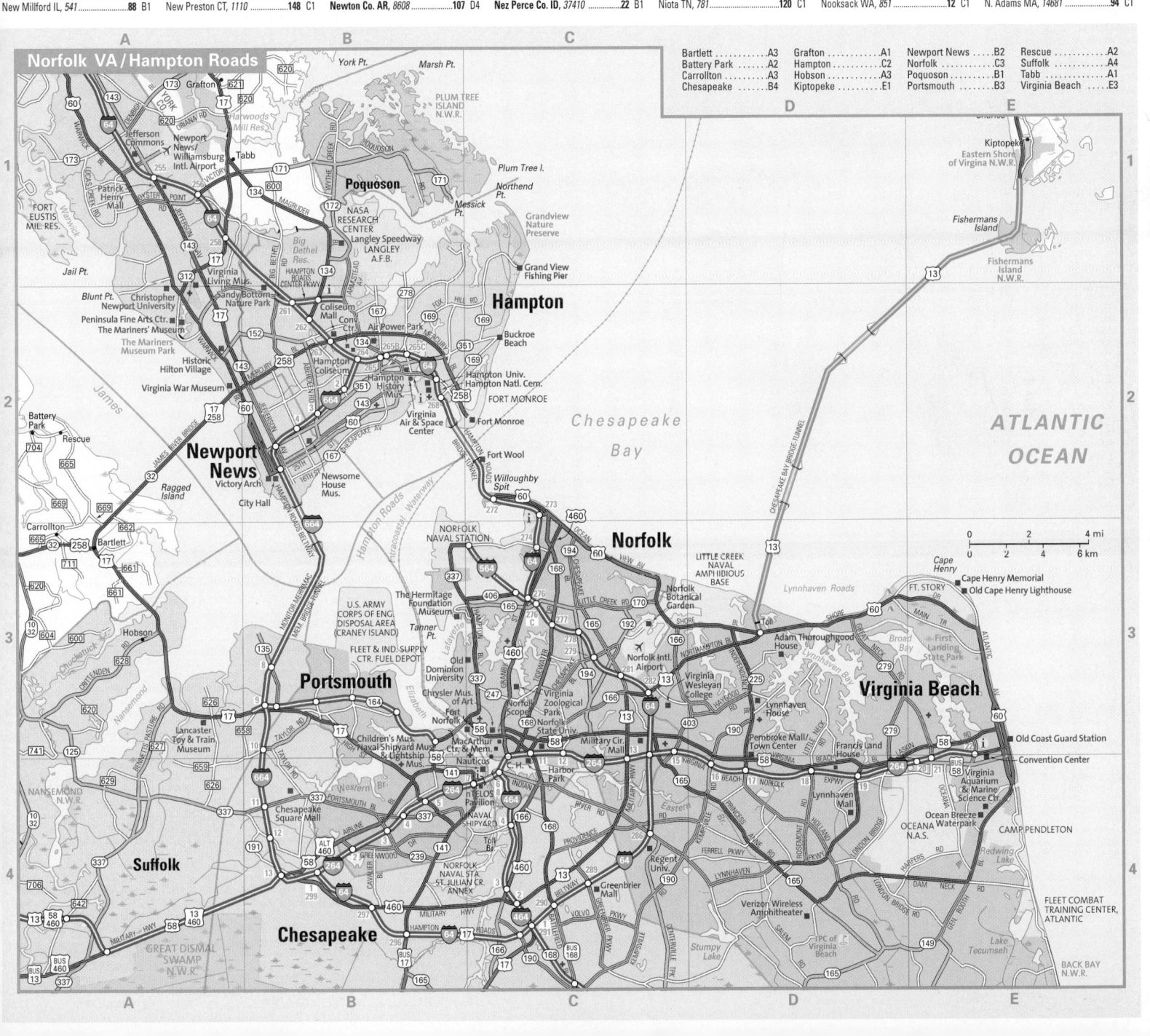

Norfolk VA / Hampton Roads

Oklahoma City OK

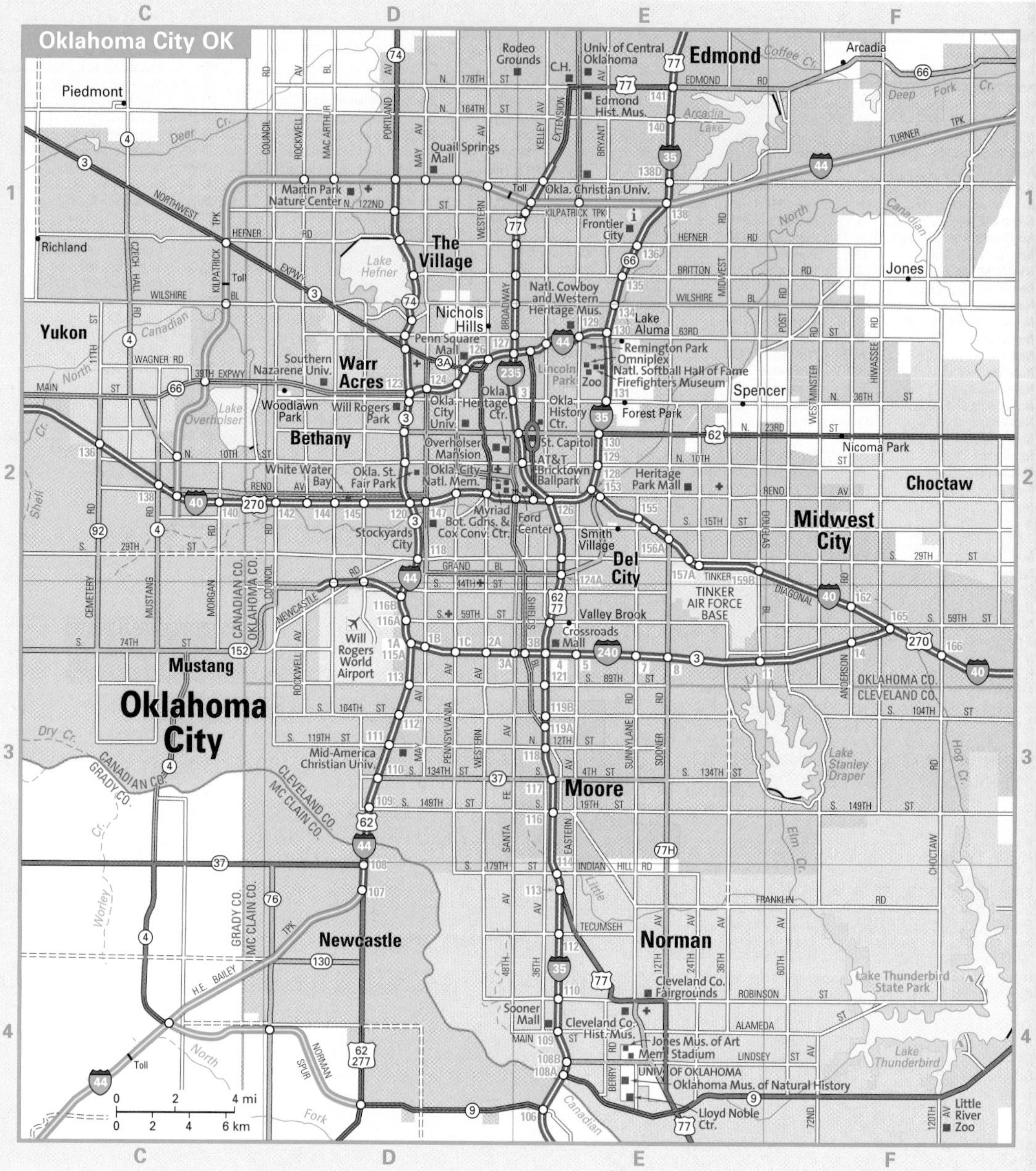

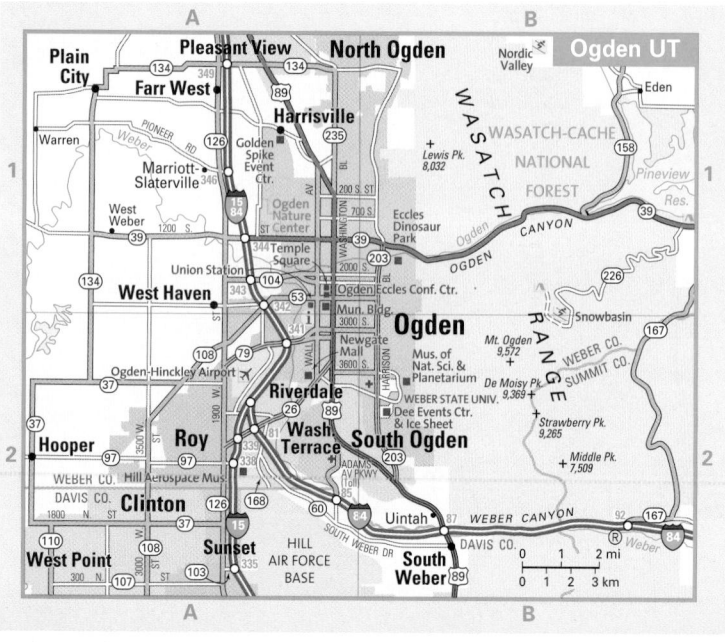

Ogden UT

Entries in **bold black** indicate counties or parishes. Entries in *bold color* indicate cities with detailed inset maps.

Northwood–Ossining 245

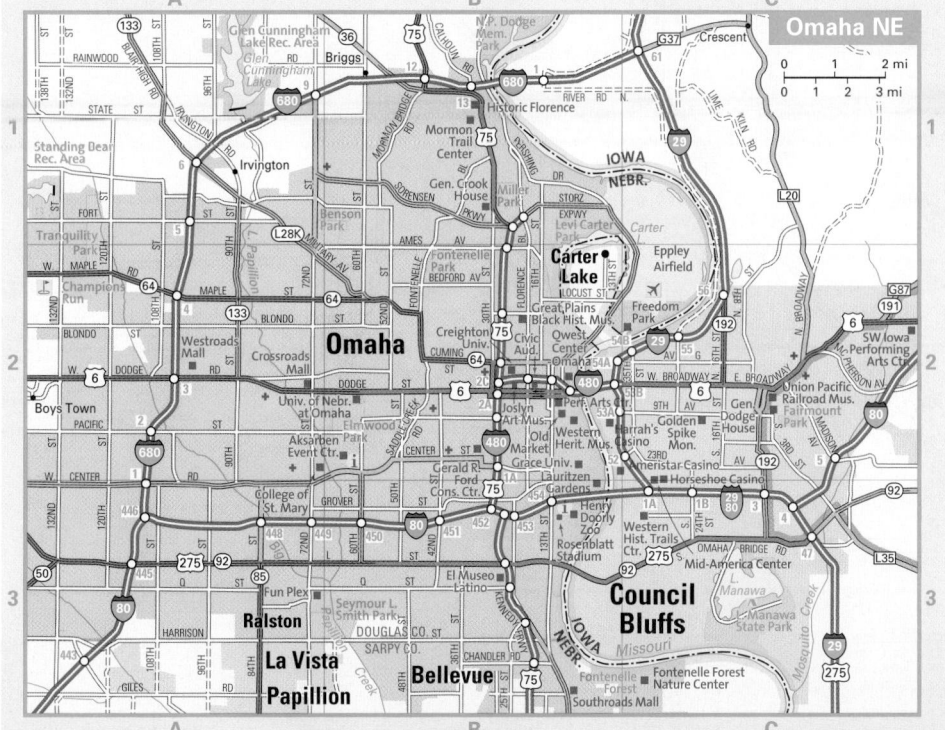

Omaha NE

Bellevue B3
Boys Town A2
Briggs B1
Carter Lake B2
Council Bluffs C3
Crescent C1
Irvington A1
La Vista A3
Omaha B2
Papillion A3
Ralston A3

Olympia WA

246 Ossipee–Palm Valley

Figures after entries indicate population, page number, and grid reference.

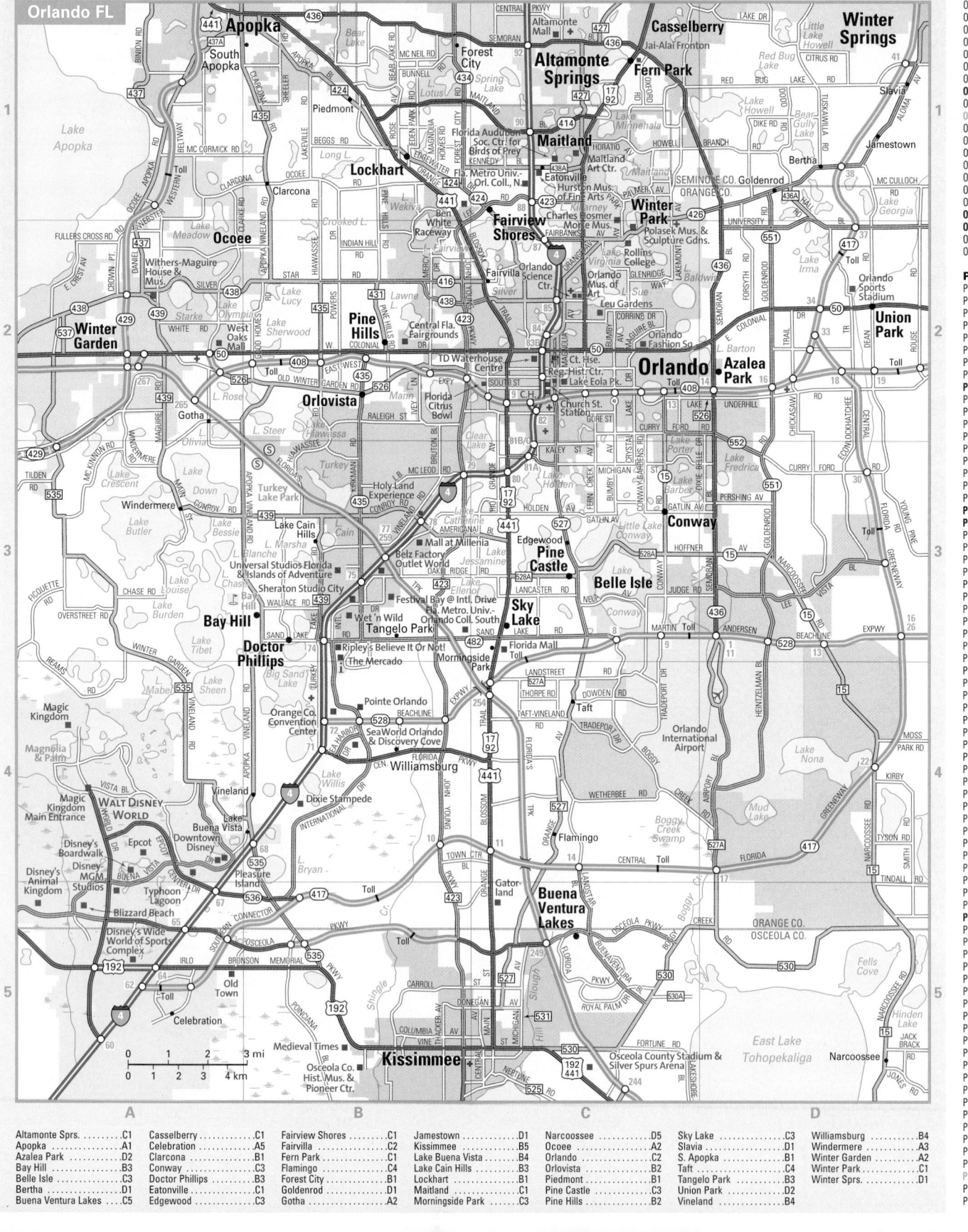

Oxnard/Ventura CA

Palm Springs CA

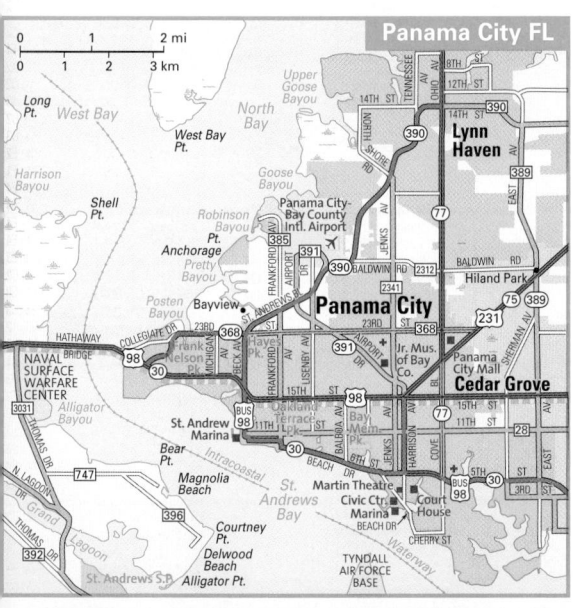

Panama City FL

Pensacola FL

Bellview	A1
Brent	B1
Brownsville	B2
Ensley	A1
Ferry Pass	B1
Goulding	B1
Gulf Breeze	B2
Myrtle Grove	A2
Pensacola	B1
Pleasant Grove	A2
Warrington	A2
W. Pensacola	A1

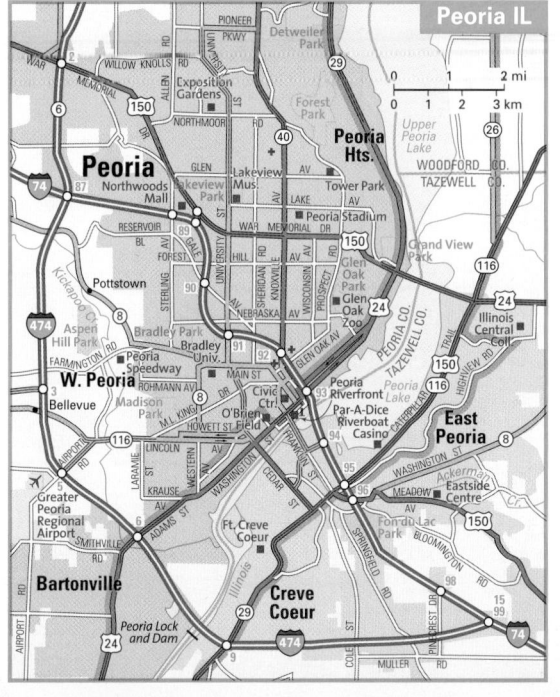

Peoria IL

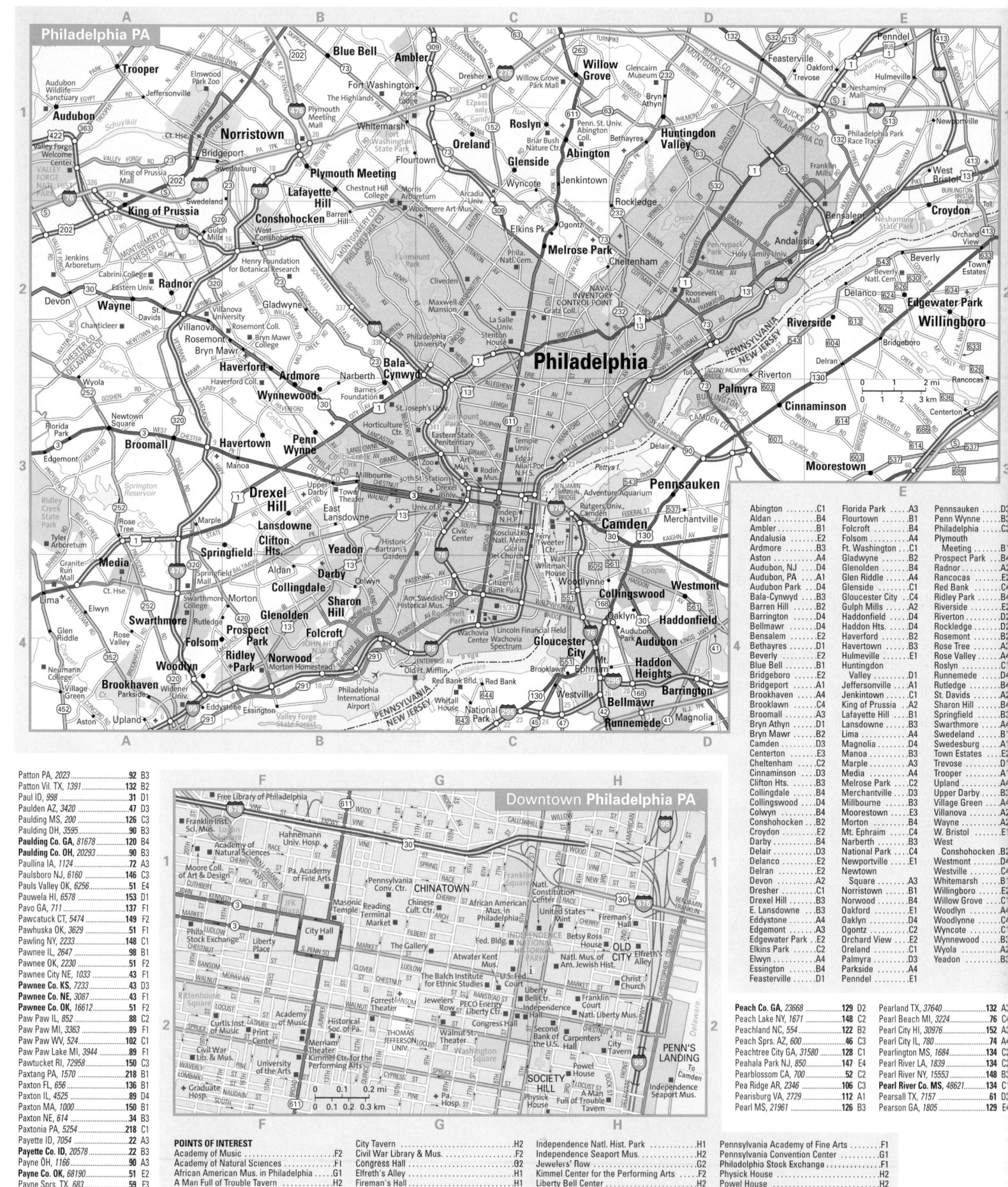

Phoenix AZ

Sun City West · Peoria · Scottsdale · Surprise · Sun City · Youngtown · El Mirage · Phoenix · Paradise Valley · Fountain Hills · Glendale · Litchfield Park · Goodyear · Avondale · Tolleson · Cashion · Laveen · Guadalupe · Tempe · Mesa · Gilbert · Chandler · Komatke · Queen Creek

Downtown Phoenix AZ

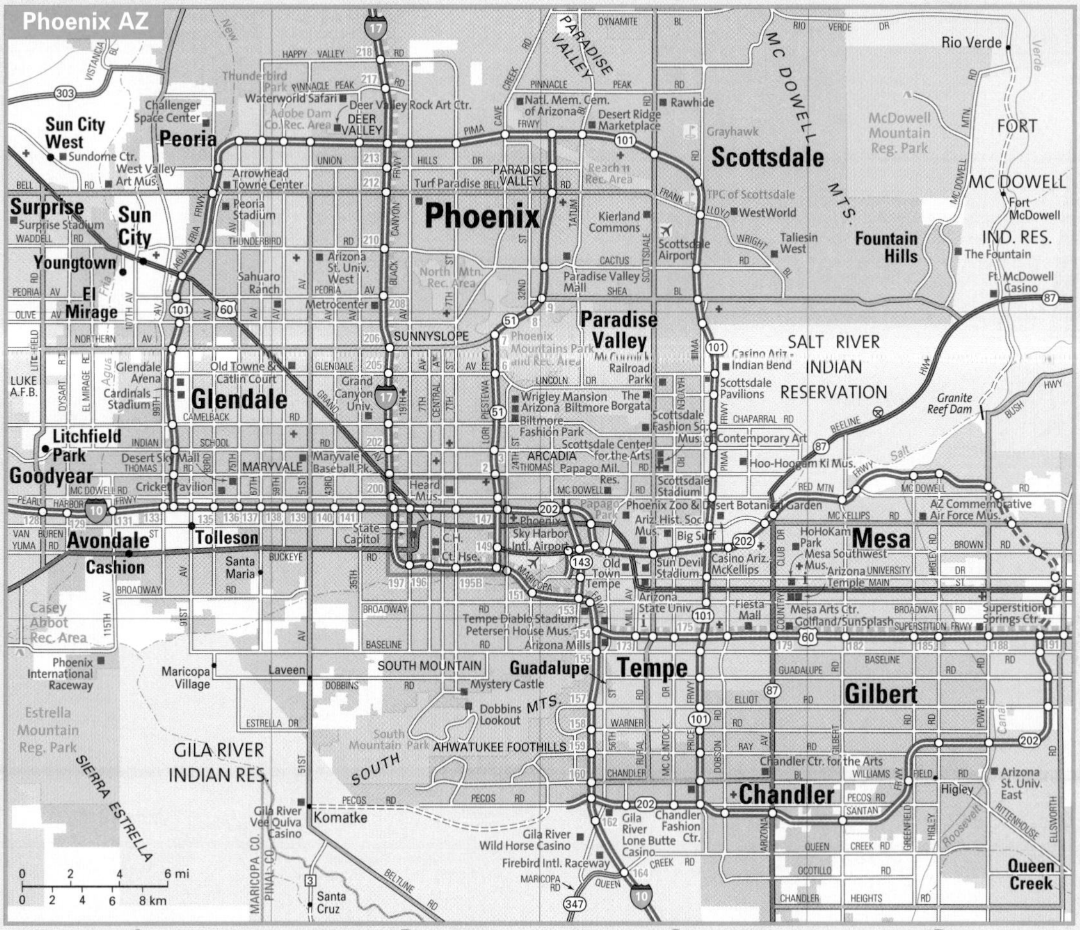

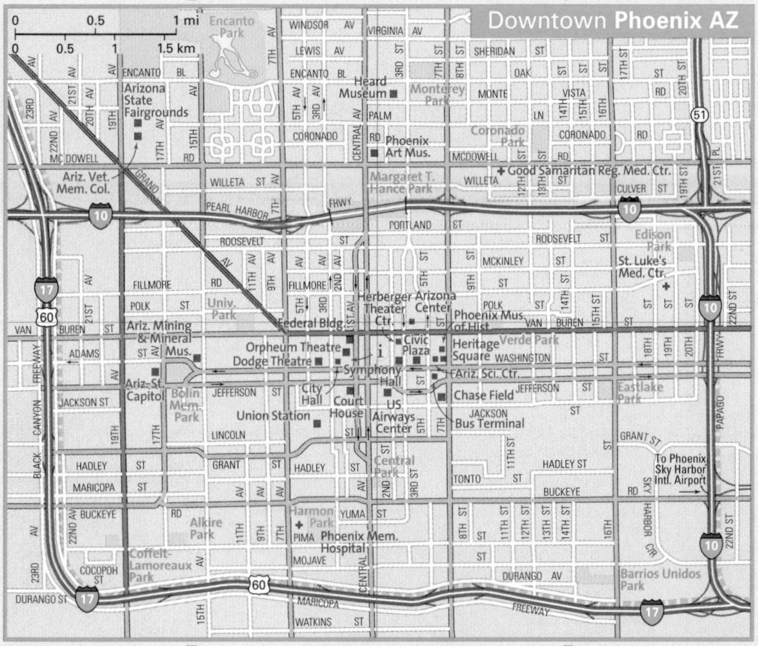

POINTS OF INTEREST

Arizona Center F1	Dodge Theatre D2
Arizona Mining & Mineral Mus. E2	Heard Mus. F1
Arizona Science Center F2	Herberger Theater Center F2
Arizona State Capitol E2	Heritage Square F2
Arizona State Fairgrounds E1	Orpheum Theatre E2
Arizona Veterans Memorial Coliseum .. E1	Phoenix Art Mus. E1
Chase Field F2	Phoenix Mus. of Hist. F2
City Hall E2	Symphony Hall F2
Civic Plaza F2	Union Station F2
	US Airways Center F2

Pierre SD

Pierre · Ft. Pierre

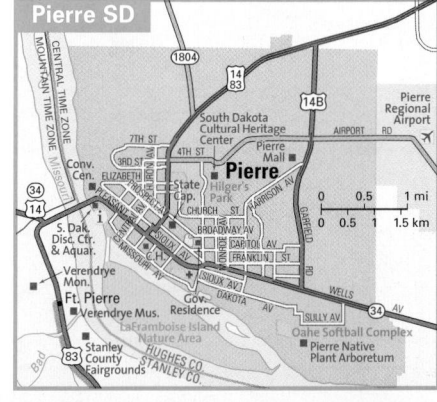

Pico Rivera CA, 63428 ....**228** E3
Picture Rocks PA, 693 ....**93** E2
Piedmont AL, 5120 ....**120** A4
Piedmont CA, 10952 ....**259** C2
Piedmont MO, 1992 ....**108** A2

Piedmont OK, 3650 ....**51** E2
Piedmont SC, 4684 ....**121** E2
Piedmont SD, 700 ....**25** D2
Piedmont WV, 1014 ....**102** B2
Pierce CO, 884 ....**33** E4

Pierce ID, 617 ....**14** C4
Pierce NE, 1774 ....**35** E2
Pierce City MO, 1385 ....**106** C2
Pierceton IN, 695 ....**89** F2
Pierce Co., 884 ....**33** E4

Pierce Co. ND, 4675 ....**18** C2
Pierce Co. WA, 700820 ......**12** C4
Pierce Co. WI, 36804 ....**67** E4
Pierce Co. GA, 15636 ....**129** F4
Pierce Co. NE, 7857 ....**35** E2

Pierre Part LA, 3239 ....**134** A3
Pierson FL, 2596 ....**139** D4
Pierson IL, 653 ....**98** B3
Pierz MN, 1277 ....**66** C2
Pierre SD, 13876 ....**26** C3

Pigeon MI, 1207 ....**76** C2
Pigeon Cove MA, 1700 ....**151** F1
Pigeon Forge TN, 5083 ......**111** D4
Pigeon LA, 600 ....**134** A2
Pike Co. AL, 29605 ....**128** A4

Pike Co. AR, 11303 ....**117** C
Pike Co. GA, 13688 ....**128** C
Pike Co. IL, 17384 ....**98** A
Pike Co. IN, 12837 ....**89** D
Pike Co. KY, 68736 ....**111** E

Pike Co. MS, 38940 ....**127** D
Pike Co. MO, 18351 ....**97** D
Pike Co. OH, 28709 ....**101** D
Pike Co. PA, 46302 ....**93** F
Pikesville MD, 29123 ....**144** C

Piketon OH, 1907 ....**101** D
Pikeville KY, 6295 ....**111** E
Pikeville NC, 719 ....**123** E
Pikeville TN, 1781 ....**120** D
Pilot Grove MO, 723 ....**97** C

Pilot Knob MO, 697 ....**108** A
Pilot Mtn. NC, 1281 ....**112** A
Pilot Pt. TX, 3538 ....**59** F
Pilot Rock OR, 1532 ....**21** E
Pilot Sta. AK, 550 ....**154** E

Pima AZ, 1989 ....**55** E
Pima Co. AZ, 843746 ....**54** C
Pinal Co. AZ, 179727 ....**55** D
Pinardville NH, 5779 ....**81** F
Pinch WV, 2811 ....**101** F

Pinckard AL, 667 ....**128** B
Pinckney MI, 2141 ....**76** B
Pinckneyville IL, 5464 ....**98** B
Pinconning MI, 1386 ....**76** B
Pine AZ, 1931 ....**47** E

Pine Beach NJ, 1950 ....**147** A
Pine Bluff AR, 55085 ....**117** D
Pinebluff NC, 1109 ....**122** C
Pine Bluffs WY, 1153 ....**33** F
Pine Bush NY, 1539 ....**148** A

Pine City MN, 3043 ....**67** D
Pine Co. MN, 26530 ....**64** C
Pinecrest FL, 600 ....**140** C
Pinecrest FL, 19055 ....**233** A
Pineda FL, 1100 ....**141** E

Pinedale WY, 1412 ....**32** A
Pine Forest TX, 632 ....**132** C
Pine Grove CA, 650 ....**36** C
Pine Grove PA, 2154 ....**146** A
Pine Grove WV, 571 ....**101** F

Pine Grove Mills PA, 1141 ....**92** C
Pine Haven WY, 222 ....**25** E
Pine Hill AL, 966 ....**127** E
Pine Hill NJ, 10880 ....**146** C
Pine Hills FL, 41764 ....**246** B

Pinehurst ID, 1661 ....**14** E
Pinehurst MA, 6941 ....**151** E
Pinehurst NC, 9706 ....**122** C
Pinehurst TX, 4266 ....**132** A
Pinehurst TX, 2274 ....**132** C

Pine Island MN, 2337 ....**73** D
Pine Island NY, 700 ....**148** A
Pine Island TX, 849 ....**61** F
Pine Island Ctr. FL, 1721 ...**214** A
Pine Knoll Shores NC, 1524 ...**115** D

Pine Knot KY, 1680 ....**110** C
Pineland FL, 444 ....**142** C
Pineland TX, 980 ....**124** C
Pine Lawn MO, 4204 ....**256** E
Pine Level NC, 1313 ....**123** E

Pinellas Co. FL, 921482 ...**140** B
Pinellas Park FL, 45658 .....**140** B
Pine Mtn. GA, 1141 ....**128** C
Pine Plains NY, 1412 ....**94** B
Pine Pt. ME, 600 ....**82** B

Pine Prairie LA, 1087 ....**133** E
Pine Ridge SC, 1593 ....**122** A
Pine Ridge SD, 3171 ....**34** A
Pine River MN, 928 ....**64** A
Pinesdale MT, 742 ....**15** D

Pinetop-Lakeside AZ, 3582 ...**47** E
Pinetops NC, 1419 ....**113** E
Pinetown DE, 1100 ....**145** E
Pine Valley CA, 1501 ....**53** D
Pine Valley NY, 950 ....**93** E

Pineview GA, 532 ....**129** D
Pineville KY, 2093 ....**110** C
Pineville LA, 13829 ....**125** E

City index (Pittsburgh area)

Acmetonia D1
Aspinwall C1
Avalon A1
Baldwin C3
Bellevue B1
Ben Avon A1
Ben Avon Hts. A1
Bethel Park B3
Blawnox C1
Braddock C2
Braddock Hills C2
Brentwood B3
Bridgeville A3
Broughton B3

Carnegie A2
Castle Shannon ...B3
Chalfant D2
Cheswick D1
Churchill D2
Coraopolis A1
Crafton A2
Cuddy A3
Dormont B3
Dravosburg C3
Duquesne D3
E. McKeesport ...D3
E. Pittsburgh D2
Edgewood C2

Emsworth A1
Etna C1
Evergreen B1
Ewingsville A2
Forest Grove A1
Forest Hills C2
Fox Chapel C1
Glassport C3
Glenfield A1
Glenshaw C1
Green Tree B2
Groveton A1
Haysville A1
Heidelberg A3

Homestead C2
Ingram A2
Kenmawr A1
Kirwan Hts. A3
Liberty C3
McKeesport D3
McKees Rocks B1
Millvale B1
Monroeville D2
Moon Run A2
Morgan A2
Mt. Lebanon B3
Mt. Oliver B2
Munhall C3

N. Braddock C2
Oakmont D1
Osborne A1
Penn Hills C2
Pennsbury Vil. A2
Perrysville B1
Pitcairn D2
Pittock A2
Pittsburgh B2
Pleasant Hills C3
Plum D1
Port Vue C3
Presto A3
Rankin C2

Rennerdale A2
Rosslyn Farms A2
Sandy Creek D1
Sharpsburg C1
Springdale D1
Stewartsville D3
Swissvale C2
Sygan A3
Thornburg A2
Trafford D2
Turtle Creek D2
Upper St. Clair ...A3
Verona D1
Wall D3

W. Homestead C2
W. Mifflin C3
W. Park A1
W. View B1
Whitaker C2
Whitehall B3
White Oak D3
Wilkinsburg C2
Wilmerding D3

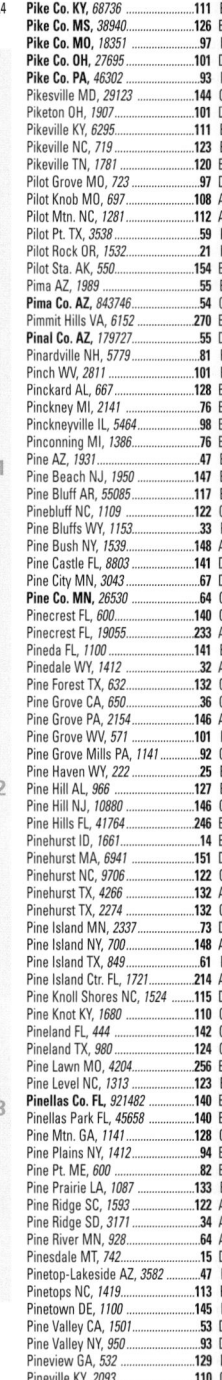

Pittsburgh PA

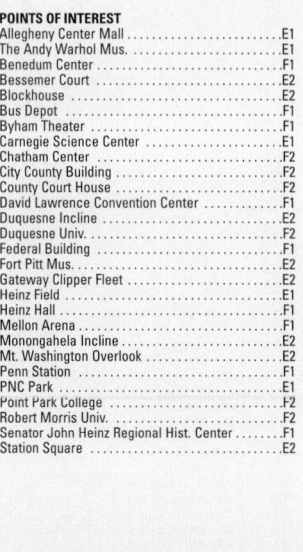

Downtown Pittsburgh PA

POINTS OF INTEREST
Allegheny Center Mall E1
The Andy Warhol Mus. E1
Benedum Center E2
Bessemer Court E2
Blockhouse E2
Bus Depot F1
Byham Theater F1
Carnegie Science Center E1
Chatham Center F2
City County Building F2
County Court House F2
David Lawrence Convention Center F1
Duquesne Incline E2
Duquesne Univ. F2
Federal Building F1
Fort Pitt Mus. E2
Gateway Clipper Fleet E2
Heinz Field E1
Heinz Hall F1
Mellon Arena F1
Monongahela Incline E2
Mt. Washington Overlook E2
Penn Station F1
PNC Park E1
Point Park College F2
Robert Morris Univ. F2
Senator John Heinz Regional Hist. Center ...F1
Station Square E2

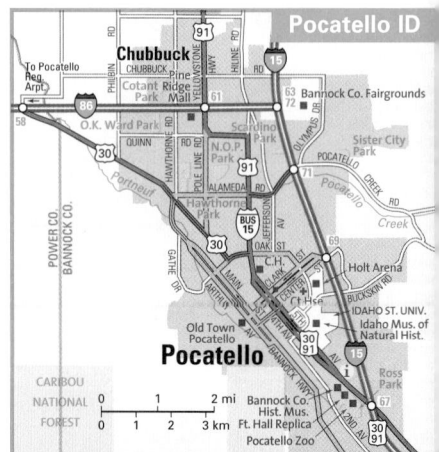

Pocatello ID

Portland ME inset index

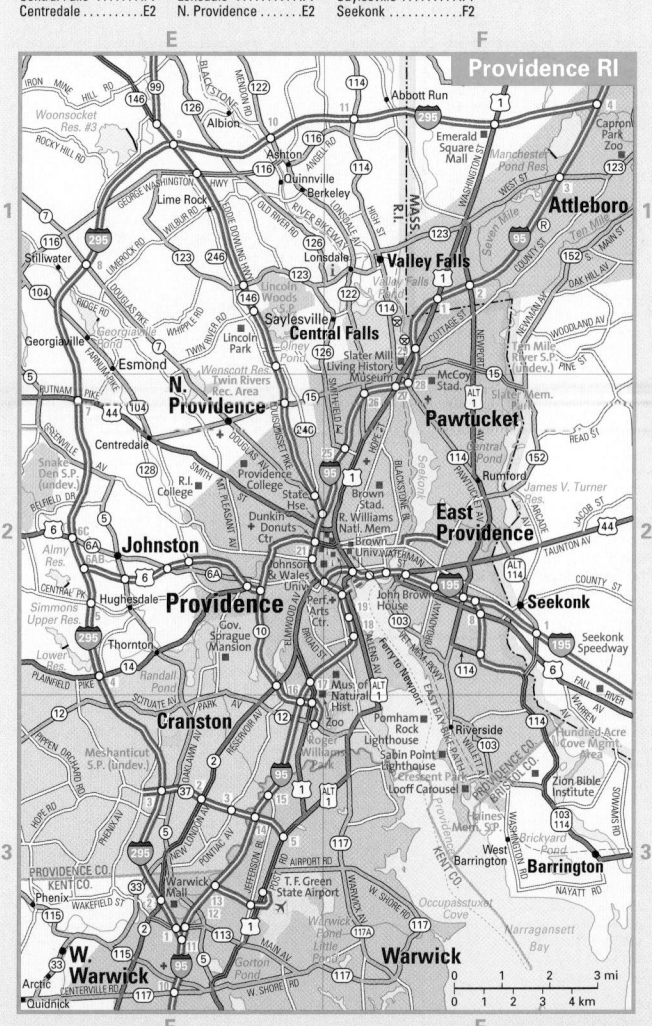

Providence RI inset index

Portland OR inset index

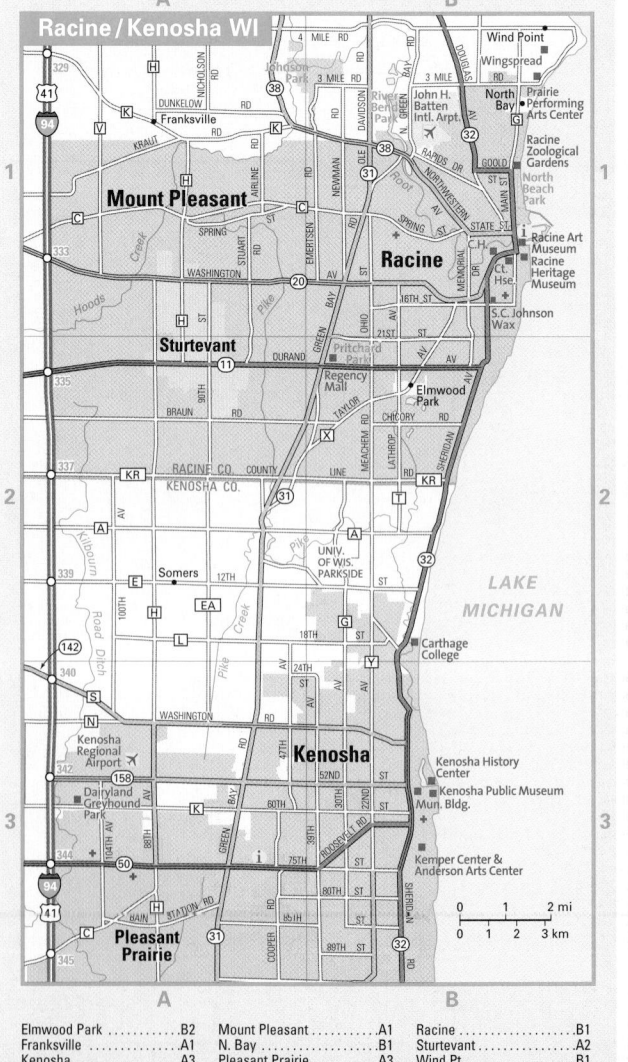

■ Entries in **bold black** indicate counties or parishes. Entries in *bold color* indicate cities with detailed inset maps.

Quincy–Renova **253**

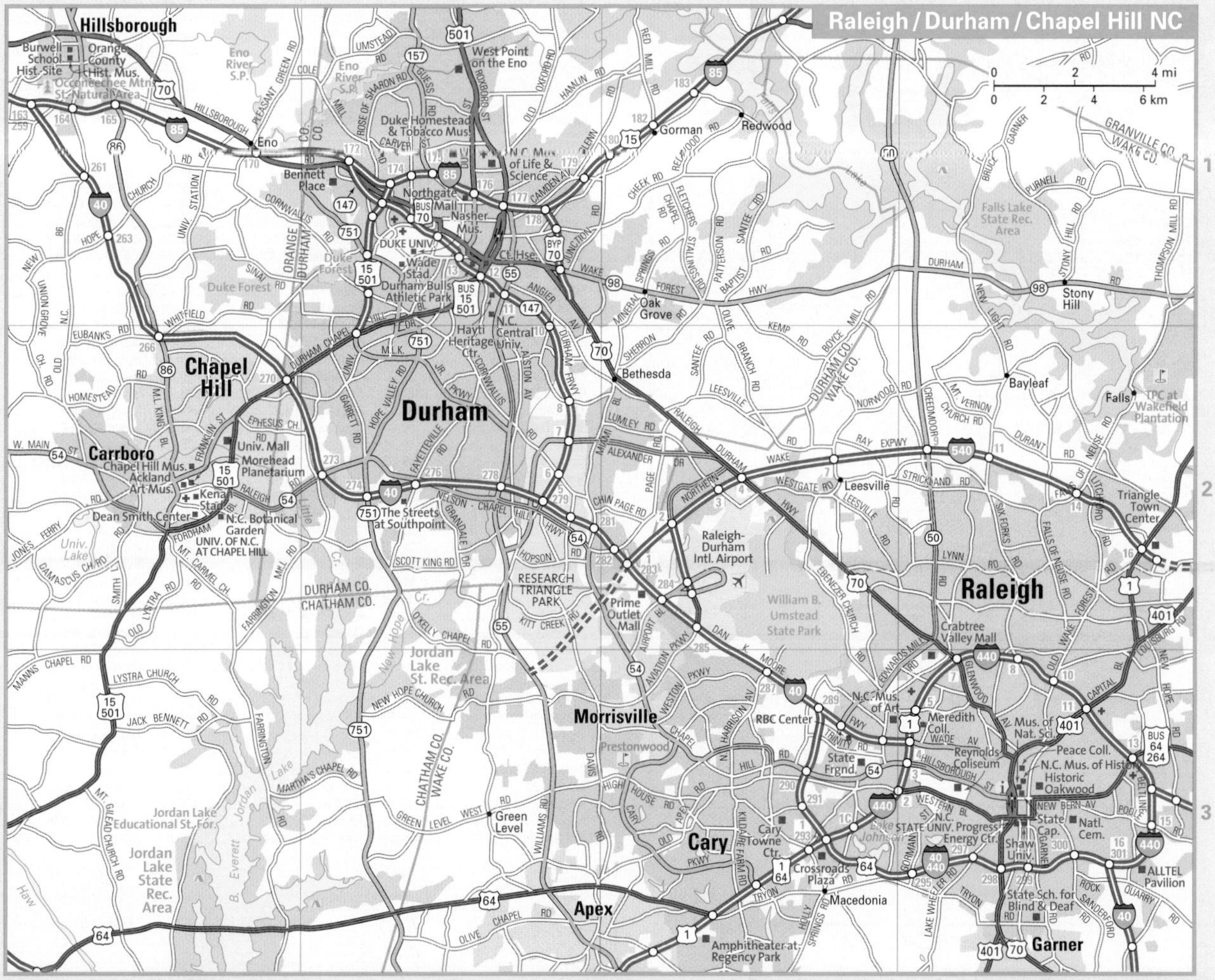

Raleigh / Durham / Chapel Hill NC

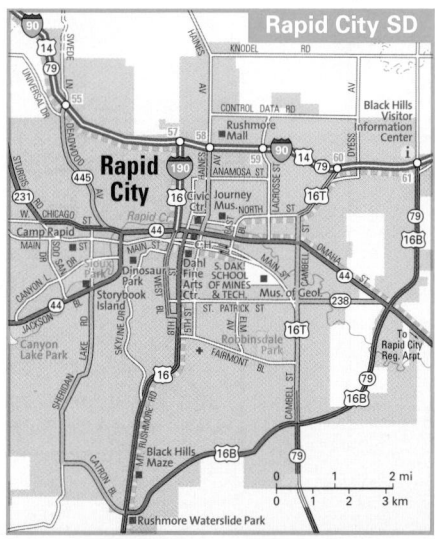

Rapid City SD

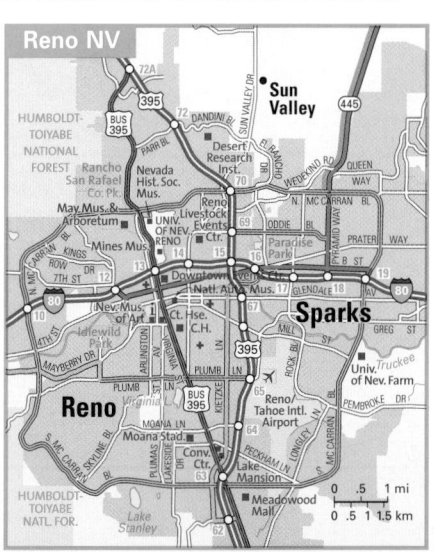

Reno NV

Richmond VA (map index)

Atlee ... B1	Chamberlayne Farms ... B1	Glen Allen ... B1
Bellwood ... B3	Chesterfield ... B3	Greendale ... B1
Bensley ... B3	E. Highland Park ... B1	Highland Sprs. ... B1
Bon Air ... A2	Fair Oaks ... C2	Hunton ... B1
Borkeys Store ... C1		Lakeside ... B1
Centralia ... A3		Laurel ... B1

Mechanicsville ... C1	Rivermont ... C3
Midlothian ... A2	Sandston ... C2
Newmans ... C1	Seven Pines ... C2
Old Cold Harbor ... C1	Short Pump ... A1
Pearsons Corner ... C1	Studley ... C1
Richmond ... B2	Varina ... C2

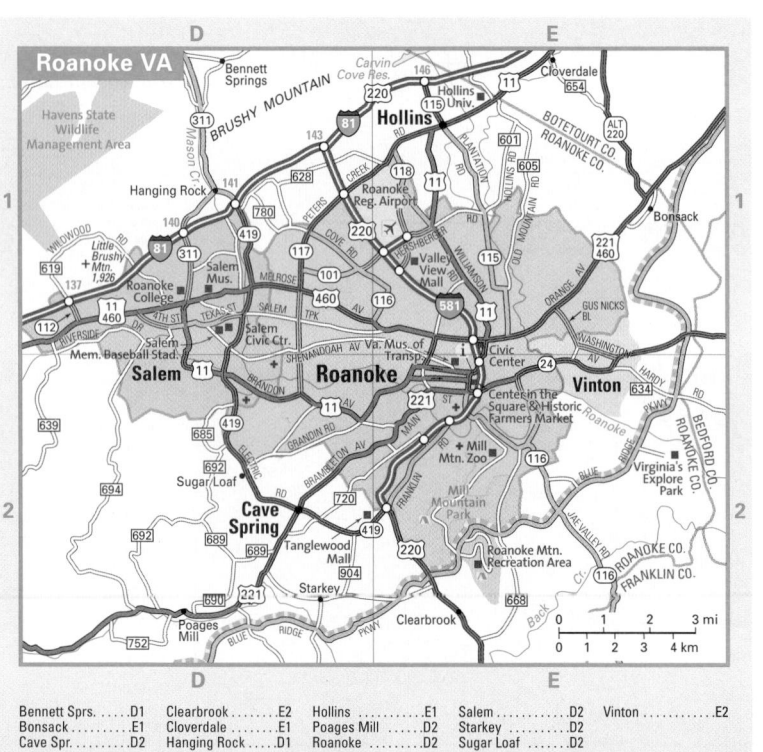

Roanoke VA (map index)

Bennett Sprs. ... D1	Clearbrook ... E2	Hollins ... E1	Salem ... D2	Vinton ... E2
Bonsack ... E1	Cloverdale ... E1	Poages Mill ... D2	Starkey ... D2	
Cave Spr. ... D2	Hanging Rock ... D1	Roanoke ... D2	Sugar Loaf ... D2	

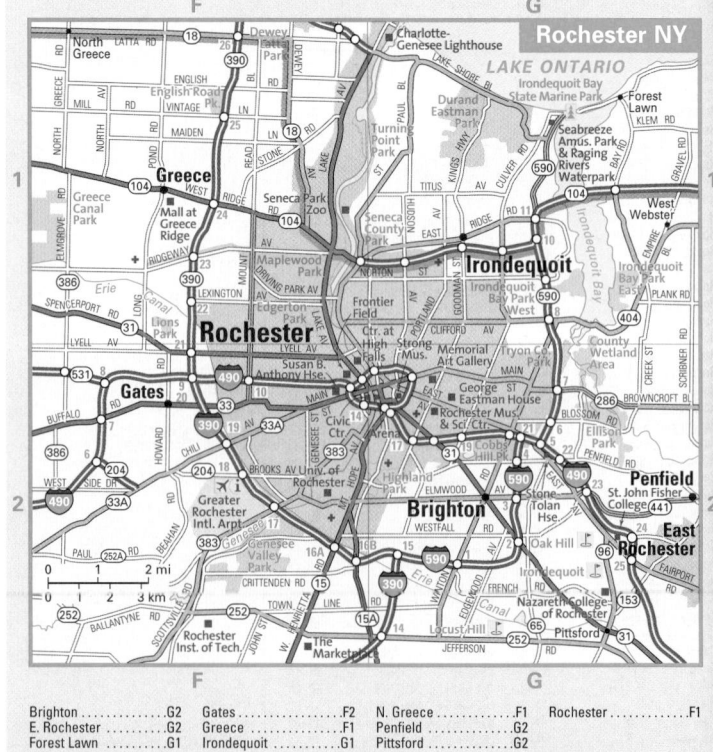

Rochester NY (map index)

Brighton ... G2	Gates ... F2	N. Greece ... F1	Rochester ... F1
E. Rochester ... G2	Greece ... F1	Penfield ... G2	
Forest Lawn ... G1	Irondequoit ... G1	Pittsford ... G2	

Entries in **bold black** indicate counties or parishes. Entries in *bold color* indicate cities with detailed inset maps.

River Edge–Rusk **255**

Rockford IL

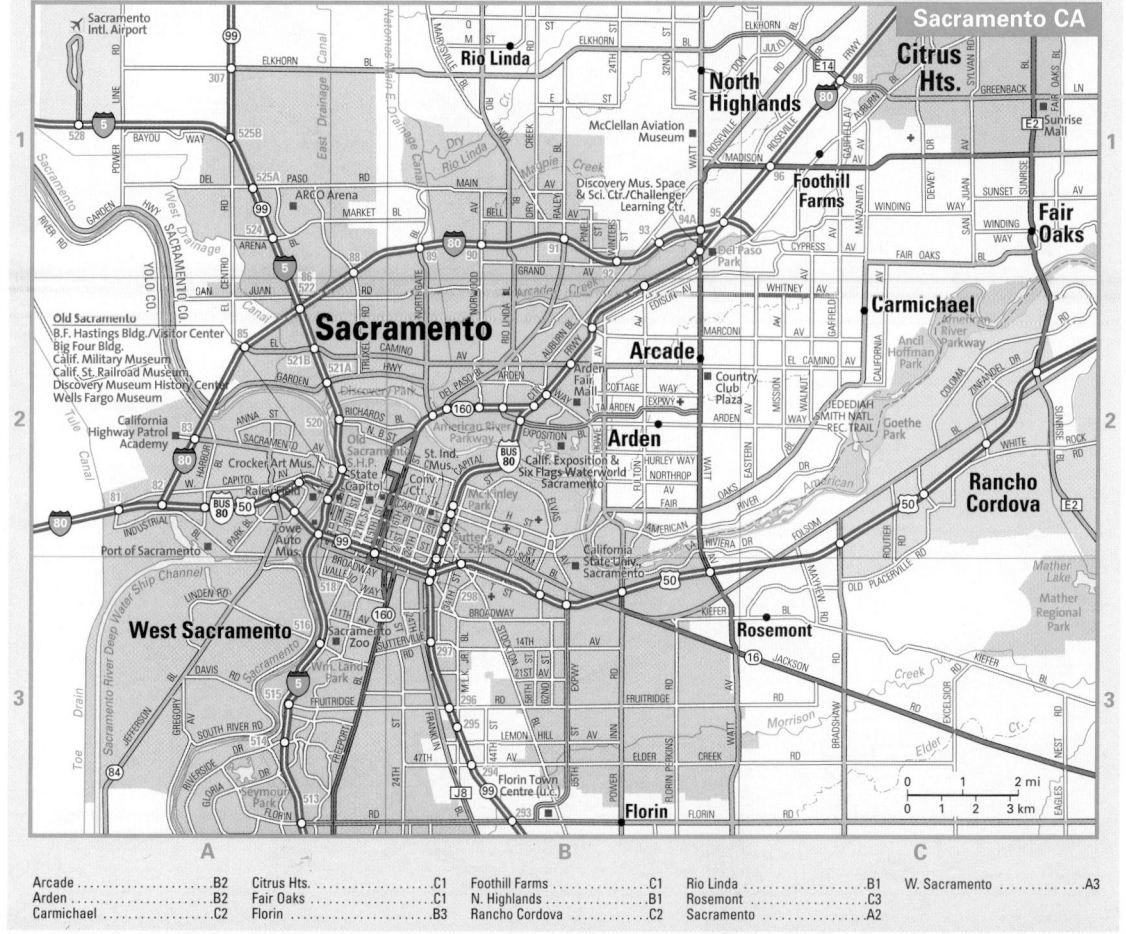

Sacramento CA

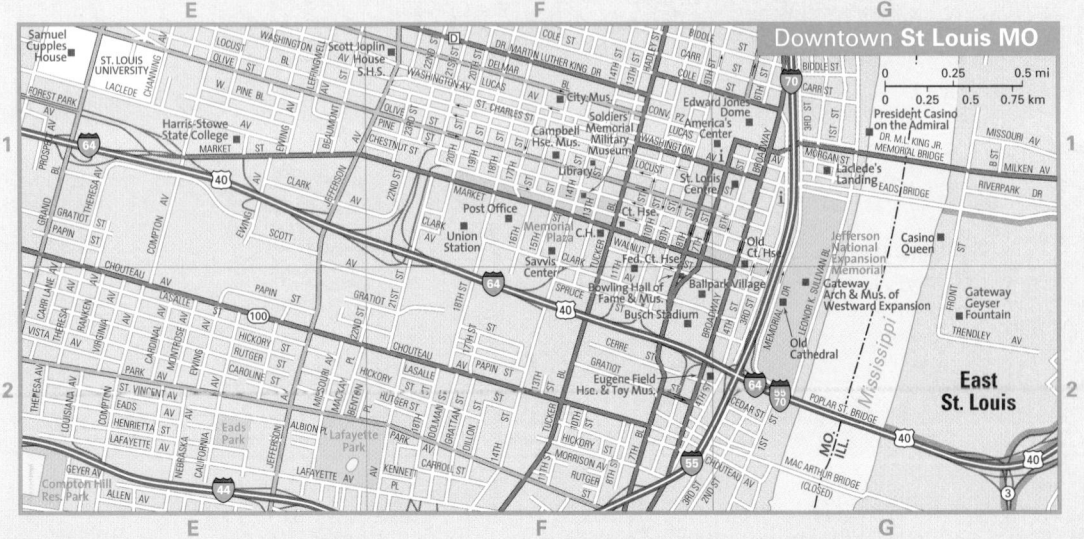

St Louis MO

Downtown St Louis MO

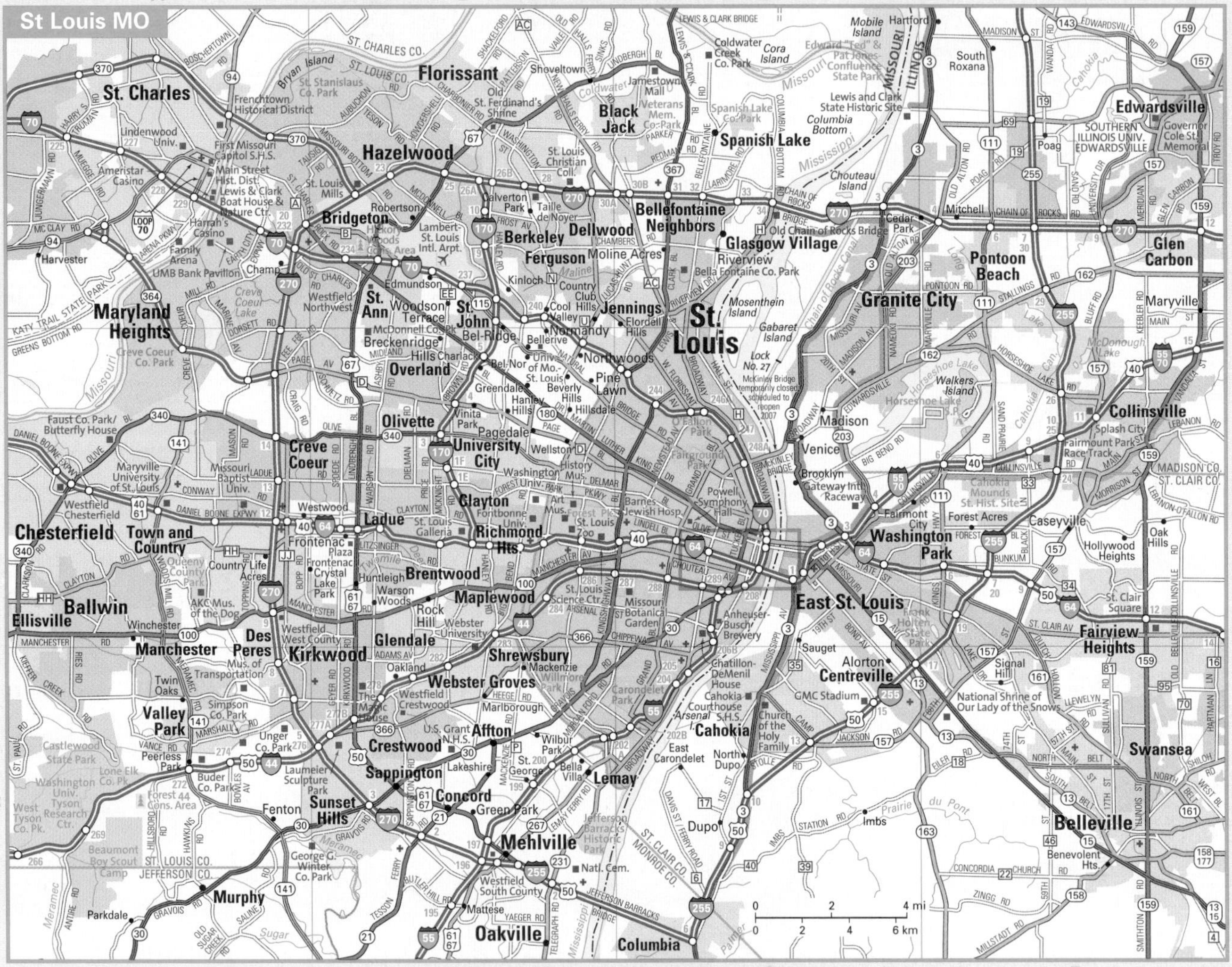

Entries in **bold black** indicate counties or parishes. Entries in **bold color** indicate cities with detailed inset maps.

Sag Harbor–St Charles Parish **257**

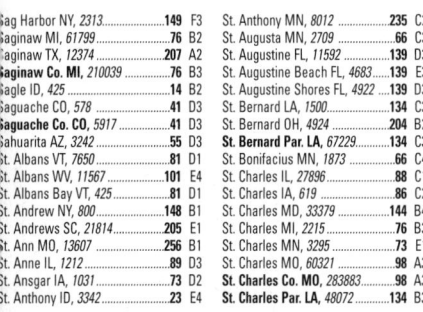

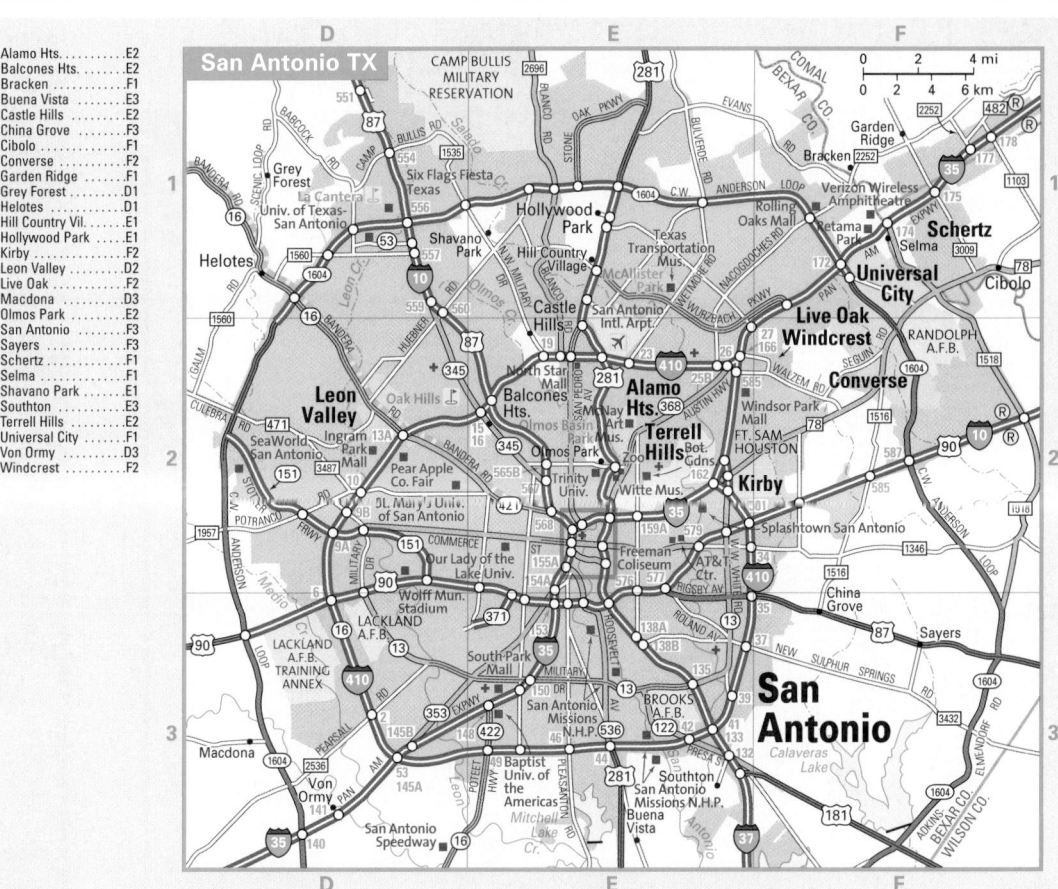

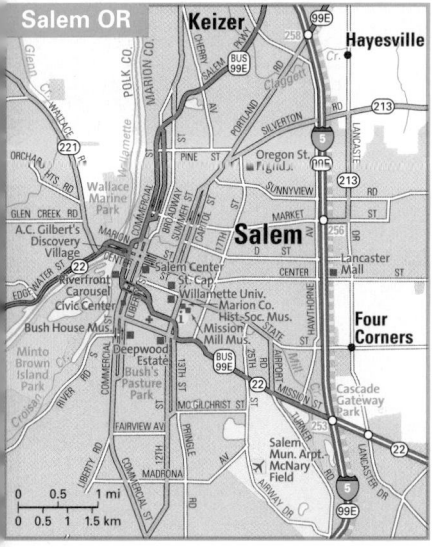

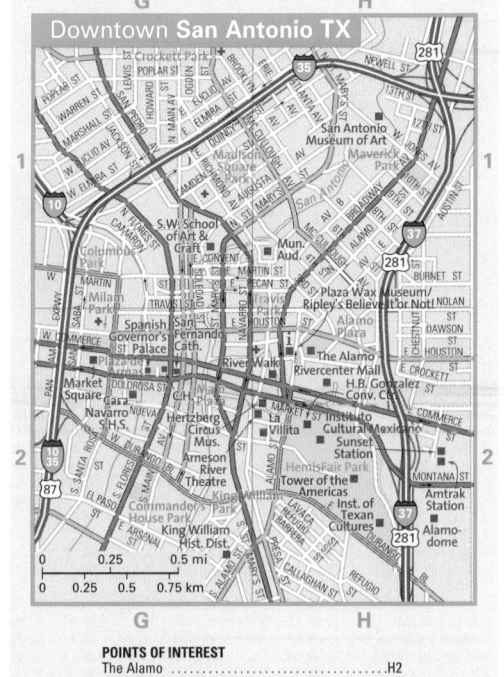

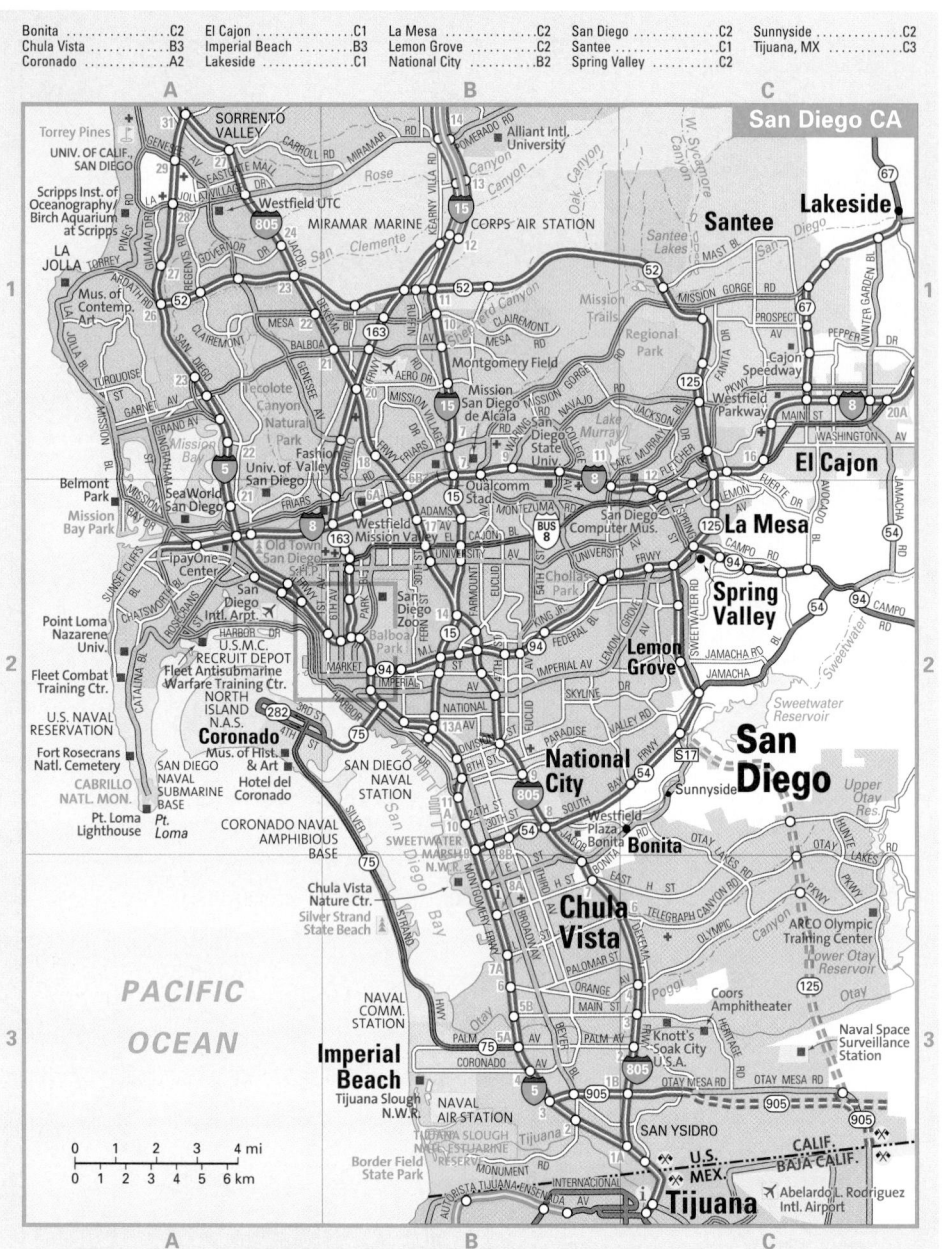

San Diego CA

PACIFIC OCEAN

POINTS OF INTEREST

Automotive Mus. E1	San Diego Aerospace Mus. E1
Balboa Park E1	San Diego Aircraft Carrier Museum ..D2
Balboa Stadium E2	San Diego Convention Center ...D2
Casa del Prado E1	San Diego Hall of Champions ...E1
Children's Mus. D2	San Diego Intl. Arpt. D1
Civic Center D2	San Diego Mus. of Art E1
Computer Museum E2	San Diego Museum of Man E1
Copley Symphony Hall D1	San Diego Natural Hist. Mus. ...E1
County Court House D1	San Diego Zoo E1
Firehouse Mus. D2	Santa Fe Depot D2
Gaslamp Quarter & W. H. Davis House ..E2	Seaport Village D2
The Globe Theatres E1	Spanish Village Art Center E1
House of Hospitality E1	Sports Mus. E1
Maritime Mus. D1	Spreckels Organ Pavilion E1
Mus. of Contemporary Art, San Diego ..D2	Spreckels Theatre D2
PETCO Park D2	Starlight Bowl E1
Reuben H. Fleet Science Center ..E1	Timken Mus. of Art E1
	Villa Montezuma E2

Downtown San Diego CA

Entries in **bold black** indicate counties or parishes. Entries in **bold color** indicate cities with detailed inset maps.

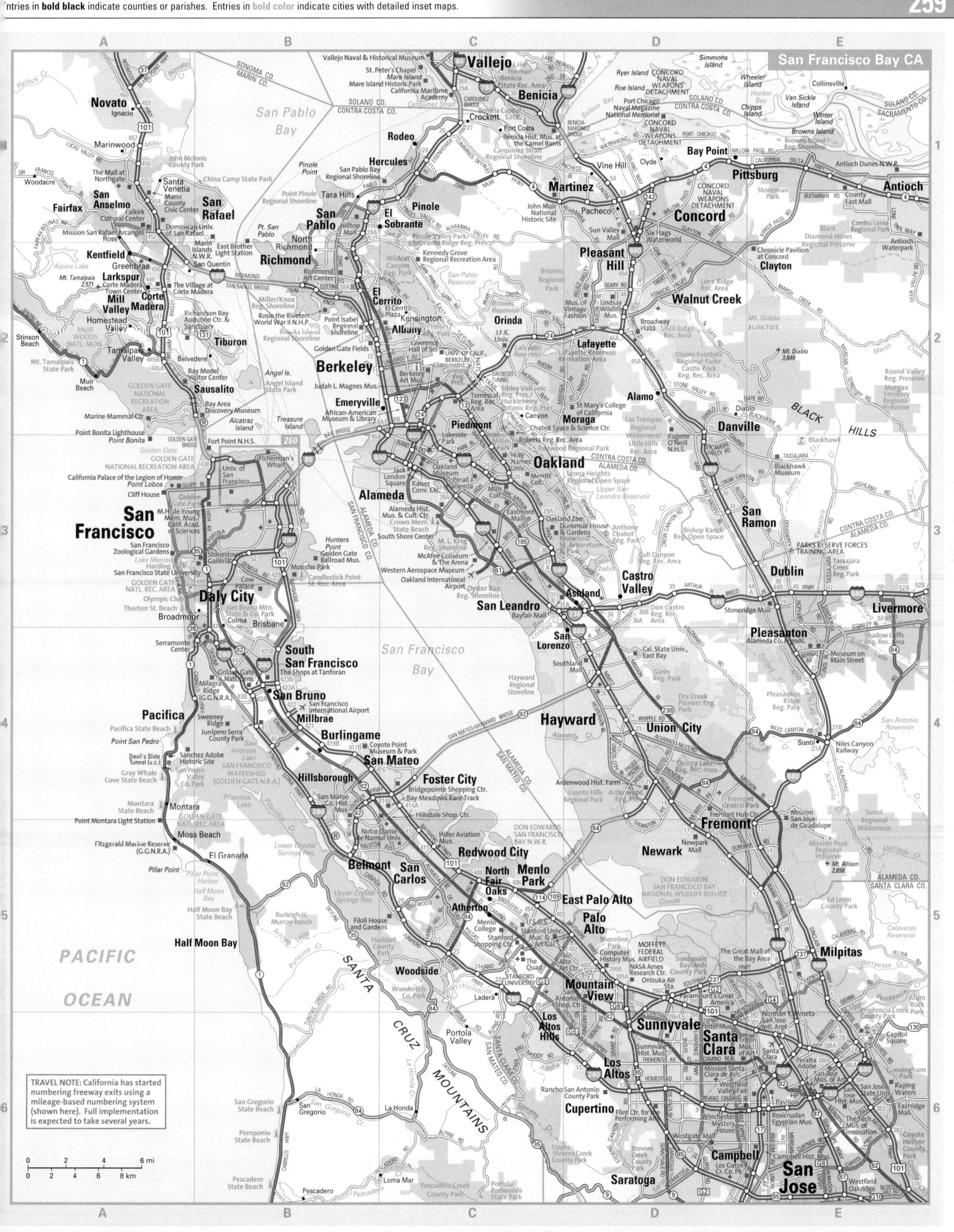

San Francisco Bay CA

TRAVEL NOTE: California has started numbering freeway exits using a mileage-based numbering system (shown here). Full implementation is expected to take several years.

PACIFIC OCEAN

San Pablo Bay

San Francisco Bay

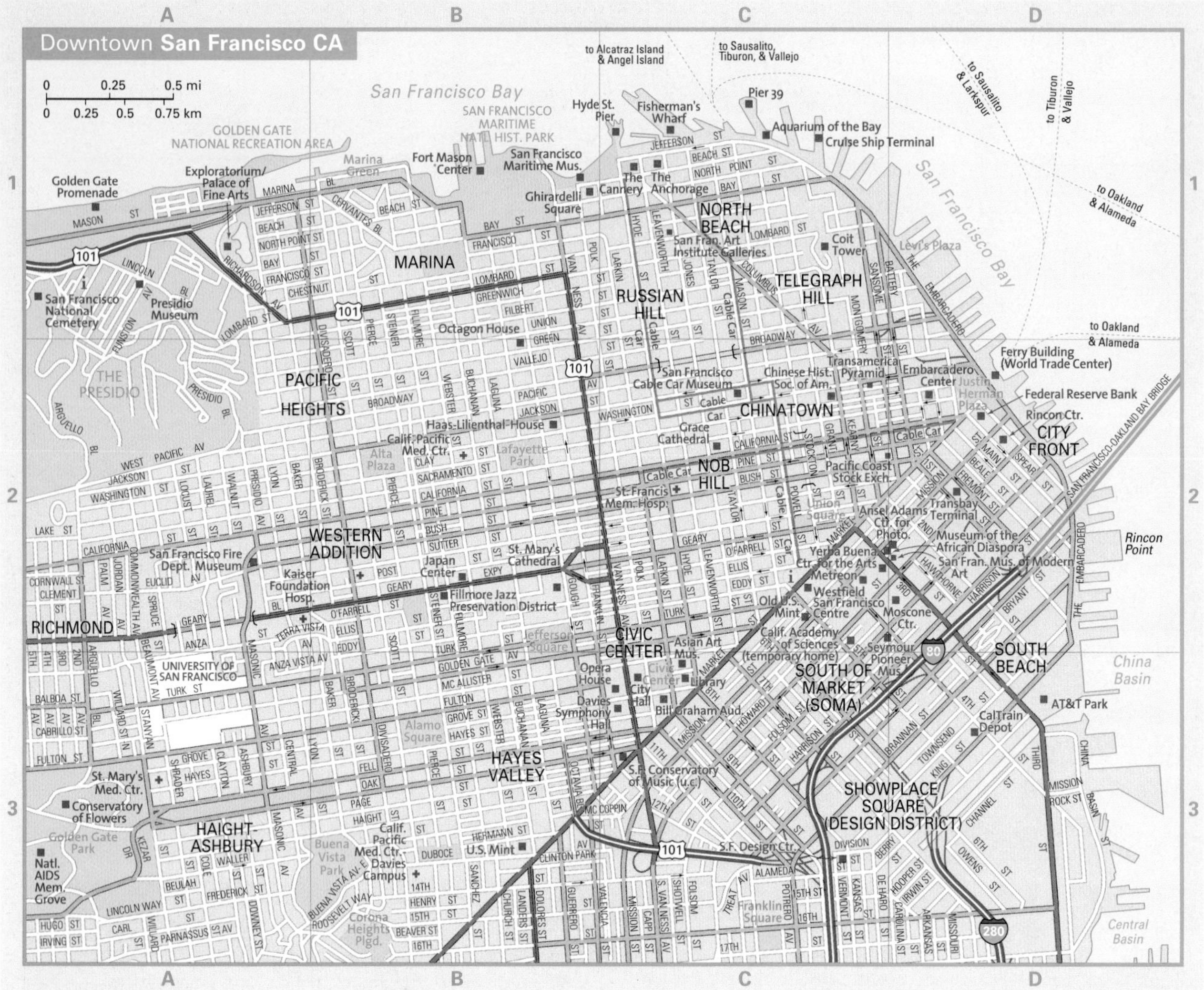

Downtown San Francisco CA

[Map of Downtown San Francisco with grid columns A–D and rows 1–3, showing neighborhoods including MARINA, PACIFIC HEIGHTS, RUSSIAN HILL, TELEGRAPH HILL, NORTH BEACH, CHINATOWN, NOB HILL, WESTERN ADDITION, RICHMOND, CIVIC CENTER, HAYES VALLEY, HAIGHT-ASHBURY, SOUTH OF MARKET (SOMA), SOUTH BEACH, CITY FRONT, THE PRESIDIO, and San Francisco Bay.]

POINTS OF INTEREST

The Anchorage	C1
Ansel Adams Center for Photography	D2
Aquarium of the Bay	C1
Asian Art Museum	C3
AT&T Park	D3
Bill Graham Auditorium	C3
The Cannery	C1
Chinese Hist. Society of America	C2
City Hall	C3
Coit Tower	C1
Conservatory of Flowers	A3
Cruise Ship Terminal	C1
Davies Symphony Hall	C3
Embarcadero Center	D2
Exploratorium/Palace of Fine Arts	A1
Fillmore Jazz Preservation District	B2
Fisherman's Wharf	C1
Fort Mason Center	B1
Ghirardelli Square	C1
Golden Gate Natl. Rec. Area	A1
Golden Gate Park	A3
Golden Gate Promenade	A1
Grace Cathedral	C2
Haas-Lilienthal House	B2
Hyde Street Pier	C1

Japan Center	B2
Levi's Plaza	D1
Metreon	C2
Moscone Center	D2
National AIDS Memorial Grove	A3
Octagon House	B2
Old U.S. Mint	C2
Opera House	C3
Pier 39	C1
The Presidio	A2
Presidio Mus.	A1
Rincon Center	D2
St. Mary's Cathedral	B2
San Francisco Art Institute Galleries	C1
San Francisco Cable Car Mus.	C2
San Francisco Fire Dept. Mus.	A2
San Francisco Maritime Mus.	B1
San Francisco Maritime Natl. Hist. Park	B1
San Francisco Mus. of Modern Art	D2
San Francisco Natl. Cemetery	A1
Seymour Pioneer Museum	C2
Transamerica Pyramid	C2
U.S. Mint	B3
Univ. of San Francisco	A3
Westfield San Francisco Centre	C2
Yerba Buena Center for the Arts	C2

Santa Barbara CA

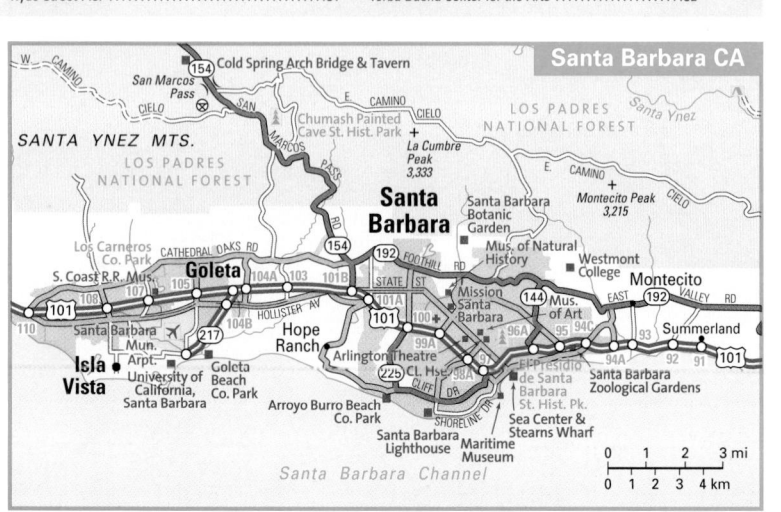

Santa Fe NM

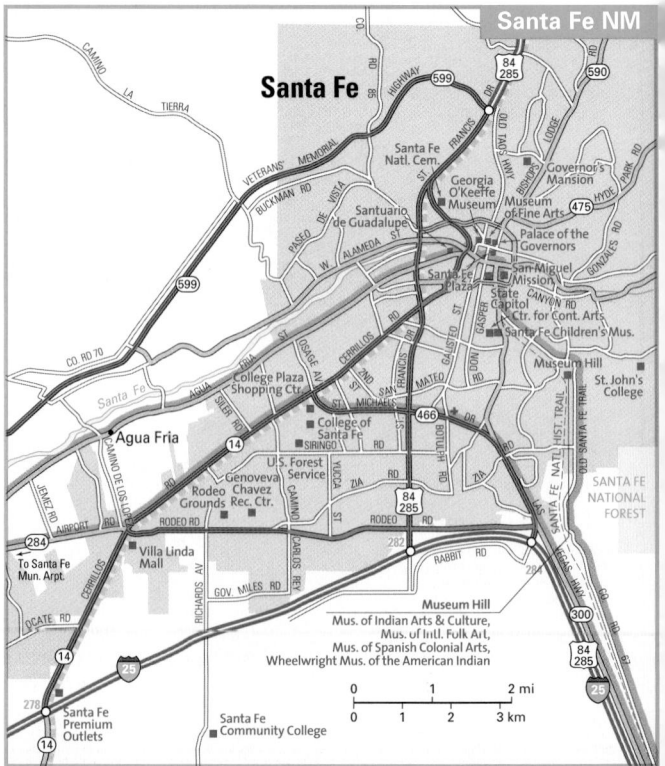

Entries in **bold black** indicate counties or parishes. Entries in ***bold color*** indicate cities with detailed inset maps.

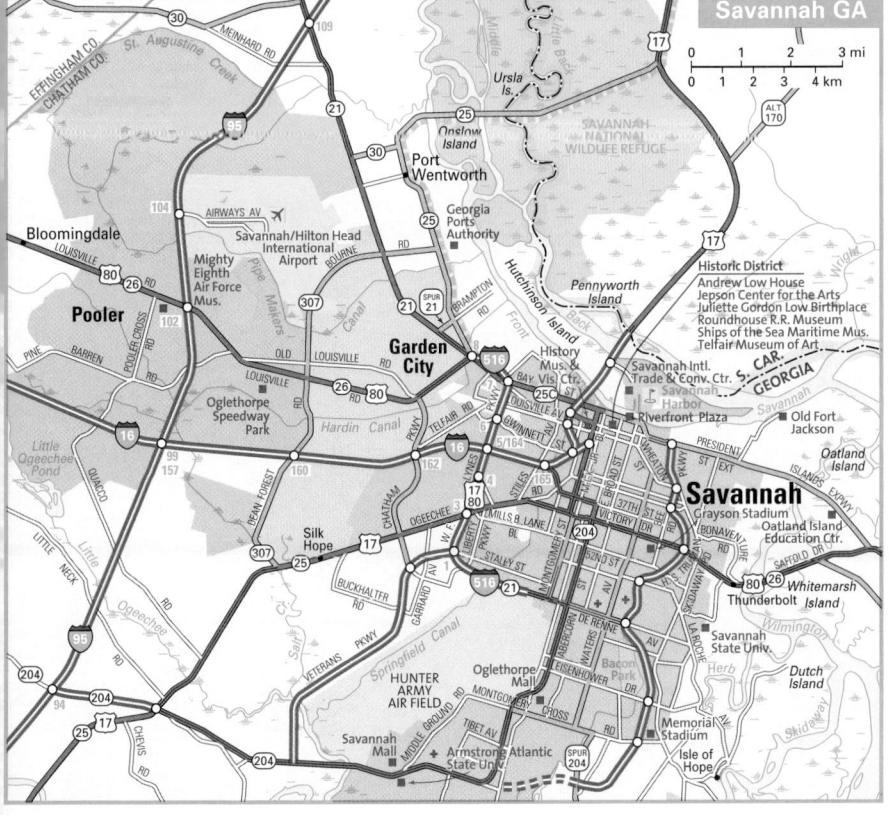

Savannah GA

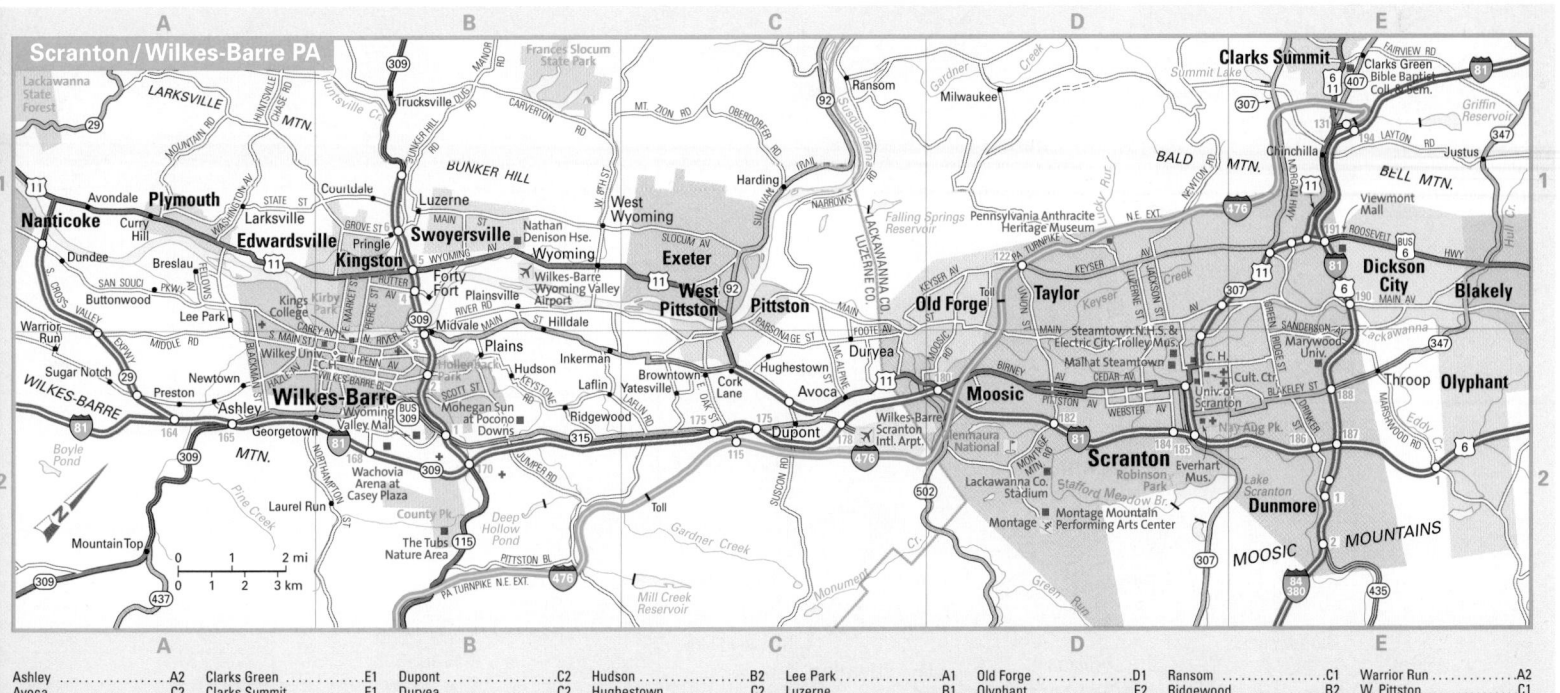

Scranton / Wilkes-Barre PA

Seattle / Tacoma WA

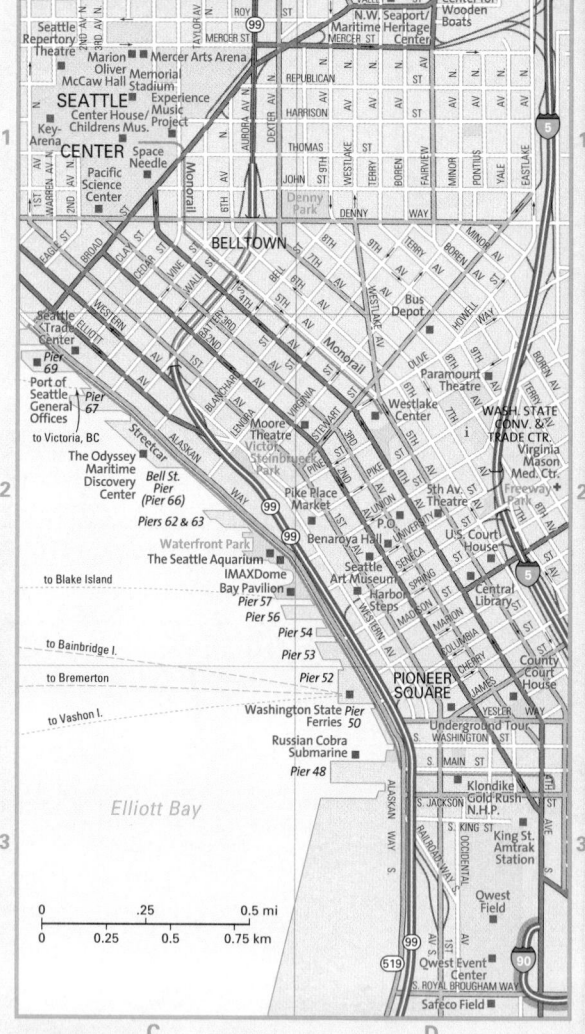

Downtown Seattle WA

POINTS OF INTEREST

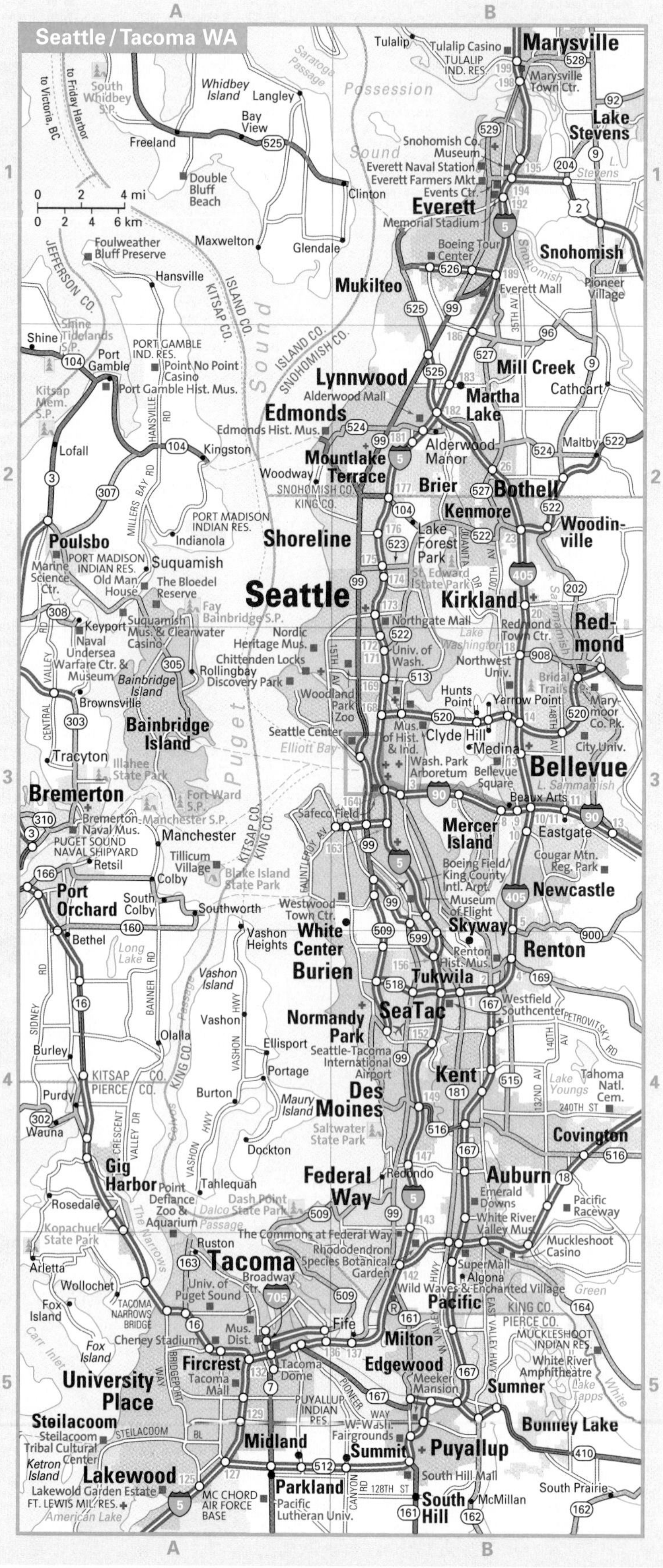

Entries in **bold black** indicate counties or parishes. Entries in **bold color** indicate cities with detailed inset maps.

Sentinel–Slater 263

Sentinel OK, 859 .... 51 D3
Sequatchie Co. TN, 11370 .... 120 B1
Sequim WA, 4334 .... 12 B2
Sequoyah Co. OK, 38972 .... 116 B1
Sergeant Bluff IA, 3321 .... 35 F2
Sergeantsville NJ, 650 .... 147 D1
Sesser IL, 2128 .... 98 C4
Setauket NY, 15931 .... 149 D3
Seth Ward TX, 1926 .... 50 A4
Seven Corners VA, 8701 .... 270 B4
Seven Fields PA, 1986 .... 92 A3
Seven Hills OH, 12080 .... 204 F3
Seven Lakes NC, 3214 .... 122 C1
Seven Mile OH, 678 .... 100 B2
Seven Pts. TX, 1145 .... 59 F3
Severance CO, 597 .... 33 E4
Severn MD, 35076 .... 144 C2
Severna Park MD, 28507 .... 144 C2
Sevier Co. AR, 15757 .... 116 C3
Sevier Co. TN, 71170 .... 111 D4
Sevier Co. UT, 18842 .... 39 E2
Sevierville TN, 11757 .... 111 D4
Seville OH, 2160 .... 91 E3
Sewanee TN, 2361 .... 120 A1
Seward AK, 2830 .... 154 C3
Seward NE, 6319 .... 35 F4
Seward Co. KS, 22510 .... 42 B4
Seward Co. NE, 16496 .... 35 E4
Sewaren NJ, 2780 .... 240 A6
Sewell NJ, 3400 .... 146 C4
Sewickley PA, 3902 .... 92 A4
Seymour CT, 15454 .... 149 D2
Seymour IN, 18101 .... 99 F2
Seymour IA, 810 .... 87 D3
Seymour MO, 1834 .... 107 D2
Seymour TN, 8850 .... 110 C4
Seymour TX, 2908 .... 58 C1
Seymour WI, 3335 .... 68 C4
Seymourville LA, 2200 .... 134 A2
Shabbona IL, 929 .... 88 C1
Shackelford Co. TX, 3302 .... 58 C2
Shadeland IN, 1682 .... 89 E4
Shady Cove OR, 2307 .... 28 B1
Shady Pt. OK, 848 .... 116 B1
Shady Rest CT, 550 .... 148 C1
Shady Side MD, 5559 .... 144 C3
Shadyside OH, 3675 .... 101 F1
Shady Spr. WV, 2078 .... 111 F1
Shafter CA, 12736 .... 45 D4
Shaker Hts. OH, 29405 .... 91 E2
Shakopee MN, 20568 .... 66 C4
Shalimar FL, 718 .... 136 B2
Shallotte NC, 1381 .... 123 D4
Shallowater TX, 2086 .... 58 A1
Shamokin PA, 8009 .... 93 E3
Shamokin Dam PA, 1502 .... 93 D3
Shamrock TX, 2029 .... 50 C3
Shandon CA, 986 .... 44 C4
Shannock RI, 900 .... 150 C4
Shannon GA, 1682 .... 120 B3
Shannon IL, 854 .... 88 B1
Shannon MS, 1657 .... 119 D3
Shannon Co. MO, 8324 .... 107 F2
Shannon Co. SD, 12466 .... 26 A4
Shannon Hills AR, 2005 .... 117 E2
Shannontown SC, 4100 .... 122 B4
Sharkey Co. MS, 6580 .... 126 A2
Sharon CT, 800 .... 94 B2
Sharon MA, 5941 .... 151 D2
Sharon PA, 16328 .... 91 F2
Sharon SC, 421 .... 122 A2
Sharon TN, 988 .... 108 C3
Sharon WI, 1549 .... 74 C4
Sharon Hill PA, 5468 .... 248 B4
Sharon Sprs. KS, 835 .... 42 B2
Sharon Sprs. NY, 547 .... 79 F4
Sharonville OH, 13804 .... 100 B2
Sharp Co. AR, 17119 .... 107 F4
Sharpes FL, 3415 .... 141 E1
Sharpsburg MD, 691 .... 144 A1
Sharpsburg NC, 2421 .... 113 E4
Sharpsburg PA, 3594 .... 250 C1
Sharpsville IN, 618 .... 89 F4
Sharpsville PA, 4500 .... 91 F2
Sharptown MD, 649 .... 145 E4
Shasta Co. CA, 163256 .... 28 C3
Shasta Lake CA, 9008 .... 28 C4
Shattuck OK, 1274 .... 50 C2
Shavano Park TX, 1754 .... 257 E1
Shaver Lake CA, 705 .... 45 D2
Shaw MS, 2312 .... 118 A4
Shawanee TN, 2865 .... 111 D3
Shawano WI, 8298 .... 68 C4
Shawano Co. WI, 40664 .... 68 C4
Shawnee KS, 47996 .... 96 B2
Shawnee OH, 608 .... 101 E1
Shawnee OK, 28692 .... 51 F3
Shawnee Co. KS, 169871 .... 96 A2
Shawneetown IL, 1410 .... 109 D1
Shawsville VA, 1029 .... 112 B2
Sheboygan WI, 50792 .... 75 D2
Sheboygan Co. WI, 112646 .... 74 C2
Sheboygan Falls WI, 6772 .... 75 D2
Sheep Sprs. NM, 237 .... 48 A2
Sheffield AL, 9652 .... 119 E2
Sheffield IL, 946 .... 88 B2
Sheffield IA, 930 .... 73 D3
Sheffield MA, 750 .... 94 B2
Sheffield PA, 1268 .... 92 B2
Sheffield Lake OH, 9371 .... 91 D2
Shelbiana KY, 600 .... 111 E1
Shelbina MO, 1943 .... 97 E1
Shelburn IN, 1268 .... 99 E2
Shelburne VT, 1700 .... 81 D2
Shelburne Falls MA, 1951 .... 94 C1
Shelby IA, 696 .... 86 A2
Shelby MI, 1914 .... 75 E2
Shelby MS, 2926 .... 118 A4
Shelby MT, 3216 .... 15 E2
Shelby NE, 690 .... 35 E3
Shelby NC, 19477 .... 121 F1
Shelby OH, 9821 .... 91 D3
Shelby Co. AL, 143293 .... 127 F1
Shelby Co. IL, 22893 .... 98 C2
Shelby Co. IN, 43445 .... 99 F1
Shelby Co. IA, 13173 .... 86 A1
Shelby Co. KY, 33337 .... 100 A4
Shelby Co. MO, 6799 .... 97 E1
Shelby Co. OH, 47910 .... 90 B4
Shelby Co. TN, 897472 .... 118 B1
Shelby Co. TX, 25224 .... 124 C3
Shelbyville IL, 4971 .... 98 C2
Shelbyville IN, 17951 .... 99 F1
Shelbyville KY, 10085 .... 100 A4
Shelbyville MO, 682 .... 97 E1
Shelbyville TN, 16105 .... 119 F1
Sheldon IL, 1232 .... 89 D3
Sheldon IA, 4914 .... 35 F1
Sheldon MO, 529 .... 106 C1
Sheldon TX, 1831 .... 220 D2
Shelley ID, 3813 .... 23 E4
Shell Knob MO, 1393 .... 106 C3
Shell Lake WI, 1309 .... 67 E2
Shellman GA, 1166 .... 128 C4
Shell Pt. SC, 2856 .... 130 C2
Shell Rock IA, 1298 .... 73 D4
Shellsburg IA, 938 .... 87 E1
Shelly PA, 1200 .... 146 C1
Shelter Island NY, 1234 .... 149 E3
Shelter Island Hts. NY, 981 .... 149 E3
Shelton CT, 38101 .... 149 D2
Shelton NE, 1140 .... 35 D4
Shelton WA, 8442 .... 12 B3
Shenandoah IA, 5546 .... 86 A3
Shenandoah PA, 5624 .... 93 E3
Shenandoah TX, 1503 .... 132 A2
Shenandoah VA, 1878 .... 102 C3
Shenandoah Co. VA, 35075 .... 102 C3
Shepherd MI, 1536 .... 76 A2
Shepherd TX, 2029 .... 132 B2
Shepherdstown WV, 803 .... 103 D2
Shepherdsville KY, 8334 .... 100 A4
Sherando VA, 665 .... 102 C4
Sherborn MA, 1200 .... 150 C1
Sherburn MN, 1082 .... 72 B2
Sherburne NY, 1455 .... 79 E4
Sherburne Co. MN, 64417 .... 66 C3
Sheridan AR, 3872 .... 117 E3
Sheridan CA, 750 .... 36 C2
Sheridan CO, 5600 .... 209 B4
Sheridan IL, 2411 .... 88 C2
Sheridan IN, 2520 .... 89 F4
Sheridan MI, 705 .... 76 A3
Sheridan MT, 659 .... 23 E2
Sheridan OR, 3570 .... 20 B2
Sheridan WY, 15804 .... 25 D3
Sheridan Co. KS, 2813 .... 42 C1
Sheridan Co. MT, 4105 .... 17 E1
Sheridan Co. NE, 6198 .... 34 A2
Sheridan Co. ND, 1710 .... 18 C3
Sheridan Co. WY, 26560 .... 25 D2
Sherman IL, 2871 .... 98 B1
Sherman MS, 548 .... 118 C3
Sherman NY, 714 .... 92 A1
Sherman TX, 35082 .... 59 F1
Sherman Co. KS, 6760 .... 42 B2
Sherman Co. NE, 3318 .... 35 D3
Sherman Co. OR, 1934 .... 21 D2
Sherman Co. TX, 3186 .... 50 A2
Sherrard IL, 694 .... 88 A2
Sherrill NY, 3147 .... 79 E3
Sherrills Ford NC, 941 .... 112 A4
Sherwood ND, 255 .... 18 B1
Sherwood OH, 801 .... 90 B2
Sherwood OR, 11791 .... 20 B2
Sherwood WI, 1550 .... 74 C1
Sherwood Manor CT, 5689 .... 150 A2
Sheyenne ND, 318 .... 19 D3
Shiawassee Co. MI, 71687 .... 76 B4
Shickshinny PA, 959 .... 93 E3
Shidler OK, 520 .... 51 F1
Shields MI, 6590 .... 76 B2
Shillington PA, 5059 .... 146 A2
Shiloh NJ, 534 .... 145 F1
Shiloh OH, 721 .... 91 D3
Shiloh OH, 11272 .... 208 D1
Shiloh PA, 10192 .... 275 E1
Shiner TX, 2070 .... 61 E3
Shinglehouse PA, 1250 .... 92 C1
Shingle Sprs. CA, 2643 .... 36 C3
Shingletown CA, 2222 .... 28 C4
Shinnecock Hills NY, 1749 .... 149 E3
Shinnston WV, 2295 .... 102 A2
Shiocton WI, 954 .... 74 C1
Ship Bottom NJ, 1384 .... 147 E4
Shipman IL, 655 .... 98 B2
Shippensburg PA, 5586 .... 103 D1
Shiprock NM, 8156 .... 48 A1
Shipshewana IN, 536 .... 89 F2
Shiremanstown PA, 1521 .... 218 A2
Shirley IN, 806 .... 100 A1
Shirley MA, 1427 .... 95 D1
Shirley NY, 25395 .... 149 D4
Shishmaref AK, 562 .... 154 B2
Shively KY, 15157 .... 99 F4
Shoals IN, 807 .... 99 E3
Shoemakersville PA, 2124 .... 146 A1
Shokan NY, 1252 .... 94 A2
Shonto AZ, 568 .... 47 E1
Shore Acres NJ, 4500 .... 147 E3
Shoreacres TX, 1488 .... 132 B3
Shoreham MI, 860 .... 89 E1
Shoreham Beach MD, 1300 .... 144 C3
Shoreline WA, 53025 .... 12 C3
Shoreview MN, 25924 .... 235 C1
Shorewood IL, 7686 .... 88 C2
Shorewood MN, 7400 .... 66 C4
Shorewood WI, 13763 .... 234 D2
Shorewood Hills WI, 1732 .... 231 A2
Short Beach CT, 5100 .... 149 D2
Shortsville NY, 1320 .... 78 C3
Shoshone ID, 1398 .... 30 C1
Shoshone Co. ID, 13771 .... 14 B3
Shoshoni WY, 635 .... 32 C1
Show Low AZ, 7695 .... 47 F4
Shreve OH, 1582 .... 91 D3
Shreveport LA, 200145 .... 124 C2
Shrewsbury MA, 31640 .... 150 C1
Shrewsbury MO, 6644 .... 256 B3
Shrewsbury NJ, 3590 .... 147 E2
Shrewsbury PA, 3378 .... 103 E1
Shrub Oak NY, 1812 .... 148 B2
Shubuta MS, 651 .... 127 D3
Shullsburg WI, 1246 .... 74 A4
Shungopavi AZ, 632 .... 47 E2
Shuqualak MS, 562 .... 127 D1
Sibley IA, 2796 .... 72 A2
Sibley LA, 1098 .... 125 D2
Sibley Co. MN, 15356 .... 66 C4
Sicily Island LA, 453 .... 125 F3
Sicklerville NJ, 6000 .... 147 D4
Sidell IL, 626 .... 99 D1
Sidman PA, 973 .... 92 B4
Sidney IL, 1062 .... 99 D1
Sidney IA, 1300 .... 86 A3
Sidney MT, 4774 .... 17 F3
Sidney NE, 6282 .... 34 A3
Sidney NY, 4068 .... 79 E4
Sidney OH, 20211 .... 90 B4
Sidon MS, 672 .... 126 B1
Sierra Blanca TX, 533 .... 57 D4
Sierra Co. CA, 3555 .... 37 D1
Sierra Co. NM, 13270 .... 56 B2
Sierra Madre CA, 10578 .... 228 E2
Sierra Vista AZ, 37775 .... 55 E4
Siesta Key FL, 7150 .... 140 B4
Signal Hill CA, 9333 .... 228 D4
Signal Mtn. TN, 7429 .... 120 B1
Sigourney IA, 2209 .... 87 E2
Sigurd UT, 430 .... 39 E2
Sikeston MO, 16992 .... 108 B2
Silas AL, 529 .... 127 D3
Siler City NC, 6966 .... 112 C4
Siletz OR, 1133 .... 20 B3
Silica OH, 1100 .... 90 C2
Siloam Sprs. AR, 10843 .... 106 B3
Silsbee TX, 6393 .... 132 C2
Silt CO, 1740 .... 40 C1
Silters NY, 600 .... 94 B1
Silver Bay MN, 2068 .... 65 D3
Silver Bow Co. MT, 34606 .... 23 E1
Silver City NM, 10545 .... 55 F2
Silver City NC, 1146 .... 122 C2
Silver Cliff CO, 512 .... 41 D3
Silver Creek MO, 608 .... 106 B2
Silver Creek NE, 441 .... 35 E3
Silver Creek NY, 2896 .... 78 A4
Silverdale PA, 1001 .... 146 C2
Silverdale WA, 15816 .... 12 C3
Silver Grove KY, 1215 .... 100 B2
Silverhill AL, 616 .... 135 E2
Silver Hill MD, 33515 .... 270 E4
Silver Lake IN, 546 .... 89 F3
Silver Lake KS, 1358 .... 96 A2
Silver Lake MA, 1000 .... 151 E2
Silver Lake MN, 761 .... 66 C4
Silver Lake NC, 5788 .... 123 E3
Silver Lake OH, 3019 .... 188 B1
Silver Lake WI, 2341 .... 74 C4
Silver Ridge NJ, 1211 .... 147 E3
Silver Spr. MD, 76540 .... 144 B3
Silver Sprs. FL, 6400 .... 139 D4
Silver Sprs. NV, 4708 .... 37 E2
Silver Sprs. NY, 844 .... 78 B4
Silver Sprs. Shores FL, 6690 .... 139 D4
Silverthorne CO, 3196 .... 41 D1
Silverton CO, 531 .... 40 C4
Silverton NJ, 9200 .... 147 E3
Silverton OH, 5178 .... 204 B2
Silverton OR, 7414 .... 20 C2
Silverton TX, 771 .... 50 B4
Silvis IL, 7269 .... 208 C2
Simi Valley CA, 111351 .... 52 B2
Simla CO, 663 .... 41 F2
Simmesport LA, 2239 .... 133 F1
Simms MT, 373 .... 15 E3
Simonton TX, 718 .... 61 F2
Simpson LA, 583 .... 125 D4
Simpson Co. KY, 16405 .... 109 F2
Simpson Co. MS, 27639 .... 126 B3
Simpsonville KY, 1281 .... 100 A4
Simpsonville MD, 4400 .... 144 B2
Simpsonville SC, 14352 .... 121 F2
Simsboro LA, 684 .... 125 E2
Simsbury CT, 5603 .... 94 C3
Sinclair WY, 423 .... 32 C2
Sinclairville NY, 665 .... 78 A4
Sinking Spr. PA, 2639 .... 146 A2
Sinton TX, 5676 .... 61 E4
Sioux Ctr. IA, 6002 .... 35 F1
Sioux City IA, 85013 .... 35 F1
Sioux Co. IA, 31589 .... 35 F1
Sioux Co. NE, 1475 .... 33 F1
Sioux Co. ND, 4044 .... 26 B1
Sioux Falls SD, 123975 .... 27 F4
Sioux Rapids IA, 720 .... 72 A3
Sippewisset MA, 950 .... 151 E4
Sipsey AL, 552 .... 119 F4
Siren WI, 988 .... 67 E2
Siskiyou Co. CA, 44301 .... 28 C3
Sisseton SD, 2572 .... 27 F1
Sissonville WV, 4399 .... 101 E3
Sister Bay WI, 886 .... 69 D3
Sister Lakes MI, 1000 .... 89 F1
Sisters OR, 959 .... 21 D3
Sistersville WV, 1588 .... 101 F1
Sitka AK, 8835 .... 155 D4
Six Mile SC, 553 .... 121 E2
Skagit Co. WA, 102979 .... 12 C2
Skagway AK, 862 .... 155 D3
Skamania Co. WA, 9872 .... 12 C4
Skaneateles NY, 2616 .... 79 D3
Skellytown TX, 610 .... 50 B3
Skiatook OK, 5396 .... 51 F1
Skidaway Island GA, 6914 .... 130 C3
Skidmore TX, 1013 .... 61 E4
Skidway Lake MI, 3147 .... 76 B1
Skippack PA, 2889 .... 146 C2
Skokie IL, 63348 .... 89 D1
Skowhegan ME, 6696 .... 82 C1
Sky Lake FL, 5651 .... 246 C3
Skyline AL, 843 .... 120 A2
Skyway WA, 13977 .... 262 B4
Slater IA, 1306 .... 86 C1
Slater MO, 2083 .... 97 D2
Slater SC, 2228 .... 121 E2

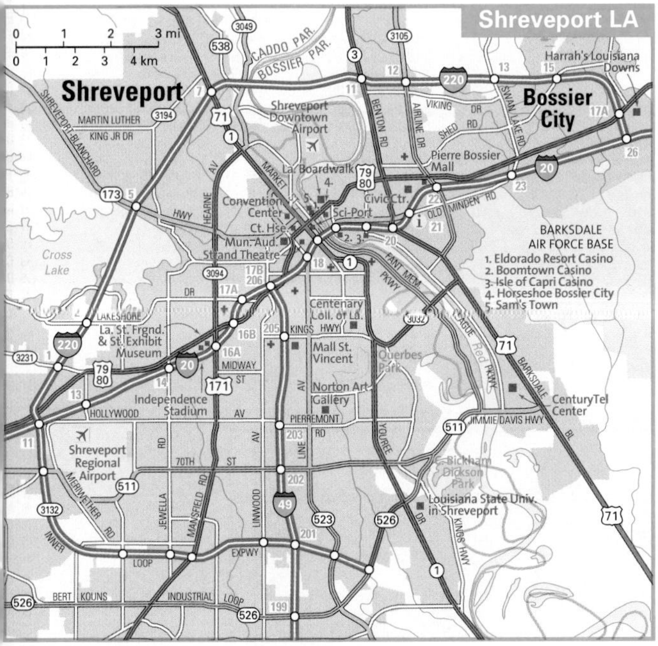
Shreveport LA
0 1 2 3 mi
0 1 2 3 4 km
Shreveport
Bossier City
Harrah's Louisiana Downs
Shreveport Downtown Airport
Pierre Bossier Mall
Louisiana Boardwalk
Convention Center
Civic Ctr.
Sci-Port
Ct. Hse.
Mun. Aud.
Strand Theatre
BARKSDALE AIR FORCE BASE
1. Eldorado Resort Casino
2. Boomtown Casino
3. Isle of Capri Casino
4. Horseshoe Bossier City
5. Sam's Town
Cross Lake
La. St. Frgnd. & St. Exhibit Museum
Centenary Coll. of La.
Mall St. Vincent
Norton Art Gallery
Independence Stadium
CenturyTel Center
Shreveport Regional Airport
Louisiana State Univ. in Shreveport
CADDO PAR.
BOSSIER PAR.

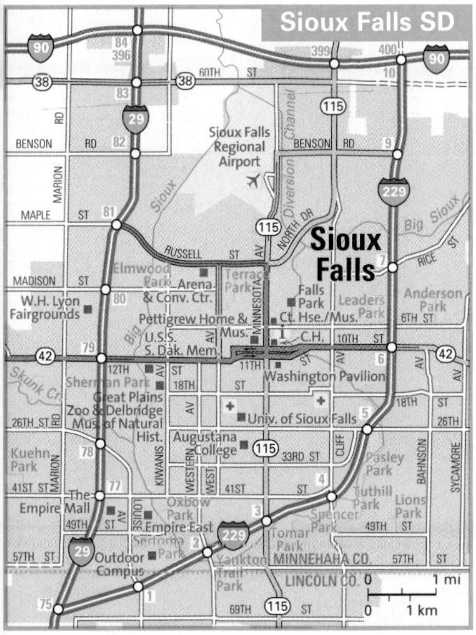
Sioux Falls SD
Sioux Falls
Sioux Falls Regional Airport
W.H. Lyon Fairgrounds
Elmwood Park
Arena & Conv. Ctr.
Terrace Park
Falls Park
Pettigrew Home & Mus.
U.S.S. S. Dak. Mem.
Washington Pavilion
Great Plains Zoo & Delbridge Mus. of Natural Hist.
Univ. of Sioux Falls
Augustana College
Empire Mall
Empire East
Outdoor Campus
MINNEHAHA CO.
LINCOLN CO.
0 1 mi
0 1 km

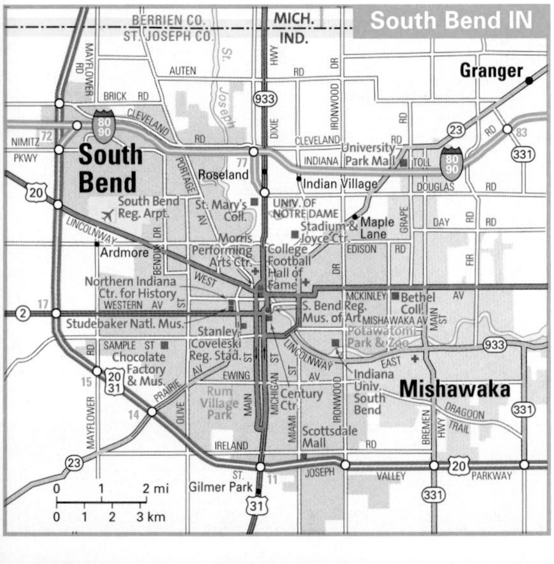
South Bend IN
BERRIEN CO.
ST. JOSEPH CO.
MICH.
IND.
Granger
South Bend
Roseland
University Park Mall
Indian Village
South Bend Reg. Arpt.
St. Mary's Coll.
UNIV. OF NOTRE DAME
Stadium & Joyce Ctr.
Maple Lane
Ardmore
Morris Performing Arts Ctr.
College Football Hall of Fame
Northern Indiana Ctr. for History
Studebaker Natl. Mus.
S. Bend Mus. of Art
Bethel Coll.
Potawatomi Park & Zoo
Stanley Coveleski Reg. Stad.
Chocolate Factory & Mus.
Rum Village Park
Century Ctr.
Indiana Univ. South Bend
Mishawaka
Scottsdale Mall
Gilmer Park
0 1 2 mi
0 1 2 3 km

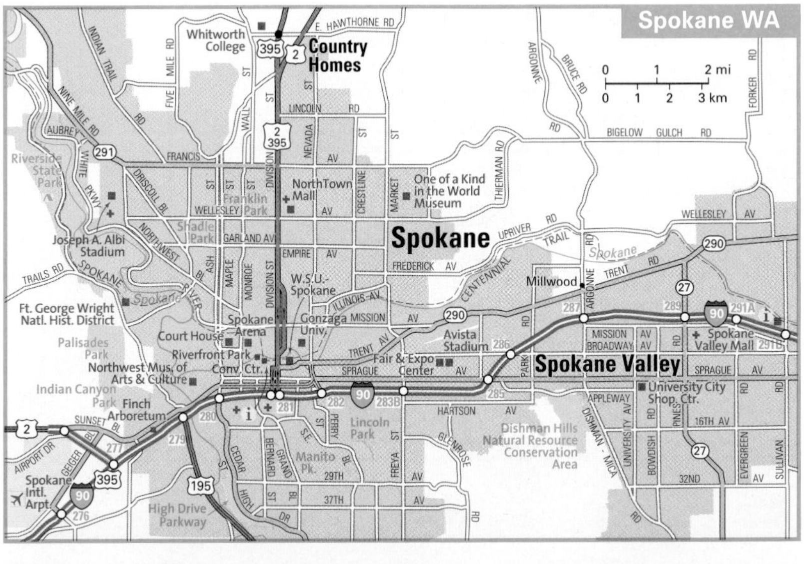
Spokane WA
0 1 2 mi
0 1 2 3 km
Whitworth College
Country Homes
Riverside State Park
NorthTown Mall
One of a Kind in the World Museum
Spokane
Joseph A. Albi Stadium
Millwood
W.S.U.-Spokane
Gonzaga Univ.
Ft. George Wright Natl. Hist. District
Court House
Spokane Arena
Riverfront Park
Conv. Ctr.
Northwest Mus. of Arts & Culture
Fair & Expo Center
Avista Stadium
Spokane Valley
Spokane Valley Mall
University City Shop. Ctr.
Indian Canyon Park
Finch Arboretum
Lincoln Park
Manito Pk.
Dishman Hills Natural Resource Conservation Area
Spokane Intl. Arpt.
High Drive Parkway

Springfield IL

Springfield MA

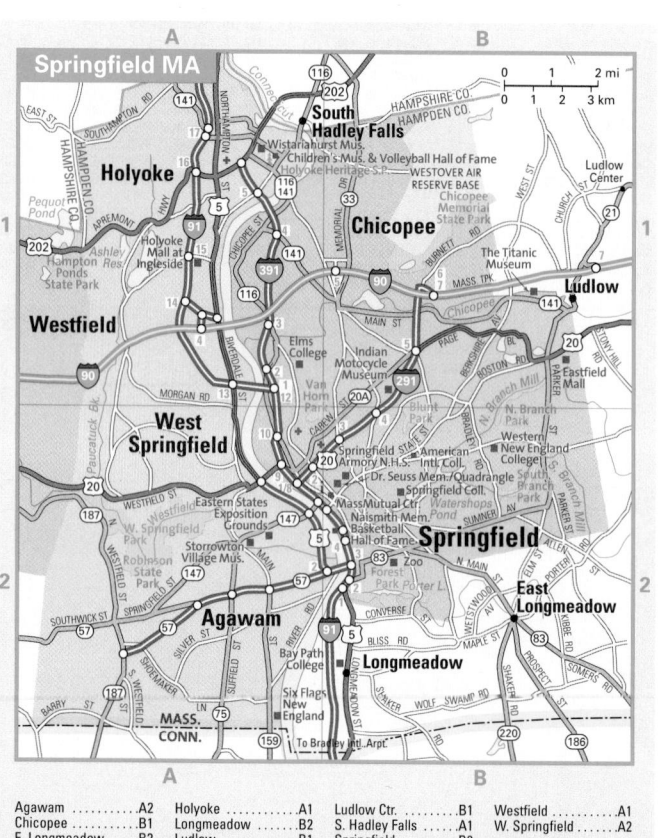

Springfield MO

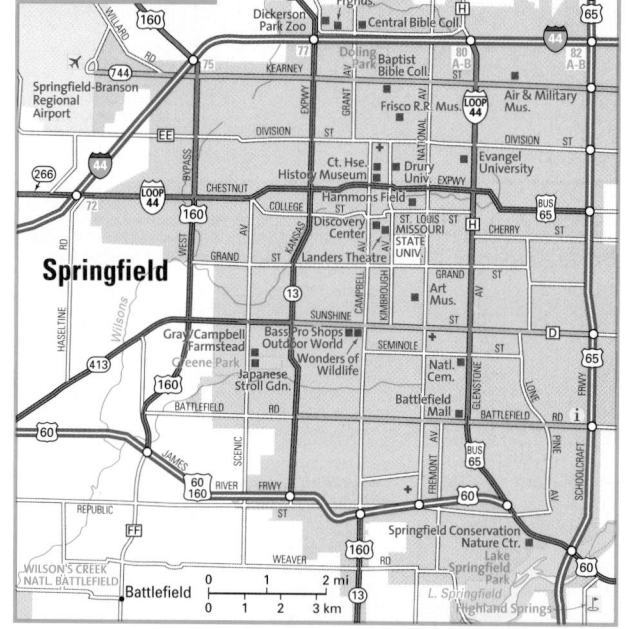

Stamford CT

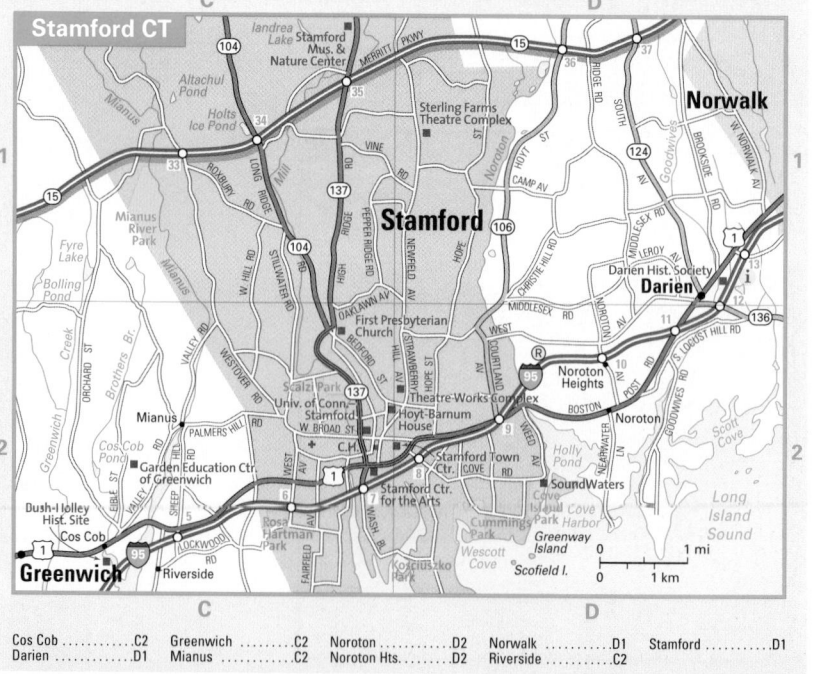

Entries in **bold black** indicate counties or parishes. Entries in **bold color** indicate cities with detailed inset maps.

South Lebanon–Stillmore 265

Syracuse NY

Stockton CA

Tallahassee FL

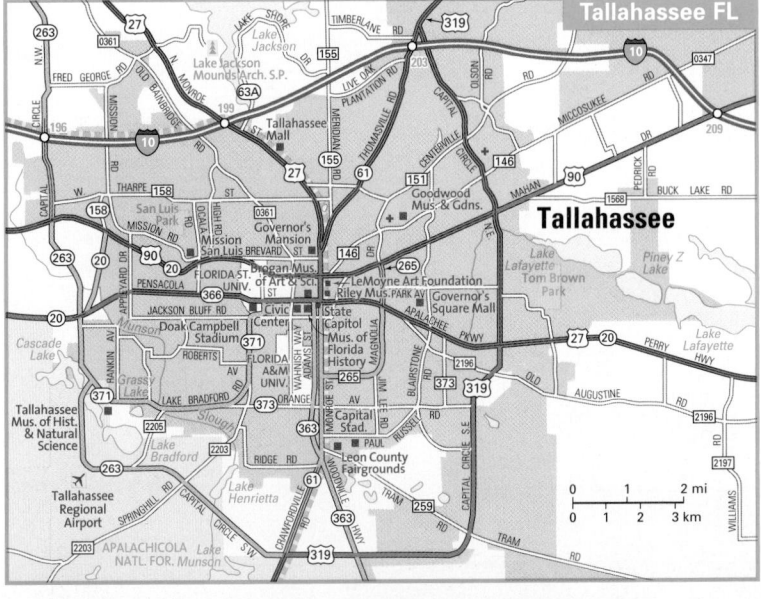

Tampa/St Petersburg FL

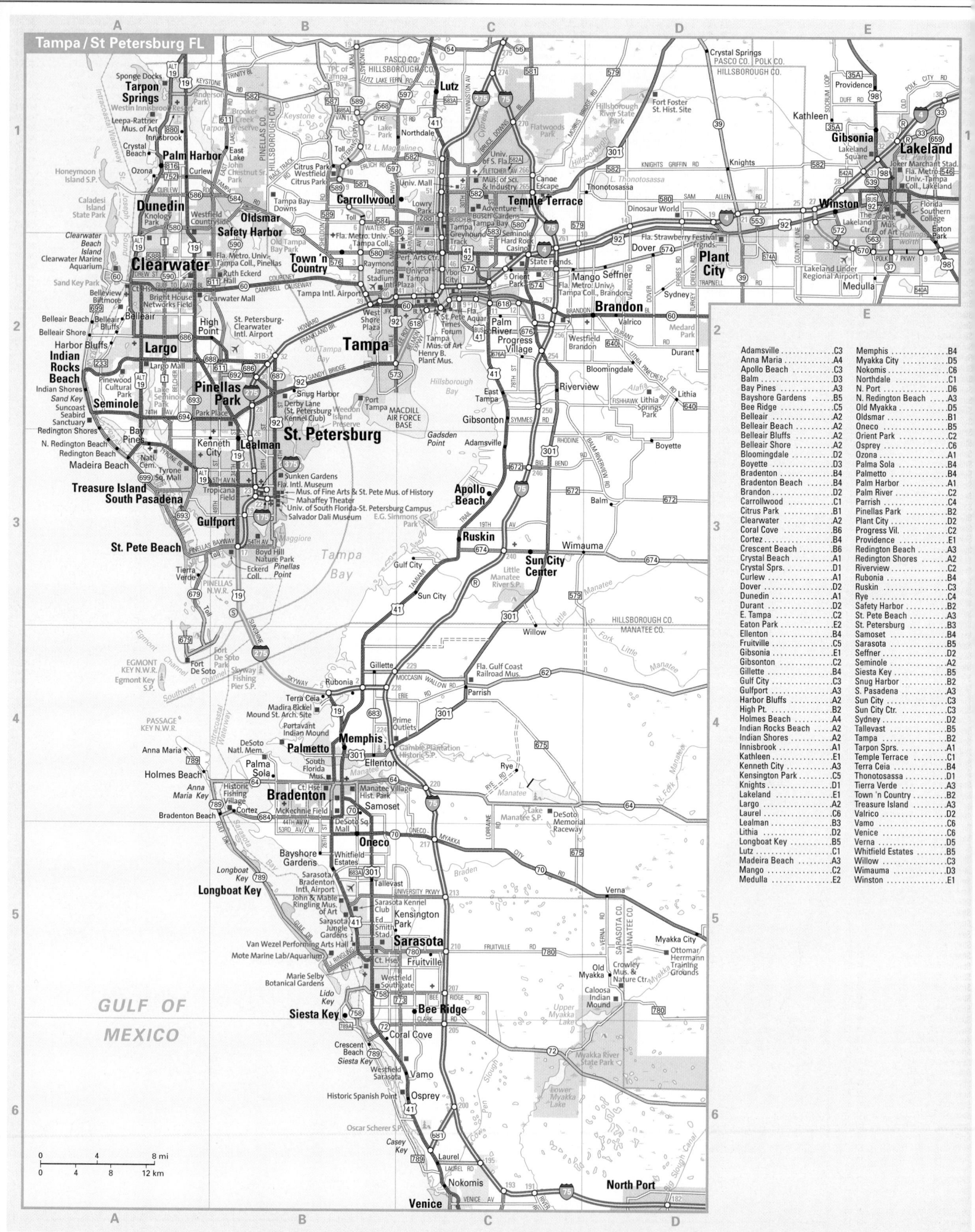

Stillwater ME, 1600 ... 83 D1
Stillwater MN, 15143 ... 67 D3
Stillwater NY, 1644 ... 94 B1
Stillwater OK, 39065 ... 51 F2
Stillwater Co. MT, 8195 ... 24 B1
Stilwell KS, 1200 ... 96 B3
Stilwell OK, 3276 ... 106 B4
Stimson Crossing WA, 773 ... 12 C2
Stinnett TX, 1936 ... 50 B2
Stinson Beach CA, 751 ... 259 A2
Stites ID, 226 ... 22 B1
Stockbridge GA, 9853 ... 120 C4
Stockbridge MA, 900 ... 94 B2
Stockbridge MI, 1260 ... 76 B4
Stockbridge WI, 649 ... 74 C1
Stockdale TX, 1398 ... 61 E3
Stock Island FL, 4410 ... 142 C4
Stockton CA, 243771 ... 36 C3
Stockton IL, 1926 ... 74 A4
Stockton KS, 1558 ... 43 D2
Stockton MN, 682 ... 73 E1
Stockton MO, 1960 ... 106 C1
Stockton NJ, 560 ... 146 C1
Stockton UT, 443 ... 31 E4
Stockton Sprs. ME, 550 ... 83 D2
Stockville NE, 36 ... 34 C4
Stoddard WI, 815 ... 73 F2
Stoddard Co. MO, 29705 ... 108 B2
Stokes Co. NC, 44711 ... 112 B3
Stokesdale NC, 3267 ... 112 B3
Stoneboro PA, 1104 ... 92 A2
Stone Co. AR, 11499 ... 107 E4
Stone Co. MS, 13622 ... 135 D1
Stone Co. MO, 28658 ... 107 D3
Stonega VA, 475 ... 111 D2
Stoneham MA, 22219 ... 151 D1
Stone Harbor NJ, 1128 ... 104 C4
Stone Mtn. GA, 7145 ... 120 C4
Stone Park IL, 5127 ... 203 C4
Stone Ridge NY, 1173 ... 94 B3
Stoneville NC, 1002 ... 112 B3
Stonewall LA, 1668 ... 124 C3
Stonewall MS, 1149 ... 127 D3
Stonewall OK, 465 ... 51 F4
Stonewall Co. TX, 1693 ... 58 B2
Stonewood WV, 1815 ... 102 A2
Stoney Creek Mills PA, 5900 ... 146 B2
Stonington CT, 1032 ... 149 F2
Stonington IL, 960 ... 98 C1
Stonington ME, 850 ... 83 D2
Stony Brook NY, 13727 ... 149 D3
Stony Creek CT, 900 ... 149 E2
Stony Pt. NY, 11744 ... 148 B2
Stony Pt. NC, 1380 ... 112 A4
Storey Co. NV, 3399 ... 37 D2
Storm Lake IA, 10076 ... 72 A4
Stormstown PA, 1602 ... 92 C3
Storrs CT, 10996 ... 150 B3
Story WY, 887 ... 25 D3
Story City IA, 3228 ... 86 C1
Story Co. IA, 79981 ... 86 C1
Stottville NY, 1355 ... 94 B2
Stoughton MA, 11200 ... 151 D2
Stoughton WI, 12354 ... 74 B3
Stoutsville OH, 581 ... 101 D1
Stover MO, 968 ... 97 D3
Stow OH, 32139 ... 91 E2
Stowe PA, 3585 ... 146 B2
Stowe VT, 500 ... 81 E2
Stowell TX, 1572 ... 132 C3
Strafford MO, 1845 ... 107 D2
Strafford Co. NH, 112233 ... 81 F4
Straitsville CT, 1000 ... 149 D1
Strasburg CO, 1402 ... 41 E1
Strasburg IL, 603 ... 98 C2
Strasburg ND, 549 ... 26 C1
Strasburg OH, 2310 ... 91 E4
Strasburg PA, 2800 ... 146 A3
Strasburg VA, 4017 ... 102 C2
Stratford CA, 1264 ... 44 C3
Stratford CT, 49976 ... 149 D2
Stratford IA, 746 ... 72 C4
Stratford NJ, 7271 ... 146 C3
Stratford OK, 1474 ... 51 F4
Stratford TX, 1991 ... 50 A2
Stratford WI, 1523 ... 68 A4
Stratham NH, 1000 ... 82 A4
Strathmoor Vil. KY, 625 ... 230 E2
Strathmore CA, 2584 ... 45 D3
Strathmore NJ, 6740 ... 147 E1
Stratmoor Hills CO, 6650 ... 205 D2
Stratton CO, 669 ... 42 A2
Stratton ME, 425 ... 82 B1
Stratton NE, 396 ... 42 B1
Strawberry AZ, 1028 ... 47 E4
Strawberry Pt. IA, 1386 ... 73 E4
Strawn TX, 739 ... 59 D3
Streamwood IL, 36407 ... 203 B3
Streator IL, 14190 ... 88 C3
Streetsboro OH, 12311 ... 91 E2
Stroh IN, 700 ... 90 A2
Stromsburg NE, 1232 ... 35 E3
Strong AR, 651 ... 125 E1
Strong ME, 550 ... 82 B1
Strong City KS, 584 ... 43 F3
Stronghurst IL, 896 ... 87 F3
Strongsville OH, 43858 ... 91 E2
Stroud OK, 2758 ... 51 F2
Stroudsburg PA, 5756 ... 93 F3
Strum WI, 1001 ... 67 F4
Struthers OH, 11756 ... 91 F3
Stryker OH, 1406 ... 90 B2
Stuart FL, 14633 ... 141 E4
Stuart IA, 1712 ... 86 B2
Stuart NE, 625 ... 35 D1
Stuart VA, 961 ... 112 B3
Stuarts Draft VA, 8367 ... 102 C4
Sturbridge MA, 2047 ... 150 B2
Sturgeon MO, 944 ... 97 E2
Sturgeon Bay WI, 9437 ... 69 D4
Sturgis KY, 2030 ... 109 D1
Sturgis MI, 11285 ... 90 A1
Sturgis SD, 6442 ... 25 F3
Sturtevant WI, 5287 ... 74 C4
Stutsman Co. ND, 21908 ... 19 D3
Stuttgart AR, 9745 ... 117 F3
Suamico WI, 950 ... 68 C4
Subiaco AR, 439 ... 116 C1
Sublette KS, 1592 ... 42 B4
Sublette Co. WY, 5920 ... 32 A1
Sublimity OR, 2148 ... 20 C2
Succasunna NJ, 12569 ... 148 A3
Sudan TX, 1039 ... 57 F1
Sudbury MA, 2300 ... 150 C1
Suffern NY, 11006 ... 148 B2
Suffield CT, 1244 ... 150 A2
Suffolk VA, 63677 ... 113 F3
Suffolk Co. MA, 689807 ... 151 D1
Suffolk Co. NY, 1419369 ... 149 D3
Sugar City ID, 1242 ... 23 E4
Sugar Creek MO, 3839 ... 224 D3
Sugarcreek OH, 2174 ... 91 E4
Sugarcreek PA, 5331 ... 92 A2
Sugar Grove IL, 3909 ... 88 C1
Sugar Grove PA, 613 ... 92 B1
Sugar Grove VA, 741 ... 111 F2
Sugar Hill GA, 11399 ... 120 C3
Sugar Land TX, 63328 ... 132 A3
Sugarland Run VA, 9400 ... 144 A3
Sugar Loaf NY, 700 ... 148 A2
Sugar Notch PA, 1023 ... 261 A2
Suisun City CA, 26118 ... 36 B3
Suitland MD, 33515 ... 144 B3
Sulligent AL, 2151 ... 119 D4
Sullivan IL, 4326 ... 98 C1
Sullivan IN, 4617 ... 99 E2
Sullivan MO, 6351 ... 97 F4
Sullivan WI, 688 ... 74 C3
Sullivan City TX, 3998 ... 63 E4
Sullivan Co. IN, 21751 ... 99 E2
Sullivan Co. MO, 7219 ... 87 D4
Sullivan Co. NH, 40458 ... 81 E4
Sullivan Co. NY, 73966 ... 94 A2
Sullivan Co. PA, 6556 ... 93 E2
Sullivan Co. TN, 153048 ... 111 E3
Sullivans Island SC, 1911 ... 131 D2
Sully IA, 904 ... 87 D2
Sully Co. SD, 1556 ... 26 C3
Sulphur LA, 20512 ... 133 D2
Sulphur OK, 4794 ... 51 F4
Sulphur Rock AR, 421 ... 107 F4
Sulphur Sprs. AR, 671 ... 106 B3
Sulphur Sprs. TX, 14551 ... 124 A1
Sultan WA, 3344 ... 12 C3
Sumas WA, 960 ... 12 C1
Sumiton AL, 2665 ... 119 F4
Summerdale AL, 655 ... 135 E2
Summerfield NC, 7018 ... 112 B3
Summerland Key FL, 600 ... 143 D4
Summers Co. WV, 12999 ... 112 A1
Summerside OH, 5523 ... 204 C2
Summersville MO, 544 ... 107 F2
Summersville WV, 3294 ... 101 F4
Summerton SC, 1061 ... 122 B4
Summertown TN, 800 ... 119 E1
Summerville GA, 4556 ... 120 B3
Summerville SC, 27752 ... 131 D1
Summit AR, 586 ... 107 E3
Summit IL, 10637 ... 203 D5
Summit KY, 3400 ... 101 D3
Summit MS, 1428 ... 126 B4
Summit NJ, 21131 ... 148 A4
Summit SD, 281 ... 27 F2
Summit WA, 8041 ... 262 B5
Summit Co. CO, 23548 ... 41 D1
Summit Co. OH, 542899 ... 91 E3
Summit Co. UT, 29736 ... 31 F4
Summitville IN, 1090 ... 89 F4
Sumner IL, 1022 ... 99 D3
Sumner IA, 2106 ... 73 E3
Sumner MS, 407 ... 118 B3
Sumner WA, 8504 ... 12 C3
Sumner Co. KS, 25946 ... 51 E1
Sumner Co. TN, 130449 ... 109 F3
Sumrall MS, 1005 ... 126 C4
Sumter SC, 39643 ... 122 B4
Sumter Co. AL, 14798 ... 127 E2
Sumter Co. FL, 53345 ... 140 C1
Sumter Co. GA, 33200 ... 129 D3
Sumter Co. SC, 104646 ... 122 B4
Sun LA, 471 ... 134 C1
Sunapee NH, 750 ... 81 E4
Sunbright TN, 577 ... 110 B3
Sunburst MT, 415 ... 15 E1
Sunbury OH, 2630 ... 91 D4
Sunbury PA, 10610 ... 93 D3
Sun City AZ, 38309 ... 54 C1
Sun City CA, 17773 ... 53 D3
Sun City Ctr. FL, 16321 ... 140 C3
Sun City West AZ, 26344 ... 249 A1
Suncook NH, 5362 ... 81 F4
Sundance WY, 1161 ... 25 F3
Sunderland MD, 1400 ... 144 C4
Sunderland MA, 850 ... 150 A1
Sundown TX, 1505 ... 57 F1
Sunfield MI, 591 ... 76 A4
Sunfish Lake MN, 504 ... 235 D3
Sunflower MS, 696 ... 118 A4
Sunflower Co. MS, 34369 ... 118 A4
Sun Lakes AZ, 11936 ... 54 C2
Sunland Park NM, 13309 ... 56 C4
Sunman IN, 805 ... 100 A2
Sunnybrook MD, 2300 ... 144 C1
Sunny Isles Beach FL, 15315 ... 233 C3
Sunnyside UT, 404 ... 39 F1
Sunnyside WA, 13905 ... 13 E4
Sunnyslope CA, 4437 ... 229 H3
Sunnyvale CA, 131760 ... 36 B4
Sunol CA, 1332 ... 259 E4
Sun Prairie WI, 20369 ... 74 B3
Sunray TX, 1950 ... 50 A2
Sunrise FL, 85779 ... 143 E1
Sunrise Beach TX, 704 ... 61 D1
Sunset LA, 2352 ... 133 F2
Sunset UT, 5204 ... 244 A2
Sunset Beach NC, 1824 ... 123 D4
Sunset Hills MO, 8267 ... 256 B3
Sun Valley ID, 1427 ... 22 C4
Superior AZ, 3254 ... 55 D2
Superior CO, 9011 ... 209 B1
Superior MT, 893 ... 14 C3
Superior NE, 2055 ... 43 E1
Superior WI, 27368 ... 64 C4
Superior WY, 244 ... 32 B2
Supreme LA, 1119 ... 134 A3
Suquamish WA, 3510 ... 262 A2
Surf City NJ, 1442 ... 147 E4
Surf City NC, 1393 ... 123 E3
Surfside FL, 4909 ... 233 C4
Surfside Beach SC, 4425 ... 123 D4
Surfside Beach TX, 763 ... 133 E4
Surgoinsville TN, 1484 ... 111 D3
Suring WI, 605 ... 68 C4
Surprise AZ, 30848 ... 54 C1
Surrey ND, 917 ... 18 B2
Surry VA, 262 ... 113 F2
Surry Co. NC, 71219 ... 112 A3
Surry Co. VA, 6829 ... 113 F2
Susan VA, 475 ... 113 F1
Susan Moore AL, 721 ... 119 F3
Susanville CA, 13541 ... 29 D4
Susquehanna PA, 1690 ... 93 F1
Susquehanna Co. PA, 42238 ... 93 E2
Sussex NJ, 2145 ... 148 A2
Sussex VA, 125 ... 113 E2
Sussex WI, 8828 ... 74 C3
Sussex Co. DE, 156638 ... 145 F4
Sussex Co. NJ, 144166 ... 148 A2
Sussex Co. VA, 12504 ... 113 E2
Sutcliffe NV, 281 ... 37 D1
Sutherland IA, 707 ... 72 A3
Sutherland NE, 1129 ... 34 B3
Sutherlin OR, 6669 ... 20 B4
Sutter CA, 2885 ... 36 B2
Sutter Co. CA, 78930 ... 36 B2
Sutter Creek CA, 2303 ... 36 C3
Sutton AK, 1080 ... 154 C3
Sutton MA, 650 ... 150 C2
Sutton NE, 1447 ... 35 E4
Sutton WV, 1011 ... 101 F3
Sutton Co. TX, 4077 ... 60 B1
Suttons Bay MI, 589 ... 69 F4
Suwanee GA, 8725 ... 120 C3
Suwannee Co. FL, 34844 ... 138 B2
Swain Co. NC, 12968 ... 121 D1
Swainsboro GA, 6943 ... 129 F2
Swampscott MA, 14412 ... 151 D1
Swannanoa NC, 4132 ... 121 E1
Swann Keys DE, 700 ... 145 F4
Swanquarter NC, 275 ... 115 E3
Swansboro NC, 2663 ... 115 D4
Swansea IL, 10579 ... 98 B3
Swansea SC, 533 ... 122 A4
Swanton OH, 3307 ... 90 B2
Swanton VT, 2548 ... 81 D1
Swan Valley ID, 213 ... 23 F4
Swarthmore PA, 6170 ... 146 C3
Swartz LA, 4247 ... 125 F2
Swartz Creek MI, 5102 ... 76 B3
Swayzee IN, 1011 ... 89 F4
Swea City IA, 642 ... 72 B2
Swedesboro NJ, 2055 ... 146 C4
Sweeny TX, 3624 ... 132 A4
Sweet Briar VA, 750 ... 112 C1
Sweet Grass Co. MT, 3609 ... 24 A1
Sweet Home OR, 8016 ... 20 C3
Sweetser IN, 906 ... 89 F3
Sweet Sprs. MO, 1628 ... 97 D3
Sweetwater FL, 14226 ... 143 E2
Sweetwater TN, 5586 ... 120 C1
Sweetwater TX, 11415 ... 58 B3
Sweetwater Co. WY, 37613 ... 32 B2
Swepsonville NC, 922 ... 112 C4
Swift Co. MN, 11956 ... 66 A3
Swifton AR, 871 ... 107 F4
Swifts Beach MA, 2700 ... 151 E3
Swift Trail Jct. AZ, 2195 ... 55 E2
Swiftwater PA, 800 ... 93 F3
Swink CO, 696 ... 41 F3
Swisher IA, 813 ... 87 E1
Swisher Co. TX, 8378 ... 50 A4
Swissvale PA, 9653 ... 250 C2
Switzer WV, 1138 ... 111 E1
Switzerland Co. IN, 9065 ... 100 B3
Swoyersville PA, 5157 ... 93 E2
Sycamore GA, 496 ... 129 D4
Sycamore IL, 12020 ... 88 C1
Sycamore OH, 914 ... 90 C3
Sycaway NY, 3000 ... 188 E2
Sykesville MD, 4197 ... 144 B1
Sykesville PA, 1246 ... 92 B3
Sylacauga AL, 12616 ... 128 A1
Sylva NC, 2435 ... 121 D1
Sylvan Beach NY, 1071 ... 79 E3
Sylvania AL, 1186 ... 120 A2
Sylvania GA, 2675 ... 130 B2
Sylvania OH, 18670 ... 90 C2
Sylvan Lake MI, 1735 ... 210 B1
Sylvan Lake NY, 1200 ... 148 C1
Sylvan Shores FL, 2424 ... 141 D3
Sylvan Sprs. AL, 1465 ... 195 D2
Sylvester GA, 5990 ... 129 D4
Symsonia KY, 450 ... 109 D2
Syosset NY, 18544 ... 148 C3
Syracuse IN, 3038 ... 89 F2
Syracuse KS, 1812 ... 42 B3
Syracuse NE, 1762 ... 35 F4
Syracuse NY, 147306 ... 79 D3
Syracuse OH, 879 ... 101 E2
Syracuse UT, 9398 ... 31 E3

T

Tabor IA, 993 ... 86 A3
Tabor SD, 417 ... 35 E1
Tabor City NC, 2509 ... 123 D3
Tacna AZ, 555 ... 54 A2
Tacoma WA, 193556 ... 12 C3
Taft CA, 6400 ... 52 B1
Taft FL, 1938 ... 246 C4
Taft TX, 3396 ... 61 E4
Tahlequah OK, 14458 ... 106 B4
Tahoe City CA, 1761 ... 37 D2
Tahoka TX, 2910 ... 58 A2
Taholah WA, 824 ... 12 A3
Takoma Park MD, 17299 ... 270 D2
Talbot Co. GA, 6498 ... 128 C2
Talbot Co. MD, 33812 ... 145 D3
Talbott TN, 1400 ... 111 D4
Talbotton GA, 1019 ... 128 C2
Talco TX, 570 ... 124 B1
Talcottville CT, 4500 ... 150 A3
Talent OR, 6066 ... 28 B2
Taliaferro Co. GA, 2077 ... 121 E4
Talihina OK, 1211 ... 116 B2
Talkeetna AK, 772 ... 154 C3
Talladega AL, 15143 ... 120 A4
Talladega Co. AL, 80321 ... 128 A1
Tallahassee FL, 150624 ... 137 E2
Tallahatchie Co. MS, 14903 ... 118 B4
Tallapoosa GA, 2789 ... 120 B4
Tallapoosa Co. AL, 41475 ... 128 B1
Tallassee AL, 4934 ... 128 A2
Tallevast FL, 1100 ... 266 B5
Talleyville DE, 6300 ... 146 B3
Tallmadge OH, 16390 ... 91 E3
Tallula IL, 638 ... 98 B1
Tallulah LA, 9189 ... 126 A2
Talmage CA, 1141 ... 36 A2
Talmo GA, 477 ... 121 D3
Taloga OK, 372 ... 51 D2
Talty TX, 1028 ... 59 F2
Tama IA, 2731 ... 87 D1
Tama Co. IA, 18103 ... 87 D1
Tamalpais Valley CA, 10691 ... 259 A2
Tamaqua PA, 7174 ... 93 E3
Tamarac FL, 55588 ... 143 E1
Tamaroa IL, 740 ... 98 B4
Tamms IL, 724 ... 108 C2
Tampa FL, 303447 ... 140 B2
Tampico IL, 772 ... 88 B2
Taney Co. MO, 39703 ... 107 D3
Taneytown MD, 5128 ... 103 E1
Tangelo Park FL, 2430 ... 246 B3
Tangent OR, 933 ... 20 B3
Tangier VA, 604 ... 114 B2
Tangipahoa LA, 747 ... 134 B1
Tangipahoa Par. LA, 100588 ... 134 B1
Tanner AL, 900 ... 119 F2
Tannersville PA, 1000 ... 93 F3
Tanque Verde AZ, 16195 ... 55 D3
Tantallon MD, 7900 ... 144 B4
Taos MO, 870 ... 97 E3
Taos NM, 4700 ... 49 D1
Taos Co. NM, 29979 ... 49 D1
Tappahannock VA, 2068 ... 103 E4
Tappan NY, 6757 ... 148 B3
Tappen ND, 210 ... 18 C4
Tara Hills CA, 5332 ... 259 B1
Tarboro NC, 11138 ... 113 E4
Tarentum PA, 4993 ... 92 A3
Tariffville CT, 1371 ... 150 A3
Tarkiln RI, 950 ... 150 C2
Tarkio MO, 1935 ... 86 A4
Tarpon Sprs. FL, 21003 ... 140 B2
Tarrant City AL, 7022 ... 119 F4
Tarrant Co. TX, 1446219 ... 59 E2
Tarrytown NY, 11090 ... 148 B3
Tasso TN, 1300 ... 120 B1
Tatamy PA, 930 ... 93 F3
Tate Co. MS, 25370 ... 118 B2
Tattnall Co. GA, 22305 ... 129 F3
Tatum NM, 683 ... 57 F2
Tatum TX, 1175 ... 124 B2
Taunton MA, 55976 ... 151 D3
Tavares FL, 9700 ... 140 C1
Tavernier FL, 2173 ... 143 E4
Tawas City MI, 2005 ... 76 B1
Taylor AL, 1898 ... 136 C1
Taylor AZ, 3176 ... 47 F4
Taylor AR, 566 ... 125 D1
Taylor MI, 65868 ... 90 C1
Taylor NE, 207 ... 35 D2
Taylor PA, 6475 ... 261 D1
Taylor TX, 13575 ... 61 E1
Taylor Co. FL, 19256 ... 137 F3
Taylor Co. GA, 8815 ... 129 D2
Taylor Co. IA, 6958 ... 86 B3
Taylor Co. KY, 22927 ... 110 B1
Taylor Co. TX, 126555 ... 58 C3
Taylor Co. WV, 16089 ... 102 A2
Taylor Co. WI, 19680 ... 67 F3
Taylor Creek FL, 4289 ... 141 E4
Taylor Lake Vil. TX, 3694 ... 132 B3
Taylor Mill KY, 6913 ... 204 B3
Taylors SC, 20125 ... 121 F2
Taylors Falls MN, 951 ... 67 D3
Taylors Sprs. IL, 583 ... 98 B2
Taylorsville IN, 936 ... 99 F2
Taylorsville KY, 1009 ... 100 A4
Taylorsville MD, 900 ... 144 B1
Taylorsville MS, 1341 ... 126 C3
Taylorsville NC, 1799 ... 111 F4
Taylorsville UT, 57439 ... 257 A2
Taylortown NJ, 1200 ... 148 A3
Taylortown NC, 845 ... 122 C1
Taylorville IL, 11427 ... 98 B1
Tazewell TN, 2165 ... 111 D3
Tazewell VA, 4206 ... 111 F2
Tazewell Co. IL, 128485 ... 88 B4
Tazewell Co. VA, 44598 ... 111 F2
Tchula MS, 2332 ... 126 B1
Tea SD, 1742 ... 27 F4
Teague TX, 4557 ... 59 F4
Teaneck NJ, 39260 ... 148 B3
Teaticket MA, 1907 ... 151 E4
Teays WV, 2400 ... 101 E3
Tecumseh MI, 8574 ... 90 B1
Tecumseh NE, 1716 ... 35 F4
Tecumseh OK, 6098 ... 51 F3
Teec Nos Pos AZ, 799 ... 48 A1
Tega Cay SC, 4044 ... 122 A2
Tehachapi CA, 10957 ... 52 C1
Tehama CA, 432 ... 36 B1
Tehama Co. CA, 56039 ... 36 B1
Tekamah NE, 1892 ... 35 F2
Tekoa WA, 826 ... 14 B3
Tekonsha MI, 712 ... 90 A1
Telfair Co. GA, 11794 ... 129 E3
Telford PA, 4680 ... 146 C2
Tell City IN, 7845 ... 99 E4
Teller Co. CO, 20555 ... 41 E2
Tellico Plains TN, 859 ... 120 C1
Telluride CO, 2221 ... 40 B3
Temecula CA, 57716 ... 53 D3
Tempe AZ, 158625 ... 54 C1
Temperance MI, 7757 ... 90 C1
Temple GA, 2383 ... 120 B4
Temple OK, 1146 ... 51 E4
Temple PA, 1400 ... 146 B1
Temple TX, 54514 ... 59 E4
Temple City CA, 33377 ... 228 E2
Temple Hills MD, 7792 ... 270 E5
Temple Terrace FL, 20918 ... 140 C2
Templeton CA, 4687 ... 44 C4
Templeton MA, 800 ... 95 D1
Tenafly NJ, 13806 ... 148 B3
Tenaha TX, 1046 ... 124 C3
Tenants Harbor ME, 500 ... 82 C3
Tenino WA, 1447 ... 12 C4
Tennent NJ, 1100 ... 147 E2
Tennessee Ridge TN, 1334 ... 109 D3
Tennille GA, 1505 ... 129 E1
Tensas Par. LA, 6618 ... 125 F3
Ten Sleep WY, 304 ... 24 C3
Tequesta FL, 5273 ... 141 F4
Terra Alta WV, 1456 ... 102 B2
Terra Bella CA, 3466 ... 45 D4
Terrace Hts. WA, 6447 ... 13 D4
Terrace Park OH, 2273 ... 204 C2
Terrebonne OR, 1469 ... 21 D3

Harbor View ... B1
Holland ... A2
Lime City ... B2
Maumee ... A2
Moline ... B2
Northwood ... B2
Oregon ... B1
Ottawa Hills ... A1
Perrysburg ... A2
Rossford ... B2
Stony Ridge ... B2
Sylvania ... A1
Toledo ... A1
Walbridge ... B2

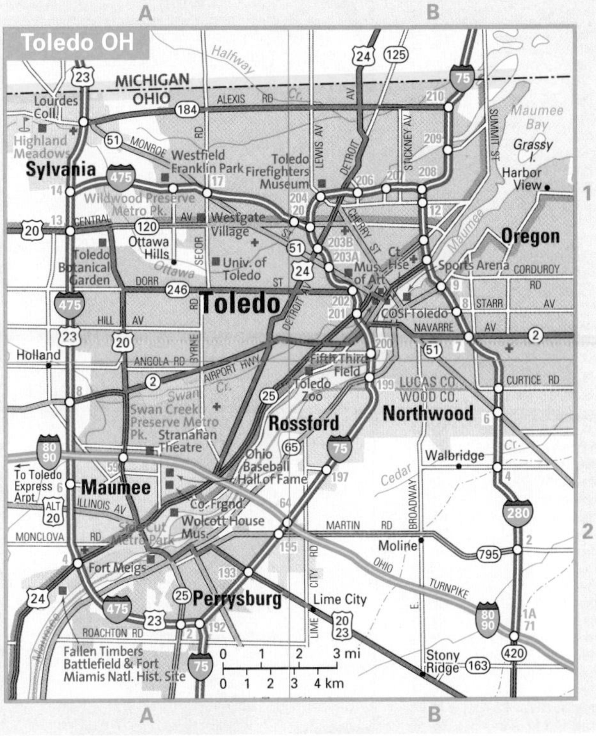
Toledo OH
A
B
1
2
MICHIGAN
OHIO
Sylvania
Toledo
Oregon
Ottawa Hills
Holland
Maumee
Rossford
Northwood
Walbridge
Perrysburg
Lime City
Moline
Stony Ridge
Harbor View
Maumee Bay
Fallen Timbers Battlefield & Fort Miamis Natl. Hist. Site
Fort Meigs
Toledo Zoo
Swan Creek Preserve Metro Pk.
Wildwood Preserve Metro Pk.
Toledo Botanical Garden
Univ. of Toledo
Sports Arena
Fifth Third Field
Ohio Baseball Hall of Fame
To Toledo Express Arpt.
LUCAS CO.
WOOD CO.
0 1 2 3 mi
0 1 2 3 4 km

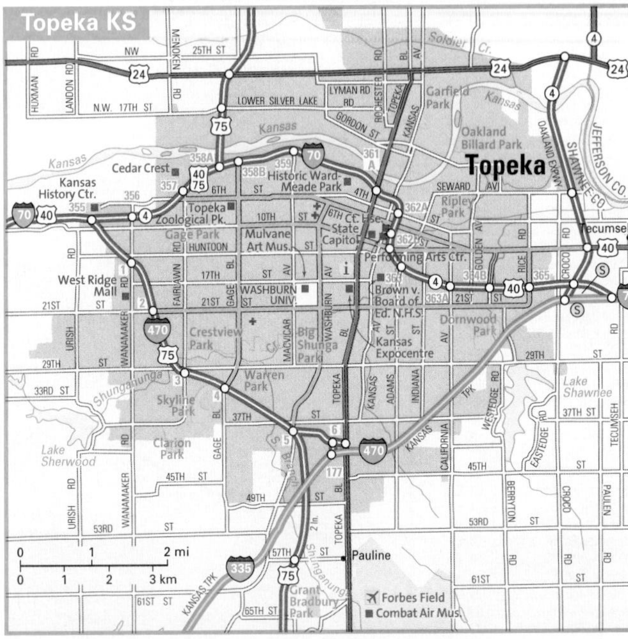
Topeka KS
Topeka
Kansas
Soldier Cr.
Garfield Park
Oakland Billard Park
Cedar Crest
Kansas History Ctr.
Historic Ward-Meade Park
Topeka Zoological Pk.
Gage Park
Mulvane Art Mus.
State Capitol
Performing Arts Ctr.
West Ridge Mall
Washburn Univ.
Brown v. Board of Ed. N.H.S.
Dornwood Park
Crestview Park
Big Shunga Park
Kansas Expocentre
Warren Park
Skyline Park
Clarion Park
Lake Sherwood
Lake Shawnee
Tecumseh
Pauline
Forbes Field
Combat Air Mus.
SHAWNEE CO.
JEFFERSON CO.
0 1 2 mi
0 1 2 3 km

Terrebonne Par. LA, *104503* 134 A4
Terre Haute IN, *59614* 99 E2
Terre Hill PA, *1237* 146 A2
Terrell TX, *13606* 59 F2
Terrell Co. GA, *10970* 128 C4
Terrell Co. TX, *1081* 60 A2
Terrell Hills TX, *5019* 257 E2
Terry MS, *664* 126 B3
Terry MT, *611* 17 E4
Terry Co. TX, *12761* 57 F2
Terrytown LA, *25430* 134 B3
Terrytown NE, *646* 33 F2
Terryville CT, *5360* 149 D1
Terryville NY, *10589* 149 D3
Tesuque NM, *909* 49 D2
Teton ID, *569* 23 F4
Teton Co. ID, *5999* 23 F4
Teton Co. MT, *6445* 15 E3
Teton Co. WY, *18251* 24 A3
Tetonia ID, *247* 23 F4
Teutopolis IL, *1559* 98 C2
Tewksbury MA, *28851* 95 E1
Texarkana AR, *26448* 116 C4
Texarkana TX, *34782* 116 C4
Texas MA, *1300* 150 B2
Texas City TX, *41521* 132 B4
Texas Co. MO, *23003* 107 E1
Texas Co. OK, *20107* 50 A1
Texhoma OK, *935* 50 A1
Texico NM, *1065* 49 F4
Thatcher AZ, *4022* 55 E2
Thaxton MS, *513* 118 C3
Thayer IL, *750* 98 B1
Thayer KS, *500* 106 A1
Thayer MO, *2201* 107 F3
Thayer Co. NE, *6055* 35 E4
Thayne WY, *341* 31 F1
The Colony TX, *26531* 59 F2
The Dalles OR, *12156* 21 D2
Thedford NE, *211* 34 C2
The Hills TX, *1492* 61 E1
Theodore AL, *6811* 135 E2
The Pinery CO, *7253* 41 E1
The Plains OH, *2931* 101 E2
Theresa NY, *812* 79 E1
Theresa WI, *1252* 74 C2
Thermal CA, *1400* 53 E3
Thermalito CA, *6045* 36 C1
Thermopolis WY, *3172* 24 C4
The Village OK, *10157* 51 E3
The Vil. of Indian Hill OH, *5907* 204 C2
The Woodlands TX, *55649* 132 A2
Thibodaux LA, *14431* 134 A3
Thief River Falls MN, *8410* 19 F2
Thiells NY, *4758* 148 B2
Thiensville WI, *3254* 74 C3
Thomas OK, *1238* 51 D2
Thomas WV, *452* 102 B2
Thomasboro IL, *1233* 88 C4
Thomas Co. GA, *42737* 137 E1
Thomas Co. KS, *8180* 42 B2
Thomas Co. NE, *729* 34 C2
Thomaston CT, *3200* 149 D1
Thomaston GA, *9411* 128 C1
Thomaston ME, *2714* 82 C3
Thomaston NY, *2607* 241 G3
Thomasville AL, *4649* 127 E3
Thomasville GA, *18162* 137 E1
Thomasville NC, *19788* 112 B4
Thompson IA, *596* 72 C2
Thompson ND, *1006* 19 E3
Thompson Falls MT, *1321* 14 C3
Thompsons Sta. TN, *1283* 109 F4
Thompsontown PA, *711* 93 D4
Thompsonville CT, *1600* 150 A2
Thompsonville IL, *571* 98 C4
Thompsonville MI, *457* 69 F4
Thomson GA, *6828* 121 E4
Thomson IL, *559* 88 A1
Thonotosassa FL, *6091* 140 C2
Thoreau NM, *1863* 48 B3
Thorndale PA, *3561* 146 B3
Thorndale TX, *1278* 61 E1
Thorne Bay AK, *557* 155 E4
Thornton AR, *517* 117 E4
Thornton CA, *850* 36 C3
Thornton CO, *82384* 41 E1
Thornton TX, *525* 59 F4
Thorntown IN, *1562* 89 E4
Thornville OH, *731* 101 D1
Thornwood NY, *5980* 148 B2
Thorofare NJ, *1500* 146 C3
Thorp WI, *1536* 67 F4
Thorsby AL, *1820* 127 F1
Thousand Oaks CA, *117005* 52 B2
Thousand Palms CA, *5120* 53 E3
Thrall TX, *710* 61 E1
Three Bridges NJ, *850* 147 D1
Three Forks MT, *1728* 23 F1
Three Oaks MI, *1829* 89 E1
Three Pts. AZ, *5273* 55 D3
Three Rivers CA, *2248* 45 D3
Three Rivers MA, *2939* 150 A2
Three Rivers MI, *7328* 89 F1
Three Rivers TX, *1878* 61 D4
Three Way TN, *1375* 108 C4
Throckmorton TX, *905* 59 D2
Throckmorton Co. TX, *1850* 59 D2
Throop PA, *4010* 261 E2
Thurmont MD, *5588* 144 A1
Thurston OH, *555* 101 D1
Thurston Co. NE, *7171* 35 F2
Thurston Co. WA, *207355* 12 C4

Tiana NY, *2200* 149 E3
Tiburon CA, *8666* 259 B2
Tice FL, *4538* 142 C1
Tickfaw LA, *617* 134 B2
Ticonderoga NY, *2800* 81 D3
Tidioute PA, *792* 92 B2
Tierra Amarilla NM, *90* 48 C1
Tierra Verde FL, *3574* 266 A3
Tieton WA, *1154* 13 D4
Tiffin IA, *975* 87 E1
Tiffin OH, *18135* 90 C3
Tift Co. GA, *38407* 129 E4
Tifton GA, *15060* 129 E4
Tigard OR, *41223* 20 C2
Tigerton WI, *764* 68 B4
Tignall GA, *653* 121 E4
Tijeras NM, *474* 48 C3
Tiki Island TX, *1016* 132 B4
Tilden IL, *922* 98 B4
Tilden NE, *1078* 35 E2
Tilden TX, *500* 61 D4
Tilghman MD, *854* 145 D4
Tillamook OR, *4352* 20 B2
Tillamook Co. OR, *24262* 20 B1
Tillman Co. OK, *9287* 51 D4
Tillmans Corner AL, *15685* 135 E2
Tillson NY, *1709* 94 B3
Tilton IL, *2976* 89 D4
Tilton NH, *3231* 81 F4
Tiltonsville OH, *1329* 91 F4
Timber Lake SD, *443* 26 C2
Timberlake VA, *10683* 112 C1
Timberon NM, *309* 57 D2
Timberville VA, *1739* 102 C3
Timmonsville SC, *2315* 122 C3
Timpson TX, *1094* 124 C3
Tinley Park IL, *48401* 89 D2
Tinton Falls NJ, *15053* 147 E2
Tioga LA, *1500* 125 E4
Tioga ND, *1125* 18 A2
Tioga PA, *622* 93 D1
Tioga TX, *754* 59 F1
Tioga Co. NY, *51784* 93 E1
Tioga Co. PA, *41373* 93 D1
Tionesta PA, *615* 92 A2
Tippah Co. MS, *20826* 118 C2
Tipp City OH, *9221* 100 B1
Tippecanoe Co. IN, *148955* 89 E4

Bakersville B1	Fallsington A2	Mercerville B1	Trenton B2
Ewing A1	Lawrenceville B1	Morrisville A2	W. Trenton A1
Ewingville A1	Lewisville B1	Slackwood B1	White Horse B2

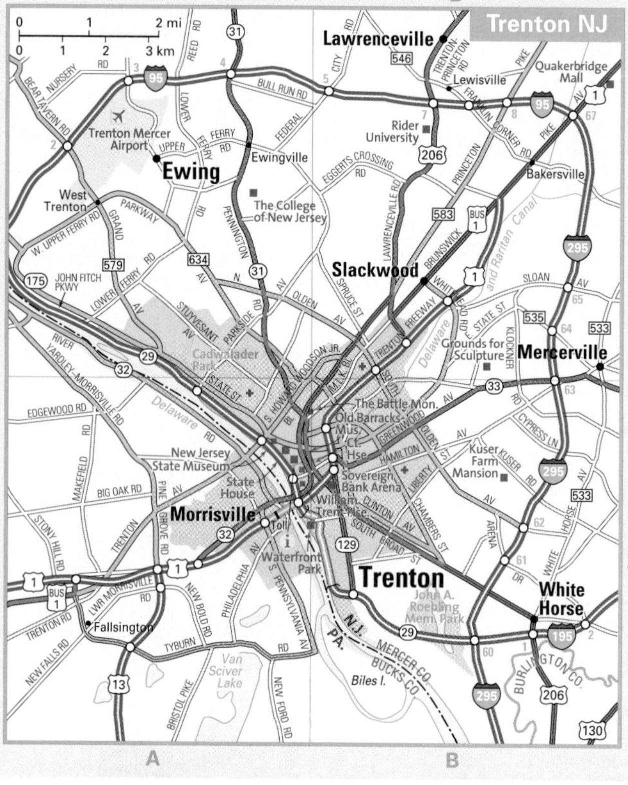

Trenton NJ
A
B
1
2
0 1 2 mi
0 1 2 3 km
Lawrenceville
Lewisville
Quakerbridge Mall
Rider University
Trenton Mercer Airport
Ewing
Ewingville
Bakersville
West Trenton
The College of New Jersey
Slackwood
Mercerville
Cadwalader Park
Grounds for Sculpture
The Battle Mon.
Old Barracks Mus.
New Jersey State Museum
State House
Sovereign Bank Arena
Kuser Farm Mansion
Morrisville
Trenton
Waterfront Park
John A. Roebling Mem. Park
White Horse
Fallsington
Van Sciver Lake
Biles I.
Delaware

Tipton CA, *1790* 45 D3
Tipton IN, *5251* 89 F4
Tipton IA, *3155* 87 F1
Tipton MO, *3261* 97 D3
Tipton OK, *916* 51 D4
Tipton PA, *1225* 92 C3
Tipton Co. IN, *16577* 89 F4
Tipton Co. TN, *51271* 118 B1
Tiptonville TN, *2439* 108 B3
Tishomingo OK, *3162* 51 F4
Tishomingo Co. MS, *19163* 119 D2
Tiskilwa IL, *787* 88 B2
Titonka IA, *584* 72 C3
Titus Co. TX, *28118* 124 B1
Titusville FL, *40670* 141 E1
Titusville NJ, *800* 147 D2
Titusville PA, *6146* 92 A2
Tiverton RI, *7282* 151 D4
Tivoli NY, *1163* 94 B2
Toano VA, *1400* 113 F1
Toast NC, *1922* 112 A3
Tobaccoville NC, *2209* 112 A3
Toccoa GA, *9323* 121 D2
Todd Co. KY, *11971* 109 E2
Todd Co. MN, *24426* 66 B1
Todd Co. SD, *9050* 34 C1
Togiak AK, *809* 154 B3
Tohatchi NM, *1037* 48 A2
Tok AK, *1393* 155 D2
Toksook Bay AK, *532* 154 B3
Toledo IL, *1166* 99 D2
Toledo IA, *2539* 87 D1
Toledo OH, *313619* 90 C2
Toledo OR, *3472* 20 B3
Toledo WA, *653* 12 C4
Tolland CT, *800* 150 A3
Tolland Co. CT, *136364* 149 E1
Tolles CT, *650* 149 D1
Tolleson AZ, *4974* 249 A2
Tolono IL, *2700* 99 D1
Toluca IL, *1339* 88 B3
Tomah WI, *8419* 74 A1
Tomahawk WI, *3770* 68 B3
Tomball TX, *9089* 132 A2
Tom Bean TX, *941* 59 F1
Tombstone AZ, *1504* 55 E3
Tome NM, *2211* 48 C4
Tom Green Co. TX, *104010* 58 C4
Tomkins Cove NY, *1400* 148 B2
Tompkins Co. NY, *96501* 79 D4
Tompkinsville KY, *2660* 110 A3
Toms River NJ, *86327* 147 E3
Tonalea AZ, *562* 47 E2
Tonasket WA, *994* 13 E1
Tonawanda NY, *16136* 78 A3
Tonganoxie KS, *2728* 96 B2
Tonica IL, *685* 88 B2
Tonkawa OK, *3299* 51 E1
Tonopah NV, *2627* 37 F3
Tontitown AR, *942* 106 C4
Tooele UT, *22502* 31 E4
Tooele Co. UT, *40735* 31 D4
Tool TX, *2275* 59 F3
Toole Co. MT, *5267* 15 F1
Toombs Co. GA, *26067* 129 F3
Toomsboro GA, *622* 129 E2
Topeka IN, *1159* 89 F2

Topeka KS, *122377* 96 A2
Toppenish WA, *8946* 13 D4
Topsfield MA, *2826* 151 F1
Topsham ME, *6271* 82 B3
Topton PA, *1948* 146 B1
Toquerville UT, *910* 39 D4
Tornado WV, *1111* 101 E4
Tornillo TX, *1609* 56 C4
Toronto OH, *5676* 91 F4
Toronto SD, *202* 27 F3
Torrance CA, *137946* 52 C3
Torrance Co. NM, *16911* 49 D4
Torreon NM, *297* 48 B2
Torreon NM, *244* 48 C4
Torrington CT, *35202* 94 C3
Torrington WY, *5776* 33 F2
Totowa NJ, *9892* 240 A1
Toughkenamon PA, *1375* 146 B3
Toulon IL, *1400* 88 B3
Towaco NJ, *2700* 148 A3
Towanda KS, *1338* 43 F4
Towanda PA, *3024* 93 E1
Towaoc CO, *1097* 40 B4
Tower MN, *479* 64 C3
Tower City ND, *252* 19 E4
Tower City PA, *1396* 93 E4
Tower Hill IL, *609* 98 C2
Tower Lakes IL, *1310* 203 B1
Town and Country MO, *10894* 256 A2
Town Creek AL, *1216* 119 E2
Towner ND, *574* 18 C2
Towner Co. ND, *2876* 19 D1
Town Line NY, *2521* 78 B3
Town 'n Country FL, *72523* 266 B2
Town of Pines IN, *798* 89 E2
Towns Co. GA, *9319* 121 D2
Townsend DE, *346* 145 E1
Townsend MA, *1043* 95 D1
Townsend MT, *1867* 15 F4
Towson MD, *51793* 144 C1
Tracy CA, *56929* 36 C4
Tracy MN, *2268* 72 A1
Tracy City TN, *1679* 120 A1
Tracyton WA, *3267* 262 A3
Traer IA, *1594* 87 E1
Trafalgar IN, *1798* 99 F2
Trafford AL, *523* 119 F4
Trafford PA, *3236* 250 D3
Trail Creek IN, *2296* 89 E2
Traill Co. ND, *8477* 19 E3
Trainer PA, *1901* 146 C3
Tramway NC, *750* 122 C1
Tranquillity CA, *813* 44 C3
Transylvania Co. NC, *29334* 121 E1
Trappe MD, *1146* 145 D4
Trappe PA, *3210* 146 B2
Trapper Creek AK, *423* 154 C3
Traskwood AR, *548* 117 E3
Travelers Rest SC, *4099* 121 E2
Traver CA, *732* 45 D3
Traverse City MI, *14532* 69 F4
Traverse Co. MN, *4134* 27 F1
Travis Co. TX, *812280* 61 E1
Treasure Co. MT, *861* 17 D4
Treasure Island FL, *7450* 140 B3
Trego Co. KS, *3319* 42 C2
Tremont IL, *2029* 88 B4

Tremont PA, *1784* 146 A1
Tremonton UT, *5592* 31 E3
Trempealeau WI, *1319* ......73 F
Trempealeau Co. WI, *27010* 67 F4
Trent SD, *254* 27 F4
Trenton FL, *1617* 138 C3
Trenton GA, *1942* 120 B2
Trenton IL, *2610* 98 B3
Trenton KY, *419* 109 E3
Trenton MI, *19584* 90 C1
Trenton MO, *6216* 86 C4
Trenton NE, *507* 42 B1
Trenton NJ, *85403* 147 D2
Trenton NC, *206* 115 D3
Trenton OH, *8746* 100 B2
Trenton TN, *4683* 108 C4
Trenton TX, *662* 59 F1
Trenton UT, *449* 31 E2
Trent Woods NC, *4192* 115 D3
Treutlen Co. GA, *6854* 129 F2
Trevorton PA, *2010* 93 E3
Trevose PA, *6525* 146 C2
Trexlertown PA, *1000* 146 B1
Treynor IA, *950* 86 A2
Trezevant TN, *901* 108 C4
Triadelphia WV, *817* 91 F4
Triana AL, *458* 119 F2
Triangle VA, *5500* 144 A4
Tribes Hill NY, *1024* 94 A1
Tribune KS, *835* 42 B3
Tri-City OR, *3519* 28 B1
Trigg Co. KY, *12597* 109 D3
Tri-Lakes IN, *3925* 90 A2
Trilby FL, *850* 140 C1
Trimble CO, *650* 40 B4
Trimble TN, *728* 108 C3
Trimble Co. KY, *8125* 100 A3
Trimont MN, *754* 72 B2
Trinidad CO, *9078* 41 E4
Trinidad TX, *1091* 59 F3
Trinity AL, *1841* 119 F2
Trinity NC, *6690* 112 B4
Trinity TX, *2721* 132 A1
Trinity Co. CA, *13022* 28 B4
Trinity Co. TX, *13779* 132 B1
Trion GA, *1993* 120 B2
Tripoli IA, *1310* 73 E4
Tripp SD, *711* 35 E1
Tripp Co. SD, *6430* 26 C4
Triumph LA, *3358* 134 C4
Trona CA, *650* 45 E4
Trooper PA, *6061* 146 C2
Trophy Club TX, *6350* 207 B1
Tropic UT, *508* 39 E4
Trotwood OH, *27420* 100 B1
Troup TX, *1949* 124 B3
Troup Co. GA, *58779* 128 C1
Trousdale Co. TN, *7259* 109 F3
Trout Creek MT, *261* 14 C3
Troutdale OR, *13777* 20 C2
Troutdale VA, *1230* 111 F3
Trout Lake WA, *494* 21 D1
Troutman NC, *1592* 112 A4
Trout Valley IL, *599* 203 A1
Troutville VA, *432* 112 B1
Trowbridge Park MI, *2012* 69 D1
Troy AL, *13935* 128 A3

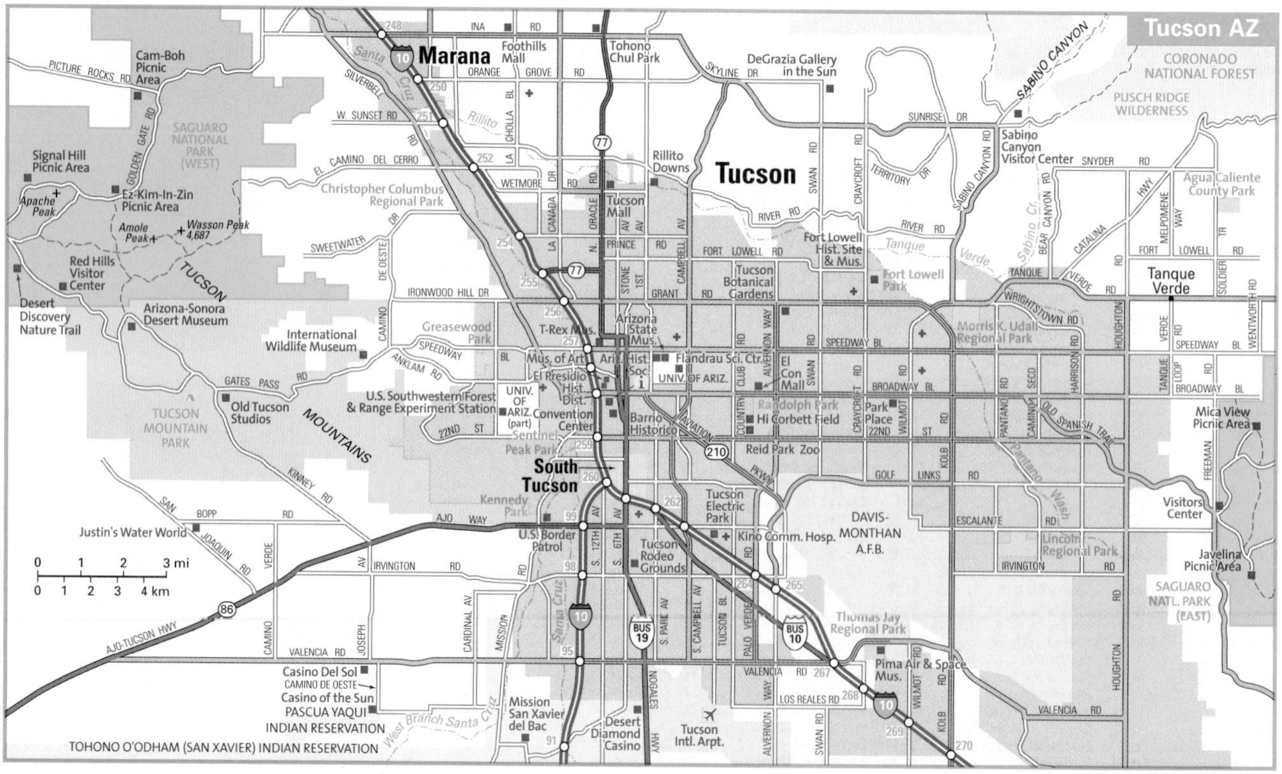

Tucson AZ
Marana
Foothills Mall
Tohono Chul Park
DeGrazia Gallery in the Sun
CORONADO NATIONAL FOREST
PUSCH RIDGE WILDERNESS
Cam-Boh Picnic Area
SAGUARO NATIONAL PARK (WEST)
Signal Hill Picnic Area
Christopher Columbus Regional Park
Rillito Downs
Tucson
Sabino Canyon Visitor Center
Agua Caliente County Park
Apache Peak
Ez-Kim-In-Zin Picnic Area
Amole Peak
Wasson Peak 4,687
Tucson Mall
Fort Lowell Hist. Site & Mus.
Red Hills Visitor Center
TUCSON
Tucson Botanical Gardens
Fort Lowell Park
Tanque Verde
Desert Discovery Nature Trail
Arizona-Sonora Desert Museum
Greasewood Park
T-Rex Mus.
Arizona State Mus.
Morris K. Udall Regional Park
International Wildlife Museum
Mus. of Art
Ariz. Hist. Soc.
Flandrau Sci. Ctr.
UNIV. OF ARIZ.
El Con Mall
El Presidio Hist. Dist.
U.S. Southwestern Forest & Range Experiment Station
UNIV. OF ARIZ. (part)
Convention Center
Old Tucson Studios
TUCSON MOUNTAIN PARK
MOUNTAINS
Barrio Historico
Randolph Park
Hi Corbett Field
Park Place
Mica View Picnic Area
Sentinel Peak Park
Reid Park Zoo
South Tucson
Kennedy Park
Tucson Electric Park
DAVIS-MONTHAN A.F.B.
Visitors Center
Justin's Water World
U.S. Border Patrol
Kino Comm. Hosp.
Lincoln Regional Park
Tucson Rodeo Grounds
Javelina Picnic Area
SAGUARO NATL. PARK (EAST)
0 1 2 3 mi
0 1 2 3 4 km
Thomas Jay Regional Park
Casino Del Sol
Casino of the Sun
PASCUA YAQUI INDIAN RESERVATION
Pima Air & Space Mus.
Mission San Xavier del Bac
Desert Diamond Casino
Tucson Intl. Arpt.
TOHONO O'ODHAM (SAN XAVIER) INDIAN RESERVATION

Entries in **bold black** indicate counties or parishes. Entries in **bold color** indicate cities with detailed inset maps.

Tulsa OK

Vicksburg MS

Waco TX

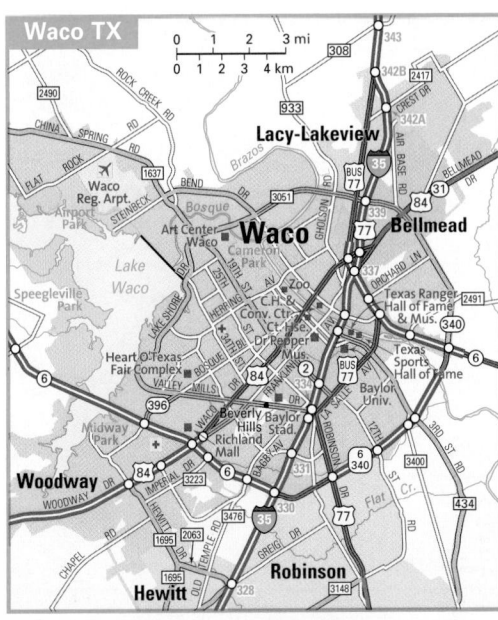

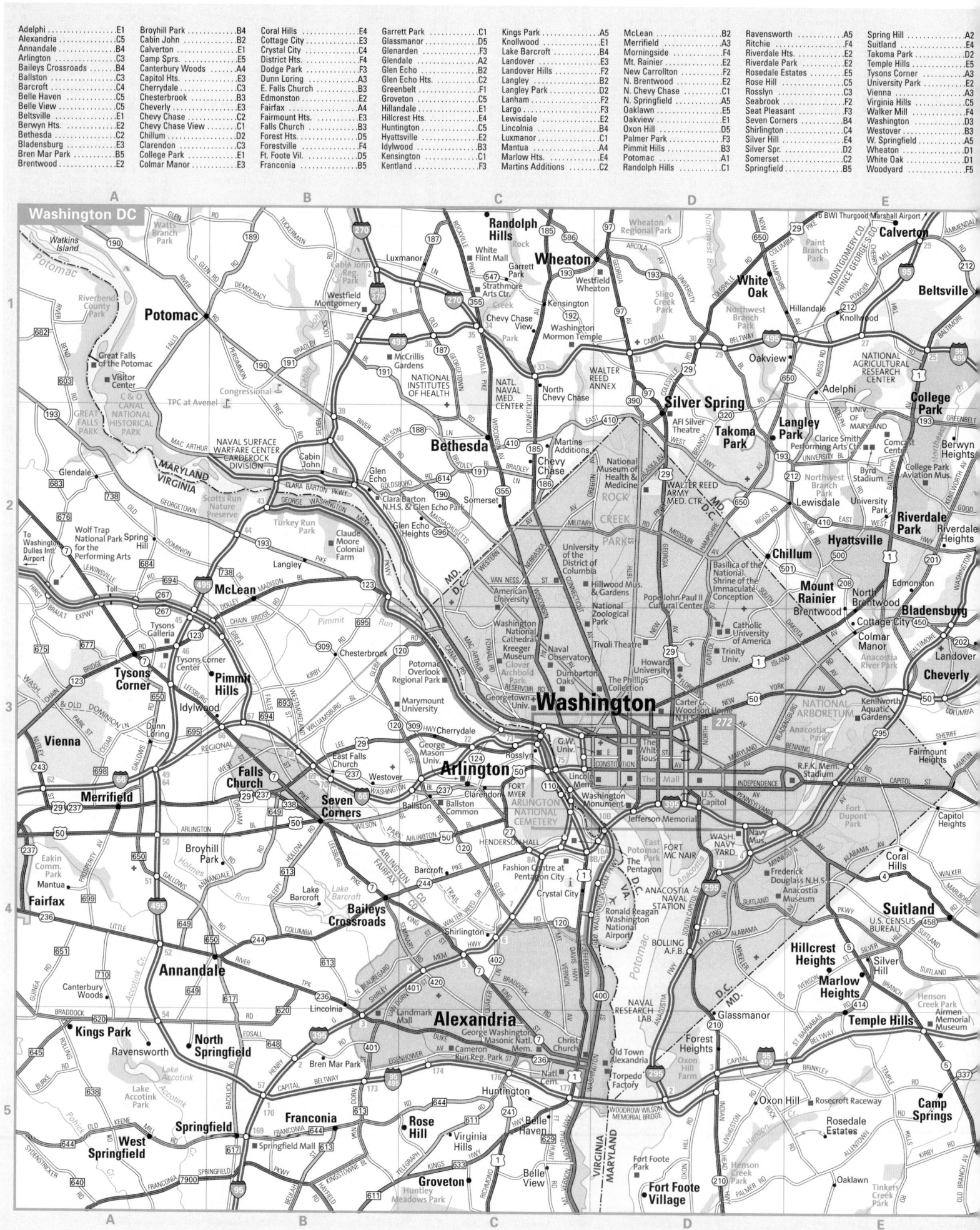

Entries in **bold black** indicate counties or parishes. Entries in **bold color** indicate cities with detailed inset maps.

Vermilion Parish–Waynesboro 271

POINTS OF INTEREST

Entries in **bold black** indicate counties or parishes. Entries in **bold color** indicate cities with detailed inset maps.

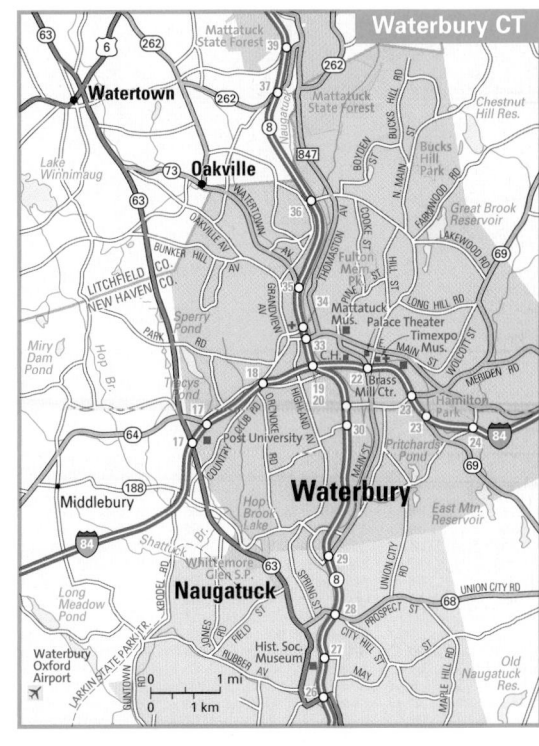

Waterbury CT

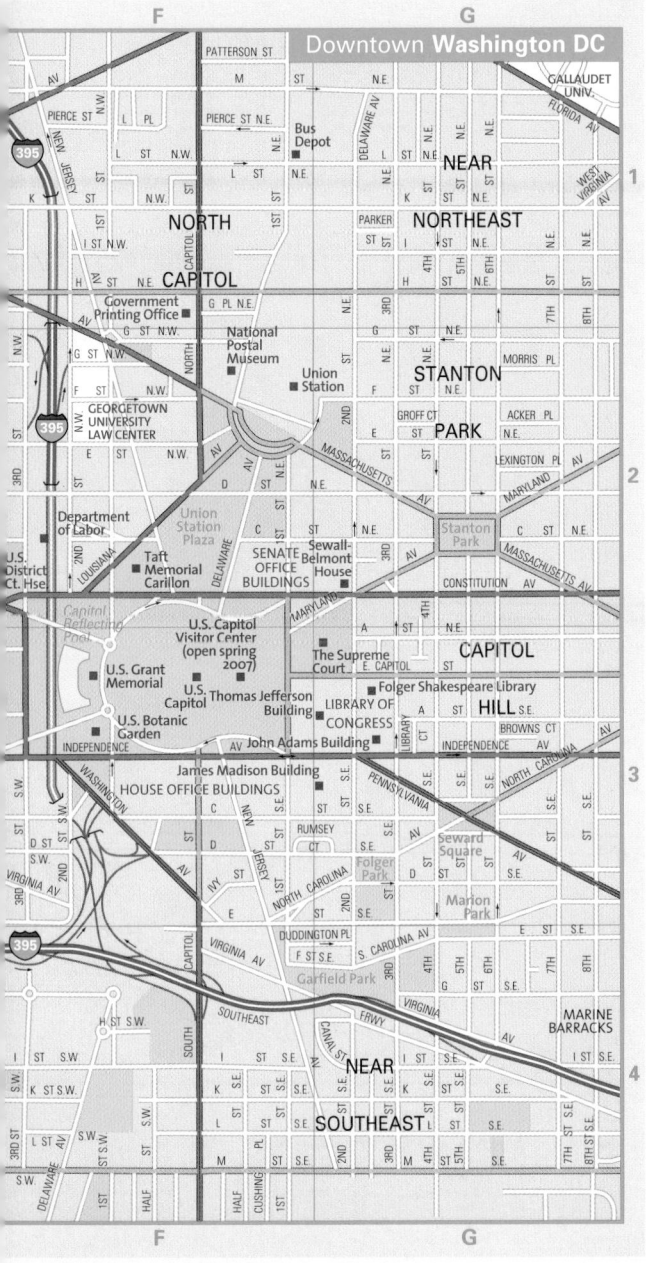

Downtown Washington DC

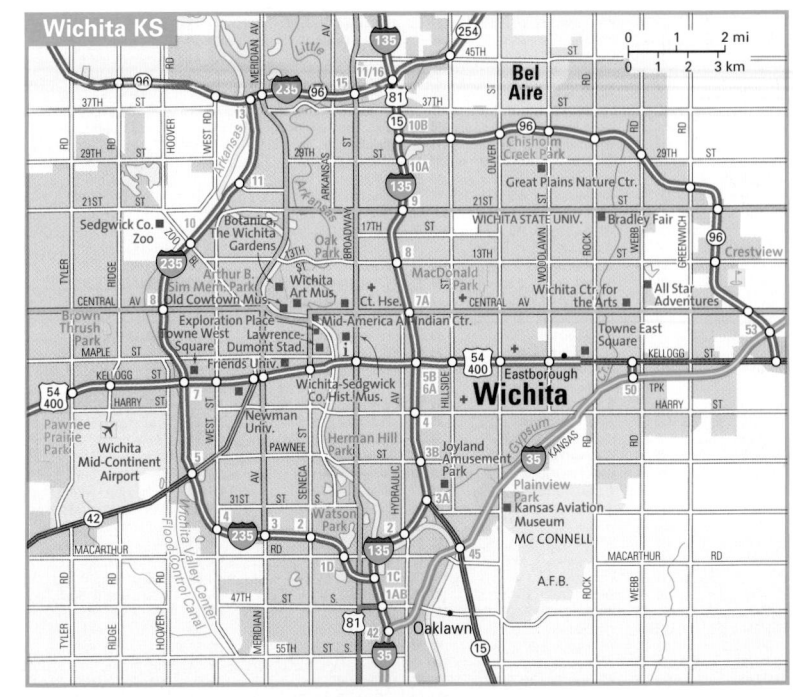

Wichita KS

Williamsburg VA

Wilmington DE

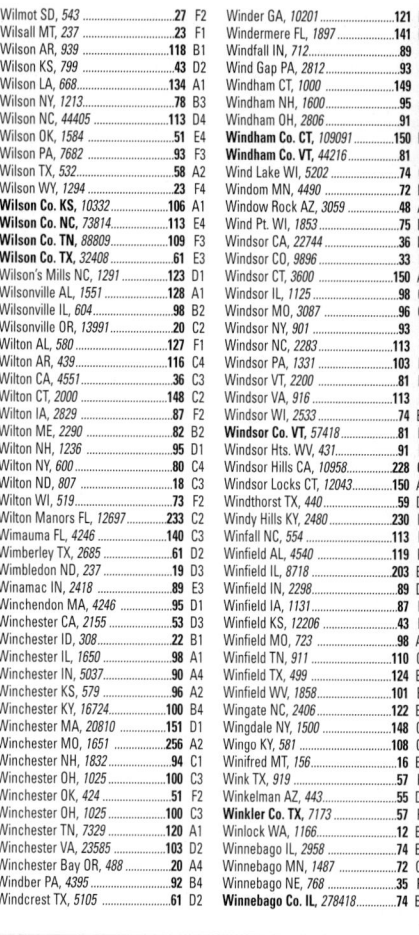

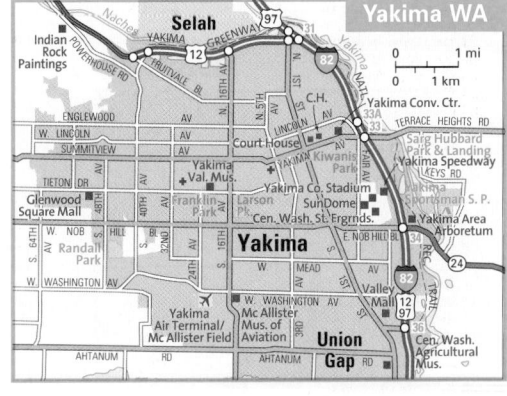

Auburn C2
Bramanville D2
Chaffinville C1
Cherry Valley C2
Dorothy Pond D2
E. Millbury D2
Edgemere D2
Leicester C2
Millbury D2
Morningdale D1
Pondville C2
Rochdale C2
Stoneville C2
Worcester C1

Worcester MA

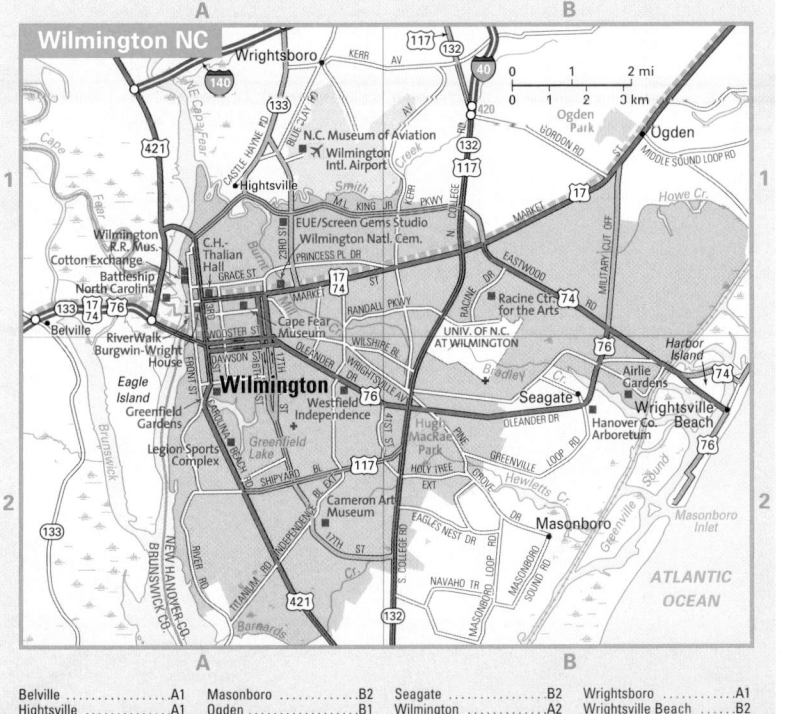

Wilmington NC

Belville A1
Hightsville A1
Masonboro B2
Ogden B1
Seagate B2
Wilmington A2
Wrightsboro A1
Wrightsville Beach ...B2

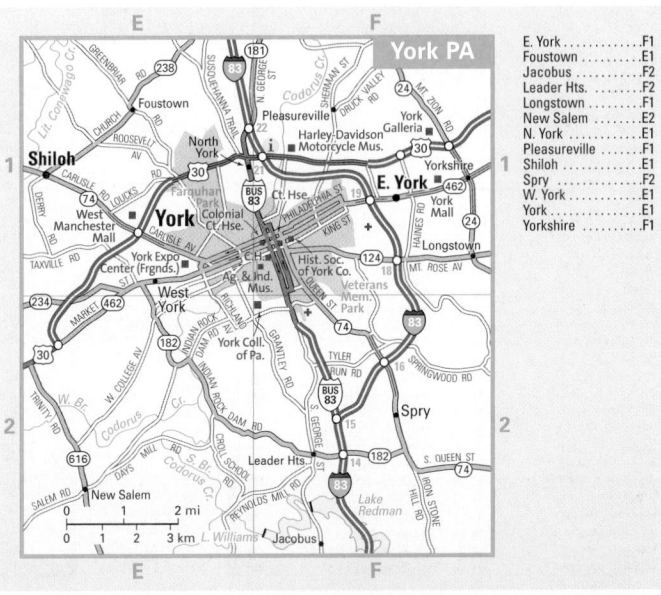

Yakima WA

York PA

E. York F1
Foustown E1
Jacobus F2
Leader Hts. F2
Longstown F1
New Salem E2
N. York E1
Pleasureville E1
Shiloh F2
Spry F2
W. York E1
York F1
Yorkshire F1

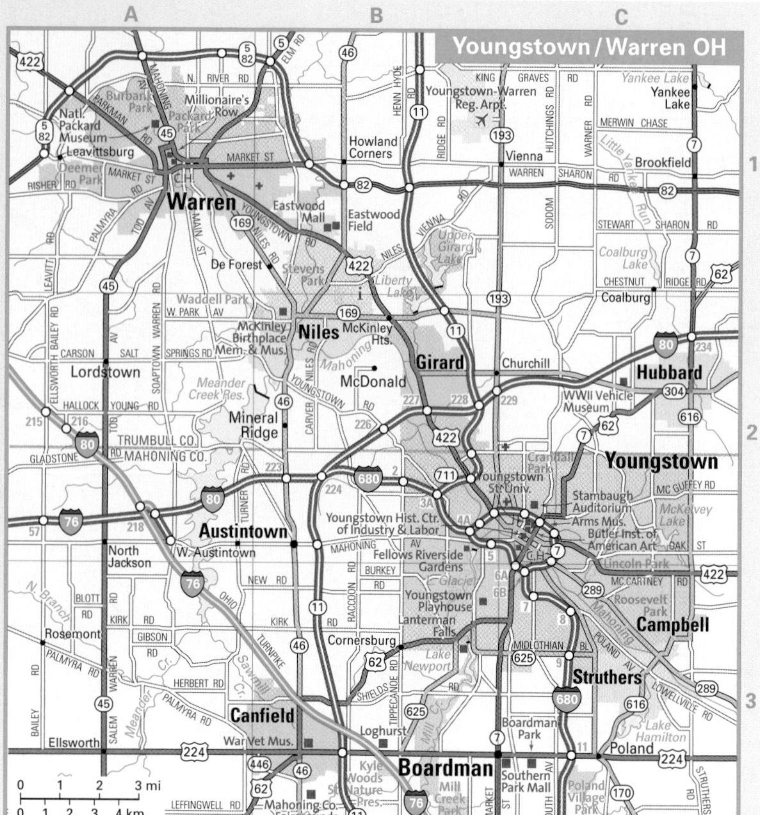
Youngstown / Warren OH
Warren
Niles
Girard
Hubbard
Youngstown
Austintown
Campbell
Struthers
Canfield
Boardman
Lordstown
McDonald
Mineral Ridge
Brookfield
Vienna
Howland Corners
Youngstown-Warren Reg. Arpt.
Yankee Lake
Poland
Leavittsburg
De Forest
Churchill
Coalburg
Cornersburg
Ellsworth
Rosemont
North Jackson
W. Austintown
Eastwood Mall
Mill Creek Park
Southern Park Mall
Mahoning Co. Fairgrounds
0 1 2 3 mi
0 1 2 3 4 km

Austintown B2	Cornersburg B3	Lordstown A2	Rosemont A3
Boardman B3	De Forest B1	McDonald B2	Struthers C3
Brookfield C1	Ellsworth A3	McKinley Hts. B2	Vienna C1
Campbell C3	Girard B2	Mineral Ridge B2	Warren A1
Canfield B3	Howland Corners B1	Niles B2	W. Austintown A2
Churchill C2	Hubbard C2	N. Jackson A2	Yankee Lake C1
Coalburg C1	Leavittsburg A1	Poland C3	Youngstown C2

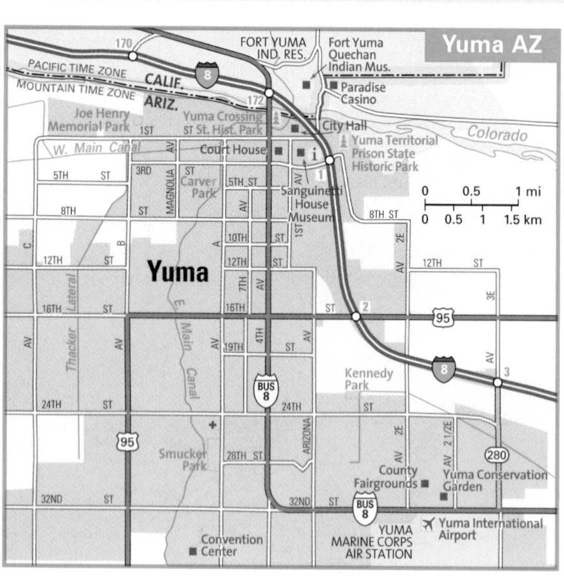
Yuma AZ
FORT YUMA IND. RES.
Fort Yuma Quechan Indian Mus.
PACIFIC TIME ZONE
MOUNTAIN TIME ZONE
CALIF.
ARIZ.
Paradise Casino
Joe Henry Memorial Park
Yuma Crossing St. Hist. Park
City Hall
Colorado
Court House
Yuma Territorial Prison State Historic Park
Carver Park
Sanguinetti House Museum
Yuma
Kennedy Park
Smucker Park
County Fairgrounds
Yuma Conservation Garden
Convention Center
YUMA MARINE CORPS AIR STATION
Yuma International Airport
0 0.5 1 mi
0 0.5 1 1.5 km

Wycombe PA, *650*....................**146** C2
Wykoff MN, *460*....................**73** E2
Wylie TX, *15132*....................**59** F2
Wymore NE, *1656*....................**43** F1
Wynantskill NY, *3018*....................**188** E2
Wyncote PA, *3046*....................**248** C1
Wyndmere ND, *533*....................**27** F1
Wynne AR, *8615*....................**118** A1
Wynnewood OK, *2367*....................**51** E4
Wynona OK, *531*....................**51** F1
Wyocena WI, *668*....................**74** B2
Wyodak WY, *125*....................**25** E3
Wyola MT, *186*....................**24** C2
Wyoming DE, *1141*....................**145** E2
Wyoming IL, *1424*....................**88** B3
Wyoming IA, *626*....................**87** F1
Wyoming MI, *69368*....................**75** F3
Wyoming MN, *3048*....................**67** D3
Wyoming NY, *513*....................**78** B3
Wyoming OH, *8261*....................**204** B1
Wyoming PA, *3221*....................**261** B1
Wyoming RI, *475*....................**150** C4
Wyoming Co. NY, *43424*....................**78** B4
Wyoming Co. PA, *28080*....................**93** E2
Wyoming Co. WV, *25708*....................**111** F1
Wyomissing PA, *11155*....................**146** A2
Wythe Co. VA, *27599*....................**112** A2
Wytheville VA, *7804*....................**112** A2

X

Xenia IL, *407*....................**98** C3
Xenia OH, *24164*....................**100** C1

Y

Yachats OR, *617*....................**20** B3
Yacolt WA, *1055*....................**20** C1
Yadkin Co. NC, *36348*....................**112** A3
Yadkinville NC, *2818*....................**112** A4
Yah-Tah-Hey NM, *580*....................**48** A2
Yakima WA, *71845*....................**13** D4
Yakima Co. WA, *222581*....................**13** D4
Yakutat AK, *680*....................**155** D3
Yalaha FL, *1175*....................**140** C1
Yale MI, *2063*....................**76** C3
Yale OK, *1342*....................**51** F2
Yalesville CT, *3600*....................**149** D1
Yalobusha Co. MS, *13051*....................**118** B3
Yamhill OR, *794*....................**20** B2
Yamhill Co. OR, *84992*....................**20** B2
Yampa CO, *443*....................**40** C1
Yancey Co. NC, *17774*....................**111** E4
Yanceyville NC, *2091*....................**112** C3
Yankeetown FL, *629*....................**138** C4
Yankton SD, *13528*....................**35** E1
Yankton Co. SD, *21652*....................**35** E1
Yaphank NY, *5025*....................**149** D3
Yardley PA, *2498*....................**147** D2
Yardville NJ, *9208*....................**147** D2
Yarmouth ME, *3560*....................**82** B3
Yarmouth MA, *2100*....................**151** F3
Yarmouth Port MA, *5395*....................**151** F3
Yarnell AZ, *645*....................**47** D4
Yarrow Pt. WA, *1008*....................**262** B3
Yates Ctr. KS, *1599*....................**96** A4
Yates City IL, *725*....................**88** A3
Yates Co. NY, *24621*....................**78** C4
Yatesville GA, *408*....................**129** D1
Yatesville PA, *649*....................**261** C2
Yavapai Co. AZ, *167517*....................**47** D4
Yazoo City MS, *14550*....................**126** B2
Yazoo Co. MS, *28149*....................**126** B2
Yeadon PA, *11762*....................**146** C3
Yeagertown PA, *1035*....................**93** D3
Yell Co. AR, *21139*....................**117** D2
Yellow House PA, 475....................**146** B2
Yellow Medicine Co. MN, *11080*..**66** A4
Yellow Sprs. MD, *1100*....................**144** A1
Yellow Sprs. OH, *3761*....................**100** C1
Yellowstone Co. MT, *129352*....................**24** C1
Yellville AR, *1312*....................**107** E3
Yelm WA, *3289*....................**12** C4
Yemassee SC, *807*....................**130** C2
Yerington NV, *2883*....................**37** E2
Yerkes KY, *500*....................**111** D2
Yermo CA, *900*....................**53** D1
Yoakum TX, *5731*....................**61** E3
Yoakum Co. TX, *7322*....................**57** F2
Yoder WY, *169*....................**33** F2
Yoe PA, *1022*....................**103** E1
Yolo CA, *550*....................**36** B2
Yolo Co. CA, *168660*....................**36** B2
Yoncalla OR, *1052*....................**20** B4
Yonkers NY, *196086*....................**148** B3
Yorba Linda CA, *58918*....................**229** F3
York AL, *2854*....................**127** D2
York NE, *8081*....................**35** E4
York NY, *450*....................**78** C3
York PA, *40862*....................**103** E1
York SC, *6985*....................**122** A2
York Beach ME, *1400*....................**82** B4
York Co. ME, *186742*....................**82** B4
York Co. NE, *14598*....................**35** E4
York Co. PA, *381751*....................**103** E1
York Co. SC, *164614*....................**122** A2
York Co. VA, *56297*....................**113** F2
York Harbor ME, *3321*....................**82** B4
York Haven PA, *809*....................**93** E4
Yorkshire NY, *1403*....................**78** B4
Yorkshire VA, *6732*....................**144** A3
York Sprs. PA, *574*....................**103** E1
Yorktown IN, *4785*....................**89** F4
Yorktown NY, *14891*....................**148** B2
Yorktown TX, *2271*....................**61** E3
Yorktown VA, *203*....................**113** F2
Yorktown Hts. NY, *7972*....................**148** B2
York Vil. ME, *2000*....................**82** B4
Yorkville IL, *6189*....................**88** C2
Yorkville OH, *1230*....................**91** F4
Young AZ, *561*....................**47** E4
Young Co. TX, *17943*....................**59** D2
Young Harris GA, *604*....................**121** D2
Youngstown NY, *1957*....................**78** A3
Youngstown OH, *82026*....................**91** F3
Youngstown PA, *400*....................**92** B4
Youngsville LA, *3992*....................**133** F2
Youngsville NC, *651*....................**113** D4
Youngsville PA, *1834*....................**92** B1
Youngtown AZ, *3010*....................**249** A1
Youngwood PA, *4138*....................**92** A4
Yountville CA, *2916*....................**36** B3
Ypsilanti MI, *22362*....................**90** C1
Yreka CA, *7290*....................**28** C2
Yuba City CA, *36758*....................**36** C2
Yuba Co. CA, *60219*....................**36** C2
Yucaipa CA, *41207*....................**53** D2
Yucca Valley CA, *16865*....................**53** E2
Yukon OK, *21043*....................**51** E3
Yulee FL, *8392*....................**139** D2
Yuma AZ, *77515*....................**53** F4
Yuma CO, *3285*....................**42** A1
Yuma Co. AZ, *160026*....................**54** A2
Yuma Co. CO, *9841*....................**34** A4
Yutan NE, *1216*....................**35** F3

Z

Zacata VA, *450*....................**103** E4
Zachary LA, *11275*....................**134** A1
Zanesville IN, *602*....................**90** A3
Zanesville OH, *25586*....................**101** E1
Zap ND, *231*....................**18** B3
Zapata TX, *4856*....................**63** D3
Zapata Co. TX, *12182*....................**63** D3
Zavala Co. TX, *11600*....................**60** C3
Zavalla TX, *647*....................**132** C1
Zearing IA, *617*....................**87** D1
Zeb OK, *498*....................**106** B4
Zebulon GA, *1181*....................**128** C1
Zebulon KY, *700*....................**111** E1
Zebulon NC, *4046*....................**113** D4
Zeeland MI, *5805*....................**75** F3
Zeigler IL, *1669*....................**98** C4
Zelienople PA, *4123*....................**92** A3
Zephyr Cove NV, *1649*....................**37** D2
Zephyrhills FL, *10833*....................**140** C2
Zia Pueblo NM, *646*....................**48** C3
Ziebach Co. SD, *2519*....................**26** B2
Zillah WA, *2198*....................**13** E4
Zimmerman MN, *2851*....................**66** C3
Zion IL, *22866*....................**75** D4
Zion KY, *550*....................**109** E1
Zion PA, *2054*....................**92** C3
Zion Crossroads VA, 375....................**102** C4
Zionsville IN, *8775*....................**99** F1
Zolfo Sprs. FL, *1641*....................**140** C3
Zumbrota MN, *2789*....................**73** D1
Zuni Pueblo NM, *6367*....................**48** A3
Zwolle LA, *1783*....................**125** D4

PUERTO RICO

Aceitunas PR, *1688*....................**187** D1
Adjuntas PR, *4980*....................**187** D1
Aguada PR, *3871*....................**187** D1
Aguadilla PR, *16776*....................**187** D1
Aguas Buenas PR, *4368*....................**187** E1
Aguilita PR, *4922*....................**187** E1
Aibonito PR, *9269*....................**187** E1
Añasco PR, *5880*....................**187** D1
Arecibo PR, *9318*....................**187** E1
Arroyo PR, *7244*....................**187** E1
Bajadero PR, *3877*....................**187** E1
Barceloneta PR, *4253*....................**187** E1
Barranquitas PR, *2910*....................**187** E1
Bayamón PR, *203499*....................**187** E1
Betances PR, *835*....................**187** D1
Boquerón PR, *1218*....................**187** D1
Cabo Rojo PR, *10610*....................**187** D1
Caguas PR, *88680*....................**187** E1
Camuy PR, *4013*....................**187** D1
Canóvanas PR, *8069*....................**187** F1
Carolina PR, *168164*....................**187** F1
Cataño PR, *30071*....................**187** E1
Cayey PR, *19940*....................**187** E1
Cayuco PR, *1284*....................**187** D1
Ceiba PR, *6277*....................**187** E1
Ceiba PR, *3698*....................**187** E1
Ciales PR, *3082*....................**187** E1
Cidra PR, *4881*....................**187** E1
Coamo PR, *12356*....................**187** E1
Coco PR, *5803*....................**187** E1
Comerío PR, *4478*....................**187** E1
Comunas PR, *2027*....................**187** F1
Coquí PR, *3590*....................**187** E1
Corazón PR, *2925*....................**187** E1
Corozal PR, *11444*....................**187** E1
Coto Norte PR, *1381*....................**187** E1
Daguao PR, *1488*....................**187** F1
Dorado PR, *12747*....................**187** E1
Duque PR, *1529*....................**187** F1
El Mangó PR, *1979*....................**187** F1
Esperanza PR, *1092*....................**187** F1
Fajardo PR, *33286*....................**187** F1
Florida PR, *5652*....................**187** E1
Guánica PR, *9247*....................**187** D1
Guayabal PR, *2377*....................**187** E1
Guayama PR, *21624*....................**187** E1
Guayanilla PR, *5110*....................**187** D1
Guaynabo PR, *78806*....................**187** E1
Gurabo PR, *9046*....................**187** F1
Hatillo PR, *5321*....................**187** D1
Hormigueros PR, *12444*....................**187** D1
Humacao PR, *20682*....................**187** F1
Isabela PR, *12818*....................**187** D1
Jagual PR, *1402*....................**187** E1
Jayuya PR, *3516*....................**187** E1
Jobos PR, *3475*....................**187** E1
Juana Diaz PR, *9505*....................**187** E1
Juncos PR, *8978*....................**187** F1
Lajas PR, *5036*....................**187** D1
La Parguera PR, *1141*....................**187** D1
La Plena PR, *1036*....................**187** E1
Lares PR, *7042*....................**187** D1
Las Marías PR, *1823*....................**187** D1
Las Marías PR, *988*....................**187** D1
Las Piedras PR, *6352*....................**187** F1
Levittown PR, *30140*....................**187** E1
Loíza PR, *4123*....................**187** F1
Los Llanos PR, *2301*....................**187** E1
Luquillo PR, *7947*....................**187** F1
Manatí PR, *16173*....................**187** E1
Maricao PR, *1123*....................**187** D1
Maunabo PR, *2075*....................**187** F1
Mayagüez PR, *78647*....................**187** D1
Moca PR, *4757*....................**187** D1
Mora PR, *1857*....................**187** D1
Morovis PR, *2285*....................**187** E1
Naguabo PR, *4432*....................**187** F1
Naranjito PR, *1931*....................**187** E1
Orocovis PR, *909*....................**187** E1
Palmarejo PR, *1087*....................**187** D1
Palomas PR, *1742*....................**187** D1
Patillas PR, *4091*....................**187** E1
Peñuelas PR, *6712*....................**187** D1
Playita PR, *2192*....................**187** F1
Pole Ojea PR, *1829*....................**187** D1
Ponce PR, *155038*....................**187** E1
Potala Pastillo PR, *3819*....................**187** E1
Puerto Real PR, *6166*....................**187** D1
Punta Santiago PR, *5803*....................**187** F1
Quebrada PR, *1130*....................**187** D1
Quebradillas PR, *5319*....................**187** D1
Rafael Capó PR, *1863*....................**187** D1
Rincón PR, *1436*....................**187** D1
Río Grande PR, *13467*....................**187** F1
Sabana Eneas PR, *1847*....................**187** D1
Sabana Grande PR, *8784*....................**187** D1
Sabana Hoyos PR, *1823*....................**187** E1
Salinas PR, *6141*....................**187** E1
San Antonio PR, *6456*....................**187** D1
San Antonio PR, *2300*....................**187** D1
San Germán PR, *12033*....................**187** D1
San Isidro PR, *8071*....................**187** F1
San Juan PR, *421958*....................**187** E1
San Lorenzo PR, *8947*....................**187** F1
San Sebastián PR, *11598*....................**187** D1
Santa Isabel PR, *6993*....................**187** E1
Santo Domingo PR, *3633*....................**187** D1
Tallaboa PR, *1150*....................**187** D1
Toa Alta PR, *4368*....................**187** E1
Trujillo Alto PR, *50841*....................**187** E1
Utuado PR, *9887*....................**187** E1
Vázquez PR, *2297*....................**187** E1
Vega Alta PR, *11755*....................**187** E1
Vega Baja PR, *28811*....................**187** E1
Vieques PR, *4325*....................**187** F1
Villalba PR, *4388*....................**187** E1
Yabucoa PR, *6636*....................**187** F1
Yauco PR, *19609*....................**187** D1
Yaurel PR, *1468*....................**187** E1

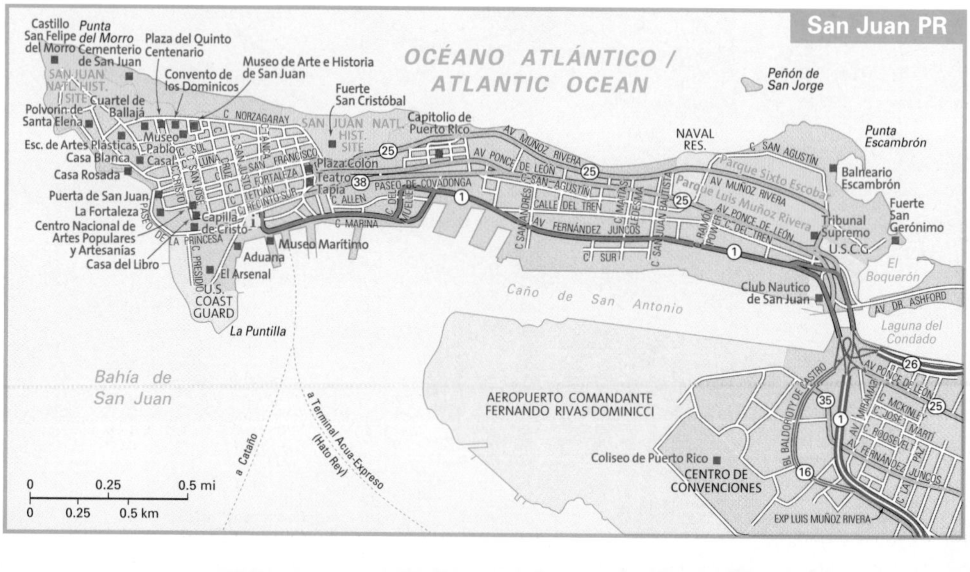
San Juan PR
OCÉANO ATLÁNTICO / ATLANTIC OCEAN
Castillo San Felipe del Morro
Punta del Morro
Plaza del Quinto Centenario
Cementerio de San Juan
SAN JUAN NATL. HIST. SITE
Convento de los Dominicos
Museo de Arte e Historia de San Juan
Fuerte San Cristóbal
Capitolio de Puerto Rico
Polvorín de Santa Elena
Cuartel de Ballajá
Esc. de Artes Plásticas
Casa Blanca
Museo Pablo Casals
Casa Rosada
Puerta de San Juan
La Fortaleza
Centro Nacional de Artes Populares y Artesanías
Casa del Libro
Capilla de Cristo
Plaza Colón
Teatro Tapia
Aduana
Museo Marítimo
El Arsenal
U.S. COAST GUARD
La Puntilla
NAVAL RES.
Peñón de San Jorge
Punta Escambrón
Balneario Escambrón
Fuerte San Gerónimo
Parque Sixto Escobar
Parque Luis Muñoz Rivera
Tribunal Supremo
U.S.C.G.
El Boquerón
Club Nautico de San Juan
Caño de San Antonio
Laguna del Condado
Bahía de San Juan
a Cataño
a Terminal Acua-Expreso (Hato Rey)
AEROPUERTO COMANDANTE FERNANDO RIVAS DOMINICCI
Coliseo de Puerto Rico
CENTRO DE CONVENCIONES
0 0.25 0.5 mi
0 0.25 0.5 km

Abbotsford–Clinton 277

Entries in **bold color** indicate cities with detailed inset maps.

CANADA

Abbotsford BC, *115463* 163 D3
Aberdeen SK, *534* 165 F1
Acton ON, *7767* 172 C2
Acton Vale QC, *7299* 175 D3
Adstock QC, *1629* 175 E2
Airdrie AB, *20382* 164 C2
Air Ronge SK, *955* 160 B3
Ajax ON, *73753* 173 D2
Aklavik NT, *632* 155 D1
Alban ON, *1084* 170 C3
Albanel QC, *2455* 176 B3
Alberta Beach AB, *762* 158 C4
Alberton PE, *1115* 179 E3
Aldergrove BC, *11910* 163 D3
Alexandria ON, *3369* 174 B3
Alfred ON, *1348* 174 B3
Alix AB, *825* 164 C2
Allan SK, *679* 165 F2
Alliston ON, *9679* 172 C1
Alma QC, *25918* 176 C3
Almonte ON, *4659* 174 A3
Altona MB, *3434* 167 E4
Amherst NS, *9470* 180 C1
Amherstburg ON, *20339* 172 A4
Amos QC, *13044* 171 E1
Amqui QC, *6473* 178 B1
Ange-Gardien QC, *1994* 175 D3
Angus ON, *9722* 172 C1
Annapolis Royal NS, *550* 180 B3
Antigonish NS, *4754* 181 E1
Arborg MB, *959* 167 E3
Arcola SK, *532* 166 C4
Armagh QC, *1603* 175 F1
Armstrong BC, *4256* 164 A3
Arnold's Cove NL, *1024* 183 E4
Arnprior ON, *7192* 174 A3
Arthur ON, *2284* 172 C2
Asbestos QC, *6580* 175 E3
Ascot Corner QC, *2342* 175 E3
Ashcroft BC, *1788* 163 E1
Asquith SK, *574* 165 F2
Assiniboia SK, *2483* 166 A4
Athabasca AB, *2415* 159 D3
Athens ON, *1026* 174 A4
Atholville NB, *1381* 178 C2
Atikokan ON, *3560* 168 C4
Aurora ON, *40167* 173 D2
Austin QC, *1201* 175 D3
Avondale NL, *701* 183 E4
Ayer's Cliff QC, *1102* 175 D3
Aylesford NS, *807* 180 C2
Aylmer ON, *7126* 172 C3
Aylmer QC, *36085* 174 B3
Ayr ON, *3636* 172 C3
Baddeck NS, *907* 181 F1
Badger NL, *906* 183 D3
Baie-Comeau QC, *23079* 177 D2
Baie-du-Febvre QC, *1135* 175 D2
Baie-Ste-Anne NB, *1600* 179 D3
Baie-St-Paul QC, *7290* 176 C4
Baie Verte NL, *1492* 183 D2
Balcarres SK, *622* 166 B3
Balgonie SK, *1239* 166 B3
Balmoral NB, *1836* 178 C2
Bancroft ON, *4089* 171 E4
Banff AB, *7135* 164 B3
Barraute QC, *2010* 171 E2
Barrhead AB, *4213* 158 C3
Barrie ON, *103710* 173 D1
Barry's Bay ON, *1259* 171 E4
Bas-Caraquet NB, *1689* 179 D2
Bashaw AB, *825* 164 C1
Bassano AB, *1320* 165 D3
Bathurst NB, *12924* 179 D2
Battleford SK, *3820* 159 F4
Bay Bulls NL, *1014* 183 F4
Bayfield ON, *909* 172 B2
Bay Roberts NL, *5237* 183 E4
Beachburg ON, *870* 174 A3
Beamsville ON, *9047* 173 D3
Beauceville QC, *6261* 175 E2
Beauharnois QC, *6387* 174 C3
Beaumont AB, *7006* 159 D4
Beaumont QC, *2153* 175 E1
Beaupré QC, *2761* 175 E1
Beausejour MB, *2772* 167 F3
Beauval SK, *843* 159 F2
Beaverlodge AB, *2110* 157 F1
Beaverton ON, *3065* 173 D1
Bécancour QC, *11051* 175 D2
Bedford NS 181 D3
Bedford QC, *2667* 175 D4
Beechville NS, *2312* 181 D3
Beeton ON, *3822* 173 D2
Beiseker AB, *838* 164 C2
Bella Bella BC, *1253* 156 C4
Belledune NB, *1923* 178 C2
Bellefeuille QC, *14066* 174 C3
Belleville ON, *45986* 173 E1
Belmont ON, *1819* 172 B3
Beloeil QC, *19053* 175 D3
Benito MB, *415* 166 C2
Bentley AB, *1035* 164 C2
Beresford NB, *4414* 179 D2
Berthierville QC, *3939* 175 D2
Bertrand NB, *1269* 179 D2
Berwick NS, *2282* 180 C2
Betsiamites QC, *1625* 178 A1
Bible Hill NS, *5741* 181 D2
Bienfait SK, *786* 166 C4
Biggar SK, *2243* 165 F2
Big River SK, *741* 159 F3
Binscarth MB, *445* 166 C3
Birch Hills SK, *957* 160 B4
Birchy Bay NL, *612* 183 E2
Birtle MB, *715* 167 D3
Bishop's Falls NL, *3688* 183 D3
Bissett MB, *243* 167 F3
Black Diamond AB, *1866* 164 C3
Blackfalds AB, *3042* 164 C2
Black Lake QC, *4109* 175 E2
Blacks Hbr. NB, *1082* 180 A2
Blackville NB, *1015* 178 C4
Blaine Lake SK, *508* 160 B4
Blainville QC, *36029* 174 C3
Blairmore AB, *1993* 164 C4
Blanc-Sablon QC, *1201* 183 D1
Blenheim ON, *4795* 172 B4
Blind Bay BC, *2464* 163 F1
Blind River ON, *3969* 170 B3
Blue Mts. ON, *6116* 172 C1
Bluewater ON, *6919* 172 B2
Blyth ON, *987* 172 B2
Bobcaygeon ON, *2854* 173 E1
Bois-Blanc NB, *857* 179 D2
Boischatel QC, *4303* 175 E1
Boissevain MB, *1495* 167 D4
Bolton ON, *20553* 173 D2
Bon Accord AB, *1532* 159 D4
Bonaventure QC, *2756* 179 D2
Bonavista NL, *4021* 183 E3
Bonnyville AB, *5709* 159 E3
Borden-Carleton PE, *798* 179 E4
Bothwell ON, *1002* 172 B3
Botwood NL, *3221* 183 D2
Bouctouche NB, *2426* 179 D4
Bourget ON, *1005* 174 B3
Bowden AB, *1174* 164 C2
Bowen Island BC, *2957* 163 D3
Bow Island AB, *1704* 165 D4
Bowmanville ON, *32556* 173 D2
Bowser BC, *1307* 162 C3
Bowsman MB, *320* 166 C2
Boyle AB, *836* 159 D3
Bracebridge ON, *13751* 171 D4
Bradford ON, *16978* 173 D2
Bradford-W. Gwillimbury ON, *22228* 173 D1
Bragg Creek AB, *678* 164 C3
Brampton ON, *325428* 173 D2
Brandon MB, *39716* 167 D4
Brant ON, *31669* 172 C3
Brantford ON, *86417* 172 C3
Brantville NB, *1153* 179 D3
Bridgenorth ON, *2279* 173 E1
Bridgetown NS, *1035* 180 B3
Bridgewater NS, *7621* 180 C3
Brigham QC, *2250* 175 D3
Brighton ON, *9449* 173 E2
Brigus NL, *784* 183 E4
Bristol NB, *719* 178 B4
Broadview SK, *669* 166 C3
Brochet MB, *226* 161 D1
Brockville ON, *21375* 174 B4
Bromont QC, *4808* 175 D3
Bromptonville QC, *5571* 175 E3
Brooklin ON, *5789* 173 D2
Brooklyn NS, *1078* 180 C4
Brooks AB, *11604* 165 D3
Brookside NS, *1286* 181 D3
Brownsburg-Chatham QC, *6770* 174 C3
Bruderheim AB, *1202* 159 D4
Bruno SK, *571* 166 B2
Brussels ON, *1143* 172 B2
Buchans NL, *877* 183 D3
Buckingham QC, *11668* 174 B3
Buffalo Creek BC, *701* 157 F4
Buffalo Lake AB, *722* 157 F1
Buffalo Narrows SK, *1137* 159 F2
Burford ON, *1841* 172 C3
Burgeo NL, *1782* 182 C4
Burin NL, *2470* 183 E4
Burk's Falls ON, *940* 171 D4
Burlington ON, *150836* 173 D3
Burnaby BC, *193954* 163 D3
Burns Lake BC, *1942* 157 D2
Burnt Islands NL, *801* 182 C4
Bury QC, *1171* 175 E3
Cabano QC, *3213* 178 A2
Cache Creek BC, *1056* 163 E1
Caledon ON, *50595* 172 C2
Caledon East ON, *1974* 172 C2
Caledonia ON, *8582* 172 C3
Caledon Vil. ON, *1651* 172 C2
Calgary AB, *878866* 164 C3
Calmar AB, *1902* 159 D4
Cambridge NS, *723* 180 C2
Cambridge ON, *110372* 172 C3
Cambridge-Narrows NB, *654* 180 B1
Campbellford ON, *3675* 173 E1
Campbell River BC, *28456* 162 B2
Campbellton NB, *7798* 178 C2
Camperville MB, *524* 167 D2
Camrose AB, *14854* 159 D4
Canal Flats BC, *709* 164 B3
Candle Lake SK, *503* 160 B4
Canmore AB, *10792* 164 B3
Canning NS, *811* 180 C2
Cannington ON, *2007* 173 D1
Canora SK, *2200* 166 C2
Canso NS, *992* 181 F2
Cantley QC, *5898* 174 B3
Cap-aux-Meules QC, *1659* 179 F3
Cap-Chat QC, *2913* 178 C1
Cap-de-la-Madeleine QC, *32534* 175 D2
Cape Breton Reg. Mun. NS, *105968* 181 F1
Cape St. George NL, *926* 182 C3
Caplan QC, *2010* 179 D2
Cap-Pele NB, *2266* 179 E4
Capreol ON, *3471* 170 C3
Cap-St-Ignace QC, *3204* 175 F1
Cap-Santé QC, *2571* 175 E1
Caraquet NB, *4442* 179 D2
Carberry MB, *1513* 167 D4
Carbonear NL, *4759* 183 E4
Cardigan PE, *382* 179 F4
Cardinal ON, *1739* 174 B4
Cardston AB, *3475* 164 C4
Carleton Place ON, *9083* 174 A3
Carleton-St-Omer QC, *4010* 178 C2
Carlisle ON, *2180* 172 C2
Carlyle SK, *1260* 166 C4
Carmacks YT, *431* 155 D3
Carman MB, *2831* 167 E4
Carmanville NL, *798* 183 E2
Carnduff SK, *1017* 166 C4
Caronport SK, *1040* 166 A3
Carrot River SK, *1017* 160 C4
Carseland AB, *662* 164 C3
Carstairs AB, *2254* 164 C2
Cartwright MB, *304* 167 D4
Cartwright NL, *629* 183 F1
Casselman ON, *2910* 174 B3
Cassidy BC, *978* 162 C3
Castlegar BC, *7002* 164 A4
Castor AB, *935* 165 D2
Catalina NL, *995* 183 E3
Causapscal QC, *2634* 178 B1
Cavendish PE, *267* 179 E4
Cawston BC, *1013* 163 F3
Cayuga ON, *1643* 172 C3
Cedar BC, *4440* 162 C3
Central Saanich BC, *15348* 163 D4
Centreville NS, *1047* 180 C2
Centreville-Wareham-Trinity NL, *1146* 183 E3
Chalk River ON, *975* 171 E3
Chambly QC, *20342* 175 D3
Chambord QC, *1693* 176 B3
Champlain QC, *1623* 175 D2
Chandler QC, *2817* 179 D1
Channel-Port aux-Basques NL, *4637* 182 C4
Chapais QC, *1795* 176 A2
Chapleau ON, *2832* 170 B2
Charlesbourg QC, *70310* 175 E1
Charlie Lake BC, *1727* 158 A2
Charlo NB, *1449* 178 C2
Charlottetown PE, *32245* 179 E4
Charny QC, *10507* 175 E1
Chase BC, *2460* 163 F1
Châteauguay QC, *41003* 174 C3
Château-Richer QC, *3442* 175 E1
Chatham ON, *44156* 172 B4
Chatham-Kent ON, *107341* 172 A4
Chemainus BC, *2706* 162 C3
Chertsey QC, *4112* 174 C2
Chesley ON, *1880* 172 B1
Chester NS, *1590* 180 C3
Chestermere AB, *3414* 164 C3
Chesterville ON, *1498* 174 B4
Chéticamp NS 181 E3
Chetwynd BC, *2591* 157 E1
Chibougamau QC, *7922* 176 A2
Chicoutimi QC, *60008* 176 C3
Chilliwack BC, *62927* 163 E3
Chipman NB, *1432* 178 C4
Christina Lake BC, *1035* 164 A4
Churchbridge SK, *796* 166 C3
Chute-aux-Outardes QC, *1968* 177 D2
Clair NB, *863* 178 A3
Clairmont AB, *1481* 157 F1
Clarence-Rockland ON, *19612* 174 B3
Clarenville NL, *5104* 183 E3
Claresholm AB, *3622* 164 C4
Clarington ON, *69834* 173 D2
Clarke's Beach NL, *1257* 183 E4
Clark's Hbr. NS, *944* 180 B4
Clermont QC, *3078* 176 C4
Clinton ON, *3117* 172 B2

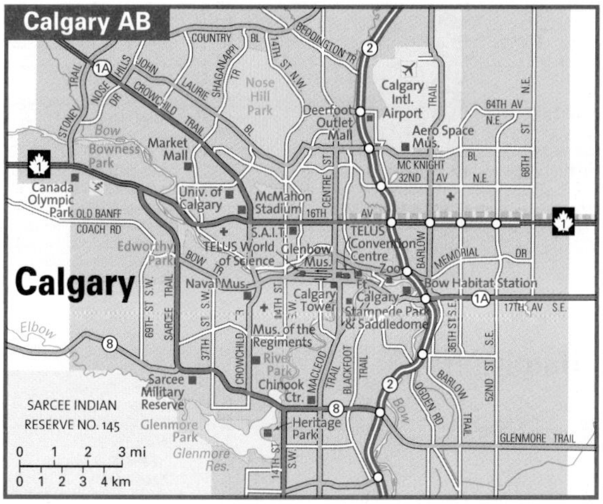
Calgary AB
Calgary
Calgary Intl. Airport
Nose Hill Park
Deerfoot Outlet Mall
Aero Space Mus.
Market Mall
Bowness Park
Canada Olympic Park
Univ. of Calgary
McMahon Stadium
S.A.I.T.
TELUS World of Science
Glenbow Mus.
TELUS Convention Centre
Zoo
Bow Habitat Station
Naval Mus.
Calgary Tower
Ft. Calgary
Stampede Park & Saddledome
Mus. of the Regiments
Chinook Ctr.
Sarcee Military Reserve
SARCEE INDIAN RESERVE NO. 145
Glenmore Park
Glenmore Res.
Heritage Park
GLENMORE TRAIL
0 1 2 3 mi
0 1 2 3 4 km

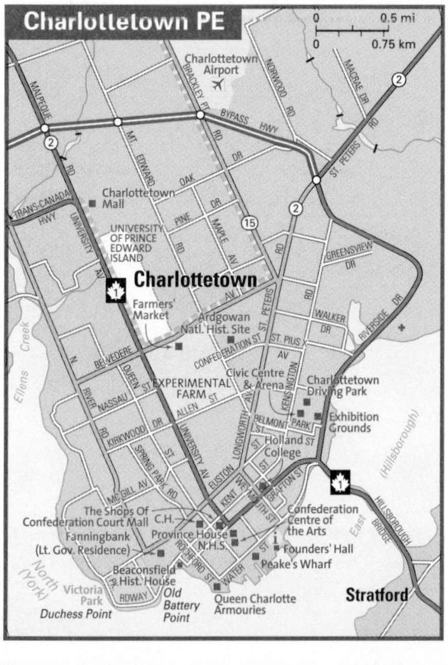
Charlottetown PE
Charlottetown Airport
Charlottetown
Charlottetown Mall
UNIVERSITY OF PRINCE EDWARD ISLAND
Farmers' Market
Ardgowan Natl. Hist. Site
Civic Centre & Arena
Charlottetown Driving Park
EXPERIMENTAL FARM
Exhibition Grounds
Holland College
Confederation Centre of the Arts
Founders' Hall
Peake's Wharf
The Shops Of Confederation Court Mall
Province House N.H.S.
Fanningbank (Lt. Gov. Residence)
Beaconsfield Hist. House
Victoria Park
Old Battery Point
Queen Charlotte Armouries
Duchess Point
Stratford
Ellens Creek
0 0.5 mi
0 0.75 km

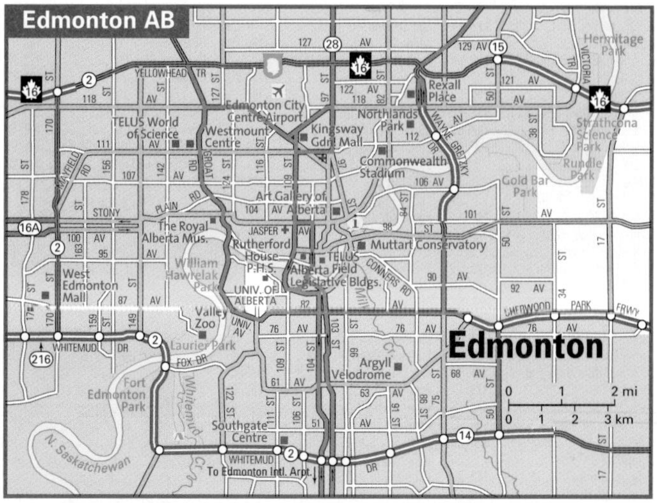
Edmonton AB
Edmonton
Edmonton City Centre Airport
Rexall Place
Northlands Park
Kingsway Gdn. Mall
Westmount Centre
TELUS World of Science
Commonwealth Stadium
Art Gallery of Alberta
Hermitage Park
Strathcona Science Park
Rundle Park
Gold Bar Park
The Royal Alberta Mus.
William Hawrelak Park
Rutherford House P.H.S.
Alberta Field Legislative Bldgs.
Muttart Conservatory
UNIV. OF ALBERTA
West Edmonton Mall
Valley Zoo
Laurier Park
Argyll Velodrome
Fort Edmonton Park
Southgate Centre
To Edmonton Intl. Arpt.
N. Saskatchewan
0 1 2 mi
0 1 2 3 km

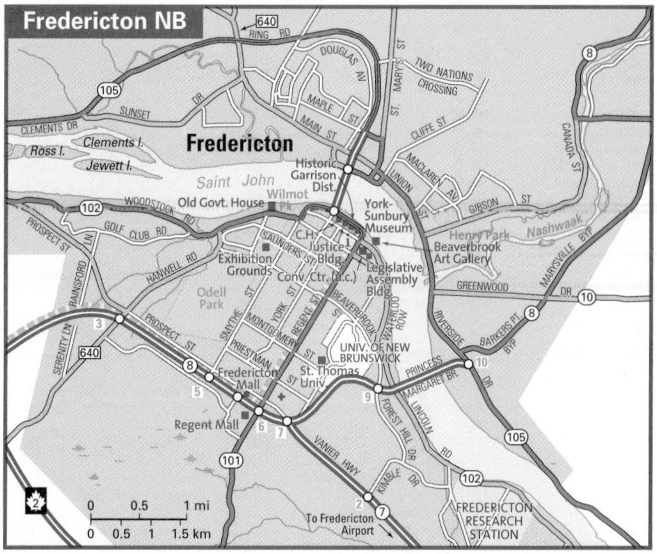
Fredericton NB
Fredericton
Saint John
Clements I.
Jewett I.
Ross I.
Historic Garrison Dist.
Old Govt. House
Wilmot Pk.
York-Sunbury Museum
Beaverbrook Art Gallery
Nashwaak
C.H.
Justice Bldg.
Exhibition Grounds
Conv. Ctr.
Legislative Assembly Bldg.
Odell Park
UNIV. OF NEW BRUNSWICK
St. Thomas Univ.
Fredericton Mall
Regent Mall
To Fredericton Airport
FREDERICTON RESEARCH STATION
0 0.5 1 mi
0 0.5 1 1.5 km

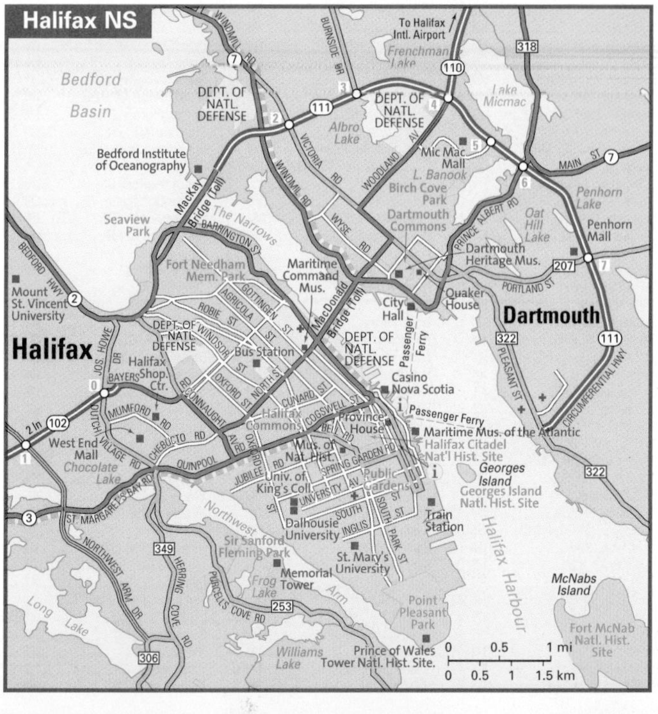
Halifax NS
Halifax
Dartmouth
To Halifax Intl. Airport
Bedford Basin
Frenchman Lake
DEPT. OF NATL. DEFENSE
Lake Micmac
Albro Lake
Bedford Institute of Oceanography
Mic Mac Mall
Birch Cove Park
Dartmouth Commons
Seaview Park
The Narrows
Penhorn Lake
Penhorn Mall
Oat Hill Lake
Dartmouth Heritage Mus.
Fort Needham Mem. Park
Maritime Command Mus.
Quaker House
Mount St. Vincent University
City Hall
Bus Station
Halifax Shop. Ctr.
Casino Nova Scotia
Halifax Commons
Province House
Passenger Ferry
Maritime Mus. of the Atlantic
Halifax Citadel Nat'l Hist. Site
West End Mall
Chocolate Lake
Mus. of Nat. Hist.
Public Gardens
Univ. of King's Coll.
Dalhousie University
St. Mary's University
Georges Island Natl. Hist. Site
Train Station
Sir Sandford Fleming Park
Memorial Tower
Frog Lake
Northwest Arm
Long Lake
Point Pleasant Park
Williams Lake
Prince of Wales Tower Natl. Hist. Site
Halifax Harbour
McNabs Island
Fort McNab Natl. Hist. Site
0 0.5 1 mi
0 0.5 1 1.5 km

Hamilton ON

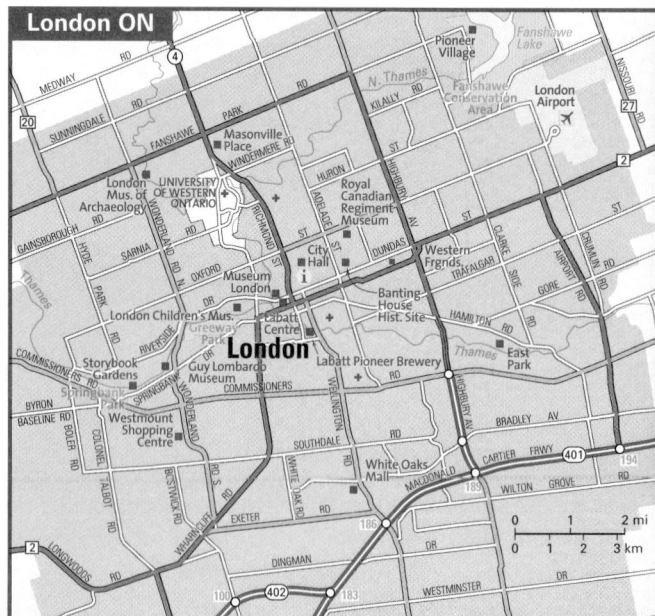

London ON

Entries in **bold color** indicate cities with detailed inset maps.

L'Isle-Verte–Port Dover **279**

Montréal QC

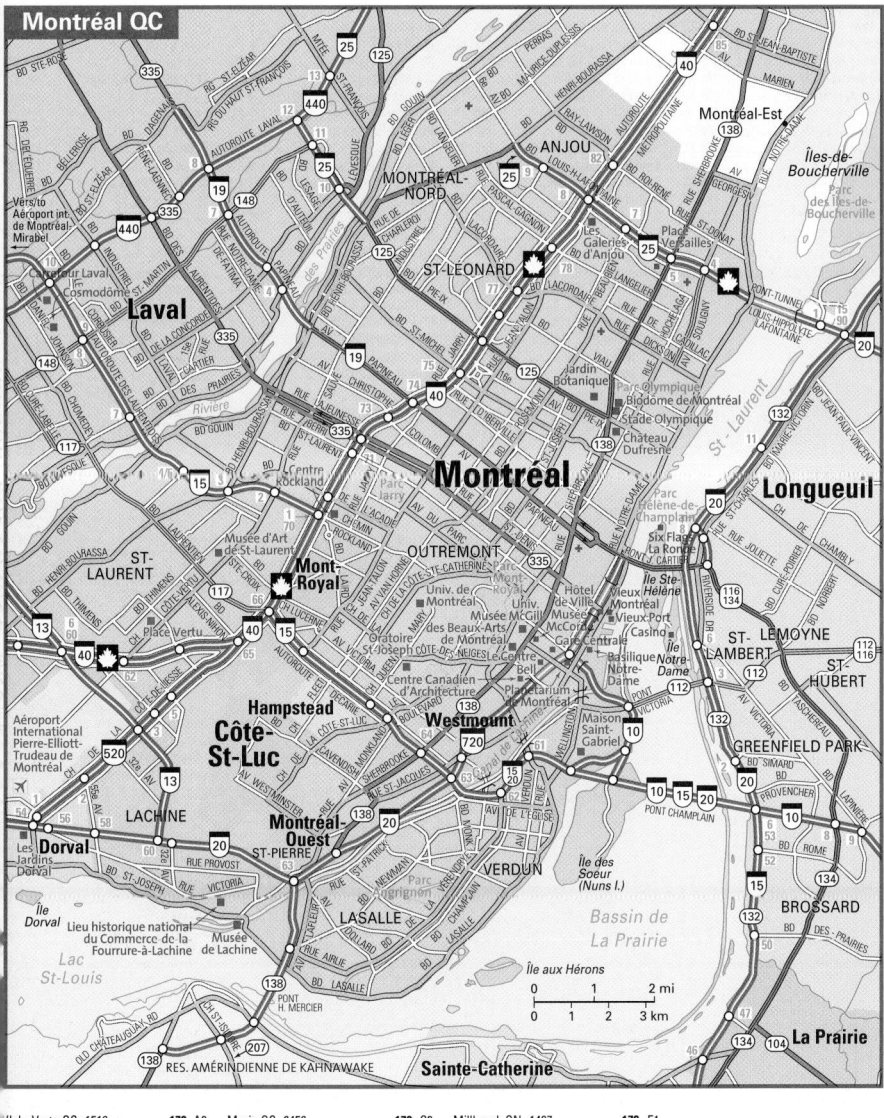

Ottawa ON

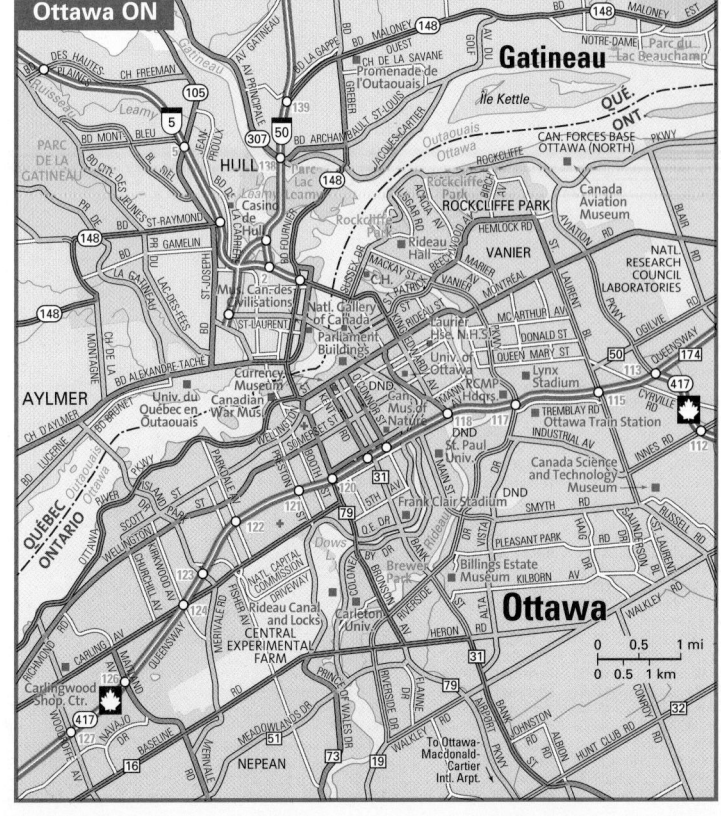

Murdochville QC, 1171.....179 D1
Murray Hbr. PE, 357.....179 F4
Murray River PE, 435.....179 F4
Musgrave Hbr. NL, 1294.....183 E2
Musgravetown NL, 640.....183 E3
Nackawic NB, 1042.....180 A1
Naicam SK, 761.....160 B4
Nakusp BC, 1698.....164 A3
Nanaimo BC, 73000.....162 C3
Nanoose Bay BC, 4723.....162 C3
Nantes QC, 1424.....175 E2
Nanton AB, 1841.....164 C3
Napanee ON, 7760.....173 F1
Napierville QC, 3073.....174 C3
Naramata QC, 1791.....163 F3
Nauwigewauk NB, 1508.....180 B2
Neepawa MB, 3325.....167 D3
Neguac NB, 1697.....179 D3
Neilburg SK, 3346.....159 F4
Nelson BC, 9298.....164 B4
New Aiyansh BC, 716.....156 B1
New Carlisle QC, 1431.....179 D2
New Glasgow NS, 9432.....181 D2
New Hamburg ON, 7003.....172 C3
New Hazelton BC, 750.....156 C1
New Liskeard ON, 4906.....171 D2
Newmarket ON, 65788.....173 D2
New Maryland NB, 4284.....180 A1
Newport QC, 1808.....179 E1
New Richmond QC, 3760.....178 C2
New Tecumseth ON, 26141.....172 C2
New Victoria NS, 1049.....181 F1
New Waterford NS, 10185.....181 F1
New-Wes-Valley NL, 2832.....183 E2
Niagara Falls ON, 78815.....173 D3
Niagara-on-the-Lake ON, 13839.....173 D3
Nicholas Denys NB, 1034.....178 C2
Nicolet QC, 7928.....175 D2
Nigadoo NB, 983.....179 D2
Nipawin SK, 4275.....160 C4
Nipigon ON, 1964.....169 E3
Niverville MB, 1921.....167 E4
Nobleton ON, 3472.....173 D2
Nominingue QC, 2064.....174 B2
Norfolk ON, 60847.....172 C3
Normandin QC, 3524.....176 B3
Norman's Cove-
Long Cove NL, 852.....183 E4
Norman Wells NT, 666.....155 E2
Norris Arm NL, 843.....183 E2
Norris Pt. NL, 786.....182 C2
N. Battleford SK, 13692.....159 F4
N. Bay ON, 52771.....171 D3
N. Cowichan BC, 26148.....162 C4
Northeastern Manitoulin
and the Islands ON, 2531.....170 C4
N. Perth ON, 12055.....172 C2
N. Rustico PE, 637.....179 E4
N. Saanich BC, 10436.....163 D4
N. Sydney NS.....181 F1
N. Tetagouche NB, 973.....178 C2
N. Vancouver BC, 44303.....163 D3
Norway House MB, 456.....161 E4
Norwich ON, 2510.....172 C3

Norwood ON, 1653.....173 E1
Notre Dame
de Lourdes MB, 619.....167 E4
Notre-Dame-
des-Érables NB, 958.....179 D2
Notre-Dame-des-Pins QC, 1030..175 E2
Notre-Dame-
du-Bon-Conseil QC, 1453.....175 D2
Notre-Dame-du-Lac QC, 2152.....178 A2
Notre-Dame-du-Laus QC, 1382..174 B2
Notre-Dame-
du-Mont-Carmel QC, 5055.....175 D2
Notre-Dame-du-Nord QC, 1109..171 D2
Notre-Dame-
du-Portage QC, 1172.....178 A2
Nouvelle QC, 1960.....178 C2
Noyan QC, 1093.....175 D4
Oak Bay BC, 17798.....163 D4
Oak Lake MB, 359.....167 D4
Oakville ON, 144738.....173 D2
Oka QC, 3194.....174 C3
Okanagan Falls BC, 1971.....163 F3
Okotoks AB, 11664.....164 C3
Old Perlican NL, 714.....183 E3
Olds AB, 6607.....164 C2
O'Leary PE, 860.....179 E4
Oliver BC, 4224.....163 F3
Omemee ON, 1310.....173 E1
Onaping ON, 4104.....170 C3
108 Mile Ranch BC, 2441.....157 F4
150 Mile House BC, 1142.....157 F4
100 Mile House BC, 1739.....157 F4
Onoway AB, 847.....159 D4
Orangeville ON, 25248.....172 C2
Orillia ON, 29121.....173 D1
Ormstown QC, 3647.....174 C3
Oromocto NB, 8843.....180 B1
Orono ON, 1666.....173 D2
Osgoode ON, 1831.....174 B3
Oshawa ON, 139051.....173 D2
Osler SK, 823.....165 F1
Osoyoos BC, 4295.....163 F3
Ottawa ON, 774072.....174 B3
Outlook SK, 2129.....165 F2
Owen Sound ON, 21431.....172 C1
Oxbow SK, 1132.....166 C4
Oxford NS, 1132.....181 D1
Oyen AB, 1020.....165 E2
Pabos QC, 1427.....179 D1
Pabos Mills QC, 1452.....179 D1
Paisley ON, 1033.....172 B1
Palmarolle QC, 1527.....171 D1
Palmerston ON, 2518.....172 C2
Papineauville QC, 2247.....174 B3
Paquetville NB, 667.....179 D2
Paradise NL, 9598.....183 F4
Paris ON, 9881.....172 C3
Parkhill ON, 1752.....172 B3
Parksville BC, 10323.....162 C3
Parrsboro NS, 1529.....180 C2
Parry Sound ON, 6124.....171 D4
Pasadena NL, 3133.....182 C3
Paspébiac QC, 3326.....179 D2
Peace River AB, 6240.....158 B2
Peachland BC, 4654.....163 F2

Pelham ON, 15272.....173 D3
Pelican Narrows SK, 690.....160 C3
Pelly Crossing YT, 328.....155 D2
Pemberton BC, 1637.....163 D2
Pembroke ON, 13490.....174 A3
Penetanguishene ON, 8316.....172 C1
Penhold AB, 1729.....164 C2
Pense SK, 533.....166 B3
Penticton BC, 30985.....163 F3
Percé QC, 3614.....179 E1
Perth ON, 6003.....174 A3
Perth-Andover NB, 1908.....178 B4
Petawawa ON, 14398.....171 E4
Peterborough ON, 71446.....173 E1
Peterview NL, 811.....183 D2
Petitcodiac NB, 1444.....180 C1
Petit-Matane QC, 1365.....178 B1
Petit-Rocher NB, 1966.....179 D2
Petrolia ON, 4849.....172 B3
Pickering ON, 87139.....173 D2
Picton ON, 4563.....173 F2
Pictou NS, 3875.....181 D1
Picture Butte AB, 1701.....165 D4
Pilot Butte SK, 1850.....166 B3
Pilot Mound MB, 676.....167 D4
Pinawa MB, 1500.....167 F3
Pincher Creek AB, 3666.....164 C4
Pinehouse SK, 1038.....160 B2
Pintendre QC, 6209.....175 E1
Pitt Meadows BC, 14670.....163 D3
Placentia NL, 4426.....183 E4
Plantagenet ON, 1103.....174 B3
Plaster Rock NB, 1219.....178 B3
Plessisville QC, 6756.....175 E2
Plum Coulee MB, 526.....167 E4
Plympton-Wyoming ON, 7359...172 B3
Pohénégamook QC, 3097.....178 A3
Pointe-à-la-Croix QC, 1513.....178 C2
Pointe-au-Père QC, 4171.....178 B1
Pointe-aux-Outardes QC, 1413..178 B1
Pointe-Calumet QC, 5604.....174 C3
Pointe-du-Lac QC, 6902.....175 D2
Pt. Edward ON, 2101.....172 A3
Pointe-Lebel QC, 1931.....177 D2
Pointe-Sapin NB, 627.....179 D3
Pointe-Verte NB, 1041.....178 C2
Pt. Leamington NL, 685.....183 D2
Ponoka AB, 6330.....164 C1
Ponteix SK, 550.....165 F4
Pontiac QC, 4643.....174 A3
Pont-Lafrance NB, 754.....179 D3
Pont-Landry NB, 1342.....179 D3
Pont-Rouge QC, 7146.....175 E1
Porcupine ON, 7196.....170 C1
Porcupine Plain SK, 820.....166 C1
Portage la Prairie MB, 12976.....167 E4
Port Alberni BC, 17743.....162 C3
Port Alice BC, 1126.....162 A1
Port au Choix NL, 1010.....182 C1
Port au Port East NL, 642.....182 C3
Port-Cartier QC, 6412.....177 E2
Port Colborne ON, 18450.....173 D3
Port Coquitlam BC, 51257.....163 D3
Port-Daniel-Gascons QC, 1559..179 D2
Port Dover ON, 5527.....172 C3

L'Isle-Verte QC, 1519.....178 A2
Listowel ON, 5905.....172 C2
Little Current ON, 1564.....170 C4
Lively ON, 6704.....170 C3
Liverpool NS, 2888.....180 C4
Lloydminster AB, 13148.....159 E4
Lloydminster SK, 7840.....159 E4
Lockeport NS, 701.....180 C4
Logan Lake BC, 2185.....163 E1
London ON, 336539.....172 B3
Longlac ON, 1748.....169 E3
Longue-Rive QC, 1352.....178 A1
Longueuil QC, 128016.....174 C3
Lorretteville QC, 13737.....175 E1
L'Orignal ON, 2033.....174 B3
Lorraineville QC, 1411.....171 D2
Louisbourg NS, 1071.....181 F4
Louiseville QC, 7622.....175 D2
Lourdes NL, 650.....182 C1
Lucan ON, 2010.....172 B3
Lucknow ON, 1207.....172 C2
Lumby BC, 1618.....164 A3
Lumsden NL, 622.....183 E2
Lumsden SK, 1581.....166 B3
Lunenburg NS, 2568.....180 C3
Luseland SK, 602.....165 E2
Lyster QC, 1685.....175 E2
Lynn Lake MB, 699.....161 D1
Macamic QC, 1519.....171 D1
MacGregor MB, 882.....167 E4
Mackenzie BC, 5206.....157 E1
Macklin SK, 1330.....165 E2
Madoc ON, 1730.....173 E1
Magog QC, 14283.....175 D3
Magrath AB, 1993.....165 D4
Mahone Bay NS, 991.....180 C3
Maidstone SK, 995.....159 F4
Maisonnette NB, 605.....179 D2
Malartic QC, 3704.....171 D1
Manawan QC, 1646.....174 C1
Manigotagan MB, 192.....167 F3
Manitou MB, 775.....167 E4
Manitouwadge ON, 2949.....169 E3
Maniwaki QC, 3571.....174 A2
Manning AB, 1293.....158 B1
Mannville AB, 722.....159 E4
Maple Ridge BC, 63169.....163 D3
Marathon ON, 4416.....169 E4

Maria QC, 2458.....178 C2
Marieville QC, 7240.....175 D3
Markdale ON, 1433.....172 C1
Markham ON, 208615.....173 D2
Markstay-Warren ON, 2627.....171 D3
Marmora ON, 1589.....173 E1
Marshall SK, 433.....159 E4
Martensville SK, 4365.....165 F2
Marystown NL, 5908.....183 E4
Mascouche QC, 29556.....174 C3
Mashteuiatsh QC, 1861.....176 B3
Maskinongé QC, 1087.....175 D2
Masset BC, 926.....156 A2
Masson-Angers QC, 9799.....174 A3
Matagami QC, 1939.....171 E1
Matane QC, 11635.....178 B1
Mattawa ON, 2270.....171 D3
Maxville ON, 864.....174 B3
Mayerthorpe AB, 1570.....158 C4
Mayo YT, 366.....155 D2
McAdam NB, 1513.....180 A1
McBride BC, 711.....157 F3
McCreary MB, 522.....167 D3
McLennan AB, 804.....158 B2
McWatters QC, 1815.....171 D2
Meadow Lake SK, 4582.....159 F3
Meadows NL, 676.....182 C3
Meaford ON, 10381.....172 C1
Medicine Hat AB, 51249.....165 D4
Melfort SK, 5559.....160 B4
Melita MB, 1111.....167 D4
Melocheville QC, 2449.....174 C3
Melville SK, 4453.....166 C3
Memramcook NB, 4719.....180 C1
Mercier QC, 9442.....174 C3
Merrickville-Wolford ON, 2812.....174 B4
Merritt BC, 7088.....163 E2
Merville BC, 2069.....162 C4
Messines QC, 1322.....174 A2
Métabetchouan-
Lac-à-la-Croix QC, 4198.....176 C3
Metcalfe ON, 1610.....174 B3
Metchosin BC, 4857.....163 D4
Middleton NS, 1744.....180 C3
Midland ON, 16214.....172 C1
Mildmay ON, 1191.....172 C2
Milestone SK, 542.....166 B4
Milk River AB, 879.....165 D4
Mill Bay BC, 1974.....163 D4

Millbrook ON, 1467.....173 E1
Mille-Isles QC, 1209.....174 C3
Millet AB, 2037.....159 D4
Milltown-Head of Bay
d'Espoir NL, 884.....183 D3
Milton NS, 1004.....180 C4
Milton ON, 31471.....173 D2
Milverton ON, 1707.....172 C2
Minitonas MB, 538.....167 D2
Minnedosa MB, 2426.....167 D3
Minto NB, 2776.....178 C4
Minto ON, 8164.....172 C2
Mirabel QC, 27330.....174 C3
Miracle Beach BC, 1627.....162 B2
Miramichi NB, 18508.....179 D3
Mira Road NS, 1268.....181 F1
Miscou Ctr. NB, 643.....179 D2
Miscouche PE, 766.....179 D4
Mission BC, 31272.....163 D3
Mississauga ON, 612925.....173 D2
Mississippi Mills ON, 11647.....174 A3
Mistissini QC, 1814.....176 B1
Mitchell ON, 4181.....172 B2
Moncton NB, 61046.....179 D4
Mono ON, 6922.....172 C2
Montague PE, 1945.....179 E4
Mont-Carmel QC, 1244.....176 C4
Mont-Joli QC, 5886.....178 B1
Mont-Laurier QC, 7365.....174 B2
Montmagny QC, 11750.....175 F1
Montréal QC, 1039534.....174 C3
Montrose BC, 1067.....164 A4
Moose Jaw SK, 32131.....166 B3
Moose Lake MB, 740.....161 D4
Moosomin SK, 2361.....166 C3
Morden MB, 6142.....167 E4
Morin-Heights QC, 2575.....174 C3
Morinville AB, 6540.....159 D4
Morris MB, 1673.....167 E4
Morrisburg ON, 2583.....174 B4
Mt. Albert ON, 2615.....173 D2
Mt. Brydges ON, 2221.....172 B3
Mt. Forest ON, 4584.....172 C2
Mt. Moriah NL, 700.....182 C3
Mt. Pearl NL, 24964.....183 F4
Mt. Uniacke NS.....180 C3
Mulgrave NS, 904.....181 E1
Mundare AB, 653.....159 D4
Munster ON, 1390.....174 A3

280 Port Edward–Ste-Anne-de-la-Pérade

Figures after entries indicate population, page number, and grid reference.

Québec QC

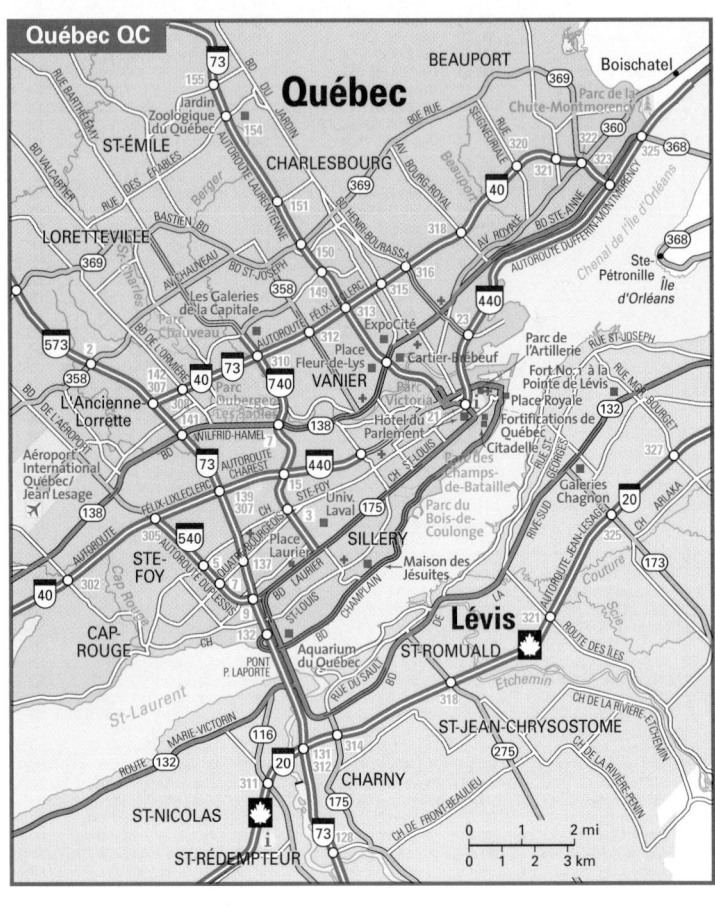

St John's NL

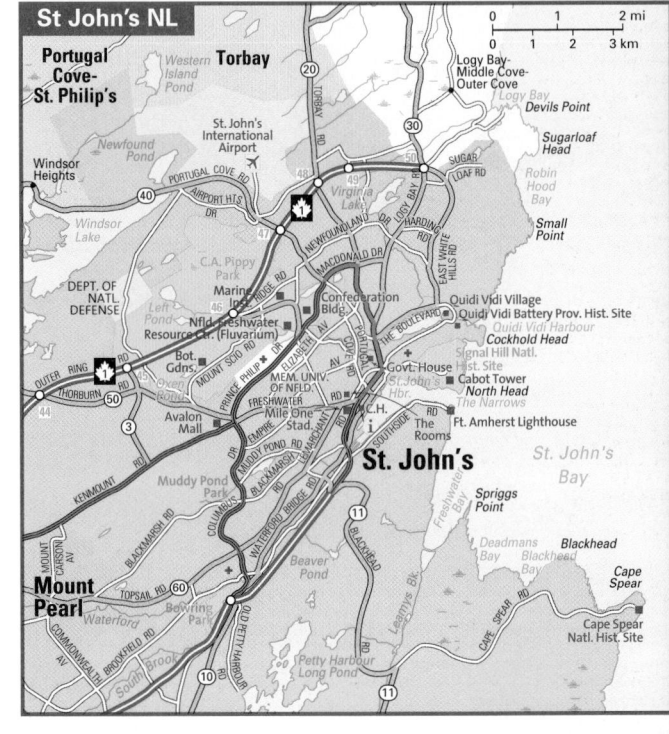

Regina SK

Saint John NB

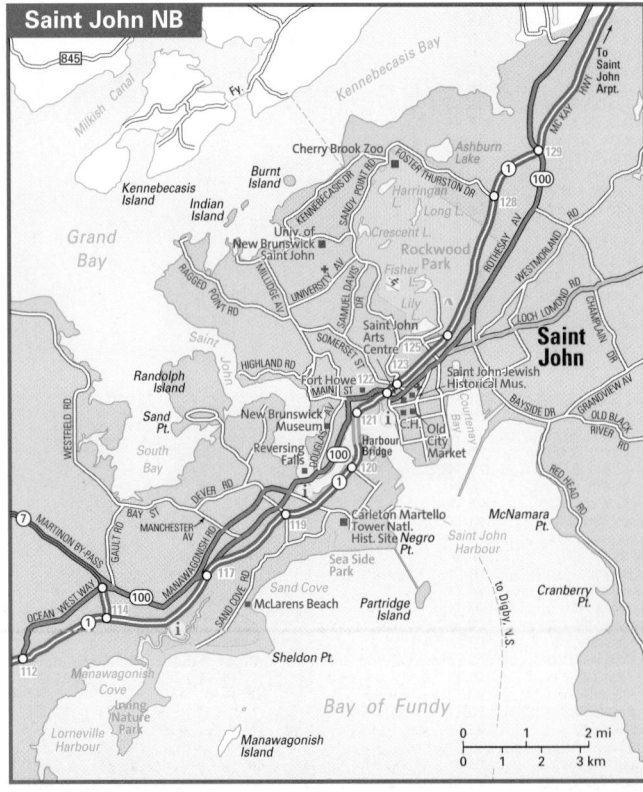

Saskatoon SK

Toronto ON

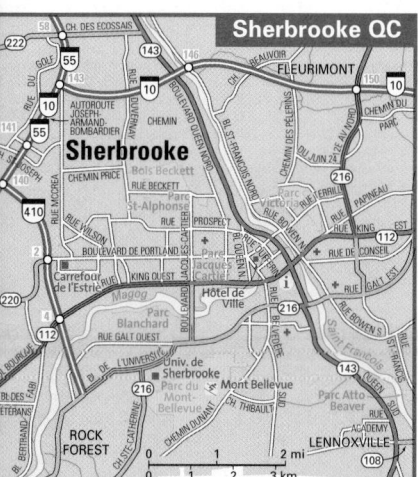

Sherbrooke QC

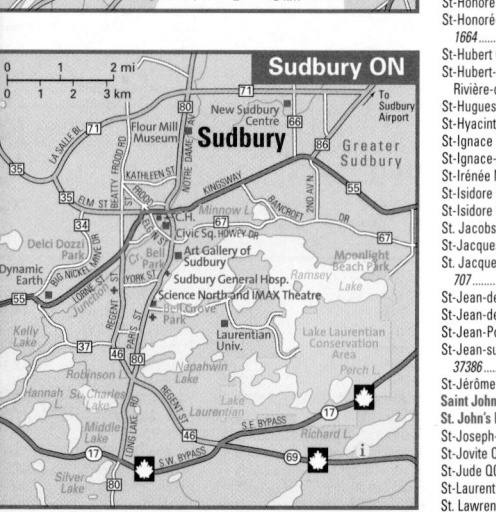

Sudbury ON

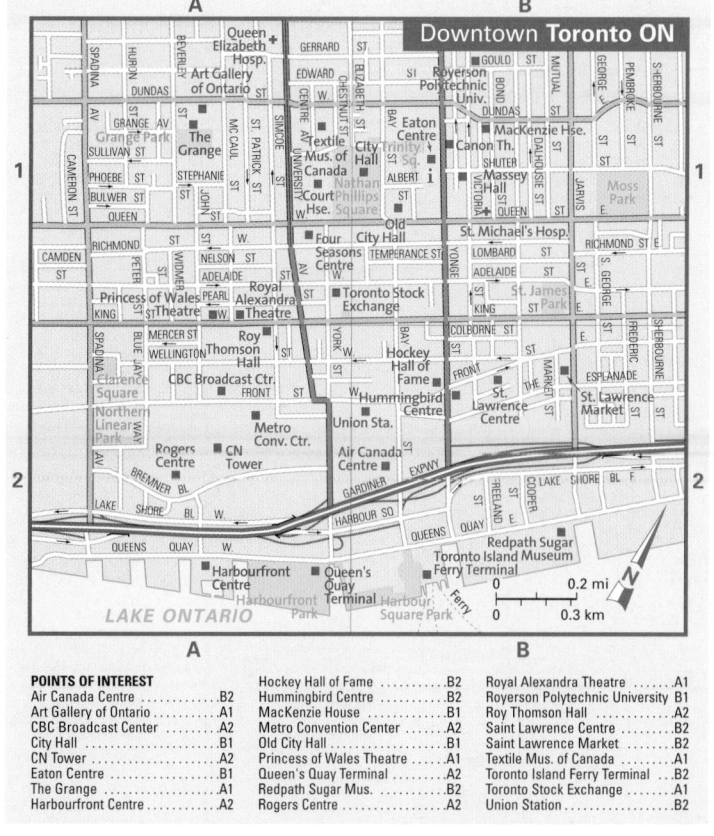

Downtown Toronto ON

POINTS OF INTEREST
Air Canada Centre B2
Art Gallery of Ontario A1
CBC Broadcast Center A2
City Hall B1
CN Tower A2
Eaton Centre B1
The Grange A1
Harbourfront Centre A2
Hockey Hall of Fame B2
Hummingbird Centre B2
MacKenzie House B1
Metro Convention Center A2
Old City Hall B1
Princess of Wales Theatre ...A1
Queen's Quay Terminal A2
Redpath Sugar Mus. B2
Rogers Centre A2
Royal Alexandra Theatre A1
Royerson Polytechnic University B1
Roy Thomson Hall A2
Saint Lawrence Centre B2
Saint Lawrence Market B2
Textile Mus. of Canada A1
Toronto Island Ferry Terminal ..B2
Toronto Stock Exchange A1
Union Station B2

St-Stanislas QC, 1076.........175 D2
St. Stephen NB, 4667.........180 A2
St-Théodore-d'Acton QC, 1544...175 D2
St. Thomas ON, 33236.........172 B3
St-Timothée QC, 8299.........175 D1
St-Tite QC, 3845.........175 D1
St-Tite-des-Caps QC, 1426.........175 E1
St-Ubalde QC, 1460.........175 D1
St-Ulric QC, 1649.........178 B1
St-Urbain QC, 1430.........176 C4
St-Valère QC, 1308.........175 D2
St-Victor QC, 2460.........175 E2
St. Walburg SK, 672.........159 F4
St-Wenceslas QC, 1132.........175 D2

Scoudouc NB, 1047.........179 D4
Seaforth ON, 2692.........172 B2
Sechelt BC, 7775.........162 C3
Sedgewick AB, 865.........165 D1
Selkirk MB, 9752.........167 E3
Senneterre QC, 3275.........171 D4
Sexsmith AB, 1653.........157 F1
Shannon QC, 3668.........175 D1
Shaunavon SK, 1775.........165 F4
Shawinigan QC, 17535.........175 D2
Shawinigan-Sud QC, 11544.........175 D2
Shawville QC, 1582.........174 A3
Shediac NB, 4892.........179 D4

Smoky Lake AB, 1011.........159 D3
Smooth Rock Falls ON, 1830.........170 C1
Snow Lake MB, 1207.........161 E2
Somerset MB, 459.........167 E4
Sorel-Tracy QC, 34194.........175 D2
Sorrento BC, 1197.........163 F1
Souris MB, 1683.........167 D4
Souris PE, 1248.........179 F4
Southampton ON, 3360.........172 B1
S. Bruce Peninsula ON, 8090.........172 B1
Southey SK, 693.........166 B3
S. Huron ON, 10019.........172 B3
S. Indian Lake MB, 808.........161 E1

Stewiacke NS, 1388.........181 D2
Stirling AB, 877.........165 D4
Stirling ON, 2149.........173 E1
Stoke QC, 2475.........175 E3
Stonewall MB, 4012.........167 E3
Stoney Pt. ON, 1316.........172 A4
Stony Mtn. MB, 1700.........167 E3
Stony Plain AB, 9589.........159 D4
Stouffville ON, 11073.........173 D2
Stoughton SK, 720.........166 C4
Strasbourg SK, 760.........166 B3
Stratford ON, 29676.........172 C2
Strathmore AB, 7621.........164 C3
Strathroy ON, 12805.........172 B3

Tofield AB, 1818.........159 D4
Tofino BC, 1466.........162 B3
Torbay NL, 5474.........183 F4
Toronto ON, 2481494.........173 D2
Tottenham ON, 4829.........173 D2
Tracadie-Sheila NB, 4724.........179 D3
Trail BC, 7575.........164 A4
Treherne MB, 644.........167 E4
Trent Hills ON, 12569.........173 E1
Trenton NS, 2798.........181 D2
Trenton ON, 1.........173 E2
Trepassey NL, 889.........183 E4
Tring-Jonction QC, 1333.........175 E2
Triton NL, 1102.........183 D2

Valemount BC, 1195.........157 F3
Val-Joli QC, 1532.........175 E3
Vallée-Jonction QC, 1882.........175 E2
Valleyview AB, 1856.........158 B3
Val-Morin QC, 2216.........174 C2
Val-Senneville QC, 2479.........171 E2
Vancouver BC, 545671.........163 D3
Vanderhoof BC, 4390.........157 D2
Vankleek Hill ON, 2022.........174 B3
Varennes QC, 19653.........175 D2
Vaudreuil-Dorion QC, 19920.........174 C3
Vauxhall AB, 1112.........165 D4
Vegreville AB, 5376.........159 D4
Venise-en-Québec QC, 1243.........175 D2

Wallaceburg ON, 11114.........172 A3
Warfield BC, 1739.........164 A4
Warman SK, 3481.........165 F2
Warwick QC, 4874.........175 D2
Wasaga Beach ON, 12419.........172 C1
Waterford ON, 2871.........172 C3
Waterloo ON, 86543.........172 C2
Waterloo QC, 3993.........175 D2
Waterville NS, 808.........180 C2
Waterville QC, 1824.........175 E3
Watford ON, 1625.........172 B3
Watrous SK, 1808.........166 B3
Watson SK, 794.........166 B2
Watson Lake YT, 912.........155 F1
Waverley NS, 934.........181 D3
Wawa ON, 3279.........169 F4
Wawanesa MB, 516.........167 D4
Wawota SK, 538.........166 C4
Wedgeport NS, 1217.........180 B4
Weedon QC, 2646.........175 E3
Welland ON, 48402.........173 D3
Wellesley ON, 1666.........172 C2
Wellington ON, 1943.........173 E2
Wellington PE, 382.........179 E4
Wembley AB, 1497.........157 F1
Wentworth-Nord QC, 1121.........174 C2
Westbank BC, 15700.........163 F2
Western Shore NS, 1015.........180 C3
Westlock AB, 4819.........159 D3
W. Lorne ON, 1458.........172 B3
W. Nipissing ON, 13114.........171 D1
W. Vancouver BC, 41421.........163 D3
Westville NS, 3879.........181 D2
Wetaskiwin AB, 11154.........159 D4
Weyburn SK, 9534.........166 B4
Wheatley ON, 1920.........172 A4
Whistler BC, 8896.........163 D1
Whitby ON, 87413.........173 D2
Whitchurch-Stouffville ON, 22008.........173 D2
White City SK, 1013.........166 B3
Whitecourt AB, 8334.........158 C4
Whitehorse YT, 19058.........155 F1
White Rock BC, 18250.........163 D3
Whitewood SK, 947.........166 C3
Wiarton ON, 2349.........172 B1
Wickham QC, 2516.........175 D2
Wikwemikong ON, 1352.........170 C1
Wilkie SK, 1282.........165 F2
Williams Lake BC, 11153.........157 D2
Winchester ON, 2427.........174 B3
Windermere BC, 1060.........164 B3
Windsor NS, 3778.........180 C2
Windsor ON, 208402.........172 A4
Windsor QC, 5321.........175 E3
Wingham ON, 2885.........172 B2
Winkler MB, 7943.........167 E4
Winnipeg MB, 619544.........167 E3
Winnipeg Beach MB, 801.........167 E3
Winnipegosis MB, 621.........167 D2
Witless Bay NL, 1056.........183 F4
Wolfville NS, 3658.........180 C2
Wolseley SK, 766.........166 C3

Anmore ....D1   Burnaby ....D2   New Westminster ...D2   N. Vancouver (DM) ......C1   Richmond ....C2   Vancouver B2
Belcarra ....D1   Coquitlam ....D2   N. Vancouver ....B1   Port Moody ....D1   Surrey ....D2   W. Vancouver A1

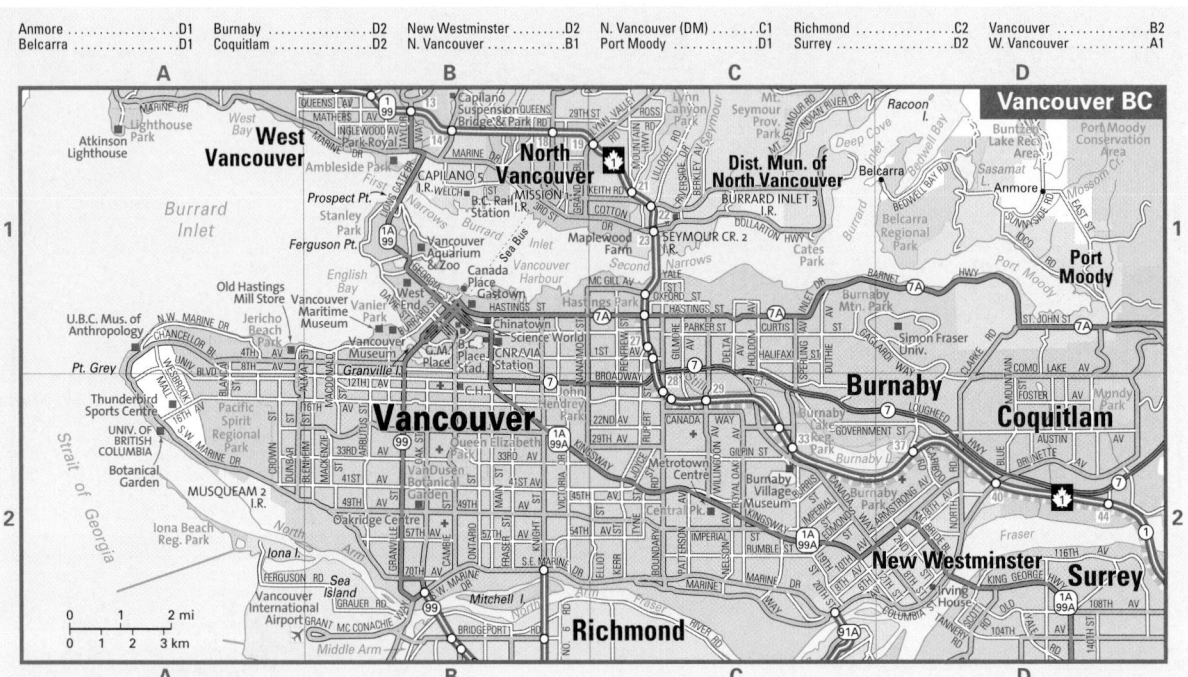

St-Zacharie QC, 2100.........175 F2
St-Zénon QC, 1180.........174 C2
St-Zotique QC, 4158.........174 C3
Salaberry-de-Valleyfield QC, 26170.........174 C3
Salisbury NB, 1954.........180 C1
Salmo BC, 1120.........164 B4

Shediac Bridge NB, 950.........179 D4
Shediac Cape NB, 787.........179 D4
Shelburne NS, 2013.........180 B4
Shelburne ON, 4122.........172 C2
Shellbrook SK, 1276.........160 B4
Sherbrooke QC, 75916.........175 E3
Sherwood Park AB, 47645.........164 C1

S. River ON, 1040.........171 D4
Spallumcheen BC, 5134.........164 A3
Spaniard's Bay NL, 2694.........183 E4
Sparwood BC, 3812.........164 C4
Spirit River AB, 1100.........157 F1
Spiritwood SK, 907.........159 F4
Springdale NL, 3045.........183 D2

Sturgeon Falls ON, 5978.........171 D3
Sturgis SK, 627.........166 C2
Sudbury ON, 103879.........170 C3
Summerford NL, 1010.........183 E2
Summerland BC, 10713.........163 F2
Summerside PE, 14654.........179 E4
Sundre AB, 2267.........164 C2

Trochu AB, 1033.........164 C2
Trois-Pistoles QC, 3635.........178 A2
Trois-Rivières QC, 46264.........175 D2
Truro NS, 11457.........181 D2
Tuktoyaktuk NT, 930.........155 D1
Tumbler Ridge BC, 1851.........157 F1
Turner Valley AB, 1608.........164 C3

Verchères QC, 4782.........174 C3
Verdun QC, 60564.........174 C3
Vermilion AB, 3948.........159 E4
Vernon BC, 33494.........164 A3
Victoria BC, 74125.........163 D4
Victoria NL, 1798.........183 E4
Victoriaville QC, 38841.........175 E2

Wood Buffalo AB, 41466.........159 D1
Woodstock NB, 5198.........178 B1
Woodstock ON, 33061.........172 C3
Woodville ON, 871.........173 D1
Wotton QC, 1568.........175
Wright QC, 1137.........174 A2
Wynyard SK, 1919.........166 B3
Wyoming ON, 2200.........172 B4
Yamachiche QC, 2631.........175 D2
Yarmouth NS, 7561.........180 B4
Yellowknife NT, 16541.........155 D1
Yorkton SK, 15107.........166 C3
Youbou BC, 727.........162 B3

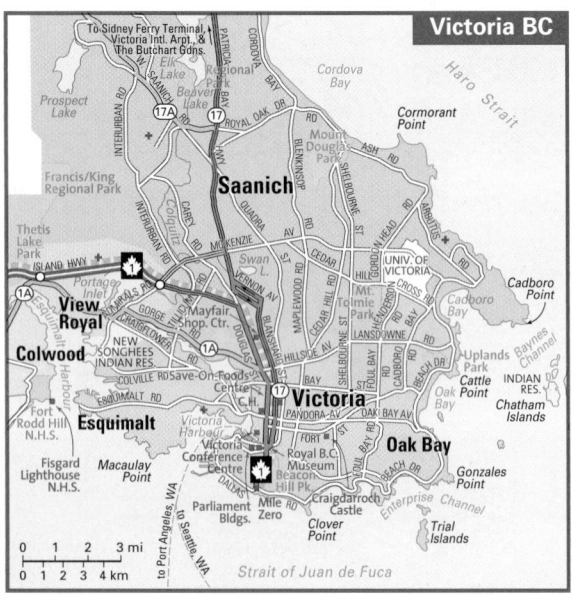

Salmon Arm BC, 15210.........163 F1
Salmon Cove NL, 746.........183 E4
Salmon River NS, 2259.........180 B4
Sandy Bay SK, 160.........160 C2
Saratoga Beach BC, 1627.........162 B2
Sarnia ON, 70876.........172 A3
Saskatoon SK, 196811.........165 F2
Saugeen Shores ON, 11388.........172 B1
Sault Ste. Marie ON, 74566.........170 B3
Sayabec QC, 1999.........178 B1
Schomberg ON, 1216.........173 D2
Scott QC, 1705.........175 E2

Shippagan NB, 2872.........179 D3
Shoal Lake MB, 801.........167 D3
Shubenacadie NS, 906.........181 D1
Sicamous BC, 2720.........164 A3
Sidney BC, 10929.........163 D1
Silver Creek BC, 1062.........163 F1
Simcoe ON, 14175.........172 C3
Sioux Lookout ON, 5336.........168 C2
Slave Lake AB, 6600.........158 C3
Smithers BC, 5414.........156 C2
Smiths Falls ON, 9140.........174 A3
Smithville ON, 3317.........173 D3

Springhill NS, 4091.........180 C1
Springside SK, 525.........166 C2
Sproat Lake BC, 1888.........162 B3
Spruce Grove AB, 15983.........159 D4
Squamish BC, 14247.........163 D2
Stanstead QC, 2995.........175 D4
Stayner ON, 3885.........172 C1
Steinbach MB, 9227.........167 E4
Stellarton NS, 4809.........181 D2
Stephenville NL, 7109.........182 C3
Stephenville Crossing NL, 1993.........182 C2
Stettler AB, 5215.........165 D2

Tweed ON, 1539.........173 E1
Twillingate NL, 2611.........183 E2
Two Hills AB, 1091.........159 E4
Ucluelet BC, 1559.........162 B3
Union Bay BC, 1167.........162 C3
Unity SK, 2243.........165 E2
Upton QC, 1986.........175 D2
Uxbridge ON, 8540.........173 D2
Val-Comeau NB, 823.........179 D3
Valcourt QC, 2411.........175 D2
Val-David QC, 3819.........174 C2
Val-des-Monts QC, 7842.........174 B3
Val-d'Or QC, 22748.........171 E2

Viking AB, 1052.........159 E4
Ville-Marie QC, 2770.........171 D2
Virden MB, 3109.........167 D4
Vulcan AB, 1762.........164 C3
Wabana NL, 2679.........183 F4
Wabasca AB, 1114.........159 D2
Wabowden MB, 497.........161 E3
Wabush NL, 1843.........177 E1
Wadena SK, 1412.........166 B2
Wainwright AB, 5117.........159 E4
Wakaw SK, 884.........165 F1
Waldheim SK, 889.........165 F1
Walkerton ON, 4970.........172 B1

Entries in **bold color** indicate cities with detailed inset maps.

Acámbaro–Zumpango del Río **283**

MEXICO

Cancún MX

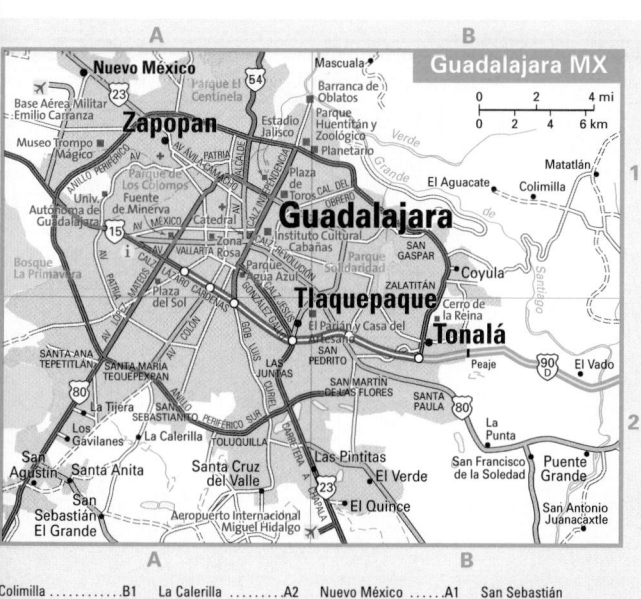

Guadalajara MX

México MX

Monterrey MX

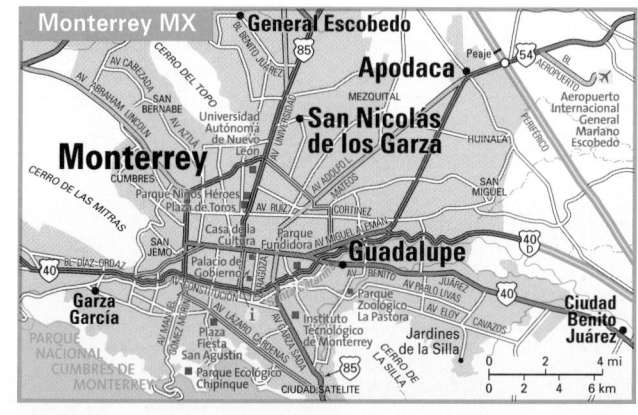

Miles

Cities listed along the diagonal (in order):

- Albany, NY
- Albuquerque, NM
- Amarillo, TX
- Anchorage, AK
- Atlanta, GA
- Baltimore, MD
- Billings, MT
- Birmingham, AL
- Bismarck, ND
- Boise, ID
- Boston, MA
- Buffalo, NY
- Calgary, AB
- Charleston, SC
- Charleston, WV
- Charlotte, NC
- Cheyenne, WY
- Chicago, IL
- Cincinnati, OH
- Cleveland, OH
- Columbus, OH
- Dallas, TX
- Denver, CO
- Des Moines, IA
- Detroit, MI
- El Paso, TX
- Halifax, NS
- Houston, TX
- Indianapolis, IN
- Jackson, MS
- Jacksonville, FL
- Kansas City, MO
- Las Vegas, NV
- Little Rock, AR
- Los Angeles, CA
- Louisville, KY
- Memphis, TN
- México, MX
- Miami, FL
- Milwaukee, WI
- Minneapolis, MN
- Mobile, AL
- Montréal, QC
- Nashville, TN
- New Orleans, LA
- New York, NY
- Oklahoma City, OK
- Omaha, NE
- Orlando, FL
- Ottawa, ON
- Philadelphia, PA
- Phoenix, AZ
- Pittsburgh, PA
- Portland, ME
- Portland, OR
- Québec, QC
- Raleigh, NC
- Rapid City, SD
- Reno, NV
- Richmond, VA
- St. Louis, MO
- Salt Lake City, UT
- San Antonio, TX
- San Diego, CA
- San Francisco, CA
- Seattle, WA
- Tampa, FL
- Toronto, ON
- Vancouver, BC
- Washington, DC
- Wichita, KS
- Winnipeg, MB

Kilometers

Milles

	Memphis, TN	México, MX	Miami, FL	Milwaukee, WI	Minneapolis, MN	Mobile, AL	Montréal, QC	Nashville, TN	New Orleans, LA	New York, NY	Oklahoma City, OK	Omaha, NE	Orlando, FL	Ottawa, ON	Philadelphia, PA	Phoenix, AZ	Pittsburgh, PA	Portland, ME	Portland, OR	Québec, QC	Raleigh, NC	Rapid City, SD	Reno, NV	Richmond, VA	St. Louis, MO	Salt Lake City, UT	San Antonio, TX	San Diego, CA	San Francisco, CA	Seattle, WA	Tampa, FL	Toronto, ON	Vancouver, BC	Washington, DC	Wichita, KS	Winnipeg, MB
Albany, NY	1214	2809	1439	929	1245	1344	230	1003	1440	151	1549	1292	1235	302	223	2561	485	270	2954	362	639	1750	2747	482	1036	2224	1953	2919	2964	2899	1290	400	3032	369	1471	1697
Albuquerque, NM	1033	1462	2155	1426	1339	1344	2172	1248	1276	2015	546	973	1934	2108	1954	466	1670	2338	1395	2321	1782	841	1020	1876	1051	624	818	825	1111	1463	1949	1841	1597	1896	707	1608
Amarillo, TX	750	1275	1834	1142	1055	1106	1888	965	993	1731	262	726	1613	1825	1671	753	1386	2054	1695	2038	1499	837	1306	1593	767	964	513	1111	1397	1763	1628	1557	1897	1612	423	1420
Anchorage, AK	4083	5010	4970	3512	3176	4511	4106	4061	4479	4389	3881	3362	4749	4012	4357	3590	4056	4690	2425	4255	4448	2980	3010	4391	3799	2939	4247	3526	3070	2252	4763	4099	2132	4290	3680	2725
Atlanta, GA	389	1753	661	813	1129	332	1241	242	473	869	944	989	440	1160	782	1868	676	1197	2647	1373	396	1511	2440	527	549	1916	1000	2166	2618	2705	455	958	2838	636	989	1580
Baltimore, MD	933	2423	1109	805	1121	1013	564	716	1142	192	1354	1168	904	523	104	2366	246	520	2830	696	309	1626	2623	152	841	2100	1671	2724	2840	2775	960	565	2908	38	1276	1573
Billings, MT	1625	2263	2554	1175	839	2019	2093	1648	1955	2049	1227	904	2333	2029	2019	1199	1719	2352	889	2242	2110	379	960	2053	1341	548	1500	1302	1176	816	2348	1762	949	1953	1067	823
Birmingham, AL	241	1631	812	763	1079	258	1289	194	351	985	729	941	591	1225	897	1723	763	1313	2599	1438	547	1463	2392	678	501	1868	878	2021	2472	2657	606	958	2791	758	838	1531
Bismarck, ND	1337	2456	2224	767	431	1765	1685	1315	1734	1641	1136	616	2003	1621	1611	1662	1311	1944	1301	1834	1702	320	1372	1645	1053	960	1599	1765	1749	1229	2018	1354	1362	1545	934	415
Boise, ID	1954	2477	2883	1748	1465	2302	2535	1976	2234	2491	1506	1234	2662	2472	2462	993	2161	2795	432	2685	2495	930	430	2496	1628	342	1761	1096	646	500	2677	2204	633	2395	1346	1452
Boston, MA	1353	2843	1529	1100	1417	1433	313	1136	1563	215	1694	1463	1324	413	321	2706	592	107	3126	388	729	1921	2919	572	1181	2395	2092	3065	3135	3070	1380	570	3204	458	1616	1868
Buffalo, NY	927	2522	1425	642	958	1165	397	716	1254	400	1262	1005	1221	333	414	2274	217	560	2667	546	642	1463	2460	485	749	1936	1665	2632	2677	2612	1276	106	2745	384	1184	1410
Calgary, AB	2174	2944	3061	1603	1267	2602	2197	2152	2570	2480	1908	1453	2840	2103	2448	1525	2147	2781	852	2346	2539	915	1286	2482	1890	874	2182	1628	1497	679	2854	2190	559	2381	1749	816
Charleston, SC	760	2063	583	1003	1319	642	1145	543	783	773	1248	1290	379	1106	685	2184	642	1101	2948	1277	279	1824	2741	428	850	2218	1310	2483	2934	2973	434	1006	3106	539	1291	1771
Charleston, WV	606	2201	994	601	918	837	822	395	926	515	1022	952	790	759	454	2035	217	839	2610	972	313	1422	2403	322	512	1880	1344	2393	2620	2571	845	537	2705	346	953	1369
Charlotte, NC	614	1994	730	857	1173	572	1003	397	713	631	1102	1144	525	922	543	2107	438	959	2802	1135	158	1678	2595	289	704	2072	1241	2405	2759	2827	581	802	2960	397	1145	1625
Cheyenne, WY	1217	1809	2147	1012	881	1570	1799	1240	1502	1755	773	497	1926	1736	1725	1004	1425	2059	1166	1949	1758	305	959	1760	892	436	1046	1179	1176	1234	1941	1468	1368	1659	613	1132
Chicago, IL	539	2126	1382	89	409	923	841	474	935	797	807	474	1161	778	768	1819	467	1101	2137	991	861	913	1930	802	294	1406	1270	2105	2146	2062	1176	510	2196	701	728	860
Cincinnati, OH	493	2088	1141	398	714	731	815	281	820	636	863	736	920	751	576	1876	292	960	2398	972	522	1219	2191	530	350	1667	1231	2234	2407	2368	935	484	2501	517	785	1166
Cleveland, OH	742	2337	1250	443	760	981	588	531	1070	466	1073	806	1045	525	437	2085	136	751	2469	738	568	1264	2262	471	560	1738	1481	2437	2478	2413	1101	303	2547	370	995	1211
Columbus, OH	594	2189	1163	454	771	832	725	382	921	535	930	802	958	661	474	1942	190	858	2464	874	482	1275	2257	517	417	1734	1332	2300	2474	2424	1036	440	2558	416	852	1222
Dallas, TX	466	1128	1367	1010	999	639	1772	681	525	1589	209	669	1146	1708	1501	1077	1246	1917	2140	1921	1189	1077	1933	1309	635	1410	271	1375	1827	2208	1161	1441	2342	1362	367	1363
Denver, CO	1116	1709	2069	1055	924	1478	1843	1162	1409	1799	681	541	1847	1779	1744	904	1460	2102	1261	1992	1680	404	1054	1688	855	531	946	1092	1271	1329	1862	1512	1463	1686	521	1176
Des Moines, IA	720	1866	1632	378	246	1115	1165	725	1117	1121	546	136	1411	1101	1091	1558	791	1424	1798	1314	1157	629	1591	1126	436	1067	1009	1766	1807	1822	1426	834	1956	1025	390	697
Detroit, MI	752	2347	1401	380	697	991	564	541	1079	622	1062	743	1180	500	592	2074	292	838	2405	713	724	1201	2198	627	549	1675	1490	2373	2415	2350	1194	233	2483	526	984	1148
El Paso, TX	1112	1197	1959	1617	1530	1231	2363	1328	1118	2235	737	1236	1738	2300	2147	432	1893	2563	1767	2513	1834	1105	1315	1955	1242	864	556	730	1181	1944	1753	2032	2087	2008	898	1871
Halifax, NS	2058	3548	2234	1652	1969	1231	715	1841	2268	920	2400	2015	2030	823	1026	3412	1297	542	3678	584	1434	2473	3471	1277	1887	2947	2797	3646	3687	3622	2085	1045	3756	1164	2322	2089
Houston, TX	586	954	1201	1193	1240	473	1892	801	360	1660	449	910	980	1828	1572	1188	1366	1988	2381	2041	1198	1318	2072	1330	863	1650	200	1487	1938	2449	995	1561	2583	1433	608	1604
Indianapolis, IN	464	2043	1196	279	596	737	872	287	826	715	752	618	975	809	655	1764	370	1038	2280	1022	639	1101	2073	641	239	1549	1186	2122	2290	2249	990	541	2383	596	674	1047
Jackson, MS	211	1398	915	835	1151	187	1514	423	185	1223	612	935	694	1450	1135	1482	988	1550	2544	1663	783	1458	2337	914	505	1813	644	1780	2232	2612	709	1183	2746	996	771	1570
Jacksonville, FL	733	1837	345	1160	1477	410	1325	589	556	953	1291	1336	141	1286	866	2072	822	1281	2994	1457	460	1859	2787	609	896	2264	1084	2370	2822	3052	196	1187	3186	720	1337	1928
Kansas City, MO	536	1668	1466	573	441	930	1359	559	932	1202	348	188	1245	1296	1141	1360	857	1525	1805	1509	1077	710	1598	1085	252	1074	812	1695	1814	1872	1259	1028	2007	1083	192	823
Las Vegas, NV	1611	1769	2733	1808	1677	1922	2596	1826	1854	2552	1124	1294	2512	2532	2500	285	2215	2855	1188	2745	2360	1035	442	2444	1610	417	1272	337	575	1256	2526	2265	1390	2441	1276	1872
Little Rock, AR	140	1457	1190	747	814	457	1446	355	455	1262	355	570	969	1382	1175	1367	920	1590	2237	1595	889	1093	2030	983	416	1507	600	1703	2012	2305	984	1115	2439	1036	464	1205
Los Angeles, CA	1839	1853	2759	2082	1951	2031	2869	2054	1917	2820	1352	1567	2538	2806	2760	369	2476	3144	971	3019	2588	1309	519	2682	1856	691	1356	124	385	1148	2553	2538	1291	2702	1513	2146
Louisville, KY	386	1981	1084	394	711	625	920	175	714	739	774	704	863	856	678	1786	394	1062	2362	1069	564	1215	2155	572	264	1631	1125	2144	2372	2364	878	589	2497	596	705	1162
Memphis, TN		1595	1051	624	940	395	1306	215	396	1123	487	724	830	1243	1035	1500	780	1451	2382	1456	749	1247	2175	843	294	1652	739	1841	2144	2440	845	975	2574	896	597	1359
México, MX			2154	2200	2113	1426	2900	1810	1313	2619	1323	1783	1933	2838	2525	1484	2375	2941	2819	3051	2151	2365	2367	2283	1825	2135	853	1683	2233	2996	1948	2570	3139	2386	1481	2477
Miami, FL				1478	1794	727	1671	907	874	1299	1609	1654	232	1631	1211	2390	1167	1627	3312	1803	805	2176	3105	954	1214	2581	1401	2688	3140	3370	274	1532	3504	1065	1655	2246
Milwaukee, WI					337	1019	939	569	1020	894	880	514	1257	875	865	1892	564	1198	2063	1088	956	842	1970	899	367	1446	1343	2145	2186	1991	1272	607	2124	799	769	789
Minneapolis, MN						1335	1255	886	1337	1211	793	383	1573	1192	1181	1805	881	1515	1727	1405	1273	606	1839	1216	621	1315	1257	2014	2055	1654	1588	924	1788	1115	637	452
Mobile, AL							1575	450	146	1203	799	1119	506	1481	1115	1662	1019	1531	2731	1707	730	1641	2545	861	688	2000	673	1960	2411	2799	521	1214	2933	970	958	1787
Montréal, QC								1094	1632	383	1625	1300	1466	121	454	2637	607	282	2963	155	871	1758	2756	714	1112	2232	2043	2931	2972	2907	1522	330	3041	600	1547	1374
Nashville, TN									539	906	703	747	686	1031	818	1715	569	1234	2405	1244	532	1269	2198	626	307	1675	954	2056	2360	2463	701	764	2597	679	748	1337
New Orleans, LA										1332	731	1121	653	1570	1245	1548	1108	1660	2663	1783	871	1643	2431	1002	690	1932	560	1846	2298	2731	668	1302	2865	1106	890	1755
New York, NY											1469	1258	1094	439	91	2481	367	313	2920	515	499	1716	2713	342	956	2189	1861	2839	2929	2864	1150	507	2998	228	1391	1665
Oklahoma City, OK												463	1388	1563	1408	1012	1124	1792	1934	1776	1237	871	1727	1331	505	1204	466	1370	1657	2002	1403	1295	2136	1350	161	1158
Omaha, NE													1433	1238	1228	1440	928	1561	1662	1451	1265	525	1455	1263	440	932	927	1630	1672	1719	1448	971	1853	1162	307	638
Orlando, FL														1427	1006	2169	963	1422	3091	1598	601	1955	2884	750	993	2360	1180	2467	2918	3149	82	1327	3283	860	1434	2025
Ottawa, ON															451	2575	545	382	2901	257	831	1696	2694	675	1050	2170	1981	2869	2910	2845	1483	268	2978	562	1485	1280
Philadelphia, PA																2420	306	419	2890	586	411	1686	2683	254	895	2160	1774	2779	2900	2835	1062	522	2968	140	1330	1633
Phoenix, AZ																	2136	2804	1335	2788	2249	1308	883	2343	1517	651	987	358	750	1513	2184	2307	1655	2362	1173	2075
Pittsburgh, PA																		690	2590	758	497	1386	2383	341	611	1859	1519	2494	2599	2534	1019	321	2668	240	1046	1332
Portland, ME																			3223	264	827	2019	3016	670	1279	2493	2189	3162	3233	3168	1478	668	3301	556	1714	1966
Portland, OR																				3114	2923	1268	578	2925	2057	771	2322	1093	638	170	3106	2633	313	2824	1775	1463
Québec, QC																					1003	1908	2905	846	1261	2381	2193	3080	3122	3057	1654	479	3190	732	1696	1523
Raleigh, NC																						1777	2716	157	825	2193	1398	2563	2894	2926	656	820	3060	265	1266	1724
Rapid City, SD																							1151	1720	963	628	1335	1372	1368	1195	1970	1429	1328	1620	712	792
Reno, NV																								2718	1850	524	1870	642	217	755	2899	2426	898	2617	1568	1867
Richmond, VA																									834	2194	1530	2684	2934	2869	805	660	3003	108	1274	1667
St. Louis, MO																										1326	968	1875	2066	2125	1008	782	2259	837	441	1075
Salt Lake City, UT																											1419	754	740	839	2375	1902	973	2094	1044	1455
San Antonio, TX																												1285	1737	2275	1195	1714	2410	1635	624	1621
San Diego, CA																													508	1271	2481	2601	1414	2720	1531	2209
San Francisco, CA																														816	2933	2643	958	2834	1784	2193
Seattle, WA																															3164	2577	140	2769	1843	1390
Tampa, FL																																1383	3297	916	1448	2039
Toronto, ON																																	2711	563	1217	1375
Vancouver, BC																																		2902	1977	1375
Washington, DC																																			1272	1566
Wichita, KS																																				956

Kilomètres

	Memphis, TN	México, MX	Miami, FL	Milwaukee, WI	Minneapolis, MN	Mobile, AL	Montréal, QC	Nashville, TN	New Orleans, LA	New York, NY	Oklahoma City, OK	Omaha, NE	Orlando, FL	Ottawa, ON	Philadelphia, PA	Phoenix, AZ	Pittsburgh, PA	Portland, ME	Portland, OR	Québec, QC	Raleigh, NC	Rapid City, SD	Reno, NV	Richmond, VA	St. Louis, MO	Salt Lake City, UT	San Antonio, TX	San Diego, CA	San Francisco, CA	Seattle, WA	Tampa, FL	Toronto, ON	Vancouver, BC	Washington, DC	Wichita, KS
México, MX	566																																		
Miami, FL	691	3466																																	
Milwaukee, WI	004	3540	2378																																
Minneapolis, MN	512	3400	2887	542																															
Mobile, AL	636	2294	1170	1640	2148																														
Montréal, QC	101	4666	2689	1511	2019	2534																													
Nashville, TN	346	2912	1459	916	1426	724	1760																												
New Orleans, LA	637	2113	1406	1641	2151	235	2626	867																											
New York, NY	807	4214	2090	1438	1948	1936	616	1458	2143																										
Oklahoma City, OK	784	2129	2589	1416	1276	1286	2615	1131	1176	2364																									
Omaha, NE	165	2869	2661	827	616	1800	2092	1202	1804	2024	745																								
Orlando, FL	335	3110	373	2023	2531	814	2359	1104	1051	1760	2233	2306																							
Ottawa, ON	000	4566	2624	1408	1918	2383	194	1659	2526	706	2515	1992	2296																						
Philadelphia, PA	665	4063	1948	1392	1900	1794	730	1316	2003	146	2265	1976	1619	726																					
Phoenix, AZ	414	2388	3846	3044	2904	2674	4243	2759	2491	3992	1628	2317	3490	4143	3894																				
Pittsburgh, PA	255	3821	1878	907	1418	1640	977	916	1783	591	1809	1493	1549	877	492	3437																			
Portland, ME	335	4732	2618	1928	2438	2463	454	1986	2671	504	2883	2512	2288	615	674	4512	1110																		
Portland, OR	833	4536	5329	3319	2779	4394	4767	3870	4285	4698	3112	2674	4973	4668	4650	2148	4167	5186																	
Québec, QC	343	4909	2901	1751	2261	2747	249	2002	2869	829	2858	2335	2571	414	943	4486	1220	425	5010																
Raleigh, NC	205	3461	1295	1538	2048	1175	1401	856	1401	803	1990	2035	967	1337	661	3619	800	1331	4703	1614															
Rapid City, SD	006	3805	3501	1355	975	2640	2829	2042	2644	2761	1401	845	3146	2729	2713	2105	2230	3249	2040	3070	2859														
Reno, NV	500	3809	4996	3170	2959	4095	4434	3537	3911	4365	2779	2341	4640	4335	4317	1421	3834	4853	930	4674	4370	1852													
Richmond, VA	356	3673	1535	1446	1957	1385	1149	1007	1612	550	2142	2032	1207	1086	409	3770	549	1078	4706	1361	253	2767	4373												
St. Louis, MO	73	2936	1953	591	999	1107	1789	494	1110	1538	813	708	1598	1689	1440	2441	983	2058	3310	2029	1327	1549	2977	1342											
Salt Lake City, UT	658	3435	4153	2327	2116	3218	3591	2695	3109	3522	1937	1500	3797	3492	3475	1047	2991	4011	1241	3831	3529	1010	843	3530	2134										
San Antonio, TX	189	1372	2254	2161	2023	1083	3287	1535	901	2994	750	1492	1899	3187	2854	1588	2444	3522	3736	3529	2249	2148	3009	2462	1558	2283									
San Diego, CA	962	2708	4325	3451	3241	3154	4716	3308	2970	4568	2204	2623	3969	4616	4471	576	4013	5088	1759	4956	4124	2208	1033	4319	3017	1213	2068								
San Francisco, CA	450	3593	5052	3517	3306	3879	4782	3797	3697	4713	2666	2690	4695	4682	4666	1207	4182	5202	1027	5023	4656	2201	349	4721	3324	1191	2795	817							
Seattle, WA	926	4821	5422	3204	2661	4504	4677	3963	4394	4608	3221	2766	5067	4578	4562	2434	4077	5097	274	4919	4708	1923	1215	4616	3419	1350	3660	2045	1313						
Tampa, FL	360	3134	441	2047	2555	838	2449	1128	1075	1850	2257	2330	132	2386	1709	3514	1640	2378	4998	2661	1056	3170	4664	1295	1622	3821	1923	3992	4719	5091					
Toronto, ON	569	4135	2465	977	1487	1953	531	1229	2095	816	2084	1562	2135	431	840	3712	516	1075	4236	771	1319	2299	3903	1062	1258	3060	2758	4185	4253	4146	2225				
Vancouver, BC	142	5051	5638	3418	2877	4719	4893	4179	4610	4824	3437	2981	5282	4792	4776	2663	4293	5311	504	5133	4924	2137	1445	4832	3635	1566	3878	2275	1541	225	5305	4362			
Washington, DC	442	3839	1714	1286	1794	1561	965	1093	1780	367	2172	1870	1384	904	225	3800	386	895	4544	1178	426	2607	4211	174	1347	3369	2631	4376	4560	4455	1474	906	4669		
Wichita, KS	61	2383	2663	1237	1025	1541	2489	1204	1432	2238	259	494	2307	2389	2140	1887	1683	2758	2856	2729	2037	1146	2523	2050	710	1680	1004	2463	2870	2965	2330	1958	3181	2047	
Winnipeg, MB	87	3985	3614	1270	727	2875	2211	2151	2824	2679	1863	1027	3258	2060	2627	3339	2143	3163	2354	2451	2774	1274	3004	2682	1730	2341	2608	3554	3529	2237	3281	2212	2212	2520	1538

TEMPERATURE CONVERSIONS			
°F	°C	°C	°F
110	43.3	40	104
100	37.8	35	95
90	32.2	30	86
80	26.7	25	77
70	21.1	20	68
60	15.6	15	59
50	10.0	10	50
40	4.4	5	41
32	0	0	32
30	-1.1	-5	23
20	-6.7	-10	14
10	-12.2	-15	5
0	-17.8	-20	-4
-10	-23.3	-25	-13
-20	-28.9	-30	-22
-30	-34.4	-35	-31
-40	-40.0	-40	-40
-50	-45.6	-45	-49

DISTANCE CONVERSIONS

MILES	KM	KM	MILES
1	1.6	1	0.6
5	8.0	2	1.2
10	16.1	5	3.1
15	24.1	10	6.2
20	32.2	15	9.3
25	40.2	20	12.4
30	48.3	25	15.5
35	56.3	30	18.6
40	64.4	40	24.9
45	72.4	50	31.1
50	80.5	60	37.3
55	88.5	70	43.5
60	96.6	80	49.7
65	104.6	90	55.9
70	112.7	100	62.1
75	120.7	110	68.4
80	128.7	120	74.6
85	136.8	130	80.8
90	144.8	140	87.0
95	152.9	150	93.2
100	160.9	160	99.4

VOLUME CONVERSIONS

GALLONS	LITERS	LITERS	GALLONS
1	3.8	1	0.26
2	7.6	2	0.5
3	11.4	3	0.8
4	15.1	4	1.1
5	18.9	5	1.3
10	37.9	10	2.6
15	56.8	20	5.3
20	75.7	30	7.9
25	94.6	40	10.6
30	113.6	50	13.2
40	151.4	75	19.8
50	189.3	100	26.4

Interstate Route
Other Route
206   Distance in Miles
332   Distance in Kilometers
4:15   Approximate Travel Time
● **Miami**   City on Distance Chart, pp. 284–285
● Fort Pierce   Other City

Distances and driving times may vary depending on actual
route traveled and driving conditions.

TOURISM INFORMATION

UNITED STATES

Alabama
Alabama Bureau of Tourism & Travel
800.252.2262, 334.242.4169
www.800alabama.com

Alaska
Alaska Travel Industry Association
800.862.5275
www.travelalaska.com

Arizona
Arizona Office of Tourism
866.275.5816, 602.374.3700
www.arizonaguide.com

Arkansas
Arkansas Dept. of Parks & Tourism
800.628.8725, 501.682.7777
www.arkansasstateparks.com

California
California Division of Tourism
800.862.2543, 916.444.4429
www.visitcalifornia.com

Colorado
Colorado Tourism Office
800.265.6723, 303.892.3885
www.colorado.com

Connecticut
Connecticut Office of Tourism
888.288.4748, 860.256.2800
www.ctvisit.com

Delaware
Delaware Tourism Office
866.284.7483, 302.739.4271
www.visitdelaware.com

District of Columbia
DC Convention and Tourism Corp.
800.422.8644, 202.789.7000 or 7030
www.washington.org

Florida
Visit Florida
850.488.5607, 888.735.2872
www.visitflorida.com

Georgia
Georgia Dept. of Industry, Trade & Tourism
800.847.4842
www.georgia.org/travel

Hawaii
Hawaii Visitors & Conv. Bureau
800.464.2924, 808.923.1811
www.gohawaii.com

Idaho
Idaho Department of Commerce
800.635.7820, 208.334.2470
www.visitid.org

Illinois
Illinois Bureau of Tourism
800.406.6418
www.enjoyillinois.com

Indiana
Indiana Tourism
800.759.9191, 317.232.8860
www.enjoyindiana.com

Iowa
Iowa Division of Tourism
888.472.6035, 515.242.4705
www.traveliowa.com

Kansas
Kansas Travel & Tourism
800.252.6727, 785.296.2009
www.travelks.com

Kentucky
Department of Tourism
800.225.8747, 502.564.4930
www.kentuckytourism.com

Louisiana
Louisiana Office of Tourism
225.342.8119
www.louisianatravel.com

Maine
Maine Office of Tourism & Film
888.624.6345, 207.624.7843
www.visitmaine.com

Maryland
Maryland Office of Tourism Develop.
877.333.4455
www.visitmaryland.org

Massachusetts
Mass. Office of Travel & Tourism
800.227.6277, 617.973.8500
www.massvacation.com

Michigan
Travel Michigan
888.784.7328, 517.373.0670
www.michigan.org

Minnesota
Minnesota Tourism
888.868.7476, 651.296.5029
www.exploreminnesota.com

Mississippi
Mississippi Dev. Authority/Tourism
866.733.6477, 601.359.3297
www.visitmississippi.org

Missouri
Missouri Division of Tourism
800.519.2100, 573.751.4133
www.visitmo.com

Montana
Travel Montana
800.847.4868, 406.841.2870
www.visitmt.com

Nebraska
Nebraska Travel & Tourism
877.632.7275, 402.471.3796
www.visitnebraska.org

Nevada
Nevada Commission on Tourism
800.638.2328, 775.687.4322
www.travelnevada.com

New Hampshire
New Hampshire Division of Travel & Tourism Development
800.386.4664, 603.271.2665
www.visitnh.gov

New Jersey
New Jersey Office of Travel & Tourism
800.847.4865, 609.777.0885
www.visitnj.org

New Mexico
New Mexico Department of Tourism
800.545.2070, 505.827.7400
www.newmexico.org

New York
New York State Division of Tourism
800.225.5697, 518.474.4116
www.iloveny.com

North Carolina
North Carolina Division of Tourism, Film & Sports Development
800.847.4862, 919.733.4171
www.visitnc.com

North Dakota
North Dakota Tourism
800.435.5663, 701.328.2525
www.ndtourism.com

Ohio
Ohio Division of Travel & Tourism
800.282.5393, 614-466-8844
www.discoverohio.com

Oklahoma
Oklahoma Dept. of Tourism & Rec.
800.652.6552, 405.230.8420
www.travelok.com

Oregon
Oregon Tourism Comm. (Travel Oregon)
800.547.7842, 503.378.8850
www.traveloregon.com

Pennsylvania
Pennsylvania Tourism Office
800.847.4872
www.visitpa.com

Rhode Island
Rhode Island Tourism Division
800.556.2484, 401.222.2601
www.visitrhodeisland.com

South Carolina
S.C. Dept. of Parks, Rec. & Tourism
888.727.6453, 803.734.1700
www.discoversouthcarolina.com

South Dakota
South Dakota Department of Tourism
800.732.5682, 605.773.3301
www.travelsd.com

Tennessee
Tenn. Dept. of Tourist Development
800.462.8366, 615.741.2159
www.tnvacation.com

Texas
Texas Dept. of Econ. Dev., Tourism Div.
800.888.8839
www.traveltex.com

Utah
Utah Office of Tourism
800.200.1160, 801.538.1030
www.utah.com

Vermont
Vermont Dept. of Tourism & Marketing
800.837.6668, 802.828.3237
www.vermontvacation.com

Virginia
Virginia Tourism Corporation
800.847.4882, 804.786.4485
www.virginia.org

Washington
Dept. of Community Trade & Economic Development Washington State Tourism Div.
800.544.1800
www.experiencewashington.com

West Virginia
West Virginia Division of Tourism
800.225.5982, 304.558.2200
www.wvtourism.com

Wisconsin
Wisconsin Department of Tourism
800.432.8747, 608.266.2161
www.travelwisconsin.com

Wyoming
Wyoming Division of Tourism
800.225.5996, 307.777.7777
www.wyomingtourism.org

Puerto Rico
Puerto Rico Tourism Company
800.866.7827, 787.721.2400
www.gotopuertorico.com

CANADA

Alberta
Travel Alberta Canada
800.252.3782, 780.427.4321
www.travelalberta.com

British Columbia
Tourism British Columbia
800.663.6000, 250.356.6363
www.hellobc.com

Manitoba
Travel Manitoba
800.665.0040
www.travelmanitoba.com

New Brunswick
Tourism Communication Center
800.561.0123, 506.444.5205
www.tourismnewbrunswick.ca

Newfoundland & Labrador
Newfoundland & Labrador Tourism
800.563.6353, 709.729.2830
www.gov.nl.ca/tourism

Nova Scotia
Tourism Nova Scotia
800.565.0000, 902.425.5781
www.novascotia.com

Ontario
Ontario Tourism
800.668.2746, 905.282.1721
www.ontariotravel.net

Prince Edward Island
PEI Tourism
800.734.7529, 902.368.4444
www.gentleisland.com

Québec
Tourisme Québec
877.266.5687, 514.873.2015
www.bonjourquebec.com

Saskatchewan
Tourism Saskatchewan
877.237.2273, 306.787.9600
www.sasktourism.com

MEXICO

Mexico Ministry of Tourism
800.446.3942
www.visitmexico.com

BORDER CROSSING INFORMATION

As of December 31, 2006, all travelers to or from Canada, Mexico, Central and South America, and the Caribbean utilizing air or sea will be absolutely required to carry a passport. On December 31, 2007, this requirement will be extended to all land border crossings.

CANADA

U.S. citizens entering Canada from the U.S. are required to present passports or proof of U.S. citizenship accompanied by photo identification. U.S. citizens entering from a third country must have a valid passport. Visas are not required for U.S. citizens entering from the U.S. for stays of up to 180 days. Naturalized citizens should travel with their naturalization certificates. Alien permanent residents of the U.S. must present their Alien Registration Cards. Individuals under the age of 18 and traveling alone should carry a letter from a parent or legal guardian authorizing their travel in Canada.

U.S. driver's licenses are valid in Canada, and U.S. citizens do not need to obtain an international driver's license. Proof of auto insurance, however, is required.

UNITED STATES (FROM CANADA)

Canadian citizens entering the U.S. are required to demonstrate proof of their citizenship, normally with a photo identification accompanied by a valid birth certificate or citizenship card. Passports or visas are not required for visits lasting less than six months; for visits exceeding six months, they are mandatory. Individuals under the age of 18 and traveling alone should carry notarized documentation, signed by both parents, authorizing their travel.

Canadian driver's licenses are valid in the U.S. for one year, and automobiles may enter free of payment or duty fees. Drivers need only provide customs officials with proof of vehicle registration, ownership, and insurance.

MEXICO

U.S. citizens entering Mexico are required to present passports or proof of U.S. citizenship accompanied by photo identification. Passports are strongly recommended. Visas are not required for stays of up to 180 days. Naturalized citizens should travel with their naturalization certificates, and alien permanent residents must present their Alien Registration Cards. Individuals under the age of 18 traveling alone, with one parent, or with other adults must carry notarized parental authorization or valid custodial documents. All U.S. citizens visiting for up to 180 days must also procure a tourist card, obtainable from Mexican consulates, tourism offices, border crossing points, and airlines serving Mexico. However, tourist cards are not needed for visits shorter than 72 hours to areas within the Border Zone (extending approximately 25 km into Mexico)

U.S. driver's licenses are valid in Mexico.

Visitors who wish to drive beyond the Baja California Peninsula or the Border Zone must obtain a temporary import permit for their vehicles. To acquire a permit, one must submit evidence of citizenship and of the vehicle's title and registration, as well as a valid driver's license. A processing fee must be paid. Permits are available at any Mexican Army Bank (Banjercito) located at border crossings or selected Mexican consulates. Mexican law also requires the posting of a refundable bond, via credit card or cash, at the Banjercito to guarantee the departure of the vehicle. Do not deal with any individual operating outside of official channels.

All visitors driving in Mexico should be aware that U.S. auto insurance policies are not valid and that buying short-term tourist insurance is mandatory. Many U.S. insurance companies sell Mexican auto insurance. American Automobile Association (for members only) and Sanborn's Mexico Insurance (800.638.9423) are popular companies with offices at most U.S. border crossings.